S0-BRD-969

N

Maryland

North Carolina

Atlantic Ocean

Chesapeake Bay

Richmond

FREDERICK
Winchester
Berryville
CLARKE
Leesburg
LOUDOUN
WARREN
Woodstock
Front Royal
FAUQUIER
SHENANDOAH
Washington
Luray
PAGE
Warrenton
Manassas Park
Manassas
PRINCE WILLIAM
DISTRICT OF COLUMBIA
ARLINGTON
Arlington
Falls Church
Fairfax
FAIRFAX
Alexandria
ROCKINGHAM
Harrisonburg
MADISON
Stanardsville
Madison
GREENE
CULPEPER
Culpeper
ORANGE
Orange
STAFFORD
Stafford
Fredericksburg
Spotsylvania
SPOTSYLVANIA
KING GEORGE
King George
WESTMORELAND
Montross
RICHMOND
ESSEX
Tappahannock
Warsaw
NORTHUMBERLAND
Heathsville
USTA
Waynesboro
Charlottesville
ALBEMARLE
Palmyra
LOUISA
Louisa
CAROLINE
Bowling Green
NELSON
Lovingston
FLUVANNA
GOOCHLAND
HANOVER
Hanover
KING WILLIAM
KING AND QUEEN
King and Queen
Saluda
MIDDLESEX
Lancaster
LANCASTER
ACCOMACK
Accomac
ERST
mherst
BUCKINGHAM
Buckingham
Cumberland
Goochland
Powhatan
POWHATAN
HENRICO
King William
New Kent
NEW KENT
Gloucester
GLOUCESTER
MATHEWS
Mathews
Eastville
NORTHAMPTON
APPOMATTOX
Appomattox
Farmville
PRINCE EDWARD
CUMBERLAND
Amelia
AMELIA
Chesterfield C.H.
CHESTERFIELD
Colonial Heights
CHARLES CITY
Charles City
JAMES CITY
Williamsburg
YORK
Yorktown
Rustburg
Hopewell
Prince George
Petersburg
PRINCE GEORGE
Surry
Newport News
Poquoson
Hampton
MPBELL
CHARLOTTE
Charlotte C.H.
NOTTOWAY
Nottoway
DINWIDDIE
Dinwiddie
SUSSEX
Sussex
ISLE OF WIGHT
Isle of Wight
Norfolk
Portsmouth
Virginia Beach
HALIFAX
Halifax
Lunenburg
LUNENBURG
Boydton
MECKLENBURG
Lawrenceville
BRUNSWICK
Emporia
GREENSVILLE
SOUTHAMPTON
Courtland
Franklin
Suffolk
Chesapeake

THE VIRGINIA
LANDMARKS REGISTER

THE VIRGINIA

PUBLISHED FOR THE VIRGINIA DEPARTMENT OF HISTORIC RESOURCES

BY THE UNIVERSITY PRESS OF VIRGINIA

CHARLOTTESVILLE AND LONDON

LANDMARKS REGISTER

FOURTH EDITION

Edited by Calder Loth

WITHDRAWN

Jefferson-Madison
Regional Library
Charlottesville, Virginia

16006114
(B)

The Board of Historic Resources gratefully acknowledges the generous assistance of the following patrons for supporting this edition of *The Virginia Landmarks Register:*

Margaret Karen Berkness

John R. Broadway, Jr.

Mr. and Mrs. M. Caldwell Butler

Mr. and Mrs. Randolph Byrd

Dominion Resources, Inc.

The Dunlevy Milbank Foundation

Mr. and Mrs. Paul Funkhouser

The Glavé Firm, Architects

Mr. and Mrs. O. Bruce Gupton

Frank Hardy, Inc., Realtors

The Eugene Holt Foundation

Mr. and Mrs. Charles S. Luck III

Mr. and Mrs. Ivor Massey, Jr.

The Preservation Alliance of Virginia

Mr. and Mrs. Charles H. Seilheimer

Don Swofford, Architect

Ulysses X. White

Anne R. Worrell

John G. Zehmer, Jr.

Anonymous

In memory of Sally White Barnes

In memory of Robert D. Kilpatrick

THE UNIVERSITY PRESS OF VIRGINIA

© 1999 by the Virginia Department of Historic Resources
All rights reserved
Printed in the United States of America

First published 1999

♾ The paper used in this publication meets the minimum requirements of the American National Standard for Information Sciences—Permanence of Paper for Printed Library Materials, ANSI Z39.48-1984.

The Virginia Devisal of Arms on the title page was presented by Queen Elizabeth II during her 1976 visit to the Commonwealth.

LIBRARY OF CONGRESS CATALOGING-IN-PUBLICATION DATA

The Virginia landmarks register / edited by Calder Loth. — 4th ed.
   p.   cm.
   Includes index.
   ISBN 0-8139-1862-6 (cloth : alk. paper)
   1. Historic sites—Virginia. 2. Virginia—History, Local.
  I. Loth, Calder, 1943– . II. Virginia. Dept. of Historic Resources.
F227.V864 1999
975.5—dc21

                              98-41522
                                  CIP

CONTENTS

THE FOURTH EDITION of *The Virginia Landmarks Register* illustrates our belief that Virginia's history is among its greatest gifts to share with the world. The abiding legacy of the Commonwealth is evident on every page and embodied in the houses, commercial structures, historic districts, Indian sites, farms, railroad depots, fishing villages, and schoolhouses scattered across the state. Not the least of these places is Jamestown. Our family spent an enlightening afternoon at the archaeological site there digging for artifacts for the Jamestown Rediscovery Project. The items we found buried in that soil helped us envision those brave men and women who founded our Commonwealth and a new nation.

Virginia's historic buildings and sites, with the stories each has to tell, remind us of the awesome responsibility of maintaining our inheritance. They educate our children and enlighten our visitors. They serve as cultural and social anchors in our communities, and they create a sense of place and beauty in our lives.

Each registered property is a touchstone that keeps us on course, reminding us of those who came before us—their values and their struggles to endure and achieve. The properties and the people who occupied them inspire us to move into the future informed, proud, and poised to fulfill our considerable potential.

James S. Gilmore III
GOVERNOR

Roxane G. Gilmore
FIRST LADY OF VIRGINIA

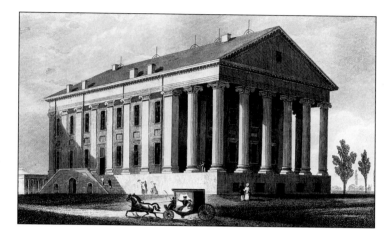

THE VIRGINIA General Assembly has charged the Virginia Department of Historic Resources with the responsibility for preparing a register of the Commonwealth's significant landmarks and for publishing that register from time to time, "setting forth appropriate information concerning those properties." This publication grows out of long hours of research, fieldwork, and consideration by the department's staff and its board, the Board of Historic Resources, over many years. While board and staff members have changed over time, an abiding interest in recognizing and promoting an appreciation for Virginia's historic, architectural, and archaeological resources has marked the work of all those who have served here. That work will continue in the years to come.

The Virginia Landmarks Register has become an effective tool for furthering the Commonwealth's interests in historic resource stewardship and careful decision making. However, the ultimate responsibility for preserving Virginia's landmarks rests with those who own them and those who make decisions affecting them. With this register the Commonwealth formally recognizes the profound debt all Virginians owe to those who own and lovingly care for this remarkable legacy and to decision makers who understand its contribution to the unique fabric of Virginia.

On behalf of our board and staff, I am pleased to present The Virginia Landmarks Register to the people of Virginia.

H. Alexander Wise, Jr.
DIRECTOR, VIRGINIA DEPARTMENT
OF HISTORIC RESOURCES

The *Virginia Landmarks Register* is published on behalf of the Virginia General Assembly under the authority of the Virginia Department of Historic Resources, H. Alexander Wise, Jr., director.

Properties are officially listed on the Virginia Landmarks Register by the Virginia Board of Historic Resources.

M. Karen Berkness, Chairman
Randolph Byrd
William M. Kelso
True F. Luck
Carter F. McNeely
Ulysses X. White
John G. Zehmer, Jr.

Virginia nominations to the National Register of Historic Places are made by the State Review Board.

Gary R. Grant, Chairman
Michael B. Barber
S. Allen Chambers
Evelyn D. Chandler
Jeffrey L. Hantman
William M. Kelso
Dennis J. Pogue
Robert G. D. Pottage III
Crandall A. Shifflett
John H. Spencer
Anne R. Worrell
John G. Zehmer, Jr.

❧ PREFACE

The Register Program

The history of Virginia is a special chapter in the American story, one embodied in the many historic buildings, structures, archaeological sites, and districts that collectively form the Commonwealth's cultural landscape. Tangible evidence of Native American occupation within the state's borders spans 16,000 years. The English colonial experiment in what is today the United States began in Virginia, at Jamestown, and ended nearby at Yorktown. Virginia was home to many of the nation's founding fathers and birthplace of eight presidents. The first Africans in English America arrived in Virginia. The state holds some of the most noted works of American historic architecture. Many of the most important engagements of the Civil War were fought on Virginia soil. More recently, scientific flight simulations leading to the first lunar landing were conducted in Virginia.

Virginia's many and varied landmarks are inseparably linked with the Commonwealth's sense of place, environmental quality, and economic health. Moreover, our rich heritage is the shared treasure of all Americans. The recognition of these facts prompted the formation in 1965 of the Virginia Advisory Legislative Council Study Commission to determine what role state government should play in safeguarding this legacy. The study commission recommended that the state take positive steps to identify and protect its historic resources, and in 1966 the General Assembly established the Virginia Historic Landmarks Commission, charging it with the task of perpetuating "those structures and areas which have a close and immediate relationship with the values upon which the State and the nation were founded."

The enabling legislation directed the commission, through its professional staff, to make a survey of the state and to designate as historic landmarks the buildings, structures, sites, and historic districts that constitute the historical, architectural, and archaeological sites of statewide or national significance. In an early meeting the commission decided that the list of designated historic landmarks would be called the Virginia Landmarks Register and that each entry in the register would be called a Virginia Historic Landmark. Since designating the first

Virginia Historic Landmark (Tuckahoe in Goochland County) in 1968, the Virginia Landmarks Register has expanded to more than 1,800 entries.

Registration is an ongoing process: the list will lengthen over the next several decades as additional places are studied and have their significance verified. Because our interpretation of Virginia history is constantly evolving, the types of places nominated to the register will inevitably become more diverse. Places formerly thought to have been commonplace or insignificant may eventually be seen as important survivals. Hence, properties that might once have been determined ineligible for registration may receive more sympathetic consideration in the future.

In 1984 the Historic Landmarks Commission was reorganized as the Division of Historic Landmarks within a newly established Department of Conservation and Historic Resources. A legislative study commission subsequently appointed by Governor Gerald L. Baliles recommended that the state's historic preservation activities be carried out by an independent agency. Thus, in 1989 the General Assembly established the Department of Historic Resources. The legislation also created the seven-member Board of Historic Resources to continue making additions to the Virginia Landmarks Register and to accept preservation easements on both registered landmarks and contributing properties in registered historic districts. Board members are appointed by the governor to serve four-year terms. The director of the Department of Historic Resources is charged by the legislation with the periodic publishing of "a complete register of designated properties setting forth appropriate information concerning those properties." The legislation further provides for places of local significance to be included in the Virginia Landmarks Register. Assisting the board with the Register program is the professional staff of the Department of Historic Resources, which includes architectural historians, archaeologists, historians, architects, and various other specialists who operate from the Richmond office and four regional offices.

Although some nominations to the Virginia Landmarks Register originate from within the department, most are generated through requests from property owners, preservation organizations, local governments, and other interested parties. A nomination report, containing detailed descriptions, a statement of significance, supporting documentation, maps, and photographs, is prepared for each place. Reports may be compiled either by the department's staff or by members of the public. Final action on a nomination rests with Board of Historic Resources. Board approval attests that a property or district is an official state historic resource.

Listing on the Virginia Landmarks Register *does not restrict* a private owner's use of his or her property. Architectural controls, such as those imposed through historic district zoning, can be established only by local governing bodies. Registration is primarily an official recognition that a place is an outstanding historic resource and is worthy of preservation. Private owners may provide legal protection for a registered landmark by voluntarily donating a historic preservation easement on the property to the Board of Historic Resources. The easement is a legal contract between the state and the grantor stipulating that the historic integrity of the landmark and its setting shall be preserved in perpetuity. The board currently holds approximately 250 easements on individually registered landmarks or contributing properties in historic districts.

Virginia and the Federal Program

The program of the Board of Historic Resources, and consequently that of the Department of Historic Resources, is closely aligned with the federal preservation program. The National Historic Preservation Act of 1966 called for the expansion of the National Register of Historic Places to include properties of state and local as well as national significance and charged the states with the responsibility of submitting nominations to the National Register. In accordance with the federal act, the director of the Department of Historic Resources is mandated by state legislation to serve as the State Historic Preservation Officer (SHPO), in which capacity he or she is responsible for maintaining liaison between the state and federal agencies and carrying out Virginia's functions within the federal preservation program.

The National Register of Historic Places is administered by the National Park Service within the Department of the Interior. Regulations governing the National Register require each state to establish a State Review Board to examine and make recommendations upon proposed nominations to the National Register. In Virginia the State Review Board members are appointed by the Virginia SHPO and must represent certain professional disciplines. The Board of Historic Resources and the State Review Board act in close cooperation so that properties listed on the Virginia Landmarks Register are, in nearly every case, nominated to the National Register of Historic Places. Because the National Park Service ordinarily accepts the nominations made by the states, the Virginia entries in the National Register of Historic Places generally include the entries in the Virginia Landmarks Register. Like the Virginia Landmarks Register, listing in the National Register of Historic Places is primarily honorific; it imposes no restrictions on the use of private property.

National Historic Landmarks

Under the authority of the Historic Sites Act of 1935, the secretary of the interior, upon recommendation by the Advisory Board on National Parks, Historic Sites, Buildings, and Monuments, may declare a property to be a National Historic Landmark (not to be confused with the National Register of Historic Places). National Historic Landmarks (NHLs) must possess overriding national significance under specific themes. The owner of a National Historic Landmark is offered a certificate and a special bronze plaque stating the designation. The Board of Historic Resources may be consulted on properties being considered for National Historic Landmark designation but does not play a direct role in the program. Approximately one hundred Virginia places have been designated National Historic Landmarks. Although they may not have received the specific designation of National Historic Landmark, most historic properties owned by the National Park Service are considered to have National Historic Landmark status.

The Fourth Edition

This fourth edition of *The Virginia Landmarks Register* is an illustrated compilation of all places officially designated as Virginia Historic Landmarks by the Virginia Board of Historic Resources and its predecessor, the Virginia Historic Landmarks Commission, from the first register meeting on November 5, 1968, through March 19, 1997. Places added to the register after March 19, 1997, while this work was in preparation, are listed in Appendix II.

Each entry in this work is followed by its archives file number. The first part of this hyphenated number is the numerical designation of the city, town, or county in which the individual property or district is located; the second part of the number is the individual survey number of the landmark within its respective city, town, or county. The archives file number is followed by two dates: the date the property or district was added to the Virginia Landmarks Register (VLR) and the date the place was listed in the National Register of Historic Places (NRHP). In those rare instances where a Virginia Historic Landmark was not listed in the National Register of Historic Places, no NRHP date is given. Those entries of special national significance that have been designated National Historic Landmarks have the notation *NHL* at the end of their entries followed by the date that designation was made. In some cases National Historic Landmarks were never officially listed in the National Register of Historic Places.

Landmarks with historic preservation easements held by the Commonwealth of Virginia, through the Board of Historic Resources, are followed by the designation *BHR Easement*. It should be noted that in a number of cases the Board of Historic Resources holds easements jointly with other agencies and organizations such as the Virginia Outdoors Foundation, the Association for the Preservation of Virginia Antiquities, or the Historic Alexandria Foundation. In the interest of saving space, joint easements holders have not been noted; however, such information is available from the Department of Historic Resources. A number of preservation easements are held on contributing properties in historic districts and are not specifically listed in this work.

Those landmarks that have been destroyed or otherwise have suffered loss of historic or architectural integrity, and thus have been officially removed from the Virginia Landmarks Register, are illustrated and briefly described in Appendix I.

The information contained in the entries for each of the landmarks herein is taken primarily from the nomination reports and research notes filed in the archives of the Department of Historic Resources. In many instances material in the nomination reports has been updated or corrected through subsequent research. Numerous additional corrections in the department's information have been made through the editorial process for this publication. Most of the entries have been reviewed by pertinent members of the department's staff. Many representatives of organizations and institutions as well as private citizens with special knowledge of landmarks in particular categories or in particular geographical regions have edited entries and have brought to light new and more accurate information in the process. Finally, wherever possible, entries have been sent to owners or custodians of individual landmarks for review and comment. The responses from scores of property owners have been especially helpful in correcting errors and bringing the entries up-to-date. Subsequent research by staff members, scholars, property owners, and other interested parties will inevitably provide information unavailable or unknown to the editor during the preparation of this work. Such material will gladly be accepted and placed in the department's archives both for reference and for use in future editions of *The Virginia Landmarks Register.*

A Cautionary Note

Most privately owned properties included in this edition of *The Virginia Landmarks Register* are not open to the public, and their privacy should be respected. Some places are open to visitors on a regular basis; others may be visited by special arrangement or on special occasions. Also, most public buildings are regularly accessible to the public. Those properties that are exhibited as museums or historic attractions have been noted, for the most part, in the entries. The most up-to-date general listing of Virginia historic properties open to the public with regularly scheduled times of visitation is maintained by the Virginia Tourism Corporation, 901 E. Byrd Street, Richmond, Virginia 23219.

ACKNOWLEDGMENTS

The Virginia Landmarks Register program involves the participation of many, many people including property owners, public officials, members of the Board of Historic Resources, and especially the dedicated staff of the Department of Historic Resources. This work does not adequately convey the amount of time the staff has spent on site visitation, research, report preparation, board presentations, and information management. The following list includes those members of the staff who have played active roles in the register program since the publication of the third edition of *The Virginia Landmarks Register* in 1986. This present work is largely the product of their labor, expertise, or direction.

Ann Miller Andrus, Anne S. Beckett, Robert A. Carter, Sarah S. Driggs, David A. Edwards, Keith T. Egloff, June A. Ellis, Leslie Giles, David K. Hazzard, James C. Hill, Robert L. Jolley, John R. Kern, Thomas S. Klatka, Julie Vosmik Langan, Monica S. Lawrence, Elizabeth Hoge Lipford, Deidre McCarthy, Hugh C. Miller, H. Bryan Mitchell, the late Jeffrey M. O'Dell, John Orrock, Margaret T. Peters, J. Daniel Pezzoni, John S. Salmon, M. Catherine Slusser, E. Randolph Turner III, Mary Ruffin Viles, Marc C. Wagner, and Joseph S. White III.

Certain members of the staff have rendered exceptional service to the editor in the preparation of this work. Their support has involved providing editorial assistance, taking photographs, writing entries, providing special technical support or advice, and/or offering general encouragement throughout the process. These patient and generous people merit special recognition:

Anne S. Beckett, Robert A. Carter, Suzanne K. Durham, David H. Dutton, Keith T. Egloff, David K. Hazzard, James C. Hill, Robert L. Jolley, John R. Kern, Kathleen S. Kilpatrick, Thomas S. Klatka, Monica S. Lawrence, Elizabeth Hoge Lipford, Margaret T. Peters, Nina K. Pierce, Mary Harding Sadler, John S. Salmon, M. Catherine Slusser, Susan E. Smead, E. Randolph Turner III, Mary Ruffin Viles, Marc C. Wagner, John E. Wells, Deborah B. Woodward, and especially David A. Edwards for the many excellent photographs that he took expressly for this work.

The editor expresses his particular gratitude to the following individuals around the state who kindly read and edited portions of the manuscript for areas in which they have special knowledge and expertise. Their willing and generous assistance is heartily appreciated.

J. Francis Amos, Franklin County
Charles E. Brownell, Virginia Commonwealth University
Martha Caldwell, James Madison University
Mary Calos, Hopewell
Martha C. Carter, Spotsylvania Historical Association
S. Allen Chambers, Lynchburg
Edward A. Chappell, Colonial Williamsburg Foundation
Richard T. Couture, Longwood College
Kerri Culhane, Virginia Commonwealth University
Jean Federico, Historic Alexandria
William Frazier, Historic Staunton Foundation
Leah Freiwald, Historic Green Springs, Inc.
Peter Dun Grover, Association for the Preservation of Virginia Antiquities
Gary Grant, Danville
Peter Hodson, University of Portsmouth
Emily Gordon Honts, Botetourt County Historical Society
Mary Ellen Howe, Chesterfield County
Maral Kalbian, Clarke County
George Kegley, Roanoke
Nanci King, Washington County
Clara S. Lambeth, Bedford Historical Society
K. Edward Lay, University of Virginia School of Architecture
Anne Carter Lee, Franklin County
John G. Lewis, Winchester
Col. B. B. Manchester, Gloucester Historical Society
Martha W. McCartney, James City County
Ann McCleary, Weyers Cave
Stephen L. McMaster, Richmond
Ann L. Miller, Virginia Department of Transportation Research Council
Michael Miller, City of Alexandria
Robert L. Montague III, Middlesex County
John Mouring, NASA, Langley Research Center
Janet Murray, Colonial Williamsburg Foundation
Ashley M. Neville, Hanover County
The late L. Floyd Nock III, Accomack County
Daniel Pezzoni and Leslie Giles, Landmark Preservation Associates
Robert G. D. Pottage III, Halifax County
John V. Quarstein, Virginia War Museum, Newport News
Bettie Byrd St. Clair, Tazewell County
Douglas W. Sanford, Mary Washington College
Pamela Simpson, Washington and Lee University
John H. Verrill, Eastern Shore of Virginia Historical Society
R. Dulaney Ward, Jr., City of Petersburg
Edwin Watson, Fredericksburg Area Museum
Camille Wells, University of Virginia School of Architecture
Betsy White, Washington County
Gary Williams, Sussex County
Sandra Williams, Wise County
Richard Guy Wilson, University of Virginia School of Architecture
Gibson Worsham, Montgomery County
John G. Zehmer, Jr., Historic Richmond Foundation

Thanks are also due to Howell W. Perkins of the Virginia Museum of Fine Arts for his diligence in making available many handsome photographs from the museum's archives; to Shawn Kneher for his computer skills in formatting and editing the original scanned manuscript; to Stephanie Brown for invaluable assistance in assembling the manuscript and illustrations in final form; to Melanie Kielb for special assistance in proofreading; to Sara Beth Bearss who undertook the prodigious task of preparing the index; and to Emily J. Salmon and John S. Salmon for the final proofreading of the manuscript.

The editor further extends his profound thanks to the over six hundred persons who are owners, custodians, stewards, or trustees or are in other ways associated with individual landmarks who kindly and promptly reviewed entries for specific properties. These people, regrettably too numerous to list, offered invaluable assistance by providing updated information, correcting errors of fact, improving wording, catching typographical errors, or reassuring the editor that the entry was otherwise acceptable. Many were especially generous in providing additional material, new research, and new illustrations, all of which will be deposited in the department's archives. Sundry landmark owners were also most cooperative in permitting the editor and other department staff members access to their properties to obtain updated photographs for this work.

The editor acknowledges also the numerous professional consultants who over the years have been engaged by property owners to prepare register reports. Their professional expertise has served to sustain the high standards of the register program and has increased our knowledge and appreciation of Virginia's many historic resources.

Lastly, the editor wishes to express his gratitude for the many intangible contributions made by John Melville Jennings and the late Mary Douthat Higgins to the Virginia Department of Historic Resources and its work from the very beginning. Their knowledge and love of Virginia have been invaluable assets to the register program.

THE VIRGINIA
LANDMARKS REGISTER

ACCOMACK COUNTY

Named for the Indian tribe that occupied the Eastern Shore at the time of settlement, the present county of Accomack was formed from Northampton County about 1663. The county seat is Accomac.

ACCOMAC HISTORIC DISTRICT. This Eastern Shore community has been a judicial center for over three centuries. The settlement, originally called Matompkin, grew up around John Cole's tavern where court was first held in the 1670s. It became the county seat by 1690. The town was laid out adjacent to the court square in 1786 and was known as Drummond or Drummondtown because it was on land that had been owned by Richard Drummond. Renamed Accomac in 1893, the town has evolved gently; its quiet, tree-shaded streets preserve numerous 18th- and 19th-century regional building types, both high-style and vernacular. Outstanding Federal houses include the Seymour house and the brick St. James' rectory. Other noteworthy structures are Seven Gables, The Haven, and the Francis Makemie Presbyterian Church (shown). The colonial courthouse was replaced in 1899 by the present sober Victorian structure designed by Bartholomew F. Smith. The district contains approximately 150 buildings. *(160–20) VLR: 12/16/80; NRHP: 07/21/82.*

ARBUCKLE PLACE, *Assawoman.* Originally called Assawoman, this venerable dwelling was renamed in the 20th century for Edward Arbuckle who acquired the property in 1797. The house may incorporate portions of a ca. 1723 one-room settlement house owned by Comfort Taylor Ewell, but most or all of the existing fabric appears to have been put up in 1774 by Alexander Stockley II for his son Joseph. The dwelling is the sole early remnant of the once-thriving port of Assawoman. With its steep gable roof and brick ends, Arbuckle Place is a classic example of the region's colonial vernacular architecture. The date 1774, the Stockleys' initials, and the mason's initials are inscribed on the east chimney. The interior has a hall-parlor plan and features finely detailed paneling that relates directly to a school of locally made furniture. During the Revolutionary War the local militia mustered in the yard here. *(01–66) VLR: 12/17/85; NRHP: 05/22/86.*

ASSATEAGUE COAST GUARD STATION, *Assateague Island.* Welcome facilities for both seamen and holiday makers, U.S. Coast Guard stations operated as lifesaving posts. The standard station incorporated living quarters for the lifesaving crews, a lookout tower, a boathouse—usually capable of handling two or more boats—and launchways for the speedy dispatch of crews to those in distress. Established in 1922, the Assateague station was one of a chain of such facilities along the Atlantic coast, most of which were replaced after World War II by more efficient rescue systems. Decommissioned in 1967, the station has since been transferred by the Coast Guard to the National Park Service. This interesting relic of nautical history is now part of the Assateague Island National Seashore and is currently used for seasonal housing. *(01–172) VLR: 02/20/73.*

BOWMAN'S FOLLY, *Accomac vicinity.* This stately Federal mansion was built for John Cropper, Jr., entrepreneur, Revolutionary War general, and politician. Cropper sited his home on an artificial mound on Folly Creek so that it would have a good vantage across the wide stretches of water and seaside marshes. Replacing an earlier structure, the house was completed ca. 1815 on a tract held by Cropper's wife's family since 1664. With its tall, brick-ended main section and trailing service wings built in the typical Eastern Shore style of big house, little house, colonnade, and kitchen, the complex exhibits the combination of architectural sophistication and rural domesticity characteristic of early Eastern Shore gentry seats. Distinctive touches on the little-altered house include the Palladian windows and the carvings of stars and shells under the eaves. Two of its outbuildings, a wooden dovecote and a wainscoted privy, are unusual in their fine detail. *(01–02) VLR: 05/13/69; NRHP: 11/12/69.*

ASSATEAGUE LIGHTHOUSE, *Assateague Island.* Few buildings more appropriately merit the term *landmark* than lighthouses. These singular structures stand as conspicuous and necessary focal points along the nation's coasts. Festively banded in red and white, the Assateague Lighthouse has operated as a nautical guide for the south end of Assateague Island since it was first lighted on October 1, 1867, replacing an earlier but inadequate tower built in 1831. Standing 129 feet from base to light, the lighthouse is built of brick with tapered walls. A modern automatic system has replaced its original light mechanism, a Fresnel lens imported from France, which is now on display at the Oyster and Maritime Museum in the town of Chincoteague. The lighthouse is maintained by the U.S. Coast Guard. *(01–78) VLR: 04/17/73; NRHP: 06/04/73.*

CORBIN HALL, *Horntown vicinity.* Commanding a sweeping view across Chincoteague Bay atop terraced grounds, this plantation house is perhaps the most academic example of Georgian architecture on Virginia's Eastern Shore. Its Flemish bond brick walls are accented by rubbed-brick belt courses, gauged-brick lintels, and two Palladian windows. Inside is a wealth of original woodwork, including a fully paneled parlor and a Georgian stair. The dominant interior feature is a tall stair-hall arch framed by fluted pilasters set on pedestals. The house was built for George Corbin on land purchased by his father in 1745. The construction date of 1787 is assumed from two inscribed bricks. Corbin Hall's proximity to the Maryland border and its similarity to contemporary Maryland Eastern Shore architecture suggest that the house may have been constructed by Maryland craftsmen. *(01–07) VLR: 04/18/72; NRHP: 11/09/72.*

DEBTORS' PRISON, *Accomac.* This landmark in the Accomack County courthouse complex is the county's oldest public building and a relic of the archaic custom of incarcerating debtors. The austere little structure was built in 1783 as a jailer's residence and was converted to a debtors' prison in 1824, when iron bars and heavy oak batten doors were added. It served as a debtors' prison until 1849. It was built in the southeast corner of the jail yard with the north wall of the building forming one section of the yard's wall. The jail and the wall were demolished by the county in 1909, and custody of the debtors' prison was given to the Drummondtown Branch of the Association for the Preservation of Virginia Antiquities. The building has since undergone renovation and now serves as a local history museum. *(160–09) VLR: 06/15/76; NRHP: 11/07/76.*

HOPKINS & BRO. STORE, *Onancock.* This bracketed and weatherboarded Victorian building on the Onancock waterfront housed a business founded in 1842 by Capt. Stephen Hopkins. Selling general goods, the business remained in the hands of the Hopkins family until 1965. Although the building has been moved a short distance, it retains the relation to the waterfront it enjoyed when the store was a commercial and maritime trading center for the town as well as the Eastern Shore's bayside. The interior has most of its 19th-century fittings and illustrates the maritime mercantilism of a small Chesapeake region town. Detailed records of the establishment are preserved in the Virginia Historical Society. The Hopkins family deeded the property to the Association for the Preservation of Virginia Antiquities, and it is currently used as a restaurant. *(273–02) VLR: 05/13/69; NRHP: 11/12/69.*

THE HERMITAGE, *Craddockville vicinity.* Although built on an unpretentious scale, The Hermitage has the architectural quality characteristic of the Eastern Shore's larger residences. With its chevroned-brick gables, dormer windows, symmetrical facade, and balanced proportions, the house is an excellent example of Virginia's early gentry architecture, exhibiting both quaintness and formality. It is also among the best-preserved houses of its type in the area, retaining a richly decorated parlor chimneypiece and a Georgian stair with molded handrail and turned balusters. The Hermitage was constructed in two stages between 1769 and 1787 by Emmanuel Bayly, a member of a prominent Eastern Shore family. Bayly conducted a notably successful farming operation here, raising corn, oats, flax, cattle, sheep, and hogs. The house preserves its rural setting. *(01–21) VLR: 11/18/80; NRHP: 06/28/82.*

KERR PLACE, *Onancock.* Onancock's patrician mansion is regarded as the consummate representative of the Eastern Shore's legacy of fine-quality Federal architecture. Gracefully proportioned and highlighted by a pedimented entrance pavilion, the house was begun in 1799 for John Shepherd Ker (later Kerr), an enterprising merchant, banker, and shipping magnate. Construction of the house was completed before his death in 1806. The spacious entrance hall has a finely executed stair. The three principal rooms are embellished with classical-style composition ornaments in the manner of those manufactured by Robert Wellford of Philadelphia. In 1960 the Eastern Shore of Virginia Historical Society acquired the house and two acres. Kerr Place is now the society's headquarters and a museum of the cultural heritage of this distinctive area of the state. The gardens were restored by the Garden Club of Virginia in 1981. *(273–03) VLR: 12/02/69; NRHP: 02/26/70.*

MASON HOUSE, *Guilford vicinity.* A compact colonial manor house, the Mason house is an important and rare example of the transition from the Jacobean style to the Georgian as revealed in Virginia vernacular architecture. The treatment of the front and rear walls as paneled bays is a unique survival. Although later painted over, those panels without openings are set off by a diaper pattern in glazed-header bricks. These are among the state's few remaining examples of colonial-period diaper work. The history of the house has not been precisely documented, but it probably was built after 1722 when the property was acquired by William Andrews. A striking interior feature is the Jacobean-style closed-string stair with symmetrical turned balusters and pulvinated stringer frieze. The house long stood abandoned and deteriorating but was repaired and stabilized in the early 1990s and awaits further restoration. *(01–29) VLR: 09/17/74; NRHP: 11/21/74.*

OLD MERCANTILE BUILDING, *Accomac.* A landmark in the center of Accomac's historic district, this rare example of Federal commercial architecture was erected as a store in 1816 by the brothers Richard and John Bayly. In 1819 they sold the building to Michael Higgins and Alexander Mc-Collom who operated a mercantile business for a number of years under the name of Higgins and McCollom. Stucco was added to the facade in 1899 when the building was converted to a bank, a use it kept until 1963. The Eastern Shore of Virginia Chamber of Commerce purchased the building in 1972 and restored it for its headquarters. It now houses private offices. Despite its changes of function, the building has suffered few significant alterations. Architectural refinements include the modillion cornices, a lunette gable window, and stuccoed lintels. *(160–13) VLR: 05/21/74; NRHP: 07/23/74.*

ONANCOCK HISTORIC DISTRICT. Snugly situated on Onancock Creek, four miles inland from the Chesapeake Bay, Onancock was founded in 1680 and was Accomack's first county seat. It has remained an active port for Virginia's Eastern Shore since the late 17th century. The town was laid out in an irregular grid of fifty acres. Gradually expanded, it now has a population of about 1,700 and retains a slow-paced, small-town ambience. The historic district contains a rich variety of architectural styles spanning some 200 years. The buildings range from waterfront vernacular structures to the high-style Federal mansion Kerr Place. Five 19th-century frame churches lining Market Street proclaim the long-standing importance of worship here. The commercial area is characterized by a medley of mercantile buildings, most of which date after a 1900 fire. Roomy frame houses with front porches are spread along the residential streets. *(273–01) VLR: 04/22/92; NRHP: 10/08/92.*

PITTS NECK, *New Church vicinity.* The Pitts Neck dwelling house, probably built before 1756 for Robert Pitt IV, is one of the Eastern Shore's more prominent mid-18th-century plantation residences. An interesting feature of the formal five-bay facade is the scrolled soffit of the molded-brick doorway, a motif common on Georgian buildings in England but exceptionally rare in America. The doorway and other brickwork details combine with the interior paneling and an earlier wing with a T-shaped chimney to make the house a document of colonial building motifs. Now somewhat isolated, the plantation was once the scene of much activity. In the 18th century the Pitt family operated a tobacco warehouse at the plantation's Pocomoke River landing, which remained a regular stop for Chesapeake Bay steamers as late as 1924. *(01–38) VLR 02/17/76; NRHP 10/21/76.*

ST. GEORGE'S EPISCOPAL CHURCH, *Pungoteague.* Known as Pungoteague Church until 1800 when its name was changed to St. George's to conform to its parish name, this much-changed building is the only colonial church remaining in Accomack County. According to the vestry book, Severn Guttridge built the church in 1763. It originally had a Latin-cross plan with a hipped gambrel roof and a rounded apse which resulted in the early nickname "Ace of Clubs Church." Abandoned in 1812 but later restored, the building was so mutilated by Union troops during the Civil War that only the north and south walls—the ends of the transepts—could be salvaged in 1880 when it was rehabilitated. The south wall, now the present facade, survives as a masterful example of glazed-header Flemish bond brickwork. *(01–40) VLR: 06/02/70; NRHP: 09/15/70.*

ST. JAMES' EPISCOPAL CHURCH, *Accomac.* An architectural highlight of the town of Accomac, St. James' Church was built between 1838 and 1843 with bricks salvaged from the colonial St. James' Chapel, which stood two miles south of town. With its Greek Doric portico and entablature with continuous guttae, the church is an interesting regionalized interpretation of the Greek Revival style. Of primary interest are the rare trompe l'oeil painted decorations on the interior walls and ceiling. The apsidal arch, with its false-perspective vaulting, and the other painted embellishments combine to make a skillful image that indeed work to "fool the eye." The creator of this ambitious undertaking was Jean G. Potts, an itinerant artist who later became the keeper of the Cape Charles Lighthouse. Another noteworthy interior feature is a divided stair leading to the rear gallery. The church bell was cast in Spain in 1816. *(160–05) VLR: 11/05/68; NRHP: 06/11/69.*

SCARBOROUGH HOUSE ARCHAEOLOGICAL SITE, *Davis Wharf vicinity.* On Scarborough Gut, now a silted cove of Occohannock Creek, this colonial archaeological site is believed to be the location of Occohannock House, the seat of Edmund Scarborough. Scarborough was Speaker of the Virginia House of Burgesses at the assembly of 1645–46 and the Eastern Shore's largest 17th-century landholder. Subsurface features and heavy artifact density indicate that the site remains essentially intact. Shown is a fragment of Rhenish stoneware salvaged by Department of Historic Resources archaeologists during test digs to determine the site's extent and integrity. More extensive excavation and research should yield new information about 17th- and 18th-century Eastern Shore cultural patterns that could provide valuable information about other areas in eastern Virginia where official records have been destroyed. *(01–64) VLR: 01/18/83; NRHP: 05/16/85.*

SHEPHERD'S PLAIN, *Pungoteague vicinity.* Completed in the third quarter of the 18th century, the Shepherd's Plain dwelling is a two-story Georgian mansion built for Edward Ker, an Accomack County planter and politician. Its architectural interest is heightened by the rare rusticated quoins employed on the brick ends and in the gables. The Gibbs-type rusticated surround on an end window is Virginia's only example of this motif in brick. Also noteworthy is the large quantity of original interior woodwork, especially the parlor paneling with its chimneypiece framed by pilasters set on pedestals. A stately Georgian stair dominates the hall. These architectural details demonstrate the proficiency of Eastern Shore craftsmen in executing sophisticated designs based on illustrations in 18th-century English pattern books. The handsome architectural character has been brought out through a long-term restoration by its present owners. *(01–32) VLR: 10/21/80; NRHP: 06/28/82.*

WESSELS ROOT CELLAR, *Hallwood vicinity.* This simple brick structure is possibly a unique example of a decorated outbuilding built solely to serve as a root cellar. It is believed to have been constructed sometime after 1768 when William Wessels acquired the property and erected a house for himself. Wessels's home burned in 1937, but his root cellar survived and continues to serve its original function. Most colonial root cellars were contained within the foundations of other buildings; this example is unusual for being freestanding and for having its gable decorated with a pattern of glazed-header bricks. *(01–76) VLR: 12/02/69; NRHP: 02/26/70.*

WHARTON PLACE, *Mappsville vicinity.* John Wharton, a maritime merchant and native of Accomack County, had this Federal mansion constructed shortly after he purchased the property in 1798. Wharton made his new home the headquarters of his various business interests and maintained a landing for his ships on Assawoman Creek, within sight of the house. With its graceful exterior proportions, lavish use of marble trimmings, and rich interior plasterwork and woodwork, Wharton Place is one of Virginia's outstanding examples of the Federal style, appearing somewhat uncomfortably urbane in its isolated rural setting. Of special note are its mantels trimmed with applied classical-style composition ornaments signed by Robert Wellford of Philadelphia. Wellford supplied ornaments for fine houses throughout the eastern seaboard, basing his designs on contemporary English examples. *(01–50) VLR: 04/18/72; NRHP: 11/03/72.*

ALBEMARLE COUNTY

This Piedmont county was named for William Anne Keppel, second earl of Albemarle and governor of the Virginia colony from 1737 to 1754. It was formed from Goochland County in 1744, with part of Louisa County added later. The county seat is Charlottesville.

ARROWHEAD, *Red Hill vicinity.* A rambling old homestead, Arrowhead began as a country Greek Revival residence built in 1851 for Henry Carter Moore, a local farmer. The house was expanded in 1857 and again in the early 1900s soon after the Rev. Edgar Woods acquired the property. Woods, a descendant of one of the county's first settlers, founded Pantops Academy in Charlottesville and wrote what is still one of Virginia's most respected local county histories, *Albemarle County in Virginia* (1901). His son, Samuel Baker Woods, to whom Arrowhead was transferred in 1892, was an attorney and orchardist. He served as Charlottesville's first 20th-century mayor and was first president of the Virginia Horticultural Society. Preserved on the property is an important collection of early outbuildings. The kitchen outbuilding may date from the 1820s when Dr. Charles E. and Frances E. Meriwether owned the property. *(02–195) VLR: 04/17/91; NRHP: 07/09/91.*

ASH LAWN—HIGHLAND, *Simeon vicinity.* James Monroe, U.S. senator, governor of Virginia, minister to France, England, and Spain, secretary of state, and fifth president of the United States, purchased this farm, originally named Highland, in 1793. Monroe's friend and mentor Thomas Jefferson selected the house site, within view of Jefferson's Monticello. Monroe completed the simple farmhouse, the western portion of the present building, in 1799. Calling the house his "castle cabin," he added to it over the next twenty years. The Monroe family left Highland in 1823; it was sold in 1826. Part of the east portion burned around 1840, and Parson John E. Massey built a two-story addition on its site in 1882. Opened as a museum by philanthropist Jay Winston Johns, the property is now owned by the College of William and Mary and commemorates Monroe's Albemarle County residency. *(02–99) VLR: 01/16/73; NRHP: 08/14/73.*

BELLAIR, *Carters Bridge.* A classic expression of the restrained Georgian style favored by many of Virginia's gentry, Bellair was built sometime between 1794 and 1817 for the Rev. Charles Wingfield, Jr., a landowner, public official, and Presbyterian pastor. Wingfield sold Bellair in 1822 to Martin Dawson, a businessman and merchant who promoted the development of the Rivanna Navigation Company. Dawson willed much of his estate to the University of Virginia and the State Literary Fund. The Rev. Walker Timberlake, a Methodist minister who also was involved in various business endeavors, purchased the farm in 1843. In the 1930s architect Marshall Wells, a designer of Georgian Revival residences in the Charlottesville area, renovated and expanded the house. Sensitive to the building's historic importance, Wells retained much of the original interior trim. Architect Floyd Johnson made further additions in the 1960s. *(02–02) VLR: 12/11/91; NRHP: 10/15/92.*

BLENHEIM, *Blenheim vicinity.* Blenheim's low, stretched-out Gothic Revival dwelling house, built ca. 1846, was the seat of Andrew Stevenson, who served as Speaker of the House of Representatives, ambassador to Great Britain, and rector of the University of Virginia. With its numerous outbuildings, including a colonnaded "book house," or library and what was perhaps a chapel, Blenheim is a striking if somewhat naive expression of Romantic Revivalism in central Virginia. The book house is one of the state's few detached plantation libraries. The property was originally part of a 9,350-acre land grant of 1730 to John Carter, secretary of the colony and son of Robert ("King") Carter. John Carter's son, Edward Carter, built a large H-shaped house here before 1799 which has disappeared; but its site, just to the north of the present house, is potentially of archaeological significance. *(02–05) VLR: 12/16/75; NRHP: 05/17/76.*

BLUE RIDGE FARM, *Greenwood vicinity.* The central portion of this grand country house was built ca. 1870 for William B. Smith on a farm owned in the 18th century by the Epperson family. Between 1923 and 1927 Mr. and Mrs. Randolph Ortman retained the well-known architect William Lawrence Bottomley to make additions and refinements. Bottomley skillfully transformed the dwelling into a masterpiece of the Georgian Revival style. Several of his trademark features here are the high-quality brickwork and woodwork, the open staircase, and a progression from light to dark interior spaces. Especially noteworthy is the elegant detailing of the Georgian-style trim in the principal rooms. Richmond landscape architect Charles F. Gillette was responsible for the parklike grounds and English-style gardens that take advantage of sweeping views of the countryside. The combination of Bottomley's and Gillette's talents resulted in one of Virginia's most beautiful country estates. *(02–498) VLR: 02/20/90; NRHP: 01/25/91.*

BUCK MOUNTAIN CHURCH, *Earlysville vicinity.* Although it has been moved, this simple house of worship, untouched by stylistic devices or symbolic trappings, is a rare surviving example of the wooden Anglican parish churches scattered through Virginia during the colonial period. Placed in the foothills of the Blue Ridge Mountains to serve Fredericksville Parish, the church was begun in 1747, five years after the parish was formed. Abandoned after the disestablishment, the building was used for Baptist services from 1801 until it was reacquired by a rejuvenated Episcopal congregation in 1833. In 1859 the church was moved two miles east of the original location. It once was thought that the length was reduced during the relocation, but the present building retains the approximate dimensions specified by the parish vestry in 1745. Most of the framing along with some early beaded weatherboards and interior trim were reused. *(02–145) VLR: 08/15/72.*

CARRSBROOK, *Carrsbrook subdivision, Charlottesville vicinity.* Carrsbrook is a provincial adaptation of the Palladian-style five-part house. It was built in the 1780s for Capt. Thomas Carr, a wealthy planter and soldier and the half brother of Dabney Carr, Thomas Jefferson's brother-in-law and close friend. In 1794 Thomas Carr sold Carrsbrook to Wilson Cary Nicholas who in 1798 allowed the property to be occupied by Peter Carr, Dabney Carr's son and Jefferson's ward and nephew. Peter Carr lived here until his death in 1815. Because of Jefferson's connections with the Carrs and his fondness for Palladian forms, it is thought that he influenced the design. Its proportions, however, veer too far from classical standards for Jefferson to have exercised a direct hand in the final product. The house is interesting from the standpoint of 18th-century building technology for retaining virtually all of its original fabric. *(02–11) VLR: 07/21/81; NRHP: 07/08/82; BHR EASEMENT.*

CASA MARIA, *Greenwood vicinity.* The extensive gardens at Casa Maria were designed by Charles F. Gillette, one of Virginia's most talented and productive landscape architects of the first half of the 20th century. The gardens, some of the most ambitious and best-maintained of his many projects, are notable for their stone walls, boxwood allées, azaleas, and numerous specimen trees. They were commissioned in 1919 by Mary Williams, sister of Susan Bueck Massie, who owned the adjacent Rose Hill, which also has Gillette gardens. Tradition has it that Gillette also designed the Mediterranean-style house, built 1920–22, which, if true, would make it his only architectural work. Mrs. Williams died in 1920, and the house and gardens were completed by Mrs. Massie's daughter, Ella Williams Smith, and her husband, Gordon Smith. William Lawrence Bottomley designed an addition to the house in 1928. The original exterior pink color was restored during a 1991–92 renovation. *(02–829) VLR: 04/17/90; NRHP: 12/28/90.*

CASTLE HILL, *Cismont vicinity.* The earliest portion of this two-part house is a traditional colonial frame dwelling, built in 1764 by Dr. Thomas Walker, an early explorer of the West. Here in 1781 Walker's wife delayed the British colonel Banastre Tarleton to give the patriot Jack Jouett enough time to warn Thomas Jefferson and the Virginia legislators of Tarleton's plan to capture them. The stately brick portion, an example of Jeffersonian classicism by master builder John M. Perry, was erected in 1823–24 for William Cabell Rives, minister to France, U.S. senator, and Confederate congressman. Columned conservatories were added in 1844 by William B. Phillips. Rives's granddaughter Amélie, wife of the Russian painter Prince Pierre Troubetzkoy, was a novelist and playwright. She and her husband made Castle Hill their home in the early decades of the 20th century. The house is set off by its extensive gardens and landscaped grounds. *(02–12) VLR: 11/16/71; NRHP: 02/23/72.*

THE CEDARS, *Greenwood vicinity.* Maintaining a strong presence along the scenic U.S. Highway 250, The Cedars exhibits an interesting blending of the Greek Revival style with the local Jeffersonian classicism. The entablature, window trim, and interior woodwork employ Greek profiles; however, the oversize gleaming white trim against red brick and the use

of Chinese railings harken back to Jeffersonian works. The house was built in the 1850s for Col. John S. Cocke, a relative of John Hartwell Cocke of Bremo. It has had a long and colorful history, serving variously as a residence, a boys' school, a Civil War hospital, and possibly a tavern. In 1902 the house was purchased by Chiswell Dabney Langhorne of nearby Mirador, who used the basement for gaming rooms; for many years the house was known as the "casino." Complementing the house is an adjacent galleried kitchen–servants' quarter. *(02–86) VLR: 04/18/89; NRHP: 12/27/90.*

CHRIST EPISCOPAL CHURCH, GLENDOWER, *Keene vicinity.* The influence of Thomas Jefferson's interpretation of classical architecture is demonstrated in numerous Piedmont buildings erected by master carpenters and masons he had employed at the University of Virginia. No more engaging example of the Jeffersonian idiom survives than this small but sophisticated country church erected in 1831–32 in southern Albemarle County. Called by Bishop William Meade a "neat and excellent brick church," the building is the work of William B. Phillips, a Jeffersonian workman who designed and built a variety of houses and public buildings in his mentor's mode. A hallmark of Phillips's buildings is his near-flawless Flemish bond brickwork, especially conspicuous at Christ Church. Phillips's mastery of the classical vocabulary is evident in the academically correct Doric entablature and in the temple-form proportions of the building itself. The church continues to serve St. Anne's Parish. *(02–14) VLR: 03/02/71; NRHP: 07/02/71.*

CLIFFSIDE, *Scottsville vicinity.* Cliffside, sited on a steep hill overlooking the town of Scottsville, is a boldly detailed expression of Piedmont Virginia Federal architecture. Profiting from Scottsville's rise to prosperity in the antebellum period as a canal and turnpike town, Gilly M. Lewis, a local doctor and millowner, built Cliffside as his residence in 1835. The unusually well preserved house is distinguished by its large scale, ambitious but somewhat provincial exterior detailing, and robust interior woodwork. As with many of the region's early 19th-century houses, the crisply white classical trim is set off by red brick walls. Cliffside served as Gen. Philip Sheridan's headquarters during the Union raid of Scottsville in March 1865 and also as the quarters of Gen. George A. Custer. *(02–16) VLR: 10/20/81; NRHP: 09/16/82.*

CLIFTON, *Shadwell vicinity.* Clifton was the home of Thomas Mann Randolph, Jr. (1768–1828), son-in-law of Thomas Jefferson, who served as governor of Virginia and as a congressman. The original portion of the rambling, much-evolved structure was built by Randolph in the first quarter of the 19th century to be the hub of the never-to-be port of North Milton. Randolph and several partners planned the town adjacent to the Milton Canal to support the agricultural and commercial development occurring in the area and to compete with the then prosperous but now extinct community of Milton across the Rivanna. Originally Randolph's warehouse, the house later became his residence. His office outbuilding remains on the grounds. The house was considerably expanded by later owners and now serves as a country inn. The present portico replaces a 19th-century one-story veranda. *(02–155) VLR: 06/21/88; NRHP: 11/02/89.*

COBHAM PARK, *Cobham vicinity.* Established in the 1850s, Cobham Park is preeminent among Virginia's antebellum estates. The grounds are laid out in the tradition of English romantic landscaping, with sloping lawns and clumps of trees informally arranged to make pleasing vistas. The property originally was the summer home of William Cabell Rives, Jr., second son of William Cabell Rives of Castle Hill. The house, built ca. 1855, shows unusually early Georgian Revival influences, having the character of an 18th-century mansion. It was executed by E. S. McSparren, an English master carpenter who also worked at Grace Church, Cismont. The cynosure of the interior is the flying spiral staircase, a carpentry tour de force. The estate was purchased in the early part of this century by the Peter family of Tudor Place, Washington, D.C., and served as the Peters' country home until the 1970s. *(02–153) VLR: 01/15/74; NRHP: 07/18/74.*

COCKE'S MILL AND MILLER'S HOUSE, *North Garden vicinity.* The ruins of Cocke's Mill and the associated miller's house are located against a steep wooded hill next to the splashing Hardware River. The original complex was established in the 1790s by James Powell Cocke of Edgemont. The date of the miller's house is uncertain, but it was probably built soon after the mill. The vernacular structure is one of only a handful of early millers' residences in the region and Albemarle County's only two-story stone miller's house. Cocke's Mill was known as Johnston's Mill after 1880 and remained in commercial operation into the 1930s. Subsequently neglected, the building apparently burned in the 1940s, leaving its stone foundations, dam, millrace, and cut-stone arches, all giving a hint of the mill's scale and fine construction. The miller's house is now a private residence. *(02–186) VLR: 08/15/89; NRHP: 12/06/90.*

CROSSROADS TAVERN, *Crossroads.* Crossroads Tavern was built sometime in the 1820s by the Morris family to serve travelers along the Staunton and James River Turnpike. An excellent representative of the simple vernacular hostelries that once dotted Virginia's roadways, the brick building preserves the long front porch that was a common feature of these buildings. A 19th-century English traveler in Virginia noted that the taverns "all resemble each other, having a porch in front, the length of the house." The tavern has survived virtually unaltered, providing a little-disturbed picture of early 19th-century travel-related architecture. Adding interest to the property is the survival of the daybook of C. C. Sutherland who served as the taverner in the 1850s. Behind the tavern is a two-level summer kitchen built into the slope of the hill. Recently restored, Crossroads Tavern is now a bed-and-breakfast inn. *(02–614) VLR: 05/15/84; NRHP: 08/16/84.*

COVE PRESBYTERIAN CHURCH, *Covesville.* The congregation of this rural Presbyterian church traces its origins to 1747 when Presbyterians arrived in the region. Its first church was a simple log structure which was replaced by a brick building in 1809. The brick church was severely damaged by a storm in 1880 which necessitated significant rebuilding. Many of the original bricks were used in the repairs to the walls, and a steep new roof was constructed. The resulting edifice is a picturesque example of late 19th-century rural Gothic Revival architecture essentially unaltered from the time of its completion. The interior preserves many of its original fittings and furnishings including interesting exposed roof trusses and a rear gallery—all that was left of an original three-sided gallery following the storm damage. The church continues to serve the Covesville-area Presbyterians. *(02–705) VLR: 04/18/89; NRHP: 11/02/89.*

D. S. TAVERN, *Ivy vicinity.* D. S. Tavern is one of Albemarle County's few remaining early ordinaries and the only one in the region to preserve its original bar cage. Tradition holds that the tavern marks the site of the D. S. Tree and the zero milepost of the Three-Notched Road, a principal artery from Richmond to the Shenandoah Valley in the 18th and 19th centuries. "D. S." is said to stand for David Stockton, who blazed the trail from Williamsburg and carved his initials on the tree. It could also stand for D. S. (Dissenters) Presbyterian Church, which stood in this area. The log section may have been constructed as a claims house. This one-room structure evolved with additions into an ordinary, functioning as such from the late 18th century until 1850. Chief Justice John Marshall held title to the property from 1810 to 1813. *(02–231) VLR: 08/16/83; NRHP: 09/29/83.*

EAST BELMONT, *Keswick vicinity.* The original portion of this historic dwelling is the frame rear wing erected around 1811 by John Rogers. Known as "Farmer John," Rogers, along with Thomas Jefferson, James Madison, James Monroe, and Robert McCormick (father of Cyrus Hall McCormick, inventor of the reaper), was a founding member of the Albemarle Agricultural Society and organized the county's first agricultural fair. The society was successful in extricating the Piedmont from its dependency on tobacco growing. At East Belmont, Rogers pioneered in soil conservation methods and establishing new crops. He also served Thomas Jefferson as overseer at Monticello. The brick portion of the house was built ca. 1834–35 by Rogers's son, John Rogers, Jr. The late Federal structure is set off by its fine brickwork and two-level portico. The brickwork is said to have been executed by Rogers's slave, Lewis Level, who also built several other houses in the vicinity. *(02–23) VLR: 10/18/95.*

EDGEHILL, *Shadwell vicinity.* In view of Monticello, Edgehill was the home of Thomas Jefferson Randolph, favorite grandson of Thomas Jefferson. The stately brick house was built for Randolph in 1828, his family having outgrown the 1799 frame house built for his father, Thomas Mann Randolph, Jr., husband of Jefferson's daughter Martha. The house was designed and built by the University of Virginia builders William B. Phillips and Malcolm F. Crawford, who continued the Jeffersonian style into the antebellum period. Specific Jeffersonian features are the Tuscan porch with Chinese lattice railing and the Tuscan entablatures. In 1829 Mrs. Thomas Jefferson Randolph opened a small school in the 1799 dwelling, which had been moved a short distance to make way for the present house. The school was continued by her daughters until 1896. The main house was gutted by fire in 1916 but was sympathetically rebuilt within the original walls. *(02–26) VLR: 06/15/82; NRHP: 09/09/82.*

EDGEMONT, *South Garden vicinity.* Edgemont was built ca. 1796 for Col. James Powell Cocke, a justice of Henrico County who moved to Albemarle County for its healthful climate as he suffered from malaria. Although the design is often credited to Thomas Jefferson, firm documentation for Jefferson as architect is yet to be established. Nonetheless, the Jeffersonian influence is strongly evident in the hybrid French and Palladian scheme he advocated for domestic architecture. The otherwise modest dwelling achieves sophistication through the use of careful siting, porticoed facade, and graceful proportions. The flanking dependencies are linked to the main house by tunnels similar to Monticello's arrangement. Edgemont stood almost forgotten for many years but was brought to light in 1936 by Charlottesville architect Milton L. Grigg, who directed its extensive restoration in 1938 for Dr. Graham Clark and later in 1946 for William Snead. The terraced gardens were restored in 1981. *(02–87) VLR: 09/16/80; NRHP: 11/28/80.*

EDNAM, *Ivy Road, Farmington vicinity.* Completed ca. 1905 for Edwin O. Meyer, a New York importer, Ednam is an assertive example of the turn-of-the-century Colonial Revival style, which made free use of a variety of classical forms for inventive compositions. The architect was D. Wiley Anderson, a native of Albemarle County who operated one of Richmond's most productive firms, specializing in impressive residences. With its stately portico, classical detailing, and elaborate interiors, the house presents a grandiose "Southern" image which was considered appropriate for its location. From the standpoint of social history, Ednam represents the influx of well-to-do northerners into Piedmont Virginia beginning in the late 19th century. Attracted by the scenic countryside and sociable lifestyle, they purchased old estates or established new ones, often building pretentious houses in what they regarded to be the local gentry idiom. *(02–560) VLR: 12/16/80; NRHP: 07/08/82.*

EMMANUEL EPISCOPAL CHURCH, *Greenwood vicinity.* Since its founding in the mid–19th century, Emmanuel Episcopal Church has served parishioners living on western Albemarle County estates, among them the Langhorne family at nearby Mirador. Nancy Langhorne, later Lady Astor, became involved with the congregation's mission work in the early 20th century. In 1911, along with her brothers and sisters, she commissioned the fashionable Washington architect and former Albemarle County resident Waddy B. Wood to remodel the original ca. 1863 Greek Revival country church into a very learned adaptation of Virginia's colonial ecclesiastical architecture. The project was essentially a complete rebuilding, and the outcome, especially the finely crafted interior fittings, is an exemplar of the refinement and craftsmanship associated with the best of the Colonial Revival style. Among those buried in the churchyard is Lady Astor's niece, Nancy Lancaster, noted interior designer. *(02–399) VLR: 01/20/81; NRHP: 07/08/82.*

ESMONT, *Esmont vicinity.* This Jeffersonian-style country house was built ca. 1816 for Dr. Charles Cocke, nephew of James Powell Cocke of Edgemont and cousin of John Hartwell Cocke of Bremo. Although Cocke corresponded with Jefferson, no documentation has surfaced to indicate that the statesman-architect had a hand in the design. It has, instead, been attributed to the Jeffersonian builder William B. Phillips. With its Doric entablatures and stuccoed columns, contrasting with red brick walls and green louvered blinds, the house illustrates the Jeffersonian interpretation of classicism. Except for the lengthening of the porch, Esmont stands essentially as built. Its interior preserves rich appointments, including a parquet hall floor, ornamental plaster ceilings, Philadelphia marble mantels, and silver-plated locks. *(02–30) VLR: 05/17/77; NRHP: 05/06/80.*

ESTOUTEVILLE, *Keene vicinity.* Chief among the architectural works designed and built by Thomas Jefferson's workmen is this grand country house, the creation of James Dinsmore, an Irish master builder who had worked for Jefferson at both Monticello and the University of Virginia. The unusually large dwelling, set off by a monumental Tuscan portico on each front, was begun in 1827 and completed in 1830 for John Coles III, member of a family responsible for several of the county's substantial houses. Working from ancient Roman precedent as interpreted in the books of Andrea Palladio, Dinsmore produced a masterpiece in what may be regarded as America's first native academic style. With its porticoed facades and lofty interiors, few buildings better meet Jefferson's ideal of an architecturally refined seat suitable for the young Republic's landed families or so well conform to the popular image of a patrician southern homestead. *(02–32) VLR: 04/19/77; NRHP: 01/30/78.*

FARMINGTON, *Farmington Country Club, Charlottesville vicinity.* Thomas Jefferson designed the elongated octagonal wing of this Albemarle County home for his friend George Divers. Dominated by a Tuscan portico and bull's-eye windows, the wing was completed in 1802 following Jefferson's drawings, preserved in the Massachusetts Historical Society. The original section, a typical late Georgian side-passage dwelling, probably was erected ca. 1785 after Divers purchased the property. In 1927 the house, along with its extensive service buildings and some 350 acres of farmland, was sold to Farmington, Inc., a development company that converted the property into a country club. The club remodeled the interior of the Jefferson section by removing partitions and floor levels installed in 1852–54 by Gen. Bernard Peyton, making the wing into a single grand reception room. Although the building has received extensive additions, the historic portion preserves much of its early flavor. *(02–35) VLR: 07/07/70; NRHP: 09/15/70.*

FAULKNER HOUSE, *2201 Old Ivy Road, Charlottesville.* This stately country house is noteworthy as an Albemarle County antebellum work with alterations by a designer well versed in the region's classical idiom. Erected in 1855–56, it was enlarged and remodeled in 1907 by Washington, D.C., architect Waddy B. Wood. The original center section was first the home of Addison Maupin, keeper of one of the four "hotels," or dining halls, at the University of Virginia in the 1850s. The most noted resident was U.S. Senator Thomas S. Martin, leader of Virginia's powerful Democratic party machine in the early 1900s. Purchased by the university in 1963, the building was given its current name to honor the Nobel Prize–winning novelist William C. Faulkner, who—though he never lived in this building—taught at the university in the 1950s and 1960s. Since 1975 the house has been the headquarters of the White Burkett Miller Center of Public Affairs. *(02–146) VLR: 03/20/84; NRHP: 05/03/84.*

GALLISON HALL, *24 Farmington Drive, Farmington County Club.* Designed by Lynchburg architect Stanhope Johnson, Gallison Hall is one of the state's important 20th-century country houses. Dramatically approached through ornamental iron gates, down a tree-lined drive, the many-sectioned mansion presents an idealized image of Virginia's colonial style. The original owners, Mr. and Mrs. Julio Suarez-Galban, spent many years touring Virginia's historic homes, noting their favorite features, and had Johnson incorporate these into the design. Specific references to Westover, Stratford Hall, Shirley, Gunston Hall, the Nelson house, and Gadsby's Tavern are thus found in various parts of the house. Conspicuous exterior elements are the clustered chimney stacks based on those at Bacon's Castle. The attention to detail is evident not only in the design but in the fine craftsmanship of the exterior masonry and interior woodwork. Virginia landscape architect Charles F. Gillette designed Gallison Hall's garden. *(02–808) VLR: 02/20/90; NRHP: 12/28/90.*

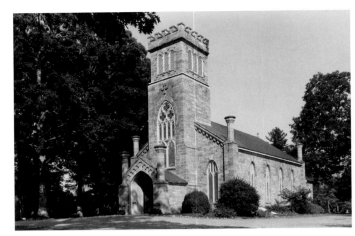

GRACE EPISCOPAL CHURCH, *Cismont.* This much-admired specimen of the earlier, more picturesque interpretation of the Gothic Revival is the only known Virginia work of William Strickland, a leading American architect of the first half of the 19th century. Strickland is better known for his monumental Greek Revival works such as the Tennessee Capitol; Grace Church, built ca. 1847, is a rare example of his Gothic style. The church was commissioned by Judith Walker Rives of nearby Castle Hill. Strickland's original drawings are preserved at the University of Virginia. The original interior woodwork, executed by E. S. McSparren, an English master carpenter, was destroyed by fire in 1895. The church was soon rehabilitated with a new roof, new interior, and chancel addition. Its walls and tower remain essentially as designed. *(02–43) VLR: 02/17/76; NRHP: 10/21/76.*

GUTHRIE HALL, *Esmont vicinity.* Guthrie Hall is perhaps Albemarle County's largest and most architecturally individual country mansion among those resulting from the influx of plutocrats into the area around the turn of the 20th century. With its porticoes, loggias, quadrant wings, and conspicuous wide arch framing the entrance, the massive house combines Georgian Revival, Palladian, and rustic influences. Its construction incorporates concrete floors and concrete walls whose exterior surfaces are embedded with quartz stone. Guthrie Hall was erected ca. 1901 for John Guthrie Hopkins, a Scottish-born, self-made copper magnate who came to Virginia to pursue his hobby of restoring old houses. The house was designed by Frederick Hill, an architect with the firm of McKim, Mead, and White; the engineer was Fred Kennedy. In addition to the finely appointed interiors of the main house, the estate boasted a bowling alley as well as a private railroad station. *(02–355) VLR: 03/17/81; NRHP: 09/23/82.*

HIGH MEADOWS, *Scottsville vicinity.* A mix of local vernacular forms, High Meadows has long been an architectural reference point on the former Staunton and James River Turnpike, just north of Scottsville. The earlier brick section of the two-part dwelling was constructed in 1831–32 by Peter White, who surveyed Scottsville and was also a farmer. White's 1853 taxes also list him as the owner of seven slaves and a piano. Around 1883 Charles B. Harris, a Scottsville merchant, added a two-story brick section with Italianate cornice and cross-gable roof. The two sections are joined by an unusual longitudinal passage rather than the more traditional hyphen. The older section preserves original paint, and the newer section has original grained woodwork. The house was restored in 1985 for use as a country inn. *(02–1020) VLR: 04/15/86; NRHP: 05/30/86.*

MALVERN, *Taylor's Gap vicinity.* The detailing, refined proportions, and finely crafted brickwork combine to make Malvern one of the area's most polished works of the Federal style. Lending it individuality is the side-passage plan with a formal three-bay facade on the gabled south end, which originally had an entrance. The main cornice is treated with a series of pendants, a detail likely inspired by an illustration in Asher Benjamin's *Country Builder's Assistant* (1797). The highlight of the interior is a delicate Federal stair with its unsupported upper flight. The house was built ca. 1800 by Mehan Mills, son-in-law of Jack Jouett. Mills owned Malvern until 1811; from 1812 to 1891 it was the property of the White family. A later owner was Benjamin Wheeler, a mayor of Charlottesville, who lived here from 1902 to 1910. Architectural historian Clay Lancaster directed the 1968 restoration of Malvern. *(02–92) VLR: 04/28/95; NRHP: 08/04/95.*

LONGWOOD, *Earlysville vicinity.* Longwood is situated on part of a 1,250-acre land patent obtained in 1735 by John Henry, father of Patrick Henry. The builder and construction date of the original section are both uncertain, but it may have been built by John Michie as early as 1765. Longwood's first recorded owner is John Michie's grandson, James Michie, Jr. (1791–1846), known as "Beau Jim," who is buried here. With its two-story, single-pile format and simple interior woodwork, the house is a representative example of the area's mid-level gentry housing. Wings were added in the early 19th century. The west wing housed a store and post office operated by James Michie, Jr. In 1940 Longwood was purchased by Gen. and Mrs. Philip Peyton who modernized the house. On the grounds is the former Longwood School, a small frame building built ca. 1900 as a schoolhouse for black children. *(02–380); VLR: 06/19/96; NRHP: 10/18/96.*

MICHIE TAVERN, *Route 53, Charlottesville vicinity.* Michie Tavern is an 18th-century hostelry originally located on Buck Mountain Road in the northern part of Albemarle County. The structure was disassembled and rebuilt at its present site near Monticello in 1927–28 by Mrs. Mark Henderson to serve as a museum for her collection of antique furniture, taking advantage of visitor traffic to Monticello. This effort marked an early manifestation not only of American antiquarianism but of Virginia's tourism industry, an important aspect of the Virginia economy developed in the 1920s and spurred by increased leisure time and the proliferation of automobiles. In 1932 the tavern was purchased by Milton L. Grigg, a noted restoration architect, who used it as his office. For the past several decades the tavern and various buildings since moved to or built on the property have served as a museum and restaurant complex. *(02–93) VLR: 02/17/93.*

MIDWAY, *Millington vicinity.* Nestled in the hills of western Albemarle County with the Blue Ridge Mountains as backdrop, this beautifully placed old manor house is a historic feature of the countryside for which the county is noted. The two-part dwelling's two-level gallery, stepped parapets, and superb Flemish bond brickwork are all distinguishing features. The facade brickwork preserves its red paint and penciled, or white-painted, joints. The interior retains most of its original woodwork. Although the property was part of a large grant to the Rodes family and was occupied by them in the colonial period, the various sections of the house appear to date from around 1800 or later. Hemp and flax, in addition to the usual crops, were grown here by the Rodeses. Midway's formal garden was laid out in 1936 by Richmond landscape architect Charles F. Gillette; the garden was restored in 1993. *(02–143) VLR: 09/19/78; NRHP: 02/31/79; BHR EASEMENT.*

MIRADOR, *Greenwood vicinity.* Completed by 1842 for James M. Bowen, Mirador was the childhood home of Lady Astor, the first woman member of Parliament. Born Nancy Witcher Langhorne, she moved to Mirador with her family in 1892 at the age of twelve and lived here intermittently until she moved to England upon her marriage to Waldorf Astor in 1906. Throughout her long, eventful life, Lady Astor maintained pride in her Virginia origins and returned to Mirador for frequent visits. Mirador is also identified with Lady Astor's sister Irene, wife of illustrator Charles Dana Gibson and prototype of his fashionable "Gibson Girl" of the 1890s. The mansion today is largely the product of an extensive 1920s remodeling undertaken for Lady Astor's niece Nancy Perkins Tree (later Nancy Lancaster), an internationally recognized interior designer. Architect William Adams Delano transformed the Federal plantation dwelling into a grandly appointed country house. *(02–100) VLR: 09/16/82; NRHP: 04/07/83.*

MILLER SCHOOL OF ALBEMARLE, *Batesville vicinity.* Miller School's complex of High Victorian Gothic buildings was provided through the will of Samuel Miller (1792–1869) to serve the children of Albemarle's poor. Miller, a county native, was born into poverty and made a fortune in the tobacco and grocery business in Lynchburg. The school, developed on one of Miller's farms, pioneered in industrial education, emphasizing both manual labor and classic liberal education. The institution's architectural focal point, Old Main, was begun in 1874. Architects Albert Lybrock and D. Wiley Anderson of Richmond created a grand statement in the weighty, richly ornamented Gothic style popularized by the English critic John Ruskin. It and the Arts Building and superintendent's house were erected under the supervision of C. E. Vawter, the school's first superintendent. Still a functioning educational facility, Miller School continues to stress craft education and academics. *(02–174) VLR: 04/17/73; NRHP: 02/15/74.*

MONTICELLO, *Route 53, Charlottesville vicinity.* Reflecting the genius and versatility of its creator, Thomas Jefferson's Monticello is a monument to a scrupulous interest in architecture, landscaping, agriculture, and domestic comforts. The remarkable house, one of America's most famous, is filled with ingenious devices and mementos of this revered founding father. Jefferson began his dwelling on the "Little Mountain" after leveling the top in 1768. He worked on it for over forty years, altering and enlarging it as his taste developed, calling it "my essay in architecture." Before 1795 the house had a Palladian-influenced tripartite form with two-level porticoes. When an extensive revision was finished in 1809, it had become a twenty-one-room amalgam of Roman, Palladian, and French architectural ideals, a unique statement by one of history's great individuals. The Thomas Jefferson Memorial Foundation has maintained Monticello as a place of pilgrimage for millions since 1923. *(02–50) VLR: 09/09/69; NRHP: 10/15/66; NHL: 12/19/60; WORLD HERITAGE LIST.*

MONTICOLA, *Howardsville vicinity.* With its hillside site above the village of Howardsville, overlooking the James River valley, Monticola preserves a romantic image of antebellum gentility. The Greek Revival mansion, its glowing white portico, cornices, and corner pilasters set off by red brick walls, was built in 1853 for Daniel James Hartsook, an entrepreneurial merchant, banker, and planter, who made a fortune in Howardsville when the community prospered from its situation along the James River and Kanawha Canal. Union troops raided Howardsville in 1865 and destroyed many of Hartsook's businesses. Monticola was also raided but not damaged. Hartsook subsequently moved to Richmond where he rebuilt his fortune. In 1887 the estate was purchased by Richmond tobacconist and diplomat Emil Otto Nolting, who modified the portico and added the north semicircular porch. The interior, which has generally plain Greek Revival woodwork in its high-ceilinged rooms, has been little changed. *(02–51) VLR: 04/18/89; NRHP: 06/22/90.*

MORVEN, *Simeon vicinity.* Morven was originally part of a large grant made to William Champe Carter in colonial times. William Short, who served as Thomas Jefferson's secretary in France and later as minister to the Netherlands, purchased Morven in 1796. Short's modest frame house is now the farm office. The main residence was built in 1821 by Martin Thacker for the planter David Higginbotham, also a friend of Jefferson. Jefferson had drafted a plan with three octagonal bays for Higginbotham the year before, but it was not used. The ideal image of a patrician Virginia homestead, the five-bay structure, fronted by a dwarf Tuscan portico, combines late Georgian with Roman Revival overtones. In 1926 Morven was purchased by Mr. and Mrs. Charles A. Stone, who established a noted thoroughbred stud farm here. Morven's much-admired formal garden was restored under the direction of Annette Hoyt Flanders in 1930. *(02–54) VLR: 02/20/73; NRHP: 04/24/73.*

MOUNT FAIR, *Brown's Cove vicinity.* Situated to command broad vistas of the panoramic landscape of Brown's Cove, Mount Fair's dwelling is a handsome specimen of builders' Greek Revival adapted for a Virginia gentry residence. The little-altered weatherboarded house was built ca. 1848 employing trim and details based on illustrations in Asher Benjamin's *Practical House Carpenter* (1830). A distinguishing feature is the balustraded lantern admitting daylight to the attic stairwell. The house originally served an 800-acre estate belonging to William T. Brown who built the present structure on the site of his father's house, which burned in 1846. Brown owned some thirty slaves and raised a variety of livestock and crops at Mount Fair. In 1930 Mount Fair became the home of Edmund S. Campbell, first dean of the University of Virginia School of Architecture. *(02–97) VLR: 08/21/90; NRHP: 12/28/90; BHR-MANAGED EASEMENT.*

MOUNT IDA, *Scottsville vicinity.* One of Virginia's most intriguing late Georgian plantation houses, Mount Ida was built ca. 1795 for William Cannon, a captain in the Buckingham County militia. Its original plan was unusual, consisting of a side passage and a large parlor, with flanking one-story wings. The parlor's ambitious Georgian trim is some of the state's most richly detailed architectural woodwork. The pedimented mantelpiece and crosseted overpanel are unique in Virginia. A two-story section replacing the east wing was added in the mid–19th century, giving the facade a generalized symmetry. The present low hipped roof uniting the two sections dates from this enlargement. In 1996–97 the house was carefully dismantled and moved from its original site in Buckingham County to a similar rural site in southern Albemarle County where it was painstakingly reconstructed, reusing virtually all of its early fabric. *(02–5001) VLR: 10/14/86; NRHP: 04/27/87.*

MOUNTAIN GROVE, *Esmont vicinity.* Mountain Grove shares with a number of other Piedmont dwellings a tripartite Palladian scheme, an architectural format derived from 18th-century English pattern books. Situated in the scenic Green Mountain area, the house was built in 1803–4 for Benjamin Harris, an Albemarle County soldier and magistrate. Although its proportions and detailing are somewhat provincial, the house is reminiscent of Jefferson's earliest designs for Monticello and reflects the sophistication of its builder in abandoning the usual Georgian rectangular plan for a more architectonic scheme. Of special interest is Mountain Grove's untouched interior, which includes paneled wainscoting, carved mantels, and two sets of stairs with turned balusters. The woodwork is important for preserving its early painted folk decoration consisting of graining on the wainscoting and an overmantel painted with marbleizing, tassels, swags, and stippling. *(02–95) VLR: 05/20/80; NRHP: 09/08/80.*

PIEDMONT FARM, *Greenwood vicinity.* In the shadow of the Blue Ridge, Piedmont Farm was originally the property of Michael Woods who sold it to his son-in-law, William Wallace, a Scotch-Irish immigrant who arrived in this county in 1734. Active in the county's early political and economic life, Wallace also was instrumental in bringing the first Presbyterian minister, the Rev. Sam Black, to the region. Wallace family tradition holds that the earliest portion of the two-part house was built for Wallace in the second half of the 18th century. The later portion, a typical example of the county's antebellum vernacular, was built about 1832 and employs penciled Flemish bond brickwork, molded-brick cornices, and two exceptional Greek Revival mantels. Nearby are a log smokehouse, log slave kitchen (later a laundry), and the ruins of the chimney and hearth of a former kitchen. *(02–114) VLR: 12/11/90; NRHP: 02/01/91.*

PINE KNOT, *Glendower vicinity.* Pine Knot was the country retreat of Theodore and Edith Roosevelt and their children from May 1905 to May 1908, while he was president of the United States. The property, which consisted of fifteen wooded acres and a simple, then unfinished, two-story dwelling, was purchased by Mrs. Roosevelt from William N. Wilmer, a family friend and owner of nearby Plain Dealing. After making changes to the interior, Mrs. Roosevelt added one or perhaps both stone chimneys and the "piazza" with untrimmed cedar posts supporting the roof. At this rustic sanctuary the president enjoyed the pleasures of nature: hiking, hunting, riding, birdwatching, and viewing the distant Blue Ridge foothills. On one visit the family was joined by the naturalist John Burroughs. Now owned by the Theodore Roosevelt Association, Pine Knot is being prepared for limited public visitation. *(02–617) VLR: 04/19/88; NRHP: 02/01/89; BHR EASEMENT.*

PLAIN DEALING, *Keene vicinity.* Few of Albemarle County's historic estates can match Plain Dealing in architectural interest and pastoral beauty. The earliest section of the H-shaped house was built ca. 1761 for John Biswell. The main portion was erected in 1789 for Samuel Dyer, a merchant and planter. Dyer named the estate after a motto affixed to his store located nearby. The parlor woodwork, with its arched closets, pedimented chimneypiece, and stop-fluted pilasters, is among the most elaborate examples of provincial late Georgian trim in the region. The Wilmer family, who owned Plain Dealing from 1855 to the mid-1930s, entertained such visitors as Robert E. Lee and Theodore Roosevelt here. From 1944 to 1952 Plain Dealing was the home of Princess Djordjadze (born Audrey Emery), who was previously married to Grand Duke Dmitri of Russia, one of the assassins of the monk Rasputin. *(02–65) VLR: 05/17/77; NRHP: 05/06/80.*

THE RECTORY, *Keene vicinity.* One of several historic properties situated in the countryside near Keene, The Rectory was built soon after 1848 when the land was acquired by St. Anne's Parish to serve as the rectory of nearby Christ Episcopal Church. In keeping with the moderation expected in clerical lifestyle, the house is a plain two-story wooden structure in builders' Greek Revival style. Pleasantly set within spacious, old-fashioned grounds at the junction of two county roads, the house stands on the site of a country store and wagon stop known as Dyer's Store, built before 1787. The store's foundation forms part of The Rectory's cellar. The Rectory remained the property of St. Anne's Parish until sold in 1917. Now a private residence, the house has since been expanded. *(02–1831) VLR: 08/21/91; NRHP: 11/07/91.*

REDLANDS, *Carters Bridge vicinity.* The original Redlands estate of 9,350 acres was granted in 1730 to John Carter, son of Robert ("King") Carter. The mansion was begun ca. 1792 for Robert Carter on a site chosen for its views. Erected by builder Martin Thacker, Redlands is one of the Commonwealth's most important Federal-period landmarks. Its stately but restrained exterior contrasts with a rich interior. The lofty oval-ended drawing room and adjacent rooms are embellished with carved detailing based on designs in pattern books by the English architect William Pain. The trim is similar to work in several other Piedmont houses and probably was executed by Lynchburg artisans. In the early 20th century the Carter family engaged Baltimore architect Howard Sill to make improvements that included replacing missing dormers, adding the front porch, and installing Pain-style mantels on the second floor. *(02–67) VLR: 09/09/69; NRHP: 11/12/69.*

SCOTTSVILLE HISTORIC DISTRICT. Scottsville began in 1732 when Edward Scott, a Goochland burgess, patented 550 acres just west of the future town. The community prospered, reaching its apogee in the early 19th century with the opening of the James River and Kanawha Canal. Scottsville soon became an important flour market. Its decline began in 1865 when Union general Philip Sheridan's troops pillaged the place, wrecking the canal and destroying commercial buildings. Scottsville never really recovered, and its stymied growth preserved its historic character. Some one hundred old buildings remain, almost half dating before the Civil War, including Classical Revival churches and a broad range of vernacular houses. The former Scottsville Christian Church (shown) was built in 1846 and now houses the Scottsville Museum. The small house next door was the home of Dr. James Turner Barclay, the church's first minister. *(298–24) VLR: 04/20/76; NRHP: 07/30/76.*

SEVEN OAKS FARM, *Greenwood vicinity.* Seven Oaks Farm is one of the numerous historic estates along U.S. Route 250 in the Greenwood neighborhood. The main residence, a frame Greek Revival dwelling, was built ca. 1847–48 for Dr. John Bolling Garrett. The monumental Ionic portico was added in 1906. An interesting landmark at Seven Oaks is a double-pen log house, built ca. 1769 for Samuel Black, who kept a tavern here whose patrons included George Rogers Clark, Meriwether Lewis, and William Clark. Also on the property are numerous early outbuildings including an 18th-century smokehouse, a hexagonal icehouse, a dairy, a greenhouse, barns, and a carriage house. In this century the property was briefly owned by relatives of the Langhorne family of nearby Mirador. Their famous Langhorne kinswoman, Lady Astor, stayed at Seven Oaks during her Virginia visits to her sister-in-law Mrs. Graham Harris. *(02–71) VLR: 06/20/89; NRHP: 12/26/89.*

SHACK MOUNTAIN, *Charlottesville vicinity.* Its name derived from the Shackelford family, Shack Mountain is regarded as the most distinctive architectural work of Sidney Fiske Kimball (1881–1955), the leading figure of America's first generation of architectural historians. This gemlike Jeffersonian-style house was built in 1935–36 as Kimball's retirement home. Kimball is credited with nurturing a scholarly interest in American buildings and promoting Thomas Jefferson as a major figure in the nation's architectural development. He was also the founder of the University of Virginia School of Architecture and a pioneer in the restoration of historic landmarks, taking an active role in Colonial Williamsburg, Monticello, Stratford, Gunston Hall, and numerous National Park Service properties. As an art historian he gained fame as director of the Philadelphia Museum of Art. Kimball wanted Shack Mountain, with its Jeffersonian format, to demonstrate the viability of a regional architectural tradition. *(02–200) VLR: 06/15/76; NRHP: 09/01/76; NHL: 10/05/92; BHR EASEMENT.*

SOUTHWEST MOUNTAINS RURAL HISTORIC DISTRICT. Extending from the Orange County line to the outskirts of Charlottesville, with the Southwest Mountains forming its spine, this 31,000-acre district includes some of the Piedmont's most pristine and scenic countryside. Characterized by undulating pastures, winding roadways, forested hills, and small hamlets, the district contains a broad range of 18th-, 19th-, and early 20th-century rural architecture, reflecting the evolving cultural patterns of more than 250 years of settlement. Although known primarily for historic estates with fine dwellings such as Castle Hill, Cobham Park, and Cloverfields, many of the district's structures are the products of a continuous vernacular building tradition. Several Afro-American settlements also lie in the area. Scattered throughout the district is a remarkable range of farm buildings including early barns, granaries, corncribs, stables, and sheds. A strong sense of community pride has enabled preservation of the district's pastoral character. *(02–1832) VLR: 08/21/91; NRHP: 02/27/92.*

SPRING HILL, *Ivy vicinity.* Illustrating a distinct regional personality, this Federal-period farm complex is a blending of various Albemarle County vernacular building traditions. The brick portion was built in the late 18th century. The house evolved to its present irregular form through alterations and expansions beginning in the early 19th century with a two-story frame addition. The hilltop property includes a ca. 1765 brick homestead later expanded to serve as quarters for farmhands. Also on the grounds are a dairy and a kitchen. Spring Hill's owners have included Michael Woods, an early settler who lived here from 1737 to 1748; Clifton Rodes, a county magistrate and brother-in-law of Jack Jouett; Thomas Wells, a trustee appointed in 1814 (with Thomas Jefferson) to oversee the founding of the Albemarle Academy; and Charles Harper, cofounder of Charlottesville's first circulating library. Spring Hill was also the childhood home of architect Waddy B. Wood (1869–1944). *(02–140) VLR: 04/19/83; NRHP: 11/12/83.*

SUNNY BANK, *South Garden vicinity.* Nestled in the hilly countryside of southern Albemarle County, Sunny Bank's residence was begun ca. 1797 as an imposing if somewhat provincial version of the Palladian tripartite scheme introduced to the region with the first version of Monticello. Its original outline was obscured in the early 19th century when the wings were raised to two stories. The original two-level portico emphasizes the provincial character by having supports that appear more as turned posts than academically proportioned columns. Most of the original interior woodwork remains, including a narrow winding stair with turned balusters. On the property are several original outbuildings and an early geometric garden with boxwood-bordered beds. The first occupant of Sunny Bank was Andrew Hart, son of a Scottish clergyman, who became an Albemarle County planter and merchant. Many generations of Harts have lived here since. *(02–96) VLR: 04/20/76; NRHP: 12/12/76.*

SUNNYFIELDS, *Simeon.* At the base of Monticello Mountain, Sunnyfields was originally a 522-acre plantation established in the 1830s by William B. Phillips, a prominent Virginia-born master mason. The house was presumably designed and built by Phillips for his own residence. In 1818 Phillips was selected by Thomas Jefferson to serve as a principal builder for the University of Virginia, the largest state building project of its time. Phillips was the brickmason for the Rotunda, the Anatomical Theater, Pavilion X, Hotel C, many of the dormitories, and the serpentine garden walls. After completing his work at the university, Phillips continued his career by building several county courthouses, including those of Madison (1830), Page (1833), Greene (1838), and possibly Caroline (ca. 1830). These buildings, including Sunnyfields, incorporate the fine brickwork and academically correct classical detailing for which Phillips is known. On the grounds is a long servants' quarter and the remains of a large terraced garden. *(02–480) VLR: 04/21/93; NRHP: 06/10/93.*

WILLIAM WALKER HOUSE, *Warren.* The stylistic influence of Thomas Jefferson is evident in this diminutive (32 by 34 feet) dwelling built in 1803 for William Walker, a merchant in the canal village of Warren. The house exhibits the subtle and sophisticated simplicity that characterizes Jefferson's smaller works such as the dependencies at Monticello, which, like the Walker house, are one story above a high basement and fronted by a simple pedimented portico. The main floor has 12-foot ceilings and employs a center hall with flanking rooms. The salon, extending the width of the north end, was originally partitioned into two rooms. The house was constructed by William Walker's brother James who worked for Jefferson both as a millwright and carpenter. The early lines of the house were long hidden by a large front porch added in the 1870s which was removed in a 1970s restoration. *(02–197) VLR: 02/20/90; NRHP: 12/28/90.*

WAVERTREE HALL FARM (BELLEVUE FARM), *Batesville vicinity.* The architecture of this country house spans nearly 150 years and reflects several different periods of ownership. The 1859 core is a well-preserved mix of Greek Revival and early Italianate forms. Dominating the composition is a pedimented portico with paired columns. Brick wings with elaborate Adam-style mantels were added around 1913 by Quincy Adams Shaw II, former brother-in-law of Lady Astor. The rear wing and most of the agricultural and service buildings date from the ownership of Col. Herman Danforth Newcomb, a native of Kentucky. Beginning in 1921, he transformed the property, which he renamed Wavertree Hall Farm, into one of the county's best-known equestrian estates. Newcomb added most of the landscaping as well. An oddity of the garden is a ca. 1913 underground stone room built into one of the garden terraces and likely intended for entertainment. *(02–847) VLR: 04/17/91; NRHP: 07/09/91.*

WOODLANDS, *Hydraulic vicinity.* The original portion of this grand old manor house was built in 1842–43 for Richard Woods Wingfield, a local planter. Patrick Martin was its carpenter, and James H. Ward was the brickmason. The house was expanded in the 1890s with a large rear wing with two-level galleries. Included on the property is a rare unaltered antebellum frame barn. Woodlands is best known for its association with John Richard Wingfield, an Albemarle County native who as a Virginia state senator played a significant role in breaking the power of the Readjuster party in 1883. He also served as consul to Costa Rica from 1886 to 1889. The property remains the seat of the Wingfield family. Except for the addition of the mid-20th-century portico, little change has occurred to dilute the old-fashioned ambience of Woodlands. *(02–621) VLR: 04/18/89; NRHP: 11/02/89; BHR EASEMENT.*

WOODSTOCK HALL TAVERN, *Ivy vicinity.* One of Albemarle County's oldest structures, Woodstock Hall Tavern achieved its present appearance in 1808, a half century after the construction of the original two-room-plan dwelling. Converted to a tavern by 1783, the building is associated with the Woods family who settled in the area in the mid–18th century. The property was acquired by Richard Woods ca. 1771, and two generations of the family occupied it over nearly eighty years. Its operation as a tavern was recorded in the 1796 travel journal of the duc de La Rochefoucauld-Liancourt. The original 1757 section has retained a considerable amount of its original fabric. As one of the county's few 18th-century buildings preserving a high degree of architectural integrity, Woodstock Hall Tavern provides valuable information on traditional building practices. The building was renovated as a country inn in 1985 and became a private residence in 1995. *(02–147) VLR: 02/18/86; NRHP: 01/29/87.*

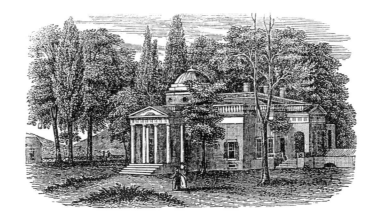

CITY OF ALEXANDRIA

Named for John Alexander, an early owner of the tract on which the town was located, this Potomac River port was established in 1749. It was incorporated as a city in 1852. From 1801 until 1846, when it was returned to Virginia, Alexandria was part of the District of Columbia.

**ALEXANDRIA CANAL TIDE LOCK ARCHAEOLOGI-
CAL SITE,** *on the Potomac River at Montgomery Street.* The seven-mile-long Alexandria Canal system linking Alexandria to Georgetown was begun in 1834 and completed in 1843. The canal's tide lock no. 4 and adjacent holding basin, the only remaining portions of the city's canal system, are relics of Virginia's industrial and transportation history, being part of a waterway that helped to bring on the economic regeneration of Alexandria in the mid–19th century. The canal, which continued in operation until 1886, connected Alexandria with the Chesapeake and Ohio Canal running inland to Cumberland, Maryland. It was used largely for transporting coal. The lock and basin had long been filled in but were restored in recent years as a point of interest in the city's waterfront park development. *(100–99) VLR: 11/20/79; NRHP: 01/15/80.*

ALEXANDRIA CITY HALL, *300 block of Cameron Street.* Perhaps the state's boldest example of the Second Empire style, the dark brick Alexandria City Hall was designed in 1871 by Washington architect Adolph Cluss. The elongated composition is dominated by its central pavilion with a massive square dome, a scheme that recalls the Louvre in Paris. The building occupies the site of the 1817 city hall designed by Benjamin Henry Latrobe that burned in 1871. Cluss incorporated into his design a clock tower based on the one that had graced Latrobe's work. The building originally had town offices on the upper floors and market stalls in arcades below. The stalls have been removed, and the building now functions exclusively as city offices. The interior has undergone numerous remodelings, but the Cameron Street facade remains without significant alteration. A Colonial Revival addition, filling the U-shaped courtyard, was added in the early 1960s. *(100–126) VLR: 11/15/83; NRHP: 03/08/84.*

ALEXANDRIA HISTORIC DISTRICT (OLD TOWN ALEXANDRIA). Alexandria was established in 1749 with its streets laid out in a uniform grid plan. It quickly became the principal seaport of northern Virginia, witnessing the construction of numerous mansions, town houses, churches, and commercial buildings. Surviving in the district's nearly one hundred blocks is the largest concentration of 18th- and 19th-century urban architecture in the state, constituting one of the finest historic cityscapes in the nation. Especially important are the district's many Federal town houses, including the grand row of 18th-century dwellings in the 200 block of Prince Street. A typical example of the rich variety and cohesive character of the street facades is the 300 block of Cameron Street (shown). The preservation of the district has been achieved through a variety of efforts, both public and private, begun over fifty years ago. *(100–121) VLR: 11/05/68; NHL: 11/13/66.*

BANK OF ALEXANDRIA, *North Fairfax and Cameron streets.* The largest early 19th-century bank building in the state, the Bank of Alexandria was built in 1803–7 and symbolized the importance of Alexandria as a commercial center. The bank company was established in 1792 with George Washington among its charter stockholders. After the bank failed in 1834, the building was used as a post office from 1845 to 1848, then as a hotel wing, later as a Union hospital, and finally as an apartment house. Despite changes in function, the building has survived with a surprising amount of original fabric. The exterior is embellished with finely carved stone detailing including an arched entry, window lintels, and an intricate cornice. The first floor retains Adam-style window casings, doors, and mantels. The building was restored in the late 1970s, returning it to use as a bank with apartments occupying the cashier's quarters on the upper floors. *(100–04) VLR: 04/17/73; NRHP: 06/04/73.*

ALEXANDRIA NATIONAL CEMETERY, *1450 Wilkes Street.* The Civil War dead of both sides often were buried hastily on battlefields after the action died down or in city, church, or private cemeteries. Later, while Confederate memorial societies retrieved remains for reinterment in special cemeteries or in sections of existing burial grounds, the United States established national military cemeteries as the final resting places for the Federal soldiers. Alexandria National Cemetery, because of its proximity to the defenses of Washington, D.C., was created during the war, in 1862. Buried here are U.S. soldiers who died in the Washington fortifications, or fell in such northern Virginia battles as Thoroughfare Gap, or were wounded in other engagements and died in area hospitals. The cemetery contains 4,066 marked graves (not including postwar burials). An 1887 Second Empire–style superintendent's lodge marks the entrance. *(100–138) VLR: 10/19/94; NRHP: 03/02/95.*

BAYNE-FOWLE HOUSE, *811 Prince Street.* A sumptuous example of a wealthy merchant's town house of the mid–19th century, the Bayne-Fowle house was built in 1854 for William Bayne, a commission merchant and grocer. It is one of the few buildings in Old Town Alexandria with a stone facade, although the brown sandstone has been painted for many years. Of particular interest is the richly appointed suite of reception rooms comprising one of the

grandest mid-Victorian interiors in the state. The rooms retain their 1870s gasoliers, early pier mirrors, and window cornices. The parlors are separated by a pendant arcade, the only example of this architectural device in the state. The house was occupied by Union troops during the Civil War, and in 1864 the Federal government confiscated the property for a military hospital. Original graffiti from the occupation remains on the attic walls. *(100–06) VLR: 06/17/86; NRHP: 11/06/86; BHR EASEMENT.*

CARLYLE HOUSE, *121 North Fairfax Street.* Alexandria's celebrated colonial mansion was completed in 1753 as the home of John Carlyle, a Scottish merchant who was a founding trustee of the city. Influenced by the compact early Georgian manor houses of Scotland, the Carlyle house is built of stone and employs a somewhat austere classicism. In April 1775 in Carlyle's handsome paneled parlor, Gen. Edward Braddock met with the governors of five colonies to plan the early campaigns against the French and the Indians. Though located in the heart of the city, the house was long hidden by a hotel built across its front. Demolition of the hotel and restoration of the house as a museum were undertaken as a Bicentennial project by the Northern Virginia Regional Park Authority. *(100–10) VLR: 05/13/69; NRHP: 11/12/69.*

FAIRFAX-MOORE HOUSE, *207 Prince Street.* This aristocratic dwelling is a classic example of an 18th-century Georgian side-passage town house. With its three stories and rear ell, it exemplifies the type of residence enjoyed by the city's most affluent citizens. Constructed on a lot originally owned by George William Fairfax, the house is part of the city's finest block of dwellings. The building date is uncertain; the front portion may have built by Capt. John Harper in the 1780s. From 1919 until her death in 1988, Alexandria historian and preservationist Gay Montague Moore made her home here. Mrs. Moore's rescue of the deteriorated house signaled the beginning of the preservation movement in the city. Her attention to this and many of the other historic and architectural resources of Alexandria contributed to the surrounding historic district's being named a National Historic Landmark in 1966. *(100–22) VLR: 04/17/90; NRHP: 01/17/91; BHR EASEMENT.*

CHRIST CHURCH, *North Columbus and Cameron streets.* Surrounded by its quaint old churchyard, Christ Church is a premier historic landmark in the heart of Alexandria. It was built in 1767–73 from plans by James Wren, one of colonial Virginia's few identified architects. Begun by James Parsons, "undertaker" of the construction, and completed by Col. John Carlyle, the Georgian building employs a rectangular format with two tiers of windows. Its Aquia Creek sandstone Palladian window and rusticated doorways are based on designs published by English architect Batty Langley. Inside are the original wineglass pulpit and altarpiece built against the Palladian window. The gallery was installed in 1785; the steeple was added in 1799. George Washington frequently attended services at Christ Church, and Robert E. Lee worshiped here in 1861, just before journeying to Richmond to accept command of the Army of Northern Virginia. *(100–12) VLR: 09/18/73; NRHP: 04/15/69; NHL: 04/15/70.*

GERALD R. FORD, JR., HOUSE, *514 Crown View Drive.* Gerald R. Ford, Jr., and his family lived in this typical suburban house from 1955 until August 19, 1974, ten days after he took the oath of office as president of the United States. During this period Ford represented the Michigan fifth district in Congress and served as House minority leader and later as vice president. Though the Fords maintained a Michigan residence, the Alexandria dwelling was their primary home. The house was designed for Ford by Viktors Purins of Grand Rapids. Some of the first photographs of Ford as president, calmly talking with reporters in front of his Alexandria residence, gave the nation a needed reassuring image in the wake of the Watergate scandal. The Fords sold the house upon leaving the White House. The president wrote its new owner: "Betty, the children, and I had many wonderful years in that home." *(100–165) VLR: 03/19/97; NHL 12/17/85.*

FORT WARD, *4301 West Braddock Road.* A formidable work of earthen military architecture, Fort Ward formed one of the strongest links in a chain of sixty-eight forts and batteries erected between 1861 and 1865 by the U.S. Army Corps of Engineers for the protection of the nation's capital. Guarding the approaches to Alexandria from the west and northwest on an elevated site four miles west of the city, the star-shaped earthwork was the fifth-largest fort in the system, with a perimeter of 818 yards, holding thirty-six gun emplacements and as many as 1,200 troops. During the Civil War Centennial, the city of Alexandria restored the northwest bastion and cleared both the perimeter and the outlying gun battery and rifle trench. Fort Ward today serves as a forty-five-acre historic park and museum. *(100–113) VLR: 12/15/81; NRHP: 08/26/82.*

GADSBY'S TAVERN, *Royal and Cameron streets.* In its heyday this tavern hosted some of the most noted figures of the early Republic, including George Washington, John Adams, Thomas Jefferson, James Madison, James Monroe, and Lafayette. The large three-story section, the ultimate in elegance and comfort for its time, was built by John Wise in 1792. The earlier two-story dormered section, a finely detailed example of the Georgian style, was built as an ordinary ca. 1770. John Gadsby operated the establishment from 1796 until 1808, during which period it achieved its greatest renown. Although the ballroom woodwork is now in the Metropolitan Museum of Art, the rest of the two-building complex survives little changed. Restored in the 1970s, the property is now owned by the city and is operated as a museum and restaurant. *(100–29) VLR: 09/09/69; NRHP: 10/15/66; NHL: 11/04/63.*

FRANKLIN AND ARMFIELD OFFICE, *1315 Duke Street.* From this three-story structure, one of the largest slave trades in the South was operated. The Franklin and Armfield partnership was established in 1828 and continued until 1836. At its peak the firm had agents in almost every southern city, owned a fleet of ships, and trafficked in thousands of slaves annually. The building was erected ca. 1812 as a residence for Robert Young, a brigadier general in the District of Columbia militia. While it was occupied by Franklin and Armfield, slave pens were built in the yard. The building served the slave trade until the Civil War when it was converted to a Union prison. The slave pens were removed to build new houses in the 1870s after the property was acquired by Thomas Swann, who added the mansard roof. Now renovated for offices, the building displays little hint of its notorious past. *(100–105) VLR: 10/16/79; NHL: 06/02/78.*

JONES POINT LIGHTHOUSE AND DISTRICT OF COLUMBIA SOUTH CORNERSTONE, *Jones Point Park.* The cottagelike Jones Point Lighthouse was an expression of federal concern for the improvement of inland navigation in the first half of the 19th century. Built in 1855, the plain weatherboarded structure with its light straddling its gable roof aided Potomac River shipping for seventy years. Next to the lighthouse is the south cornerstone of the District of Columbia originally laid in 1791 and replaced in 1794. The stone marks the beginning point of the 1791 survey that carved the District of Columbia from the states of Virginia and Maryland and originally included the city of Alexandria. The Virginia portions of the district were returned to the Commonwealth in 1846. The restored lighthouse is now a feature of the Jones Point Park. *(100–116) VLR: 03/18/80; NRHP: 05/19/80.*

ROBERT E. LEE BOYHOOD HOME, *607 Oronoco Street.*
A handsomely articulated example of Federal architecture, the Lee boyhood home was built in 1795 for John Potts, Jr., the first secretary of the Potomac Company. Its early 19th-century owners include William Fitzhugh, who served in the first Continental Congress. In 1811 Gen. Light-Horse Harry Lee, father of Robert E. Lee, moved his family here, and they resided here until 1816. In 1820 his widow, Ann Carter Lee, and their children again occupied No. 607. It was here that Robert E. Lee prepared for his entrance to the U.S. Military Academy. After Appomattox, Lee is said to have returned to Oronoco Street and climbed the wall to see "if the snowballs were in bloom." The little-altered building is now a museum operated by the Lee-Jackson Foundation. It is distinguished by its fine brickwork and restrained Federal woodwork. *(100–82) VLR: 12/17/85; NRHP: 06/05/86.*

LEE-FENDALL HOUSE, *614 Oronoco Street.* This extensive frame town house was erected in 1785 as the residence of Philip Richard Fendall on property purchased from Henry ("Light-Horse Harry") Lee, Fendall's stepson-in-law. Fendall was a director of the Potomac Company and a founder of the Bank of Alexandria. He married three times; all three of his wives were members of the Lee family. The house is the earliest of several neighboring Alexandria dwellings associated with the Lee family. It was remodeled in the Greek Revival style between 1850 and 1852, following its purchase by Louis A. Cazenove. Labor leader John L. Lewis, long the influential head of the United Mine Workers, made his home here from 1937 until his death in 1969. Administered by the Virginia Trust for Historic Preservation, the property is now a museum honoring the Lee family members. *(100–24) VLR: 04/17/79; NRHP: 06/22/79.*

LLOYD HOUSE, *220 North Washington Street.* Its regular proportions, Flemish bond brickwork, and refined detailing make this Washington Street house one of Alexandria's most admired and sophisticated statements of late Georgian architecture. Its formal five-bay facade is accented by an elegant pedimented doorway with traceried lunette, a feature reserved for the city's finest dwellings. John Wise, a local businessman, built the house ca. 1797 and sold it in 1810 to Jacob Hoffman, one of the city's mayors. Local educator Benjamin Hallowell operated a school in the house from 1826 to 1828. In 1832 it was sold to John Lloyd, whose family owned it until 1918. The house was twice saved by the Historic Alexandria Foundation from threatened demolition. In 1968 it was acquired by the city for preservation and has since been restored for use by the Alexandria Library as a repository for special historical collections. *(100–90) VLR: 02/17/76; NRHP: 07/12/76.*

THE LYCEUM, *201 South Washington Street.* The Lyceum was organized by Benjamin Hallowell as a scholarly society for the citizens of Alexandria. This group joined with the Alexandria Library Company and erected their headquarters in 1839, at one of the city's principal intersections. Alluding to the scholarship of the ancient Greeks, the building employs the Greek Revival style, its facade dominated by a Doric portico. Inside were a lecture hall, museum, and library. Attracting such speakers as John Quincy Adams and Caleb Cushing, the Lyceum was a flourishing institution until the Civil War. It was dissolved after the war, and the building became a residence. Threatened with demolition in 1969, it was purchased by the city and restored in 1974 for a visitors' center and museum. To echo the building's former role, a large lecture hall was constructed in the location of the original. *(100–91) VLR: 05/13/69; NRHP: 05/27/69.*

OLD DOMINION BANK BUILDING (THE ATHENAEUM), *201 Prince Street.* The Old Dominion Bank was incorporated in 1851 to serve various businesses connected with Alexandria's port. The bank's temple-form headquarters, conveniently located among the homes of the city's leading merchants, was completed in 1852 by B. H. Jenkins, carpenter, and Emanuel Francis, bricklayer. From 1870 until 1905 it housed the Citizens National Bank. Converted to a warehouse and later a church, the building has been restored as an exhibition gallery for the Northern Virginia Fine Arts Association and renamed the Athenaeum. The compact structure is a superlative application of the Greek Revival style to a small commercial building. During a recent renovation it was discovered that the smooth Doric columns were originally fluted, and they were so restored. *(100–02) VLR: 11/20/79; NRHP: 03/20/80.*

ROSEMONT HISTORIC DISTRICT. Situated in northwest Alexandria, in the shadow of the George Washington National Masonic Memorial, Rosemont is a lushly planted residential area occupying some eighty-four acres. It was developed between 1908 and 1914 by a group of Washington, Alexandria, and Philadelphia investors. The houses were built near the trolley line, allowing residents to work in Washington and live in a suburban neighborhood, a pattern repeated across the nation. While Rosemont's more than 450 houses represent the work of many architects and builders, as a group they achieve a remarkable level of cohesiveness in scale and materials and form a textbook of the era's middle-class architecture. House styles range from the picturesque coziness of Arts and Crafts and Craftsman to the staid dignity of the Colonial Revival. The street plan reflects suburban planning ideals of the early 1900s City Beautiful movement. *(100–137) VLR: 12/11/91; NRHP: 09/24/92.*

ST. PAUL'S EPISCOPAL CHURCH, *228 South Pitt Street.* Built in 1817, St. Paul's is the only surviving Gothic Revival building associated with Benjamin Henry Latrobe, America's first professional architect, and is Latrobe's only remaining work in Virginia. The extent of Latrobe's involvement is debated, but he did provide a design for the facade after construction of the church was under way. Although Latrobe was unhappy with alterations to his design made during construction, the church is a pioneering landmark of American Gothic Revival and was hailed on its completion as "an honorable monument to the taste and liberality of the congregation." Here was founded the Virginia Theological Seminary as well as the Alexandria Hospital. St. Paul's Sunday school was the first in the nation to contribute to a foreign mission. The church also has been the venue for the consecration of three Episcopal bishops and continues to serve an active parish. *(100–104) VLR: 04/16/85; NRHP: 05/09/85.*

STABLER-LEADBEATER APOTHECARY MUSEUM, *105–107 South Fairfax Street.* In 1792 Edward Stabler, a Quaker pharmacist, started a family apothecary business which operated continuously until it closed in 1933. In 1796 the business moved permanently to 107 South Fairfax Street, a building erected between 1774 and 1785. Among its customers were Martha Washington, Drs. James Craik and Elisha Cullen Dick, James Monroe, and Robert E. Lee. The brick building's three-bay, three-story exterior is typical of Alexandria's Federal architecture. Its curved-window shop front is a conjectural reconstruction by Thomas T. Waterman. The fanciful Gothic Revival shelves inside, a mid-19th-century alteration, are a stunning and rare example of the style's use for a shop interior. Now a museum, the apothecary's collections include, in addition to furnishings and fixtures, archival material, pharmaceutical equipment, and herbs, all kept intact by the Stabler-Leadbeater firm. *(100–106) VLR: 03/17/81; NRHP: 11/24/82.*

TOWN OF POTOMAC HISTORIC DISTRICT. This section of modern-day western Alexandria includes most of the former town of Potomac, consisting of six subdivisions—Del Ray, Del Ray II, St. Elmo, Abingdon, Hume, and parts of Mount Vernon. St. Elmo and Del Ray, platted in 1894 by Ohio developers Charles E. Wood and William Harmon, were incorporated in 1908 to form the town. The district exemplifies an early planned suburban community intended to serve commuters along railroad and trolley lines. Most of the area's ensuing growth was based on transportation expansion. Many of the residents were government employees who regularly commuted to Washington. Others worked at the nearby Potomac Yards, a primary railroad switching facility, and walked to work. The town flourished independently until it was annexed by Alexandria in 1930. A representation of generally modest residential architecture from the 1890s to 1941 survives. Several houses are mail-order structures. *(100–136) VLR: 12/11/91; NRHP: 09/10/92.*

VIRGINIA THEOLOGICAL SEMINARY (PROTESTANT EPISCOPAL THEOLOGICAL SEMINARY IN VIRGINIA), *3737 Seminary Road.* Virginia's Episcopal theological seminary was established in 1823 and acquired its site overlooking downtown Alexandria in 1827. Its growth over subsequent decades is represented by several outstanding Victorian buildings; chief among them is Aspinwall Hall of 1859, a major example of American mid-19th-century institutional work, designed by Baltimore architect Norris G. Starkweather. For its exterior Starkweather blended elements of the Italianate and Romanesque styles into a wholly original and imposing composition topped by a fanciful multitiered wooden cupola. Adjacent is Immanuel Chapel of 1881, an expression of the richly ornamented Ruskinian or High Victorian Gothic work by Charles E. Cassell of Baltimore. The seminary grounds retain elements of a romantically landscaped park designed by Andrew Jackson Downing, his only documented Virginia work. Since its founding, the seminary has provided many prominent Episcopal clerics. *(100–123) VLR: 05/16/78; NRHP: 11/17/80.*

ALLEGHANY COUNTY

Named for the Allegheny Mountains that pass through the county, Alleghany County was formed from Bath, Botetourt, and Monroe (now in West Virginia) counties in 1822, with other parts of Monroe and Bath counties added later. The county seat is Covington.

CLIFTON FURNACE, *Clifton Forge vicinity.* Located in Rainbow Gap, one of the Commonwealth's outstanding natural formations, Clifton Furnace was a major center of ironmaking, a principal industry of mid-19th-century Virginia. The site was in operation as early as 1822, and the present cold-blast charcoal furnace, a stone structure tapering in a gentle curve toward the top, was erected in 1846 by William Lyle Alexander, the forge's owner. The furnace went out of blast in 1854, although iron production continued at the site until it was completely abandoned in 1877. The stone furnace, now owned by the Virginia Department of Transportation, is the only remnant of this once-busy place. The nearby city of Clifton Forge, originally called Williamson's Station, takes its name from this early industrial site. *(03–19) VLR: 02/15/77; NRHP: 08/16/77.*

HUMPBACK BRIDGE, *Callaghan vicinity.* Humpback Bridge is the nation's only surviving curved-span covered bridge and is the oldest covered bridge in Virginia. Although the present bridge was long thought to have been built in 1835, more recent research has revealed that it was completed in 1857 and is the successor to several earlier bridges at this Dunlap's Creek crossing, all destroyed by floods. The bridge and its predecessors were part of the James River and Kanawha Turnpike, the principal highway of western Virginia. The 100-foot span has no middle support, and the center point of the floor and roof is 8 feet higher than the ends, giving the bridge its distinctive hump. The bridge was bypassed in 1929 and stood derelict until 1953 when it was purchased by the Virginia Department of Transportation and restored as part of a scenic wayside. *(03–02) VLR: 11/05/68; NRHP: 10/01/69.*

LONGDALE FURNACE HISTORIC DISTRICT. The complex of buildings, structures, and sites making up the village of Longdale Furnace are the tangible remains of an extensive mining and manufacturing operation. Industrial activity began here in 1827 when Lexington builder and entrepreneur John Jordan and his partner John Irvine built a cold-blast iron furnace here which they named Lucy Selina Furnace after their respective wives. The operation was continued by Jordan's sons but was purchased in 1869 by William Firmstone and his partner Ario Pardee and named the Longdale Iron Company. They redeveloped the site as Virginia's foremost hot-blast coke-fired furnace. A community of workers' dwellings, managers' houses, and related buildings sprang up to service the activity. The company was dissolved in 1914. Many of the buildings disappeared, but Longdale still maintains a vestige of its former character. *(03–338) VLR: 04/28/95; NRHP: 08/03/95.*

MASSIE HOUSE, *Falling Spring vicinity.* In Falling Spring Valley, with a backdrop of wooded mountains, the Massie house is Alleghany County's chief example of the Federal style and is probably the area's oldest formal dwelling. The two-story house with pedimented gables was completed in 1826 for Henry Massie, a planter who served as one of Alleghany's first magistrates. The decorative fanlight entrance incorporates Massie's initials in its tracery. Its interior woodwork includes a finely executed stair, cupboards, mantels, and wainscoting. The property is still owned by the Massie family, and the house is currently undergoing restoration after standing unoccupied for many years. *(03–11) VLR: 12/16/80; NRHP: 07/08/82.*

MILTON HALL, *Callaghan vicinity.* Nestled among the mountains in a remote corner of western Virginia, Milton Hall stands as an expression of the renewed British interest in New World real estate, especially in the southern states, in the years just after the Civil War. This distinctly English-looking Gothic villa was erected in 1874 for William Wentworth Fitzwilliam, Viscount Milton, whose wife brought him to Alleghany County for his health. Presenting an exotic contrast to its surroundings, Milton Hall was a late use of the Gothic Revival, illustrating the lingering popularity of the style among the British after it passed from fashion for rural residences in this country. The handsomely preserved house is currently used as a bed-and-breakfast inn. *(03–08) VLR: 01/20/81; NRHP: 07/26/82.*

OAKLAND GROVE PRESBYTERIAN CHURCH, *Selma vicinity.* An endearingly simple house of worship, Oakland Grove Church is the oldest-known church building in Alleghany County and is regarded as one of the county's chief historic landmarks. The congregation began as a mission of the Covington Presbyterian Church. The construction of the brick church building ca. 1847 coincided with a religious reawakening among area Presbyterians, when six churches in the Montgomery Presbytery enjoyed "a few seasons of refreshing." The church was converted to a Confederate hospital in the Civil War, and a number of soldiers are buried in its cemetery. Oakland Grove is the mother church of several nearby Presbyterian churches but is now used only for special services. The building has never been modernized; its original pews, gallery, and furnishings are intact, and it is still illuminated by kerosene lamps. *(03–04) VLR: 12/16/80; NRHP: 07/08/83.*

PERSINGER HOUSE, *Covington vicinity.* One of the earliest of Alleghany County's pioneer dwellings, this house was built by Jacob Persinger, member of a settler family. Persinger as a child was captured by the Indians and later adopted an Indian-style life. Mary Kimberlin, whom he married in 1778, refused to live as an Indian, so he built her the present house, reported to be the finest in the county at the time. The house was enlarged to its present form with its two-level gallery ca. 1888. The original log section is an interesting vernacular structure retaining numerous original interior features including a finely joined vertical board partition with beveled joints. It has a hall-parlor plan, a standard one for 18th-century Virginia vernacular dwellings. *(03–18) VLR: 12/16/80; NRHP: 07/08/82.*

SWEET CHALYBEATE SPRINGS, *Sweet Chalybeate.* This spa complex is a relic of the 19th-century days when the fashionable world of the North and South came to the mineral springs of western Virginia to "take the waters and play the marriage market." Known since the 18th century, Sweet Chalybeate was developed in 1836 into a commercial resort which lasted until 1918. Although some of the buildings are neglected and deteriorating, the relatively complete collection of mid- and late 19th-century pavilions and cottages attests to the popularity of the resort and provides a poignant picture of a Virginia spa. The springs themselves, claimed to contain the strongest carbonated mineral waters in the nation, still flow freely from the limestone bluff. Chalybeate is a type of mineral water impregnated with salts of iron. *(03–07) VLR: 10/16/73; NRHP: 01/21/74.*

AMELIA COUNTY

Formed from Prince George and Brunswick counties in 1734, this southern Piedmont county was named for Princess Amelia Sophia Eleanora, daughter of King George II. The county seat is Amelia.

DYKELAND, *Chula vicinity.* Dykeland has evolved through alterations and additions to reflect three distinct architectural styles: colonial, Federal, and country Italianate. The earliest section, an 18th-century cottage, was erected on land granted to the Rev. George Robertson and, according to tradition, stood a quarter of a mile north. It was moved and added to another former Robertson property known as Flat Creek Plantation. The house was enlarged ca. 1838 after its purchase by Lewis E. Harvie. The resulting two-story, three-bay section was further expanded in 1856–57 when Harvie added the Italianate wing and veranda. Harvie became president of the Richmond and Danville Railroad in 1856, an enterprise he helped establish in 1847. Harvie also represented Amelia County in the House of Delegates and was an ardent secessionist in the Virginia State Convention of 1861. Dykeland's 19th-century outbuildings include a kitchen, a smokehouse, and a dairy. *(04–09) VLR: 03/17/87; NRHP: 05/08/87.*

EGGLESTETTON, *Chula vicinity.* Dominated by a broad gambrel roof, Egglestetton is a quintessential example of Virginia's rural colonial architecture and is typical of the dwellings occupied by the early gentry of the region. The interior boasts unusually fine paneled walls and other ornamental details. Adding to its architectural sophistication is the pairing of the windows rather than spacing them evenly across the facade. The Eggleston family owned the property as early as 1747; the present house was built in the 1760s for Joseph Eggleston, Jr., who served as a major in the Continental army and was later elected to Congress. An inventory taken at his death shows that Eggleston maintained a substantial library here. The house was restored in the 1970s. *(04–05) VLR: 06/17/75; NRHP: 03/28/80.*

FARMER HOUSE, *Deatonville vicinity.* Dating from the early 1820s, the Farmer house is a large wood-frame I-house probably erected for Nelson Farmer whose family patented the property before 1750. Characterized by a center-passage, single-pile plan, the I-house was a popular form of two-story house design for comfortably situated but not wealthy planters of middle Virginia. The form was derived from the symmetrical 18th-century Georgian style and spread through the South and Middle West in the 19th century. The Farmer house stands out from numerous contemporaries because it preserves nearly all of its original fabric, including beaded weatherboards, front porch, stair, Federal mantels, and other trim. The tall chimneys show the high standard of workmanship achieved by the region's masons. The house stood in deteriorated condition for many years but was restored in the 1970s. *(04–43) VLR: 04/18/78; NRHP: 11/17/78.*

HAW BRANCH, *Amelia vicinity.* This outstanding example of Southside Virginia Federal architecture, one of the finest plantation houses in the region, received its present form in the early 19th century under its owner John Tabb, a delegate, whose father, Thomas Tabb, assembled the plantation before 1745. An earlier house was incorporated in the west wing. The property's name was derived from the nearby stream lined with hawthorn trees. A striking feature of the house is its elaborate interior woodwork carved with regionally interpreted Adamesque motifs, including urns, swags, hawthorn blossoms, and sunbursts. Haw Branch passed by inheritance to Tabb's daughter and descended thereafter to daughters. The Haw Branch grounds preserve a row of early outbuildings, all with clipped-gable roofs. The house was restored by a descendant of Thomas Tabb who purchased the property in 1965. *(04–02) VLR: 10/17/72; NRHP: 04/02/73.*

SAILOR'S (ALSO SAYLER'S) CREEK BATTLEFIELD, *Rice vicinity.* On April 6, 1865, Sayler's Creek (the Union forces mistakenly called it Sailor's Creek) was the site of the last major battle between the armies of generals Robert E. Lee and Ulysses S. Grant before Lee's surrender at Appomattox. Some 8,000 Confederates—the largest number of soldiers ever captured in combat in North America—were taken prisoner here. The Union success led to the final downfall of Lee's army three days later. In reporting his victory to President Lincoln (by way of General Grant), Gen. Philip Sheridan wrote, "If the thing is pressed, I think that Lee will surrender." Lincoln replied, "Let the thing be pressed." Engagements at Hillsman's Farm, Marshall's Crossroads, and Lockett's Farm constituted the battle's main actions. The Hillsman house (shown) and the Lockett house are part of the interpretive sites within the Sailor's Creek Battlefield Historical State Park. *(04–19) VLR: 10/16/84; NRHP 02/04/85; NHL: 02/04/85.*

ST. JOHN'S EPISCOPAL CHURCH, GRUB HILL, *Chula vicinity.* Consecrated in 1852 by Bishop William Meade, this church was a product of the reactivation of the Episcopal denomination in rural Virginia during the mid–19th century. It is on the site of a colonial church known simply as Grub Hill Church, a name derived from the "Grub Hill" slave quarters of the Tabb family, who gave the land for the building. The present church, a country builder's version of the Gothic Revival, has an honest simplicity that yet evokes admiration. It remains relatively unaltered and is enhanced by a quiet rural setting. The principal interior furnishings, including an ornamented triptych, are the signed work of a woodcarver, H. Jacob, completed in 1870. Owned by the trustees of Christ Episcopal Church, Amelia, St. John's is used for occasional summer services. *(04–07) VLR: 04/18/78; NRHP: 11/16/78.*

WIGWAM, *Chula vicinity.* Wigwam was the home of William Branch Giles (1762–1830), who served Virginia in both the U.S. House of Representatives and the U.S. Senate and was elected governor in 1827. Giles was also a member of the convention that revised the Virginia constitution in 1829–30. His Amelia County seat preserves its unusually attractive two-part dwelling, the original portion of which is the 18th-century rear ell. The story-and-a-half front section was added in 1815 and contains highly individualized Federal woodwork. Giles began a boys' school at Wigwam ca. 1825. A school was continued here after its purchase by the Harrison family. The house survived without significant alteration but stood unoccupied for many years. It underwent a major restoration in 1990–94. *(04–03) VLR: 05/13/69; NRHP: 11/25/69.*

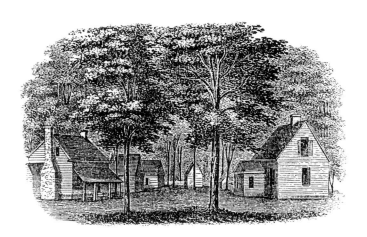

AMHERST COUNTY

Named for Maj. Gen. Jeffery Amherst, British commander in North America during the latter part of the French and Indian War and governor of the Virginia colony from 1759 to 1768, this central Piedmont county was formed from Albemarle County in 1761. Its county seat is Amherst.

BEAR MOUNTAIN INDIAN MISSION SCHOOL, *Crawford's Store vicinity.* The Monacan Indians have regarded Bear Mountain as the spiritual center of their community for hundreds of years. A small group of Monacans survived the encroachment of Europeans into their territory and has remained in the Amherst area since the early 1700s. The principal landmark here, the ca. 1870 log school, was originally built for church services for Indian people. Because Virginia's racial segregation laws excluded Monacans from public schooling, several Amherst citizens established an Episcopal mission at the site in 1908. The mission included the log school building, a new church, and a mission worker's house. A fire in 1930 left only the schoolhouse intact. From the early 1900s until 1964 when integration made it obsolete, the school provided a seventh-grade education for several hundred Monacan people. The building now belongs to the Monacan Indian Nation, Inc. *(05–230) VLR: 09/18/96; NRHP: 02/21/97.*

FORT RIVERVIEW, *Madison Heights vicinity.* A Confederate fortification located six miles east of Lynchburg, Fort Riverview is strategically situated atop a steep ridge overlooking the James River. This well-preserved defensive work contains artillery emplacements that defended the land approach as well as the river—both downstream to the east and upstream toward the Six-Mile Bridge of the former South Side Railroad. Little documentation exists concerning the fort, which probably was constructed in 1864 when the Union army's Maj. Gen. David Hunter threatened Lynchburg. This lack of written evidence increases the importance of the archaeological record, which fortunately remains intact. Besides the fortification itself, other features on the property include the trace of an old road leading to the river and fifty small piles of stone of unknown purpose scattered down the southern slope of the hill. *(05–185) VLR: 04/18/89; NRHP: 11/16/89.*

GEDDES, *Clifford vicinity.* The oldest portion of this venerable example of Piedmont vernacular architecture was built ca. 1762 for Hugh Rose, the third son of Anglican clergyman and diarist Robert Rose, with whom the house is traditionally associated. A militia colonel who represented Amherst County both in the field and in the General Assembly during the Revolution, Hugh Rose is best remembered as the friend of Thomas Jefferson who sheltered Jefferson's family at Geddes after the 1781 British raid on Charlottesville. The unusual form of the house, created by the early 19th-century addition of the passage and two west rooms, was carried out by Rose descendants, who have continued to own the property to the present. *(05–07) VLR: 10/19/82; NRHP: 02/24/83.*

MOUNTAIN VIEW FARM, *Clifford vicinity.* Mountain View Farm includes a late 18th-century house built for Col. Hugh Rose. The house was moved in 1831 from Spencer's Mountain (now Geddes Mountain) to a site not far away in order to be more convenient to the newly constructed stagecoach road linking Philadelphia with North Carolina. In 1833 the property was purchased by Dr. Paul Carrington Cabell, a prominent area physician, who erected the outbuildings including a doctor's office, a smokehouse, a well house, and a combination icehouse and carriage house. Mountain View Farm was acquired around 1858 by Lynchburg philanthropist Samuel Miller who intended to use the property for the cultivation of the medicinal herb horehound. Miller died in 1859 before his venture came to fruition. With its collection of six outbuildings, Mountain View Farm preserves an image of a traditional Piedmont rural complex of the mid–19th century. *(05–11) VLR: 09/18/96; NRHP: 09/03/97.*

HITE STORE, *Lowesville vicinity.* Hite Store has served the general merchandise needs of the Lowesville community since its construction in 1869. The business was started as a partnership of Henry Loving and Nathan Taliaferro. The building was designed to hold living quarters for the storekeeper, and from around 1876 to the 1990s it housed a post office. The Lowesville Academy operated here in the 1890s, and the building later underwent alterations to accommodate boarders. In 1902 the property was purchased by Camilla J. Hite and Mary C. Thornton, and it remained in Hite family ownership until 1991. The country Greek Revival structure is among the state's earliest and more architecturally refined general stores. In addition to dispensing merchandise, stores such as this became important social gathering places. While the majority of the state's old general stores now stand abandoned, Hite Store remains an active commercial establishment. *(05–58) VLR: 03/19/97; NRHP: 06/06/97.*

RED HILL, *Pedlar Mills vicinity.* This imposing Federal mansion was built from profits amassed by Charles Ellis through various mercantile ventures. Ellis, whose family had owned the property since the 1750s, formed a partnership with Richmond businessman John Allan, foster father of Edgar Allan Poe. Completed in 1825, Red Hill was the home of Charles Ellis's younger brother, Richard Shelton Ellis, who managed the family's Amherst properties. The Adamesque detailing and formality of the spacious plan suggest that the Ellises were familiar with the grand Federal town houses then being erected in Richmond. The spiral stair is based on a design in Owen Biddle's *Young Carpenter's Assistant* (1810), a work sold in Richmond. From 1869 to 1898 Red Hill was owned by the Presbyterian preacher and architect Robert Lewis Dabney. The 20th-century portico replaced an earlier porch. *(05–14) VLR: 03/18/80; NRHP: 06/09/80.*

SWEET BRIAR COLLEGE HISTORIC DISTRICT,
Amherst vicinity. Founded in 1901 through the bequest of Indiana Fletcher Williams, this nationally renowned liberal arts college for women boasts a distinguished complex of buildings by Ralph Adams Cram, one of America's foremost architects. During his long career Cram produced a remarkable body of work, all of impeccable quality. His collegiate commissions include West Point Chapel, Princeton Chapel, and the campuses of Rice Institute and the University of Richmond. Appointed Sweet Briar's architect in 1901, Cram departed from his usual Gothic Revival scheme and produced an elegant Georgian-style layout realized in part between 1902 and 1942. In establishing the school's image, Cram was influenced by Virginia's Georgian architecture. He stated, "History, tradition, and architectural style predetermined the course to follow." Richmond landscape architect Charles F. Gillette provided the parklike setting for Cram's scheme. The district consists of twenty-two contributing buildings. *(05–219) VLR: 01/15/95; NRHP: 03/30/95.*

SWEET BRIAR HOUSE, *Sweet Briar College, Amherst vicinity.* Elijah Fletcher, publisher of the *Lynchburg Virginian* and mayor of the city, purchased this early 19th-century farmhouse in 1825 for a weekend retreat. His wife, Maria Crawford Fletch-

er, renamed it Sweet Briar for the wild roses here. In 1851 the Fletchers transformed the plain Federal house into a major expression of the Italian Villa style, adding square towers, veranda, and arcaded portico. The design, based on one by Richard Upjohn published in Andrew Jackson Downing's *Architecture of Country Houses* (1850), may have been the choice of Fletcher's daughter, Indiana, whom Fletcher credited with the project. Indiana Fletcher Williams inherited Sweet Briar and directed in her will that the property was to become a school for young women. Sweet Briar College thus received its charter in 1901. The house since has served as the home of the college's presidents. *(05–18) VLR: 07/07/70; NRHP: 09/15/70.*

WINTON, *Clifford.* This late Georgian farmhouse was built in the 1770s for Joseph Cabell, who served with distinction as an officer in the Revolutionary War and was elected to various public offices. Cabell sold Winton in 1779 to Samuel Meredith, who likewise was a distinguished military and civic leader. Meredith was married to Patrick Henry's sister and brought the patriot's mother, Sarah Winston Syme Henry, to live at Winton. Mrs. Henry died here in 1784 and was buried in the Winton cemetery. The house received its portico and entablature when its exterior was remodeled in the early 20th century. The interior, however, preserves its original robust but localized Georgian woodwork, a striking feature of which is the drawing room chimneypiece decorated with pilasters and pediment. The original Georgian stair survives as well. The property is now a country club. *(05–21) VLR: 11/20/73; NRHP: 05/02/74.*

APPOMATTOX COUNTY

This rural central Virginia county was formed in 1854 from parts of Buckingham, Prince Edward, Charlotte, and Campbell counties. The Appomattox River, which rises here, is also the source of the county's name, deriving from an Indian tribe who lived near the river's mouth. The county seat is Appomattox.

APPOMATTOX COURT HOUSE NATIONAL HISTORIC PARK, *Appomattox Court House.* At this remote settlement, after four years of bloodshed, heroism, and extraordinary military ingenuity, Gen. Robert E. Lee, his retreat blocked, surrendered his army to Gen. Ulysses S. Grant on Palm Sunday, 1865. Lee's capitulation in effect ended the Civil War. The two commanders met in the home of Wilmer McLean where Lee accepted Grant's generous surrender terms. After the surrender and the removal of the county seat, the village almost vanished. The courthouse was destroyed, and the McLean house was taken down for exhibition at a world's fair. The village has since been restored as a historic shrine by the National Park Service, and important lost buildings were reconstructed. The complex, including some 900 acres of battlefield, is now maintained as a memorial to the moment that reunited the nation. *(06–33) VLR: 07/06/71; NRHP: 10/15/66.*

PAMPLIN PIPE FACTORY, *Pamplin.* At one time the largest clay pipe factory in America, supplying a national and international market with one million pipes a month as late as 1935, the Pamplin Pipe Factory preserves not only its large round kiln and connected chimney but the archaeological remains of several consecutive periods of clay pipe manufacture. Clay pipes, similar to those used by Virginia Indians in prehistoric times, were made here on a regular commercial basis until the factory closed in 1952. The property is now a museum. Further study and archaeological examination could reveal additional information on the evolution of pipe-manufacturing technology. It also may determine whether there is truth in the folk tradition that pipe making occurred on the site as early as the European-aboriginal contact period. *(277–02) VLR: 06/17/80; NRHP: 06/17/80.*

ARLINGTON COUNTY

The smallest Virginia county, Arlington County was first known as Alexandria County and was established in 1847 from that part of the District of Columbia ceded back to Virginia in 1846. Before being ceded to the federal government in 1791, the area was part of Fairfax County. The present name, given in 1920, honors Arlington, the Custis-Lee family estate, now the Arlington National Cemetery.

ARLINGTON HOUSE, THE ROBERT E. LEE MEMORIAL, *Arlington National Cemetery.* This columned mansion overlooking the nation's capital is best remembered as the home of Robert E. Lee from the time of his marriage to Mary Custis until the plantation was confiscated by the federal government during the Civil War and used for burials. It was begun in 1803 for Mary Custis Lee's father, George Washington Parke Custis, step-grandson of George Washington, and completed in 1818. The resulting composition, designed by George Hadfield, second architect of the U.S. Capitol, is one of the nation's boldest expressions of the Greek Revival. In 1874 Secretary of War Edwin Stanton ordered that a national cemetery be formally established on the Arlington plantation. The house remained the headquarters of the Arlington National Cemetery until 1928 when Congress established it as the Robert E. Lee Memorial. Arlington House was transferred to the National Park Service in 1933. *(00–01) VLR: 07/06/71.*

ARLINGTON POST OFFICE, *3118 North Washington Street.* Built in 1937, the Arlington Post Office was the county's first federal building and represented an important milestone in the development of Arlington from an agglomeration of disparate suburban villages to the urban community it is today. A modernistic interpretation of Georgian classicism, the deftly handled composition was designed by Louis A. Simon, supervising architect of the Department of the Treasury. The building is also an exemplar of the fine quality and attention to detail given to federal works in the 1930s, structures intended to instill pride in the institutions of government. The exterior is distinguished by its elegant domed portico. The interior murals of traditional Virginia scenes by Washington, D.C., artist Auriel Bessemer are important survivors of the depression-era program of enhancing federal projects with works of art. *(00–70) VLR: 08/13/85; NRHP: 02/07/86.*

BALL-SELLERS HOUSE, *5620 3rd Street South.* Most of the simple, often crude dwellings of the average colonial Virginian have disappeared; the finer houses that remain tend to give a misleading picture of the more typical lifestyle of the 18th century. A rare surviving example of such elementary housing is the Ball-Sellers house, tucked in the Glencarlyn neighborhood of Arlington. The tiny one-room dwelling probably was built by John Ball before his death in 1766 and is now a wing of a 19th-century house. The rustic log construction and rare surviving clapboard roof, one of the most rudimentary of early roof coverings, both hidden under later fabric, tell that many Virginians lived far from luxuriously. The house was later owned by William Carlin, an Alexandria tailor whose clientele included George Washington. This singular architectural document is now owned and preserved by the Arlington Historical Society. *(00–09) VLR: 06/17/75; NRHP: 07/17/75.*

BARCROFT COMMUNITY HOUSE, *800 South Buchanan Street.* The development of the Barcroft neighborhood began around 1892 after the subdivision of the Frank Corbett farm. More intense growth came a few years later when the area was advertised as a commuter town with "fresh country air." The need for a neighborhood civic gathering place was soon felt, and in 1908 the Methodists erected a small wood-frame structure to serve as a church and community building. Barcroft simultaneously recognized a need for additional educational facilities, so the school board leased the building for $10. Regular classes were held here until 1924. In 1914 the building became the headquarters of the Barcroft School and Civic League. It later became known officially as the Barcroft Community House and was used for church services by various denominations. This neighborhood landmark is still owned and maintained for public benefit by the Barcroft School and Civic League. *(00–40) VLR: 04/28/95; NRHP: 07/28/95.*

BANNEKER SW-9 INTERMEDIATE BOUNDARY STONE OF THE DISTRICT OF COLUMBIA, *18th and Van Buren streets.* One of the original forty boundary stones, this sandstone marker, standing only fifteen inches high, was set in 1792 to mark the westernmost point of the District of Columbia, which originally included what is now Arlington County. The district's boundaries were surveyed by Maj. Andrew Ellicott with the assistance of Benjamin Banneker (1731–1806), a black mathematician and scientist who in 1792 began an almanac, producing all of its mathematical and astronomical calculations. Banneker also became an early advocate of civil rights, requesting Thomas Jefferson to use his influence to end official prejudice against blacks. This boundary stone has come to symbolize the achievements of a gifted black individual during a time when even the most educated whites were skeptical of blacks' intellectual competence. *(00–15) VLR: 02/15/77; NHL: 05/11/76.*

BOUNDARY MARKERS OF THE DISTRICT OF COLUMBIA, *Arlington County line.* The stones marking the boundary of the District of Columbia were set in 1791 following the survey of Maj. Andrew Ellicott and his assistant, Benjamin Banneker, a free black mathematician and scientist. Cut from Aquia sandstone, the markers were spaced approximately one mile apart. The intermediate stones originally stood 2 feet high; the corner stones were 3 feet high. Of the total of forty stones marking the district's ten-mile boundary, fourteen were in Virginia; Virginia's surviving twelve are included in this designation. Their condition varies: some

preserve original inscriptions, while others have been reduced to stumps. In 1915 the Daughters of the American Revolution erected iron fences around each of the markers. The Virginia portion of the district retroceded to the Commonwealth in 1846, and the Virginia markers now roughly define the western boundaries of Arlington County. *(00–22) VLR: 08/21/90; NRHP: 02/01/91.*

CARLIN HALL, *5711 4th Street, South.* A fanciful piece of late Victorian civic architecture, Carlin Hall was built in 1892 for the Carlin Hall Association. The hall was central to the Glencarlyn neighborhood, the earliest planned suburban subdivision in Arlington County, begun in 1887 and originally called Carlin Springs. Until 1920 the building served as a meeting place for the civic association and the local Episcopal congregation. Dances and other social events were also held here. The building is the work of a local carpenter, Theodore Bailey, who mixed stock materials for the exterior embellishment of the cross-shaped structure. The property was donated to the local school board in 1920 after the Glencarlyn School was destroyed by fire. It served as the community school until 1953 when it was returned to the Carlin Hall Association. In 1962 the association deeded the property to Arlington County for a recreational and cultural center. *(00–39) VLR: 06/16/93; NRHP: 08/12/93.*

CHERRYDALE VOLUNTEER FIRE HOUSE, *3900 North Lee Highway.* Though devoid of architectural embellishment, this plain structure has been a community amenity since its completion in 1921 for the newly developed commuter suburb of Cherrydale. Cherrydale was one of several such suburbs, including Ballston and Barcroft, that sprang up in Arlington County in the early decades of the 20th century. The Cherrydale Volunteer Fire Department was formed in 1898 but had no specific firehouse until the present one, Arlington County's first permanent firehouse, was built. The building was paid for by the purchase of individual bricks. President and Mrs. Woodrow Wilson each purchased a brick during a fund-raising drive. The firehouse also offered space for a movie theater, specialty shop, and community center. The structure, a prototype of other area firehouses, continues to serve its original function, now part of the consolidated Arlington County system. *(00–44) VLR: 04/28/95; NRHP: 07/28/95.*

COLONIAL VILLAGE, *Wilson Boulevard, Lee Highway, and North Veitch Street.* Built in four phases between 1935 and 1940, the sprawling Colonial Village complex exemplifies the early application of innovative garden-city planning to low-density superblock development for low- and middle-income renters. The complex is also an early illustration of the clustering of apartment units around spacious landscaped courtyards, the separation of pedestrian and automotive routes, and the use of an interior greenbelt and staggered setbacks for increased ventilation and light. The nation's first large-scale Federal Housing Administration project of insured rental housing, Colonial Village was a model for subsequent FHA-backed projects. Developed by Gustave Ring, Colonial Village since has served as a prototype for many of America's town-house developments. The first three phases were designed by Harvey H. Warwick of Washington, D.C. Francis L. Koenig designed the fourth phase. *(00–13) VLR: 09/16/80; NRHP: 12/09/80.*

CHARLES RICHARD DREW HOUSE, *2505 1st Street, South.* Charles Richard Drew, M.D. (1904–1950), was one of the pioneers of American medicine. This Afro-American physician's research and discoveries concerning  blood plasma on the brink of World War II led to saving the lives of thousands of American soldiers. Born in Washington, D.C., Drew received the degree of Doctor of Medicine and Master of Surgery from McGill University in Montreal. He later taught at Howard University and attended graduate school at Columbia University. Upon graduating from Columbia in 1940, Dr. Drew became America's first black to receive a Doctor of Science degree in surgery. At Columbia, Drew and his aides made the breakthrough discovery that with proper preparation blood plasma could be safely stored almost indefinitely, making plasma immediately available to victims on the battlefield. The Arlington dwelling was Dr. Drew's home between 1920 and 1930. *(00–16) VLR: 02/15/77; NHL: 05/11/76.*

FORT MYER HISTORIC DISTRICT. First called Fort Whipple, Fort Myer was originally part of the network of defenses protecting Washington during the Civil War. A signal school was started here in 1869 under Gen. Albert J. Myer, for whom the fort was named after he died in 1880. The fort evolved into a cavalry post in 1887 and eventually became a permanent army post. Within the landscaped complex is a collection of late 19th- and early 20th-century residential quarters and administration buildings. Most important of the post's numerous structures is the row of imposing residences erected in the 1890s lining Grant Avenue. Here are the official quarters of the army chief of staff, the air force chief of staff, and the chairman of the Joint Chiefs of Staff. Test flights conducted at Fort Myer by Orville Wright in 1909 led to the army's adoption of the airplane as a military weapon. *(00–04) VLR: 06/19/73; NHL: 11/28/72.*

THE GLEBE, *4527 17th Street, North.* Fairfax Parish's original glebe house was built in 1773 on land purchased by the parish in 1770. One of its occupants was David Griffith, George Washington's chaplain at Valley Forge. The house burned in 1808, and in 1815 Wallis Jones built the wing of the present house, possibly using the glebe house bricks. From 1836 to 1846 The Glebe was owned by John Peter Van Ness, a former mayor of Washington. The next owner was the sculptor Clark Mills, best known for his equestrian statue of Andrew Jackson in Washington's Lafayette Park. Mills erected the octagonal section in the 1850s for his studio, one of Virginia's best examples of the eight-sided buildings advocated by theorist Orson Squire Fowler. From 1870 to 1878 The Glebe was the residence of the diplomat and statesman Caleb Cushing; in 1926 it became the home of state senator Frank Ball. The property is now the headquarters of the National Genealogical Society. *(00–03) VLR: 07/06/71; NRHP: 02/23/72.*

HUME SCHOOL, *1805 South Arlington Ridge Road.* This Queen Anne–style building was designed by Washington architect B. Stanley Simmons and was built in 1891. Prompted by reforms in education and heightened by municipal support for more sophisticated, often monumental structures, local governments gradually replaced the small wooden schoolhouses of the 19th century with commodious and frequently stylish structures, of which the Hume School is a particularly fine example. Its sophisticated detailing and distinctive tower have made it a landmark since it first opened. The school was named for Frank Hume, an early civic and educational leader in Arlington County. Although it closed in 1956, public regard for the school, the oldest standing school building in Arlington County, prompted its being deeded to the Arlington Historical Society for use as a museum of local history. *(00–11) VLR: 02/26/79; NRHP: 06/18/79.*

THE PENTAGON, *Jefferson Davis Highway and Interstate Highway 395.* One of the world's most famous buildings, the Pentagon has become the symbol of U.S. military might and America's position as a world superpower. The building grew out of a need to centralize the War Department units. Spurred on by the outbreak of World War II, planning commenced in 1941, and a site near Arlington National Cemetery was chosen. War Department architects G. Edwin Bergstrom and David J. Witmer designed what was to be the world's largest office building, containing some 6,240,000 square feet. The distinctive five-sided structure was built in the remarkably short period of sixteen months in 1941–42, in time to accommodate the wartime command. The main elevations employed the stripped classicism then in vogue for governmental architecture. The vast building still houses the U.S. Department of Defense, serving as the command center of the mightiest military force in history. *(00–72) VLR: 04/18/89; NRHP: 07/27/89; NHL: 10/05/92.*

QUARTERS 1, *Fort Myer.* Completed in 1899 as one of a series of officers' dwellings, this capacious twenty-one-room brick mansion has been the residence of all the army chiefs of staff since 1908 when Maj. Gen. J. Franklin Bell became the first chief of staff to make his home at Fort Myer. He was succeeded by Gen. Leonard Wood, who resided here from 1910 to 1914. The modified Queen Anne structure has been little changed since its completion. Its long front porch gives a homey, hospitable air to the quarters of the commander of the world's dominant military force. Its later occupants have included generals George C. Marshall, Omar N. Bradley, Douglas MacArthur, and Dwight D. Eisenhower. The house is conspicuously located at the end of Grant Avenue with a splendid view of the nation's capital. Signaling its official status is a pair of Fort McNair cannons flanking the entrance. *(00–05) VLR: 06/19/73; NHL: 11/28/72.*

WASHINGTON NATIONAL AIRPORT AND SOUTH HANGAR LINE (RONALD REAGAN WASHINGTON NATIONAL AIRPORT), *Mount Vernon Memorial Highway.* Washington National Airport represents a milestone in American aviation architecture, technology, and New Deal government initiatives. Although born of wartime need, National was the first federally constructed commercial airport in the country designed for civilian flight. The terminal building, opened in 1941, was initially designed by Howard Lovewell Cheney with subsequent participation by Charles M. Goodman and Harbin S. Chandler, Jr., and is a landmark of stripped classicism. Its footprint, plan, massing, and control tower for many years served as a model for airport design. The South Hangar Line, built in stages between 1941 and 1948, represents an important technological advance in hangar construction, using long-span steel construction, structural concrete, and combination sliding-leaf and canopy hangar doors. With many of its original features and details intact, National remains a proud gateway to the nation's capital. *(00–45) VLR: 06/27/95: NRHP: 09/12/97.*

AUGUSTA COUNTY

Formed from Orange County in 1738 with its government established in 1745, this broad, largely agricultural Shenandoah Valley county was named in honor of Augusta of Saxe-Gotha, wife of Frederick Louis, Prince of Wales, and mother of King George III. The county seat is Staunton.

JAMES ALEXANDER HOUSE, *Spottswood vicinity.* The James Alexander house and adjacent springhouse are the core remnants of one of Augusta County's more distinctive early vernacular farm complexes. In view of thousands of travelers daily passing on Interstate Highway 81, the buildings preserve a glimpse into the past, revealing the flow of Central European–inspired architectural traditions to the area from Pennsylvania. The house, built ca. 1827, integrates the Continental two-level bank form with the Georgian plan and detailing of eastern Virginia. The more purely regional springhouse employs similar two-level bank siting and limestone construction typical of Pennsylvania German architecture. The exterior fireplace on the springhouse, one of the few surviving examples of this utilitarian form, was used in such household and farm chores as butchering, laundering, soapmaking, and apple butter cooking. *(07–604) VLR: 06/16/81; NRHP: 09/16/82.*

AUGUSTA COUNTY TRAINING SCHOOL, *Cedar Green, Staunton vicinity.* Despite efforts to provide free public schooling for all Virginia children, racial segregation usually resulted in blacks receiving second-rate facilities. Augusta County was no exception. In the 1910s and 1920s, white students were accommodated in up-to-date, brick-built consolidated schools, but the hardly comparable black consolidated school, the Augusta County Training School, was not built until 1938. Originally called Cedar Green School, the frame building had only three rooms. Even then blacks contributed much of the land and labor. The school's focus was on vocational rather than academic education, offering mainly carpentry and manual arts. Integration caused it to close in 1964. The main building has since been converted into an American Legion hall. The shop building remains relatively unaltered. *(07–755) VLR: 12/11/84; NRHP: 06/19/86.*

AUGUSTA MILITARY ACADEMY, *Fort Defiance.* Founded by Confederate veteran and state delegate Charles Summerville Roller by 1874, Augusta Military Academy, until it closed in 1984, was the oldest military preparatory school in the Commonwealth. The school's dominant architectural feature is the stuccoed Main Barracks, designed by T. J. Collins and Sons of Staunton in a battlemented Gothic style and completed in 1915. The prototype was Alexander Jackson Davis's Barracks at the Virginia Military Institute. In the wake of World War I and Gen. John J. Pershing's report to Congress in 1920 recommending the early military training of American youth, the Augusta Military Academy formed the nation's first Junior Reserve Officers Training Corps and later achieved an international reputation for excellence in the field of secondary-level military education. Vacant since its closing, the complex faces an uncertain future. *(07–241) VLR: 09/16/82; NRHP: 02/10/83.*

AUGUSTA STONE CHURCH, *Fort Defiance.* Built in 1749 under the supervision of its pastor John Craig, Augusta Stone Church is the oldest standing Virginia church west of the Blue Ridge Mountains and the oldest Presbyterian church in continuous use in the Commonwealth. Craig was Virginia's first settled Presbyterian pastor and organized the Presbyterian church in Augusta County to serve its Scotch-Irish pioneers. In addition to being pastor of Augusta Stone Church, Craig helped found many other churches in the area. His building at Fort Defiance was a very simple rectangular meetinghouse with limestone rubble walls and a clipped-gable roof. The building was enlarged in 1921–22, receiving transepts, a lengthened sanctuary, and an entrance porch, all in compatible character. The original walls and roof form remain discernible amid the later additions. *(07–04) VLR: 02/20/73; NRHP: 05/09/73.*

BETHEL GREEN, *Greenville vicinity.* The house built by the contractor Jonathan Brown for James Bumgardner, an Augusta County farmer and distiller, is a document of mid-19th-century architecture and interior decoration, essentially undisturbed since its completion in 1857. Although the basic structure is conservative with its straightforward double-pile Georgian plan, the Gothic-style porches, fancy chimney stacks, and Italianate bracketed cornice make the house a stylish amalgam of contemporary architectural modes. Of exceptional interest is the Victorian interior, especially the parlors, which preserve their original textiles, furniture, and other decorations. The scrolled wallpaper, floral carpeting, and heavy silk curtains well illustrate the rich palette and mixed patterns characteristic of antebellum taste. Bills and receipts for most of the interior decorations survive in the family papers. The property remains in the ownership of Bumgardner's descendants. *(07–126) VLR: 05/18/82; NRHP: 08/26/82.*

BLACKROCK SPRINGS ARCHAEOLOGICAL SITE, *Blackrock Gap, Shenandoah National Park.* A large and functionally complex prehistoric site at the head of Paine Run near the crest of the Blue Ridge, the Blackrock Springs site contains datable material spanning the centuries from about 5500 to 1000 B.C. The intensive analysis of over 3,000 artifacts by University of Virginia archaeologists has revealed a heretofore unknown aspect of Archaic culture, represented by six separate but contemporary artifact clusters, each indicating a single occupation by a small group. Comparative study of

the Blackrock Springs site and two other prehistoric sites lying at the base of the mountain on Paine Run will allow archaeologists to explore problems of altitudinal variation and its effect on intergroup contact and Archaic cultural ecology. *(07–1149) VLR: 09/16/82; NRHP: 12/13/85.*

CHAPEL HILL, *Mint Spring vicinity.* The blending of academic with vernacular architectural traditions lends this Valley farmhouse a vibrancy usually lacking in stylistically purer works. Its vernacular I-house form is overlaid with such formal features as a pedimented entrance pavilion, three-part windows with stuccoed arches, and a fanlight doorway, all boldly and freely interpreted standard Federal forms. Adding interest is the interior woodwork with its exaggerated moldings, much of which preserves early graining and marbleizing. The hall is dominated by a graceful spiral stair. In the parlor is a rare set of vividly colored French scenic wallpaper with border and wainscot papers. The paper, entitled "Le Petit Décor," was first published in 1815 and depicts idyllic garden scenes. Several early outbuildings remain in the curtilage. The house was completed by 1834 for John Knight Churchman on property he purchased in 1826 and remains the home of Churchman's descendants. *(07–12) VLR: 07/18/78; NRHP: 11/16/78; BHR EASEMENT.*

COINER HOUSE, *Crimora vicinity.* Colorful graining, marbleizing, and polychromy, as well as elaborately stylized woodwork, were popular decorative treatments of the Shenandoah Valley homes of farmers of German origin. The Coiner house, built ca. 1825, holds one of the least-altered and most spectacular examples of such decoration yet discovered, installed in a deceptively plain brick I-house, as was often the case. The boldness of the colors and the imagination and skill with which the mantels, doors, stair, and other trim are executed serve to make the rooms a fascinating document of American folk art. The parlor mantel is embellished with neoclassical motifs of urns and sunbursts so stylized and elaborated that they bear little resemblance to the pattern-book Federal designs that inspired them. Typical of early brick houses of the area, the house walls employ Flemish bond and a molded-brick cornice. *(07–224) VLR: 06/21/77; NRHP: 03/30/78.*

CLOVER MOUNT (STONEHOUSE FARM), *Greenville vicinity.* Clover Mount is one of the earliest and best-preserved examples of a small group of vernacular stone houses built around 1800 in southern Augusta County. The discovery of early 19th-century stenciling throughout the interior provides one of Virginia's richest records of this appealing form of folk decoration. Stenciling was popular in the area, but few examples survive; Clover Mount's scheme is the most extensive recorded in the central Shenandoah Valley to date. The patterns include vertical bands of geometric and floral motifs ranging from tulips to pinwheels. Abstract border designs are used along the ceilings, around the doorframes, and lining the chair rails. The house was constructed in two sections for Robert Tate, a farmer of Scotch-Irish descent, and was completed by 1803. Tate acquired the property in 1775 and built the house to replace an earlier one. *(07–606) VLR: 06/16/81; NRHP: 09/16/82.*

CRAIGSVILLE SCHOOL, *Railroad Avenue, Craigsville.* Reflecting the formality of a Georgian mansion, the Craigsville School is a stately example of Augusta County's first phase of the larger consolidated public schools, visually proclaiming a complete break with the frame two- and three-room county schools of earlier decades. The building, opened in 1917, employed the same two-story, center-passage design as the original portion of the Weyers Cave School, including a small octagonal cupola. The school originally housed all grades, from first grade through high school. Craigsville was a growing community in the early 20th century. Its development was spurred by lumber and quarrying industries, coupled with a portland cement factory. The town acquired a fully equipped high school in 1932, and the older structure was relegated to handling elementary grades until it closed in 1968. It remained vacant until 1984 when it was sympathetically remodeled for apartments. *(07–1146) VLR: 12/11/84; NRHP: 02/27/85.*

CRIMORA SCHOOL, *Crimora.* The large window areas and spreading gable roofs of the Crimora School offer a friendly, humane contrast to the unlovable, fortresslike public schools of recent decades. Still providing a welcoming atmosphere for area children, the school is perhaps the county's best-preserved example of the central-auditorium-plan facilities developed by the State Department of Education's Division of School Buildings. The original plan, dated May 1927, is "Design 14-B," which incorporates a combination auditorium and gymnasium for its core with four large classrooms adjacent. The design proved so popular that only two schools with differing plans were subsequently built in the county until the Division of School Building's services were discontinued in the 1940s. Population growth in Crimora required additions, but the original modified bungalow character was maintained. The building now serves as a community center. *(07–964) VLR: 12/11/84; NRHP: 02/27/85.*

DEERFIELD SCHOOL, *Deerfield.* Reflecting the unhurried lifestyle of Augusta County's remote Deerfield Valley, this plain wooden schoolhouse, opened in 1937, preserves the character of an early rural consolidated school. The building is also one of the county's last two examples of the central-auditorium-plan school, a type characterized by projecting classroom wings framing a combined gymnasium and auditorium entered directly from the front door. The plan was introduced to the county by the state's Division of School Buildings in 1923 and was continued into the late 1930s after a halt in school construction brought on by the depression. The building departed from the norm by being of frame construction rather than brick. The school remains remarkably unchanged despite nearly sixty years of use. *(07–1154) VLR: 12/11/84; NRHP: 06/19/85.*

ESTALINE SCHOOLHOUSE, *Estaline.* With its blending of a simple form with more modern features, the Estaline Schoolhouse reflects the final expression of the one-room schoolhouse.

Opened in 1909, the plain gable-roofed structure is one of the last one-room schoolhouses built by the county. Because of the popularity of its teacher, the school remained in service long after most one-room schoolhouses closed, continuing until after World War II. Among its more modern features are the large windows, for light and ventilation, and a separate cloakroom. The classroom was finished with horizontal board sheathing. A low platform for the teacher's desk formerly stood opposite the entry. After its closing, the county rented the building and finally sold it in 1974. Though relatively unchanged since the busy days when the minds of the county youth were nurtured here, this landmark schoolhouse now stands idle. *(07–524) VLR: 12/11/84; NRHP: 02/27/85.*

FOLLY, *Mint Springs vicinity.* This compact Classical Revival plantation residence, set off by its outbuildings, old-fashioned gardens, and rural setting, is the focus of an ensemble uniquely Virginian. The house was begun in 1818 for Joseph Smith, a planter who served in the House of Delegates and was a member of the Virginia Constitutional Convention of 1850–51. Although the one-story, porticoed format echoes Thomas Jefferson's designs, no documentation suggests that Jefferson was directly involved. Smith, however, likely would have been acquainted with Jefferson's works and could have been inspired to imitation. The house survives unchanged except for the removal of one of its three porticoes for a west wing. Folly's serpentine garden wall is the state's only early 19th-century example of this unusual form. Its prototype, Jefferson's walls at the University of Virginia, have been rebuilt. Folly remains in the ownership of Smith's descendants. *(07–15) VLR: 09/18/73; NRHP: 10/25/73.*

GLEBE BURYING GROUND, *Swoope vicinity.* In 1749 the Anglican Augusta Parish purchased 200 acres in the western part of the county to serve both as income-producing glebe lands and as the site of a church and parsonage. The threat of Indian attack forced the parishioners to build in Staunton instead. Numerous burials, however, took place at the glebe, thus beginning one of the earliest cemeteries west of the Blue Ridge. Its oldest legible stone is dated 1770. The parish sold the glebe in 1802, but the cemetery remained in use throughout the 19th century. The various markers show the influence of English, Scotch-Irish, and German funerary art traditions. The oldest stones are slabs. Many of the upright stones are decorated with a German-style six-point compass star. The burying ground is now owned by the county and is maintained by the Augusta County Historical Society. *(07–1150) VLR: 03/16/82; NRHP: 10/01/85.*

GLEBE SCHOOLHOUSE, *Swoope vicinity.* This rare mid-19th-century one-room schoolhouse is on the former glebe of the colonial Augusta Parish. The simple gabled structure is in a form that was standard for rural schoolhouses of the period. It departs from the norm, however, by employing brick rather than wood construction, illustrating the Shenandoah Valley's strong masonry tradition. The school was most likely built as a private schoolhouse by the Thompson family around 1850. It was identified as Glebe Schoolhouse no. 19 on the 1884 Hotchkiss map of this section of Augusta County, indicating that it was a public school by then. The building was converted to a private residence when the county schools were consolidated in the early 20th century. Now empty, it stands in its remarkably beautiful setting, a relic of a vanishing aspect of rural America. *(07–706) VLR: 12/11/84; NRHP: 02/27/85.*

HANGER MILL, *Churchville vicinity.* Hanger Mill is an excellent and unaltered example of a mid-19th-century gristmill, a building type approaching near extinction. Scores of such mills once dotted the region, serving the Shenandoah Valley's flourishing wheat industry. The mill was constructed around 1860 for Jacob Hanger, a descendant of German settlers who came to the Valley before the Revolution. It is one of the few mills in Augusta County to escape the wanton burning in 1864 by Union troops under Gen. Philip Sheridan who systematically attempted to destroy the agricultural economy of the Shenandoah Valley. Its stone foundation, gable roof, heavy mortise-and-tenon framing, and four-level height are common elements of mills erected in the mid–19th century. The mill continued in operation until 1940. Most of its early machinery is intact. *(07–1211) VLR: 08/21/91; NRHP: 11/08/91.*

HARNSBERGER OCTAGONAL BARN, *Mount Meridian.* Built ca. 1867 under the direction of local carpenter William Evers, this interesting-looking structure reflects the infiltration of popular architectural theories into the agricultural community of Augusta County after the Civil War. Although it was likely inspired by octagonal building styles popularized by the writer and theorist Orson Squire Fowler, the Harnsberger barn did not copy Fowler's pattern-book designs directly. The builder instead combined these new ideas with more traditional local barn-building concepts, integrating the novel shape with the older bank barn form. The barn is still in regular use. *(07–37) VLR: 12/16/80; NRHP: 07/08/82.*

INTERVALE, *Churchville vicinity.* One of western Augusta County's most ambitious Federal-period farmhouses, Intervale was built ca. 1819 for Jonathan Shirley. The exterior employs the plain I-house form, a house type generally associated with farmers of English and Scotch-Irish extraction. The interior, however, boasts a vibrant decorative style of woodwork favored by the region's German element. The woodwork, which features carved eagles on three of the mantels, is the handiwork of Christian Bear, a joiner of German descent who came to the area from York, Pa. Intervale's stair also reflects a German influence with its heart designs carved into the brackets. Shirley sold Intervale in 1841 to the Shuey family who remained here for the next 100 years. In 1885 Theodore Shuey remodeled the exterior in the Colonial Revival style, adding the front porch and a dormered gambrel roof. *(07–18) VLR: 12/11/84; NRHP: 02/14/85.*

LONG GLADE FARM, *Spring Hill vicinity.* In the heart of Augusta County's idyllic countryside, Long Glade Farm boasts a finely preserved antebellum complex, the main feature of which is a brick dwelling built in 1848–52 for William Howell. A traditional Valley I-house with an original ell, the house has a stretcher-bond facade and a molded-brick cornice typical of the area. The front porch and interior woodwork are countrified versions of Greek Revival details extracted from architectural pattern books. Early graining remains on the hall woodwork. Near the house are two original outbuildings, a brick meat house and a two-story brick servants' house. An assortment of farm buildings, including a large late 19th-century bank barn, complete the assemblage. In 1972 Long Glade was purchased by Georgia S. Vance, a nationally recognized authority on dried flower arrangements. The farm's extensive flower garden is Mrs. Vance's creation. *(07–276) VLR: 10/18/95; NRHP: 01/22/96.*

MIDDLEBROOK GRADE SCHOOL AND HIGH SCHOOL, *Middlebrook.* These tall brick buildings, on a hill above the village of Middlebrook, are symbols of advances in rural public school facilities and expressions of local pride. The grade school was built in 1916 to accommodate the growing population of this prosperous turnpike town. The building was a community project with local residents contributing money, labor, and materials. It originally held high school grades, but additional growth necessitated a new high school building by the early 1920s. The high school was thus erected next door in 1923 and also was accomplished largely through local effort. The standardized building plans were adapted to meet the village's desire to have space for community gatherings. Instead of the usual large multipurpose room, the school had separate spaces for a gymnasium, an auditorium, and a community center. School consolidation led to the closing of both schools in 1967. *(07–686) VLR: 12/11/84; NRHP: 02/27/85.*

MIDDLEBROOK HISTORIC DISTRICT. Nestled in the Augusta County countryside south of Staunton, along Route 252—the historic Middlebrook Road—Middlebrook is one of the oldest villages in the region. Its linear plan preserves a grouping of 19th-century vernacular architecture still arranged according to the original town plat. Settlement began in the 1790s by Scotch-Irish immigrants, soon followed by German settlers. The first lots were sold by William and Nancy Scott in 1799. The rows of closely spaced dwellings and stores lining the main road maintain the character of the village as it appeared during the height of its prosperity in the 1880s. A variety of archaeological sites complements the architectural record and also documents black settlement at the west end of the village. Growth halted in the early 20th century when the Middlebrook Road ceased to be a major traffic artery. *(07–236) VLR: 07/21/81; NRHP: 02/10/83.*

HANNAH MILLER HOUSE, *Mossy Creek vicinity.* This small stone house has as its precedent the Continental bank house, a form employed to take advantage of hilly sites. The dwelling type was introduced to America by settlers of German extraction. The house stands on part of the tract owned by Henry Miller's Mossy Creek Iron Furnace. Built in 1814 for Henry Miller's widow Hannah, it is an early example of a *Stöckli,* a Swiss-German term for a small house set aside for retired parents. Such housing for the elderly, although common among the Pennsylvania Germans, was unusual in Virginia. The original portion consists of one room on each level with a plain interior. Attached to one side is an early 20th-century frame wing. The house stood unoccupied for many years but is undergoing a long-term rehabilitation. *(07–269) VLR: 12/19/78; NRHP: 05/24/79.*

HENRY MILLER HOUSE, *Mossy Creek vicinity.* On a hillside site next to the county road, this late 18th-century limestone farmhouse, one of the earliest large houses in the region, was erected for Henry Miller, a local iron manufacturer. Miller's nearby Mossy Creek furnace produced a wide range of household utensils and supplied cannonballs and arms during the Revolutionary War. His house reflects the amalgamation of British and Germanic building traditions that occurred in the region toward the end of the century. The stonework and floor plan are Germanic in style, while the general outline of the house and the placement of the chimney on the end of the house show a Georgian influence. A brick wing was added to the building's west end in the early 19th century. Most of the robust original woodwork of the older section survives. *(07–70) VLR: 02/21/78; NRHP: 05/23/79.*

MILLER-HEMP HOUSE, *Middlebrook vicinity.* The murals in the 1884 Miller-Hemp house are the region's most extensive and best-preserved demonstration of the craft of a 19th-century rural itinerant painter. The wide variety of decoration shows the creativity and broad repertoire of local artist Green Berry Jones, who signed and dated his work June 17, 1892. Large, brightly painted landscape and hunting scenes, along with vignettes containing popular figures such as Buffalo Bill, line the central hallway. Wood-grained doors and marbleized mantels with stenciled designs highlight the second-floor rooms. An amusing feature is the labeling of each room above its hall doorway. Although several other examples of Jones's artistry remain in the county, none equals the Miller-Hemp house. Like much of the Shenandoah Valley interior painting, Jones's work is a contrast to a plain exterior. *(07–638) VLR: 06/16/81; NRHP: 07/08/82.*

HENRY MISH BARN, *Middlebrook vicinity.* Erected ca. 1849 for Henry Mish, a native of York County, Pa., who settled in Virginia in 1839, this brick and frame structure illustrates the diffusion of the forebay bank barn from southeastern Pennsylvania into the Shenandoah Valley. Although the form became standard in Augusta County during the 19th century, this is one of the few pre–Civil War examples to have survived the Valley barn-burning campaigns by Union forces. Lending distinction to the Mish barn are the decorative brick lattice ventilators in the gable ends, also a feature prevalent in Pennsylvania barns. Most of the interior fittings have been removed or rearranged, but the heavy truss framing is intact. The barn has remained in continous use on this family farm, which also includes a mid-19th-century brick farmhouse, log tenant house, and several outbuildings. *(07–122) VLR: 12/14/82; NRHP: 02/10/83.*

MOFFETT'S CREEK SCHOOLHOUSE, *Newport.* The Augusta County School Board purchased this parcel next to the Mount Herman Cemetery in 1873 and erected a one-room school the same year. This was the first year of the county's program to acquire older private schools and to build new ones in its effort to develop a countywide free public school system. The growth of the village of Newport necessitated the addition of a second room in 1890. The school thus became one of twenty-two two-room graded schools in the county. The school was succeeded by a larger facility in 1923, and the property was sold to the Mount Herman Lutheran Church the following year. The building is still in use by the church's cemetery association, and its basic form has not changed, making it a reminder of the simple accommodation of rural education before the turn of the century. *(07–547) VLR: 12/11/84; NRHP: 02/27/85.*

MOUNT PLEASANT, *Spring Hill vicinity.* This venerable stone dwelling may have been erected as early as the 1760s by John Archer following his purchase of the property in 1763. In 1786 the place was acquired by Col. George Moffett, a Revolutionary War hero. Colonel Moffett's militia distinguished themselves at the 1780 battle of King's Mountain, N.C.; in 1781 they fought under Gen. Nathanael Greene in the battle of Cowpens, S.C. Colonel Moffett returned to Augusta County after the Revolution and served as one of the first trustees of what later became Washington and Lee University. The hall-parlor dwelling is a characteristic example of traditional Shenandoah Valley domestic architecture, exhibiting little academic influence. It was acquired by the Dunlap family in 1826, during whose tenure the interior was remodeled. On the property is a collection of farm buildings of various dates. The house has recently been restored. *(07–24) VLR: 04/18/89; NRHP: 10/30/89.*

MOUNT MERIDIAN SCHOOLHOUSE, *Mount Meridian.* The one-room country school is an American icon. Though an educational facility could hardly be more rudimentary, thousands of these humble structures provided the fundamentals of education to America's children for over a century. Built in 1885, the Mount Meridian Schoolhouse is among the few remaining and least-altered of the numerous one-room schools that dotted the county in the late 19th century. It was constructed by the Middle River School Board and was expanded to two rooms by 1890. Like most, the building was heated by a central stove and never had interior plumbing. The school closed in 1908 and was sold into private ownership. It was rented as a dwelling in the 1930s and 1940s but now stands unused in a cow pasture. The extra classroom has since been removed, returning the building to its original form. *(07–996) VLR: 12/11/84; NRHP: 02/27/85.*

MOUNT SIDNEY SCHOOL, *Mount Sidney.* Built in 1912 by the Staunton contractor Charles Fretwell, the Mount Sidney School is Augusta County's only remaining vestige of the first stage of school consolidation occurring in 1900–1915. These larger school buildings were a great leap from the simple one- and two-room buildings, most of which were without plumbing or electricity. The majority of the first consolidated schools were wood-frame, and nearly all of them have been razed. Mount Sidney is the county's only documented brick school of this period. The area's growing student population required an addition in 1921. In the 1950s the high school students were transferred to Weyers Cave. The school continued as an elementary school until 1967 when it was closed. Subsequently converted into apartments, the building nonetheless remains an important milestone in the county's educational history. *(07–1155) VLR: 12/11/84; NRHP: 02/27/85.*

MOUNT TORRY FURNACE, *Sherando vicinity.* Mount Torry, established in 1804, was one of the many iron furnaces in operation in the mountains of western Virginia during the 19th century. Shut down in 1854, it was reopened seven years later to supply pig iron to Richmond's Tredegar Iron Works for Confederate armaments. Tredegar purchased the furnace in 1863 to control its iron supply, but Union troops raided the site in 1864 and put it out of operation. Unlike many of the region's furnaces, Mount Torry was put back into blast after the Civil War and remained in production until 1892 when it was finally abandoned. Now preserved by the U.S. Department of Agriculture Forest Service as part of the George Washington and Jefferson National Forests, the tapered stone structure is a relic of an important 19th-century Virginia industry. *(07–871) VLR: 07/17/73; NRHP: 02/25/74.*

MOUNT ZION SCHOOLHOUSE, *Stokesville vicinity.* Providing no more than was absolutely necessary for basic elementary schooling in a rural area, the Mount Zion schoolhouse is nonetheless Augusta County's least-altered two-room schoolhouse built as such. It was completed in 1876 and remained in use as a public school until 1942. By 1880 it served sixty-five pupils with an average daily attendance of thirty-four. In its last years of operation, only one classroom, serving grades one through four, was in use. Grades five through seven were bused to a neighboring consolidated school, and their former classroom was used for storing wood and the water bucket. The building was sold by the county in 1948 and converted into a residence, but with little change to the exterior. It currently stands unoccupied. *(O7–1165) VLR: 12/11/84; NRHP: 02/27/85.*

NEW HOPE ELEMENTARY SCHOOL, *New Hope.* Built in 1925, the New Hope School was among the first modern high schools in Augusta County and is the best-preserved example of the first group of central-auditorium-plan consolidated schools of the 1920s. New Hope's design conforms to one of the state Division of School Building's standard plans, "18-F Special," an expanded version of the "18-F," entitled "Standard One-Story Eight-Room School, Unexcavated." The revised plan incorporated many of the new specialized spaces suggested for modern high schools including a library, office, stage, and home economics room. The nontraditional architecture reflects the emerging emphasis on functional design for public works. The school was built by the Eustler Brothers of Grottoes, who also built three similar schools for the county. The building was converted into an elementary school in 1947, when the modernistic front canopy was added. The building has stood unused since 1994. *(07–1087) VLR: 12/11/84; NRHP: 02/27/85.*

NORTH RIVER ELEMENTARY SCHOOL, *Moscow vicinity.* Although converted to an elementary school in 1968–69, the North River School is a landmark in Virginia public education as Augusta County's, and indeed the state's, first consolidated high school. Opened in 1936, the school grew out of a concern for the crowding and inadequate facilities in the many small high schools in the various districts. Better road conditions made such a centralized high school possible, and North River represented a consolidation of the high school classes of four districts, leaving elementary classes in the existing buildings. Employing the central-auditorium plan, the new school was a straightforward design, one provided by the state Division of School Buildings. It included a library, offices, laboratory, and home economics department. Agricultural classes were taught in a detached building. The school was enlarged in 1942, but the original three-part facade remains essentially unchanged. *(07–1153) VLR: 12/11/84; NRHP: 02/27/85.*

OLD PROVIDENCE STONE CHURCH, *Spottswood vicinity.* This simple Presbyterian meetinghouse was erected in 1793 to serve a congregation founded a half century earlier. It remained in service until 1859 when its congregation outgrew it and built a larger structure nearby. The building was subsequently used as a school, residence, general store, and finally a social hall. It was gutted by fire in 1959, but its congregation gave it some semblance of its original appearance with the replacement of its roof and windows. Its exterior now serves to illustrate the plain character of the Shenandoah Valley's early stone meetinghouses. Buried in its cemetery are the parents of Cyrus McCormick, inventor of the reaper, and the parents of J. A. E. Gibbs, inventor of an early sewing machine. *(07–25) VLR: 08/15/72; NRHP: 12/05/72.*

PAINE RUN ARCHAEOLOGICAL SITE, *near Paine Run Rockshelter, Shenandoah National Park.* A functionally varied prehistoric site with high artifact density, this small area along the bank of Paine Run probably served as a staging ground for Indians' seasonal movement into the Blue Ridge in Archaic times. The site was discovered in 1976 as part of a systematic survey of Paine Run undertaken by the Laboratory of Archaeology of the University of Virginia. Abundant comparative data from this and other Paine Run sites offer archaeologists an almost unparalleled opportunity to investigate the effects of altitude on prehistoric hunting and domestic patterns on the western face of the mountains. Its high frequency of red jasper artifacts is unique in the Shenandoah National Park and suggests early Paleo-Indian occupation (9500 to 8000 B.C.) of the site. *(07–1148) VLR: 09/16/82; NRHP: 12/13/85.*

PAINE RUN ROCK-SHELTER ARCHAEOLOGICAL SITE, *beside Paine Run, Shenandoah National Park.* Rockshelters along streams provided handy protection and shelter for Indians for many centuries. Representing at least 3,000 years of periodic small-scale occupation, the Paine Run rockshelter provides local evidence of stylistic and technological evolution in prehistoric stone projectile points and ceramics preserved here. It and the other prehistoric sites identified by University of Virginia archaeologists in a 1976 survey of this area of the Shenandoah National Park demonstrate that the region was most heavily populated during the Late Archaic–Early Woodland periods but was little used in Late Woodland times. The site thus helps document that a major change in lifestyle occurred in the Blue Ridge before the coming of the Europeans. *(07–1147) VLR: 09/16/82; NRHP: 12/13/85.*

LEWIS SHUEY HOUSE, *Swoope vicinity.* The Lewis Shuey house is a rare example in Augusta County of an 18th-century house showing the influence of German Rhenish–style construction. Built of logs sheathed in weatherboards, it possesses one of the county's two known *Flurküchenhaus* floor plans, a German-type plan that consists of three rooms around a central chimney with a corner stair. It also has the county's only known German-style common-rafter roof system with heavy underframe. One of the three rooms, the *Küche* or kitchen, preserves its original 6-foot-wide cooking fireplace. Original exposed framing members such as summer beams are seen throughout the interior. The house was built ca. 1795–1800 for Lewis Shuey, a veteran of the Revolutionary War, whose grandfather had immigrated to Pennsylvania from the Rhineland in 1732, and who himself moved from Pennsylvania to western Augusta County in 1795. *(07–700) VLR: 03/16/82; NRHP: 02/10/83.*

SUGAR LOAF FARM, *Arbor Hill vicinity.* Named for Sugar Loaf Mountain, a conical hill dominating the property, Sugar Loaf Farm is an impressive early 19th-century farm complex. The property was acquired by the Summers family in the 1770s. By 1830 David Summers had built the existing primary buildings—the farmhouse, the miller's house, and the gristmill. These substantial brick structures demonstrate a high level of craftsmanship and incorporate details, such as molded-brick cornices and corbeled chimneys, characteristic of the region's early vernacular architecture. The original part of the house has a hall-parlor plan with a ca. 1870 I-house addition. The mill, the county's only surviving brick mill, originally had machinery operating on the principles of Oliver Evans, an 18th-century mill designer. Various other farm buildings and the sites of vanished structures add to the interest of this well-tended estate. *(07–32) VLR: 04/17/91; NRHP: 07/09/91.*

VALLEY RAILROAD STONE BRIDGE, *Jolivue vicinity.* This graceful example of masonry engineering is a relic of the now abandoned Valley Railroad line between Staunton and Lexington. The four-arch bridge across Folly Mills Creek was erected in 1884 and is maintained as a scenic landmark for travelers along Interstate Highway 81 by the Virginia Department of Transportation. The bridge is built with rough-faced granite ashlar with smooth-face ashlar employed in the soffits of the arches. The arches are supported on gently tapered stone piers. The Valley Railroad was later absorbed by the Baltimore and Ohio Railroad. This branch was discontinued in 1942, and the tracks have since been removed. *(07–41) VLR: 09/17/74; NRHP: 11/19/74.*

TINKLING SPRING PRESBYTERIAN CHURCH, *Fishersville vicinity.* Founded in the late 1730s, Tinkling Spring Church houses the second oldest Presbyterian congregation in the Shenandoah Valley. The pioneering preacher John Craig was its first pastor. The present building, the third to serve its worshipers, was designed and built under the direction of its incumbent minister, Robert Lewis Dabney, who was the architect of several churches in the state. Dabney described his design, executed in 1850, as "the plainest Doric denuded of all ornaments." The chaste building, distinguished by its portico *in antis,* is similar to the chapel Dabney designed for Hampden-Sydney College. Its no-nonsense character appealed to Calvinist austerity and influenced the architecture of a number of Virginia's Presbyterian churches. Among the early families of the Tinkling Spring community were the Prestons, the Breckenridges, and the Johnstons, whose members lie buried in the cemetery. *(07–33) VLR: 01/16/73; NRHP: 04/11/73.*

VERONA SCHOOL, *Verona.* The three-room public school marked an advance in rural education in Virginia counties in the early 20th century. Its predecessor one-room school evolved into the two-room school in the 1880s. The two-room schools were usually divided into the primary room serving grades one through three and the secondary room for grades four through seven. The three-room school included a room often used for high school grades. Although the Augusta County School Board built a number of three-room schools, the 1911 Verona School is the only one remaining. Here, however, only grades one through five were taught. The plan consisted of two classrooms flanking a center hall, with the third classroom in an ell. The school closed in the 1940s. Around 1956 the building was moved back from the highway and converted into a residence for a motel manager. *(07–1299) VLR: 12/11/84; NRHP: 02/27/85.*

WALKER'S CREEK SCHOOLHOUSE, *Newport vicinity.*
Though remodeled and expanded through conversion into a
private residence, this barely noticeable little building is one of
the oldest remaining schoolhouses in Augusta County and is
the only known school of log construction. At the time of the
establishment of the free public school system in 1870, Augusta
County had 115 log schools; the number dwindled to 10 by
1890. Built in the 1850s, the Walker Creek School was purchased
for $30 by the county school board in 1873 and functioned as a
one-room school until the consolidation of area public schools
in the early 1900s. The property was sold by the school board in
1948 for $155. The building's nearly square plan reflects the
form commonly used for one-room schools. *(07–539) VLR:
12/11/84; NRHP: 02/27/85.*

WEST VIEW SCHOOL, *Weyers Cave vicinity.* A landmark
along one of the county's many scenic country roads, the West
View schoolhouse was built as a one-room school in 1875, during Augusta County's first wave of school construction after the
Underwood Constitution of 1869 mandated a free public
school system. The completely plain structure displays the dimensions and frame construction that characterized these early
free schools. The school was enlarged to two rooms in 1890.
West View continued to serve its rural neighborhood until 1917
when area schools were consolidated into the new Weyers Cave
School. The building was sold into private ownership in 1929
and has since been used for storage. Remarkably unchanged,
the interior preserves original board sheathing on walls and
ceiling, never painted or whitewashed. Simple wooden shelves
still line the central wall. *(07–426) VLR: 12/11/84; NRHP: 02/27/85.*

WEYERS CAVE SCHOOL, *Weyers Cave.* In an effort to provide fully equipped modern schools, Augusta County in the
early 1900s began a program of consolidating one- and two-
room schools, replacing them with finely appointed new buildings. Begun in 1916, the Weyers Cave School illustrates one of
the first major accomplishments of the consolidation program.
The stately structure is a vivid contrast to the tiny country
schools that originally served the county. Weyers Cave played
a leading role in the development of the county's vocational
education program. It became one of the county's two Smith-
Hughes agricultural high schools, instituting a four-year agricultural program in 1926. In 1927 the Weyers Cave students organized the Future Farmers of Virginia, a club that in 1928
evolved into the nationwide organization, Future Farmers of
America. The school was doubled in size in 1924. Closed in
1994, the buildings are now used by a religious organization.
(07–1156); VLR: 12/11/84; NRHP: 02/23/85.

BATH COUNTY

Noted for its many mineral springs, Bath County was named for Bath, England, also famed for its spa. It was formed in 1790 from Augusta, Botetourt, and Greenbrier (now in West Virginia) counties. The county seat is Warm Springs.

HIDDEN VALLEY (WARWICKTON), *Bacova vicinity.* This formal Greek Revival mansion, its facade dominated by an Ionic portico, takes its name from its matchless setting in a narrow, remote valley of the Allegheny Mountains through which the Jackson River flows. The house, originally called Warwickton, was built ca. 1857 for Judge James Warwick, grandson of Jacob Warwick, Indian fighter and pioneer settler of Bath County. Most of the polished academic detailing was adapted from designs in Asher Benjamin's *The Practical House Carpenter* (1830), thus illustrating how builders, even in the farther reaches of the South, made use of this popular Boston pattern book. In 1965 the house and surrounding lands were acquired by the U.S. Forest Service. The house has since been leased and privately restored as an inn. *(08–04) VLR: 12/02/69; NRHP: 02/26/70.*

DOUTHAT STATE PARK, *Millboro vicinity.* Encompassing over 4,000 acres of scenic mountain lands, Douthat State Park was the first of six state parks established in Virginia by the Civilian Conservation Corps (CCC) in the period 1933–42. Associated with the nationwide public works programs of the New Deal, the Douthat project offered gainful employment to 600 men of three CCC companies during its nine years of development. The CCC program sought to conserve natural and scenic resources while providing healthy retreats for visitors. Architectural and engineering highlights of the park are the fifty-five-acre lake with its dam and spillway, as well as the guest lodge and the original complex of twenty-five guest cabins. These buildings, with their high-quality craftsmanship, were published as models of rustic park architecture. The spirit of the park's original plans has been carefully maintained by the Virginia Department of Conservation and Recreation. *(08–136) VLR: 06/17/86; NRHP: 09/20/86.*

HIDDEN VALLEY ROCKSHELTER, *Bacova vicinity.* This native American archaeological site consists of an irregularly shaped overhang approximately 90 feet by 10 feet. The shelter is formed within the Oriskany sandstone formation and lies along the west bank of the Jackson River about 20 feet above the normal river flow. The shelter area contains the stratified remains of human occupation from the Late Archaic (3000 B.C.) through the Late Woodland periods (A.D. 1600). The wide variety of projectile points and ceramic types found here reflects subtle shifts in several cultures through time. The excellent state of the preservation of the site's floral and faunal materials offers an opportunity to study western Virginia subsistence patterns spanning the last 2,000 to 3,000 years. *(08–137)* *VLR: 12/17/85; NRHP: 07/22/86.*

THE HOMESTEAD, *Hot Springs.* Hot Springs has been accommodating visitors since 1766 when a small hotel, known as the Homestead, was built here. It was replaced by a large wooden hotel, erected in stages in the 19th century, which burned in 1901. Only the 1892 spa building, designed by Yarnell and Go-

forth, and several cottages survived. Its replacement, the present Homestead Hotel, is a prodigious Colonial Revival work by Elzner and Anderson of Cincinnati. The landmark central tower was added in 1929 by Warren and Wetmore of New York. The Olmstead Brothers of Boston landscaped the Homestead's grounds in the 1920s. Following Pearl Harbor, the hotel was used for the internment of 363 Japanese nationals. The International Food Conference, a precursor of the United Nations, was held here in 1943. The Homestead continues as an internationally known resort; its celebrated golf course preserves what is said to be the nation's oldest first tee in continuous use. *(08–25)* *VLR: 03/20/84; NRHP: 05/03/84; NHL: 07/17/91.*

OLD STONE HOUSE (ROBERT SITLINGTON HOUSE), *Millboro Springs vicinity.* Erected in the 1790s for Robert Sitlington, a settler who took a leading role in the organization of the county, this fieldstone vernacular farmhouse is one of the oldest dwellings in Bath County. Standing in an area containing few examples of stone architecture, the house shows the influence of the Germanic building practices typical of the Shenandoah Valley. In a conscious effort to imitate the solid two-story houses of the well-established Valley settlements, Sitlington was attempting to bring a sense of stability and permanence to his far-western home on the Cowpasture River. The facade porches were added in the late 19th century. Most of the original woodwork was removed during a 1920s remodeling. The house underwent a restoration in the early 1980s. *(08–105)* *VLR: 12/14/82; NRHP: 02/10/83.*

WARM SPRINGS BATHHOUSES (THE JEFFERSON POOLS AT WARM SPRINGS), *Warm Springs.* One of the country's oldest spas, Warm Springs has been visited by travelers seeking its curative benefits since the mid–18th century and was used by Indians before that. The two simple wooden bathhouses, one for men, the other for women, are rare survivals of a bygone era of Virginia's social and medical history and are still used for their original purpose. The octagonal men's bathhouse, perhaps the nation's oldest spa building, traditionally dates from 1761 although much of its fabric likely has been renewed. The claim of Jeffersonian design has not been documented. The twenty-sided women's bathhouse dates to the early 19th century. Both structures frame the clear bubbling pools of warm water and are open to the sky. The spa is owned by the Homestead Hotel in nearby Hot Springs and is a featured amenity for the Homestead's guests. *(08–07) VLR: 11/05/68; NRHP: 10/08/69.*

WARM SPRINGS MILL, *Warm Springs.* Also known as Miller's Mill, the Warm Springs Mill is the only remaining early gristmill in Bath County. A settlement with a mill has existed at this famous thermal spring since colonial times. The original mill here was observed by pioneer explorer Simon Kenton in 1771. The present mill, a replacement of a 19th-century mill, was erected after H. H. Miller's purchase of the property in 1901. The mill is typical of commercial gristmills of its period—a three-story, gable-roofed frame structure with an overshot Fitz waterwheel. It ceased operation in 1971 and was subsequently converted into a restaurant. The adjacent blacksmith shop and hardware store, part of the mill complex, were remodeled for retail use and lodging. Nearly all of the mill's machinery is intact. *(08–22) VLR: 02/16/88; NRHP: 09/11/89.*

CITY OF BEDFORD

Originally known as Liberty, Bedford became the Bedford county seat in 1782 when the court was moved here from New London. It was incorporated as a town in 1839. The name was changed to Bedford City in 1890 and to Bedford in 1912. It was incorporated as a city in 1969.

AVENEL, *413 Avenel Avenue.* Bedford's premier historic residence, Avenel was begun in 1835 for Frances Steptoe Burwell and William M. Burwell, son of William A. Burwell, secretary to Thomas Jefferson. William M. Burwell served in the Virginia legislature and was an emissary to Mexico. His prominence in the local political scene made Avenel a focal point of Bedford social life. An articulate blend of Federal and Greek Revival styling, the house exemplifies how skilled local craftsmen used designs from pattern books such as Asher Benjamin's *Practical House Carpenter* (1830) to embellish the interior. An interesting treatment is the division of the interior into two nearly equal halves, each with its own formal staircase. Originally the nucleus of a plantation, the house is now part of a turn-of-the-century residential neighborhood. In 1985 Avenel was acquired by the Avenel Foundation, which has since restored the house for public use. *(141–01) VLR: 12/11/91; NRHP: 01/30/92; BHR EASEMENT.*

BEDFORD HISTORIC DISTRICT. The Bedford Historic District, encompassing residential, commercial, and industrial areas, contains some 240 structures, displaying 19th- and 20th-century architectural styles and preserving a placid image of small-town America. Originally named Liberty, Bedford has served as the county seat and economic hub of Bedford County since 1782. Its situation on an early turnpike between Lynchburg and Salem and on the principal line of the old Virginia and Tennessee Railroad contributed to Bedford's 19th-century prosperity. Bedford was also a major center of tobacco manufacturing, ranking in 1881 as the state's fifth-largest producer of tobacco. The late Victorian character of the business section results from a rebuilding following a disastrous fire in 1884. Notable individual structures include the Greek Revival Presbyterian church, the 1912 Spanish Colonial Revival public school, and the stately 1930 Georgian Revival county courthouse designed by Clarence Henry Hinnant. *(141–73) VLR: 08/21/84; NRHP: 10/04/84.*

BEDFORD HISTORIC MEETING HOUSE, *153 West Main Street.* This simple Greek Revival structure, built in 1838 as the first Methodist church in Liberty (now Bedford), survives as the community's oldest religious edifice. The Methodists outgrew the little church by 1886 and sold it to the Episcopal Diocese as a house of worship for former slaves. It was reconsecrated as St. Philip's Episcopal Church, and its parishioners soon opened a day school which educated the town's black children until a black public school was established. The church was vacated when Bedford's black and white Episcopal congregations merged in 1968. The Bedford Historical Society acquired the building in 1969 and subsequently restored it for its headquarters. With its fine brickwork, pedimented roof, and pilastered belfry, the building is architecturally related to a number of antebellum churches scattered from Bedford to Southwest Virginia. *(141–05) VLR: 09/20/77; NRHP: 01/31/78; BHR EASEMENT.*

BURKS-GUY-HAGAN HOUSE, *520 Peaks Street.* The fanciful Burks-Guy-Hagan house, with its romantically landscaped grounds focusing on the Peaks of Otter, exemplifies the Victorian suburban villa. As defined by the 19th-century architectural writer Andrew Jackson Downing, the villa was "the most refined house of America—the home of its most leisurely and educated class of citizens." Like many of the villa designs published by Downing and others, the Burks-Guy-Hagan house has a picturesque silhouette accented by a central tower. It was built in 1884 for Judge Martin P. Burks, who became dean of the Washington and Lee University School of Law and later a justice of the Virginia Supreme Court of Appeals. He was also the author of Burks's *Pleading and Practice.* Local educator James R. Guy, ancestor of the present owners, purchased the property in 1907. *(141–27) VLR: 09/17/85; NRHP: 12/19/85; BHR EASEMENT.*

BEDFORD COUNTY

Named for John Russell, fourth duke of Bedford, an English statesman involved with colonial affairs, this Piedmont county in the shadow of the Peaks of Otter was formed from Lunenburg County in 1753, with parts of Albemarle and Lunenburg counties added later. The county seat is Bedford.

BELLEVUE, *Forest vicinity.* Placed to command long vistas of Bedford County's landscape, this patrician homestead is associated with educator and Confederate politician James Philemon Holcombe. The original house was built in two phases (1824 and 1840). After the Civil War, Holcombe established a private high school here. Bellevue High School prospered in the late 19th century, catering primarily to the sons of well-to-do families. In 1870 William Richardson Abbott joined Bellevue as associate principal, becoming headmaster after Holcombe's death in 1873. Competition from free public schools forced Bellevue's closing in 1909. Owned by Abbott descendants until 1995, the property still retains a dormitory building known as The Inkstand. Bellevue's original Federal-period section preserves its early 19th-century character. The antebellum portion has woodwork derived from designs in Asher Benjamin's *Practical House Carpenter* (1830). Several early outbuildings, an old garden, and a family cemetery remain on the grounds. *(09–03) VLR: 08/15/89; NRHP: 12/19/90.*

BROOK HILL FARM, *Forest vicinity.* An architectural hybrid, Brook Hill Farm's residence is distinct from the traditional architecture of the region yet references it in a number of details. The low profile and wide verandas make the house appear to be a product of the Deep South or even Texas, drawing influence from the Bungalow-Craftsman style. The design, however, was likely produced by its original owner, Graham Webb, a woman from Tennessee, who created a dwelling specifically for her taste. Completed in 1904, the house was occupied by Mrs. Webb and her husband Samuel. The Webbs sold the farm, called by them Rowncevilla, in 1909 to the Coleman family who erected a schoolhouse here for their children. The house remains little altered and retains noteworthy interior finishes, including inlaid floors, Greek Revival–style and Federal-style mantels, a spindle frieze, and an ornamental pressed-tin ceiling. *(09–318) VLR: 09/18/96; NRHP: 06/06/97.*

CIFAX RURAL HISTORIC DISTRICT. Centered around the tiny settlement of Cifax, in a scenic area of Bedford County, this 1,800-acre rural historic district defines a cultural landscape reflecting the region's two-century agricultural history. The tangible elements of its evolution include a network of tree-lined roads and 19th- and early 20th-century houses and farm structures dotting the hillsides. The dwellings and their dependencies consist of those of prosperous landowners along with simpler residences of farmers and laborers. Sprinkled among the farms are early schools and churches that served all levels of society. The focal point of Cifax is a Greek Revival farmhouse (shown) erected ca. 1855 for Anderson Poindexter, member of one of the area's leading families. Also within the district is a historic black settlement known as Scotchbroom City. *(09–254) VLR: 08/21/91; NRHP: 02/20/92.*

ELK HILL, *Forest vicinity.* The fertile soil of Bedford County spawned numerous fine farms in the late 18th century. One of the oldest, Elk Hill, preserves its Federal dwelling house built ca. 1797 for Waddy Cobbs, uncle of Nicholas Hamner Cobbs, the first rector of St. Stephen's Episcopal Church. Elk Hill's Flemish bond brickwork, formally spaced openings, and refined interior woodwork are evidence of the county's early architectural sophistication. The carved decorations on the mantels are adapted from illustrations in pattern books by the English architect William Pain. The farm was later owned by three generations of the Nelson family and was visited by their relative Thomas Nelson Page, a noted southern author who did some writing here. The house was restored in 1928 by Lynchburg architect Preston Craighill, who added the Federal-style porches. A small brick office, contemporary with the main house, stands nearby. *(09–06) VLR: 11/21/72; NRHP: 04/02/73; BHR EASEMENT.*

FANCY FARM, *Kelso Mill.* Fancy Farm's five-bay brick mansion with its pedimented gable ends ranks with Virginia's grandest examples of late Georgian domestic architecture. The exterior elevation and much of the interior detailing are based on illustrations in William Pain's *Practical Builder,* an 18th-century English pattern book. The architecturally elegant parlor is decorated with an elaborate chimneypiece, flanking arches, and Ionic pilasters. The house was built by Andrew Donald, a Scottish merchant, after his purchase of the property in 1794. As suggested by its name, Donald's new residence outshone its more modest neighbors and set a standard for the area. During the Civil War, Fancy Farm was occupied by Union general David Hunter. In 1921 the property was purchased by Sir George Sitwell, Bart., of the English literary family, for his nephew Capt. Herbert FitzRoy Sitwell. The house underwent extensive renovation in the late 1960s. *(09–07) VLR: 07/06/71; NRHP: 01/07/72.*

HOPE DAWN, *Boonesboro vicinity.* In a pastoral setting above the James River, this compact early 19th-century farmhouse is a refined and well-preserved example of Piedmont Virginia's Federal vernacular. Its finely crafted details and balanced proportions illustrate the high standards maintained by builders even for modest houses in relatively remote areas. Noteworthy features are the original porches, the Flemish bond brickwork, and the finely detailed Federal mantels based on designs in Owen Biddle's *The Young Carpenter's Assistant* (1805). The construction date is uncertain. The house may have been standing when the property was acquired in 1827 by Dr. Howell Davies, a Lynchburg druggist, who used Hope Dawn as a country home. Preserved in front of the house is a short section of the old Bethel Road, an early turnpike. The road still has its original stone retaining walls and dressed-stone gateposts. *(09–43) VLR: 09/17/74; NRHP: 10/09/74; BHR EASEMENT.*

LOCUST LEVEL, *Montvale.* Built in the 1820s, this brick house illustrates the high degree of architectural refinement common in many of Bedford County's early dwellings. Although basically an I-house, it is set off by a finely detailed doorway surround, modillion cornice, precise brickwork, and bold interior woodwork including a fine stair. The house was built for Paschal G. Buford (1791–1875), one of 19th-century Bedford County's largest landowners and developers. Buford was also an agronomist and a county justice. He is remembered locally for being responsible for securing a top rock from the Peaks of Otter from which a block was cut and sent as Virginia's contribution to the Washington Monument. In 1863 Locust Level served as a retreat for Gen. Robert E. Lee's wife and two daughters. On the property are the ruins of the 18th-century Henry Buford house, 19th-century outbuildings, and a family cemetery. *(09–18) VLR: 08/21/90; NRHP: 12/21/90.*

MOUNT AIRY, *Browntown vicinity.* An object of considerable antiquarian interest, Mount Airy was built ca. 1797 for Col. Thomas Leftwich, whose family subsequently built three similar houses in the county, each with a peculiar one-story wing that protruded from the facade. Mount Airy's wing was demolished ca. 1955, but the dwelling retains much of its bold late Georgian woodwork inside and out. Prominent on the exterior is the hefty modillion cornice. Inside is a wealth of original trim including paneled wainscoting, doors, cupboards, and mantels. Despite the loss of the original wing and subsequent later additions, the two-story core retains its hall-parlor plan. Thomas Leftwich settled in the area about 1752. He was active in the French and Indian War and the American Revolution. His fifty years of public service included a term as county justice and a seat in the Virginia General Assembly. *(09–221) VLR: 10/16/90; NRHP: 12/19/90.*

NEW LONDON ACADEMY, *New London vicinity.* Founded in 1795, the New London Academy is the only public secondary school in Virginia to operate under a charter from the General Assembly. Begun as a classical school for boys, it was established at its present location by 1797 and has operated continuously since that time. By the late 1880s it had become affiliated with the public school system and is currently an elementary school. The academy's oldest building, erected to replace an earlier frame building, is a simple but formal Greek Revival structure built 1837–39. It has continued in use in varying capacities to the present day. Marred by alterations over the years, its exterior was carefully restored to its original appearance in the early 1980s. Also on the property is an original kitchen outbuilding used as a museum of the academy's history. *(09–47) VLR: 12/21/71; NRHP: 04/13/72.*

OLD RECTORY, *Forest vicinity.* Preserving a commanding presence in the rolling farmland of western Bedford County, this country house was built ca. 1787 for Waddy Cobbs who later built the house at nearby Elk Hill. The T-shaped dwelling originally had a Palladian tripartite scheme with a two-story temple-form center section and one-story wings. The wings were raised to two stories in the antebellum period. As with a number of other area Federal houses, the woodwork has details based on illustrations in architectural pattern books by William Pain. From 1828 to 1904 the house was a center of local social life as the rectory of St. Stephen's Episcopal Church, which was founded by Nicholas Hamner Cobbs, nephew of Waddy Cobbs. The Doric portico was added soon after the house was returned to use as a private residence. *(09–56) VLR: 09/16/73; NRHP: 07/24/73.*

POPLAR FOREST, *Forest vicinity.* "The best dwelling house in the state" is how Thomas Jefferson described his Bedford County hermitage. Begun in 1806 on land inherited from his wife and completed by his death in 1826, this unique work demonstrates Jefferson's fascination with octagons. Its form is octagonal, three major rooms are elongated octagons, and the privies, tucked behind earthen mounds, are miniature domed octagons. The house was set in an elaborate villa landscape at the heart of a 4,800-acre plantation. Jefferson escaped the bustle of Monticello by visiting Poplar Forest several times a year. Here he found the peace to think, to study, and to read. After a fire in 1845, the house was rebuilt within its walls. It remained a private residence until the 1980s. In 1984 it was purchased by the Corporation for Jefferson's Poplar Forest, which is overseeing a meticulous restoration to Jefferson's original design. *(09–27) VLR: 05/13/69; NRHP: 11/12/69; NHL: 11/11/71.*

ROTHSAY, *Forest vicinity.* This architecturally refined residence was built in 1914 on the site of a Federal-period house that burned. The design represents an accomplished melding of the Georgian Revival and Craftsman styles popular during the early twentieth century. The Lynchburg firm of Heard and Cardwell designed a 1918 addition and likely designed the main part as well. Defining features are the spreading hipped roof, symmetrical facade, and unaltered interior woodwork. A garden terrace, designed by Washington landscape architect George E. Burnap in 1918, joins a combined dovecote–garden seat, a pump house, and several ancillary structures. Lynchburg architect Stanhope Johnson designed the gateposts. Behind the house are farm buildings viewed against a panoramic backdrop of the Blue Ridge Mountains. Rothsay was built for Octavius Loxley Clark Radford (1870–1935), who maintained here one of the largest and most progressive farming operations in the county. The property is owned by his descendants. *(09–65) VLR: 02/28/92; NRHP: 10/30/92.*

ST. STEPHEN'S EPISCOPAL CHURCH, *Forest vicinity.* St. Stephen's Church was established in 1824 by the Rev. Nicholas Hamner Cobbs, a Bedford County native, who was instrumental in bringing about a revival of the near-dormant Episcopal denomination in western Virginia. Cobbs later became bishop of Alabama. The congregation outgrew its original church and replaced it in 1844 with the present brick structure. A plain but refined Greek Revival building, the church is typical of the many antebellum houses of worship erected in the region by various denominations. Distinguishing features are the temple form with its pedimented gable, the triple-hung sash, and Flemish bond brickwork. From 1853 to 1858 St. Stephen's was served by the Rev. Richard Hooker Wilmer who also followed Cobbs as bishop of Alabama. The land on which the church is situated was originally part of Poplar Forest and was given to the parish by Anne Irving Moseley. *(09–29) VLR: 08/13/85; NRHP: 11/07/85.*

THREE OTTERS, *Bedford vicinity.* One of Virginia's most imaginative examples of country rural Greek Revival domestic architecture, this dwelling illustrates how the classical architectural vocabulary could be adapted to embellish fully modern, specifically American forms. Abel Beach Nichols, a Connecticut merchant, settled in Virginia in 1820 and built the house some ten years later. Although its designer-builder has not been identified, much of the detailing, inside and out, was faithfully reproduced from Asher Benjamin's *The Practical House Carpenter* (1830), a popular pattern book of the period. A unique feature is the series of small windows in the metopes that, when opened, form a ventilation system. Other features of interest include the marbleized stair, the Flemish bond brickwork, and the ruins of an original brick chicken house. *(09–31) VLR: 07/07/70; NRHP: 09/15/70.*

WOODBOURNE, *Forest vicinity.* Although built in three stages over a span of some forty years, this stucco and wood-frame plantation house presents an architecturally unified composition of pleasing proportions and shows Piedmont Federal architecture at its provincial best. The east wing, dating from the 1780s, is the earliest section. The stuccoed center pavilion with its classical pediment was added ca. 1810 and the west wing in the 1820s. The interior of the center section is marked by richly carved woodwork with designs freely adapted from contemporary architectural pattern books. Of particular interest is the first-floor mantel with its carved drapery swags and cornucopias. Woodbourne was erected on land purchased from Thomas Jefferson, who acquired it through his wife, Martha Wayles Skelton Jefferson. The house was built for William Radford and remains the property of his descendants. *(09–33) VLR: 04/17/73; NRHP: 07/02/73.*

BLAND COUNTY

Probably named for Richard Bland, a Virginia Revolutionary patriot, this sparsely populated mountainous county was formed in 1861 from Giles, Wythe, and Tazewell counties. The county seat is Bland.

MOUNTAIN GLEN, *Ceres vicinity.* A visual anchor in time, this antebellum homestead is nestled in a hollow on the lower slopes of Walker Mountain, overlooking the valley watered by the North Fork of the Holston River. The core of the complex is a two-story frame house built about 1850 for John Respass, son of John Frederick Respass, one of the area's early settlers. The house is said to have been constructed by John Lock, a Tennessee builder. In addition to farming, John Respass was a minister in the Reformed church. The complex includes a picturesque medley of 19th- and early 20th-century outbuildings and farm buildings. Mountain Glen was continuously occupied by members of the Respass and Hudson families until 1997. Unchanged by the present owner, the place preserves the air of a gentry family farm. *(10–39) VLR: 08/15/89; NRHP: 01/24/91.*

SHARON LUTHERAN CHURCH AND CEMETERY, *Ceres vicinity.* The Sharon complex was established by Lutherans who were a branch of the large German settlement of Wythe County. The first church here was built in 1821. The cemetery contains a significant number of boldly carved Germanic gravestones, documenting the artistry and rich folk culture of these settlers. The fifty to sixty surviving stones relate stylistically to those in early Lutheran cemeteries in both Wythe and Tazewell counties. These thick sandstone slabs are decorated on both sides and make use of standard Germanic motifs such as eight-petaled flowers, hearts, vines, and abstract geometrical shapes. The present church was built ca. 1883 to replace the 1821 church and retains a little-altered Eastlake-style interior. The Lutherans shared both this church and its predecessor with a Presbyterian congregation until 1911 when the latter group built its own structure. *(10–40) VLR: 11/21/78; NRHP: 02/01/79.*

BOTETOURT COUNTY

Named for Norborne Berkeley, baron de Botetourt, Virginia's royal governor from 1768 to 1770, this pastoral as well as mountainous western Virginia county was formed from Augusta County in 1769, with part of Rockbridge County added later. The county seat is Fincastle.

ANNANDALE, *Rocky Point vicinity.* Patented in the 18th century by Benjamin Estill, Annandale is a large and prosperous farm situated along the James River in a remote corner of Botetourt County. The present house was built in 1835 for Richard H. Burks, a successful planter who ran the place with some sixty-four slaves, growing tobacco and wheat. The completion of the James River and Kanawha Canal along his property in 1851 enabled Burks to ship his crops directly to market. Though an accomplished example of country Greek Revival, the general form of the house follows a traditional Georgian format with double-pile plan, three-bay facade, and hipped roof. The Grecian qualities are restricted to details such as the Greek fret window lintels and symmetrical architrave door and window frames. The parlor has an ornamental plasterwork cornice and ceiling medallion. An unusual hexagonal brick smokehouse is an original outbuilding. *(11–41) VLR: 12/09/92; NRHP: 02/11/93.*

BESSEMER ARCHAEOLOGICAL SITE, *Bessemer vicinity.* On the bottomlands of the James River, the Bessemer archaeological site has features dating to the 14th century A.D. Evidence of two distinct but overlapping Indian cultures has been identified, including an indigenous Dan River–phase palisaded village and an intrusive Page-phase village, whose people migrated from the north. The site also preserves well-defined remains of rectangular and circular houses, storage pits, and human burials, along with floral and faunal remains. Further archaeological investigation should add to the knowledge of the region's prehistoric community organization and cultural interactions. *(11–188) VLR: 09/16/82; NRHP: 12/15/84.*

BRECKINRIDGE MILL, *Fincastle vicinity.* Breckinridge Mill is a remnant of the grain and milling industry that figured significantly in the economy of antebellum Virginia. One of the oldest mills in the region, the multilevel brick structure was erected in 1822 by James Breckinridge, a leading Federalist politician and landowner of southwestern Virginia, who lived in a mansion (destroyed) nearby. The fine quality of the mill's construction is shown in the Flemish bond brickwork. Like most of Virginia's early gristmills, Breckinridge Mill stood abandoned for many years after the introduction of modern milling establishments. The building received a new lease on life when it was sympathetically converted to apartments in 1980. The mill replaced an 1804 mill also erected by Breckinridge. *(11–187) VLR: 05/20/80; NRHP: 07/30/80.*

CALLIE FURNACE, *Glen Wilton vicinity.* Callie Furnace is a late example of the iron furnaces that dotted the mountains of western Virginia in the 19th century. It was constructed in 1873 by D. S. Cook, who named it after his wife, Caroline Wilton Cook. A high-grade iron ore was mined on the property, and the pig iron produced here was transported by rail to waiting mills in Ohio and Pennsylvania. The furnace went out of blast after 1884 but remains in a good state of preservation. The gently tapered stone structure is typical of area furnace design and rises 33 feet above the firebox. It was fueled first with charcoal but was modified in 1875 to use coke. The structure is now within the George Washington and Jefferson National Forests and is maintained by the U.S. Department of Agriculture Forest Service. *(11–65) VLR: 07/17/73; NRHP: 01/21/74.*

FINCASTLE HISTORIC DISTRICT. Named for Lord Fincastle, son of Virginia's last royal governor, Lord Dunmore, this county-seat village was founded in 1772 and was one of the last civilized outposts for pioneers moving west through the Valley of Virginia. The town's grid plan was laid out by William Preston, the county surveyor. Many of the earliest buildings have been lost through devastating fires, although several streets retain weatherboarded log dwellings. The gleaming spires of three antebellum churches: St. Mark's Episcopal (1837); the Methodist church (1840); and the Presbyterian church, an 18th-century structure remodeled as a Greek Revival building in 1849, punctuate the leafy streets. Another important spire is that on the county courthouse, originally built in 1845–48 and reconstructed after a fire in 1970. One of the most picturesque historic towns in western Virginia, Fincastle preserves its setting of rolling farmland and surrounding mountains. *(218–51) VLR: 05/13/69; NRHP: 11/17/69.*

LOONEY MILL CREEK ARCHAEOLOGICAL SITE, *Buchanan vicinity.* This tract near the junction of Looney Creek and the James River contains archaeological sites of both prehistoric and historic interest. Intensive Indian settlement during the Late Woodland period (A.D. 900–1600) was confirmed by excavations uncovering human burials, storage pits, and post molds suggesting a house pattern. Robert Looney established his homestead here in 1742, and his place, known as Looney's Mill or Looney's Ferry, was visited by many settlers traveling on the adjacent Great Road on their way west. Historic features include a colonial ditch and a stone foundation with a brick addition, presumed to have belonged to Robert Looney's residence. *(11–184) VLR: 04/19/77; NRHP: 08/03/78.*

NININGER'S MILL (TINKER MILL), *Daleville vicinity.*
When Peter Nininger built this brick mill on Tinker Creek in
1847, he was continuing a milling tradition in Botetourt County that began with the county's first settlers. Beside the Pittsyl-
vania-Franklin-Botetourt Turnpike, which connected the farmlands of western Virginia with bustling Southside markets, the
mill operated for decades as a quasi-public utility, offering one
of the rural economy's most important services. Like most of
Virginia's old gristmills, Nininger's Mill was forced out of business because of an inability to compete with the modern
milling complexes. The mill was converted to a restaurant in
1968, but some of the original machinery was preserved. The
structure is now a private residence. A late 19th-century overshot metal wheel remains in place on the north wall. *(11–57)*
VLR: 05/20/80; NRHP: 07/30/80.

PHOENIX BRIDGE, *Route 685, Eagle Rock vicinity.* In an
undisturbed scenic setting, the Phoenix Bridge is the most decorative of Virginia's fast-disappearing metal-truss bridges. Its

manufacturer, the Phoenix Bridge Company of Phoenixville,
Pa., was a leading prefabricator of wrought-iron bridges in the
late 19th century. The technology of metal bridge construction
made possible a greatly improved transportation network for
rural America after the Civil War. The Phoenix Bridge is a pin-
connected structure incorporating a Pratt through truss. It employs the special Phoenix post, a compression member composed of four flanged segments riveted together. The whole is
decorated with Gothic motifs including finials, quatrefoils, and
trefoils. The bridge was built in 1887 and moved to its present
site spanning Craig Creek in 1903 where it served as a railroad
bridge. It was converted to highway use in 1961. *(11–95) VLR:*
02/18/75; NRHP: 06/10/75.

PROSPECT HILL, *Fincastle.* On the summit of a steep
grassy hill, this late Federal farmhouse, one of the principal historic landmarks of Botetourt County, commands panoramic
views of mountains, farmland, and the village of Fincastle.
Built ca. 1837–38 for John Gray, the county sheriff, the exterior
has a two-level portico and rare flush-board siding. Especially
noteworthy are the entrance fanlight and pediment lunette
with their lively intersecting tracery. The interior is decorated
with marbleizing and wood graining. The stenciled band in the
west parlor is a decorative device rarely surviving in Virginia
houses of the period. Local artistry is also evident in the carved
stair brackets and carved facia of the stair landing. The one-
story wings are later additions. *(11–185) VLR: 09/18/79; NRHP:*
12/28/79; BHR EASEMENT.

ROARING RUN FURNACE, *Eagle Rock vicinity.* Typical of the scores of iron furnaces that were sprinkled through the hills and mountains of western Virginia is Roaring Run Furnace, a single-stack, hot-blast charcoal furnace built of large squared stones. It was constructed in 1832, rebuilt in 1845, and rebuilt again early in the Civil War. Most of the pig iron produced during its last years was shipped to Richmond for use by the Tredegar Iron Works in manufacturing arms. The furnace was abandoned after the war, and the property was later incorporated into what is now the George Washington and Jefferson National Forests. The structure is preserved as a point of interest by the U.S. Department of Agriculture Forest Service. *(11–63) VLR: 06/15/76; NRHP: 03/21/83.*

SANTILLANE, *Fincastle.* This antebellum mansion occupies an elevated site just outside of Fincastle, making it one of the architectural highlights of the pastoral landscape around the county seat. The property was long owned by the Hancock family; however, the present imposing Greek Revival house was built in the 1830s for Henry Bowyer, formerly an officer in Washington's army and clerk of the court of Botetourt County for forty-three years. The house is known for its finely crafted brickwork, lofty rooms, and an unusually wide stair hall. The tall portico, added in the 20th century, replaces an earlier porch. In recent years Santillane was the home of R. D. Stoner, also a longtime clerk of the court and the author of *A Seed-Bed of the Republic* (1962), a history of Botetourt County and Southwest Virginia. *(11–32) VLR: 01/15/74; NRHP: 07/24/74.*

VARNEY'S FALLS DAM AND LOCK, *Rocky Point vicinity.* As with other surviving structures of the James River and Kanawha Canal system, this complex, consisting of a guard lock, guard wall, dam abutment, and towpath culvert, displays the artistry of the stonemason. The construction was supervised by skilled Scottish and Irish masons, although much of the labor was local, possibly slave. The structures are also the best-preserved canal remnants of the fifty-mile stretch between Lynchburg and Buchanan. Constructed between 1851 and 1858, this section flourished as a travel and trade artery until the Civil War. It returned to use after the war but was dealt a crippling blow in the flood of 1877. The canal company's assets were purchased by the Richmond and Alleghany Railroad in 1880, and the Varney's Falls section was displaced by the railroad in 1881. The complex is now in private ownership. *(11–68) VLR: 08/18/93; NRHP: 10/14/93.*

WHEATLAND MANOR, *Fincastle vicinity.* Wheatland Manor is among the most substantial and well-finished antebellum residences in Botetourt County. Although the Federal-style interior woodwork is relatively understated, the later two-tier Doric gallery shows builder's Greek Revival at its finest. The house was built in the 1820s when the brothers Joel, Jesse, and Silas Rowland jointly owned the property. Deputy sheriff Rufus Pitzer purchased the house along with a gristmill and a sawmill from Silas Rowland's son in 1851. Pitzer dressed up the facade by adding the gallery. It was also during Pitzer's ownership that a half-mile-long limestone retaining wall was constructed along the county road. After the Civil War, Wheatland Manor was home to Jacob Cronise, the county's leading cattle farmer. The house is currently undergoing restoration. *(11–38) VLR: 10/09/91; NRHP: 02/06/92.*

WILOMA, *Fincastle vicinity.* Wiloma is an architecturally successful blending of traditional area forms with pattern-book detailing. The main body of the dwelling is a Valley of Virginia I-house, a popular vernacular house type in the first half of the 19th century. Fronting the house is a provincial interpretation of a two-level Greek Revival portico, a device frequently used in the region to give houses architectural dignity. Many elements of the interior woodwork, especially the mantels, are directly adapted from illustrations in the pattern books of Boston architect Asher Benjamin. The house was built in 1848 for Morgan Utz, a Fincastle merchant who served as a ruling elder in the Fincastle Presbyterian Church and a trustee of Botetourt Seminary. Unspoiled rural scenery reinforces the historic character of this dignified old house. *(11–39) VLR: 10/18/83; NRHP: 11/22/85.*

WILSON WAREHOUSE, *Washington and Lower streets, Buchanan.* Buchanan's Wilson Warehouse is a relic of western Virginia's antebellum prosperity. It was built in 1839 as a combined dwelling, warehouse, and store for John S. Wilson, whose business activities prospered with the completion of the adjacent James River and Kanawha Canal as far as Buchanan in 1851. The urbane Greek Revival structure is set off by stepped gables, an architectural feature often used on commercial buildings of the period to protect the end of the roof from fire. The structure retains its original hardware, doorbell, and third-floor cargo wheel. Restored in 1928 by Lynchburg architect Stanhope Johnson, the building, now known as the Community House, is owned by the Buchanan Town Improvement Society. It is used as both a residence and a venue for special meetings and events. *(180–06) VLR: 07/19/77; NRHP: 01/26/78.*

CITY OF BRISTOL

Straddling the Virginia-Tennessee state line, the Virginia portion of this Southwest Virginia community originally was called Goodson, for Samuel Goodson, its founder. It was established in 1850 and incorporated as a city in 1890 with its name changed to Bristol to conform to that of its Tennessee neighbor.

BRISTOL RAILROAD STATION, *State and Washington streets.* Occupying a conspicuous location on the edge of Bristol's commercial district, the Bristol Railroad Station, originally known as the Bristol Union Railway Station, was constructed in 1902. The stone and brick structure is one of a series of depots built before World War I by Norfolk and Western Railroad employees for the company's rapidly expanding system. The contractor was John Pettyjohn of Lynchburg; George Pettyjohn, his brother, was supervisor of construction. Successfully blending Romanesque and European vernacular idioms, the building, with its authoritative hipped-roof end pavilion, exhibits a degree of architectural sophistication rarely found in the passenger stations of other medium-size Virginia cities. The station stood unoccupied for several years after the termination of passenger service and was converted to a shopping mall in the 1980s. *(102–11) VLR: 09/16/80; NRHP: 11/28/80.*

BRISTOL SIGN, *East State Street.* The most identifiable landmark of the twin cities of Bristol, Virginia, and Bristol, Tennessee, is the large electric slogan sign spanning the state line on State Street. Constructed of structural steel, the sign measures 60 by 35 feet and weighs two and one-half tons. It was donated in 1910 by Henry L. Dougherty, head of Dougherty and Company of New York, owner of Bristol's electric company. It originally was placed atop the Virginia-Tennessee Hardware Co. building but was relocated to its present site in 1915. In 1921 the slogan was changed from "Push! . . . That's Bristol" to "Bristol . . . A Good Place to Live." The sign was restored in 1982 and remains a much-admired expression of civic pride for two cities with a special common history. *(102–02) VLR: 06/21/88; NRHP: 09/08/88.*

KING-LANCASTER-MCCOY-MITCHELL HOUSE, *54 King Street.* A structure made interesting by its accretions, this complex dwelling on Solar Hill overlooking downtown Bristol is named for the families who constructed its various sections. Col. James King, an Irish immigrant and founder of the first ironworks in Tennessee, built the original I-house core around 1820. John J. Lancaster, a New York banker, aquired the property in 1874 and added an Italianate extension in 1881. In 1891 H. E. McCoy purchased the estate and commissioned the architectural firm of Beaver, Hoffmeister, and Mould of Bristol, Tenn., to remodel the house, adding the front porch and a rear wing. Joseph D. Mitchell made the final changes in 1903, which included an interior remodeling and service ell. The interiors preserve an elegant turn-of-the-century character with light fixtures, finishes, and appointments of the period. *(102–19) VLR: 04/20/94; NRHP: 07/29/94.*

VIRGINIA HIGH SCHOOL, *501 Piedmont Avenue.* The expertly handled classical design of Virginia High School, currently Virginia Middle School, is a demonstration of the community pride once expressed in the architecture of public educational facilities. Such buildings dignified their respective functions and lent identity and character to their communities. The school was designed by local architect Clarence B. Kearfott, who embellished the facade with a monumental Ionic portico. Completed in 1915, the building originally served white children from grades five on. The school today is a middle school open to all. The building has also served as a venue for many club and civic gatherings throughout its history. Defense preparedness classes were held here during World War II. *(102–30) VLR: 12/04/96; NRHP: 02/21/97.*

VIRGINIA INTERMONT COLLEGE, *Moore and Harmeling streets.* Virginia Intermont College was founded in 1884 to meet the demands of local Baptists to have higher education available to the women of the region. The school began in Glade Spring as Southwest Virginia Female Institute under the guidance of the Rev. J. R. Harrison. The massive main building, constructed after the institution's move to Bristol in 1891, was designed by Walter P. Tinsley. With its blending of Queen Anne and Romanesque references, this architectural landmark displays the aggressive eclecticism of the era. Contrived to accommodate a number of functions under one roof, the building's plan reflects normative 19th-century academic planning. Upon completion of the work, Tinsley retired from practice and became a Baptist minister. The school is now open to both men women. *(102–14) VLR: 08/21/84; NRHP: 10/04/84.*

BRUNSWICK COUNTY

Along the state's southern border, this rural county was named for the duchy of Brunswick-Lüneburg, one of the German possessions of King George I. It was formed from Prince George County in 1720 and organized in 1732. It was later enlarged with parts of Surry and Isle of Wight counties. The county seat is Lawrenceville.

BRUNSWICK COUNTY COURT SQUARE, *Lawrenceville.* With its Greek Doric courthouse, Confederate monument, clerk's office, and jail, Brunswick County's court square has the essential ingredients of a 19th-century Virginia county seat. The tree-shaded grouping serves as the focus of town and county activity. Lawrenceville was established as the county seat in 1814. By 1853 a new courthouse was required, and a contract was let to E. R. Turnbull and Robert Kirkland to provide a building based on the courthouse in adjacent Mecklenburg County. Like its model, the new building was temple form, but instead of a hexastyle Roman Ionic portico, Trumbull and Kirkland gave their structure a tetrastyle portico in the Greek Doric order, thus creating one of Southside Virginia's few Greek Revival court structures. The one-story clerk's office was designed by M. J. Dimmock of Richmond and was built in 1893. *(251–01) VLR: 11/19/74; NRHP: 12/31/74.*

FORT CHRISTANNA ARCHAEOLOGICAL SITE, *Lawrenceville vicinity.* This tract overlooking the Meherrin River contains the archaeological remains of Fort Christanna, begun in 1714 by Governor Alexander Spotswood to house an Indian school and trading center and to serve as a defense against unfriendly tribes. Within the tract are the sites of a Sapony Indian village complex, home of approximately 300 Indians who chose to remain here after the House of Burgesses voted in 1718 to abandon maintenance of the fort. Also here is the site of a residence of Lieutenant Governor Spotswood, built to encourage settlement of what was then a remote frontier area. Other 18th-century sites probably are located within the area. The worn remains of what are believed to be the fort's earthworks are now covered with trees and undergrowth. *(12–08) VLR: 11/20/79; NRHP: 07/16/80.*

GHOLSON BRIDGE, *Route 715, Lawrenceville vicinity.* Virginia's many metal-truss bridges are fast being replaced by sturdier though less visually appealing spans of concrete. Among the several examples selected for landmark designation because of rarity of type or aesthetic qualities is Gholson Bridge spanning the Meherrin River in central Brunswick County. The bridge is important from an engineering standpoint as the oldest multispan metal bridge in the state. It was constructed in 1884 by the Wrought Iron Bridge Company of Canton, Ohio, and consists of two Pratt through trusses set on random ashlar sandstone piers. The wrought-iron trusses consist of top chords and end posts that are two upright channels connected with cover plates and stay plates. Decorative details include cast-metal caps with the construction date. Above each portal is a plaque identifying the builder. *(12–80) VLR: 11/15/77; NRHP: 05/05/78.*

HOBSON'S CHOICE, *Alberta vicinity.* Erected in 1794, this multisection, one-story plantation dwelling is a provincial interpretation of the five-part Palladian scheme popularized by designs illustrated in Robert Morris's *Select Architecture* of 1755, an English pattern book that influenced various colonial and Federal-period Virginia houses. One of Brunswick County's few 18th-century brick houses, Hobson's Choice was originally the home of Dr. Richard Feild, an Edinburgh-educated physician well known for his expertise in botany and astronomy. Feild served as editor of the *Petersburg Commercial Advertiser* and the *Intelligencer.* He also was a member of the electoral col-

leges that put Thomas Jefferson and James Madison in the White House. Except for the addition of the 20th-century front porch, the house survives without significant alteration. The interior is embellished with paneled mantels and wainscoting. *(12–13) VLR: 11/20/79; NRHP: 03/18/80.*

ROCKY RUN UNITED METHODIST CHURCH, *Danieltown vicinity.* Characterized by a simple dignity, this wooden church is a demonstration of the eye for design that can be found in even the most rural areas of the state. Erected in 1857, the Classical Revival structure is the handiwork of a Lynchburg builder ironically named Thomas Jefferson. The name *Thos Jefferson* is carved in the base of the east porch column. According to a letter published in the *Richmond Advocate* in 1857, he secured plans for the church from a Methodist church in either Petersburg or Richmond. The same letter noted that construction funds were donated by Col. Isham Trotter, whose parents were among the first Methodists in Brunswick County. Deftly handled classical elements, including a pedimented roof, corner pilasters, and dwarf Doric portico lend an assured competence to the otherwise plain structure. The church remains in regular use. *(12–29) VLR: 04/28/95; NRHP: 07/07/95.*

SAINT PAUL'S COLLEGE, *Lawrenceville.* The Saul Building, Principal's Residence, and Memorial Chapel embody the
evolution of this pioneering historically black institution from
a one-room parochial school to a liberal arts college. Saint
Paul's was established in 1883 by an Episcopal deacon, the Rev.
James Solomon Russell (1857–1935), who was born a slave. Russell trained at Petersburg's Bishop Payne Divinity School. Assigned to Lawrenceville, Russell found a community where
"race prejudice seemed rampant and public opinion indifferent
if not actually hostile." By February 1883 a chapel was built, and
a parochial school soon was organized. A small school building
was later erected with funds from the Rev. James Saul of Philadelphia. In 1888 Saint Paul's Normal and Industrial School
was founded. The Queen Anne–style Principal's Residence was
built in 1900. The Memorial Chapel (shown) was completed in
1904. In 1957 the name was officially changed to Saint Paul's
College. *(251–03) VLR: 03/20/79; NRHP: 06/27/79.*

WOODLANDS, *White Plains vicinity.* This plantation house
was remodeled from an 1831–33 Federal I-house built by the
Brodnax family into a porticoed Romantic Revival mansion, a
transformation influenced both by regional example and published design. Alexander J. Brodnax adapted the floor plan
from a plan in Philadelphia architect Samuel Sloan's *The Model
Architect.* The 1860 edition owned by Brodnax, with his penciled notations on Design LVII, plate XC, was passed down
among family possessions. Family tradition has it that the airy
portico, somewhat Italianate in character, was inspired by the
Doric portico of Berry Hill in Halifax County. Several of the
1860 features, especially moldings and brackets, show a stylistic
similarity to the works of Jacob Holt, a Southside builder-
architect. The powerful composition remains one of the most
impressive vestiges of antebellum patrician lifestyle in the region. *(12–38) VLR: 02/16/82; NRHP: 07/08/82.*

BUCHANAN COUNTY

Occupying the heart of Southwest Virginia's coalfields, Buchanan County was named for President James Buchanan. It was formed in 1858 from Tazewell and Russell counties. The county seat is Grundy.

BUCHANAN COUNTY COURTHOUSE, *Grundy.* The Renaissance Revival courthouse at Grundy indicates the importance given to law and order when the area was experiencing its early coal-mining rush. Built of rough-faced locally quarried stone, this is the fourth courthouse to serve Buchanan County since its formation in 1858. Its slender corner clock tower lends distinction to the building as well as the town. The courthouse was designed by Frank P. Milburn of Washington, D.C., and completed in 1906. Milburn's firm was responsible for several other courthouses in Southwest Virginia and also supervised the 1917 reconstruction of the Buchanan courthouse interior after it was gutted by a 1915 fire which consumed much of Grundy. The building received major additions in 1949–59 and 1984. *(229–01) VLR: 07/20/82; NRHP: 09/16/82.*

BUCKINGHAM COUNTY

Probably named either for the English shire or the duke of Buckingham, this rural, largely wooded upper James River county was formed in 1761 from Albemarle County. Its county seat is Buckingham Court House.

BRYN ARVON AND GWYN ARVON, *Arvonia.* Arvonia's two Queen Anne residences, Bryn Arvon (shown) and Gwyn Arvon, are landmarks of Virginia's slate industry and the Welsh immigrants who dominated it. The houses were built in the 1890s for the Welsh quarrymen brothers Evan and John Williams, who founded the Williams Slate Company in the 1870s and revitalized Buckingham County's slate quarries. They capitalized on a growing market after the Civil War, when new construction throughout the country created an enormous demand for roofing materials. Their houses are distinguished not only by their Welsh names but by the extensive use of slate inside and out, making them interesting demonstrations of the slater's art and serving as advertisements of the quarry's products. Although the houses are similar in design and the utilization of materials, the plan and elevation of each differ. The property includes a collection of contemporary outbuildings. *(14–05)* VLR: 08/21/90; NRHP: 01/03/91.

BUCKINGHAM COURT HOUSE HISTORIC DISTRICT. Established in 1818, this county-seat village was originally named Maysville. A simple courthouse was built just west of the settlement, but within three years a new courthouse was needed. Charles Yancy, one of the county commissioners, wrote Thomas Jefferson requesting a set of plans. Jefferson complied, and the courthouse, completed in 1822, was the state's first temple-form, porticoed courthouse. Around it developed a complex of court structures, taverns, and dwellings. Several of the buildings, most conspicuously Trinity Presbyterian Church, have a Jeffersonian character. The courthouse burned in 1869 and was rebuilt in 1873 along similar lines. Gen. Robert E. Lee and his escort passed through the village after Appomattox. Lee refused accommodation in a local tavern and pitched his tent with his men for the last time just east of town. The village preserves its 19th-century air with few modern intrusions. *(14–111)* VLR: 09/09/69; NRHP: 11/17/69.

BUCKINGHAM FEMALE COLLEGIATE INSTITUTE HISTORIC DISTRICT, *Gravel Hill.* The early movement to provide women access to higher education is symbolized in the cluster of buildings that survive from the Buckingham Female Collegiate Institute, the first chartered college for women in Virginia. Opened in 1838, the school functioned until 1863 when Civil War disruption forced the removal of the students and the eventual closing of the school. Leadership and support for the institute came primarily from Virginia Methodists who regarded the school as a female counterpart to the Randolph-Macon College for men. Although the main building was dismantled in 1906, the five remaining structures are tangible reminders of this pioneering venture. Among these are the 1853 "President's Cottage," two instructors' houses, the institute store, and the West house, a ca. 1850 frame house that served as a tavern. The buildings are now private residences. *(14–127) VLR: 03/20/84; NRHP: 10/04/84.*

CARYSWOOD, *Dillwyn vicinity.* Caryswood is on part of the vast acreage in Buckingham County owned in the 18th century by Archibald Cary, a prominent colonial public figure. The Caryswood tract, some 800 acres, eventually was inherited by Cary's descendant, Edward Trent Page, who built the present house around 1849, probably after his marriage to Bettie Coupland Nicholas of Seven Islands. The two-story frame dwelling is a typical example of the country Greek Revival architecture favored by the gentry in central and southern Virginia in the antebellum period. Though understated, such dwellings were a dignified contrast to the rustic housing of the region's simple farmers. Except for a 1915 rear wing, the house has seen almost no changes since the mid–19th century. The interior has plain but robustly molded mantels and doorframes. Its collection of outbuildings includes several slave cottages. The property remains in the ownership of the builder's kinsmen. *(14–18) VLR: 12/11/91.*

PETER FRANCISCO HOUSE (LOCUST GROVE), *Sprouses Corner vicinity.* This plain late 18th-century farmhouse was the home of Peter Francisco from 1794 until the mid-1820s. Francisco appeared on the wharf at City Point as a finely dressed abandoned youth speaking an Iberian dialect. Speculated to be of noble origin, he was raised by Anthony Winston. He grew to a young man of exceptional physical stature, and in 1776 he enlisted in the Revolutionary army. The stories of his wartime feats have become part of Virginia folklore. He is reputed to have carried a 1,100-pound cannon and to have routed a squadron of Tarleton's cavalry and captured their horses. Francisco worked as a blacksmith after moving to Buckingham County. He later served as doorkeeper in the State Capitol, where his funeral was held in 1831. Francisco's home has been restored by the Society of the Descendants of Peter Francisco. *(14–97) VLR: 01/18/72; NRHP: 03/16/72.*

PERRY HILL, *St. Joy vicinity.* Perry Hill is a rare example of Gothic Revival cottage architecture adapted for a central Virginia country residence. Such building types were popularized in the mid–19th century by the writings of Andrew Jackson Downing. Acceptance of the Gothic style was limited in Virginia partly because of the popularity of the Classical Revival styles that dominated architectural taste until the Civil War. Col. Thomas Moseley Bondurant, a Whig politician and publicist in Buckingham County, built the house for his daughter and son-in-law ca. 1851–52. The house is said to have been named in honor of Oliver Hazard Perry, a naval hero of the War of 1812. Typical of the style, Perry Hill has Gothic windows with Y-mullions, pointed gables decorated with sawn-work bargeboards, and clustered chimney stacks. The rectangular outline and symmetrical plan are influenced by traditional Virginia house design. *(14–19) VLR: 07/31/80; NRHP: 10/30/80.*

SEVEN ISLANDS ARCHAEOLOGICAL AND HISTORIC DISTRICT, *Arvonia vicinity.* Located near the confluence of the James and Slate rivers, this plantation contains both prehistoric and historic components. A large Woodland-period site (A.D. 900–1600), reflecting use of a riverine environment, is the principal prehistoric feature. Five other archaeological sites, located in upland settings, trace the more diffuse adaptive use of the land mostly during the Archaic period (8000–1000 B.C.). The primary historic structure is a plain Greek Revival dwelling erected ca. 1847 for John Scott Nicholas III on the site of a colonial house built by his grandfather. During the Civil War the plantation supplied wheat, cattle, and horses (including J. E. B. Stuart's large black mount) to the Confederate government. Confederate wounded also were cared for here. To temper economic hardship after the war, the family established a school known as Seven Islands Academy and erected a wing for dormitory space. *(14–23) VLR: 04/17/91; NRHP: 07/03/91.*

STANTON FAMILY CEMETERY, *Diana Mills vicinity.* Started in 1853, the Stanton family cemetery is a very rare example of a burying ground established by free blacks before the Civil War. The Stantons were one of the few extended free black families living in rural Virginia at the height of the slavery period. The unfenced plot contains at least thirty-six marked burials, a large number for Afro-American family cemeteries, and likely holds a number of unmarked burials. Many of the graves have simple uninscribed headstones and footstones of the local slate. The cemetery was originally part of a forty-six-acre farm purchased in 1853 by Nancy and Daniel Stanton. Although the family moved from the homestead in 1930, it retained ownership of the land and the cemetery and continued family burials here. The last occurred in 1941 when Harriet Stanton Scott, granddaughter of Nancy and Daniel Stanton, was interred. *(14–52) VLR: 02/17/93; NRHP: 04/29/93.*

WOODSIDE, *Buckingham Court House vicinity.* This boldly scaled house was completed in 1860 for William M. Swoope. With its tall proportions and generous moldings, Woodside is a freely interpreted expression of the Greek Revival, exhibiting little influence from the popular architectural pattern books of the day. The facade is given articulation by use of a pedimented central pavilion and the flanking bay windows. The floor plan is a synthesis of a Palladian tripartite composition and a Georgian center-passage plan. Much of the interior woodwork survives, including pine floors and molded baseboards in every room. All of the mantels are believed to be original except for the marble parlor mantel, which, according to legend, may have come from the White House. From 1871 to 1873 Woodside was the home of Nicholas F. Bocock, a prominent local lawyer, and it remained Bocock family property until 1882. *(14–41) VLR: 12/09/92; NRHP: 11/16/93.*

CITY OF BUENA VISTA

This community on the Maury River grew up on the site of the Buena Vista iron furnace. The furnace apparently took its name from the Mexican War battle won by Gen. Zachary Taylor in 1847. Buena Vista was established in 1889 and became a city in 1892.

GLEN MAURY (PAXTON PLACE), *Glen Maury Park.* With its naive use of academic architectural forms and details, Glen Maury is a provincial though visually appealing attempt by a local builder to achieve a formal Classical Revival mansion. The local vernacular forms such as the molded-brick cornices and I-plan blend well with classical elements such as the pedimented portico and round-arch windows. Of particular interest are the boldly carved mantels, which are also regional interpretations of academic late Georgian forms. Built ca. 1831, the house was first owned by Elisha Paxton, a plantation farmer. Now owned by the city of Buena Vista, whose downtown is immediately across the Maury River, Glen Maury farm is a municipal park. The Paxton House Historical Society, formed in 1997, is raising funds to restore the house as a social, educational, and historical center. *(103–04) VLR: 05/16/78; NRHP: 05/24/79.*

OLD COURTHOUSE, *2110 Magnolia Avenue.* The former Buena Vista courthouse is a relic of the land boom that took place in the central part of Virginia's Shenandoah Valley in 1889–91. The boom, a direct result of the construction of the Norfolk and Western Railroad, contributed to the establishment of several new towns, including Buena Vista. The land company that developed Buena Vista gave credence to its activity by building in 1890 a simple but dignified Second Empire–style headquarters complete with mansard roof and tower. Two years later, when the land boom collapsed, the company sold the building to the town for use as a courthouse and municipal offices. It served Buena Vista in that capacity until 1971 when a new municipal building was built. Local citizens rescued the old building from threatened demolition and had it converted to the public library. *(103–03) VLR: 05/16/78; NRHP: 05/25/79.*

SOUTHERN SEMINARY MAIN BUILDING, *Ivy and Park avenues.* The several new towns established in the Shenandoah Valley during the land boom of 1889–91 were considered not only prime industrial and commercial sites but choice recreational areas. The scenic mountain landscape and pleasant climate, made accessible by the railroad, were the essential ingredients for large summer resorts. Of the Valley's numerous elaborate hotels built in this period, the rambling Queen Anne–style structure in Buena Vista is one of only two remaining. Designed by S. W. Foulke of New Castle, Pa., and begun in 1890, the hotel operated only briefly; the panic of 1893 forced its closing. The building was subsequently acquired by Dr. Edgar H. Rowe, who reopened it as Southern Seminary, a girls' preparatory school and junior college. The school closed in 1996, but a school under different sponsorship has since been established here. *(103–02) VLR: 12/21/71; NRHP: 04/13/72.*

❧ CAMPBELL COUNTY

Named for Gen. William Campbell, one of the heroes of the 1780 battle of King's Mountain, this southern Piedmont county was formed from Bedford County in 1781. The county seat is Rustburg.

AVOCA, *Altavista.* Designed in 1901 by Lynchburg architect John Minor Botts Lewis for Thomas and Mary Fauntleroy, Avoca is one of the state's foremost expressions of the Queen Anne style, distinguished by complex rooflines, a variety of surface treatments and window types, and numerous porches and projections. Avoca's interior has no less visual interest than the exterior. The hall is dominated by a grand staircase with a rounded balcony projecting from a landing. Avoca is also the site of an earlier dwelling, Green Level, the home of Revolutionary War patriot Col. Charles Lynch. It was on Lynch's land that area Tories were flogged by locals for allegiance to the British crown, giving rise to the term *Lynch Law.* Avoca now houses a museum and historical society. On the grounds are several outbuildings predating the present house. *(15–378) VLR: 03/16/82; NRHP: 09/16/82.*

BLENHEIM, *Spring Mills vicinity.* This outwardly unassertive house in the hilly countryside of eastern Campbell County is noted for its wealth of elaborate, provincially conceived but deftly executed woodwork. Such decoration is characteristic of the best early houses in the region. Some of the trim, particularly the stair, shows a general debt to designs in contemporary pattern books, but it is interpreted in the very free manner of the more skilled regional craftsmen. The construction date of the house is uncertain, although a sharp increase in tax assessment in 1828 suggests that the property was improved in that year for William Jones. The place acquired its present name after its purchase in 1869 by John Devereux. The house survives with few changes and remains a monument to the rural craftsman's art. Behind the house is the remnant of an early formal garden. *(15–66) VLR: 02/15/77 (EXPANDED 03/10/94); NRHP: 05/31/79; BHR EASEMENT.*

CAMPBELL COUNTY COURTHOUSE, *Rustburg.* This compact but sophisticated public building is an articulate component of Virginia's important collection of Classical Revival courthouses. With its main floor set on a high basement, the porticoed building employs the format also employed for the Pittsylvania, Patrick, and demolished Bedford County courthouses. It was completed in 1849 by John Wills. The courtroom, with its elaborate plasterwork and woodwork, is among Virginia's least-altered courtrooms of the period. Especially interesting is the aedicule above the judge's bench framing the Masonic symbol of the all-seeing eye, a unique use of this motif in a Virginia courthouse. The decorative frame is plaster, but the eye itself is realistically executed in glass. Court functions have been transferred to a modern building, and the old courthouse is being considered for alternative uses. *(15–01) VLR: 06/16/81; NRHP: 10/29/81.*

CAT ROCK SLUICE OF THE ROANOKE NAVIGATION, *Brookneal vicinity.* The Cat Rock Sluice is one of the country's best-preserved relics of a rare riverbed navigation system for bateaux. The network of sluices with their associated wing dams and towering walls was constructed by Samuel Pannill in 1827 for the Roanoke Navigation Company. The system permitted passage of poled riverboats, called bateaux, through the falls of the Staunton (Roanoke) River, opening up the river as far as Salem. The company's entire network extended for over 470 miles. The sluices, blasted through rock ledges, are paralleled by substantial stone walls called wing walls, which helped to guide the water into a single channel and provided a platform from which the boatmen could pull the bateaux through the sluice by rope. This primitive but effective system fed the early economy of southern Virginia. *(15–217) VLR: 12/20/77; NRHP: 03/25/80.*

FEDERAL HILL, *Forest vicinity.* Federal Hill, a regional interpretation of the Palladian tripartite house, was built in 1782 for James Steptoe, the second clerk of Bedford County and a lifelong friend of Thomas Jefferson. Jefferson's Bedford County retreat, Poplar Forest, is only a few miles from Federal Hill, and Jefferson visited Steptoe whenever he was in the area. It thus may have been Jefferson's guiding architectural influence that led Steptoe to employ a Palladian-derived format with a porticoed temple-form center section. Jefferson had used a similar scheme in his first designs for Monticello and continued to advocate it for the residences of friends and associates. Still standing on the grounds of Federal Hill is the second clerk's office of Bedford County, used by Steptoe throughout his long public service. *(15–03) VLR: 05/18/82; NRHP: 09/09/82.*

GREEN HILL, *Long Island vicinity.* Few plantation complexes in Virginia offer such a wide diversity of outbuildings and farm structures and provide such a complete picture of early 19th-century rural life and agricultural practices. Among the surviving outbuildings are a duck house, icehouse, kitchen, laundry, and servants' house, as well as several farm structures built of wood, brick, and stone. The nucleus of the complex is a two-story brick dwelling somewhat plain on the exterior but trimmed with ambitious provincial Federal woodwork inside. The architectural chimneypiece in the dining room is exceptional. Linking the house and outbuildings is a rare surviving network of stone walkways. Green Hill was established ca. 1800 by Samuel Pannill, who served in the General Assembly as well as on the Board of Public Works and as president of the Roanoke Navigation Company. *(15–05) VLR: 09/09/69; NRHP: 11/17/69.*

MANSION TRUSS BRIDGE, *Altavista vicinity.* With its two camelback through trusses, the Mansion Truss Bridge, crossing high above the Staunton River into Pittsylvania County, is a rare surviving type among Virginia's collection of metal-truss bridges. The bridge was constructed by the Brackett Bridge Company in 1903 and probably replaced a covered bridge. It takes its name from the 18th-century mansion of settler John Smith that stood on a hill nearby. Its stone piers have been replaced by lolly columns, steel cylinders filled with concrete. The bridge is targeted for replacement by the Virginia Department of Transportation. The fate of the bridge fabric is uncertain. *(15–218) VLR: 11/15/77; NRHP: 04/15/78.*

MOUNT ATHOS, *Kelly vicinity.* This stone ruin atop a wooded ridge overlooking the James River is of a plantation house built ca. 1800 for William J. Lewis. Its elevated site, one-story plan, classical portico, and polygonal projections have led to the speculation that its design was influenced by Thomas Jefferson, who showed partiality to all these elements in his own works. Lewis family tradition holds that Lewis and Jefferson were friends and that Jefferson advised on the house. Mount Athos was gutted by fire in 1876. The *Lynchburg Daily Virginian* noted the many valuable paintings and fine library it had contained and commented, "It is sad to see an ancient abode of so much refinement, elegance, and hospitality swept away." Archaeological investigation of the ruins and their immediate surroundings could provide additional information on this enigmatic structure. *(15–19) VLR: 02/18/75; NRHP: 07/24/75.*

SHADY GROVE, *Gladys vicinity.* Built in 1825 for Paulina Cabell Henry on land inherited from her father, Dr. George Cabell of Point of Honor in Lynchburg, Shady Grove is an example of the interpretation of highly sophisticated and academic architectural embellishments by country craftsmen. It is speculated that Mrs. Henry was attempting here to duplicate the richness of detailing found in her childhood home. The resulting interior work, the product of an unidentified artisan, is naive in its execution, possessing a charm and vitality often lacking in more academic counterparts. The neat but somewhat plain exterior likewise illustrates a blending of academic and vernacular influences. Paulina Cabell Henry was married to Spotswood Henry, a younger son of Patrick Henry. Perhaps because of Spotswood Henry's profligate lifestyle, title to the plantation remained in Paulina Henry's name. *(15–13) VLR: 05/18/82; NRHP: 08/26/82.*

SIX MILE BRIDGE, *Madison Heights vicinity.* Named for its location approximately six miles downstream from Lynchburg, this historic railroad bridge was initially completed in 1854 for the South Side Railroad, connecting Petersburg to Lynchburg. Listed by the railroad as the "First Crossing the James River," the bridge originally consisted of five stone piers supporting a superstructure of six wooden trusses for a length of 670 feet. Confederates burned the bridge in 1865 to protect Lynchburg. It was soon rebuilt with similar trusses. It was rebuilt again in 1870 when the piers were increased in height to support a wrought-iron Fink truss superstructure. The bridge was strengthened in 1886 and again in 1899 and 1920 with riveted steel Pratt-type suspended trusses. Listed as Bridge No. 58, it was abandoned in 1972, and title was transferred in 1992 by the Norfolk Southern Corp. to the Mount Athos Regional Museum and Information Center, Inc. *(15–352) VLR: 08/28/95; NRHP: 10/12/95.*

CAROLINE COUNTY

Formed in 1727 from Essex, King and Queen, and King William counties, this Middle Peninsula county, bordered by the Rappahannock River, was named for Caroline of Anspach, consort of King George II. The county seat is Bowling Green.

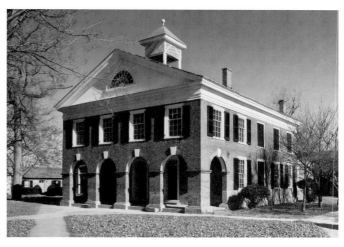

CAMDEN, *Port Royal vicinity.* This wooden mansion, one of the nation's outstanding examples of the Italian Villa style, was designed by Norris G. Starkweather of Baltimore for William Carter Pratt. The house was built on the site of an earlier Pratt house and was completed in 1859. Technologically as well as architecturally advanced, Camden was equipped with the latest conveniences including central heating, gas lighting, running water in each bedroom, inside toilets, and a shower bath. An elaborate tower was destroyed by a Union gunboat in 1863. Preserved inside are original furnishings, carpeting, and curtains, as well as Starkweather's architectural drawings. Located on the river's edge, the house served a large plantation still owned by the Pratt family. Also on the property is a contact-period Indian archaeological site which yielded two English silver medals inscribed "The King of the Machotick" and "The King of Patomeck." *(16–04) VLR: 09/09/69; NRHP: 11/17/69; NHL: 11/11/71; ARCHAEOLOGICAL ADDENDUM: 1986.*

CAROLINE COUNTY COURTHOUSE, *Bowling Green.* The Caroline County Courthouse was erected in the early 1830s to replace a courthouse that stood nearby. The architecturally sophisticated structure is highlighted by its bold Tuscan pediment and arcaded ground floor. Because of the loss of county records, the exact construction date and designer are not known, but the building's similarity to the Madison and Page County courthouses, both erected by master builders William B. Phillips and Malcolm F. Crawford, has led to the attribution of the Caroline courthouse to them. Phillips and Crawford had been employed by Thomas Jefferson at the University of Virginia where they became proficient in the classical vocabulary. They subsequently built other public buildings and houses throughout the state. Caroline's courthouse is believed to be the county's sixth courthouse. The interior underwent a modified restoration to its original configuration in the early 1970s. *(171–03) VLR: 04/17/73; NRHP: 05/25/73.*

EDGE HILL, *Woodford vicinity.* On a bluff above the Matta River, Edge Hill is the setting of two historic buildings: a brick plantation house and an antebellum academy building. The house, originally a three-bay, side-passage Federal house, was built for Rice Schooler in 1820–21. The western half was added ca. 1840. The interior of the older section has highly individualized Federal woodwork. The wood-frame, three-story academy building was erected in 1857 by Schooler's son Samuel Schooler, a scholar, writer, and military officer. Known as Edge Hill Academy, the school was founded to meet the growing demand of Virginians seeking preparation for higher education. It closed in the late 1860s, but the building, now used as a barn, nevertheless is a rare example of mid-19th-century rural school architecture. Also remaining are the sites of cabins occupied by the academy students. *(16–06) VLR: 12/14/82; NRHP: 02/10/83; BHR EASEMENT.*

GREEN FALLS, *Wright's Fork.* Though Green Falls is obviously a dwelling of great age, its construction date is uncertain. Claims have been made that the house was built in 1710. Architectural evidence, however, points to a date in the second or third quarter of the 18th century. The house thus could have been the building that served as Johnston's Tavern for which Thomas Johnston was issued a tavern license in 1747. It later was used as a store and post office. Robert Wright acquired the property in 1800 and added the south wing around 1808. The house is set off by its tall proportions and side-passage plan. Its exterior is dominated by the massive brick chimneys. On the second and third floors 18th-century trim survives, and the 1808 wing preserves its original trim. An 18th-century smokehouse is on the grounds. Seen across the fields, the house presents a memorable picture of Tidewater's early cultural landscape. *(16–34) VLR: 03/19/97; NRHP: 05/23/97.*

GAY MONT, *Port Royal vicinity.* Gay Mont, on a terraced ridge above the Rappahannock River valley, preserves an extensively documented historic garden. The garden was the creation of John Hipkins Bernard, who during an 1818 visit abroad became impressed by French landscape and garden design. Upon his return he laid out a geometric garden, the shrubbery-lined gravel paths of which are intact. Bernard ordered many plants and seeds from Europe, records of which survive in the Bernard papers. Gay Mont's house, built ca. 1800 for Port Royal merchant John Hipkins by Richard and Yelverton Stern, burned in 1959, but the 1820 stuccoed wings and Tuscan colonnade added by Bernard, Hipkins's grandson, survived and were incorporated into the reconstructed house. Gay Mont was owned by Bernard descendants until 1976 when it was deeded to the Association for the Preservation of Virginia Antiquities with a life tenancy for the donors. *(16–32) VLR: 01/18/72; NRHP: 05/19/72; BHR EASEMENT.*

HAZELWOOD ARCHAEOLOGICAL SITE, *Port Royal vicinity.* Hazelwood was the home plantation of agrarian political economist John Taylor of Caroline, a champion of Jeffersonian Republicanism. Taylor wrote keenly perceptive political pamphlets. His *Inquiry into the Principles and Policy of the Government of the United States* (1814) was a significant contribution to American political science. Taylor also wrote essays about his experiments with improved agricultural methods at Hazelwood, published in book

form as *The Arator* in 1813. The main house at Hazelwood, erected in the mid–18th century and added to by Taylor, was destroyed by fire during the Civil War. An 1816 insurance policy of the Mutual Assurance Society shows the house to have been a two-story brick structure with lower wings connected by hyphens. Archaeological excavation could yield new insights on a major historic plantation complex. Hazelwood's fields continue to be farmed. *(16–58) VLR: 06/19/73; NRHP: 01/11/74.*

LIBERTY BAPTIST CHURCH, *Fort A. P. Hill.* This rural site has been used for religious purposes since 1796 when the Liberty Baptist meeting erected a frame church here. For the first half of the 19th century, the majority of Liberty's members were black—mostly slaves who attended services with their masters. The present brick church was built in 1850. The plain gable-roof structure follows a standard form used for numerous meetinghouses, both brick and frame, built through the Virginia countryside for over a century. Common features are the two entrances and an upper tier of windows to light an interior gallery. Liberty's sober dignity was a reflection of the meeting's strict moral code, which forbade dancing, nonattendance, and intemperance. The church served the Baptists until 1941 when the property was incorporated into the A. P. Hill Military Reservation, now Fort A. P. Hill. Since 1942 it has been the post chapel. *(16–69) VLR: 06/19/96.*

OLD MANSION, *Bowling Green.* Part of a land grant of 1670, the plantation on which this venerable colonial manor house is located originally was called Bowling Green after the green sward before the entrance. The name was changed to Old Mansion when its owner, Maj. John Hoomes, donated property for the courthouse and permitted the newly formed county seat to take the name of his estate. The house, with its fine brickwork, hipped dormers, original sash, jerkinhead roof, and interior paneling, preserves a romantic image of a prosperous colonial Virginia plantation seat. A later gambrel-roof rear wing adds to its interest. The cedar-lined lawn stretching from the front is the remnant of a colonial racetrack. South of the house are the earth terraces of a large early garden. George Washington and his troops camped on the property during the Revolutionary War. *(16–5010) VLR: 11/05/68; NRHP: 11/17/69; BHR EASEMENT.*

PORT ROYAL HISTORIC DISTRICT. This tiny Rappahannock River community was a thriving tobacco port during colonial times. Named for Thomas Roy's tobacco warehouse, the town was established in 1744. It prospered through the early 19th century but declined with the advent of the railroads. Thus bypassed by progress, Port Royal remains almost entirely within its original boundaries and preserves the appearance of an early Tidewater river town. Lining its several grid-plan streets are some thirty 18th- and early 19th-century buildings, including the unusual mid-19th-century Greco-Gothic St. Peter's Episcopal Church and its colonial rectory. The numerous vacant lots are likely rich with the archaeological evidence of vanished buildings. Prominent residents included the 18th-century teacher and clergyman Jonathan Boucher; George Fitzhugh, author and prophet of the industrialized South; the Confederate nurse Capt. Sally Tompkins; and 20th-century architectural historian Thomas T. Waterman. *(284–47) VLR: 12/02/69; NRHP: 02/16/70.*

PROSPECT HILL, *Rappahannock Academy vicinity.* Prospect Hill was built ca. 1842 as the country home of Falmouth merchant Basil Gordon. With its elaborately traceried entrance, precise Flemish bond brickwork, and stone trimmings, the house displays unusually fine craftsmanship. The use of a double-pile Georgian plan and high hipped roof indicates the architectural conservatism of many of the area's wealthier residents and their lack of concern about keeping up with styles in fashion elsewhere in the country. The house is located amid beautiful landscaped grounds on a high ridge overlooking the unspoiled rural scenery of the Rappahannock River valley. *(16–19) VLR: 09/21/76; NRHP: 12/12/76.*

RIVERVIEW, *Water Street, Port Royal.* A blending of the Georgian and Greek Revival styles, this Port Royal dwelling illustrates the lag in architectural fashion between the urban and rural environments. It was built ca. 1845 by John Bernard Lightfoot, a farmer and lawyer. Lightfoot was active in local affairs, serving as town council secretary, trustee for the Rappahannock Academy, and vestryman of St. Peter's Church. Port Royal was a target for the Union army during the Fredericksburg campaign, and on December 4, 1862, Union gunboats fired on the town, damaging Riverview. In 1865, ten days after he shot President Abraham Lincoln, John Wilkes Booth was found by members of the Lightfoot family and invited to take shelter at Riverview. Booth declined and was later killed at the nearby Garret farm. The Lightfoots remained at Riverview into the 1890s. The famed Confederate nurse Capt. Sally Tompkins purchased the property in 1896. *(283–03) VLR: 04/20/94; NRHP: 07/29/94*

SANTEE, *Corbin vicinity.* A landmark of the Rappahannock River valley, Santee was originally the seat of Battaile Fitzhugh, whose ancestors had lived in the area since the late 17th century. The earlier section of the two-part house is a two-story frame ell, built by Fitzhugh in the late 18th century. The brick front section, an example of regional Federal style, was added in the early 19th century. The ell has since had its siding removed to expose its brick nogging. Behind the house is a substantial kitchen outbuilding. The property passed to Fitzhugh's daughter Patsy, wife of Samuel Gordon of Kenmore. During Gordon's tenure Stonewall Jackson and his troops camped on the grounds. Gordon requested that the soldiers not cut Santee's trees for firewood, and today the huge oaks and other trees form one of the most impressive plantation parks in the state. *(16–23) VLR: 10/21/75; NRHP: 05/07/79.*

SPRING GROVE, *Oak Corner vicinity.* Its stuccoed walls, bracketed cornice, and square cupola make this imposing pile an excellent example of the Italian Villa style advocated for the southern states by the architectural theorist Andrew Jackson Downing. The present house, at least the third on the site, was built in 1856 for Daniel Coleman DeJarnette, whose family had owned the property since the 18th century. DeJarnette served in the Virginia House of Delegates, the U.S. Congress, and the Confederate Congress. Spring Grove's interior has heavy molded classical woodwork with its original painted graining. Other interior embellishments include a curved stair, plasterwork ceiling medallions, and marble mantels. The house is still owned by the DeJarnette family and has undergone repair after being unoccupied for a long period. The architect of this highly sophisticated mansion is yet to be discovered. *(16–25) VLR: 9/21/76; NRHP: 12/12/76.*

TOWNFIELD, *Port Royal.* At the northeast corner of Port Royal, on the banks of the Rappahannock, Townfield is a rambling wooden dwelling enlarged and embellished through a succession of owners, making it a fascinating document of the art of the Virginia housewright over the period of a century. The original portion was built for Robert Gilchrist, a Scottish merchant and holder of various public offices, who acquired the property in 1744. The house was expanded on its north end in 1796 by James Robb. It probably was then that the "Port Royal porch," an enclosed extension of the main passage, was added to the north front. A two-story wing, perpendicular to the original part, was added by Philip Lightfoot in the 1830s. An elaborate architectural chimneypiece in the original section was probably part of the 1790s alterations. *(238–15) VLR 04/20/94; NRHP: 07/29/94; BHR EASEMENT.*

TRAVIS LAKE HISTORIC DISTRICT, *Fort A. P. Hill.* Set within the vast Fort A. P. Hill, this district consists of 150 acres of mostly wooded terrain around Travis Lake, a large 18th-century millpond. A gristmill and sawmill were operated here from the 1890s until 1920 by Francis Marion Travis. The serene quality of the area attracted Washington patent attorney Charles M. Thomas who purchased the lake and surrounding acreage in 1937. Here Thomas and his wife constructed a rustic retreat later known as The Lodge. The commodious log structure is in the tradition of the camps established in the Adirondacks by wealthy individuals in the late 19th century. The Thomases' haven was incorporated into the A. P. Hill Military Reservation (now Fort A. P. Hill) in 1941. The Lodge served as an officers' club and today is a retreat for both military personnel and civilians. *(16–349–23) VLR: 06/19/96.*

CARROLL COUNTY

Named in honor of Charles Carroll of Carrollton, a Maryland signer of the Declaration of Independence, this mountainous Southwest Virginia county was formed from Grayson County in 1842. Part of Patrick County was added later. The county seat is Hillsville.

CARROLL COUNTY COURTHOUSE, *Hillsville.* The principal landmark of the county-seat town of Hillsville, the Carroll County Courthouse combines two traditional courthouse forms: the arcaded front and the porticoed temple form with flanking wings. Both forms were widely employed by Jeffersonian workmen in Piedmont and Southside Virginia. They had long passed out of fashion when local builder Col. Ira B. Coltrane designed and executed the Carroll County Courthouse in 1870–75, imaginatively placing a Doric portico in front of an arcaded ground floor. Coltrane gave the building additional visual character by using Italianate brackets in the pediment and placing above it an octagonal cupola with a fancy pinnacle. The county's second courthouse, it was the scene of the Hillsville massacre of March 14, 1912, in which five persons, including the presiding judge, were killed in a courtroom battle involving the Allen family. *(237–01) VLR: 09/15/81; NRHP: 07/08/82.*

SIDNA ALLEN HOUSE, *Fancy Gap vicinity.* This capricious, if provincial, expression of the Queen Anne style was briefly the home of the notorious Sidna Allen. Allen was a member of the so-called Allen Clan that was involved in the gory Hillsville massacre of 1912. In a barrage of gunfire in the courtroom during the trial of Allen's brother Floyd, several people, including the judge and court officials, were killed. Sidna Allen, although he claimed innocence, was found guilty of participating and was sentenced to thirty-five years in prison but was pardoned after serving thirteen years. The house, finished only a year before the shooting, was designed by Allen and his wife. It was built by Preston Dickens, a local carpenter, with Allen assisting. Allen dreamed of owning the finest house in Carroll County, and the house was his dream come true until it was confiscated by the state after his conviction. *(17–05) VLR: 01/15/74; NRHP: 07/15/74.*

SNAKE CREEK FARM, *Snake Creek Community.* Although sparsely populated today, Carroll County was even more remote in 1910 when farmer James F. Martin built his residence in a narrow valley bordering Snake Creek. The thirteen-room house, the county's most modern dwelling at the time, was in the fashionable Queen Anne style with a complex roofline, projecting three-part bay, and wraparound front porch with spindle frieze. The gables were decorated with up-to-date pressed-metal shingles. Inside, Martin opposed convention and had every room completely sheathed in tongue-and-groove boards, ceilings included. The house was also the first in the area to have indoor plumbing and electricity. On the grounds is a two-room schoolhouse built before 1907 and incorporated into the county school system in 1916. Martin's second wife, Nettie, taught at the school from about 1939 until 1955 when it closed and reverted to her ownership. *(17–08) VLR: 08/21/90; NRHP: 01/11/91.*

CHARLES CITY COUNTY

Named for Prince Charles, later King Charles I, this largely rural Tidewater county was one of Virginia's eight original shires, established by 1634. Its county seat is Charles City.

BELLE AIR, *Charles City vicinity.* The original five-bay portion of this modest plantation house illustrates in its form and construction details the transition from 17th-century building methods to 18th-century ones. The exposed interior framing with summer beam and the heavy closed-string stair railing are characteristic of the 17th century. The symmetrical facade and center-passage floor plan are harbingers of standard 18th-century forms. The three-bay western section was added ca. 1800. Because of the destruction of Charles City County records, Belle Air's construction date is difficult to document. Daniel Clarke purchased the property in 1662, and the house could have been built for him or his progeny. Whatever its date, Belle Air is a unique surviving example in Virginia of a wooden house with postmedieval-type exposed interior framing. It is also likely the oldest plantation dwelling along Virginia's historic Route 5. *(18–36) VLR: 01/15/74; NRHP: 07/18/74.*

BERKELEY, *Charles City vicinity.* One of America's most historic estates, Berkeley was originally settled in 1619 as Berkeley Hundred but was wiped out in the Indian attack of 1622. The property was purchased by the Harrison family in 1691. The present mansion, built in 1726 by Benjamin Harrison IV, is among the earliest of the great Georgian plantation dwellings that became the foci of colonial Virginia's economic, cultural, and social life. Berkeley was the birthplace of Harrison's son Benjamin Harrison V, signer of the Declaration of Independence. His son William Henry Harrison, ninth president of the United States, also was born at Berkeley. Berkeley was pillaged by Benedict Arnold during the Revolutionary War and was occupied by the Army of the Potomac under Maj. Gen. George B. McClellan in 1862. Restored by its longtime owner the late Malcolm Jamieson, the plantation is now a much-visited historic attraction. *(18–01) VLR: 07/06/71; NRHP: 04/13/72; NHL: 11/11/71; BHR EASEMENT.*

LOTT CARY BIRTH SITE, *Charles City vicinity.* For two centuries this late 18th-century vernacular dwelling has been recognized as the birthplace of Lott Cary (1780–1829), the first black American missionary to Africa and a founding father of Liberia. The house is the only remnant of the plantation of John Bowry, on which Cary was born a slave. Cary lived here until 1804 when Bowry hired him out to a Richmond tobacco manufacturer. Cary taught himself to read and write and eventually purchased his freedom. He was ordained a Baptist minister and became active in the African Missionary Society and the American Colonization Society. With support from the American Baptist Board of Foreign Missions, he journeyed to Liberia where he founded the Providence Baptist Church of Monrovia and helped establish native schools. Cary died unaware that he had been elected governor of the colony. *(18–61)* VLR: 05/20/80; NRHP: 07/30/80.

EAGLE'S NEST, *Walker Store vicinity.* On a high bluff overlooking the Chickahominy River, Eagle's Nest is a small but carefully crafted planter's house built between 1700 and 1729. Its brickwork is distinctive for employing English bond with all glazed headers, which give the walls a striped appearance. Like the Adam Thoroughgood house, Eagle's Nest has one interior end chimney and one exterior end chimney. The latter is set off by tiled weatherings and a set-back T-shaped stack. The original roof was destroyed in the early 20th century when the house was raised to two stories. In 1979 the property was acquired for a game preserve by the Department of Game and Inland Fisheries. The house with a small tract was subsequently conveyed to the Association for the Preservation of Virginia Antiquities and was sold to private owners in 1981 whereupon it underwent a meticulous restoration. *(18–37)* VLR: 07/17/73; NRHP: 08/17/73.

CHARLES CITY COUNTY COURTHOUSE, *Charles City.* Named for Prince Charles, later King Charles I, the Charles City Corporation was established in 1618 and became Charles City County in 1642. Earlier courthouses were located at City Point and then Westover. The present courthouse was erected in the 1750s following the imposition in 1748 and 1749 of a special levy for the construction of a new court building. After its completion, the court made payments to Col. Richard Bland, a builder. The compact edifice is one of Virginia's six remaining arcaded colonial courthouses. The similarity of the brickwork to that at nearby Westover suggests that the two buildings shared brickmasons. The courthouse was rifled by Union troops during the Civil War, and many early records were lost. The arcade was later enclosed to provide additional space. The courthouse still serves its original use after two and a half centuries. *(18–05)* VLR: 09/09/69; NRHP: 11/17/69.

EDGEWOOD AND HARRISON'S MILL, *Charles City vicinity.* The storybook Gothic Revival house at Edgewood is an architectural contrast to the area's noted colonial plantation houses. It was built around 1854 for Richard S. Rowland of New Jersey, who moved here to operate the mill that stands just behind the house. The mill, an 18th-century structure, was originally owned by Benjamin Harrison V of nearby Berkeley and was visited during the Revolution by British troops led by Benedict Arnold. It was largely rebuilt in the early 19th century to accommodate updated machinery. During the Peninsula campaign of 1862 Confederate cavalry leader Gen. J. E. B. Stuart found refreshment at the Rowland house. Two weeks later part of Maj. Gen. George B. McClellan's Army of the Potomac encamped at Edgewood. A familiar landmark along historic Route 5, Edgewood has been restored to serve as an inn. *(18–58)* VLR: 12/14/82; NRHP: 02/10/83.

EPPES ISLAND, *Charles City vicinity.* Eppes Island has been occupied by successive generations of the Eppes family since 1624, making it the oldest farm in Virginia, and possibly the nation, in continuous ownership by the same family. Initially settled as part of a land grant to Francis Eppes, the island was part of Shirley Hundred, one of the more prosperous of the Virginia Company settlements. An archaeological investigation of Eppes Island undertaken by the Virginia Department of Historic Resources in 1984 revealed a series of sites dating from the early 17th century into the 18th century. An important prehistoric site of the Archaic and Woodland periods was found at the same time. The ca. 1790 Eppes dwelling stands on the island's western end. Despite extensive gravel mining in recent years, additional archaeological resources are believed to remain. *(18–33) VLR: 05/13/69; NRHP: 11/12/69.*

GLEBE OF WESTOVER PARISH, *Ruthville vicinity.* Built between 1720 and 1757 during the tenure of the Rev. Peter Fontaine, the Westover glebe house served the clergymen of its venerable parish until 1805 when the General Assembly required the sale of Virginia's church lands. Like other extant glebe houses, Westover's exhibits the fine masonry and careful proportions employed in the churches with which they were associated. Many of the glebe houses were retrimmed after their sale into private ownership, indicating either that they originally were very simply appointed or had fallen into bad condition by the time of their sale. This blending of architectural periods is discernible at Westover glebe house, where the Federal trim in the windows, entrance, and interior contrasts with the mid-18th-century brick walls, neatly laid in glazed-header Flemish bond. *(18–09) VLR: 03/18/75; NRHP: 06/05/75.*

EVELYNTON, *Charles City vicinity.* Designed by W. Duncan Lee (1884–1952), one of Virginia's most proficient Colonial Revival architects, Evelynton is a masterful adaptation of 18th-century Virginia architectural forms for a modern country residence. The house was completed in 1937 for Mr. and Mrs. John Augustine Ruffin, Jr., whose family had owned the property since 1847. The Ruffins' interest in the region's colonial dwellings led to their collaboration on the design. References to such well-known landmarks as Westover, Shirley, Carter's Grove, and Gunston Hall are evident in the composition, particularly in the splendid interior woodwork. The historic atmosphere is enhanced by the building's placement on an old site, with scenic views from a terraced lawn across the marshy Herring Creek. The property was the scene of a fierce skirmish during the Seven Days' battles of June 1862 during which the original dwelling was destroyed by Union soldiers. *(18–64) VLR: 06/21/88; NRHP: 08/17/89.*

GREENWAY, *Charles City vicinity.* John Tyler, tenth president of the United States, was born at Greenway on March 29, 1790. Amid a cluster of outbuildings, the dormered residence is typical of the many lesser plantation houses erected in Virginia during the second half of the 18th century. It was built around 1776 for Tyler's father, Judge John Tyler, governor of Virginia 1808–11, who is buried here. The future president lived at Greenway until his marriage to Letitia Christian. He returned in 1821 and made Greenway his home during his own tenure as governor in 1825–27. Tyler sold Greenway in 1829 and eventually purchased nearby Sherwood Forest, where he lived until his death. The unpretentious but formally proportioned dwelling has survived practically unchanged. The interior preserves original woodwork, including paneled chimneypieces. The complex is one of the many landmarks along Virginia's historic Route 5. *(18–10) VLR: 09/09/69; NRHP: 11/17/69.*

HARDENS, *Granville vicinity.* Originally patented in 1638 to Elizabeth Grayne and farmed as a separate unit for nearly three and a half centuries, Hardens is a James River estate that formerly served as a subsidiary farm, or quarter, of Shirley plantation. The property at one time was called Hardings or Hardings Landing. An 1818 survey and plat show a dwelling in the approximate location of the present house. A typical example of mid-19th-century Virginia's rural vernacular architecture, the main part of the existing frame house was erected in 1846 by Hill Carter of Shirley for his son Lewis Warrington Carter and may incorporate sections of an earlier structure. Hardens was acquired by David Walker Haxall in 1852 to supply lumber for his family's extensive Richmond milling operations. During the Civil War the place served as a Union communications station and camp for Maj. Gen. George B. McClellan in 1862. *(18–45) VLR: 12/15/81; NRHP: 02/10/83.*

AARON HILTON ARCHAEOLOGICAL SITE, *Milton vicinity.* This site includes the remains of a simple domicile built between 1870 and 1877 for Aaron Hilton (1832–1916), a respected former slave of the Lewis-Douthat and Selden families. An anonymous writer in 1915 described Hilton as "one of the landmarks of Charles City County," saying that he was an authority on the care of sheep and that neighboring farmers relied on him for advice on all occasions. In 1877 Hilton was able to realize a primary ambition of freedmen by purchasing a five-acre parcel, the tract where he had built his house. Because written records of freedmen's domestic lifestyles are uncommon, the archaeological remains of Hilton's house, accompanied by unusually substantive documentation, give the site particular significance for providing information on a neglected facet of Virginia social history. Tests by Virginia Department of Historic Resources archaeologists in 1993 confirmed the site's location. *(18–246) VLR: 12/04/96; NRHP: 02/21/97.*

KITTEWAN, *Charles City vicinity.* Barely touched by modernization, this weatherboarded old dwelling, overlooking Weyanoke Peninsula's marshy Kittewan Creek, typifies the colonial period's medium-size plantation house. Although unpretentious on the exterior, its interior is embellished with full paneling and other trim that would be noteworthy in a much larger house. The tract on which Kittewan is located was included in property acquired by Governor George Yeardley in 1618. The construction date of the house is uncertain, but in the late 18th century it was the home of Dr. William Rickman, who was appointed by the Continental Congress in 1776 to be in charge of Virginia hospitals during the Revolutionary War. Dr. Rickman died at Kittewan in 1783. During the Civil War, Kittewan was occupied by the Union troops under Gen. Philip Sheridan. *(18–13) VLR: 09/20/77; NRHP: 12/28/79.*

MOUNT STIRLING, *Providence Forge vicinity.* William Jerdone, one of Charles City County's wealthiest planters, built Mount Stirling in 1851. An exceptional example of high-style Greek Revival architecture, the house was erected at a time when few major plantation dwellings were being built in eastern Virginia. Untouched by change, the mansion, with its balustraded parapet, dwarf Ionic portico, and neat brickwork, is a rural five-bay version of the three-bay Greek Revival town houses that formerly filled downtown Richmond. Its architectural formality is reinforced by its visual dominance of its landscaped setting. Original hardware, mantels, and woodwork display the fine craftsmanship of Mount Stirling's builders, who probably had Richmond connections. A frame kitchen building dating from a preceding 18th-century plantation complex is the only remaining dependency. The plantation was occupied by Union troops in 1862 and again in 1864. *(18–15) VLR: 12/09/92; NRHP: 02/04/93.*

NORTH BEND, *Charles City vicinity.* In its present form North Bend is among the county's few examples of builders' Greek Revival. The original portion was built in 1819 for John Minge, member of one of the county's landed families. In 1843 North Bend was acquired by Thomas H. Wilcox who in 1853–55 transformed the vernacular dwelling into a double-pile Greek Revival plantation house, using decorative details based on designs in Asher Benjamin's architectural pattern books. Some of the woodwork retains original painted wood graining and marbleizing. Although updated with the remodeling, the five-bay, hipped-roof scheme maintained a traditional Georgian format. In 1865 North Bend was used as the headquarters of Union general Philip Sheridan before his 30,000 men crossed the James River to join the siege of Petersburg. Included on the plantation are several early farm buildings, a dairy, and a smokehouse. *(18–65) VLR: 07/21/87; NRHP: 08/21/89.*

PINEY GROVE, *Binns Hall vicinity.* This otherwise unprepossessing vernacular dwelling has had a complicated structural history, making it an instructive example of evolutionary expansion. The earliest portion began as a 1790 log corncrib on the plantation of Furneau Southall, deputy sheriff of Charles City County. This rare survival of log construction in this area was transformed into a general merchandise store in 1820. The store was expanded in 1853 by John S. Stubblefield, Southall's grandson, who added a single-cell frame wing. Piney Grove Store served this part of rural Charles City County for some eighty-five years. Such general stores were often gathering places and played an important role in 19th-century social life. In 1905 the structure was further expanded with a two-story frame section, and the whole building became a residence. Piney Grove has recently undergone a restoration that sensitively maintains the structure's layers of history. *(18–63) VLR: 06/18/85; NRHP: 11/26/85.*

POPLAR SPRINGS, *Ruthville vicinity.* The Poplar Springs dwelling house was once the center of a 312-acre plantation owned by Joseph Vaiden. It was situated on the busy Old Main Road that formerly connected Charles City to Williamsburg. The Vaidens established a settlement here called Vaiden's Crossroads, one of several crossroads communities serving both travelers and the county's inland population. The original section, built in 1809 by Joseph Vaiden's son Jacob, was a single-pile, side-passage dwelling, which, though tiny, was not unusual for middling landholders. Jacob Vaiden's son Robert enlarged the house in 1840–44, making it a symmetrical three-bay dwelling. He also added a story-and-a-half wing. The interior retains simple painted woodwork and six-panel doors with H-L hinges, brass knobs, and iron box locks. Two bricks on the west chimney, inscribed "IV 1809" and "RJV 1840," document the dates of the two parts. *(18–18) VLR: 03/10/94; NRHP: 08/30/94.*

THE ROWE, *Rustic vicinity.* On the bank of the James River, The Rowe is one of an architecturally sophisticated group of late 18th-century three- and five-part houses adapted from Palladian models as interpreted in 18th-century English architectural pattern books. The north wing predates the rest of the house and may have been in existence before 1779 when the property was owned by David Minge. The house apparently was expanded to its present form by Minge's son George Hunt Minge before his death in 1808. Following the precedent of Williamsburg's Finney house, The Rowe features a three-bay, two-story, pedimented center section flanked by lower wings. The format provides a convincing formality for what is otherwise a small house. The Rowe is currently unoccupied and in deteriorated condition. *(18–20) VLR: 11/15/77; NRHP: 03/28/80.*

SHERWOOD FOREST, *Charles City vicinity.* John Tyler purchased this plantation in his native Charles City County in 1842 while serving as tenth president of the United States, making it his home from 1845 until his death in 1862. To the original 18th-century house, Tyler added wings, hyphens, and attached dependencies. The western hyphen contained a ballroom and connected to Tyler's office. The additions resulted in a unified facade, 300 feet in length. Inside, the house was embellished with woodwork based on pattern-book designs by Minard Lafever. Its parlor wallpaper, ordered from France, was reproduced when the house was restored in the 1970s. Before becoming president, Tyler had served Virginia as congressman, governor, and U.S. senator, and he was a member of the Confederate Congress at his death in 1862. His home, one of many nationally significant landmarks along Virginia's historic Route 5, remains the home of Tyler's descendants. *(18–21) VLR: 09/09/69; NRHP: 10/15/66; NHL: 07/04/61.*

UPPER SHIRLEY, *Charles City vicinity.* The 1868–70 house at Upper Shirley was a secondary residence on the Shirley plantation, seat of the Carter family. Built by Hill Carter for his son William Fitzhugh Carter at a time when few houses were erected in Virginia because of the deprivations of the Civil War, the original portion was constructed by A. H. Marks and Brothers of Petersburg. The walls were laid with bricks taken from a large 18th-century bedroom house that formed part of the original architectural complex at Shirley. Under the ownership of the Edmund Saunders family, the house was enlarged in 1890–91 to nearly twice its original size and became one of the first homes in this rural county to incorporate modern turn-of-the-century conveniences. The house enjoys a romantic setting on the bank of the James. *(18–26) VLR: 12/15/81; NRHP: 10/29/82.*

SHIRLEY, *Charles City vicinity.* Shirley was patented in 1660 by Edward Hill, ancestor of the present owners. The formally arranged complex well illustrates the village air of a major colonial plantation but with special attention given to the placement and architectural treatment of the subordinate structures. The mansion, forecourt dependencies, barns, and two vanished three-story bedroom houses were built ca. 1738 following the marriage of Elizabeth Hill, heiress of Shirley, to John Carter, son of Robert ("King") Carter. The mansion was remodeled in the 1770s by Charles Carter who installed the rich interior woodwork and added the porticoes. The porticoes were modified in 1831. The stately complex, along with its accumulation of family furnishings and portraits, presents one of the most memorable pictures of the continuity of Virginia's plantation society. Ann Hill Carter, wife of Light-Horse Harry Lee and mother of Robert E. Lee, was born at Shirley in 1773. *(18–22) VLR: 11/05/68; NRHP 10/01/69; NHL: 04/15/70.*

UPPER WEYANOKE, *Charles City vicinity.* Archaeological investigations at Upper Weyanoke, a James River plantation, reveal an almost unbroken succession of settlements from the late 17th to the late 19th century. The principal historic structure is an early 19th-century brick cottage, probably built by John Minge as a dependency for a vanished larger house. The tiny two-room dwelling has been extended with modern wings, but the original configuration remains clearly discernible. Also on the grounds, but not related to the brick cottage, is a Greek Revival dwelling completed in 1859 for Robert Douthat. The generously proportioned but very plain two-story house has a side-passage plan and has long stood unoccupied. More detailed study of Upper Weyanoke's archaeological remains and their relationship to the standing structures should provide much information relating to three centuries of plantation life here. *(18–14) VLR: 09/16/80; NRHP: 12/09/80.*

WESTOVER, *Charles City vicinity.* Westover is perhaps the nation's premier example of colonial Georgian architecture as well as one of Virginia's earliest and grandest plantation mansions. It was built ca. 1730 by William Byrd II, who helped survey the Virginia–North Carolina border and founded the city of Richmond. Westover's stately air, graceful proportions, pedimented entrances, and paneled interiors have come to symbolize the high level of architectural quality attained during the colonial era. Complementing the house are original gardens and outbuildings as well as three sets of English wrought-iron gates. The plantation remained in the Byrd family until 1817. In 1899 it was purchased by Mrs. Clarise Sears Ramsey who engaged the New York restoration architect William H. Mesereau to modernize the house and to add the hyphens. Mesereau also designed the library dependency, built on the site of Byrd's library, destroyed during the 1862 Union occupation. *(18–27)* VLR: 09/09/69; NRHP:10/15/66; NHL 10/09/60; BHR EASEMENT.

WEYANOKE, *Charles City vicinity.* Weyanoke Peninsula has seen human occupation for 8,000 years and contains numerous prehistoric and colonial archaeological sites. In the contact period Weyanoke was inhabited by the Weyanoke Indians, one of the largest groups in the Powhatan chiefdom. An English settlement begun in 1619 was wiped out in the Indian attack of 1622. Joseph Harwood established a small settlement here by the 1650s. The present house was erected in 1798 for Fielding Lewis by John Stubbs, a Gloucester County housewright. The two-story dwelling, enlarged in this century with dormers and wings, is a finely crafted example of Georgian plantation architecture and features a Chinese lattice stair railing. Lewis, a nephew of Fielding Lewis of Kenmore, was a pioneer in scientific farming methods. Union general Philip Sheridan's troops occupied Weyanoke in 1864, and 15,000 Union soldiers marched toward Petersburg over a pontoon bridge here. *(18–29)* VLR: 09/21/76; NRHP: 03/10/80.

WESTOVER CHURCH, *Charles City vicinity.* Established as early as 1625, Westover Parish is one of the oldest church units in the country. The first church stood just upriver from Westover plantation but was replaced by the present, more centrally located brick church in 1731. Its rectangular form was favored for the colony's smaller ecclesiastical buildings. Westover Church served the families of the great plantations of Charles City County, and presidents William Henry Harrison, Benjamin Harrison, and John Tyler worshiped here. As a result of the disestablishment, the building stood abandoned beginning in 1805 for nearly thirty years. It was returned to service but was later desecrated by Union troops during the Civil War. Repaired after the war, it has continued in active use since. The molded-brick entrance was restored in 1956, and the clipped-gable roof was returned to its original form in 1969. *(18–28)* VLR: 08/15/72; NRHP: 12/05/72.

WOODBURN, *Charles City vicinity.* Woodburn was erected for John Tyler, tenth president of the United States, and occupied by him while he served as a congressman and as governor of Virginia. Tyler purchased the tract in 1813 and built the house shortly afterwards. In 1831 he sold it to his brother Wat H. Tyler. The house, described by John Tyler as a "decent and comfortable dwelling," is a provincial version of the tripartite Palladian house, a form popular in the South during the late 18th and early 19th centuries. The form consists of a two-story, gable-fronted center section flanked by one-story wings. Unlike more formal versions, Woodburn lacks classical proportions and details, but it maintains the form's bold outline. The house preserves plain but handsome interior woodwork as well as three early outbuildings. Woodburn is undergoing long-term restoration by its present owner, a Tyler descendant. *(18–52)* VLR: 04/19/77; NRHP: 12/12/78.

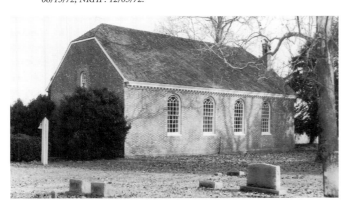

CHARLOTTE COUNTY

Formed from Lunenburg County in 1764, this southern Piedmont county was named for Charlotte of Mecklenburg-Strelitz, consort of King George III. Its county seat is Charlotte Court House.

CHARLOTTE COUNTY COURTHOUSE, *Charlotte Court House.* Charlotte County's courthouse was built in 1822–23 from plans by Thomas Jefferson. Henry Carrington, one of the Charlotte commissioners, was so impressed by Jefferson's design for the Buckingham County Courthouse that he persuaded Charlotte County to adopt it. The temple-form scheme with its Tuscan portico fulfills Jefferson's ambition to have local governmental institutions housed in models of educated architectural taste. The building was constructed by John Percival who bid on work at the University of Virginia but apparently was never employed there. While it is unclear whether Jefferson supplied a separate set of plans for the Charlotte courthouse, the courthouse as constructed differed from its Buckingham counterpart in several relatively minor aspects. Quintessentially Virginian with its red brick and white classical trim, the courthouse inspired several other court structures in the southern Piedmont and is still in regular use. *(185–01) VLR: 02/19/80; NRHP: 05/07/80.*

CHARLOTTE COURT HOUSE HISTORIC DISTRICT. Virginia's courthouse villages are among the most distinctive and appealing features of the Commonwealth's cultural landscape. Charlotte County's tiny county seat is among the best preserved of these communities. Bordered by its two principal streets is the courthouse square, on which are Thomas Jefferson's 1822–23 temple-form courthouse, two county clerk's offices, the registrar's office, the county jail, and a Civil War monument. Across the road is a row of mid-19th-century brick commercial buildings, each echoing the courthouse with a pedimented roof. One of the district's oldest structures is the Brick Tavern, an imposing country Federal hostelry built about 1820. Prominent residences include Diamond Hill, an 1840 Greek Revival dwelling, and the W. B. Ramsey house, a vernacular house with Gothic Revival flourishes. Two farms, Wynyard and Villeview, make up the western half of the historic district. *(185–23) VLR: 10/19/94; NRHP: 02/08/95.*

GREENFIELD, *Charlotte Court House vicinity.* Greenfield was the plantation of Isaac Read (1739–1777), member of the House of Burgesses and of the Virginia conventions of 1774 and 1775. Read was mortally wounded while serving as an officer in the Revolutionary War. The plain but formal dwelling he erected ca. 1771 is the oldest two-story frame house in Charlotte County. Its symmetrical five-bay facade, modillion cornice, and one-story wings give the building a commanding presence amid its rolling pastoral landscape. The Georgian stair, early mantels, and paneled wainscoting combine with the stately exterior to present a picture of 18th-century sophistication and prosperity in this thinly populated rural area. Adding to this image are the remnants of an extensive early formal garden. Greenfield remains the home of Read descendants. *(19–08) VLR: 10/17/72; NRHP: 04/02/73; BHR EASEMENT.*

MULBERRY HILL, *Randolph vicinity.* Judge Paul Carrington, a distinguished jurist and a leader in Virginia's movement from colony to commonwealth, made his home at Mulberry Hill in his later years. During the colonial period Carrington was a local justice and represented the county in the House of Burgesses. In the Revolutionary period he served on the 1776 committee that framed the Virginia Declaration of Rights. From 1789 to 1801 he was a justice on Virginia's newly created Court of Appeals. His residence, overlooking the Roanoke River valley, blends two periods of construction. The facade incorporates as its center section the late 18th-century gable end of the original house. Flanking it are two-story early 19th-century wings. On the grounds is an unusually complete set of early outbuildings including Judge Carrington's office. The property also preserves a family graveyard and traces of a large formal garden. *(19–24) VLR: 10/17/72; NRHP: 03/20/73.*

RED HILL, *Brookneal vicinity.* Patrick Henry, "Orator of the Revolution," assembled this isolated Charlotte County plantation through successive purchases of alluvial bottomlands and undulating countryside, making it his final home. Here he built a modest frame dwelling with a complement of outbuildings including his law office. The house, later incorporated into a larger structure, was destroyed by fire in 1919, but its original irregular form has since been reconstructed. Henry's simple law office remains intact. Nearby is the family cemetery containing the graves of the Revolutionary patriot and his second wife, Dorothea Dandridge Henry. The property remained in the ownership of Henry family descendants until 1944 when it was purchased by the Patrick Henry Memorial Foundation, which has since developed the property as a museum. *(19–27) VLR: 09/18/73; NRHP: 02/14/78.*

ROANOKE PLANTATION, *Randolph vicinity.* Few men have been as closely identified with a homeplace as John Randolph has with his Roanoke plantation. So attached was he to this large tract with its hilly pastures and rich bottomlands that he came to be styled John Randolph of Roanoke. A brilliant orator, Randolph used his talent in becoming a leading member of the House of Representatives and later the U.S. Senate where he opposed any challenge to the vested interests of the South, especially slavery. Randolph lived simply at Roanoke; his house was hardly more than a cottage. With its outbuildings, the place looked more like a rustic village than the grandiose seats of the South he championed. Although the acreage has been reduced and the original dwelling house destroyed, the plantation still evokes the presence of this colorful planter-statesman. *(19–29) VLR: 09/19/72; NRHP: 04/11/73.*

STAUNTON HILL, *Brookneal vicinity.* A striking exception to the normally conservative dwellings of Virginia's plantation aristocracy is this castellated Gothic-style mansion that architect John E. Johnson designed for Staunton Hill, the vast estate of Charles Bruce. The design is based on a plate in an English work by Thomas Kelly, *Designs for Cottage and Villa Architecture* (1829). The romantic qualities of Staunton Hill, completed in 1850, are seen primarily in the crenellated parapets, polygonal corner towers, and delicate marble veranda. The dwelling stands as a significant expression of both the exoticism and the historicism that would permeate American architecture for the balance of the century. In recent years Staunton Hill was the country home of Charles Bruce's grandson David K. E. Bruce, a noted diplomat who served as the U.S. ambassador to Great Britain and France and as America's first envoy to the Peoples' Republic of China. *(19–30) VLR: 11/05/68; NRHP: 10/01/69.*

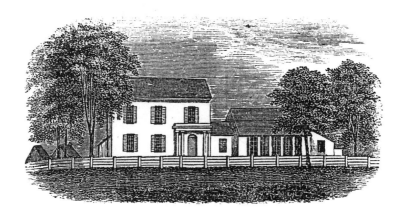

CITY OF CHARLOTTESVILLE

The county seat of Albemarle County, Charlottesville was named for Charlotte of Mecklenburg-Strelitz, consort of King George III. It was established in 1762 and became a city in 1888.

ALBEMARLE COUNTY COURTHOUSE HISTORIC DISTRICT. The principal feature of this compact quarter is Court Square, a focus of county activity since it was laid out in 1762. In the early 1800s it was not unusual to see Thomas Jefferson conversing here with James Madison and James Monroe. On the square is the county courthouse of 1803, which also served originally as a community church where Jefferson sometimes attended services. Around the square sprang up mid-19th-century law offices, residences, and taverns among which are the former Swan Tavern and the former Eagle Tavern. The 1851 Classical Revival town hall was purchased by Jefferson M. Levy, then the owner of Monticello, and converted into the Levy Opera House in 1887. Next to the courthouse is the equestrian statue of Stonewall Jackson, unveiled in 1921. Except for the multistoried Monticello Hotel building, the district maintains a consistent scale and architectural harmony. *(104–57) VLR: 01/18/72; NRHP: 06/30/72.*

BROOKS HALL, *University Avenue, University of Virginia grounds.* Providing a provocative contrast to the classicism of its neighboring Jeffersonian buildings, Brooks Hall is one of only two examples of late 19th-century eclecticism represented on the University of Virginia grounds. The building was donated in 1875 by Lewis Brooks, a Rochester, N.Y., philanthropist, and was among the earliest and best-equipped natural history museums in the country. Its exhibits included fossils presented to Thomas Jefferson from the Lewis and Clark expedition. Completed in 1877, Brooks Hall was designed by John R. Thomas, also of Rochester, who combined motifs of various historic styles into a wholly novel and airy composition. Symbolizing the building's original function is the series of carved heads of wild animals on its keystones. Thomas's original drawings for Brooks Hall are preserved in the university's archives. *(104–63) VLR: 02/15/77; (WITHIN THE NHL UNIVERSITY OF VIRGINIA HISTORIC DISTRICT).*

CHARLOTTESVILLE AND ALBEMARLE COUNTY COURTHOUSE HISTORIC DISTRICT. Charlottesville has been a regional political center since becoming the county seat in 1762. In addition to its associations with Thomas Jefferson and the University of Virginia, the city is significant for the diversity of its 19th- and early 20th-century architecture. The heart of the district is the courthouse square, containing the courthouse and several 19th-century brick offices. Also in the district is an archetypical late 19th-century main street which was made into a pedestrian mall in the 1970s. Architectural highlights are the former public library, the former post office, and the former railroad station, all employing a learned classicism. Adjacent industrial buildings and several adjoining residential neighborhoods complete the district. Scattered through the area are various Federal and Greek Revival houses. While not devoid of intrusions, the district gives Charlottesville's downtown a strong sense of historical continuity. *(104–72) VLR: 11/18/80; NRHP: 07/28/82.*

THE FARM (JOHN A. J. DAVIS HOUSE), *1201 East Jefferson Street.* This carefully articulated dwelling is one of the many Jeffersonian-style structures built by skilled workmen formerly involved with the construction of the University of Virginia. Although the builders here are undocumented, the similarity of the house to known works by William B. Phillips and Malcolm Crawford makes an attribution plausible. The Jeffersonian influence is seen mainly in the classical detailing, the Tuscan portico, and the Chinese railing. The house was competed in 1827 for Charlottesville attorney John A. J. Davis. In 1830 Davis became law professor at the University of Virginia where, in 1840, he was shot dead by a student. In 1865 the house served as a headquarters for Union general George A. Custer. George R. B. Michie, founder of the local Michie Publishing Co., purchased the house in 1909. The place fell into disrepair in the 1980s but was restored in 1993. *(104–002) VLR: 03/20/96; NRHP: 10/21/82 (UPDATED 11/07/96).*

GEORGE ROGERS CLARK MONUMENT, *University and Jefferson Park avenues.* The monument to Albemarle County native George Rogers Clark, "Conqueror of the Northwest," is the fourth of four works of public sculpture commissioned from members of the National Sculpture Society by Charlottesville philanthropist Paul Goodloe McIntire. McIntire engaged Robert Ingersoll Aitken to create a heroic-size bronze group that portrays a mounted Clark with members of his expedition confronting an Indian chief and members of his party. The sculpture was cast by the Gorham Company and was erected in 1921. A masterful and complex work of art, the monument reflects the influence of the City Beautiful movement. McIntire departed here from his usual practice of donating monuments to the city and presented the Clark sculpture to the University of Virginia. *(104–252) VLR: 06/19/96; NRHP: 05/16/97.*

THOMAS JONATHAN JACKSON SCULPTURE, *Jackson Park, Fourth and Jefferson streets.* Adjacent to the Albemarle County Courthouse, the equestrian statue of Thomas Jonathan ("Stonewall") Jackson is the third of four monuments given by philanthropist Paul Goodloe McIntire for the embellishment of his native city. Such civic works of art were essential ingredients of the City Beautiful movement, a turn-of-the-century effort to enhance America's cities with public amenities of fine design. Charlottesville's much-praised Lewis and Clark monument encouraged

McIntire to commission the eminent sculptor Charles Keck to produce this additional work. Though a monument to Jackson was contemplated as early as 1897, not until Keck's statue was unveiled in 1921 was the ambition fulfilled. Keck portrayed Jackson riding into battle on Little Sorrel. Carved on the granite pedestal are allegorical figures of Faith and Valor. The work is considered one of the nation's finest equestrian monuments. *(104–251) VLR: 06/19/96; NRHP: 05/16/97.*

ROBERT EDWARD LEE SCULPTURE, *Lee Park, First and Jefferson streets.* With the exception of Richmond, no Virginia city can boast a more important collection of public sculpture than Charlottesville. The principal pieces of this body of work are the four sculptures donated by local philanthropist Paul Goodloe McIntire. For the Lee monument, McIntire created a place worthy of a likeness of the Confederacy's most distinguished general when in 1917 he purchased a block in the heart of downtown. Now known as Lee Park, it was the first of four public parks that McIntire gave to the city. The equestrian statue was commissioned from sculptor Henry Shrady that same year. Shrady died before completing the work, and it was finished by Leo Lentelli in 1924. The powerful composition stands on an oval pedestal of pink granite designed by Virginia-born architect Walter Dabney Blair. *(104–264) VLR: 06/19/96; NRHP: 05/16/97.*

MOREA, *209 Sprigg Lane.* In the shadow of Thomas Jefferson's "Academical Village," Morea is the only surviving dwelling built by a member of the University of Virginia's original faculty. Erected in 1835, the singular structure was originally the home of John Patton Emmet, the university's first professor of natural history. Born in Ireland, Emmet was the son of Irish nationalist Thomas Addis Emmet. He attended West Point and later studied medicine in New York City, gaining a reputation as a scientist and an inventor. The dwelling displays a number of affinities to Jefferson's architecture and was likely erected by university workmen although Emmet wrote that it was "contrived by myself." Morea was acquired by a group of university alumni and friends and donated to the university in 1960 for its official guesthouse. Its name is derived from *Morus multicaulis,* the Chinese mulberry tree that Emmet grew here while experimenting with silkworm culture. *(104–44) VLR: 03/20/84; NRHP: 05/03/84.*

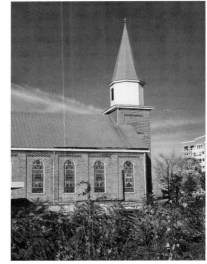

MOUNT ZION BAPTIST CHURCH, *105 Ridge Street.* Mount Zion Baptist Church evokes the struggle by Charlottesville's Afro-Americans to establish a viable community following Emancipation. Blacks required institutions that were truly their own, and the churches filled that need by serving not only as houses of worship but as social centers, theaters, and meeting places dealing with the affairs of the black community. The Mount Zion congregation was organized in 1867 and met in private houses until a Ridge Street house was donated to serve as a permanent home. It was replaced by a wooden church in 1875. The congregation outgrew the building and replaced it with the present brick structure in 1884. Embellished in the 1890s with its steeple, stained-glass windows, and pipe organ, the church became a symbol of the growing importance of Charlottesville's black community. Local tradition assigns its design to George Wallace Spooner, a Charlottesville architect. *(104–181) VLR: 06/19/91; NRHP: 10/15/92.*

OAK LAWN, *Cherry Avenue and Ninth Street.* This accomplished example of Jeffersonian Palladianism is one of the many structures in the region whose architecture was influenced by builders who adopted Thomas Jefferson's distinctive style while working on his projects. The three-part house, with its pedimented center section and flat-roof Tuscan portico, was built in 1822 for Nimrod Bramham, a merchant who served in the House of Delegates. The design and construction are attributed to James Dinsmore, a Scotch-Irish master carpenter brought to Charlottesville by Jefferson to assist with the building of Monticello and later the University of Virginia. After Bramham's death in 1847, Oak Lawn was sold to James Fife, an influential Baptist minister who in 1823 helped organize the Baptist General Convention. Born in Scotland, Fife served as Richmond's city engineer before moving to Charlottesville. *(104–31) VLR: 04/17/73; NRHP: 05/25/73.*

THE ROTUNDA, *University of Virginia.* The Rotunda is the most important individual architectural work of Thomas Jefferson, who, had he pursued no other activity, would be considered one of America's leading architects. Designed when he was over seventy and completed in 1826, the Rotunda was the principal element of Jefferson's scheme for the University of Virginia. Jefferson modeled it after the Pantheon in Rome, which he considered to be the most perfect example of what he called "spherical" architecture. He divided the first two levels into suites of oval rooms for lecture halls. The domed top floor, with its ring of paired Composite columns, served as the university's library. The Rotunda was gutted by fire in 1895. New York architect Stanford White designed a new interior, which departed from Jefferson's plan, and added the north portico. The White interior was removed in a mid-1970s attempt to recreate the Jeffersonian interior. *(104–56) VLR: 09/09/69; NRHP: 10/15/66; NHL: 12/21/65.*

RUGBY ROAD–UNIVERSITY CORNER HISTORIC DISTRICT. Covering some twenty blocks north of the University of Virginia grounds, this tightly developed neighborhood contains academic, commercial, and residential buildings associated with the university during the period before World War II. Most date to the boom years between 1890 and 1930 when the student population quadrupled. Noteworthy university structures are Madison Hall, Carr's Hill (the university president's house), Fayerweather Gymnasium, and Bayly Museum, all in various classical idioms. Clustered along leafy streets is a variety of residential buildings including some twenty-three fraternity houses and various apartment houses, many of which also emulate the university's classical tradition. Among the more architecturally distinguished fraternity houses is the grouping on Rugby Road, known as the Quadrangle, as well as a range of columned structures along Madison Lane. The era also produced the colorful strip of commercial buildings along University Avenue known as the Corner. *(104–130, 133) VLR: 11/15/83; NRHP: 02/16/84.*

"THEIR FIRST VIEW OF THE PACIFIC" (MERIWETHER LEWIS AND WILLIAM CLARK SCULPTURE), *West Main Street at Ridge Street.* This sculptural group depicts Albemarle County native Meriwether Lewis and William Clark, whose father was from Albemarle County, at the climax of their famous 1803–6 expedition to explore the Louisiana Purchase. Shown with them is their Indian guide Sacagawea. Erected in 1919, the group is the work of the nationally prominent sculptor Charles Keck, member of the National Sculpture Society. The monument is the first of four commemorative sculptures commissioned by Charlottesville philanthropist Paul Goodloe McIntire to adorn his native city. Though not on the scale of many heroic sculptures, Keck's monument is an able representative of the figurative style of outdoor statuary produced by members of the society. Their work formed an important component of the turn-of-the-century City Beautiful movement. *(104–273) VLR: 06/19/96; NRHP: 05/16/97.*

UNIVERSITY OF VIRGINIA HISTORIC DISTRICT. Thomas Jefferson's design for the center of today's sprawling university is internationally regarded as one of the outstanding accomplishments of American architecture. Between 1814 and 1826 Jefferson designed and supervised the construction, created the curriculum, and selected the library and faculty. Jefferson's concept was an "Academical Village" where students lived in close proximity to the professors and their classes. Flanking an elongated terraced lawn open to the south, ten pavilions housed the professors, each building in a different architectural order intended for instruction. The students occupied the colonnaded dormitories and outer ranges. At the head stood the domed library, the Rotunda. A fire in 1895 destroyed the Rotunda; its rebuilding and the closing of the south end with Cabell, Rouss, and Cocke halls were the work of Stanford White. Other significant buildings include Brooks Hall, 1877; the Chapel, 1889; and the Amphitheater, 1921. *(104–42) VLR: 10/06/70; NRHP: 11/20/70; NHL: 11/11/71; WORLD HERITAGE LIST.*

JOHN VOWLES HOUSE, *1111 and 1113 West Main Street.* The three-bay town house at 1111 West Main Street is presumed to be the handiwork of James Dinsmore, a Scotch-Irish master builder who with John Neilson was brought by Thomas Jefferson from Philadelphia to work on Monticello and later the University of Virginia. Along with Jefferson's and other commissions, Dinsmore speculated in Charlottesville real estate. In 1818 he purchased lots on Main Street and apparently built this town house following his sale of the lot to John Vowles, a painter and glazier who had also worked at the university. Although lacking the monumental classicism of Jefferson's designs, the house has the fine brickwork, sophisticated proportions, and academic moldings associated with buildings by Jefferson's workmen. A nearly identical town house was attached to the Vowles house about 1830. Both buildings have served a variety of uses in their long history. *(104–40) VLR: 10/18/88; NRHP: 11/02/89.*

WERTLAND STREET HISTORIC DISTRICT. A genteel residential quarter between the University of Virginia and downtown Charlottesville, this compact district is defined by approximately thirty freestanding dwellings, mostly ca. 1900. Wertland Street takes its name from the family of William Wertenbaker, appointed by Thomas Jefferson to serve as the university's second librarian, a post he held for over fifty years. Wertenbaker's 1830 brick I-house at 1301 Wertland Street is the oldest house in the district. Its grounds originally extended to Main Street. The formerly semirural area began to be developed in the 1880s as one of several neighborhoods serving members of the university community. By the early 1900s more than fifteen houses had been built, primarily on Wertland Street. Today, though adjacent to the bustle of a large university and a commercial corridor, the neighborhood preserves a hint of the quiet, reassuring ambience of pre–World War I America. *(104–136) VLR: 12/11/84; NRHP: 02/14/85.*

CITY OF CHESAPEAKE

Named for the Chesapeake Bay, this sprawling, largely rural municipality was formed in 1963 by a merger of Norfolk County and the city of South Norfolk, both of which thereby became extinct.

DISMAL SWAMP CANAL, *Deep Creek.* Traversing the vast swamp from which it takes its name, the Dismal Swamp Canal is a twenty-two-mile channel between Deep Creek and the village of South Mills, N.C. The 100-foot-wide waterway was originally dug between 1793 and 1805 by the Dismal Swamp Canal Company to connect the Southern Branch of the Elizabeth River with the Pasquotank River in North Carolina. Excavated by hand labor under difficult swamp conditions, the canal was an early engineering achievement that provided an inland link between the two states. It eventually became part of the Intracoastal Waterway. The canal is recognized as a National Historic Civil Engineering Landmark by the American Society of Civil Engineers. Included in the canal complex are two lift locks built in 1940–41, two steel bascule drawbridges dating from 1933–34, and three water-level control spillways. *(131–35) VLR: 02/16/88; NRHP: 06/06/88.*

GREAT BRIDGE BATTLE ARCHAEOLOGICAL SITE, *off Route 168 between Great Bridge and Oak Grove.* The first pitched battle of the Revolution in Virginia was fought on December 9, 1775, at the Great Bridge, a wooden causeway across 360 yards of marsh and open water of the Southern Branch of the Elizabeth River, south of Norfolk. Lord Dunmore, the royal governor, had a British garrison here to protect this approach to Norfolk. The bloody engagement proved to be a victory for the patriots. The British abandoned their fortified position at this strategic point and eventually were forced to evacuate Norfolk because it could not be defended from the south. Artifacts of this engagement likely survive in the marshes adjacent to the bridge site. *(131–23) VLR: 01/05/71; NRHP: 03/28/73.*

SOUTH NORFOLK HISTORIC DISTRICT. South Norfolk began as a section of Berkeley, an 1880s streetcar suburb established across the Eastern Branch of the Elizabeth River from Norfolk. From the first, South Norfolk offered housing to employees at nearby rail yards and factories. By 1902 the community had a population of some 2,000. By the late 1920s most of the houses now within the neighborhood were in place. Although South Norfolk achieved second-class city status, the area was eventually incorporated into the present city of Chesapeake. The district is characterized by closely spaced free-standing houses on a grid of streets. Also included are several churches, a school, and a small business district. The houses are mostly simple builders' versions of popular early 20th-century styles, nearly all of wood-frame construction, and nearly all with a front porch, a necessity during the area's hot summers. *(131–55) VLR: 12/08/87; NRHP: 01/27/89.*

WALLACETON, *3509 George Washington Highway South.* This unassuming mid-19th-century building was originally built as a store to serve the employees of the Wallace Company, a lumber company, as well as the residents of Wallaceton, a settlement on the Dismal Swamp Canal. The original section, built of vertical juniper logs, was made into a residence for John G. Wallace after the Civil War. In 1888 the Irish poet John Boyle O'Reilly visited Wallaceton and wrote: "We stopped at Mr. Wallace's, in the Dismal Swamp,—one of the largest and most beautiful farms in America . . . it was hard to realize, from our refined surroundings, and the gracious hospitality we were enjoying, that we were within the very heart of the Dismal Swamp." The widening of the canal in the 1910s necessitated moving the building approximately 100 feet. The house remains the property of the Wallace family. *(131–379) VLR: 03/10/94; NRHP: 05/19/94.*

CHESTERFIELD COUNTY

Formed from Henrico County in 1749, Chesterfield County was named for Philip Dormer Stanhope, fourth earl of Chesterfield, British statesman and diplomat. The county seat is Chesterfield Court House.

AZUREST SOUTH, *Virginia State University, Ettrick.* Azurest South was designed by Amaza Lee Meredith (1895–1984), one of the country's first black female architects, as her own residence and studio. The compact, clean-lined dwelling, built in 1939, is among the Commonwealth's few mature examples of the International Style, a design approach which developed in Germany after World War I and espoused a complete break with traditional architecture. Meredith was a professor at Virginia State University, founding and chairing the Fine Arts Department in the early 1930s. For the bathroom and kitchen of Azurest South, Meredith designed vividly colored and patterned floors, walls, and ceilings. The living room mantel is a stylish Art Deco design. In addition to homes in Virginia and Texas, Meredith designed Azurest North, a vacation community for Afro-Americans at Sag Harbor on Long Island. Azurest South is now owned by the Virginia State University Alumni Association. *(20–5245–36) VLR: 10/20/93; NRHP: 12/30/93.*

BELLONA ARSENAL, *Midlothian vicinity.* An iron foundry was established here in 1814 by Maj. John Clarke and was served by the Chesterfield coal mines. Three years later Clarke was instrumental in having the federal government establish an arsenal adjacent to the foundry. Named for the Roman goddess of war, Bellona Arsenal was used for storing munitions produced in Clarke's foundry. The arsenal was abandoned in 1832, but the foundry survived and eventually was leased by the Confederate government for the production of ordnance. Today, four of the arsenal's eight major buildings remain. Three of these, grouped around a quadrangle, have been converted to residences. Nearby stands a roofless 90-foot-long granite powder magazine. Also on the property are the ruins of two smaller buildings and several archaeological sites. The whole assemblage is one of the state's most significant early 19th-century industrial complexes. *(20–06) VLR: 01/05/71; NRHP: 05/06/71.*

BELLWOOD, *Defense General Supply Center, Bellwood.* Known originally as Sheffields and later as Auburn Chase, Bellwood was a working farm from the early 17th century until 1941. The two-story dwelling, erected ca. 1790 by wealthy planter Richard Gregory, is a characteristic example of the wooden Georgian architecture favored by Virginia planters of the time. In May 1864 Confederate general P. G. T. Beauregard made the house his headquarters. It also served as a meeting place between Beauregard and President Jefferson Davis. James Bellwood bought the property in 1887 and turned it into a model farm, its products winning acclaim at the 1914 Pacific International Exposition. The U.S. Army purchased Bellwood in 1941 and activated the Richmond General Depot. Although the house has been adapted as an officers' club, much of its early fabric is intact. An elk herd established by Bellwood is maintained on an adjacent twenty-acre reserve. *(20–07) VLR: 06/19/73; NRHP: 12/12/78.*

BON AIR HISTORIC DISTRICT. The sultry, sooty atmosphere of the South's late 19th-century cities encouraged urban dwellers to escape the insufferable summers by going to mountain or waterside resorts. It also spurred development of more convenient retreats in the cities' wooded fringes. With its salubrious name, Bon Air was begun in 1877 by the Bon Air Land and Improvement Company in a sylvan section of Chesterfield County convenient by rail to downtown Richmond. Financial problems in the late 1910s ended Bon Air's role as a resort, but its proximity to the city and the ascendancy of the automobile enabled it to evolve into a distinctive residential suburb. Its principal artery, Buford Road, is still lined with gaily ornamented Victorian cottages. A reminder of the former resort character is the 1881–82 Bon Air Hotel annex (shown). Though now surrounded by suburban sprawl, Bon Air maintains its village ambience. *(20–5084) VLR: 04/19/88; NRHP: 11/15/88.*

BRIDGE AT FALLING CREEK, *U.S. Route 1/301 (Jefferson Davis Highway) at Falling Creek.* Nestled in a wayside park between the busy north- and southbound lanes of U.S. Route 1/301, the Bridge at Falling Creek is one of only twelve known masonry-arched turnpike bridges remaining in the state. It was built in 1823 as a component of the Manchester-Petersburg Turnpike. In his 1829 report to the Board of Public Works, Dr. James Henderson, the company's president, described the bridge with enthusiasm: "The bridge at Falling Creek is considered in this part of the world to be a structure of some elegance." Built by William Carter of Richmond, the bridge was one of five in the turnpike system. It was removed from service in 1931 upon the completion of the southbound lane of U.S. Route 1/301. The wayside was developed in 1934 with the cooperation of the Chesterfield Garden Club. *(20–135) VLR: 08/28/95; NRHP: 10/12/95.*

CASTLEWOOD, *Chesterfield Court House.* The neo-Palladian style popularized in 18th-century England is evident in the massing of Castlewood, a five-part house conspicuously located at Chesterfield Court House. Although a unified composition, the house was erected in stages of uncertain sequence. The middle section probably was built ca. 1816 for Parke Poindexter, clerk of the court. The south wing may be part of the initial construction, but its elaborate, highly individualized woodwork dates from the 1830s and matches that at Norwood in Powhatan County. The north wing, with its gouged-work mantel, appears to predate the rest of the house and apparently was moved from elsewhere. Castlewood has had numerous owners. From 1860 to 1872 it was used by Methodists for traveling ministers. It was converted to a bank in 1977. In 1992 it was acquired for preservation by Chesterfield County and now is used for county offices. *(20–14) VLR: 06/15/76; NRHP: 11/21/76.*

CHESTER PRESBYTERIAN CHURCH, *3424 West Hundred Road, Chester.* Now the chapel of the recently expanded Chester Presbyterian Church, this simple Gothic Revival structure has served the Chester community for some 120 years. The church was built in 1880 almost singlehandedly by Martin T. Grove, one of a group of northern fortune seekers who brought their families to the Chester area following a rumor that Gen. Benjamin Butler had left behind a buried military chest containing $80,000. They discovered no money, but some became founding members of Chester Presbyterian Church in 1878. The church was at times a temporary meeting place for Methodists and Baptists. It was moved to its present location from the original site on Winfree Road in 1951. In 1995 the building was repositioned and renovated to become the focal point of a new sanctuary complex. The original pews are still in use. *(20–5088) VLR: 06/15/76; NRHP: 11/21/76.*

CHESTERFIELD COUNTY COURTHOUSE AND COURTHOUSE SQUARE, *Chesterfield.* Chesterfield County's courthouse square has been the location of the county seat since the county was formed in 1749. The site was chosen because of its situation near the county's geographic center, and because it was at the intersection of five roads. The colonial courthouse was demolished in 1917 despite early preservation sentiment. The 1918 courthouse that replaced it was designed by J. T. Skinner of Petersburg and built by the Vaughan Construction Co. of Shawsville. A competent essay in the Colonial Revival style, its general form, with its portico and octagonal cupola, recalls the colonial James City County Courthouse in Williamsburg. Also in the tree-shaded square is the 1828 clerk's office, the 1889 clerk's office, and the 1892 jail. A replica of the 1749 courthouse, built in 1976–77, houses the Chesterfield County Museum. *(20–277) VLR: 10/09/91; NRHP: 08/18/92.*

DINWIDDIE COUNTY PULLMAN CAR, *Hallsboro Yard, County Line Road, Midlothian vicinity.* A relic of the era when railroads offered luxurious, reliable travel accommodations, the *Dinwiddie County* was built in 1926 by the Pullman Company of Chicago, world-renowned manufacturer of railroad cars. Founded in 1868, the Pullman Company produced handsome, comfortable, and in some cases palatial, rolling stock. It became so successful that Pullman became a generic name for sleeping cars. The *Dinwiddie County,* originally named the *Mount Atlas,* is an excellent representative of the heavy-weight, all-steel sleeper and is one of two known surviving cars of its type. It differed from standard sleeping cars by having an observation lounge. In 1950 it was assigned to exclusive use by the Norfolk and Western Railway Co. The Pullman Company sold the car to the Old Dominion Chapter of the National Railway Historical Society in 1965. *(20–23) VLR: 04/17/91; NRHP: 07/03/91.*

EPPINGTON, *Winterpock vicinity.* Eppington was originally the home of Francis Eppes, a cousin of Martha Jefferson, wife of Thomas Jefferson. The house is set deep in the timber-farm region of western Chesterfield County, along the Appomattox River. After Martha Jefferson's death, the Eppes family cared for two of Jefferson's daughters at Eppington while their father was serving as minister to France. Jefferson visited Eppington on several occasions; during one of his stays, he received an invitation from President George Washington to serve as secretary of state. The wood-frame house has had a complex evolution. Its center portion was built ca. 1770, and the wings were added ca. 1790. The interior is embellished with unusually fine paneling. Donated to the county by the Cherry family in 1989, the house is now exhibited as a museum by the Chesterfield County Department of Parks and Recreation. *(20–25) VLR: 09/09/69; NRHP: 11/12/69; BHR EASEMENT.*

FALLING CREEK IRONWORKS ARCHAEOLOGICAL SITE, *Bellwood vicinity.* The Falling Creek Ironworks is ac- knowledged to be the first successful iron production facility in English North America. From the earliest period of the Vir- ginia venture, the exploitation of natural commodities was a principal objective of the Virginia Company of London. A par- ty of workers succeeded in completing a portion of the iron- works in 1620 and produced a sample of iron that same year. During the Indian attack of 1622, twenty-seven persons were slain at the ironworks, and the facility was destroyed. Opera- tions were never reestablished. Extensive documentation through various surveys and test excavations has determined that the site is still relatively intact. Its various features, de- posits, and artifacts hold important information on one of the nation' earliest industrial sites. *(20–63) VLR: 01/15/95; NRHP: 03/29/95.*

HALLSBOROUGH TAVERN, *Midlothian vicinity.* Travelers on the old Buckingham Road (now U.S. Route 60) were served by this rambling wooden tavern throughout most of the 19th century. The building was constructed in three stages begin- ning in the last quarter of the 18th century and ending in 1832, when the two-story east wing was completed. Much of the original fabric in each section is intact, and traces of a former hipped roof and unusual false-plate construction can be seen in the west wing, the oldest section, which formerly held the taproom. The tavern's first owners were the Michaux family, descendants of area Huguenot settlers. From 1826 to 1972 the property was owned by the Spears family. Union soldiers raid- ed the tavern during the Civil War, stealing horses and meat. Restoration by subsequent owners has assured the preservation of this venerable landmark. *(20–30) VLR: 12/18/79; NRHP: 03/17/80.*

HENRICUS HISTORICAL PARK (HENRICO SITE), *601 Coxendale Road, Chester vicinity.* The unhealthy position of Jamestown inspired the establishment of a new town in a more salubrious, easily defended place upriver. In 1611 Sir Thomas Dale selected Farrar's Island, naming it Henrico or Henricus in honor of Prince Henry. The ambitious plans for a new capital along with a college for Indians here did not mature. By 1619 only "three old houses and a ruinated church" remained. The place was abandoned altogether after the Indian attack of 1622. The town site was probably destroyed by earthmoving under- taken in 1864 by Union troops to shorten the course of the riv- er. What remains of the island's tip is now part of Henricus Historical Park, established by Chesterfield County and the Henricus Foundation in 1986. The church is commemorated by a cross erected in 1911 and the university by an obelisk erected in 1910. *(20–709) VLR: 12/21/71; NRHP: 04/13/72.*

MAGNOLIA GRANGE, *Chesterfield Court House.* This brick plantation house, prominently situated across from the county courthouse, was built for William Winfree in 1823. It is the county's most sophisticated example of the Federal style and is noted for its elaborate woodwork and ornamental ceiling medallions. The design source for the medallions was Asher Benjamin's *American Builder's Companion* (1806), an architec- tural pattern book widely used by Virginia builders. The simi- larity of the trim to that in other Virginia Federal mansions, notably Hampstead, Horn Quarter, and Upper Brandon, sug- gests common craftsmen. The exterior displays the formality characteristic of the Federal mode, having a symmetrical five- bay facade and hipped roof. The present portico is a modern replacement of an earlier portico. The house was purchased by Chesterfield County in 1984 and is now exhibited as a museum by the Chesterfield County Historical Society. *(20–74) VLR: 11/20/79; NRHP: 03/17/80.*

OLIVE HILL, *Matoaca vicinity.* Dominated by a monumental pedimented roof, this large plantation house, set on terraces above the Appomattox River, was built between 1755 and 1770 by Roger Atkinson, a public-spirited entrepreneur and letter writer, for his eldest son and namesake. The house is interesting for its unusual plan and for the quantity of original fabric it preserves. Still intact are its molded weatherboards, window sash, louvered shutters, and paneled woodwork. A striking interior feature is the complex Chinese lattice stair rail, which may have been inspired by the Chinese stair in Battersea across the Appomattox River in Petersburg. The pedimented roof appears to be an early 19th-century alteration, replacing a conventional gable roof. The house, a fine demonstration of the architectural dignity that could be achieved in wood construction, was restored after World War II. *(20–49) VLR: 12/17/74; NRHP: 04/03/75.*

SWIFT CREEK MILL, *U.S. Route 1, Colonial Heights vicinity.* Milling operations were conducted at this Swift Creek site from the mid–17th century into the 1950s. The present brick structure, the lower portion of a formerly taller building, dates mostly from 1852 when the property was acquired by the Swift Creek Manufacturing Company, but its massive stone foundations may incorporate fabric of the original mill erected by Henry Randolph ca. 1660. Civil War action centered around the mill on May 10, 1864, when Gen. Benjamin Butler attempted a crossing of Swift Creek in a move against Gen. George Pickett's Confederate troops on the north bank. In 1964 the building was adapted into a restaurant and playhouse, preserving much original fabric including three large grinding stones in their original casings. Adjacent is a mid-19th-century mill store, a rare surviving example of this type of ancillary structure. *(20–81) VLR: 09/18/73; NRHP: 01/11/74.*

TRABUE'S TAVERN, *Midlothian vicinity.* Trabue's Tavern stands amid the sprawling suburban development of Chesterfield County as a relic of Midlothian's busy coal-producing era. Characteristic of Southside Virginia's vernacular architecture, the house has had a complex evolution. The oldest part, the west wing, reputedly was built ca. 1730, but the final form of the house was not achieved until an enlargement and remodeling ca. 1815. The first owners, the Trabues, descendants of area Huguenot settlers, owned and operated several nearby coalpits. Their home served as an ordinary patronized by travelers and miners alike. On the grounds are several early outbuildings, survivors of what was formerly an unusually large collection of service structures. *(20–55) VLR: 02/18/75; NRHP: 06/10/75.*

VAWTER HALL AND OLD PRESIDENT'S HOUSE, VIRGINIA STATE UNIVERSITY, *College Avenue, Ettrick.* The 1908 Vawter Hall and the Old President's House of 1907 constitute the historic core of the oldest state-supported college for blacks in the United States. The school was chartered in 1882 as the Virginia Normal and Collegiate Institute, following up on a pledge of the Readjuster party, led by William Mahone, to establish a state institute of higher learning for blacks. The first buildings have disappeared, but Vawter Hall and the Old President's House today symbolize the historic continuity of the institution. A dignified but austere brick structure, Vawter Hall is in the plain academic style of the era and originally housed administrative offices, a bookstore, a cafeteria, and an auditorium. The modified Queen Anne–style former president's house now contains offices. Vawter Hall's architect was Harrison Waite of Petersburg who likely also designed the Old President's House. *(20–5246, 5247) VLR: 02/19/80; NRHP: 05/07/80.*

CLARKE COUNTY

Honoring George Rogers Clark (who spelled his name without the e), conqueror of the Northwest Territory, this Shenandoah Valley county was formed from Frederick County in 1836 with part of Warren County added later. The county seat is Berryville.

ANNEFIELD, *Boyce vicinity.* This elegantly finished mansion is one of Virginia's grandest works of Federal architecture. Erected ca. 1790, Annefield was the home of Matthew Page, who named the place for his wife, Anne Randolph Meade Page, sister of Bishop William Meade. Annefield was later owned by Thomas Carter, whose son William Page Carter was a Virginia poet. Mary Ann Custis, wife of Robert E. Lee, was born at Annefield in 1808 while her mother was visiting here. The house epitomizes the high architectural quality of the plantation houses built in Virginia's northern counties by members of Tidewater families who moved into this fertile region in the late 18th century. The delicate Ionic portico and its Chinese lattice railing are set off by the rugged limestone walls. The elaborate woodwork and composition ornaments of its spacious interiors are based on designs in 18th-century English pattern books by William Pain. *(21–02) VLR: 09/09/69; NRHP: 11/17/69.*

BERRYVILLE HISTORIC DISTRICT. Berryville began as a colonial crossroads settlement known as Battletown. It expanded in the early 1800s after the construction of turnpikes linking Berryville to trade between Winchester and Alexandria. The town became the county seat when Clarke County was formed from Frederick in 1836. The arrival of the Shenandoah Valley Railroad in 1879 secured Berryville's role as a processing and shipping center for the lower Shenandoah Valley. Preserved in the district is a fine range of commercial, residential, governmental, religious, and industrial buildings associated with nearly all periods in the town's development. These structures, particularly the tidy old houses lining its tree-shaded residential streets, preserve an image of small-town America. Principal landmarks are the 1836 courthouse and the 1857 Italianate Grace Episcopal Church. The 1810 Sarah Stribling house, long the Battletown Inn, and the adjacent Jonathan Smith house (shown) are conspicuous buildings of the Federal period. *(168–12) VLR: 06/17/87; NRHP: 11/03/87.*

BETHEL CHURCH, *Bethel.* A remarkably unchanged old meetinghouse in a timeless rural setting, Bethel Memorial Church is among Virginia's many important historic resources that still are essentially unknown to the general public. The property on which it stands was the site of a log Quaker meetinghouse. This had fallen into ruin when the Baptists purchased the property in 1808. They built the present church in 1833–36, a work of conspicuous simplicity, echoing the denomination's nonconformist character. Of great interest is the interior with its three-sided gallery supported by slender columns on both levels. Stark from the absence of religious symbolism, the room has the flavor of early New England meetinghouses, though recent examinations have revealed evidence of decorative painting. The congregation vacated the building in 1930. It is now owned and maintained by a private foundation and used on special occasions. *(21–35) VLR: 04/18/89; NRHP: 02/07/91.*

BLANDY EXPERIMENTAL FARM, *Millwood vicinity.* Designated the State Arboretum of Virginia in 1986, the Blandy Experimental Farm began in 1926 when Graham F. Blandy, a New York stockbroker, bequeathed a 712-acre portion of his estate The Tuleyries to the University of Virginia to be used to educate boys "in the various branches" of farming. Since then the farm has educated both students and the public in botany, genetics, horticulture, and agriculture and has established one of the largest collections of specimen trees and shrubs in the eastern United States. The farm is administered from the Quarters building, the original section of which is the former slave quarters of The Tuleyries. The property is organized into three sections: the arboretum, commercial farming areas, and research areas. The arboretum is a noteworthy example of picturesque landscaping. *(21–550) VLR: 09/15/92; NRHP: 11/12/92.*

BURWELL-MORGAN MILL (MILLWOOD MILL), *Millwood.* This carefully restored, fully operational exhibition mill is the historic focal point of the tiny town of Millwood. The massive gabled structure is an important facet of the region's agricultural history, a relic of an era when the area's many productive farms were served by large commercial gristmills. The mill was begun in 1782 by Col. Nathaniel Burwell of nearby Carter Hall. Burwell's partner in the enterprise was Gen. Daniel Morgan, the Revolutionary War hero who settled just west of Millwood. The building's original portion is built of native limestone; the wooden third story was added after 1872 when the mill was acquired by T. M. Eddy and A. H. Garvin. Restoration of the mill, including the considerable quantity of early machinery, was undertaken in the 1960s by the Clarke County Historical Association. Its grounds have been landscaped by the Garden Club of Virginia. *(21–23) VLR: 09/09/69; NRHP: 11/17/69.*

CARTER HALL, *Millwood.* With its stately architecture and landscaped park, Carter Hall presents an idealized image of the patrician South. The house was erected in the late 1790s for Col. Nathaniel Burwell, originally of Carter's Grove, James City County. The heroic Ionic portico was added in 1814 by Burwell's son George. In 1862 Stonewall Jackson set up headquarters here, using the park as his campground. The plantation was purchased in 1930 by pharmaceutical magnate Gerard Lambert, who commissioned New York architect Harrie T. Lindeberg to undertake an extensive remodeling. Lindeberg removed a cupola and had the stucco removed from the stone walls. The Georgian-style woodwork and flying spiral stair are also Lindeberg's design. The beautiful park provides one of Virginia's most impressive landscape settings for a historic house. Carter Hall is now the headquarters of the People to People Health Foundation, also known as Project HOPE. *(21–12) VLR: 06/19/73; NRHP: 07/24/73.*

COOL SPRING BATTLEFIELD, *Shenandoah River near the West Virginia line.* The Cool Spring Battlefield encompasses the theater of Clarke County's most significant Civil War battle. The sanguinary event took place here on July 18, 1864, along both sides of the Shenandoah River in the northeast corner of the county. It occurred after Gen. Jubal Early's daring raid against Washington in the summer of 1864. Union troops pursued Early from Washington, D.C., and clashed here, with Early successfully holding off further advance. Early's raid proved politically embarrassing for the Lincoln administration and obligated General Grant to rethink his western strategy, leading to the establishment of the Union's Middle Military Division under Gen. Philip Sheridan. Sheridan eventually defeated Early at the battle of Cedar Creek in October 1864. The 4,064-acre Cool Spring Battlefield preserves the general rural character it had in 1864, including its network of farms and roads. *(21–976) VLR: 12/06/95; NRHP: 06/06/97.*

FARNLEY, *White Post vicinity.* Named for the Quaker family who established the farm in the 18th century, Farnley was developed into a prosperous plantation by the Hay family. William Hay, an attorney born in Scotland and later a resident of Williamsburg and Richmond, purchased the property in 1808. Around 1815 he built a plain brick house which still stands. James Hay, his son, married into the locally prominent Burwell family and built Farnley's principal residence, a grand late Federal mansion begun ca. 1832. Dominating the surrounding pastoral landscape, the stuccoed dwelling has a stately exterior, bold interior woodwork, and an unusual wraparound veranda on the rear. Attached to the house is a series of service structures. On a knoll nearby is a rare two-story stone slave quarters. One of the county's numerous historic estates, Farnley is now a noted pony farm. *(21–30) VLR: 12/13/88; NRHP: 11/02/89; BHR EASEMENT.*

FAIRFIELD, *Berryville vicinity.* Fairfield is one of the largest of several houses erected in the late 18th century by members of the Washington family on their extensive holdings in the lower Shenandoah Valley. Most of these properties are now in West Virginia. Fairfield follows the symmetrical, rectangular format typical of Virginia's Tidewater Georgian houses but is built of native limestone. It was completed ca. 1770 for Warner Washington, whose first cousin George Washington visited here on numerous occasions. The dormers and terminal wings were added in this century by the Richardson family, who acquired the property in 1830. The one-story connecting wings are part of the original construction. The house preserves its original Georgian stair and paneled woodwork. The handsome grounds have terraced gardens. Fairfield's unusually large brick and stone barn probably was built in the early 19th century. *(21–29) VLR: 12/02/69; NRHP: 02/26/70.*

GLENDALE FARM, *Charlestown Pike and Crums Church Road.* Glendale Farm is an antebellum farm complex set in the pastoral landscape of northwestern Clarke County. Its unusually large-scale brick farmhouse was built ca. 1847 for Archibald Bowen. The interior preserves distinctive provincial Greek Revival woodwork. An original kitchen-laundry outbuilding stands nearby. An important feature of the property is a rare Appalachian-type double-crib log barn. This impressive structure is composed of massive timbers employing V-notching. Bowen is said to have been a Union sympathizer, which if true might explain why the barn was not destroyed during the Civil War when Union troops obliterated many other barns in the Shenandoah Valley. Although no fighting took place here, the house served as a field hospital for both sides. Several other early farm buildings remain on the property. *(21–34) VLR: 01/15/95; NRHP: 03/17/95.*

GREENWAY COURT, *White Post vicinity.* Thomas Fairfax, sixth Baron Fairfax of Cameron (1693–1781), was the proprietor of a five-million-acre grant of northern Virginia lands inherited from his mother, daughter of Lord Culpeper. Fairfax set up residence at Greenway Court in 1752 in order to manage this vast holding firsthand. He lived in what was a hunting lodge, replaced in 1828 by the present brick farmhouse. Of the original complex, only the modest stone land office, porter's lodge, and a plank "powder house" remain, all probably dating from the 1760s. George Washington, who began his career as a surveyor for Lord Fairfax, was a frequent visitor at Greenway Court. While the three earliest buildings are significant survivors of Fairfax's establishment, the grounds likely hold a rich store of archaeological data relating to what is the region's premier colonial site. *(21–28) VLR: 09/09/69; NRHP 10/15/66; NHL: 10/09/60.*

GREENWAY RURAL HISTORIC DISTRICT. One of Virginia's most scenic cultural landscapes, this rural historic district contains roughly thirty square miles of connecting historic farms. Unlike other areas of western Virginia, Clarke County was settled by members of landed families from the Tidewater who brought here an appreciation for stylish architecture and the means to build fine country seats. Leading families who established plantation complexes include the Carters, Burwells, and Meades. Among the district's outstanding individually registered plantation houses are Saratoga, Long Branch, The Tuleyries, and Farnley. The district takes its name from Greenway Court, the country seat of Lord Fairfax. Scattered among the large estates is a collection of vernacular dwellings, mills, country churches, and schoolhouses, all connected by a network of scenic roadways. The area remains almost entirely in agricultural use, though horse breeding has replaced much of the more traditional farming. *(21–963) VLR: 08/18/93; NRHP: 11/04/93.*

GUILFORD, *White Post vicinity.* Maj. Isaac Hite, Jr., of Belle Grove in Frederick County, built this stately brick mansion between 1812 and 1820 for his son, James Madison Hite. The exterior was modified in the 1830s by the addition of the Ionic portico, the front doorway, and the rear wing. The otherwise academic portico employs curious octagonal column shafts that may have resulted from a misreading of instructions on how to build a column; such instructions usually showed in plan an octagonal configuration of boards as a structural core. Guilford's interior remains unchanged and features decorative Federal mantels and grained trim and doors. A rare survival is the painted checker pattern on the floorboards of the second-floor hall. On the grounds is a contemporary two-story brick servants' quarter. An 1846 advertisement in the *Alexandria Gazette and Virginia Advertiser* described Guilford as "one of the most desirable estates in the Valley." *(21–39) VLR: 12/09/92; NRHP: 02/04/93.*

HUNTINGDON, *Boyce.* Originally called The Meadow, Huntingdon is a farm of rolling pastures bordered with the region's distinctive stone walls. The commodious, formally proportioned limestone farmhouse was erected in 1830 by John Evelyn Page, third son of John and Maria Horsmanden Byrd Page. Page's parents moved to the area in 1784, during the generation-long migration by members of landed Tidewater families to property held in the state's northern counties. Both the original five-bay house and the single-pile ell added ca. 1840 remain unaltered from their time of construction, preserving original late Federal woodwork. The farm, as well as the entire area, was the scene of considerable Civil War activity from 1862 to 1864, and earthworks remain in the front field. Union troops burned Huntingdon's large barn in 1862, but the house escaped damage. An original smokehouse and ice pit survive. *(21–188) VLR: 09/19/78; NRHP: 05/25/79.*

JOSEPHINE CITY SCHOOL, *301-A Josephine Street, Berryville.* Built in 1882 to serve the Afro-American community of Josephine City, this plain two-room structure is a rare example of a Reconstruction-era schoolhouse for blacks and is a testament to the early efforts of Clarke County's blacks to improve their educational facilities. The building was erected with contributions of labor and money from the local black citizenry and was one of only seven Afro-American schools in Clarke County at the time. It served as an elementary school until 1930 when it was moved a short distance to make way for the new Clarke County Training School. The building was then converted into the home economics cottage and so used until 1971 when it was given over to storage. Now leased by the Josephine Improvement Association, the building is being developed into a local Afro-American museum and cultural center. *(21–177) VLR: 02/14/95; NRHP: 04/07/95.*

LONG BRANCH, *Millwood vicinity.* This stately Classical Revival mansion is one of the few remaining residential works designed—at least in part—by Benjamin Henry Latrobe. Latrobe sent plans to Robert Carter Burwell in 1811, several months after Burwell's builder had begun the foundations. The porticoes—one Doric and one Ionic—were added after 1842 by Hugh Mortimer Nelson when the house was extensively remodeled. The elegant Greek Revival woodwork, also added by Nelson, is based on designs by Minard Lafever published in *The Beauties of Modern Architecture* (1835). Although remodeled, the house remains, as noted by architectural historian Talbot Hamlin, "an important monument in American architecture." In 1986 Long Branch was purchased by Baltimore textile executive Harry Z. Isaacs who restored the house and established a foundation which exhibits the place as a museum. The restoration included the construction of the crenellated west wing, a replica of the early east wing. *(21–95) VLR: 11/05/68; NRHP: 10/01/69.*

LONG MARSH RUN RURAL HISTORIC DISTRICT. Incorporating some sixteen square miles of farmland in north-central Clarke County, between the West Virginia line and Route 7, this rural historic district is one of the least-disturbed and most scenic agricultural landscapes in the lower Shenandoah Valley. The district contains several large estates, both 18th-century and antebellum, associated with the county's early settlers, the Washington family being most prominent among them. In addition to sustaining much of the 19th-century fabric of the county's gentry agrarian economy, the district also includes three small Afro-American communities as well as many small late 19th-century farms, country churches, and schools, along with several mills and mill sites. While diversification of the local economy in the 20th century meant a shift away from wheat to apple orchards, cattle, and horses, large landholdings have remained the district's predominant land-use pattern. *(21–967) VLR: 06/19/96; NRHP: 11/04/96.*

LUCKY HIT, *White Post vicinity.* A component of Clarke County's outstanding collection of Federal plantation houses, Lucky Hit was built in 1791 by Col. Richard Kidder Meade, an aide-de-camp to George Washington. Meade gave the property its unusual name because he purchased it sight-unseen and considered himself "lucky" to have chosen such beautiful land. Lucky Hit was

the childhood home of William Meade, the noted 19th-century Episcopal bishop of Virginia. The house is distinctive for having five bays on both its facade and its ends. The ends are given a formality by the use of pedimented gables. Most of the original Federal woodwork and early hardware remains on the interior. On the grounds are two original outbuildings: a summer kitchen and privy. From 1947 to 1973 the property was owned by Alexander Mackay-Smith who modernized the house and added the west wing. *(21–45) VLR: 06/16/93; NRHP: 08/12/93.*

MEADEA, *White Post.* Meadea was the birthplace of Bishop William Meade, who helped bring about the revival of the Episcopal church in 19th-century Virginia. Built before 1784, the house is a rare example of an early log structure in the area. The property was originally part of a 50,212-acre tract owned jointly by Robert Burwell, George Washington, and Fielding Lewis. A portion was later sold to Col. Richard Kidder Meade, an aide-de-camp to Washington. The Meade family, from whom the property takes its name, lived here until their larger home, Lucky Hit, was completed in 1791. The property remained in the family until the turn of the 20th century and today is once again owned by a Meade descendent. The present center passage and west chamber probably were added in the 19th century. The 20th-century lean-to replaced an early kitchen. *(21–18) VLR: 06/16/93; NRHP: 02/08/95.*

NORWOOD, *Berryville vicinity.* An elegant but restrained essay in a rural Federal idiom, Norwood is situated at the end of a maple-shaded lane amid immaculately maintained grounds. The house is on what was originally part of a 1760 land patent from Thomas, Lord Fairfax, and was built around 1819 for Lewis Neill who inherited the property from his grandfather. Although expanded with later wings, the original two-story core with its exceptionally large windows, unusual transverse hall, and spacious double parlors remains little changed. Nearly all of the original woodwork is intact, including the wooden Federal mantels based on Philadelphia marble prototypes. The property was given its present name by William D. McGuire who purchased the farm in 1858. Norwood is one of the county's few important Federal houses to have been built by descendants of Irish settlers from Pennsylvania rather than members of Tidewater Virginia families of English descent. *(21–57) VLR: 08/17/94; NRHP: 09/30/94.*

OLD CHAPEL, *Boyce vicinity.* Constructed of limestone rubble, this austere little structure is considered the earliest Episcopal church building west of the Blue Ridge Mountains. It was built in 1793 under the patronage of Nathaniel Burwell of Carter Hall, replacing a log church of 1747 which stood nearby. The congregation left Old Chapel in 1834 for a new church in Millwood. It is still maintained by its parish with a special service held here once a year. Most of the original interior woodwork is intact, including the pulpit and box pews. Among the cemetery's many graves of individuals bearing distinguished Tidewater Virginia surnames are those of Edmund Randolph and Nathaniel Burwell. The Episcopal bishop William Meade began his ecclesiastical career as a lay reader at Old Chapel. *(21–58) VLR: 11/21/72; NRHP: 04/02/73.*

OLD CLARKE COUNTY COURTHOUSE, *North Church Street, Berryville.* Clarke County's historic courthouse belongs to Virginia's collection of Roman Revival courthouses, the prototypes for which were Thomas Jefferson's public buildings. With its tetrastyle Tuscan portico of wood and stucco set against red brick walls, the courthouse follows the Jeffersonian formula of classical forms and details rendered in native materials. The ornamented cupola houses the bell used to call the court to session. The building was erected by David Meade, younger brother of Bishop William Meade, soon after Clarke County was formed from Frederick County in 1836. Although the exterior survives relatively unchanged, the courtroom was altered around the turn of the century when its axis was shifted, with the bench moved from the east to the south wall. Included on the square are the jail, sheriff's office, and former clerk's office. A new county courthouse, erected in 1977, stands nearby. The historic courthouse is now designated the General District Court Building. *(168–01) VLR: 09/16/82; NRHP: 07/07/83.*

RIVER HOUSE, *Millwood vicinity.* Originally known as Ferry Farm for its location next to Berry's Ferry, one of the Shenandoah River's busiest 19th-century ferry crossings, this massive house is an outstanding example of Shenandoah Valley stone architecture. It was built around 1820 by William Nelson Burwell, son of Col. Nathaniel Burwell of Carter Hall. Constructed of irregular-coursed limestone rubble, the two-story I-house is a blending of vernacular and Georgian forms. Most of its original Federal woodwork is intact. Remaining on the property is a smokehouse and a rare three-part servants' quarters. During the Civil War, Berry's Ferry was used heavily by both Confederate and Union troops, and the house is said to have served as a field hospital. The Gilpin family gave the house its present name when they acquired it in the 1940s. River House is now a bed-and-breakfast inn. *(21–64) VLR: 10/20/93; NRHP: 12/23/93.*

SARATOGA, *Boyce vicinity.* Revolutionary War soldier Daniel Morgan had this Georgian mansion begun in 1779 while he was on leave from the war. He named it in honor of the battle of Saratoga in which he had distinguished himself as a military leader. The house probably was constructed by Hessian soldiers held prisoner in nearby Winchester. Recalled to active service in 1780, Morgan was made a brigadier general and won a brilliant victory against the British at Cowpens in South Carolina. In the antebellum period Saratoga was the home of Philip Pendleton Cooke, Virginia story writer and poet. It was later occupied by his brother, John Esten Cooke, historical novelist and biographer. The house is a distinguished example of the large stone plantation houses erected in the lower Shenandoah Valley in the late 18th century. The little-changed interior preserves paneled woodwork. On the farm are several early outbuildings. *(21–70) VLR: 12/02/69; NRHP: 02/26/70; NHL: 11/07/73; BHR EASEMENT.*

SCALEBY, *Millwood vicinity.* A monument to affluence, this splendid mansion is one of Virginia's most ambitious manifestations of the American Country House movement. Emulating the stately homes of England, a proper country seat required a mansion of a scale and design sufficient to inspire awe. Complementary heroic gates, formal gardens, and parklike grounds were all necessary ingredients of the formula. With its forthright classicism and red brick walls, Scaleby evokes a more American than European image though its scale is European. It was designed by Howard Sill of Baltimore for Mr. and Mrs. Henry Brook Gilpin and built in 1909–11. Hattie Newcomer Gilpin was a Baltimore heiress who in 1907 decided to establish a country estate in fashionable Clarke County. She named the place Scaleby after her husband's ancestral home in England. Owned by the Gilpin family until 1986, the estate has since undergone extensive renovation. *(21–86) VLR: 04/17/90; NRHP: 12/28/90.*

SOLDIER'S REST, *Berryville.* Its setting and layers of historic associations place Soldier's Rest among Clarke County's premier landmarks. George Washington visited the farm in 1748 while surveying for Lord Fairfax. The present house was built ca. 1780 for William and Rebecca Morton. Revolutionary War hero Gen. Daniel Morgan owned the property briefly in 1800, a fact that has made Soldier's Rest the subject of much local lore. In the 1810s it was purchased by War of 1812 veteran Col. Griffin Taylor who probably gave the place its present name. An interesting and unusual survivor of the lower Shenandoah Valley's early domestic architecture, the exterior has changed little since it was sketched by James E. Taylor, an illustrator accompanying Union general Philip Sheridan. The interior has undergone various modifications but preserves much early trim and hardware. Especially notable are the delicate Federal stair and the individually detailed dining room mantel. *(21–73) VLR: 03/20/96; NRHP: 05/23/96; BHR EASEMENT.*

THE TULEYRIES, *Boyce vicinity.* This grand estate was formed ca. 1833 by Joseph Tuley, Jr., who inherited a fortune amassed by his father in the tanning business. So impressive were the results of Tuley's expenditures here that he gave the place a name alluding to the French royal palace the Tuileries, as well as to his own. The estate is dominated by a huge late Federal mansion fronted by a Corinthian portico and crowned by a cupola. Inside are a domed entrance, sweeping curved stair, and other fine appointments. The spacious park includes a complex of architecturally individual service buildings. After Tuley's death The Tuleyries was acquired by Upton L. Boyce, an attorney for the Norfolk and Western Railway Co. In 1903 it was purchased by Graham F. Blandy of New York. The house was carefully restored in the late 1980s by the diplomat Orme Wilson, Jr., Blandy's nephew by marriage. *(21–82) VLR: 07/06/71; NRHP: 08/07/72.*

WICKLIFFE CHURCH, *Berryville vicinity.* This rural church is set off by its gaunt stepped-parapet gables and the pair of small Doric columns composing a naive but effective interpretation of a portico *in muris.* Wickliffe Church was built in 1846 to replace an earlier church that burned. The church served the Episcopal families in the northeastern part of Clarke County, many of whom were descendants of prominent Tidewater families. It preserved the name of its predecessor church, which honored John Wycliffe, the first to translate the Bible into English. Declining membership resulted in the merger of the church with Grace Episcopal Church, Berryville, in 1918. Still a consecrated house of worship, the building is used for an annual homecoming service. This simple interior remains almost untouched by the liturgical reforms of the late 19th century, exhibiting the low-church proclivities of Virginia's gentry. *(21–89) VLR: 01/15/95; NRHP: 03/17/95.*

WHITE POST HISTORIC DISTRICT. The crossroads village of White Post grew up around the whitewashed wooden marker that Thomas, Lord Fairfax, had erected in the 1760s to point the way to Greenway Court, the nearby estate from which he managed his vast proprietary holdings. The octagonal post that gives the town its name has been replaced several times, but its form has been maintained as a village landmark and symbol of community identity for over two centuries. Bishop William Meade, who led the 19th-century revival of the Episcopal church in Virginia, was born in White Post. The village today is a visually cohesive grouping of some twenty-one residences, two churches, and several commercial structures in local vernacular styles, ranging in date from the 1790s to the 1920s. The principal architectural landmark, the 1875 Bishop Meade Memorial Church, is a rugged work of country Gothic Revival. *(21–66) VLR: 08/16/83; NRHP: 09/29/83.*

CITY OF CLIFTON FORGE

Named for John Clifton's Iron Furnace in the nearby Iron Gate Gorge, this railroad town was established in 1861 and incorporated in 1884. It became a city in 1906.

CLIFTON FORGE COMMERCIAL HISTORIC DISTRICT. Originally known as Williamson, Clifton Forge developed in the 1850s in the narrow strip between the Jackson River and the Virginia Central Railroad tracks. The railroad later became part of the Chesapeake and Ohio system, which in 1878 built a roundhouse here, a project that spurred the incorporation of the town in 1884. Concentrated growth occurred after 1890 when Clifton Forge became a major division point on the rail line and saw development of extensive rail yards for the assembly of coal trains. This historic district includes what has served as the community's commercial quarter since the 1880s. The Y-shaped area is focused primarily along Main Street and East Ridgeway Street, which are distinguished by two- and three-story small-town commercial facades. Also in the district are the 1896 C&O freight depot and the 1906 C&O office building. *(105–17) VLR: 08/21/91; NRHP: 01/28/92.*

CITY OF COLONIAL HEIGHTS

This modern city on the heights above the Appomattox River takes its name from the fact that the marquis de Lafayette placed his artillery, known as the Colonials, here to shell British positions in Petersburg in 1781. The community was established in 1910 and became a city in 1948.

3 IN.
8 CM

CONJURER'S FIELD ARCHAEOLOGICAL SITE, *Conduit Road.* Situated on the west bank of the Appomattox River, on what was formerly a plantation known as Conjurer's Neck, this site contains deposits relating to an Indian village of the Middle and Late Woodland periods (500 B.C.–A.D. 1600). Excavations in 1966 and 1967 revealed well-preserved cultural features such as refuse-filled pits and human burials. The diverse ceramic fragments provide data for studies on cultural interactions between peoples living in the Piedmont, on the coastal plain, and along the fall line. Shown is a sampling of projectile points. *(106–20) VLR: 12/12/89; NRHP: 10/25/90.*

ELLERSLIE, *Longhorne Drive.* The Ellerslie estate was established in 1839 by David Dunlop and his wife, Anna Mercer Minge Dunlop. A native of Ayr, Scotland, Dunlop became one of the leaders of Virginia's tobacco industry. His castellated mansion was designed in 1856 by Robert Young, a Belfast architect, and was surrounded by romantically landscaped grounds

of unusual elaboration. The mansion was hit by Federal cannon fire during the battle of Swift Creek, May 9, 1864, and later served as Gen. P. G. T. Beauregard's headquarters. Gen. Johnson Hagood's South Carolina Brigade also used the estate as a rest camp during September 1864, following action along the Weldon railroad. Dunlop's grandson employed the Richmond firm of Carneal and Johnston to remodel the mansion in 1910 in the more fashionable Bungaloid mode. The spreading hipped roof and dormers replaced the original flat roof, but the basic mass of the house and the tower are original. *(106–01) VLR: 09/18/73; NRHP: 12/04/73.*

FORT CLIFTON ARCHAEOLOGICAL SITE, *Conduit Road.* Part of the complex system of defensive Confederate earthworks situated for the protection of both Richmond and Petersburg, Fort Clifton was built in early May 1964 and named for the house that stood nearby. As soon as it was completed, the fort came under attack from five Union gunboats supporting Federal troops engaged at Swift Creek. One gunboat was crippled by return fire, and the others withdrew. Fort Clifton was attacked twice more, on June 10 and 16, but to no effect. An impressively large and well-preserved example of Confederate fortifications, Fort Clifton is today owned by the city of Colonial Heights. *(106-05) VLR: 10/21/80; NRHP: 02/03/81.*

OAK HILL, *151 Carroll Avenue.* Oak Hill, on the heights above the Appomattox River overlooking Petersburg, is an architecturally interesting one-story Federal plantation house. The front section of the H-shaped dwelling is an elongated octagon of unusual refinement, having triple-hung sash and rich Federal detailing similar to that found in many early Petersburg houses. The shape of this section apparently was inspired by the house at Violet Bank, the plantation immediately to the east. Both plantations have since been developed with 20th-century housing. Oak Hill was originally called Archer's Hill and was used for a gun emplacement by General Lafayette during the Revolution. The house was built for Thomas Dunn in 1825–26. *(106-04) VLR: 04/16/74; NRHP: 07/30/74.*

VIOLET BANK, *Royal Oak Avenue.* This compact and surprisingly sophisticated dwelling is distinguished by its three-part bays, intricate Federal woodwork, and Adamesque plasterwork ceilings. The plasterwork, some of the finest Federal-period plaster ornamentation in the state, is based on designs published in Asher Benjamin's *American Builder's Companion* (1806). Originally the home of Thomas Shore, the present house dates from 1815 and replaces an earlier structure destroyed by fire. The three-part bays relate the house to a series of Richmond town houses inspired by designs of Benjamin Henry Latrobe. Latrobe visited Shore in 1796 and may have influenced the appearance of Shore's future house. Violet Bank was used as a headquarters for Gen. Robert E. Lee in 1864, and it was here that Lee learned of the explosion at the Crater. It is now a local history museum owned by the city of Colonial Heights. *(106–03) VLR: 04/16/74; NRHP: 07/30/74.*

CITY OF COVINGTON

Named for Peter Covington, an early settler, this mountain community on the Jackson River, the county seat of Alleghany County, was established in 1818 and incorporated as a town in 1833. It became a city in 1953.

COVINGTON HISTORIC DISTRICT. Covington was laid out along the Jackson River in 1818 and became the county seat in 1822. The historic district is primarily commercial in character and includes most of the land in the original forty-acre grid. A full range of small-town architectural types can be found here, from the 1910 county courthouse designed by Charles M. Robinson to blocks of typical "Main Street" commercial structures. Also in the district are two small residential neighborhoods along Locust and Riverside streets. At least six antebellum buildings survive, but most of the district's fabric dates from 1890 to 1940, a period of urbanization brought on by the 1890 consolidation of the Chesapeake and Ohio Railroad and the establishment of several large industries, most notably the West Virginia Pulp and Paper Co. Industrial development was effectively pursued by the Covington Improvement Company, established in 1890. *(107–25) VLR: 08/21/90; NRHP: 02/21/91.*

FUDGE HOUSE, *620 Parklin Drive.* For almost two centuries this much-expanded dwelling was home to the Fudge family. The Fudges were from Rockingham County and of German descent; their name was originally Futch. The property was acquired by brothers Christian and Conrad Fudge in 1795. Around 1798 Conrad Fudge built a two-story log house that is the core of the present dwelling. He substantially enlarged the house in the 1820s, adding a large brick section and new chimneys. His son Andrew inherited the property in 1849; he farmed the land and operated a distillery in addition to serving as the county clerk. Andrew's son Joseph and three of his brothers fought in the Civil War, serving in the Stonewall Brigade. Joseph inherited the property and further enlarged the house in 1897, giving it a Victorian character. The current owner purchased the house from the Fudge heirs in 1991. *(107–23) VLR: 02/17/93; NRHP: 04/29/93.*

CRAIG COUNTY

Nestled in the mountains of Southwest Virginia, Craig County was named for Robert Craig, a 19th-century congressman. It was formed from Botetourt, Roanoke, Giles, and Monroe (now in West Virginia) counties in 1851 and subsequently enlarged. The county seat is New Castle.

CRAIG HEALING SPRINGS, *Craig Springs.* Craig Healing Springs is a collection of nearly thirty early 20th-century resort buildings representative of the architecture of Virginia's more modern mountain spas. Developed as a resort between 1909 and 1920 by the Craig Healing Springs Company, the complex flourished with the advent of automobile travel in the years between the two world wars but declined in popularity with changes in travel and vacation patterns in the 1950s. The Christian Church (Disciples of Christ) in Virginia purchased the property in 1960 and has adapted the generally plain wooden buildings for use as a camp and conference center while carefully maintaining the grounds and buildings as well as many of the original furnishings. *(22–04) VLR: 12/16/80; NRHP: 07/21/82.*

NEW CASTLE HISTORIC DISTRICT, *New Castle.* This secluded mountain community preserves one of the Commonwealth's noted antebellum court complexes. The courthouse was built in 1851 when New Castle became the county seat. Using a portico and tripartite scheme, the building was modeled after Botetourt County's courthouse. Union troops passed through during the Civil War and are said to have left saber cuts on the courtroom balustrade. Adjacent is a country Greek Revival building containing the jail and sheriff's residence. Across from the square is the antebellum Central Hotel with its two tiers of galleries, one of the period's larger county-seat taverns. These court-related structures attracted enterprise and became the nucleus of a commercial center and a residential area. The typical New Castle commercial building is a two-story frame store with a false-front parapet and large display windows. *(268–13) VLR: 09/18/73 (EXPANDED 04/21/93); NRHP: 10/25/73.*

CULPEPER COUNTY

Formed from Orange County in 1749, Culpeper County probably was named for Thomas Culpeper, second Baron Culpeper of Thoresway, governor of Virginia from 1677 to 1683, whose family long held proprietary rights in the Northern Neck. The county seat is Culpeper.

BURGANDINE HOUSE, *807 South Main Street, Culpeper.* The Burgandine house has long been considered to be Culpeper's oldest dwelling. Architectural evidence suggests that as originally built, it was a story-and-a-half structure put up in the late 18th century or the first part of the 19th century and was probably a laborer's residence. The original core employs log construction, a building material not unusual for area vernacular houses. It later received a porch and was covered with weatherboards. A wing (since removed) was added in the mid–19th century. Despite other modifications, the original simple lines of the house betray its early origins. The house was donated to the town of Culpeper in 1966 and has since served as the headquarters of the Culpeper Historical Society. It underwent an extensive restoration in 1997–98. *(204–05) VLR: 12/04/96; NRHP: 03/07/97.*

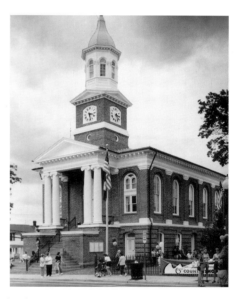

CULPEPER HISTORIC DISTRICT. The county-seat town of Culpeper is significant for its architectural cohesiveness and associations with commercial, military, political, and transportation history. Originally known as Fairfax, Culpeper was founded in 1759. Most of the commercial buildings are vernacular, Italianate, or neoclassical brick structures. The tree-shaded residential streets hold a rich variety of domestic architecture. The district's focal point is the Culpeper County Courthouse, completed in 1874 by Samuel Proctor who crowned it with a fanciful cupola. Commercial history is linked with its early roads, stagecoach routes, and the railroad. Military history is represented by the homes of Revolutionary War general Edward Stevens and Confederate general Ambrose Powell Hill. The town served as a staging area and hospital center for armies of both sides in the Civil War. Though a growing community, Culpeper preserves a typically American small-town ambience. *(204–20) VLR: 04/21/87; NRHP: 10/22/87.*

CULPEPER NATIONAL CEMETERY, *305 U.S. Avenue.* The Culpeper National Cemetery was established in April 1867, in a county that may have seen more Civil War combat than any other in Virginia. Several monuments commemorate the Union casualties of the battle of Cedar Mountain fought on August 9, 1862. Occupied by each army for months at a time, Culpeper County was the scene of the battle of Brandy Station on June 9, 1863, the largest cavalry battle of the war. Here also was the Union army's winter encampment of 1863–64, when Lt. Gen. Ulysses S. Grant arrived to take command. Union dead from those actions are also in the cemetery. The Second Empire–style superintendent's lodge was built in 1872 from a design by Quartermaster General Montgomery C. Meigs. In 1978 the Veterans of Foreign Wars donated adjacent land that doubled the size of the cemetery and relieved pressure on Arlington National Cemetery. *(204–69) VLR: 10/18/95; NRHP: 02/26/96.*

FARLEY, *Brandy Station vicinity.* Farley's frame mansion is among the most imposing of the plantation houses built for Tidewater families who moved to the Piedmont after the Revolution. Originally a Beverley family property called Sans Souci, the tract was purchased in 1801 by William Champe Carter of Albemarle County, who renamed it for his wife, Maria Byrd Farley Carter, and built the house soon after. With its stately facade marked by three pedimented pavilions, the house is an impressive Virginia interpretation of English neoclassicism. Inside is a formal suite of four reception rooms with original woodwork. In 1863 Farley was purchased by Franklin P. Stearns, a Vermont-born businessman. That same year the house was commandeered by Gen. John Sedgwick for a Union headquarters during the 1863–64 winter encampment. Farley stood empty for many years but was meticulously restored in the 1980s. *(23–05) VLR: 10/21/75; NRHP: 05/06/76.*

ELMWOOD, *Boston vicinity.* A forthright example of country Italianate architecture, Elmwood has the added distinction of preserving interior painted decorations executed in the 1870s by Joseph Dominick Phillip Oddenino. Oddenino was born in 1831 in Italy where he designed patterns for linen in a family business. He emigrated to America in 1862 and served as a musician in the Union army. Following the war, he settled in the Virginia Piedmont because it reminded him of his native Italy. Here he earned a living painting architectural decorations using the medium of fresco. His commissions included Mitchells Presbyterian Church, Hebron Lutheran Church in Madison County, and the Culpeper County Courthouse. The decorations in Elmwood employ patterns of columns in the hall, panels in the parlor, and floral ceiling medallions. The house was built in 1870 for William H. Browning. Little changed since the 19th century, it remains the property of Browning's descendants. *(23–44) VLR: 06/18/85; NRHP: 01/16/86.*

GREENVILLE, *Raccoon Ford vicinity.* This massive country residence was completed by 1854 for Philip Pendleton Nalle, a local entrepreneur. The architecturally muscular dwelling is a freely interpreted Classical Revival design, having giant Doric columns, tall bracketed cornices, and heavy window entablatures.

The cornice masks a rare W-shaped roof on all but the rear elevation. Stylistically, Greenville is more akin to the antebellum mansions of the Deep South than to the generally more genteel dwellings of Virginia. It was designed by the Culpeper County lawyer, politician, and architect Jeremiah Morton, who designed several other porticoed houses in the vicinity. Greenville was caught in the midst of considerable Civil War fighting in 1863–64. So heavy was the artillery firing that the adjacent pasture was later called "cannonball field." Nalle's son, Philip Nalle, Jr., sold Greenville in 1918. Unoccupied since 1974, the house underwent restoration in 1998. *(23–09) VLR: 12/18/79; NRHP: 03/17/80.*

GREENWOOD, *1913 Orange Road, Culpeper.* During the early 19th century many rich, influential men of the western Piedmont contented themselves with small yet commodious plantation houses. Greenwood, built ca. 1823–24, possibly around an earlier section, for John Williams Green, judge of the Virginia Supreme Court, illustrates this dwelling type. With its dormered center section and one-story wings, the house shows how a standard vernacular type could be expanded and given a pleasing but unpretentious formality. The interior preserves most of its Federal woodwork. In 1825 Judge Green received the marquis de Lafayette and former president James Monroe at Greenwood during Lafayette's celebrated tour as "guest of the nation." The Civil War touched Greenwood when Federal troops occupied the house and established a gun emplacement on the grounds. *(204–70) VLR: 01/18/83; NRHP: 11/22/85.*

A. P. HILL BOYHOOD HOME, *102 North Main Street, Culpeper.* Confederate lieutenant general Ambrose Powell Hill (1825–1865) lived in the original portion of this house from age seven until 1842, when he entered the U.S. Military Academy. Hill's parents enlarged the plain Federal town house into the present Italian Villa–style building just before the Civil War, expanding its depth and adding the third story, heavy bracketed cornice, and cupola. Later altered for commercial use, the building, situated on one of the town's main intersections, remains a dominant architectural element in downtown Culpeper. A. P. Hill was one of Gen. Robert E. Lee's most valued lieutenants, assisting him in nearly every major engagement of the Army of Northern Virginia until felled on April 2, 1865, just after the siege of Petersburg, and taken to Richmond for burial. *(204–06) VLR: 06/19/73; NRHP: 10/02/73.*

HANSBOROUGH RIDGE WINTER ENCAMPMENT, *Stevensburg vicinity.* Sometimes known as the "Union's Valley Forge," the Army of the Potomac's 1863–64 winter encampment in Culpeper and Fauquier counties was the largest and most important encampment of the Civil War. Under the command of Maj. Gen. George G. Meade, and with new leadership from Lt. Gen. Ulysses S. Grant, the army of veterans and recruits that broke camp on May 4, 1864, was larger, more purposeful, and more professional than ever before. This was the army that would compel the surrender of Lee's Army of Northern Virginia. Part of the army, which was spread over some sixty miles, occupied Hansborough Ridge, a promontory two and a half miles long that dominates the southern approach to Brandy Station. From a distance, the ridge appears about as heavily forested today as it was before the winter encampment. Piles of stone mark the soldiers' hut sites. *(23–68) VLR: 10/09/91.*

HILL MANSION, *501 South East Street, Culpeper.* The Hill mansion is a sophisticated example of the Italianate style, one of the several picturesque modes popular in the 1850s. The house was completed in 1857 for Edward Baptist Hill, member of a prominent Culpeper family. The front is sheltered by an arcaded veranda, a device advocated for southern houses in this period. Other noteworthy features are the scored stucco, the elaborate porches, both cast-iron and wood, as well as interior appointments, including a broad curving stair. The house served as a Confederate hospital and was visited both by Maj. Gen. A. P. Hill, a brother of the builder, and Gen. Robert E. Lee, whose wounded son, Brig. Gen. W. H. F. ("Rooney") Lee, was nursed here. Later in the war it was used as headquarters for Union troops. *(204–02) VLR: 12/18/79; NRHP: 03/17/80.*

LITTLE FORK CHURCH, *Rixeyville vicinity.* Built in 1774–76 by William Phillips for St. Mark's Parish, Little Fork Church is one of the Piedmont's few colonial houses of worship. It replaced an earlier wooden structure that burned. The parish vestry records contain a note dated March 17, 1776, recording a payment of £5 to Edward Voss "for two plans of the brick Church." They also note payments in tobacco to William Phillips as "undertaker" of the building. In a beautiful rural setting, the rectangular church, 80 feet in length, is distinguished by its spreading hipped roof, fine brickwork, and arched windows. Although used as a stable by Union troops during the Civil War, the church retains much original interior trim, including an impressive architectural altarpiece featuring a broken pediment with Doric entablature and pilasters. Little Fork remains an active Episcopal church. *(23–13) VLR: 05/13/69; NRHP: 11/12/69.*

LOCUST GROVE, *Rapidan vicinity.* The core of this evolved dwelling is a rare example for its locale of a middling farmer's residence of the colonial period. It began as a 16-by-20-foot structure of dressed-pine planks with full-dovetail notching and may have been built as early as 1735 for William Willis. Except for beaded ceiling joists, the original interior was extremely plain. A single-room frame addition was constructed a decade or so later, and the whole was covered in weatherboarding. Mantels were added during the Federal period along with the present boxed stair, replacing the original ladder stair. The house was further expanded by four lean-to units, the last attached ca. 1840. The resulting structure illustrates the improvements in housing that accompanied the rising prosperity of area farmers. Isaac Willis, who lived here from 1774 to 1867, owned nineteen slaves, 150 head of livestock, and a "pleasure carriage." *(23–49) VLR: 08/13/85; NRHP: 10/10/85; BHR EASEMENT.*

MADDEN'S TAVERN, *Lignum vicinity.* This simple log structure is a rare relic of pre–Civil War black entrepreneurship in rural Virginia. Completed about 1840, the tavern was built, owned, and operated by Willis Madden (1800–1879), a free black, and was likely the only tavern in the region with a proprietor of Madden's race. Virginia free blacks were able to earn and keep wages and to own and operate a business but were forbidden to vote, bear arms, testify against a white person, or be educated. Madden built the tavern on property he purchased in 1835 on the Old Fredericksburg Road. The western half of the structure was Madden's family quarters, and the eastern portion consisted of a public room and a loft for overnight guests. A general store and blacksmith-wheelwright shop were also on the property. Union troops sacked the place in 1863–64. The property is still owned by Madden's descendants. *(23–29) VLR: 05/15/84; NRHP: 08/16/84.*

MITCHELLS PRESBYTERIAN CHURCH, *Mitchells.* This simple Carpenter's Gothic church contains the most elaborate example of late 19th-century folk-style trompe l'oeil frescoes in the state. Executed in the 1890s, or possibly earlier, by the Italian immigrant painter Joseph Dominick Phillip Oddenino, born in 1831 in Chieri, Torino, the artwork is a curious transplant in rural Virginia of the ancient art of fresco, a common form of interior embellishment throughout Europe. The scheme is architectonic, consisting of a Gothic arcade on the side walls and an apse flanked by pairs of twisted baroque columns. The ceiling is painted to resemble beams framing rosettes. Mitchells Church was built in 1879 under the leadership of the Rev. John P. Strider. The frescoes, along with the church, underwent complete restoration beginning in 1979. Several other examples of Oddenino's work remain in the region; Mitchells Church is the finest and most complete. *(23–51) VLR: 02/19/80; NRHP: 05/07/80.*

RAPIDAN HISTORIC DISTRICT. A tiny village bisected by the Rapidan River, though with its principal section on the Culpeper side, Rapidan began in the late 18th century as a small milling community known as Waugh's Ford. Reflecting optimism for future progress, the settlement was renamed Rapid Ann Station with the coming of the Orange and Alexandria Railroad in 1854. It was renamed Rapidan in 1886. As a strategic railroad stop and river crossing, the village saw several Civil War raids, during which most of its buildings were destroyed. The village emerged from the war as a shipping point for wood products. Its current buildings, mostly dating from the late 1800s and early 1900s, range from simple vernacular structures to large Italianate and late Victorian farmhouses. Especially significant are the two 1874 Carpenter's Gothic churches: Waddell Memorial Presbyterian Church on the Orange County side and Emmanuel Episcopal Church in Culpeper County. *(23–52) VLR: 03/17/87; NRHP: 05/08/87.*

SALUBRIA, *Stevensburg.* A classic example of American Georgian architecture, Salubria was erected in the mid–18th century by the Rev. John Thompson, rector of St. Mark's Parish. Thompson's first wife was the widow of Governor Alexander Spotswood. Upon her death, Thompson married Elizabeth Rootes, and their son, Philip Rootes Thompson, eventually inherited the property. Typical of high-style Georgian design, the exterior is distinguished by a carefully calculated proportional system and minimal architectural ornamentation. Lending the house special significance as a document of colonial artistry is its outstanding interior paneling. The parlor chimneypiece is framed by Doric pilasters that support a full Doric entablature. The property was acquired by the Hansbrough family in 1802, who named it Salubria, meaning healthful. In 1853 Salubria was bought by Robert O. Grayson, in whose family it remains. On the grounds are remnants of a large terraced garden. *(23–20) VLR: 12/02/69; NRHP: 02/16/70; BHR EASEMENT.*

ST. STEPHEN'S EPISCOPAL CHURCH, *115 North East Street, Culpeper.* The oldest church in Culpeper, St. Stephen's was built in 1821 on land donated to the parish by Brig. Gen. Edward Stevens, a local Revolutionary War hero. As originally completed, the church was a relatively plain rectangular structure. It was remodeled in 1861 when the slender steeple and entrance vestibule were added. The chancel was extended ca. 1870, and the side galleries were removed in 1884. Stained-glass windows were added toward the end of the century. Decorative wall frescoes by the Italian-born local artist Joseph Dominick Phillip Oddenino, added in the 1880s, have since been painted over. St. Stephen's was one of the area's few churches to escape Union destruction during the Civil War. The original steeple blew down in 1957, and its replacement suffered the same fate in 1990. The present steeple is a replica of the original. *(204–03) VLR: 12/06/95.*

SLAUGHTER-HILL HOUSE, *306 North West Street, Culpeper.* Maintaining connections to various phases of Culpeper's history, the Slaughter-Hill house began in the late 18th century as a one-room-plan structure built of planked log construction. A frame addition in the early 19th century doubled its size. The house was further remodeled between 1835 and 1840 when the older sections were renovated and enlarged. The core of the Slaughter-Hill house remains one of the region's rare ex-

amples of a one-room urban vernacular dwelling. It probably was built for John Jameson, who served as the county clerk from 1771 to 1810. The present name derives from Dr. Philip Slaughter, a local physician who made the mid-19th-century modifications. The Hill name is from Sarah Hill, of the locally prominent Hill family, who purchased the house in 1888 and whose daughter owned it until 1944. *(204–21) VLR: 09/20/88; NRHP: 03/16/89.*

CUMBERLAND COUNTY

Named for William Augustus, duke of Cumberland, third son of King George II, this rural upper James River county was formed from Goochland County in 1749. The county seat is Cumberland Court House.

AMPTHILL, *Cartersville vicinity.* The brick section of this two-part house above the James River was erected ca. 1835 for Randolph Harrison in the one-story classical-styled format favored by Thomas Jefferson. Jefferson sent Harrison drawings for a new house in 1815. The drawings likely provided inspiration for the porticoed section added twenty years later to an existing frame house. With its refined classical elements set off by red brick walls, the composition is a graceful statement of Jefferson's architectural ideals. Back-to-back with this brick portion is a colonial-period house, probably built by Harrison's father, Carter Henry Harrison. The frame house was enlarged when the brick section was added. Mantels copied from designs in Asher Benjamin's *Practical House Carpenter* (1830) were added to its original paneled woodwork. Several early brick service structures remain. *(24–32) VLR: 01/05/71; NRHP: 04/13/72.*

CARTERSVILLE BRIDGE RUIN, *Cartersville.* The late 19th-century composite timber and iron superstructure of this engineering landmark was built on stone piers and abutments constructed in 1822 for a covered bridge. The 843-foot bridge was one of the last major bridges of such construction across the James River. All but the two end spans were destroyed by tropical storm Agnes in 1972. These spans and the stone piers have been consciously preserved parallel to a modern replacement bridge. They compose an intriguing eye-catcher from the hilltop village of Cartersville. The state transferred title to the ruin to the Cartersville Bridge Association after the flood. *(24–53) VLR: 03/21/72; NRHP: 09/14/72.*

CARTERSVILLE HISTORIC DISTRICT. Little disturbed by modern development, this old river town enjoys a commanding presence on a bluff above the James River. Established at a ferry crossing in 1790, Cartersville boasts a variety of vernacular architectural types dating from the 18th century to the early 1900s. Noteworthy early buildings include The Deanery of the 1780s and the Glaser house and Baptist parsonage, both dating from the 1790s. An important relic of Cartersville's heyday is the rambling Cartersville Tavern built ca. 1810 and later expanded. Sprinkled through the village are three churches, a former schoolhouse, a post office, and several commercial structures. Cartersville flourished as a transportation center in antebellum times, serving traffic on the Cartersville Bridge, opened in 1822, and the James River and Kanawha Canal on the north shore. Bypassed by the railroad in 1880, Cartersville fell into dormancy, and thus it has remained. *(24–126) VLR: 04/21/93; NRHP: 06/10/93.*

CLIFTON, *Cartersville vicinity.* Revolutionary patriot Carter Henry Harrison was the original owner of Clifton. As a member of the Cumberland Committee of Safety, Harrison wrote the instructions for a declaration of independence from "any Allegiance to his Britannick Majesty," presented to the Virginia Convention of May 1776. The convention was among the first of such bodies to declare outright for American independence. Clifton originally was included in a grant willed to Thomas Randolph in 1723 by his grandfather Robert ("King") Carter. Dating from the mid-1700s, the mansion is an excellent example of the architectural formality that could be achieved in Georgian architecture using wooden construction. Wood frequently was preferred over masonry since wooden houses tended to be less damp. The house retains its early molded weatherboarding and a fine suite of paneled rooms. The rooms have later Greek Revival mantels copied from Asher Benjamin's *Practical House Carpenter* (1830). *(24–36) VLR: 04/17/73; NRHP: 06/19/73.*

CUMBERLAND COUNTY COURTHOUSE, *Cumberland.* William A. Howard, an associate of Thomas Jefferson's master builder Dabney Cosby, Sr., built the Cumberland County Courthouse in 1818. Designed in the Jeffersonian Classical style, the compact building is dominated by a finely executed Tuscan portico. The form departs from the norm by being only one story in height and by having the portico on the long side. Howard also designed the diminutive brick clerk's office east of the courthouse. Completed in 1821, the office building features a full Doric entablature and a portico with unusual octagonal columns, probably resulting from a misreading of pattern-book instructions for column construction. Also on the courthouse green are the original county jail, a 19th-century well, and a monument to the county's Confederate dead. Several prominent Virginia lawyers, including Patrick Henry, John Marshall, Edward Carrington, and Richard Randolph, practiced law here. *(24–05) VLR: 08/17/94; NRHP: 09/30/94.*

GRACE EPISCOPAL CHURCH, *Ca Ira.* Grace Church, Ca Ira, survives as a visually engaging illustration of the stylistic hybridization that occurred with Romantic Revivalism in the antebellum period. Its temple form and precise Flemish bond brickwork are an offspring of Virginia's Classical Revival tradition fostered by Thomas Jefferson, while its Greek and Gothic details were adapted from builders' pattern books. The pulpit is based on a pulpit design from Asher Benjamin's *Practical House Carpenter* (1830). The church was erected in 1840–43 by Valentine Parrish, a local master builder, and is the only remaining building of Ca Ira, a town laid out in 1787 which enjoyed brief prosperity before the Civil War. The name Ca Ira is probably derived from a French Revolutionary marching song. *(24–09) VLR: 06/17/80; NRHP: 10/30/80.*

MORVEN, *Cartersville vicinity.* This highly refined Greek Revival dwelling was built in 1820 by Randolph Harrison as a wedding present for his daughter Jane. The house was never part of a working farm but rather served as a rural retreat for its owners. Though modest in scale, Morven exhibits outstanding craftsmanship. The Flemish bond brickwork is unusually precise. The wood trim consists of academically correct Greek moldings that are incorporated in the pedimented gable ends. A classical tablet motif decorates the east gable. Unusual are the single-sash second-floor windows, each of which raises in a wall pocket behind the cornice. Architecturally harmonious rear wings were added to the original I-house in 1885 and 1895. In the shady surrounding yard are an early smokehouse and a ca. 1890 schoolhouse. The property was acquired by George W. Bogart in 1870 and remains in the ownership of his descendants. *(24–27) VLR: 12/12/89; NRHP: 12/28/90; BHR EASEMENT.*

MUDDY CREEK MILL, *Tamworth.* Erected in stages, this large merchant mill, one of the most impressive historic mills in the state, achieved its present appearance after 1792 when the mill's partners agreed to raise the building to its existing height. Combining stone, brick, and wooden construction, the building is the state's only surviving mill with two tiers of dormers, a feature sometimes employed on very large urban mills. Muddy Creek Mill operated until the 1960s, producing flour, meal, and other products. Much of the early machinery is intact, including the French millstones. The mill is part of the tiny settlement of Tamworth, which also includes the miller's house, a small brick store of ca. 1800, and a late 18th-century farmhouse, now the home of the mill's owners. Structural repairs were made to the mill in the 1980s with the assistance of a state threatened-property grant. *(24–16) VLR: 06/18/74; NRHP: 10/09/74; BHR EASEMENT.*

NEEDHAM, *Farmville vicinity.* Situated just north of Farmville on Route 45, Needham was the home of educator, jurist, and politician Creed Taylor (1766–1836). Taylor influenced national politics in 1800 when, as a presidential elector, he organized Virginia's electors to secure the election of Thomas Jefferson as president. In 1810, while residing in Richmond, Taylor became a tutor for local attorneys on "the practical part of the law." He presided over a moot court whose students included future president John Tyler, future secretary of state Abel Parker Upshur, and future U.S. senator William Cabell Rives. Taylor also served in the General Assembly both as a delegate and as Speaker of the senate. Taylor's plain Federal residence at Needham was built ca. 1802. From 1821 to 1830 he operated a law school here—Virginia's first proprietary law school. A number of Needham alumni enjoyed distinguished careers in public service. Taylor is buried on the place. *(24–30) VLR: 02/16/88; NRHP: 11/10/88.*

CHARLES IRVING THORNTON TOMBSTONE, *Cumberland State Park, Hillcrest vicinity.* Charles Irving Thornton's tombstone in the secluded Thornton family cemetery is the only tangible reminder of Charles Dickens's visit to the Commonwealth during his tour of the United States in 1842. Already regarded as a major literary figure, the author, as a favor for a Thornton family friend, composed the stone's lengthy and poignant inscription to commemorate the death of the Thornton infant in 1842. The

inscription on the simple stone begins: "THIS IS THE GRAVE of a little Child whom God in his goodness called to a Bright Eternity when he was very young." Only one other Dickens epitaph is known, that of his sister-in-law, making the Thornton inscription an especially interesting work of this towering literary figure and unique among his American writings. *(24–54) VLR: 06/17/80; NRHP: 11/25/80.*

CITY OF DANVILLE

Named for the Dan River on which the city is located, this milling center and tobacco market in southern Pittsylvania County was established in 1793. It was incorporated as a town in 1830 and as a city in 1890.

DAN RIVER INC., *situated along both sides of the Dan River in downtown Danville.* The Riverside Division buildings of Dan River Inc. represent several stages in the century-long development of one of America's major textile companies, including the firm's first cotton mill at the corner of Main and Bridge streets in downtown Danville. The complex consists of six cotton mills and a flour mill. Also in the extensive assemblage are two masonry dams, warehouses, a dye house, a machine shop, a research building, the remains of a power canal, and a number of support buildings such as boiler houses and coal bunkers. The major architectural styles range from the relatively small brick vernacular mills and outbuildings of the "cotton factory fever" of the 1880s and 1890s to the massive concrete modernist structure of the 1920s. The complex forms an important component of the industrial image of this southern manufacturing city. *(108–13) VLR: 07/20/82.*

DANVILLE MUNICIPAL BUILDING, *418 Patton Street.* The turn-of-the-century architectural movement termed the American Renaissance endowed cities and towns with grand classical works that lend a strong sense of continuity and place. A relatively late but nonetheless effective expression of this movement is the Danville Municipal Building, a tour de force of civic stagecraft. Fronted by a monumental Ionic colonnade and closing a vista on a tight site amid relatively narrow streets, the building exudes a European urbanity. It was designed by the local firm of Heard and Chesterman and completed in 1927. The project was generated by a desire to consolidate expanded municipal offices with court facilities. No less imposing is the interior, the corridors and principal rooms of which are a bold display of columns, pilasters, and other classical details. The building now houses only municipal offices. *(108–111–71) VLR: 04/28/95; NRHP: 07/21/95.*

DANVILLE NATIONAL CEMETERY, *721 Lee Street.* Established in December 1866, the Danville National Cemetery first was used to inter Union prisoners of war who died in the tobacco warehouses and factories that were converted into Danville's Confederate prisons. Most of the dead, 1,170 known and 143 unknown, were enlisted men and noncommissioned officers who succumbed to diseases ranging from pneumonia to scurvy. The cemetery also has four group burials, of sixteen U.S. Army and U.S. Army Air Force casualties of World War II. Their remains were reinterred in 1949 from cemeteries in France, Italy, and Honduras. The oblong cemetery is surrounded by a low stone wall and is entered by wrought-iron gates. The original 1870s superintendent's lodge was demolished in 1928 and replaced with the present Colonial Revival structure. *(108–54) VLR: 01/15/95; NRHP: 04/07/95.*

DANVILLE OLD WEST END HISTORIC DISTRICT. This large neighborhood immediately south of downtown boasts what is perhaps the Commonwealth's most splendid and most concentrated collection of Victorian and early 1900s residential and ecclesiastical architecture. Lining Main Street and adjacent side streets is an assemblage of the full range of architectural styles from the antebellum era to World War I. While much of Virginia was slow in recovering from the economic setbacks caused by the Civil War and Reconstruction, Danville's tobacco and textile enterprises generated great prosperity that found tangible expression in the elegant houses built by local industrialists. Most of the residential development, highlighted by several decorous churches, took place on the estate of Maj. William T. Sutherlin, whose Italian Villa–style residence is at the core of the district. After suffering several demolitions in the 1960s, this impressive district is now protected by local ordinance. *(108–56) VLR: 11/09/72; NRHP: 04/11/73.*

DANVILLE SOUTHERN RAILWAY PASSENGER DEPOT, *677 Craghead Street.* The railroad station is among the most threatened of American architectural forms. Perhaps less than 10 percent of our extant stations are used for their original function. Many that are not abandoned now serve new uses. Temporarily closed to passenger service in 1993, Danville's Southern Railway depot has found new life as a branch of the Science Museum of Virginia, with one waiting room refurbished for Amtrak passenger service. The elongated structure, decorated with fancy stepped gables, recalls the Renaissance architecture of the Low Countries. It was designed by Frank P. Milburn and completed in 1899, serving a principal stop on the Southern's Washington-to-Atlanta route. The depot burned in 1922 and was rebuilt within its original walls in modified form. A central tower was not reconstructed, and the interior was simplified. The depot is now owned by the city of Danville. *(108–58–12) VLR: 04/28/95; NRHP: 07/21/95.*

DANVILLE TOBACCO WAREHOUSE AND RESIDENTIAL HISTORIC DISTRICT. Occupying some forty blocks of the heart of the city, this district formed the economic wellspring of 19th-century Danville. The various warehouses, factories, shops, and dwellings display the city's mill-town personality and the rise of its working class. Industrial activity in Danville grew in conjunction with the development of its transportation systems and the cultivation of bright-leaf tobacco, which shaped Danville into one of the South's primary tobacco markets. The tobacco industry achieved its greatest growth in the 1870s and 1880s with the emergence of plug and twist tobacco manufacture. Today the district is composed of approximately 585 structures related to Danville's tobacco enterprise. Some thirty-seven of the buildings are factories, auction warehouses, or storage facilities, all constructed between 1870 and 1910. The residential area contains approximately 450 workers' dwellings erected between 1880 and the 1930s. *(108–58) VLR: 03/18/80; NRHP: 07/08/82.*

DOWNTOWN DANVILLE HISTORIC DISTRICT. This twenty-five-acre urban historic district encompasses the core of southern Virginia's leading tobacco- and textile-manufacturing city. The district has been the commercial and administrative heart of Danville from the 1790s to the present. Spread through the area are retail establishments, banks, hotels, theaters, lodges, and several tobacco factories built from the 1870s through the 1920s. The city's prosperity and the importance of the activities these buildings housed are reflected in the architectural sophistication and often monumental scale of this urban fabric. The high-rise Masonic Building and the Hotel Danville, both dating from the 1920s, still dominate the skyline. At least ten buildings, the Municipal Building and U.S. Post Office among them, were designed by local architect J. Bryant Heard. Despite gaps, the wide range of styles here lends much visual variety to the streetscapes. *(108–111) VLR: 06/16/93; NRHP: 08/12/93.*

HOTEL DANVILLE, *600 Main Street.* An elegant component of Danville's central business district, this neo-Adamesque high-rise building was erected in 1927 to house the city's leading hostelry. The structure is representative of the wave of finely appointed, thoroughly modern hotels put up in medium-size and large cities across the country in the 1920s. The architect of the carefully articulated composition was H. A. Underwood & Co. of Raleigh, N.C. The owner and developer was the firm of Clements, Chism, and Parker, Inc. Founded in the 1880s, the company was Danville's largest retail furniture enterprise and occupied the greatest amount of commercial space in the hotel. The western portion of the building originally housed a motion picture theater and included Danville's first commercial radio station. The complex also incorporates a section of Danville's 1890 municipal building and city market. The hotel closed in 1975 and was rehabilitated for housing in 1982–83. *(108–27) VLR: 10/16/84; NRHP: 12/06/84.*

MAIN STREET UNITED METHODIST CHURCH, *767 Main Street.* Recalling the somber medieval buildings of northern Italy, Danville's "Mother Church of Methodism" is among the most ambitious works of Victorian architecture in a city famed for such works. The Romanesque Revival composition is dominated by an 87-foot-high campanile replete with bartizans, machicolations, and arcades. These same elements embellish the facade, the front of a vast sanctuary. The church was begun in 1865 and initially completed by the contractor Henry Exall in 1873. Subsequent large churches in the neighborhood inspired the Methodists to remodel their church into a much grander statement. The work, undertaken in 1890–91, resulted in the present facade and tower, attributed to the architect William M. Poindexter. The contractor was J. R. Pleasants. The completed work is, among other things, a masterpiece of Victorian brickwork. The adjacent 1923 educational building was designed by J. Bryant Heard of Danville. *(108–63) VLR: 10/16/90; NRHP: 12/06/90.*

PENN-WYATT HOUSE, *862 Main Street.* A symbol of Danville's 19th-century affluence, the Penn-Wyatt house is the city's most exuberant example of Victorian residential architecture. The original owner, James Gabriel Penn, came to Danville in 1868 and established himself as a tobacco commission merchant. By 1876 he could afford to build the most extravagant of the many showy houses on Main Street. Penn's continued prosperity is reflected in the improvements made in 1887 and 1894. The resulting structure thus exhibits a range of late 19th-century stylistic influences. The most noteworthy addition is the front porch with its two-tiered belvedere. Consistent with the exterior is the ornate interior, which retains many of its fittings including intricately carved woodwork, stained-glass windows, and a variety of light fixtures. Penn's widow sold the house in 1934 to the Wyatt family, who owned it until 1977. *(108–03) VLR: 10/17/78; NRHP: 09/07/79.*

SUTHERLIN HOUSE (DANVILLE MUSEUM OF FINE ARTS AND HISTORY), *975 Main Street.* This Italian Villa–style mansion was built in 1857–58 for Maj. William T. Sutherlin, a member of the Virginia Convention of 1861 and later chief quartermaster for Danville. The design is attributed to architect Frank G. Clopton. On April 2, 1865, when the Confederate government evacuated Richmond, Danville was chosen for a temporary capital. During the week of April 3–10, 1865, the Sutherlins opened their home to President Davis and members of his cabinet. Here Davis signed his last official proclamation as president of the Confederacy and presided over the last official cabinet meeting. Davis and the remnants of his fugitive government left Danville on April 10 for Greensboro, N.C., and their "flight into oblivion." Typical of the Italian Villa style, Sutherlin's house has a stepped-back facade, bracketed cornice, and square tower. It now serves as a museum and cultural center. *(108–06) VLR: 05/13/69; NRHP: 11/17/69.*

DICKENSON COUNTY

This mountainous coal-mining Southwest Virginia county was formed from Russell, Wise, and Buchanan counties in 1880. It was named for William J. Dickenson, delegate from Russell County at the time the county was formed. The county seat is Clintwood.

DICKENSON COUNTY COURTHOUSE, *Clintwood.* The Dickenson County Courthouse is a Colonial Revival landmark in the heart of the Commonwealth's coalfields. The courthouse was originally built in 1894. The construction of the Carolina, Clinchfield, and Ohio Railway in 1915 initiated increased coal mining and timbering in the area and created significant prosperity. That same year the courthouse underwent extensive improvements with the present facade constructed from the design of Roanoke architect H. M. Miller. The original 1894 section was razed in 1972 and replaced by a modern wing. The courtroom on the second floor behind the three arched windows was left intact. *(196–01) VLR: 07/20/82; NRHP: 09/16/82.*

DINWIDDIE COUNTY

This rural Southside country was named for Robert Dinwiddie, lieutenant governor of the Virginia colony from 1751 to 1758. It was formed from Prince George County in 1752. The county seat is Dinwiddie.

BURLINGTON, *Matoaca vicinity.* The wood-frame, double-pile plantation dwelling of this Appomattox River property is an exemplar of colonial Virginia's domestic architecture. Characteristic elements of the style used here include the symmetrical arrangement of bays, weatherboarded walls, pedimented dormers, and brick end chimneys. Burlington's paneled wainscoting, with a row of panels above the chair rail, is similar to that in several other Dinwiddie County houses, suggesting common craftsmen. An important original feature is the architectural corner cupboard decorated with Doric pilasters, arched doors, and semidomed interior. Other noteworthy elements are the paneled chimneypiece and the walnut stair rail with turned balusters. Destruction of the Dinwiddie records hinders documentation of the property. An 1802 insurance policy, however, shows its owner then was Robert Pleasants. It was later owned by the Friend family for over a hundred years. *(26–01) VLR: 10/21/75; NRHP: 04/30/76.*

BURNT QUARTER, *Five Forks.* The earliest portion of this venerable plantation house was built in the mid–18th century for Robert Coleman. The plantation subsequently passed through marriage to the Peterson, Goodwyn, and Gilliam families to the current owners. Evolved to its present form by additions and changes, the rambling frame structure has interior woodwork in Georgian, Federal, and Greek Revival styles. The plantation, one of the oldest continuously operated farms in the region, derives its name from British colonel Banastre Tarleton's burning of a grain quarter on one of his marauding expeditions during the Revolutionary War. On April 1, 1865, the property became the scene of fierce fighting during the battle of Five Forks. The house was used as a Union headquarters. A series of family portraits, slashed by the soldiers, still hangs unrepaired on the parlor walls. *(26–25) VLR: 09/09/69; NRHP: 11/25/69.*

DINWIDDIE COUNTY COURTHOUSE, *Dinwiddie.* Since its completion in 1851, this simple Greek Revival public building has been the architectural focal point for this Southside county seat, formerly known as Dinwiddie Court House. It was described as a "very neat and tasty building" when first opened, doing "great credit to the builder." The courthouse was remodeled in 1858 when its interior was divided into two floors and the courtroom was relocated on the upper level. In March 1865 Union general Philip Sheridan, leading his troops in a drive on Petersburg, was checked temporarily near the courthouse by Maj. Gen. George E. Pickett. The next day, April 1, the two commanders clashed again at Five Forks where the Union victory compelled Lee to evacuate his army from Petersburg and Richmond. The courthouse received its Doric portico in 1933 through federal government assistance. *(26–04) VLR: 02/20/73; NRHP: 03/21/73; BHR EASEMENT.*

FIVE FORKS BATTLEFIELD, *Five Forks.* The decisive battle of Five Forks, fought April 1, 1865, took its name from the junction of five county roads that became the focus of intense conflict. The defeat of Confederate forces sent here to protect Gen. Robert E. Lee's last supply line forced the Southern commander to abandon his defense of Richmond and Petersburg and begin his retreat west. Eight days later Lee was outflanked by Gen. Ulysses S. Grant and surrendered his army at Appomattox. The Five Forks junction, next to Burnt Quarter plantation, retains the rural, open setting it had during the Civil War. Much of the battlefield is now a unit of the Petersburg National Battlefield. *(26–103) VLR: 09/09/69; NRHP: 10/15/66; NHL: 12/19/60.*

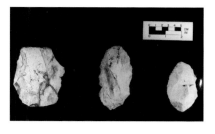

GOOSENECK FIELD (CONOVER) ARCHAEOLOGICAL SITE, *Stony Creek vicinity.* Some of the earliest Native America occupation of Virginia occurred during the Paleo-Indian period, at least ca. 9500 to 8000 B.C. Clearly identifiable sites relating to this period are extremely rare because of the low population density in those remote times. Also, sites of such antiquity are very subtle and apt to have been disturbed over the centuries. The Conover site is one of Virginia's few currently recognizable locations yielding diverse Paleo-Indian artifacts, including lithic tool types and manufactured by-products. The presence of maintenance and processing tools in various stages of reduction, along with stone flakes, has led to the conclusion that the site was used as a quarry-related base camp or maintenance station. A significant number of the site's artifacts are in the archaeological collections of the Virginia Department of Historic Resources. *(26–121) VLR: 06/21/83; NRHP: 03/28/85.*

MANSFIELD, *Matoaca vicinity.* This plantation house is one of a group of noteworthy dwellings associated with Roger Atkinson (1725–1798), a Petersburg tobacco merchant and land speculator. Atkinson purchased the property in the 1760s and apparently added the two-story section to an existing early 18th-century story-and-a-half dwelling. During the 1830s Mansfield was owned by Hugh A. Garland, a biographer of John Randolph of Roanoke, who operated a girls' school here. With its ambitious interior woodwork and unusual form, Mansfield is one of several neighboring plantation houses that bear the mark of highly accomplished craftsmen. The drawing room paneling and the Georgian stair are some of the finest colonial woodwork in the county. Mansfield's historic setting was significantly compromised in recent years when scores of small houses were built on the surrounding fields. *(26–12) VLR: 12/16/75; NRHP: 05/28/76.*

MAYFIELD, *3348 West Washington Street, Petersburg vicinity.* Mayfield, the oldest brick house in Dinwiddie County, is a classic expression of formal mid-18th-century Virginia architecture. Its distinguishing features include a clipped-gable roof, symmetrical five-bay facades, and paneled interior. The earliest documented owner was Robert Ruffin, who lived here until 1769. Later it belonged to Thomas Tabb Bolling and then to the Goodwyn family. Gen. Robert E. Lee watched the final action at Petersburg from Mayfield before the retreat that ended at Appomattox. In 1882 the property became the site of Central State Hospital. The house, long hidden from public view by surrounding hospital buildings, was spared demolition in 1969 when it was moved intact one mile to its present site on the edge of the hospital property. It has since been restored and is now an inn. *(26–27) VLR: 05/13/69; NRHP: 11/12/69; BHR EASEMENT.*

SAPONY EPISCOPAL CHURCH, *DeWitt vicinity.* From 1763 to 1801 Sapony was served by the Rev. Devereux Jarrett, a proponent of Methodism within the Anglican, and later Episcopal, church. Jarrett was one of Virginia's few Anglican clerics to be affected by the Great Awakening. His several religious revivals were described in his *Brief Narrative of the Revival of Religion in Virginia* (1778). A monument to Jarrett and his wife stands inside the church. Sapony was built in 1725–26 by Edward Colwell. Tradition has it that the building partially collapsed after a service in 1869, but it was soon repaired. It was further remodeled in 1896–98. Despite these changes, much colonial fabric remains, including window sash, paneled wainscoting, and sections of the original pews and communion rail. A rare survival is the colonial holy table. Although a landmark of American Methodism, Sapony has remained in the Bath Episcopal Parish and has been designated a shrine church. *(26–19) VLR: 10/21/75; NRHP: 04/30/76.*

ROSE BOWER, *Bolster's Store vicinity.* Constructed between 1818 and 1826, Rose Bower's dwelling house is the nucleus of an early 19th-century plantation owned and farmed by the Rose family since its establishment. The complex of outbuildings and farm buildings represents a continuum of domestic and agricultural activity. Some of the crops grown historically at Rose Bower—tobacco, corn, cotton, peanuts, hay, and wheat—are still grown here today. The house itself has undergone few alterations. The plain exterior is still clad with original beaded weatherboards. The interior has a hall-parlor plan with an enclosed stair. The parlor is embellished with an interesting provincial Federal chimneypiece and a rare built-in china cabinet with original glass doors. Some of the woodwork preserves original grained and marbleized decorative painting. *(26–90) VLR: 12/11/90; NRHP: 02/05/91.*

WALES, *Petersburg vicinity.* Built for Howell Briggs (1709–1775), a militia captain, magistrate, and vestryman, Wales is one of the most architecturally distinctive plantation houses in Southside Virginia. Howell Briggs's son Gray Briggs (ca. 1731–1807), born at Wales, served in the House of Burgesses and made Wales his home after completing his term in the assembly. The original ca. 1730 portion of the house is a simple hall-parlor dwelling. This core was expanded ca. 1752 into a five-part structure 104 feet long. The treatment of the wings with half-hipped roofs is unique in Virginia. The house has since undergone remarkably few changes; the exterior preserves its early weatherboarding, window sash, shutters, and doors. Inside, nearly all of the original woodwork remains including the architectural chimneypiece in the west-wing parlor. This elegant room is a demonstration of the refined taste exhibited by some of the leading families in outlying areas. *(26–24) VLR: 11/19/74; NRHP: 12/23/74.*

WILLIAMSON ARCHAEOLOGICAL SITE, *Dinwiddie vicinity.* This archaeological site consists of a very large and rare quarry workshop of Paleo Indians dating to before 9000 B.C. The twenty-acre site has yielded thousands of artifacts including fluted points, scrapers, knives, burins, hammers, and workshop debris. Most of the points and tools are made of chert, taken from a local outcrop. One of these chert projectile points is shown here. The site is among the largest of its type and age located thus far in North America. Occupying a plateau overlooking Little Cattail Run, the site currently consists of cultivated farmland with some adjacent woodland. *(26–35) VLR: 05/13/69; NRHP: 12/02/69.*

CITY OF EMPORIA

Formed in 1887 from a merger of Hicksford and Belfield, the Greensville county seat was named for Emporia, Kansas, hometown of a business associate of the local delegate. The charter was revoked in 1888, but the town was reincorporated in 1892. It became a city in 1967.

GREENSVILLE COUNTY COURTHOUSE COMPLEX, *South Main Street.* Greensville County's courthouse square, which has served as the location of the county's seat of government since 1787, preserves three buildings of architectural interest. The main element, the courthouse, was built in 1831 by Daniel Lynch as a plain three-part Palladian structure and was embellished in the early 20th century with an Ionic portico. The excellently documented clerk's office was constructed in 1894 by the Southern Fireproof Company after the plans of Reuben Shireffs. The former Greensville Bank building of 1900, now the county administrator's office, contains a remarkable interior of locally produced decorative stamped sheet metal. The square was the scene of military action in the Civil War when Gen. Wade Hampton, CSA, undertook to defend the railroad bridge across the Meherrin, General Lee's link to Southern supply sources. *(109–02) VLR: 09/16/82; NRHP: 07/21/83.*

H. T. KLUGEL ARCHITECTURAL SHEET METAL WORK BUILDING, *135 Atlantic Street.* The facade of the H. T. Klugel building is one of the landmarks of Emporia and probably the state's most original example of the use of galvanized architectural sheet metal. This singular work was fabricated in 1914 to ornament the newly built headquarters of H. T. Klugel's metalworks firm, founded in 1902. The facade served to advertise the rich decorative elements manufactured within. Unlike most firms, Klugel did not produce a catalog but designed each piece to order with emphasis on style and craftsmanship. Other local examples of his work include the cornice of the Old Merchants and Farmers Bank and the interior paneling of the county office building. The business has since been sold by the Klugel family, but its operation continues under new ownership, still making use of many of Klugel's machines and patterns. *(109–05) VLR: 11/21/72; NRHP: 04/02/73; BHR EASEMENT.*

OLD MERCHANTS AND FARMERS BANK BUILD-ING, *South Main Street.* The Old Merchants and Farmers Bank Building, completed in 1902, is a miniature version of the commercial structures that gave turn-of-the-century America's main streets architectural dignity. Even such a small structure could project a sense of monumentality through the use of a mansard roof and a fancy sheet-metal cornice, in this case manufactured locally by H. T. Klugel. The cornice is a demonstration of how a rich architectural effect could be achieved with minimal cost and effort. The building was used as a bank until 1920 and as a law office until the mid-1940s. It then became the local library. In 1978 Greensville County deeded the building to the Greensville Historical Society. It was dedicated as a local history museum in 1994. *(109–08) VLR: 11/21/78; NRHP: 05/07/79.*

VILLAGE VIEW, *221 Briggs Street.* Surrounded by spacious, parklike grounds, Village View is Emporia's outstanding example of Federal architecture. The imposing house features a refined main stair, richly ornamented mantels, and unusual scrollwork decoration in the main entry's fanlight and sidelights. Village View was built in the 1790s for James Wall, member of a prominent local family. It was purchased in the 1820s from Wall's heirs by Nathaniel Land who made improvements to the house before his marriage to Maria Pendleton Woodlief in 1830. The house served as a Confederate headquarters during the Civil War; generals W. H. F. Lee, Wade Hampton, and Matthew Butler met in the parlor. After the war William Henry Briggs operated a boys' academy here. In 1986 Village View was donated by the Briggs family to the Village View Foundation, which has since restored the house for public exhibition and use. *(109–04) VLR: 11/18/80; NRHP: 09/16/82.*

ESSEX COUNTY

On the Rappahannock River side of the Middle Peninsula, Essex County probably was named for the English shire. It was formed from the extinct Rappahannock County in 1692. The county seat is Tappahannock.

BLANDFIELD, *Caret vicinity.* Robert Beverley II, member of one of Virginia's great landed families, began planning this plantation mansion in the late 1760s. Although the house was ready for occupancy by 1774, Beverley continued construction and the ordering of furniture over the next twenty years. The resulting five-part structure is a highly competent interpretation of English Palladianism and represents colonial American house building at its grandest. The center section is highlighted by pedimented pavilions and is flanked by connected two-story dependencies framing a wide forecourt, all constructed with exceptionally fine brickwork. Both the exterior and the floor plan follow illustrations in James Gibbs's *Book of Architecture* (1728). In 1844 the original woodwork was replaced with plain Greek Revival trim. Blandfield was sold by the Beverleys in 1983 to Mr. and Mrs. James C. Wheat, Jr., who undertook a meticulously researched restoration, reconstructing the interior's 18th-century appearance. *(28–05) VLR: 05/13/69; NRHP: 11/12/69.*

BROOKE'S BANK, *Loretto vicinity.* The diminutive proportions of this colonial plantation house may result from the fact that it was built for a woman, Sarah Taliaferro Brooke, who supervised its construction. Completed in 1751, the rectangular house, with its formal lines, fine brickwork, and spreading hipped roof, is a classic example of Virginia's Georgian architecture. An unusual note is the diamond patterning formed by glazed headers in the two massive chimneys. The highlight of the interior is the broad center-passage arch framing an original curved stair. Delicate late Georgian trim was added to the woodwork in the principal rooms. The house was shelled by the Union gunboat *Pawnee* in the Civil War, but the damage was not extensive. After years of neglect, Brooke's Bank was restored in the 1930s. A museum-quality restoration, including the replacement of the 1930s wings, took place in 1995–98. *(28–07) VLR: 06/01/71; NRHP: 09/28/71; BHR EASEMENT.*

CHERRY WALK, *Dunbrooke vicinity.* The outbuildings, farm buildings, and residence at Cherry Walk form an unusually complete Tidewater plantation complex of the middling class, providing a rare, essentially undisturbed picture of a vanished lifestyle. With its gambrel roof, plain interior, and unadorned brick walls, the dwelling house is a characteristic example of late 18th-century eastern Virginia architecture, built ca. 1795 for Carter Croxton, whose family had settled here in 1739. The outbuildings include two dairies, a smokehouse, a privy, and a kitchen. The farm buildings consist of an early frame barn, a plank corncrib, and a late 19th-century blacksmith shop. The buildings, erected over a long span of time, illustrate various rural construction techniques. The entire complex has been carefully restored by its present owners. *(28–08) VLR: 12/14/82; NRHP: 02/10/83; BHR EASEMENT.*

ELMWOOD, *Loretto vicinity.* The wealth and influence of the Garnetts is manifest in Elmwood, one of Virginia's most ambitious colonial mansions. Muscoe Garnett, whose family had been prominent in county affairs since the 17th century, had the house built ca. 1774. The austere formality of the 100-foot facade contrasts with the highly ornamented interior woodwork, some of the finest of the late colonial period. The drawing room is especially grand, having scrolled pediments and Ionic pilasters decorating the doorways and chimneypiece based on designs published by Abraham Swan. The house was partially remodeled in the Italianate style in 1852 by Muscoe R. H. Garnett, a Confederate statesman. After standing empty for many years, Elmwood was restored in the 1950s by a descendant of the builder. Complementing the house is a large formal garden and park. A collection of rare early farm buildings stands on the lowlands. *(28–11) VLR: 06/02/70; NRHP: 09/15/70; BHR EASEMENT.*

GLEBE HOUSE OF ST. ANNE'S PARISH, *Champlain vicinity.* The St. Anne's Parish glebe house is one of the finest and probably the oldest of Virginia's colonial glebe houses, of which barely a dozen survive. Glebe houses were built on church lands used for the support of the parish. The houses were sometimes rented; more often they served as rectories. It is not unusual for glebe houses to display architectural quality equal to their churches, especially in the brickwork. The St. Anne's glebe house probably was begun around the same time as the nearby 1719 Vauter's Church, for the brickwork is very similar. The diarist the Rev. Robert Rose, who came here in 1725, was its first occupant. The property was sold by its parish as the result of the disestablishment and became a private residence known as Cloverfield. It had stood vacant since the 1960s, but by 1998 a restoration was underway. *(28–14) VLR: 11/19/74; NRHP: 03/03/75.*

GLENCAIRN, *Chance vicinity.* This informal old planter's house, a landmark to passing motorists on nearby U.S. Route 17, was constructed with rare framing techniques, which offer important clues to early Virginia building technology. The oldest portion of the house began ca. 1730 as a one-room dwelling with exposed ceiling joists and exposed framing for an exterior cornice. This elementary dwelling was expanded to its present form with its long rear porch in the fourth quarter of the 18th century, during the ownership of the Waring family. The shed dormers likely date from a mid-19th-century renovation. An oddity of the plan of the later section is the exceptionally wide center passage. The house long stood in a state of neglect but was carefully restored in the late 1970s. *(28–15) VLR: 02/21/78; NRHP: 05/14/79.*

LINDEN, *Champlain vicinity.* Built on an unusually generous scale, Linden was completed ca. 1825 for Lewis Brown who inherited this inland farm from his father, Merriday Brown, a watchmaker and planter. With its three-bay, side-hall plan, the house is an interesting adaptation of the Federal town house form for a country residence. While there was no practical reason for this scheme in a rural areas, it nevertheless was employed intermittently for farmhouses during the Federal period. The house has fine-quality brickwork and retains much of its early woodwork, including mantels, staircases, and pine flooring. The name of the property probably was derived from the large, now very old, linden trees that stand directly in front of the house. On the grounds are an early graveyard and the remnants of a terraced garden. *(28–24) VLR: 12/11/91; NRHP: 10/15/92.*

PORT MICOU, *Loretto vicinity.* A relic of the days when the Rappahannock River was a main transportation artery for both people and commerce, the Port Micou complex consists of a granary-warehouse and a small dwelling probably built as an overseer's house. Named for Paul Micou, a Huguenot who began purchasing property here in 1697, Port Micou was a wharf complex for much of the 18th century. It was acquired by Robert Paine Waring in 1835, and the two structures were built either by Waring or his son-in-law Richard Baylor, both prosperous landowners. The large two-story granary, notable for its workmanship, originally stored wheat that was shipped to Tidewater cities. The functionally related dwelling has but one room and a passage on its main floor. Only with imagination can one picture the hum of activity that once took place at this now lonely place. *(28–274) VLR: 06/19/91; NRHP: 02/06/92.*

TAPPAHANNOCK HISTORIC DISTRICT. Tappahannock began as a village known as Hobb's Hole in the mid–17th century. The core of this Rappahannock port preserves an assemblage of 18th- and 19th-century architecture. Its focal point is the 1848 Roman Revival courthouse. Adjacent is the 1728 courthouse that was partially burned by the British in 1814 and since remodeled as a Methodist church. The 18th-century debtors' prison and ca. 1808 clerk's office stand nearby. Important houses include the mid-18th-century Ritchie house on Prince Street, the late 18th-century Brockenborough house on Water Street, now part of St. Margaret's School, and the 1850 Roane-Wright house on Duke Street. These houses respectively were the residences of three cousins, editor Thomas Ritchie, banker John Brockenborough, and Spencer Roane, members of a political circle known as the Essex Junto or Richmond Junto who helped the Jeffersonian Democratic-Republican party maintain its national dominance. *(310–24) VLR: 08/15/72; NRHP: 04/02/73.*

VAUTER'S (VAWTER'S) CHURCH, *Loretto vicinity.* The ability of the colonial mason to give articulation and dignity to an otherwise elementary structure is no better illustrated than in the brickwork of Vauter's Church. With glazed-header Flemish bond set off by rubbed-brick corners,  gauged-brick arches, and molded-and-gauged pedimented doorways, the masonry is a demonstration of early 18th-century craftsmanship. It has long been asserted that the T-shaped building was erected in two stages: the main section ca. 1719 to serve as the upper church of St. Anne's Parish and the south wing in 1731. The consistency of the brickwork, however, has led to more recent speculation that the building was erected at one time. The church underwent an interior remodeling in conjunction with the resumption of regular services in 1827, but much colonial fabric was reused. Unlike many other colonial churches, Vauter's escaped Civil War damage. *(28–42) VLR: 08/15/72; NRHP: 12/05/72.*

WHEATLAND, *Loretto vicinity.* John Saunders, a planter and merchant, had this massive frame house erected on the banks of the Rappahannock River between 1849 and 1851. The house was attached to an earlier dwelling, now the kitchen wing. With its high basement and two-tier porticoes, the main house presents a classic "southern plantation" image. In addition to his farming activities, Saunders operated a plantation wharf, known as Saunders Wharf, within sight of the house. Here he received goods for his store in Loretto, and neighboring farmers bought produce for transportation to cities. Steam packets continued to call at Saunders Wharf until 1937. The present wharf building, dating from 1916, is possibly the only such structure remaining on the Rappahannock and is now preserved as a small museum and tourist attraction. *(28–44) VLR: 09/20/88; NRHP: 12/19/90; BHR EASEMENT.*

WOODLAWN, *Millers Tavern vicinity.* Woodlawn, also known as the Trible house, is an example of the fast-disappearing single-cell domiciles built in great numbers beginning in the late 18th century. These small but well-crafted dwellings demonstrate the newly acquired ability of modest Virginia farmers to create shelters more substantial and more refined than the rude yeomen's cottages of the colonial period. The first portion of the tiny gambrel-roofed structure was constructed ca. 1816 for John Haile. The house was expanded with a lean-to addition ca. 1840 when it was acquired by George Trible. Carefully restored in the 1970s after standing empty and neglected, Woodlawn is a point of interest on U.S. Route 360, the highway connecting Richmond and Tappahannock. *(28–47) VLR: 02/21/78; NRHP: 07/16/80.*

CITY OF FAIRFAX

Originally called Providence, this former crossroads village became the Fairfax county seat in 1798. Its name was changed to Fairfax in 1859. The community was incorporated as a town in 1874 and became a city in 1961.

CITY OF FAIRFAX HISTORIC DISTRICT. The modern city of Fairfax had its origins in 1798 when the General Assembly directed that the county seat be relocated near the county's geographic center. The site, named Providence in 1805, was at the junction of the Little River Turnpike and the Ox Road. These historic routes remain heavily traveled thoroughfares through the district. Centered around the 1800 courthouse, the district includes some forty-eight buildings, six of which predate 1850. The rest are modest commercial and residential structures. An exception is the 1900 frame town hall (shown), built for community use by Joseph E. Willard, a lieutenant governor and diplomat. During the Civil War town life was subjected to constant disruption by continuous troop movements and guerrilla raids. Although now an incorporated city greatly expanded beyond its 19th-century confines, Fairfax's historic core retains a village-like character. *(151–03) VLR: 10/14/86; NRHP: 10/27/87.*

FAIRFAX COUNTY COURTHOUSE, *400 Chain Bridge Road.* The Fairfax county seat was moved to the village of Providence, now the city of Fairfax, in 1799. The new courthouse was designed by James Wren, who also designed Falls Church and Christ Church, Alexandria. Wren's courthouse combines an arcade, a feature of colonial courthouses, with the temple form, a building shape favored for Classical Revival buildings. This combination continued to be employed for Virginia courthouses into the antebellum period. During the Civil War the courthouse was used as a military outpost by both Union and Confederate soldiers. At various times it was visited by Confederate generals P. G. T. Beauregard and Joseph E. Johnston, as well as by President Jefferson Davis. The building, a reminder of this suburbanized county's link with the past, continues to house court functions. Its 1885 jail stands nearby. *(151–03–1) VLR: 10/20/73; NRHP: 05/03/74.*

FAIRFAX PUBLIC SCHOOL, *10209 Main Street.* The original section of this historic school was built in 1873, four years after the ratification of the new state constitution that provided for a statewide system of public schools. The school marked the commitment of Fairfax (then called Providence) to providing free public education to the community's elementary-level children. Like many rural schools of the period, the brick building had a gable-end front and resembled a country church. The area's growing population necessitated an expansion of the facility in 1912. The addition, which doubled the school's size, was attached perpendicular to the original section. With its hipped roof and tall paired windows, the addition has the simple dignity typical of schools of the era. The building stood vacant from the 1970s but has since been restored to serve as the Fairfax Museum and Visitors' Center. *(151–38) VLR: 04/22/92; NRHP: 10/21/92.*

RATCLIFFE-ALLISON HOUSE, *10386 Main Street.* This early 19th-century residence is representative of the simple vernacular housing once common in northern Virginia's towns and villages. It remains one of the few early structures in this now-urbanized county seat. Long known erroneously as Earps Ordinary, the house began as a one-room dwelling built in 1812 for Richard Ratcliffe, a landowner who also donated a lot for the county courthouse. The house was purchased in 1820 by Gordon and Robert Allison who expanded it and added the second story. It served as rental property until it was rescued from threatened demolition in 1920 by Dr. Kate Waller Barrett, a Virginia social worker. In 1972 Dr. Barrett's daughter, Mrs. Charles Pozer, donated the house to the city of Fairfax. It currently is being restored by the city and Historic Fairfax City, Inc., to serve as a museum interpreting the community's 19th-century lifestyle. *(151–02) VLR: 01/16/73; NRHP: 02/16/73.*

TASTEE 29 DINER, *10536 Lee Highway.* The prefabricated diner is a uniquely American form of roadside commercialism. Taking its name from U.S. Route 29, Fairfax's Tastee 29 Diner is a rare survivor of the once-numerous streamlined Moderne diners that operated across the United States. Built by the Mountain View Diner Company of Singac, N.J., the shiny, eye-catching establishment was installed on its site in July 1947. From the mid-1930s through the 1950s, the diner emerged as the ubiquitous roadside eatery, offering a comfortable atmosphere and quickly prepared home-style cooking to a new "car-mobile" society. Machine-age materials such as shining stainless steel and ceramic tile conveyed the image of cleanliness and efficiency. The beauty of machine-age precision is expressed in the sleek, rounded glass-brick corners, colored neon tubes, porcelain enamel panels, formica, and brightly colored tile. Tastee 29 Diner continues in regular operation. *(151–39) VLR: 06/17/92; NRHP: 10/29/92.*

FAIRFAX COUNTY

This northern Virginia county, accommodating many suburban communities of metropolitan Washington, D.C., was named for the sixth Baron Fairfax of Cameron, proprietor of the Northern Neck. It was formed from Prince William County in 1742. The county seat is Fairfax.

BELVOIR MANSION ARCHAEOLOGICAL SITE AND FAIRFAX GRAVE, *Fort Belvoir.* Belvoir, built 1736–41, was one of the great mansions of colonial Virginia. On a bluff overlooking the Potomac, the house was the residence of Col. William Fairfax, cousin and land agent to Thomas, Lord Fairfax. Belvoir was inherited in 1757 by Fairfax's son George William Fairfax, who accompanied George Washington during a 1748 expedition to the frontier to survey the Fairfax holdings. The house burned in 1783, and its ruins were demolished by mortar and cannon shots fired from British ships in August 1814. The site was eventually incorporated into Fort Belvoir, a major U.S. Army installation. Archaeological excavations have revealed the original configuration of the house, a conjectural reconstruction of which is shown. The foundations and associated sites are now protected by the army. The graves of Colonel Fairfax and his wife are located on the grounds. *(29–41) VLR: 07/17/73; NRHP: 06/04/73.*

CAMP A. A. HUMPHREYS PUMP STATION AND FILTER BUILDING, *U.S. Route 1, Fort Belvoir.* With its well-modulated classicism, this pump station illustrates how a time-honored architectural vocabulary can give respectability to an industrial building. The pump station was constructed in 1918 to accommodate Camp A. A. Humphreys, a U.S. Army training camp that was the predecessor of Fort Belvoir. Built to produce filtered drinking water, the facility was part of a construction program to ensure that troops, while in training, were not affected by diseases brought on by drinking impure water. The principal building, a buff-brick water filtration plant, was a project of the Army Corps of Engineers. It and its supply station provided filtered water to the camp and later Fort Belvoir until 1970. In 1986 the facility was leased to Fairfax County and was sympathetically converted into a homeless shelter. *(29–96) VLR: 06/19/96.*

CLIFTON HISTORIC DISTRICT. Established on Pope's Head Creek in southwestern Fairfax County, this tidy community sprang up between 1868 and 1910 through the impetus of New York immigrant Harrison G. Otis. Otis purchased land parcels around the depot of the Orange and Alexandria Railroad and in 1869 became postmaster of the new U.S. post office named Clifton. He promoted the settlement by opening roads, developing a sawmill, and building the Clifton Hotel, a residential and resort hostelry. In barely a decade the town had acquired churches, a school, shops, and a gristmill. By 1910 Clifton had 200 residents. Growth all but ceased after 1910 with the exhaustion of pulpwood supplies, which affected Clifton's wood product industries. With some sixty buildings Clifton today preserves a near-perfect image of an early 1900s village. Set in shady yards, its wooden houses employ a variety of straightforward vernacular forms. Picket fences abound. *(29–225) VLR: 04/16/85; NRHP: 08/15/85.*

COLVIN RUN MILL, *Colvin Run.* Constructed between 1810 and 1820, this voluminous brick structure is a survivor of the hundreds of early gristmills that once marked Virginia's countryside, enterprises essential to the state's agricultural economy. With its exterior overshot wheel, it offers a picture-book image of this rural architectural form. Its first owner and miller was most likely Philip Carper, who held the property from 1811 until 1842. The mill remained in operation through the 1930s. The realignment of the adjacent Route 7, however, disrupted the water supply, and the mill fell into disuse and disrepair. By the time the Fairfax County Park Authority purchased it in 1965, the mill was approaching ruinous condition. Painstakingly restored, with its reconstructed machinery patterned after the principles of the 19th-century mill engineer Oliver Evans, Colvin Run Mill now is a museum of early milling design and practices. *(29–08) VLR: 09/21/76; NRHP: 08/16/77.*

CORNWELL FARM, *Great Falls vicinity.* A landmark along the Georgetown Pike, Cornwell Farm's residence is a one of Fairfax County's few surviving examples of antebellum plantation architecture. Built in 1831 for John Jackson, the house displays, with its Georgian outline, the architectural conservatism prevalent among many of the region's landowners. The facade's Flemish bond brickwork is exceptionally well crafted and is comparable to that found on the finest town houses of Alexandria or Georgetown. Union soldiers bivouacked on the grounds during the Civil War, and before the restoration of the house in 1936, the names of soldiers from several northern states could be seen inscribed on the interior walls. Despite heavy suburban development in the vicinity, Cornwell Farm retains a rural setting. The place takes its present name from B. F. Cornwell, who purchased the property after the Civil War. *(29–09) VLR: 09/21/76; NRHP: 04/13/77.*

DRANESVILLE TAVERN, *Dranesville.* Framed by its brown sandstone chimneys, this hostelry is a conspicuous reminder of the days when teamsters and travelers used the Leesburg Turnpike on trips to and from Alexandria, Leesburg, and Winchester. Dating to 1823, the tavern was built in three log sections connected by "dogtrots," since enclosed with weatherboards. The building survived the Civil War years and the nearby 1862 battle of Dranesville and came to serve principally as a wagon stand for teamsters. In 1968 the Fairfax County Park Authority acquired the property and moved the building about 100 feet back from its original site to accommodate the widening of the Leesburg Turnpike (Route 7). It has since been restored and is operated as a historic property rental facility. *(29–11) VLR: 04/18/72; NRHP: 11/09/72.*

FAIRFAX ARMS, *Colchester.* During the 18th century the Potomac River creeks accommodated small port towns settled by Scottish merchants. Most became dormant as their harbors silted up. A typical case is Colchester on the Occoquan River, a town which did not survive the 18th century. A relic of this former port is the Fairfax Arms tavern, one of the settlement's only two surviving 18th-century buildings. The tavern was standing as early as 1763 when William Linton was cited for operating an ordinary on the parcel. William Thompson kept a tavern here from 1779 until his death in 1800, after which it became a private residence. The unassuming frame structure, with brick and stone chimneys, is representative of the simple vernacular style that characterized the architecture of these early ports. *(29–43) VLR: 12/19/78; NRHP: 05/21/79.*

FORT BELVOIR HISTORIC DISTRICT, *Fort Belvoir.* Named for Belvoir, the Fairfax family plantation situated here in the 18th century, Fort Belvoir encompasses a 1,500-acre tract acquired by the U.S. Army Corps of Engineers in 1912. It became the official home of the corps in 1918. Designated Fort Humphreys in 1922, the installation was renamed Fort Belvoir in 1934. The historic district contains the administrative and ceremonial core of the 1930s Army Corps Training Center campus as well as the principal residential structures built in the 1920s for officers' housing. Also in the district is a row of wooden warehouses built in 1917, the earliest structures on the post. Formally arranged brick Georgian Revival buildings with limestone trim and porticoes dominate the central campus. A multiplicity of 1930s Colonial Revival brick houses in a layout reminiscent of a garden suburb defines the senior officers' quarters. *(29–209) VLR: 03/20/96.*

FORT HUNT, *Alexandria vicinity.* Fort Hunt was part of the Endicott system of seacoast defenses erected between 1889 and 1901 to guard twenty-six major ports. As the nation's capital Washington was given priority in the construction of this system of modern concrete and earthen gun and mortar emplacements. Located at Sheridan Point overlooking the Potomac, the complex was equipped with four concrete batteries and various support structures. The fort was garrisoned until World War I, never having experienced action. In 1933 the property was transferred to the National Park Service, and the following year the Civilian Conservation Corps developed the site into a recreational area. During World War II the fort was reoccupied by the military and served as an interrogation site for captured German and Japanese officers. It was returned to the National Park Service in 1948. *(29–103) VLR: 12/18/79; NRHP: 03/26/80.*

FRYING PAN MEET-INGHOUSE, *2615 Centerville Road, Floris.* This simple meetinghouse traces its origins to 1775 when a Baptist congregation was organized at nearby Bull Run. Some of its members later wrote to Robert ("Councillor") Carter requesting his permission to build a meetinghouse on land he owned near Frying Pan Spring. Carter agreed, and the present structure,

erected by members of the congregation, was standing by 1791. The little-altered wood-frame building is in the plain vernacular favored by nonconformists. Frying Pan is one of the state's oldest surviving Baptist houses of worship where a racially integrated congregation was maintained from the very beginning. In 1984 the property was acquired by the Fairfax County Park Authority for a museum. The unusual name derives from a local legend which holds that Indians camping on the site were attacked by settlers and left behind their frying pan containing their meal. *(29–15) VLR: 12/11/90; NRHP: 02/05/91.*

GEORGE WASHINGTON MEMORIAL PARKWAY, *Arlington Memorial Bridge to Capital Beltway.* The parkway is one of America's important contributions to landscape design. Created to accommodate recreational motorists, these extended verdant parks offer constantly unfolding scenic views. The parkway concept was an outgrowth of the turn-of-the-century City Beautiful movement. Washington's McMillan Plan of 1902 called for numerous parkways linking Great Falls, Mount Vernon, the Potomac River bridges, and existing parks. The George Washington Memorial Parkway, originally including the Mount Vernon Memorial Highway, opened in 1932. Its Virginia portion today consists of the parkway's northern leg, built 1930–65 and extending over nine miles from Memorial Bridge north to the Capital Beltway. This undulating roadway continues the character of the original southern section. The project, initiated by the National Park Service and the Bureau of Public Roads, maintains the Potomac corridor's scenic beauty while making it accessible to thousands of motorists daily. *(29–218) VLR: 10/09/91; NRHP: 06/02/95.*

GUNSTON HALL, *Mason's Neck.* Gunston Hall was the home of Revolutionary patriot George Mason, author of the Virginia Declaration of Rights and much of the 1776 constitution of Virginia. Mason's home overlooking the Potomac River is one of the nation's most noted examples of colonial architecture. The compact exterior was constructed ca. 1755. The extraordinarily rich interiors including a rare Chinese-style dining room, were designed by William Buckland, a skilled English architect and joiner. The masterful carving and other detailing were crafted by William Bernard Sears, one of Buckland's artisans. The house and its extensive formal gardens present one of America's most elegant expressions of colonial taste. The property was given to the Commonwealth by Louis Hertle in 1932. Since his death in 1949, Gunston Hall has been a museum and has undergone long-term restoration under the patronage of the National Society of the Colonial Dames of America. *(29–50) VLR: 09/09/69; NRHP: 10/15/66; NHL: 12/19/60.*

HERNDON DEPOT, *Elden Street, Herndon.* A landmark in the town center, this board-and-batten depot is a surviving example of the simple railroad stations that served small communities in the last century. Twenty-one miles from Washington, D.C., Herndon was a busy commuter stop as well as a shipping point for dairy products bound for the capital around the turn of the century. A depot was here as early as 1859, when the Alexandria, Loudoun, and Hampshire Railroad was extended to Herndon. The first town council meetings were held in the building after the founding of Herndon in 1879. Rail service through the community was discontinued in the 1960s, but the building later was restored to house town offices. Since that time, the depot has been made an architectural highlight of a redesigned town square and is now a museum operated by the Historical Society of Herndon. *(29–212) VLR: 04/17/79; NRHP: 06/18/79.*

HERNDON HISTORIC DISTRICT. The core of this northern Virginia community maintains a neighborly, old-fashioned character despite its proximity to Dulles International Airport and the seemingly endless development spread across the surrounding landscape. The town sprang up around the rail depot constructed to serve the Alexandria, Loudoun, and Hampshire Railroad, which reached Herndon by 1859. The settlement received its name the previous year honoring Capt. William Lewis Herndon of Fredericksburg, skipper of a packet ship which sank off Cape Hatteras in 1857. Following the Civil War, Herndon became the loading point for area dairymen shipping milk to Washington. By 1911 the town was home for nineteen milk shippers. The electrification of the rail line that same year spurred the development of Herndon into a bedroom community. Most of the commercial area postdates a 1917 fire. The surrounding shady streets retain a wide range of modest housing types built from 1890 to 1920. *(235–03) VLR: 02/20/90; NRHP: 01/11/91.*

HOPE PARK MILL AND MILLER'S HOUSE (ROBEY'S MILL), *Pope's Head Road.* This small wooden mill and adjacent miller's house began as an adjunct to Hope Park, a large plantation. It later gained importance as a neighborhood mill, serving the needs of nearby plantations, as opposed to the larger merchant mills that served a greater area. The two buildings probably were erected ca. 1800 during the ownership of David Stuart. Caught in the crossfire of the Civil War, Hope Park Mill during the winter of 1861–62 was Post No. 3 for many Confederate units. The mill prospered once again around the turn of the century under the ownership of Frank Robey, whose death in 1906 brought an end to its commercial life. With its small pasture and wooded hillsides, the complex, which includes a smokehouse, springhouse, and cabin, all of log, preserves a vestige of early rural life in Fairfax County. *(29–64) VLR: 11/16/76; NRHP: 08/15/77.*

HUNTLEY, *Groveton vicinity.* An intriguing Federal dwelling perched on the edge of a steep hill, Huntley was built ca. 1825 as a secondary home for Thomson Francis Mason, a grandson of George Mason of Gunston Hall. The compact house has singular architectural sophistication and exhibits the refined ingenuity inherent in the buildings of the English Regency period. Although it has stood unoccupied for a long period, the house has suffered few alterations. Preserved on the grounds are several original outbuildings including a large brick-vaulted underground icehouse and an unusually large brick privy. The property is now owned by Fairfax County, which has undertaken basic repairs but has not established a permanent use. The unrestored house and grounds are periodically opened to the public. *(29–117) VLR: 03/21/72; NRHP: 11/03/72.*

LANGLEY FORK HISTORIC DISTRICT, *Langley.* The intersection commonly known as Langley Fork retains its historic identity and appearance in a region that has been subjected to intense modern development. It includes an assemblage of local vernacular buildings scattered among large leafy lots. Six structures form the nucleus of the district: the Langley Ordinary, built ca. 1850; the mid-19th-century Langley Toll House; Gunnell's Chapel, built after 1865 for a black Methodist congregation; the Friends Meeting House (shown), erected in 1853; the Mackall house, now the site of Happy Hill Country Day School; and Hickory Hill, once the residence of Robert F. Kennedy, U.S. attorney general under President John F. Kennedy. In the 19th century Langley Fork was a major turnpike junction for northern Virginia. During the Civil War, Union general McCall of the Pennsylvania Reserves made Langley Ordinary his headquarters. *(29–214) VLR: 09/16/80; NRHP: 10/19/82.*

MOOREFIELD, *Moorefield Road, Vienna.* Moorefield was the home of Jeremiah Moore (1746–1815), a pioneer Baptist preacher and reformer who was an early advocate of religious freedom and of the separation of church and state in Virginia. Moore was known to Thomas Jefferson, George Washington, George Mason, and Patrick Henry, and he encouraged their active support of his principles. His home, now surrounded by modern housing, was originally a simple wood-frame vernacular farmhouse, typical of the area, but was significantly modified in the 1950s when it was veneered with brick and had its dormers altered. Much of the original fabric remains intact beneath the later work. It is now owned by the town of Vienna, and long-term plans call for restoration to its original appearance. Pastor Moore lies buried in a family cemetery near the house. *(153–04) VLR: 09/20/77; NRHP: 04/19/78.*

MOUNT VERNON, *Alexandria vicinity.* George Washington became the proprietor of Mount Vernon in 1754 and through a series of alterations and remodelings, completed by 1787, transformed a simple farmhouse built by his father into the mansion that it is today. The composition is set off by its cupola, rusticated wooden siding, and famous portico. Every aspect of the estate—the architecture of the mansion, the decoration of its interior, the planning of the outbuildings, the layout of the gardens, and the operation of the plantation—received Washington's most careful attention. After Washington's death at Mount Vernon in 1799, the property gradually fell into disrepair. In 1858 some 200 acres of the original 8,000-acre plantation were acquired by the Mount Vernon Ladies' Association organized by Ann Pamela Cunningham. The association continues to maintain the meticulously restored complex in its matchless Potomac River setting as a shrine to the father of our country. *(29–54) VLR: 09/09/69; NRHP: 10/15/66; NHL: 12/19/60.*

MOUNT VERNON MEMORIAL HIGHWAY, *Arlington Memorial Bridge to Mount Vernon.* Opened in 1932, the Mount Vernon Memorial Highway was the first parkway project of the U.S. government and the first such road with a commemorative function explicit in its name and alignment. Engineer Jay Downer, landscape architect Gilmore D. Clarke, and arborist Henry Nye served as design consultants. All three were employees of New York's Westchester County Park Authority where they gained experience in parkway design. Embellished with its stone-faced arch bridges, concrete-slab base, beveled curbing, and lush landscaping, the parkway affords fine views of the Potomac River and points of interest along the way. Approximately fifteen miles long, the route begins at Arlington Memorial Bridge and extends south along the Potomac through Alexandria and on through riverside woodlands and meadows to Mount Vernon. It is now part of an extensive parkway system serving the nation's capital. *(29–218) VLR: 03/17/81; NRHP: 05/18/81.*

OAKTON TROLLEY STATION, *2923 Gray Street, Oakton.* The lone survivor of the trolley stations that served Fairfax County commuters in the early 1900s, the Oakton station was constructed in 1905 by the Washington and Fairfax Electric Railway Co. It was located on land sold to the company by developer Willis R. Gray who encouraged extending the line to serve his Oakton subdivision. In addition to passengers, the station was a shipping point for area florists sending fresh flowers to Washington. The station also accommodated a post office and store. The trolley service was discontinued in 1939, and the station was converted to a general store and later a boardinghouse. The tracks were eventually removed, and the station was restored as a residence in 1988. With its shady yard and wraparound porch, the homey building is a vignette of simpler times. *(29–477) VLR: 10/19/94; NRHP: 02/08/95.*

PATOWMACK CANAL AT GREAT FALLS HISTORIC DISTRICT, *Great Falls.* The Patowmack Company was organized in 1785 to make the Potomac River navigable from Georgetown to Harper's Ferry, a project designed to bring western trade to the Chesapeake region. The canal, one of the earliest in the country to have locks, was innovative from an engineering standpoint. George Washington, a prime mover in Potomac River improvements, served as the company's first president. The Patowmack Canal Corporation went bankrupt and dissolved its charter in 1826. The canal was abandoned in 1830. The section at Great Falls preserved by the National Park Service contains several locks and numerous archaeological sites relating to the canal and the town of Matildaville, which was planned to serve the canal at Great Falls but eventually disappeared. A remarkable engineering feat is the deep canal trace cut through the rock cliffs. *(29–211) VLR: 09/19/78; NRHP: 10/18/79; NHL: 12/17/82.*

POHICK CHURCH, *Fort Belvoir vicinity.* A sophisticated essay in the Georgian style, the exterior of Pohick Church, with its lack of religious symbolism, recalls the more refined dissenter chapels of 18th-century England. Erected 1769–74, the work is attributed to James Wren who designed the architecturally similar Falls Church. George Washington and George Mason served on the vestry and also may have had a hand in the design. The exterior is highlighted by Aquia stone pedimented doorways based on schemes by James Gibbs, which are likely the work of William Copein, the church's mason. The interior woodwork, executed by William Bernard Sears, was destroyed in the Civil War by Union troops who used the church as a stable. The present woodwork, a deft essay of early Colonial Revival design, is by architect Glenn Brown, who directed a restoration begun in 1901. Pohick remains an active Episcopal church. *(29–46) VLR: 11/05/68; NRHP: 10/16/69.*

ST. MARY'S ROMAN CATHOLIC CHURCH, *Fairfax Station.* Clara Barton, founder and first president of the American Red Cross, established a field hospital at St. Mary's Church in August 1862 during the second battle of Manassas. It was here that she was first noticed for her humanitarianism, heroism, and organizational ability. From St. Mary's as many as 1,000 wounded Union soldiers at a time were moved by train back to Washington. The country Gothic building was erected in 1858 to serve the Irish immigrants recruited to work on the construction of the Orange and Alexandria Railroad. Although its interior suffered as a result of its wartime use, the exterior remains little altered since its construction. *(29–169) VLR: 02/17/76; NRHP: 07/01/76.*

POPE-LEIGHEY HOUSE, *Fort Belvoir vicinity.* A monument in domestic architecture to the egalitarian faith of architect Frank Lloyd Wright, the Pope-Leighey house is the third and perhaps the most representative of Wright's Usonian houses. Wright developed the Usonian, or U.S.-onian, concept as a means of providing practical, economic housing with the quality and clarity of design he believed essential to modern American life. The house was designed in 1939 for Loren B. Pope, who lived in it until 1947 when it was sold to Mr. and Mrs. Robert A. Leighey. Threatened by highway construction, the house was dismantled and moved from Falls Church in 1965 and rebuilt under the sponsorship of the National Trust for Historic Preservation on the grounds of Woodlawn Plantation. The house, preserving most of its Wright-designed furniture, is exhibited by the National Trust as a landmark of Wrightian design and American modernity. *(29–58) VLR: 10/06/70; NRHP: 12/18/70.*

SALONA, *McLean vicinity.* With its extensive grounds, early outbuildings, and straightforward Federal architecture, Salona recalls an earlier era in Fairfax County when such rural complexes were common here. Built in 1811–12, the house first served as the home of the Rev. William Maffitt and his wife, Henrietta Lee Tuberville Maffitt. President James Madison spent the night at Salona in August 1814 after his escape from Washington during the British sack of the city. War touched Salona again in the winter of 1861–62 when the house was occupied by an element of a Vermont brigade and later by a volunteer battalion of New York troops. During the Union occupation the house was substantially damaged, but it was later restored and received its Italianate brackets and a two-story wing. Though surrounded by the busy community of McLean, Salona's tree-dotted lawn and surrounding fifty acres preserve a feeling of the area's former rural character. *(29–34) VLR: 06/19/73; NRHP: 07/24/73.*

SULLY, *Chantilly vicinity.* Richard Bland Lee, younger brother of Light-Horse Harry Lee and uncle of Robert E. Lee, had this rambling farmhouse built in 1794 and added its east wing in 1799. Lee was a founder of Phi Beta Kappa and served as the first U.S. congressman from northern Virginia. Although it is not a formal mansion, the fine quality of Sully's woodwork demonstrates the attention that was often given to less pretentious Virginia houses. Adding visual interest is the inviting piazza with its scalloped eaves. Adjacent to the house are a stone dairy, a smokehouse, and a kitchen-laundry. The latter displays a rare use of galleting (small stones inserted in the mortar joints for decoration). Sully was threatened with destruction when Dulles International Airport was built nearby. Spared through a special act of Congress, Sully is now a museum exhibited by the Fairfax County Park Authority. *(29–37) VLR: 10/06/70; NRHP: 12/18/70.*

U.S. ARMY PACKAGE POWER REACTOR, *Fort Belvoir.* Constructed in 1957, this package power reactor was the U.S. Army's first nuclear-powered generating station and the country's first water-pressurized reactor to be brought on line. As such, it was the prototype of a family of nuclear power plants under development by the Atomic Energy Commission and the Department of Defense for use by the military at remote locations. The term *package* refers to the capability of this prototype to be sent to a facility in component form and assembled on location. This feature proved revolutionary to military bases in isolated areas such as Greenland that previously depended on supply lines and storage tanks that were vulnerable to attack. The reactor also served as a training facility until it was deactivated in 1973. Although its core has been removed, the basic structure of the reactor remains little changed. *(29–193) VLR: 06/19/96.*

WOODLAWN, *Fort Belvoir vicinity.* This five-part mansion was completed in 1806 on a site overlooking lands formerly part of Mount Vernon. The plantation was the wedding gift of George Washington to Eleanor Parke ("Nelly") Custis and her husband, Lawrence Lewis, respectively Washington's ward and nephew. Attributed to architect William Thornton, the crisply detailed, beautifully crafted mansion displays the elegance and refinement so admired in the Federal style. Woodlawn eventually fell into disrepair and was acquired by a group of Quakers in 1846. Later owned by Baptists, Woodlawn was part of the Underground Railroad. In the early 20th century Elizabeth Sharpe engaged architect Edward W. Donn, Jr., to rebuild the wings and hyphens. Senator and Mrs. Oscar Underwood of Alabama lived here before its acquisition in 1948 by the Woodlawn Public Foundation. Now owned by the National Trust for Historic Preservation, Woodlawn is a museum and center for historical studies. *(29–56) VLR: 12/02/69; NRHP: 02/26/70; NHL: 08/05/98.*

CITY OF FALLS CHURCH

Falls Church was named for the colonial church erected here in 1767–69. The church was so designated because of its proximity to the Little Falls of the Potomac River. The community was established in 1850 and incorporated in 1875. It became a city in 1948.

BIRCH HOUSE, *312 East Broad Street.* The Birch house stands out as one of the few tangible reminders of Falls Church's mid-19th-century heritage. Preserving a nostalgic image of a quieter era, the house is conspicuously located on Route 7, the former Alexandria-Leesburg Turnpike. The original portion was erected as a farmhouse before 1845 and evolved to its present form by the 1870s when it received its tall gable with Gothic-style bargeboards. The house was long the home of Joseph E. Birch, who assisted in the incorporation of Falls Church as a town in 1875 and served on the first town council. In 1968 his grandson deeded the house to Historic Falls Church, Inc. It has since been restored and sold with protective covenants. *(110–10) VLR: 06/21/77; NRHP: 10/26/77.*

CHERRY HILL, *312 Park Avenue.* The former rural character of Falls Church is embodied in the farmstead that is now part of a seven-acre park in the heart of the city. On the property is a ca. 1845 Greek Revival house and a ca. 1845 frame barn. From 1870 to 1945 Cherry Hill was owned by the Joseph Riley family. Poet James Whitcomb Riley was Riley's nephew, and some of his poems include descriptions of Cherry Hill and its residents. Joseph Riley led the drive to incorporate Falls Church in 1875 and also helped start its first public school. The city purchased Cherry Hill in 1956. The house has since been restored and furnished as a museum interpreting the lifestyle of the area's prosperous antebellum farm families. The barn houses a 19th-century tool collection. *(110–04) VLR: 06/19/73; NRHP: 07/26/73.*

FALLS CHURCH, *115 East Fairfax Street.* Lending its name to the surrounding city, this colonial house of worship was preceded by a 1733 wooden church. Having determined that structure unfit to repair thirty years later, churchwardens George Washington and William Fairfax advertised for proposals. A design by James Wren was accepted, and the new church was completed under Wren's supervision in 1769. With its rectangular, two-story mass and hipped roof, Wren's scheme has the secular quality favored by low-church Anglicans. During the Revolution, American forces used Falls Church as a recruiting station. It was abandoned after the disestablishment but was returned to service in 1839. Union troops caused considerable damage when they used the building as a hospital and then as a stable. After the war the federal government awarded the parish $1,300 for damages. In 1959 the east wall was demolished for a new chancel. *(110–01) VLR: 12/02/69; NRHP: 02/26/70.*

MOUNT HOPE, *203 Oak Street.* One of the city of Falls Church's principal historic resources, Mount Hope has two distinct parts: a simple frame dwelling and a more elaborate Victorian ornamental villa, both virtually intact and joined by an infill section of uncertain date. The earlier portion was erected around 1815. The brick portion was built in 1869 by A. E. Lounsbury for William A. Duncan for $3,000, a sizable sum at the time. Tax records indicate that in 1875 the brick section was valued higher than both Gunston Hall and Woodlawn. Its exterior is distinguished by its spirited wooden detailing, particularly the balconied gable. Although the original 216-acre farm has been developed, the house and remaining half acre of land are protected by a local easement. *(110–15) VLR: 08/21/84; NRHP: 10/04/84.*

FAUQUIER COUNTY

Named for Francis Fauquier, lieutenant governor of Virginia from 1758 to 1768, this northern Virginia county, known for its numerous estates, was formed in 1759 from Prince William County. Its county seat is Warrenton.

ASHLEIGH, *Delaplane vicinity.* Brilliantly sited in Fauquier County's beautiful countryside, this Greek Revival villa was the home of Margaret Marshall, granddaughter of Chief Justice John Marshall. She received a portion of the family's Oak Hill estate and had the house built ca. 1840. Tradition has it that she designed the house herself after obtaining ideas during a trip through the Deep South. The tradition is plausible as the design is not typical of Virginia and resembles the raised one-story antebellum dwellings of Alabama and Mississippi. The house was constructed by William S. Sutton, who erected many houses in the area. The property remained the home of Margaret Marshall and her husband, John Thomas, whom she married in 1845, until 1860 when it was sold to a relative. Despite subsequent changes in ownership, Ashleigh has always been maintained as a prestigious estate. *(30–05) VLR: 02/20/73; NRHP: 08/14/73.*

BOXWOOD (GENERAL WILLIAM ["BILLY"] MITCHELL HOUSE), *Middleburg vicinity.* Gen. Billy Mitchell (1879–1936) made his home at this northern Virginia estate from 1926 until his death ten years later. During his military career, Mitchell became the foremost advocate of air power as an essential element in the nation's defense. He foresaw that the airplane would replace the battleship as the military's most effective weapon. Frustrated by the official indifference to his ideas, he accused the military establishment of an "almost treasonable administration of national defense." His resulting court-martial received nationwide attention and won him considerable public sympathy. The Fauquier County estate to which Mitchell and his wife moved after his court-martial consists of an 1826 stone house built for William Swart which the Mitchells enlarged by adding a wing. The architecturally inviting home remains essentially as it was when the famous challenger of conventional military wisdom lived here. *(30–91) VLR: 02/15/77; NHL: 12/08/76.*

BRENTMOOR (SPILMAN-MOSBY HOUSE), *173 Main Street, Warrenton.* A classic Italian Villa–style dwelling, Brentmoor was built in 1859–61 for Judge Edward M. Spilman. In his book *The Architecture of Country Houses* (1850), Andrew Jackson Downing illustrated a design resembling Brentmoor described as "a simple, rational, convenient, and economic dwelling for the southern part of the Union." The Spilman family sold the property in the 1870s to James Keith, president of the Virginia Court of Appeals. In 1875 it was purchased by John Singleton Mosby, the Confederate ranger, who with his partisans outwitted the Union army during the Civil War to the extent that much of northern Virginia was known as "Mosby's Confederacy." Mosby sold the house in 1877 to former Confederate general Eppa Hunton, who was then serving in Congress. Brentmoor was the childhood home of Eppa Hunton, Jr., a founder of the prominent Richmond law firm Hunton and Williams. *(156–14) VLR: 02/15/77; NRHP: 01/20/78.*

GERMANTOWN ARCHAEOLOGICAL SITES, *Midland vicinity.* Lieutenant Governor Alexander Spotswood brought a group of German immigrants to Germanna in Orange County in 1714 to mine and refine ore from his iron mines. The first party of colonists included mechanics from the Nassau-Siegen district of Westphalia. In 1718 twelve families dissatisfied with conditions at Germanna acquired a warrant for lands twelve miles north near the Fauquier County village of Midland. The site of the 1721 Tilman Weaver house and the adjacent Germantown Tavern site are the only identified archaeological remains of the settlement. The stones of the Weaver house chimney remain scattered amid the undergrowth. The ca. 1721 house site, together with the remains of the ca. 1780 tavern, should yield information about the home life of this early immigrant ethnic group. *(30–239) VLR: 06/15/82; NRHP: 09/16/82.*

LORETTA, *Warrenton vicinity.* Loretta exemplifies the transformation of many Fauquier County farmhouses into prestige estates by owners whose wealth came from sources other than agriculture. The house began as a conventional early 19th-century brick dwelling, built by Frances Edmonds, widow of Col. Elias Edmonds, using $5,000 her husband received for service in the Revolutionary War. John Gains, a Warrenton banker, purchased Loretta in 1907, and within a year he and his wife Cornelia transformed the house into a sophisticated Colonial Revival mansion. Gains sold Loretta in 1911 to W. W. Finley, president of the Southern Railway Company, who added the Ionic portico. Frederick Haserick bought the property in 1924. His widow left it to her son who continues to live here. The house, comfortably situated in a pastoral setting at the end of a tree-lined drive, has remained little changed since Finley's death in 1924. *(30–35) VLR: 10/20/93; NRHP: 12/23/93.*

MELROSE CASTLE, *Casanova vicinity.* On the edge of a cliff, this rugged country house is an important expression of the castellated mode of the mid-19th-century Gothic Revival. Constructed between 1857 and 1860, the house was designed by Edmund George Lind who was born and trained in England. Lind established his  practice in Baltimore in 1856. Melrose was commissioned by Dr. James H. Murray of Maryland for a large farm purchased in 1856. He named it for Melrose Abbey in Scotland, which he claimed as an ancestral home. With its battlemented stone walls, central tower, and dramatic siting, Melrose illustrates the impact on southern landed families of the 19th-century romantic movement, especially the medievalism popularized by the novels of Sir Walter Scott. Melrose was occupied by Federal troops in 1862. More recently it served as the inspiration for Mary Roberts Rinehart's mystery *The Circular Staircase* (1908). *(30–70) VLR: 09/15/81; NRHP: 02/10/83.*

THE MILL HOUSE (CHINN'S MILL), *Atoka vicinity.*
This complex of structures reflects an early gristmill operation and the area's 20th-century hunt country society. A mill was operated here by Charles Chinn as early as 1768. Leven Powell, founder of Middleburg, was responsible for many of the buildings, including the present mill, the miller's house, the cooper's house, a dairy-smokehouse, and the millowner's house (now the centerpiece of the complex). After the mill ceased operation, the property took on an entirely new aspect with its purchase by John S. Phipps, son of Henry Phipps, a partner of Andrew Carnegie and director of the United States Steel Corporation. From 1924 to 1929 Phipps enlarged the house, converted several outbuildings to guest quarters, added a stable and swimming pool, and united the complex with landscaping. Though today it is a splendid country estate, the rustic character of Chinn's dwelling has been maintained. *(30–659) VLR: 06/21/83; NRHP: 01/12/84.*

MONTEROSA (NEPTUNE LODGE), *343 Culpeper Street, Warrenton.* Monterosa was originally the home of William ("Extra Billy") Smith, two-term governor of Virginia (1846–49 and 1864–65). Smith also served in the Virginia senate, the U.S. House of Representatives, the Confederate House of Representatives, and as a major general in the Confederate army. Early in his career, Smith ran the longest mail route in the nation and was dubbed "Extra Billy" by a U.S. senator during a congressional investigation. Sharing the site with Smith's house are three outbuildings: an architecturally stylish Italianate stable built in 1847, a brick smokehouse, and a late 19th-century dwelling known as The Office. James K. Maddux, a later owner and a leader in the Warrenton Hunt, remodeled Smith's Italianate dwelling in the Colonial Revival taste, adding the portico. He also changed its name to Neptune Lodge. *(156–20) VLR: 06/19/90; NRHP: 01/25/91.*

OAK HILL, *Marshall vicinity.* Oak Hill was an early home of John Marshall, noted chief justice of the Supreme Court. The wood-frame dwelling, completed by 1773 when Marshall was seventeen, is a classic example of Virginia's colonial vernacular. John Marshall became the owner of Oak Hill in 1785 when his father, Thomas Marshall, moved to Kentucky. Although John Marshall lived mostly in Richmond and Washington, he kept his Fauquier County property, making improvements and using it as a retreat. In 1819 he built an attached Classical Revival house as a residence for his son Thomas. In 1835 Oak Hill was inherited by Thomas Marshall's son John Marshall II, whose overindulgence in hospitality forced him to sell the place to his brother Thomas. The property left the family after Thomas Marshall, Jr.'s mortal wounding in the Civil War. *(30–44) VLR: 04/17/73; NRHP: 06/18/73.*

OAKLEY, *Upperville vicinity.* Oakley's residence, which sits grandly amid the undulating pastures of the northern Virginia countryside, is a sophisticated and well-preserved country house in the Italian Villa style, which was infrequently employed in the region. Completed in 1857, the house retains a romanticism symbolic of the lifestyle of its first owner, Richard Henry Dulany. Dulany was the founder in 1853 of the Upperville Colt and Horse Show, the oldest in the country and a focal point of equestrian activity in Virginia's hunt country. Cavalry skirmishes took place on the Oakley property in the Civil War, and the house was occupied successively by Confederate and Union troops. The architecturally conspicuous rear veranda was given its intermediate balcony by a recent owner, Mrs. Archibald Cary Randolph, who maintained the estate as a leading horse farm. *(30–46) VLR: 06/15/82; NRHP: 02/24/83.*

OLD FAUQUIER COUNTY JAIL, *Courthouse Square, Warrenton.* Warrenton's former jail is a singular example of the state's early county penal architecture. The complex includes the 1808 brick jail, converted to the jailer's residence and completed in 1823, and the parallel 1823 stone jail with its high-walled jail yard. Located next to the courthouse, the jail provides a telling picture of conditions endured by inmates of such county facilities. A jail was built for the county in 1779, but it proved to be inadequate within a number of years. The more substantial brick structure was finished in 1808, and on October 24 the keys to the new jail were turned over to the sheriff. With the completion of the stone jail and its plank-lined cells, the resulting two-part building served the county until 1966. The complex is now maintained by the Fauquier County Historical Society as a county history museum. *(156–04) VLR: 02/15/77; NRHP: 01/20/78.*

UPPERVILLE HISTORIC DISTRICT. Surrounded by grand estates and scenic farmland, Upperville is a principal geographic reference point for Virginia's renowned hunt country. The linear village was laid out in 1797 by Joseph Carr along the Alexandria-Winchester Turnpike. Carr planned the lower or

western end for commerce and the upper or eastern end for residential use, with the town taking its name from the residential portion. The village's entire length preserves detached country versions of various 19th-century styles in brick, wood, and log, all shaded by masses of trees. A striking, albeit modern, accent is the 1950s Trinity Episcopal Church, in the style of a French medieval parish church. Designed by H. Page Cross of New York, the church was donated by philanthropist and parishioner Paul Mellon. Upperville is the home of the nation's oldest horse show, founded in 1853 by Richard Henry Dulany. *(400–64) VLR: 01/18/72; NRHP; 10/18/72.*

WARRENTON HISTORIC DISTRICT. From its beginnings as a colonial village, this prosperous community has been home to lawyers and politicians such as John Marshall, who practiced here; William Smith, governor of Virginia in 1846–49 and 1864–65; and Eppa Hunton, Confederate general and U.S. congressman. Known as Fauquier Court House until its incorporation in 1810, Warrenton takes its present name from Warren Academy. The community has long been noted for its beautiful setting, healthful climate, and cultivated society. As a result it boasts an exceptional collection of houses, churches, and commercial buildings in a wide range of styles. The district also preserves a number of structures associated with the Civil War, when Warrenton was variously occupied by both sides. The architectural focal point is the county courthouse, a Classical Revival building erected in 1890 on the site of an earlier courthouse. Prestigious residences line Culpeper and Falmouth streets. *(156–19) VLR: 08/16/83; NRHP: 10/13/83.*

WAVERLY, *Middleburg vicinity.* This ochre-colored mansion with its Greek Revival portico and Gothic Revival rear wing is an architectural highlight on the scenic Halfway Road connecting Middleburg and The Plains. Its core is an 18th-century stone cottage which was incorporated into the present house in antebellum times. The end chimney of the cottage remains visible behind the portico piers. With its component parts, one rustic and the others stylish, Waverly illustrates the dramatic change in lifestyle that took place for many of the county's farmers in the mid–19th century. Signaling the era when the region became popular for country estates, the house was restored in the 1940s by Mr. and Mrs. Thomas Furness, who employed Chicago architect David Adler for the project. Waverly now serves as home of the Piedmont Vineyards, one of Virginia's first modern commercial wineries. *(30–226) VLR: 09/19/78; NRHP: 03/12/79; BHR EASEMENT.*

WESTON, *Casanova vicinity.* An instructive amalgam of farm buildings, Weston was originally the residence of the Fitzhugh family. The rambling house began as a log cottage probably built for Thomas Fitzhugh around 1810. The property was purchased from the Fitzhughs by Charles Joseph Nourse in 1859. Nourse, who was reared in Georgetown, D.C., named the farm Weston in commemoration of his ancestral home Weston Hall in England. Under Nourse the house grew by steady accretion. Changes and additions made in 1860, 1870, and 1893 resulted in an L-shaped structure with Carpenter's Gothic detailing. Following Nourse's death in 1906, his widow Annie operated a school and summer camp here. During World War II the Nourse daughters maintained Weston as a hospitality center for servicemen, serving some 11,000 meals by the end of the war. Weston and its collection of outbuildings are now a farm museum owned by the Warrenton Antiquarian Society. *(30–58) VLR: 09/18/96; NRHP: 12/06/96.*

FLOYD COUNTY

This mountainous Southwest Virginia county was named for John Floyd, governor of Virginia from 1830 to 1834. It was formed from Montgomery in 1831, with part of Franklin County added later. The county seat is Floyd.

FLOYD PRESBYTERIAN CHURCH, *Floyd.* The architectural highlight of the county-seat community of Floyd, this simple Greek Revival church is a product of the 1840s Second Great Awakening, which spread Presbyterianism into southern and western Virginia. Energized by this activity, the Floyd congregation erected the present building in 1850. It was built by Henry Dillon, an Irish immigrant who grew up and trained in Charleston, S.C. After moving to Floyd County, Dillon built several buildings in the area including a now-demolished courthouse. As was the practice among country builders of the day, Dillon relied on a pattern book for many of the details, in this case *The Practical House Carpenter* (1830), by Asher Benjamin. The church, the oldest public building in the county, remained in continuous use by the Presbyterians until 1974. Since 1992 it has served as a Masonic temple. *(219–03) VLR: 12/16/75; NRHP: 05/17/76.*

ZION LUTHERAN CHURCH AND CEMETERY, *Floyd vicinity.* Floyd County's Zion Lutheran Church is a landmark to the religious history of Southwest Virginia and to the enduring cultural traditions of German pioneers who moved into the region at the end of the 18th century. Formed in 1813 to minister to the settlers north of the town of Floyd, the Zion congregation occupied three successive buildings before the present structure was erected in 1898. The pews of the present church were saved from the third meetinghouse, built in 1861. A large cemetery to the rear of the building holds a rich collection of 19th-century funerary art, including a number of German-style markers carved by local artisans. The German stones have rectangular-shouldered bodies with rounded or pointed heads. Some of the late 19th-century German stones are conical. The oldest inscribed stone in the group is dated 1817. *(31–24) VLR: 06/16/81.*

FLUVANNA COUNTY

Fluvanna County takes its name from the 18th-century appellation of the upper James River, meaning "river of Anne," in honor of Queen Anne. It was formed from Albemarle County in 1777. The county seat is Palmyra.

BREMO HISTORIC DISTRICT, *Bremo Bluff vicinity.* Bremo includes three separate estates, all created by the planter, soldier, and reformer Gen. John Hartwell Cocke (1780–1866) on his family's 1725 land grant. Still owned by Cocke's descendants, the three properties—Upper Bremo, Lower Bremo, and Recess—preserve architecturally singular dwellings and numerous associated outbuildings and farm buildings, all erected under Cocke's supervision. The principal architectural piece is the mansion at Upper Bremo, completed in 1820, one of America's foremost works of Palladian-style architecture. While strongly influenced by Thomas Jefferson's architecture, its design is the result of a collaboration between Cocke and master builder John Neilson, who worked for Jefferson at Monticello and the University of Virginia. Contrasting with the classical Upper Bremo are the Lower Bremo and Recess houses, both in a neo-Jacobean style inspired by Bacon's Castle in Surry County, a Cocke family home. *(32–02) VLR: 09/09/69; NRHP: 11/12/69; NHL: 11/11/71; BHR EASEMENT (LOWER BREMO).*

BREMO SLAVE CHAPEL, *Bremo Bluff.* This simple Gothic Revival structure was constructed in 1835 as a slave chapel for Bremo, the plantation of John Hartwell Cocke. It is the state's only known slave chapel and represents Cocke's deep concern for the religious and moral edification of slaves. He had his slaves taught to read and decided that it was his Christian duty to provide them with religious instruction. Cocke was determined that his slaves should have their own house of worship and thus had the board-and-batten structure built on what became known as Chapel Field. Cocke and his wife Louisa frequently conducted services themselves. The chapel fell into disuse after the Civil War. In 1884 it was moved to the village of Bremo Bluff to serve the local Episcopal parish. It remained a church until 1924 when converted to a parish hall for the present Grace Church. *(32–30) VLR: 12/18/79; NRHP: 03/17/80.*

FLUVANNA COUNTY COURTHOUSE HISTORIC DISTRICT, *Palmyra.* Termed by architectural historian Talbot Hamlin the "Acropolis of Palmyra," this cluster of court structures, dominated by a temple-form Greek Doric courthouse, stands grandly overlooking the surrounding village. Gen. John Hartwell Cocke of nearby Bremo, one of the five commissioners who drafted plans for both the courthouse and jail, took primary responsibility for their final appearance. The 1829 stone jail, built by John G. Hughes, is similar to the distinctive brick and stone farm buildings at Bremo. The courthouse, completed in 1831, was supervised by Walker Timberlake, a Methodist preacher-contractor. It is one of the state's few antebellum courthouses to remain without additions and retain its original interior arrangement and many original fittings. Inscribed on the stone lintel above the entrance is "THE MAXIM HELD SACRED BY EVERY FREE PEOPLE/OBEY THE LAWS." *(32–40) VLR: 01/05/71; NRHP: 09/22/71.*

GLENARVON, *Bremo Bluff vicinity.* William Galt (1755–1825), a Scottish immigrant, became a wealthy Richmond merchant and accumulated numerous plantations. He devised three in Fluvanna County, extending for some five miles along the James River, to his adopted sons James and William, Jr. They divided them evenly, naming them Point of Fork and Glenarvon, and built identical houses in 1834–35. Placed overlooking the James River and Kanawha Canal, which afforded easy access to Richmond markets, the nearly identical houses were similar in size and quality to the large Classical Revival mansions of the state capital. Both were embellished with Greek Revival porticoes on their garden elevations. Documentary resources concerning William Galt, Jr.'s comfortable life at Glenarvon are plentiful, with his books, wines, children, and frequent travels figuring prominently in his interests. The kitchen outbuilding, icehouse, and foundations of several other ancillary structures remain on Glenarvon's grounds. *(32–15) VLR: 12/16/75; NRHP: 05/28/76.*

POINT OF FORK ARSENAL ARCHAEOLOGICAL SITE, *Columbia vicinity.* One of the nation's few 18th-century arsenals, Point of Fork was established at this strategic point during the Revolution. Col. John Graves Simcoe, commander of the Queen's Rangers, raided it on June 5, 1781, in a move coinciding with Tarleton's raid on the Virginia legislature at Charlottesville. Simcoe's men destroyed the buildings and burned the supplies, leaving only the stone foundations. New buildings were erected near the site after the war, and Point of Fork was operated as a state arsenal until 1801 when it was abandoned in favor of the more centrally located arms manufactory in Richmond. During its brief period of service, Point of Fork was used for the manufacture and repair of arms and equipment and supplied material to combat the Whiskey Rebellion and to aid the Fallen Timbers campaign. *(32–26) VLR: 11/05/68; NRHP: 10/01/69.*

POINT OF FORK PLANTATION, *Columbia vicinity.* Named for its situation at the junction of the James and Rivanna rivers, Point of Fork plantation is marked by a Classical Revival mansion, one of two nearly identical houses built in 1834–35 as residences for the two adopted sons of William Galt, a prominent Richmond merchant and native of Scotland. Both James Galt's Point of Fork and William Galt's Glenarvon are exceptional examples of the plantation architecture of the upper James River region, illustrating the transition from the Federal period to the Greek Revival. The interior of each house has large, airy rooms on either side of a center hall dominated by a spiral stair. Union general Philip Sheridan set up headquarters at Point of Fork in March 1865. Point of Fork is also believed to be the site of Rassawek, principal village of the Monocan Indians. *(32–24) VLR: 04/16/74; NRHP: 08/13/74.*

CITY OF FRANKLIN

The city of Franklin started in the 1830s. The origin of the name is uncertain; it may have been named for Benjamin Franklin or for an area storekeeper named Franklin. It was a post village in 1855 and was incorporated as a town in 1876. Franklin became a city in 1961.

THE ELMS, *Clay Street.* Built by Paul D. Camp, a founder of the Camp Manufacturing Company, today's Union Camp Corporation, the Elms stands as a tangible symbol of the success of a large industrial enterprise. The lumber industry that Camp and his brothers developed in Southampton County after the Civil War revived the economy of southeastern Tidewater Virginia and also enabled the Camp family to create new cultural resources for the Franklin area in the form of schools and libraries. The spacious late Victorian house, built in 1897, exemplifies the residences erected by well-to-do small-town businessmen and community leaders in the late 19th century. Typical of such houses, it has numerous gables, a corner tower, long front porch, and decorative interior woodwork. Now owned by the Camp family foundations, the Elms is used for the management of philanthropic activities and for special functions. *(145–05) VLR: 09/15/81; NRHP: 09/09/82.*

FRANKLIN HISTORIC DISTRICT. Franklin arose between 1835 and 1840 as a village at the head of navigation on the Blackwater River. By the mid–19th century, the development of rail transportation and river commerce in southeastern Virginia made Franklin an important commercial depot for the region's agricultural products. In the late 19th century, Franklin became the headquarters of the Union Camp Corporation, a timber products industry. The majority of the buildings in the district, which includes the downtown area and adjacent residential streets, date from Franklin's economic resurgence in this period. Homey streetscapes of high-style and vernacular residences are seen throughout the large neighborhood west of the downtown. Because of a fire in 1881, most of the structures in the commercial area date from the late 19th and early 20th centuries. Examples of Italianate and Colonial Revival styles are particularly well represented in the commercial architecture of Main Street. *(145–06) VLR: 04/16/85; NRHP: 05/09/85.*

FRANKLIN COUNTY

Formed from Bedford and Henry counties in 1785, this largely rural county at the base of the Blue Ridge Mountains was named in honor of Benjamin Franklin. Its county seat is Rocky Mount.

BROOKS-BROWN HOUSE, *Dickinson.* The earliest portion of this galleried frame house was built in the 1830s and was later expanded with several additions. Its original occupant was Andrew Brooks, a Franklin County farmer who served in the Virginia House of Delegates from 1843 to 1863. The property was later acquired by Brooks's brother-in-law, William A. Brown, one of the county's leading tobacco farmers and manufacturers. Brown established a tobacco factory adjacent to the house around 1870. During the last two decades of the 19th century, the house also functioned as a stagecoach stop known as the Halfway House, a name assigned because of the property's location midway between Danville and Roanoke. A detached building on the property served as an office and later as a county polling station; its kitchen–dining room walls preserve rare 19th-century graffiti. *(33–128) VLR: 08/15/89; NRHP: 11/02/89.*

CAHAS MOUNTAIN RURAL HISTORIC DISTRICT. Skirted by U.S. Route 220, which follows the trace of the 18th-century Carolina Road, this 1,450-acre rural historic district near Boone's Mill preserves a scene that would still be familiar to the thousands of settlers who passed by on wagon and foot on their migration to western North Carolina. The scenic valley at the approaches to Maggodee Gap is dominated by Cahas Mountain, Franklin County's highest peak. Since the early 1800s the district has been home to the Boone and Taylor families who built substantial brick dwellings as well as lesser houses, including a log dwelling with a rare log purlin roof. The principal landmarks today are the 1820 John and Susan Boon house, a large Federal brick residence, and the similar Taylor-Price house. These and numerous later structures are part of the rich architectural legacy of the area's long-standing farming tradition. *(33–393) VLR: 03/20/96; NRHP: 06/07/96.*

THE FARM, *Lawndale Drive, Rocky Mount.* The Farm originally served as the ironmaster's house of the Washington Iron Works, Franklin County's first industrial enterprise. The self-sufficient 18,000-acre plantation was one of the last great iron plantations in Virginia. Franklin County's first court met here in 1786 while the house also served as an ordinary. The original portion of the house was built ca. 1779 by James Callaway. It was expanded in the 1820s and remodeled in the Greek Revival style in 1856. The property was purchased in 1823 by Peter Saunders, Jr., an ironmaster who acquired the place with his brothers. The ironworks flourished under Saunders's direction. Following flood damage in 1851, the family transformed the property into an extensive farming operation. Remaining on the grounds is the kitchen–servants' quarters outbuilding along with the office chimney and traces of other outbuildings. *(157–21) VLR: 02/21/89; NRHP: 11/02/89.*

GREER HOUSE, *206 East Court Street, Rocky Mount.* Also known as the 1861 House, the Greer house was originally the home of Dr. Thomas Bailey Greer, a well-regarded Franklin County physician. Dr. Greer was a third-generation county resident and played a significant role in local politics, as had his father and grandfather before him. He earned statewide renown for his achievements in medicine and served as a member of the first State Medical Examining Board, responsible for the formalization of the medical profession in Virginia. Dr. Greer's house was one of the community's most imposing residences at the time. Construction began in 1861 but was not completed until after the Civil War. It is architecturally significant as an example of the clean-lined builder's Greek Revival then in vogue. The doorway transoms and other details are based on designs in Asher Benjamin's *The Practical House Carpenter* (1830). *(157–23) VLR: 02/20/90; NRHP: 12/28/90*

FINNEY-LEE HOUSE, *Snow Creek vicinity.* Deep in the Franklin County countryside, the Finney-Lee house is a surprisingly refined late Federal I-house exhibiting handsomely crafted wooden trim and Flemish bond brickwork. Such dwellings, although not commonplace, were preferred by many southern Virginia gentry families in contrast to the more robust Greek Revival plantation mansions of the Deep South. The house was built in 1838–39 for Peter Finney, owner of some 3,000 acres and thirty slaves, who died shortly before its completion. In 1855 Finney's son William sold the house and 445 acres to his sister Louisa's husband, Charles C. Lee. Delicately detailed Federal ornamentation is found on the stair brackets and mantels. On the second floor is a so-called traveler's room, originally accessible only from a stair in the dining room. Among the farm buildings are two ca. 1900 tobacco barns and a tobacco packhouse. *(33–179) VLR: 03/19/97; NRHP: 05/23/97.*

HOOK-POWELL-MOORMAN FARM, *Hales Ford vicinity.* On the Lynchburg–Rocky Mount Turnpike, this plantation was settled in 1784 by John Hook, a Scottish-born merchant who built the vernacular Georgian structure here that served as his store. His residence is preserved in the core of the present farmhouse. Hook sold a wide variety of items among which were quality goods and books, an indication of a relatively sophisticated clientele for this backcountry. A savvy businessman, Hook at his death in 1808 possessed an estimated 40,000 acres and 110 slaves. The store building was moved across the turnpike and placed adjacent to an outdoor kitchen and slave quarters around 1855 when the next owner, Llewellyn H. Powell, remodeled Hook's dwelling into a country Greek Revival farmhouse. Dr. John A. Moorman purchased the property in 1879 and soon added an attached kitchen. His office and dispensary were added ca. 1890. *(33–22) VLR: 04/28/95; NRHP: 07/21/95.*

OTTER CREEK ARCHAEOLOGICAL SITE, *Ferrum vicinity.* This site includes a prehistoric settlement dating from the last half of the Late Woodland period (A.D. 1300–1600). Within the area are undisturbed prehistoric cultural features and post molds as well as well-preserved faunal and floral remains. This material holds significant information on regional environmental adaptation and settlement patterns during this period. The site's location on a remote upland spur of the Blue Ridge is highly unusual for this region and may allow it to provide data that help to identify networks of communication and trade connecting Dan River–related cultures on both sides of the Blue Ridge Mountains. The discovery of fired lumps of pottery clay suggests on-site manufacture of vessels and pipes. *(33–288) VLR: 04/16/85; NRHP: 05/09/85.*

BOOKER T. WASHINGTON NATIONAL MONUMENT, *Hardy vicinity.* Booker T. Washington, the preeminent Afro-American leader of his generation, was born a slave on the Burroughs plantation on April 5, 1856. With freedom gained following the Civil War, Washington attended Hampton Institute and later taught there. His achievements as an educator led to his being selected to establish a normal school for blacks in Alabama which became the Tuskegee Institute. As stated on his monument there, Washington "lifted the veil of ignorance from his people and pointed the way to progress through education

and industry." Washington's career was documented in his autobiography *Up from Slavery* where he described the "miserable, desolate, and discouraging surroundings" of his Franklin County birthplace. The Burroughs plantation was acquired by the National Park Service in 1957. Washington's humble origins are memorialized here with a replica of the slave cabin in which he was reared. *(33–15) VLR: 01/16/73; NRHP: 10/15/66.*

WASHINGTON IRON FURNACE, *Old Furnace Road, Rocky Mount.* Iron was made at this site by 1773 in a bloomery under the direction of John Donelson, father-in-law of President Andrew Jackson. A furnace was erected on the site and was sold in 1779 to Jeremiah Early and James Callaway who patriotically changed its name from The Bloomery to Washington Iron Works. The furnace entered into blast July 1, 1797. Three Saunders brothers bought the industry ca. 1820, and Peter Saunders, Jr., became the ironmaster. The furnace flourished; by 1836 it employed as many as a hundred workers. In 1851 a flash flood struck the furnace while in blast, exploding the interior and ending its operation until the Civil War, when it was again in use. The surviving furnace structure is a thirty-foot tapered granite pylon with its hearth and bellows openings at its base. *(157–29) VLR: 10/17/72; NRHP: 03/20/73.*

WAVERLY, *Burnt Chimney vicinity.* The stateliness that the Greek Revival style could bestow on a wooden American farmhouse, even one lacking columns, is evident in the former Burwell family homestead at Waverly. The bold, formally proportioned structure is visually dominated by the full entablature surrounding the mass. The house was built in the late 1850s for tobacco planter Armistead L. Burwell and his family. The design and construction are attributed to Seth Richardson, a local builder. Specific details, however, are adapted from designs found in the pattern books of Asher Benjamin whose works were widely used by Virginia housewrights. The interior woodwork, though plain, shows the hand of an accomplished finish carpenter. Like many of the area's other planters, the Burwells operated a factory for the manufacture of plug tobacco. From the 1940s to the 1970s the Burwells maintained a large dairy farm at Waverly. *(33–28) VLR: 06/19/96; NRHP: 11/07/96.*

WOODS-MEADE HOUSE (GREER HOUSE), *118 Maple Street, Rocky Mount.* One of the rare early landmarks of Rocky Mount, the Woods-Meade house is a vernacular dwelling with sophisticated overtones and a complex evolution. The front section was built ca. 1830 or earlier for Robert T. Woods, who served in both the Virginia House of Delegates and Virginia senate. It has distinctive masonry details including a molded-brick cornice, gauged-brick jack arches, and curious half-round brick pilasters and rounded-brick porch supports. The latter apparently were part of a one-bay portico that was later altered. Morrison Meade acquired the house in 1834 and added a frame section on the rear wall, connecting the house to a kitchen outbuilding. The two-story addition, with side porches, made a small house into a relatively commodious one. *(157–03) VLR: 10/20/81; NRHP: 07/08/82.*

FREDERICK COUNTY

Formed from Orange County in 1738, with parts of Augusta added later, this northernmost Shenandoah Valley county was named in honor of Frederick Louis, Prince of Wales, eldest son of King George II. Its county seat is Winchester.

BELLE GROVE AND CEDAR CREEK BATTLEFIELD, *Middletown.* A landmark of Federal architecture, Belle Grove was erected in 1794–97 for Maj. Isaac Hite, Jr., a Revolutionary War officer. Hite was married to Nelly Conway Madison Hite, sister of James Madison. During the planning of the house, James Madison wrote Thomas Jefferson requesting assistance. Though Jefferson suggested refinements, the house is more in the spirit of the Adam-inspired Federal architecture than Jefferson's Classical Revivalism. This is particularly evident in the interior woodwork, which has Adam-style details copied from *Pain's British Palladio* (1786). Civil War activity here culminated in the battle of Cedar Creek on October 19, 1864, when Gen. Philip Sheridan's counterattack effectively ended the Valley campaign in favor of the North. The house served as Union headquarters. A century later, Francis Welles Hunnewell bequeathed the property to the National Trust for Historic Preservation. *(34–02) VLR: 11/05/68; NHL: 08/11/69; BHR EASEMENT (CEDAR CREEK BATTLEFIELD).*

WILLA CATHER BIRTHPLACE, *Gore.* American novelist and short-story writer Willa Cather (1873–1947) was born in this plain weatherboarded log house in the tiny community of Gore west of Winchester. The next year the infant Willa was taken by her parents to live at Willow Shade nearby. In 1883 the family moved to Red Cloud, Neb., where she spent her formative years. In her writings Cather concentrated on the pioneer traditions of the Nebraska prairie and the deserts of the Southwest, emphasizing the themes of courage, struggle, and respect for the land. She received the Pulitzer Prize for her novel *One of Ours* (1922). Cather's Virginia birthplace was built in the early 19th century by her great-grandfather Jacob Seibert. It was enlarged and remodeled ca. 1850. The house was owned and occupied by her maternal grandmother, Rachel E. Boak, when her parents were married here in 1872. *(34–161) VLR: 09/21/76; NRHP: 11/16/78.*

FREDERICK COUNTY POOR FARM, *Round Hill vicinity.*
The concept of the county poorhouse developed in the late
18th century from popular assumptions about the nature of
poverty. As contrasted with the "undeserving poor," the "deserving poor" were those who could not work because of age,
physical disability, or mental condition, thus meriting public
assistance. Frederick County built its first structure to serve the
"deserving poor" in Winchester in 1793–94. By 1819 it was
thought that better care could be provided in a rural, more
self-sufficient setting. A farm was therefore purchased, and the
present complex was developed here. With its central block and
flanking residential wings, the farm's buildings are the oldest
and most intact of such public charity complexes in the state.
The facility closed in 1947. The property is now in private ownership with the buildings being used for storage. *(34–99) VLR:*
06/16/93; NRHP: 08/12/93.

HOPEWELL FRIENDS MEETING HOUSE, *Clearbrook*
vicinity. By the second quarter of the 18th century, large numbers of Pennsylvania Quakers began moving into unsettled
lands of northern Virginia and the Shenandoah Valley and
founding new communities. The Hopewell Meeting of the Religious Society of Friends was established in Frederick County
in 1734, and in 1759 the congregation replaced its first meetinghouse with the earliest portion of the present building, erected
by Thomas McClun. The limestone structure was doubled in
size in 1788–94. A schism developed within the society in 1827,
and a partition was erected through the interior, as it was in
many meetings, so that each group could have its own meeting
place. The factions reunited in 1910, and the partition was removed. Echoing the quiet sobriety of the Quakers, the plain
building, one of the oldest houses of worship west of the Blue
Ridge Mountains, remains in regular use. *(34–06) VLR: 11/15/77;*
NRHP: 03/28/80.

MONTE VISTA, *Middletown vicinity.* An eye-catcher for an
ever-constant stream of motorists on both Interstate Highway
81 and U.S. Route 11, this ambitious residence and its capacious
barn are a celebration of late Victorian architectural verve. The
house was begun in 1883 for Charles W. Heater, a Frederick
County farmer and businessman. Heater added the Monte Vista
property to the original Heater farm, Cedar Grove, scene of the
Civil War battle of Cedar Creek. With its bulk counterbalanced
by its lively roofline, including a striking dormered tower,
Heater's mansion exhibits the bravado and eclecticism that are
hallmarks of the period. The character of the facade was
changed ca. 1942 when a two-story Tuscan portico replaced the
original porch. The large bank barn, also built in 1883, is made
conspicuous by its tall cupola. *(34–14) VLR: 04/21/87; NRHP: 11/16/87.*

NEWTOWN-STEPHENSBURG
HISTORIC DISTRICT
(STEPHENS CITY). Chartered
in 1758, what is today Stephens City
is the second-oldest town in Frederick County. Originally called
Stephensburg, it was named Newtown-Stephensburg in 1879 and renamed Stephens City in 1887. The
town grew up along a major crossroads on the Valley Pike and became known for its wagon-making
trade. The nationally known Newtown wagon was manufactured
here. The community's buildings
are chronologically and stylistically
diversified: 18th-century log structures stand among buildings echo-

ing 19th-century revival styles. Typical of small Valley towns,
most dwellings here are simple vernacular types that set off a
scattering of more high-style works. The historic character is
reinforced by a lack of significant construction over the past
sixty years. During the Civil War constant troop movements
caused the town to change hands many times, six times in one
day alone, but with minimal destruction. *(304–01) VLR: 12/11/91;*
NRHP: 08/18/92.

ROSE HILL FARM, *Opequon vicinity.* In contrast to today's restless demographics, Rose Hill Farm is an attestation of family continuity. Samuel Glass, an Irish native, settled in the Opequon Creek area in 1735. Part of his extensive holdings, including the Rose Hill property, was inherited in 1797 by his grandson, Samuel. The log house that Samuel Glass II occupied here before gaining title is now the rear wing of the present house. In 1816 the farm's ownership passed to Glass's son Thomas, who built the front section by 1819. The boxy appearance of the structure, emphasized by a shallow roof and row of attic windows, is a regional architectural idiom. Fighting took place around the house during the 1862 battle of Kernstown. In 1952 the property was inherited by Julian Wood Glass, Jr., descendant of the first Samuel Glass. Now owned by the Glass–Glen Burnie Foundation, Rose Hill Farm is currently undergoing restoration. *(34–115) VLR: 06/19/96; NRHP: 02/21/97.*

ST. THOMAS'S CHAPEL, *Middletown.* A starkness and exaggerated verticality lend this village church visual presence. The rural Gothic Revival style is given full play here in the three arches of the facade and the tall pointed windows with their Y-tracery. St. Thomas's was built ca. 1835 to serve the Episcopal congregation of Middletown and was completed by 1837 when Bishop Meade officiated at a confirmation here. Episcopalians, both urban and rural, traditionally have been attentive to the architectural quality of their churches; hence it is not surprising that St. Thomas's is an effective though provincial interpretation of the Gothic style. The church was a Confederate hospital during the Civil War, and Northern troops used it as a stable. The building was closed in 1930, and in 1966 it was given over to the town of Middletown. It has since been restored as an interdenominational chapel. *(260–01) VLR: 01/16/73; NRHP: 04/11/73.*

SPRINGDALE, *Bartonville.* Springdale was originally the home of Jost Hite, the earliest European settler in the lower Shenandoah Valley. The ruins of what was probably Hite's home and tavern, built in the 1730s next to the Indian trail that became the Valley Turnpike, still stand in the yard. The present dwelling, a large stone house in the German vernacular tradition, was built in 1753 by mason Simon Taylor for Hite's son John. John Hite held numerous public positions including trustee for the town of Winchester. He was a friend of George Washington, who is recorded to have been a visitor at Springdale. Although the original limestone walls survive, the interior and exterior trim, including the portico and dormers, date from mid-19th- and early 20th-century remodelings. The house remains a prominent landmark along present-day U.S. Route 11. *(34–127) VLR: 04/21/81; NRHP: 07/08/82.*

SPRINGDALE MILL COMPLEX, *Bartonville.* Springdale Mill was erected ca. 1788 by David Brown and replaced an earlier mill established by Jost Hite. A well-preserved example of an early industrial form once common in the region, the structure is distinguished by its massive limestone walls with a corner chimney, a characteristic feature of early mill design. The mill long served the settlement of Bartonville and the surrounding rural community as a merchant mill where grain was bought and sold as well as ground. Although currently not in operation, the mill's machinery, most of which dates from the late 19th century, is intact. Included in the complex is an early stone dwelling and a log and frame house, both of which probably housed early millers. *(34–128) VLR: 03/17/81; NRHP: 07/08/82.*

SUNRISE, *Gore vicinity.* The very picture of a historic homestead, Sunrise maintains a quiet setting in the scenic landscape of western Frederick County. It is situated on Hollow Road, an unpaved 18th-century road trace. The original log portion was built after Robert Muse purchased the property in 1818. A ca. 1850 log extension gave the house a somewhat irregular five-bay facade. The exterior was weatherboarded, and the two-level porch was added at the same time. Although of simple outline, the addition was fitted with country Greek Revival trim including curious scalloped lintels over interior openings and an Asher Benjamin–style doorway. The house was further enlarged with a rear wing in 1914. The property remained in the Muse family until 1963. Its old-fashioned character has been carefully maintained by the current owners. Two late 19th-century barns and a meat house remain on the property. *(34–486) VLR: 10/19/94; NRHP: 02/08/95.*

WILLOW SHADE, *Gore vicinity.* Willow Shade was the childhood home of the renowned American author Willa Cather. The gaunt Greek Revival house was built ca. 1853 for Cather's grandfather William Cather and his wife, Emily Ann Caroline Smith Cather, both descendants of early Frederick County settlers. After Willa Cather's birth nearby in 1873, her Cather grandparents moved to Nebraska and turned Willow Shade over to her parents. There she lived until age nine when she and her parents also moved to Nebraska. In her last novel, *Sapphira and the Slave Girl* (1940), Cather immortalized Willow Shade when she wrote: "The slats of the green window shutters rattled, the limp cordage of the great willow trees in the yard was whipped and tossed furiously by the wind. I had been put in my mother's bed so that I could watch the turnpike, then a macadam road with a blue limestone facing." *(34–162) VLR: 12/12/89; NRHP: 12/18/90.*

CITY OF FREDERICKSBURG

At the falls of the Rappahannock River, this river port between Spotsylvania and Stafford counties was named for Frederick Louis, Prince of Wales, eldest son of King George II. Fredericksburg was established in 1728 and was incorporated as a town in 1782. It became a city in 1879.

BROMPTON, *Sunken Road and Hanover Street.* First known as the Marye house for John Lawrence Marye, who purchased the property in 1824, Brompton, as it was later named, figured prominently in both battles of Fredericksburg. The original core, built ca. 1838, was enlarged and remodeled during Marye's long tenure into an imposing Roman Revival dwelling with a flat-roofed Ionic portico. The steep hill known as Marye's Heights, which the house dominates, was the twice the scene of fierce combat. On December 13, 1862, Confederates repulsed heavy Union assaults with the latter suffering many casualties along the Sunken Road below the heights. The second battle of Fredericksburg was fought almost entirely on Marye's Heights. On May 3, 1863, Union general John Sedgwick seized the heights from Gen. Jubal Early. The pedimented roof was added during the repair of war damage. Brompton is now the official residence of the president of Mary Washington College. *(111–08) VLR: 05/15/79; NRHP: 07/24/79.*

THE CHIMNEYS, *623 Caroline Street.* Taking its name from its massive exterior chimneys, this conspicuously located Georgian town house, with its broad hipped roof and five-bay facade, is one of Fredericksburg's most prominent colonial dwellings. Significant among its architectural features is the unusually elaborate woodwork in the southwest parlor, which employs carved swags and garlands on the chimneypiece and latticework friezes on the window and door frames, all rare examples of colonial architectural woodcarving. The house was built ca. 1771 for John Glassell, a Scottish merchant who returned to his native land after the outbreak of the Revolution. The property served as the headquarters of the Historic Fredericksburg Foundation during the 1970s. It has since been sold and restored for use as a restaurant. *(111–15) VLR: 12/17/74; NRHP: 04/03/75; BHR EASEMENT.*

THE DOGGETT HOUSE, *303 Amelia Street.* One of Fredericksburg's most substantial and well-appointed Federal town houses, the Doggett house was built ca. 1817 for attorney Carter Littlepage Stevenson. Stevenson served for thirty-five years as Fredericksburg's Commonwealth's attorney, was president of the Farmers' Bank of Virginia, and became a delegate to the General Assembly. Stevenson sold the house in 1827 to druggist John B. Hall whose family remained here over sixty years. Dr. A. C. Doggett purchased the property in 1888. In addition to its fine interior, the house preserves its service appendages, including a kitchen–servants' quarters outbuilding. Also on the property is a rare early 19th-century office, a quaint building with a brick-pier portico situated directly on the street corner. These structures offer a glimpse into the management of prosperous urban dwelling in the early 19th century. *(111–87) VLR: 12/09/92.*

FALL HILL, *Fall Hill Avenue.* This hilltop plantation next to the falls of the Rappahannock River originally was included in the 8,000 acres of Spotsylvania County patented by Francis Thornton I ca. 1720. Francis Thornton III (1711–1749) maintained a summer residence at Fall Hill. The present house probably was built for Francis Thornton V (1760–1835) around the time of his marriage to Sally Innes in 1790. Francis Thornton V served as Spotsylvania County justice of the peace. The house was extensively remodeled in the 1840s by Francis Thornton V's granddaughter and her husband, John Roberts Taylor, who closed up several windows and replaced the woodwork. During the Fredericksburg campaign Gen. Robert E. Lee's men built a breastworks at the foot of the hill to guard the river crossing. The property, with its ancient trees, scattering of outbuildings, and panoramic view of downtown Fredericksburg, is owned by Thornton descendants. *(111–149) VLR: 04/17/73; NRHP: 06/18/73; BHR EASEMENT.*

FEDERAL HILL, *500 Hanover Street.* Federal Hill is an architecturally formal late 18th-century dwelling which illustrates the sophistication that could be achieved with wood-frame construction. It was built ca. 1795 for Robert Brooke, governor of Virginia 1794–96. Brooke called the property Federal Hill because of his strong support of the Federalist party. Consistent with the exterior is a spacious and elegant interior. The drawing room, occupying the entire north end of the first floor, features Doric pilasters, arched window alcoves, and a paneled chimneypiece with a scrolled pediment. The chimneypiece in the dining room opposite is ornamented with foliated consoles and unusual intertwining rope carving. The windows have friezes decorated with lattice carving. A rare early summerhouse with louvered sides and ogee-domed roof stands in the garden. *(111–30) VLR: 11/19/74; NRHP: 03/26/75.*

FREDERICKSBURG AND SPOTSYLVANIA NATIONAL MILITARY PARK *(also in Spotsylvania, Caroline, Orange, and Stafford counties).* Gen. Robert E. Lee's Army of Northern Virginia achieved significant victories at Fredericksburg in 1862 and Chancellorsville in 1863 but

suffered an irreparable blow with the death of Lt. Gen. Thomas J. ("Stonewall") Jackson. In 1864 the armies returned to the Fredericksburg area and met at the sanguinary battles of the Wilderness and Spotsylvania Court House. Preserved by the National Park Service in a 6,100-acre network of battlefield sites are some thirty miles of earthworks, approximately forty monuments, and several buildings including Salem Church in Spotsylvania County and the colonial mansion Chatham in Stafford County. In Fredericksburg, the Park Service has preserved much of the property lining the Sunken Road (shown), scene of some of the fiercest fighting of the first and second battles of Fredericksburg. *(111–147) VLR: 01/16/73; NRHP: 10/15/66.*

FREDERICKSBURG GUN MANUFACTORY ARCHAEOLOGICAL SITE, *Dunmore and Gunnery streets.* The Fredericksburg Gun Manufactory was established by the Virginia Convention in 1777 for the purpose of repairing and manufacturing small arms for the Revolution. The gun manufactory functioned in this strategic role until 1783, supplying arms to the regiments of numerous Virginia counties. The enterprise was run by Fielding Lewis and Charles Dick. Its stone magazine was ordered built with the same plan and dimensions as Williamsburg's powder magazine. Other structures here included a coal house, storage house, and mill-house. In 1783 the property became the site of the Fredericksburg Academy, which remained here until 1801. Located at the southern edge of the city's historic district, only fragments of foundations remain above ground today. The site, now owned by the city of Fredericksburg, should hold significant archaeological information on 18th-century American arms technology. *(111–145) VLR: 04/19/77; NRHP: 11/14/78.*

FREDERICKSBURG HISTORIC DISTRICT. Fredericksburg's historic district is a forty-block area including the original fifty-acre town site of 1728. The city began as a frontier port at the falls of the Rappahannock, serving settlers to the west. It grew as a trading center and county seat during the colonial period. Economic prosperity following the Revolution resulted in the over two hundred Federal buildings still standing. Laid out on a grid, the district comprises one of the South's outstanding historic townscapes, including fine examples of colonial, Federal, Victorian, and Colonial Revival architecture. Notable structures are the 18th-century Hugh Mercer Apothecary Shop, the 1849 Norman-style St. George's Episcopal Church, and the 1851 Gothic Revival courthouse by James Renwick (shown). Fierce fighting centered on Fredericksburg during the Civil War, but the downtown was spared extensive damage. The rehabilitation activity of recent decades has enhanced the district's historic character. *(111–132) VLR: 03/02/71; NRHP: 09/22/71.*

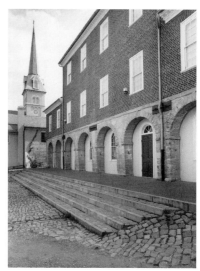

FREDERICKSBURG TOWN HALL AND MARKET SQUARE, *907 Princess Anne Street.* Fredericksburg's former town hall and connecting square is a rare Federal-period public complex. Completed in 1816, the town hall is a plain, almost domestic-appearing building. The rear elevation, set on a stone arcade, dominates the market square, a sloping space on the interior of the block. The complex follows the precedent of English town halls, which traditionally had meeting spaces above an arcaded market area. Here farmers, craftsmen, and other vendors sold their goods in the formerly open arcades of the lower level. Political leaders and social elite held public meetings, assemblies, and dances above. Businessmen rented the wings for office space. Although the market ceased with the development of produce stores, the town hall continued to house the local government until 1982. In 1988 the building was converted to a local history museum. *(111–57); VLR: 10/20/93; NRHP: 07/22/94.*

KENMORE, *1201 Washington Avenue.* One of America's most noted works of Georgian architecture, Kenmore was completed by 1776 for Fielding Lewis and his wife, Betty Washington Lewis, only sister of George Washington. Lewis was a merchant and planter as well as a Revolutionary patriot. He served in the House of Burgesses, financed the Fredericksburg Gun Manufactory, and helped organize local resistance by merchants and militia. The Lewises' mansion, with its plain but formal exterior, boasts an exceptionally elaborate interior with the finest 18th-century plasterwork ceilings and chimneypieces in the country. The dining room, one of America's most beautiful historic spaces, features an overmantel containing a plaster bas-relief with scenes from Aesop's fables. Threatened by development in 1922, the property was purchased by the Kenmore Association, which exhibits the house as a museum. On the grounds are restored gardens as well as the archaeological sites of several original outbuildings. *(111–47) VLR: 11/05/68; NRHP: 06/04/69; NHL: 04/15/70.*

JAMES MONROE LAW OFFICE (JAMES MONROE MUSEUM AND MEMORIAL LIBRARY), *908 Charles Street.* James Monroe moved to Fredericksburg in 1786 and began his law practice at this location, continuing a career in public service that would carry him on to be a U.S. senator; American minister to France, England, and Spain; governor of Virginia; secretary of state; and fifth president of the United States. The whole of Monroe's career, including his Fredericksburg practice, is memorialized in this Charles Street building, erected in several stages, ca. 1815, ca. 1836, and ca. 1850. The building stands on the site of Monroe's actual office and is itself a well-preserved example of a Federal-period office structure. The museum, owned by the Commonwealth and administered by Mary Washington College, exhibits many possessions of Monroe and his wife, Elizabeth Kortright Monroe. *(111–66) VLR: 09/09/69; NHL: 11/13/66.*

NATIONAL BANK OF FREDERICKSBURG (FARMERS' BANK OF VIRGINIA), *900 Princess Anne Street.* Erected in 1819–20 by Robert and George Ellis as the Farmers' Bank of Virginia, this Federal commercial building has served continuously as a bank except for intervals during the Civil War. The residential part, originally occupied by the bank's cashier, was the boyhood home of the 19th-century naval captain William Lewis Herndon. During the Union occupation of Fredericksburg, the bank was used as headquarters by the Union command. President Lincoln addressed troops and citizens from its steps on April 22, 1862. The Farmers' Bank failed at the end of the war, and the building became the home of the National Bank of Fredericksburg, chartered in 1865. The exterior is distinguished by its pedimented temple form and fine detailing, including stone lintels and keystones, Flemish bond brickwork, and handsome entrance. Some early trim remains within. *(111–21) VLR: 01/18/83; NRHP: 08/11/83.*

PRESBYTERIAN CHURCH OF FREDERICKSBURG, *Princess Anne and George streets.* The Presbyterian Church of Fredericksburg ranks with the Commonwealth's finest surviving examples of Jeffersonian Roman Revival works. Built in 1833, the building is dominated by a Tuscan portico *in muris* and a handsomely detailed belfry with an entablature in the Doric order of the Baths of Diocletian. Although its architect is unknown, the striking similarity of the design to the works of master builders William B. Phillips and Malcolm F. Crawford, two of the most able practitioners of Jefferson's style, strongly favors an attribution. The building survives little changed from its original appearance, even preserving many early interior features. During the Civil War the church served as a hospital for both Union and Confederate soldiers, and it was here that Clara Barton came to nurse the Union wounded after the battle of Fredericksburg in 1862. *(111–34) VLR: 05/17/83; NRHP: 03/01/84.*

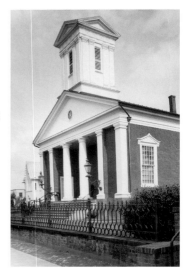

RISING SUN TAVERN, *1304 Caroline Street.* This venerable structure was built in the 1760s for Charles Washington, younger brother of George Washington, and served as his residence while he lived in Fredericksburg. In 1792 John Frazer converted the house into a tavern known as the Golden Eagle. The building was maintained for that purpose until 1823. Acquired by the Association for the Preservation of Virginia Antiquities in 1907, the building has been renovated as an 18th-century hostelry museum. Archaeological investigation in the 1970s revealed that the facade was shaded by a long porch during the time it was a tavern, and the missing feature was reconstructed. The name Rising Sun comes from an early Fredericksburg tavern sign which mistakenly was thought to have been made for this building. *(111–88) VLR: 09/09/69; NRHP: 10/15/66; NHL: 01/29/64.*

THE SENTRY BOX, *133 Caroline Street.* An elegant specimen of late Georgian architecture highlighted by a finely detailed porch, The Sentry Box was built in 1786 for Gen. George Weedon, a distinguished Revolutionary officer. During the Yorktown campaign Weedon and his Virginia troops held Lord Cornwallis in check at Gloucester Point. Later active in local government, Weedon served as mayor of Fredericksburg. He named his home "The Sentry Box" out of nostalgia for his military career. He and his wife, a sister-in-law of Gen. Hugh Mercer, invited Mercer's family to live at The Sentry Box. They left the property to the Mercers, and Confederate general Hugh Weedon Mercer was born here. The grounds later were the site of considerable Civil War activity. Despite interior modifications, the original character of the house has been maintained. In the yard is an 18th-century icehouse. *(111–95) VLR: 04/17/90; NRHP: 02/26/92.*

MARY WASHINGTON HOUSE, *1200 Charles Street.* George Washington bought this property in 1772 for his mother, Mary Ball Washington, so that she could be near her daughter Betty Lewis and her son Charles. She lived here until her death in 1789. It was at this house in March 1789 that president-elect Washington stopped to receive his mother's blessing before traveling to New York for his inauguration. It was their last farewell. The present structure consists of the building purchased by Washington and an addition he had built, as well as 19th-century additions. It was acquired by the Association for the Preservation of Virginia Antiquities in 1890 to prevent it from being taken to the Chicago World's Columbian Exposition. It was subsequently restored and furnished with period furniture, including several of Mary Washington's possessions. The garden was restored in 1968 by the Garden Club of Virginia. *(111–110) VLR: 03/18/75; NRHP: 06/05/75.*

GILES COUNTY

Named for William Branch Giles, U.S. senator from Virginia at the time of its formation in 1806, this mountainous county was made up of sections of Montgomery, Monroe (now in West Virginia), and Tazewell counties. Its county seat is Pearisburg.

GILES COUNTY COURTHOUSE, *Pearisburg.* The earliest and most prominent landmark of Pearisburg, this Federal-style building is the third courthouse to stand on the town's central public square since the county was established in 1806. The two-story central block with its delicately ornamented octagonal cupola was constructed in 1836 by Thomas Mercer and was inspired by the several courthouses built by James Toncray, particularly the 1833 Montgomery County Courthouse in Christiansburg, since demolished. In May 1862 the courthouse square became the scene of an encounter between Union and Confederate troops that is graphically recorded in the diary of Lt. Col. Rutherford B. Hayes, the commanding Union officer present and later 19th president of the United States. The courthouse has undergone various alterations; the portico was added in 1900. *(279–03) VLR: 07/20/82; NRHP: 09/09/82.*

ANDREW JOHNSTON HOUSE, *208 North Main Street, Pearisburg.* With its five-bay facade, Flemish bond brickwork, and molded-brick cornice, the Andrew Johnston house is a classic example of western Virginia Federal vernacular architecture. It was built in 1829 as the residence of Andrew Johnston who, with his brother David, was a founding settler of Giles County. In 1806 these sons of Scottish immigrants contracted to lay out the town lots of Pearisburg, the county seat. Andrew Johnston's son, Harvey G. Johnston, inherited the property upon the death of his mother in 1853. The county's principal physician, Dr. Johnston ran his practice from a small wooden building on the grounds. The practice was continued by his son, Harvey G. Johnston, Jr. In 1995 the property was deeded to the Giles County Historical Society to serve as a museum honoring the Johnston family and their contributions to the county's history. *(279–01) VLR: 12/09/92; NRHP: 02/11/93.*

PEARISBURG HISTORIC DISTRICT. The county seat of Giles County was laid out in 1806 on land donated by Col. George Pearis, an early settler. The plan established a large public square for county buildings, situated at the northeast corner of Main Street and Wenonah Avenue. A standard grid filled in the rest of the area. The district encompasses nineteen buildings located either on or in the immediate vicinity of the square. The square is dominated by the 1836 courthouse, the town's principal landmark. Other resources include the Western Hotel, built ca. 1829 as the courthouse tavern and later modified. The 1910 Christ Episcopal Church, rebuilt in the 1920s after a fire, is a striking example of the Arts and Crafts influence. The remaining buildings are a cohesive mix of late 19th- and early 20th-century commercial structures. An exception is the Art Deco facade of the 1940 Pearis Theater. *(279–12) VLR: 12/11/91; NRHP: 01/30/92.*

NEWPORT HISTORIC DISTRICT. Tucked in the narrow valley of Greenbriar Branch, at the base of Gap Mountain, the village of Newport began in the 1830s as a transportation crossroads and regional commercial center along the Cumberland Gap Turnpike. Development focused around a small industrial center consisting of a tanyard, oil mill, gristmill, and blacksmith shop. Newport also became an overnight stop for travelers along their way to area mineral springs. The establishment of the Newport Woolen Mill and the nearby Sinking Creek Furnace in the 1870s led to much new construction. Today the village consists of approximately sixty-six structures of which fifty-three are significant to its historic character. Most of the buildings are frame, freestanding dwellings or stores with decorative wooden trim. Many structures were built after 1902, when a fire destroyed most of the buildings in the heart of the community. *(35–151) VLR: 12/08/93; NRHP: 02/25/94.*

GLOUCESTER COUNTY

Between the York and the Piankatank rivers, this Tidewater county was named either for the English shire or for Henry, duke of Gloucester, third son of King Charles I. It was formed from York County in 1651. The county seat is Gloucester.

ABINGDON CHURCH, *White Marsh vicinity.* Abingdon Parish was formed in 1655 to minister to the residents of lower Gloucester County. The present church, the parish's second, was built ca. 1755 and is one of Virginia's most refined colonial structures. Making use of a cruciform plan, one reserved for more important churches, the building is set off by its superb brickwork, especially the molded-brick doorways. Although its interior was damaged by Federal troops during the Civil War and was remodeled during the course of repairs, much of the fabric is original, including the galleries, sections of wainscoting, window sash, portions of the altarpiece, and part of the pulpit. The church became inactive in the early 1800s as the result of the disestablishment. Episcopalians reoccupied the building in 1826 and have had continued services to the present. A restoration of the interior to its colonial appearance was accomplished in the 1980s. *(36–01) VLR: 07/07/70; NRHP: 09/15/70.*

ABINGDON GLEBE HOUSE, *White Marsh vicinity.* This architecturally engaging dwelling belongs to Virginia's collection of colonial glebe houses, structures built to serve their parishes either as rental property or as rectories. The house originally served Abingdon Parish, the second church of which is a short distance away, and was standing as early as 1724 when it was mentioned in a report by the rector, Thomas Hughes, to the bishop of London. Built of Flemish bond with glazed headers, the T-shaped house with its original low wings illustrates the transition from the irregular vernacular structures of the 17th century to the symmetrical houses of the Georgian period. The hipped roofs of the wings are among Virginia's earliest uses of that roof form. The house and its glebe lands were confiscated from the parish and sold during the disestablishment. The property has been in private ownership ever since. *(36–02) VLR: 07/07/70; NRHP: 09/15/70.*

AIRVILLE, *Zanoni vicinity.* Airville is endowed with particular architectural quality. The original section is a traditional gambrel-roof dwelling built perhaps as early as 1747 by the Dixon family. In 1827 the property was bought by Thomas Smith, a highly successful merchant and General Assembly delegate who had business interests extending to New York, London, and the West Indies. Smith began building the main two-story section in 1836. Completed in 1840, four months before his death, the result is a finely crafted specimen of late Federal architecture. Smith's brother, who put Airville up for sale, advertised it as a "Dwelling house of ample dimensions, finished in the neatest manner, and of the very best materials . . . fitted up with handsome Marble Mantles, and a circular Staircase of Mahogany." The estate has an outstanding complex of early outbuildings, including an icehouse and a dairy, both with conical roofs. *(36–03) VLR: 10/16/90; NRHP: 12/06/90.*

BURGH WESTRA, *Ware Neck.* An illustration in *Cottage Residences* (1842), the influential architectural pattern book by architectural theorist Andrew Jackson Downing, provided the inspiration for this romantic Tudor-style cottage. The dwelling was completed in 1851 for Dr. Philip Alexander Taliaferro, who owned a copy of Downing's book. Design III in *Cottage Residences,* the plate after which the house was modeled, was recommended by Downing for a site on a body of water. Taliaferro's house conforms to the recommendation; Burgh Westra is positioned on the west bank of Gloucester's North River. Its name is Scottish for "village of the west." The property has remained in the ownership of the builder's family to the present. The house was gutted by fire in 1983, but the walls survived, and the interior has been reconstructed. Dr. Taliaferro's personal copy of *Cottage Residences* was lost in the fire. *(36–10) VLR: 04/20/76; NRHP: 10/08/76.*

FAIRFIELD ARCHAEOLOGICAL SITE, *White Marsh vicinity.* Fairfield was an unusually large and elaborate 17th-century mansion, probably built by Lewis Burwell ca. 1692. It stood here for two centuries until it was destroyed by fire in 1897. Its external appearance, distinguished by diagonally set Jacobean chimney stacks, is well known through several early photographs, including the ca. 1892 one shown here. Archaeological investigation of the site could reveal much information about the plan, sequence of development, and architectural details of one of Virginia's oldest architecturally distinguished plantation houses. Near the house site are the sites of several outbuildings as well as what may be an earlier 17th-century residence. *(36–61) VLR: 02/20/73; NRHP: 07/16/73.*

GLOUCESTER COUNTY COURTHOUSE SQUARE HISTORIC DISTRICT, *Gloucester.* Set off by its ca. 1766 courthouse, this cluster of public buildings and offices is a classic example of a Tidewater county-seat complex. The principal county buildings are within a grassy walled area. The courthouse, although having undergone later alterations including the substitution of the present ca. 1900 portico for an earlier porch, remains among the more sophisticated of Virginia's colonial court structures. Other buildings on the square are the early 19th-century clerk's office and debtors' prison and the late 19th-century sheriff's office. Across the road stands the ca. 1770 former Botetourt Hotel, a rare example of a large colonial hostelry. It was restored in the early 1970s for county offices. On the north and south sides of the square are groupings of simple mid-19th- and early 20th-century frame law offices. *(36–21) VLR: 02/20/73; NRHP: 10/03/73.*

GLOUCESTER POINT ARCHAEOLOGICAL DISTRICT, *Gloucester Point.*

Occupying a triangular promontory extending southward into the York River, this archaeologically rich area contains a concentration of well-preserved sites spanning 300 years of Virginia history. From the beginning of the 17th century until the end of the Civil War, Gloucester Point was the focal point of concurrent commercial, domestic, and military activity. Evidence for three forts has been uncovered: a 1667 palisaded fort for protection from the Dutch, a Revolutionary War gun battery constructed by Lord Cornwallis's forces in 1781, and a Civil War fort occupied at separate times in 1862 by Union and Confederate forces. Associated with the Cornwallis fortification are the sites of a British military hospital and graveyard. Archaeologists have linked the remains of at least five domestic buildings to the Gloucester Town plat of 1707. Further research of sealed layers within the district could yield important data on colonial history. *(36–19) VLR: 04/21/87; NRHP: 06/10/85.*

GLOUCESTER WOMAN'S CLUB, *Gloucester.*

This venerable landmark at the junction of two colonial roads began in the 18th century as a one-room, side-passage structure, a common early form. Significant original interior features include its closed-string stair, wide-muntin sashes, and deep molded cornices. The building received its porches and other additions in the early 19th century. A local tradition holds that the building initially served as an ordinary. The organization of the interior spaces and certain documentary evidence point instead to the likelihood that it served as a mercantile establishment. Throughout much of the 19th century, the property was known as The Hill or Edge Hill. The building was occupied by a dressmaker and the Gloucester Agricultural Society before its purchase in 1923 by the Gloucester Woman's Club. Sympathetically maintained, it continues to serve as the club's headquarters. *(36–31) VLR: 11/20/73; NRHP: 01/24/74; BHR EASEMENT.*

HOLLY KNOLL, *Capahosic.*

Holly Knoll was the retirement home of Robert Russa Moton (1867–1940). The son of emancipated slaves, Moton rose to the position of director of military programs at his alma mater, Hampton Institute. In 1915 he succeeded Booker T. Washington as principal of the Tuskegee Institute. He served as an adviser to five U.S. presidents and also sponsored research leading to the establishment of federal centers for agricultural development and the prevention of communicable diseases. He was the keynote speaker at the dedication of the Lincoln Memorial in 1922 and wrote two internationally published books, *Finding a Way Out* and *What the Negro Thinks.* Built in 1935, his porticoed Georgian Revival house on the banks of the York River later became a site for important conferences on civil rights, education, and international relations. It is now the centerpiece of the privately owned Moton Conference Center. *(36–134) VLR: 03/16/82; NHL: 12/21/81.*

KEMPSVILLE, *Glenns vicinity.*

This colonial manor house takes its name from the Kemp family. Its construction date is uncertain, but the original portion, long the home of the Broaddus family, was likely built in the mid–18th century or earlier. The location of the house near Dragon Swamp has led to a mistaken identification of the place as Dragon Ordinary, a building which actually stood a mile away. Characteristic of colonial vernacular architecture, the house combines sophisticated detailing with an asymmetrical facade. The walls are laid in Flemish bond, and the chimneys have T-shaped stacks. Inside is a Georgian stair and a paneled chimney wall. The clapboard roof preserved under the present roof is a rare surviving example of a once-common, albeit crude, roofing type. Rarer still is a fragment of 18th-century wallpaper lining the semi-dome of the parlor cupboard. *(36–15) VLR: 09/20/77; NRHP: 12/21/78.*

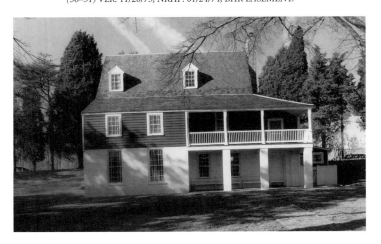

LANDS END, *Naxera vicinity.* At the tip of Robins Neck overlooking the Severn River, this brick dwelling was the home of sea captain John Sinclair, a privateer. At the outbreak of the Revolutionary War, Sinclair contributed both his ships and services to the war effort. With his small, maneuverable vessels, he was among the first to take British ships as prizes. A native of Hampton, Sinclair acquired his Gloucester County property in 1796 and built his house soon after, living here until his death in 1820. Unusually tall because of its above-grade basement (necessitated by the marshy site), the structure is a model work of late 18th-century Tidewater architecture, making use of a gambrel roof, a form employed by many Gloucester County houses of the period. The house was restored in the 1970s by historian Claude O. Lanciano, Jr. *(36–28) VLR: 09/17/74; NRHP: 11/06/74.*

LITTLE ENGLAND, *Gloucester Point vicinity.* This symmetrical plantation house, in a commanding position at the mouth of Sara's Creek, is a sophisticated example of mid-18th-century Tidewater architecture. Typical of the colony's finest dwellings, the house is very plain on the exterior, relying on its regular fenestration, geometrical proportions, and fine brickwork for aesthetic effect. In contrast to the exterior, the interior has fully paneled walls and is highlighted by architectural chimneypieces and a Georgian stair railing, all showing colonial Virginia joinery at its best. The property was granted to John Perrin in 1651; the present house was built some 100 years later by his descendant, also named John Perrin. One of the frame wings is an 18th-century addition that originally was attached to the center of the land front and was moved to the north end in the 1930s when the house was restored. *(36–30) VLR: 10/06/70; NRHP: 12/18/70.*

LOWLAND COTTAGE, *Ware Neck.* Lowland Cottage stands on land included in a 1642 grant to Thomas Curtis. Robert Bristow, Curtis's son-in-law, became the owner ca. 1665, making it his home plantation. Bristow, a prosperous merchant, maintained a wharf and storehouse here, both despoiled by Nathaniel Bacon's rebels in 1676. Bristow moved to England after the rebellion, and for the next 112 years his Virginia property was managed for him and his heirs by a series of resident agents. Circumstance suggests that the house was built by Bristow ca. 1670, but the actual date is not known. In its original form, with a center chimney, rear staircase, and exposed ceiling joists, the house was a late 17th-century vernacular type. The chimney was removed in the 19th century and replaced with end chimneys and a smaller center stack. The property likely contains archaeological sites associated with 17th-century Tidewater commerce. *(36–32) VLR: 04/06/71; NRHP: 09/22/71; BHR EASEMENT.*

WALTER REED BIRTHPLACE, *Belroi.* Dr. Walter Reed, conqueror of yellow fever, was born in 1851 in this cottage at Belroi, a county crossroad. The tiny house, a rural one-room vernacular cottage, is typical of a dwelling type once prevalent throughout Virginia's

Tidewater and Piedmont. The Reeds were using it as a temporary home until a parsonage could be completed for Reed's father, the local Methodist minister. In the aftermath of the Spanish-American War, Dr. Reed was appointed to head a commission to Cuba in 1900 to investigate the cause of yellow fever. His discovery that the disease was transmitted by mosquitoes led to its eradication. In 1926 Dr. Reed's birthplace was acquired and restored by the Medical Society of Virginia. The property was transferred to the Association for the Preservation of Virginia Antiquities in 1968. *(36–80) VLR: 04/17/73; NRHP: 09/20/73.*

ROARING SPRINGS, *Gloucester vicinity.* Named for a large spring on the property, Roaring Springs is an old Virginia homestead that has evolved through enlargements and remodelings by its various owners. The western end began as a colonial-period one-room cottage with side passage, possibly as an overseer's house for Church Hill, a Throckmorton family plantation. In 1794 it was sold to Francis Thornton, who expanded the house to its present form before 1802. Notable features of the enlargement are the stair with its beaded, diagonally set balusters and the parlor fireplace wall with its fine paneling and arched openings. The stair and paneling are very similar to woodwork in Toddsbury, also in Gloucester County, suggesting common craftsmen. The house was further remodeled in the mid–19th century when Greek Revival doors and window trim were installed. *(36–40) VLR: 08/15/72; NRHP: 09/22/72; BHR EASEMENT.*

ROSEWELL, *White Marsh vicinity.* The ruins of Rosewell conjure up an unforgettable romantic vision of colonial Virginia. Perhaps our largest colonial mansion, Rosewell was begun in 1726 for Mann Page I and likely was designed by an English-trained architect. The house remained uncompleted at Page's death but was finished by his son Mann Page II. It stood three stories high and was crowned by twin octagonal cupolas. Most of the interior woodwork was removed after the Page family sold Rosewell in 1838. Its richly carved staircases survived the alteration but were lost when the house burned in 1916. The walls, considered to be the country's finest colonial brickwork, gradually crumbled so that only portions remain. The surviving sections were stabilized after the Greaves family donated the ruins to the Gloucester Historical Society in Virginia in 1979. The property is now maintained and exhibited by the Rosewell Foundation. *(36–41) VLR: 11/05/68; NRHP: 10/01/69; BHR EASEMENT.*

SHELLY ARCHAEOLOGICAL DISTRICT, *White Marsh vicinity.* Named for the profusion of oyster shells that long appeared in the fields after plowing, Shelly holds exceptional archaeological value. The property of the Page family since the late 17th century, Shelly was acquired by John Mann in 1680 and was inherited by Mann's daughter Mary and her husband, Matthew Page, in 1694. Of particular interest is Shelly's variety of prehistoric sites, which illustrate the adaptation of the estuarine environment by Indians from the Late Archaic through the Late Woodland periods. The identification of an Indian site as that of the historic "Cantaunkack" settlement provides important evidence concerning the interaction of Indians with Europeans in the early 17th century. Various mid-17th- and 18th-century sites are preserved here as well. During the 18th century Shelly served as an ancillary farm for nearby Rosewell, the main Page family seat. *(36–73) VLR: 08/15/89; NRHP: 07/12/90; BHR EASEMENTS.*

TIMBERNECK, *White Marsh vicinity.* Timberneck, on a broad peninsula bordered by creeks flowing into the York River, was a Mann family homestead in the 17th and 18th centuries. The property was purchased ca. 1793 by John Catlett from John Page of Rosewell. The present house at Timberneck is a rambling post-Revolutionary farmhouse built for the Catletts. The two-part, two-story weatherboarded structure has well-preserved appointments including a fine stair and much original hardware. Although the later section was built in the mid–19th century, the details of the earlier portion, including the modillion cornice and pedimented porch, were repeated. With its rural setting, early smokehouse, rare 19th-century picket fence, old trees, and commanding view of the York, Timberneck is a substantially undisturbed Tidewater plantation in an area of Gloucester County undergoing suburban development. *(36–74) VLR: 06/19/79; NRHP: 09/10/79.*

TODDSBURY, *Nuttall vicinity.* This much-evolved old manor house is one of Virginia's most admired historic dwellings. The Todd family acquired the property in the late 17th century, but the original portion of the house, probably a simple side-passage structure, was most likely erected for Christopher Todd before his death in 1743. By 1782 Toddsbury was owned by Todd's grandson Philip Tabb, who added the library wing in 1784. Tabb also changed the gable roof to a gambrel roof and added the paneling and other woodwork. The paneling and stair were likely executed by the same craftsman who installed similar woodwork in nearby Roaring Springs. The house underwent an extensive renovation after 1946, when the kitchen wing was added and the porch modified. In 1957 Toddsbury became the home of Virginia preservationist Gay Montague Moore. Overlooking the North River, the house has noteworthy landscaped grounds and formal gardens. *(36–45) VLR: 09/09/69; NRHP: 11/12/69; BHR EASEMENT.*

WARE CHURCH, *Gloucester vicinity.* The large scale of this finely crafted colonial church indicates the importance of its parish, which served many of Gloucester County's leading families. The construction date is unknown; however, the building most likely was erected in the second quarter of the 18th century during the rectorship of the Rev. James Clack. Few of Virginia's colonial churches can boast more handsome or better-preserved brickwork, which here consists of Flemish bond with clear blue glazed headers and gauged brick arches. Ware is also Virginia's only rectangular colonial church served by three entrances, each with a gauged-work architectural surround. Portions of original woodwork remain on the interior. Although abandoned following the disestablishment, the church was later reoccupied by the Episcopalians and continues to serve as a parish church. *(36–48) VLR: 10/17/72; NRHP: 03/20/73.*

WARNER HALL, *Naxera vicinity.* On the Northwest Branch of the Severn River, Warner Hall is one of Gloucester County's most venerable plantations. It was established in 1642 and was the home of councillors Augustine Warner I, Augustine Warner II, John Lewis I, and John Lewis II, as well as George Washington's grandmother, Mildred Warner Washington. Washington's diary records visits here. Remaining from the colonial period are two brick dependencies probably built by John Lewis II in the mid–18th century along with the colonial mansion between them. The latter was destroyed by fire ca. 1845. On its site is a stately Colonial Revival mansion, completed ca. 1905. Among the outbuildings is a rare colonial stable of brick construction. Sites of various other buildings, possibly from the 17th century, likely remain. The walled Warner and Lewis family cemetery here is owned by the Association for the Preservation of Virginia Antiquities. *(36–49) VLR: 06/17/80; NRHP: 11/25/80.*

WHITE HALL, *Zanoni vicinity.* Built ca. 1836 by Dr. Samuel Powell Byrd, on property inherited by his wife, Catherine Corbin Fauntleroy Byrd, White Hall is the successor to an earlier brick dwelling, long the seat of the Willis family. The present house is an example of the pedimented temple-form dwelling type popular for more sophisticated early 19th-century Virginia houses. Along with such antecedents as the Finnie house in Williamsburg and the John Marshall house in Richmond, White Hall reflects the increasing interest in using classical forms to lend dignity and character. The house is a marked contrast to the unimaginative I-house, the more usual form of Virginia's rural houses, both large and small. Like many of Gloucester County's historic dwellings, White Hall is set near the water's edge, the Ware River in this case, and is approached by an impressive axial drive lined with cedars. *(36–51) VLR: 05/15/84; NRHP: 08/16/84.*

GOOCHLAND COUNTY

This pastoral Piedmont county bordering the James River was named in honor of William Gooch, lieutenant governor of Virginia from 1727 to 1749. It was formed from Henrico County in 1728. The county seat is Goochland Court House.

BOLLING HALL, *Rock Castle Road.* Organized education for the deaf in America had its origins around 1812 at this plantation when Col. William Bolling (1777–1845) brought the Scottish teacher John Braidwood here to educate his two deaf children. Braidwood was a grandson of Thomas Braidwood, a famous teacher of the deaf. Braidwood's success with the family children here led Bolling to establish the nation's first formal school for deaf children at Cobbs, an old family home in Chesterfield County. Bolling, one of the county's leading citizens, also served as colonel in charge of Goochland troops assisting in the defense of Norfolk in the War of 1812. Bolling Hall was built either for William Bolling or his father before 1799 on land that had been in the family since the early 18th century. It began as a side-passage dwelling and was later enlarged. The interior preserves original paneled fireplace walls. *(37–02) VLR: 04/06/71; NRHP: 12/27/72.*

BOLLING ISLAND, *Rock Castle vicinity.* In a rolling pastoral setting overlooking the James River, Bolling Island's plantation residence is a much-evolved structure whose earliest portion, a section of the east wing, dates from about 1771. The central brick core was built between 1800 and 1810. The entire house achieved its present appearance through a substantial remodeling carried out between 1820 and 1835 by Thomas Bolling, son of Col. William Bolling of Bolling Hall. Thomas Bolling gave the house the look of a Classical Revival villa by installing triple-hung sash and adding the portico with its Chinese lattice railing. An orangery was added to the east wing. The resulting composition has the Palladian-type tripartite scheme popularized in the region by Thomas Jefferson. Along with its three remaining dependencies, Bolling Island preserves the image of a prosperous early 19th-century family seat of the Virginia Piedmont. *(37–03) VLR: 08/15/89; NRHP: 12/27/90; BHR EASEMENT.*

ELK HILL, *George's Tavern vicinity.* The forthright Greek Revival mansion at Elk Hill illustrates a sophistication in its proportions, plan, and interior woodwork comparable to that of Richmond town houses of the period. The house was built between 1835 and 1839 for Randolph Harrison, Jr., on a portion of land formerly owned by Thomas Jefferson. Like the finer urban dwellings of Richmond, Elk Hill has a spacious rear veranda rather than the monumental front portico more typical of the Greek Revival houses of the Deep South. The principal rooms are enriched with elaborate doorways with Greek fret friezes. In 1943 Elk Hill became the country home of S. Buford Scott, a Richmond stockbroker. The house is used today for the administrative offices of Elk Hill Farm, a private, nonprofit school established in 1970 for at-risk young men. *(37–09) VLR: 10/17/78; NRHP: 02/02/79.*

HOWARD'S NECK, *Pemberton.* The centerpiece of this upper James River plantation is the refined Federal residence built ca. 1825 for Edward Cunningham, a leader in the Richmond milling industry. Cunningham's Richmond town house, the Cunningham-Archer house (demolished), was designed by Robert Mills, and Mills may have been involved at Howard's Neck. With its sophisticated proportions and rich interior appointments, including an elegant curved stair, the house shows the hand of a talented architect. Adding interest to the plantation is a full complement of outbuildings including an 18th-century "old dwelling," a kitchen, smokehouse, toolhouse, orangery, and several old farm buildings. Of special significance is a "street" of three slave houses, an exceptionally rare survival. The proximity of the quarters to the mansion suggests that they housed slaves serving the "home quarter," and not field hands. The plantation is named for Allen Howard, who acquired it in 1741. *(37–100) VLR: 11/16/71; NRHP: 02/23/72.*

GOOCHLAND COUNTY COURT SQUARE, *Goochland Court House.* Like several Piedmont county seats, the village of Goochland Court House is graced by a dignified Roman Revival courthouse designed and built by a master builder who worked under Thomas Jefferson during the construction of the University of Virginia. The Tuscan order temple-form building, completed in 1826, is the work of Dabney Cosby, Sr., who is credited with courthouses, churches, houses, and educational buildings throughout central Virginia, all displaying fine brickwork. Cosby was assisted here by Valentine Parrish who also worked on many other Piedmont structures. The courthouse is one of the few to retain its apsidal end, and the interior preserves its original gallery supported on Tuscan columns. Other early structures on the grassy square are the stone jail, brick clerk's office, Confederate monument, and brick wall, erected to keep out wandering cattle. *(37–136) VLR: 07/07/70; NRHP: 09/15/70.*

THE LOCKKEEPER'S HOUSE, *Cedar Point.* This relic of Virginia's canal era was built ca. 1836, following the opening of the Maidens-to-Lynchburg portion of the James River and Kanawha Canal. Serving lock no. 7, the stone and frame structure, with its typical center chimney,

was the scene of much activity during some thirty years of service. Horses were changed here, invoices checked, and tolls collected. The house also served as a tavern and offered simple accommodations for passengers and canalboat crews. A separate interior stair leads to the guest quarters. It passed out of service when the canal was replaced by the Richmond and Alleghany Railroad, now part of the CSX system. The tracks were laid on the towpath. It is believed to be one of only two lockkeeper's houses remaining in the state. *(37–105) VLR: 09/17/74; NRHP: 11/21/74; BHR EASEMENT.*

POWELL'S TAVERN, *River Road.* A landmark along historic River Road, Powell's Tavern has served as a tavern, stagecoach stop, and post office. Consisting of two distinct parts, the earliest section is a traditional two-story frame dwelling built around 1770 by William Powell, a Yorkshire native, who came here to manufacture bricks. His son, William, Jr., added shed wings when he acquired a license in 1808 to operate an ordinary. The front section was erected in 1820 to serve Powell's growing business. The tavern, now a private residence, was an important stopping place at the end of a first-day's journey west from Richmond. The two sections were situated so that coaches could pull in between them under a covered area. Lafayette stopped at Powell's Tavern in 1824 during his American tour. Joseph Martin wrote in his *Gazetteer of Virginia* (1836) that Powell's Tavern offered "good order and excellent accommodations." *(37–23) VLR: 04/18/72; NRHP: 04/02/73.*

ROCK CASTLE, *Rock Castle Road.* Named for a high rock bluff nearby, this James River property was patented in 1718 by Charles Fleming. Its small but sophisticated manor house was erected in the third decade of the 18th century for the patentee's son Tarleton Fleming. The house was raided in 1781 by the Fleming family's distant British cousin, Col. Banastre Tarleton, who was attempting to capture Governor Thomas Jefferson and members of the Virginia General Assembly then meeting in Albemarle County. Later encased in Victorian additions, the house was restored to its original appearance in 1935 when it was moved a few hundred feet to make way for a new house on its site. Even in its new location, Rock Castle is one of the purest examples of traditional 18th-century Virginia architecture in the Piedmont. The first floor is fully paneled and has a fine Georgian stair. *(37–54) VLR: 07/07/70; NRHP: 09/15/70; BHR EASEMENT.*

TUCKAHOE, *River Road, Richmond vicinity.* The contrasting qualities of elegance, domesticity, and remoteness, all characteristic of Virginia's colonial plantation life, are keenly felt at Tuckahoe. The plantation was one of several established by William Randolph of Turkey Island for his sons. His second son, Thomas, probably built the north wing by 1723. The south wing, connecting saloon, and carved woodwork were most likely added by Thomas's son, William Randolph, after his marriage in 1734 to Maria Judith Page of Rosewell. The woodwork is colonial artistry at its best. North of the house is a row of early outbuildings forming a rare plantation "street." In the tiny schoolhouse opposite, Thomas Jefferson attended classes when his parents, Peter and Jane Randolph Jefferson, were at Tuckahoe. Tuckahoe remained in the Randolph family until 1830. In 1935 it was acquired by Mr. and Mrs. N. Addison Baker, whose descendants live here today. *(37–33) VLR: 11/05/68; NRHP: 11/22/68; NHL: 08/11/69; BHR EASEMENT.*

WOODLAWN, *Oilville vicinity.* Elisha Leake, a Goochland miller, built this large brick dwelling in the last quarter of the 18th century after his service in the Revolutionary War. In 1806 the property was leased to John Trevillian, who, because of its convenient location on Three Chopt Road between Richmond and Charlottesville, opened a tavern here. Woodlawn was sold in 1834 to Thomas Taylor, who was later a Mexican War hero and is remembered for planting the American flag on Chapultepec Castle. The spacious old house is distinguished by its Flemish bond brickwork, stuccoed jack arches, delicate dentil cornices, and unaltered interior. Particularly interesting are the unusual two-story pent closets between the chimneys, one of which contains a secret stair. *(37–35) VLR: 07/06/71; NRHP: 12/16/71.*

GRAYSON COUNTY

Named for William Grayson, a Virginia delegate to the Continental Congress and one of Virginia's first two U.S. senators, this mountainous county was formed from Wythe County in 1792 with a portion of Patrick County added later. Its county seat is Independence.

OLD GRAYSON COUNTY COURTHOUSE, *Independence.* The center of the county seat of Independence is dominated by the architecturally fanciful former courthouse, an eclectic structure set off by its pointed corner towers and curvilinear gables. Its architect, Frank P. Milburn of Washington, D.C., designed some half-dozen courthouses in Southwest Virginia as well as courthouses in West Virginia and Kentucky. The building was completed in 1908 during the brief boom that allowed many mountain counties to erect impressive new court structures, works that served as local status symbols. The courthouse, one of several to have served the county, was threatened with demolition in the early 1980s when a new structure was built. A preservation effort resulted in its acquisition in 1983 by the 1908 Courthouse Foundation, which has undertaken a long-term rehabilitation. The building is now used for special functions. *(240–01) VLR: 06/21/77; NRHP: 01/26/78.*

OLD GRAYSON COUNTY COURTHOUSE AND CLERK'S OFFICE, *Old Town.* Grayson's county seat was established at this site in 1799. The second courthouse, a log structure, was built soon after. The diminutive clerk's office was erected in 1810. In 1833 the county commissioned James Toncray to built a brick courthouse. Toncray, a leading builder of courthouses in Southwest Virginia, constructed Wythe County's courthouse in 1818 (demolished) and Scott County's courthouse in 1829. He built courthouses for Montgomery and Floyd counties (both demolished) at the same time he was working on the Grayson structure. Toncray employed a tripartite composition, using two-story wings, for each of his courthouses. The building became a private residence after the county seat was moved to Independence. It later was used as a hotel and eventually for a barn. Both it and the clerk's office were privately restored in 1988. *(38–04, 05) VLR: 09/18/96; NRHP: 02/21/97.*

RIPSHIN, *Ripshin Road, Troutedale.* Author Sherwood Anderson (1876–1941) had this rustic but comfortable log and stone dwelling built after visiting Grayson County in 1925 and falling in love with its breathtaking unspoiled landscape. The house, completed in 1927, was designed by Anderson's architect-friend James Spratling of New Orleans. The property was named for a nearby creek. A native of Ohio, Anderson regarded Ripshin as his home and lived here until his death. Anderson's most memorable writings included *Winesburg, Ohio; Poor White; Many Marriages;* and *Memories.* These and others of his books and short stories were part of the American school of realism. While he lived at Ripshin, Anderson served as publisher, editor, and reporter for two Marion, Va., newspapers. The house, inside and out, has changed little since Anderson lived here. *(38–08) VLR: 03/02/71; NRHP: 09/22/71; NHL: 11/11/71.*

GREENE COUNTY

This rural Piedmont county was named for Gen. Nathanael Greene, Revolutionary War hero. It was formed from Orange County in 1838. The county seat is Stanardsville.

GIBSON CHAPEL MEMORIAL AND MARTHA BAGBY BATTLE HOUSE, BLUE RIDGE SCHOOL, *Dyke vicinity.* The Blue Ridge School (formerly the Blue Ridge Industrial School) was founded in 1910 by the Rev. George P. Mayo as a missionary effort of the Episcopal church to bring educational opportunities to isolated mountain communities. In 1924 Mayo determined that the school should have a chapel and boldly sought the services of Ralph Adams Cram, the nation's foremost practitioner of the Gothic style. Cram, best known for such monumental works as the West Point and Princeton University chapels, donated the Blue Ridge chapel design, listed in his log as job no. 670, 1928. The spare but deft work, executed in native fieldstone, was carried to completion in 1932 under the supervision of Charlottesville architect Stanislaw Makielski. Makielski also designed the adjacent Tudor-style Martha Bagby Battle house, built in 1934 as the headmaster's residence. *(39–41,42) VLR: 02/17/93; NRHP: 04/29/93.*

GREENE COUNTY COURTHOUSE, *Stanardsville.* The principal landmark of the tiny county seat of Stanardsville, Greene County's courthouse is a polished representative of an important group of Roman Revival courthouses scattered through Virginia's Piedmont. These works mostly were the products of various master builders who had learned the classical vocabulary from Thomas Jefferson while building the University of Virginia. This courthouse was erected in 1838 by William Donoho and William B. Phillips and follows the standard temple-form format with a properly executed Doric entablature. As originally finished, the facade had only the four pilasters; the portico was added in 1927–28. The ornamental octagonal cupola is presumably original. The courthouse was heavily damaged by fire in 1979, but the exterior survived intact. The interior has since been rebuilt. *(302–01) VLR: 12/02/69; NRHP: 02/26/70.*

LOCUST GROVE, *Amicus vicinity.* On a carefully chosen site with the Blue Ridge Mountains as backdrop, Locust Grove was built ca. 1798 for Isaac Davis, Jr. (1754–1835), a successful planter, land speculator, and slave owner who served in the Virginia House of Delegates and held various appointive county offices. Although the house lacks academic architectural character, its two stories and four-room plan made it a vivid contrast to the humble abodes common to the rustic dwellers of the Blue Ridge foothills. The exterior preserves early beaded weatherboarding and porches, and the interior, with its paneled wainscoting and paneled mantels, retains its original well-appointed character. Davis, being a public figure, used the exterior to signal his rank, with the principal rooms serving as social spaces for entertaining the public as well as friends and family. The house was restored in 1983–85. *(39–35) VLR: 06/17/87; NRHP: 09/25/87.*

OCTONIA STONE, *Stanardsville vicinity.* This rounded outcropping in the Greene County countryside marked the terminus of the westernmost boundary of the 24,000-acre Octonia Grant. The grant was made in 1722 by Lieutenant Governor Alexander Spotswood to eight Virginians: Bartholomew Yates, Lewis Latané, John Robinson, Jeremiah Clowder, Harry Beverley, Christopher Robinson, William Stanard, and Edwin Thacker. The grant, some two miles wide and twenty miles long, began in the east on the Rapidan River near Spicer's Mill in Orange County. The original grant lapsed for want of settlement and was regranted in 1729 to Robert Beverley, son of Harry Beverley. The stone is still identified by its mark, a figure eight composed of two nearly perfect circles topped by a cross. *(39–03) VLR: 06/02/70; NRHP: 09/15/70.*

GREENSVILLE COUNTY

Greensville County was named either for Gen. Nathanael Greene or for Sir Richard Grenville, leader of the Roanoke Island settlement of 1585. Situated along the North Carolina border, it was formed from Brunswick County in 1780 and later expanded. The county seat is Emporia.

ALEXANDER WATSON BATTE HOUSE, *Jarratt vicinity.* Employing forms of uncompromising simplicity, this hall-parlor dwelling is a reminder that large landowners of the early Republic oftentimes shunned architectural ostentation, concentrating on their crops rather than on domestic luxuries. Structural investigation suggests that Alexander Batte, owner of several tracts, constructed the house in two phases between 1815 and 1835, the east section being the oldest. The floor levels of the two sections do not align, and the trim of each section has subtle differences. Contrasting with the plainness of the wooden elements are the massive fieldstone chimneys and foundations that have recently been rebuilt because of deteriorated mortar. Such small houses were once a common element of the landscape, but few have survived in this region. The Batte house, together with a nearby antebellum barn, offers an intriguing look at a regional early 19th-century farmstead. *(40–02) VLR: 04/17/91; NRHP: 07/03/91.*

JOHN GREEN ARCHAEOLOGICAL SITES, *Emporia vicinity.* The John Green sites, named for a recent owner, are two adjacent and related Indian sites that are among the few in southeastern Virginia containing tested postcontact elements. Limited excavation has revealed well-preserved house patterns, human burials, and refuse-filled pits. The mixture of typical aboriginal artifacts with colonial trade items, together with floral and faunal remains, provides a rare opportunity for studying Indian settlement patterns as well as the acculturation of the interior coastal plain Indians during the period 1680 to 1730. In addition to what has been salvaged, the wide variety of pre- and postcontact-period artifacts that likely remain on the sites should aid the study of interaction between Indians of Virginia's Piedmont and Tidewater regions. A copper spoon and copper kettle (shown) are among the colonial trade items excavated. *(40–18) VLR: 05/17/83; NRHP: 05/09/85.*

SPRING HILL, *Emporia vicinity.* Although in neglected condition, Spring Hill is recognized as the finest 18th-century residence surviving in Greensville County. The construction date has not been documented, but the building was standing by 1786 when William Andrews operated a tavern here. George Washington visited the tavern in 1791 and noted it in his journal: "Breakfasted at one Andrews' a small but decent House about a mile after passing the ford (or rather the bridge) over the Meherrin river." The original portion of the house is a two-story, side-passage dwelling still sheathed with early beaded weatherboards. The passage contains an unusually fine Georgian stair with vase-and-column balusters and what may be an original grained finish. Two early outbuildings remain on the grounds. The house served as a girls' school in the mid–19th century when it was owned by Mary G. Jane Johnson. *(40–17)* *VLR: 10/15/85; NRHP: 12/02/85.*

WEAVER HOUSE, *Cowie Corner vicinity.* The Weaver house is one of Greensville County's few surviving antebellum plantation dwellings. The plain two-story structure was built between 1838 and 1840 for Jarrad Weaver on land formerly owned by the Waller family of Williamsburg. Although the house lacks the grandeur of the Tidewater plantation houses, Weaver was a prosperous landowner, owning carriages, modern farming equipment, and more than twenty slaves who tended crops of peas, oats, corn, and cotton. The house has a number of features typically associated with vernacular Southside farmhouses including what was originally a hall-parlor plan, painted wood graining, and the comparatively late use of Federal-type woodwork. The weatherboarded walls are presently covered with modern asbestos shingles; the house otherwise has suffered few alterations. *(40–06)* *VLR: 06/16/81; NRHP: 07/08/82.*

HALIFAX COUNTY

This Southside county was named for George Montagu Dunk, second earl of Halifax, president of the Board of Trade from 1748 to 1761. It was formed from Lunenburg County in 1752. Its county seat is Halifax. South Boston, formerly an independent city, has recently reverted to the county.

BERRY HILL, *South Boston vicinity.* A premier monument of the American Greek Revival, Berry Hill's imposing mansion was erected in 1842–44 for James Coles Bruce, one of Virginia's most affluent antebellum planters. John E. Johnson, a friend of the family, was the architect; Josiah Dabbs served as contractor. The house stands in a broad, semicircular landscaped park and is flanked by porticoed dependencies forming a dramatic architectural ensemble. The facade is dominated by a heroic octastyle Doric portico inspired by the Parthenon. No less impressive is the lofty interior with its grand divided stair, ornamental ceiling medallions, and imported marble mantels. A colonnaded service wing projects from the rear. This remarkably preserved plantation retains early outbuildings, both ruins and sites of slave quarters, and one of the state's largest slave cemeteries. In 1997 Berry Hill was purchased by AXA, a French-based insurance company, and converted into a training college. *(41–04) VLR: 11/05/68; NRHP: 11/25/69; NHL: 11/11/71; BHR EASEMENTS.*

BLACK WALNUT, *Clover vicinity.* This historic Southside homestead is noted for its unusually complete collection of plantation structures. Placed about the rambling frame residence are a brick kitchen, washhouse, dairy, two smokehouses, two sheds, a cool-storage building, privy, stable, barn, and slave cabin. A late 18th-century schoolhouse and a family cemetery complete the group. Together the buildings remind us of the complexity and self-sufficiency of southern plantations. Using slaves before the Civil War and hired labor afterwards, these agricultural complexes required organization and manpower. Black Walnut's dwelling was begun between 1774 and 1790 for Matthew Sims. It was expanded in the early 1800s and again in 1848. Halifax County's only Civil War engagement—the battle of Staunton River Bridge—was fought on Black Walnut property. The farm, originally one of the county's largest, is owned by Sims family descendants. *(41–06) VLR: 08/21/91; NRHP: 10/29/91.*

BRANDON PLANTATION, *Delila vicinity.* Brandon Plantation was originally the homestead of the Brandon family who settled here in the mid–18th century. The present house, a two-part vernacular dwelling, was built in 1800 and enlarged ca. 1842. The plain but forthright country Greek Revival mantels and stair in the later section are attributed to Thomas Day, a well-known black cabinetmaker of nearby Milton, N.C. Day, whose shop produced a wealth of furniture and architectural trim, has achieved national attention as a symbol of successful black entrepreneurship in a time and region where the majority of Afro-Americans were enslaved. An equally important feature at Brandon Plantation is the rare, carefully restored ca. 1800 kitchen–slave house with its unusual extended cornice. The building is an example of the fast-disappearing service structures that once were a ubiquitous feature of the southern agrarian landscape. *(41–157) VLR: 10/18/95; NRHP: 04/26/96.*

BROOKLYN TOBACCO FACTORY, *Brooklyn.* A relic of a leading Virginia industry, this plain but substantially built brick building is perhaps the state's best-preserved antebellum tobacco factory. Located in the heart of Virginia's bright-leaf tobacco belt, the three-level factory was constructed around 1855 for planters Joshua Hightower and Beverly Barksdale II, probably by the Halifax County builder Dabney Cosby, Jr. Uncommonly large for its rural location, the factory originally employed slave labor to produce plug or chewing tobacco. Tobacco for smoking and snuff was later manufactured here. The factory's whitewashed interior walls remain untouched since the enterprise folded in the 1880s. The interior also preserves various specialized workrooms and remnants of original machinery. A restoration of the long disused factory was begun in 1997. *(41–259) VLR: 10/18/95; NRHP: 01/22/96.*

BROOKLYN STORE AND POST OFFICE, *Brooklyn.* Once a defining feature of rural America, the general store is rapidly becoming an endangered architectural species. Such buildings formerly dotted the countryside with regularity. Most have vanished, however, and most remaining ones are abandoned. An unusually early example is found in the tiny hamlet of Brooklyn, built around 1850 by William Easley as the successor to an earlier establishment. Easley later was associated with Beverly Barksdale II, and after 1855 Barksdale operated the store in conjunction with his nearby Brooklyn Tobacco Factory. The business along with the post office was run by Barksdale's son when it closed in 1903. The building eventually was converted to a dwelling but with few changes to its interior, which preserves a number of its early fittings including the customized shelving in the large sales room. A rehabilitation of 1994–95 rescued the store from deterioration. *(41–07) VLR; 10/18/95; NRHP: 01/22/96.*

BUCKSHOAL FARM, *Omega vicinity.* Buckshoal Farm was the birthplace and favorite residence of William M. Tuck (1896–1983), one of Virginia's most popular 20th-century governors. Elected to that post in 1945, he is remembered for his effect on labor-management relationships. He was instrumental in the passage of the Right-to-Work Act of 1947, which eliminated union membership as a condition of employment. Tuck was elected to the U.S. Congress in 1953 where he served for sixteen years. He became known for his humorous, personable character and his direct approach to issues. His rural Southside origins were an essential facet of his engaging personality. While serving in Richmond and Washington, Tuck returned to Buckshoal Farm as often as possible "just to keep from going crazy," and here he died. The oldest part of the house is an early 19th-century log structure. It was expanded with frame additions in 1841 and 1921. *(41–108) VLR: 03/17/87; NRHP: 09/16/87.*

CARTER'S TAVERN, *Pace's vicinity.* Carter's Tavern, on Halifax County's historic River Road, is a handsomely preserved example of an early southern Virginia ordinary. With most of its original interior fabric intact, the capacious frame building provides a rare picture of the arrangement of a once-common Virginia institution. Of particular significance here is the great quantity of original graining and marbleizing on the woodwork, most of which is unusually ornate. Licenses issued in 1802 and 1804 indicate that Joseph Dodson, Jr., operated an ordinary here in what was also his residence. The place was acquired in 1807 by Samuel Carter, who enlarged the building by adding the two-story main section. Carter managed the tavern until his death in 1836. The building stood derelict for many years until 1972 when Mr. and Mrs. Robert H. Edmunds acquired the building and restored it. *(41–08) VLR: 09/17/74; NRHP: 10/11/74.*

BOWLING ELDRIDGE HOUSE, *Elmo vicinity.* This L-shaped plantation seat is characteristic of the housing favored by the majority of the region's gentry in the early 19th century. Though it lacks the stylish frills of an architect-designed dwelling, the building has an inherent sophistication derived from the use of an established architectural vocabulary of forms and proportions. The front was originally accented by a two-tier portico. The interior is highlighted by reeded woodwork, intricately carved stair brackets, and areas of original graining. The house was built ca. 1822 for Bowling Eldridge, a tobacco planter and millowner. At its peak the plantation included nearly a thousand acres, sustained by some seventy slaves. The Eldridge family sold the place in 1869, and the house suffered neglect during a century-long period of absentee landowners. The current owners, Eldridge descendants, are planning a restoration. *(41–81) VLR: 06/16/93; NRHP: 08/12/93.*

GLENNMARY, *Riverdale vicinity.* Glennmary is the work of the master builder Dabney Cosby, Sr., who assisted with the original Jeffersonian buildings at the University of Virginia. Leaving Charlottesville, Cosby continued to design and build throughout southern Virginia. As noted in his account book, Glennmary was begun in 1837 for Archibald Glenn, son of a Halifax merchant. Although a plantation dwelling, its three-bay, side-hall-plan format is more commonly seen in urban housing. Typical of Cosby's works, Glennmary employs brickwork of the highest quality. By the time it was built, Cosby had veered from the purely Roman classicism favored by Thomas Jefferson and was using Greek elements. The mantels are based on Grecian designs published by Asher Benjamin in *The Practical House Carpenter* (1830). Glennmary stood neglected for many years but was restored in the 1980s. *(41–104) VLR: 11/21/78; NRHP: 02/01/79.*

HALIFAX CHURCH AT PROVIDENCE (OLD PROVIDENCE PRESBYTERIAN CHURCH), *Providence.* This simple country church housed Halifax County's first Presbyterian congregation. Presbyterians began to spread through the southern Piedmont in the mid–18th century.

By 1830 they decided to have a more conveniently located meetinghouse and soon erected the present structure. Eschewing any prideful trappings, the little wooden building is basically an enclosed space. Its small size reflects its original membership, which numbered only twenty-six, including sixteen blacks. A singular feature of the plain interior is the horizontal plank cladding. By 1926 the congregation had outgrown the building and moved on. The church then was used as a storage barn. It became the property of the Blanks family in 1947 who in 1981 restored it as a family memorial, now in the care of the Blanks Memorial Foundation, Ltd. *(41–113) VLR: 12/08/87; NRHP: 07/07/88.*

HALIFAX COUNTY COURTHOUSE, *Halifax.* Occupying a site that has been used for court purposes since the Revolution, the 1839 Halifax County Courthouse is one of the Classical Revival court buildings erected by master builders influenced by Thomas Jefferson while constructing the University of Virginia. Its designer and builder, Dabney Cosby, Sr., along with his son, Dabney Cosby, Jr., provided Southside Virginia with a variety of architecturally literate houses, churches, and public buildings. Prior to the Halifax project, the elder Cosby had participated in the design and construction of the courthouses for Goochland, Lunenburg, and Sussex counties. As with the Sussex courthouse, Cosby abandoned the strict temple form here in favor of a T-plan. He also departed from his normal use of Roman orders and instead employed a Greek Ionic order. The courthouse was enlarged in 1904 by an extension of the rear wing. *(230–77) VLR: 12/15/81; NRHP: 09/16/82.*

THE LITTLE PLANTATION (FOURQUREAN HOUSE), *South Boston vicinity.* In the early 19th century numerous small plantations growing tobacco as the principal cash crop were established in south central Virginia. Each plantation was normally served by an unpretentious frame dwelling house surrounded by a cluster of outbuildings. The design and layout of these complexes were completely utilitarian, the buildings having little or no reference to current architectural fashions. Such modest regional units are exemplified by The Little Plantation, established in 1830 by Daniel Fourqurean and consisting of a compact vernacular dwelling where the only elegance is a marbleized stair. Its original outbuildings include a stone kitchen and a log office. In an effort to restore a picture of the area's early rural lifestyle, a recent owner has added early outbuildings, salvaged from nearby farms, to replace missing ones. *(41–37) VLR: 09/21/76; NRHP: 05/06/80.*

INDIAN JIM'S CAVE ARCHAEOLOGICAL SITE, *Brookneal vicinity.* A natural formation on the banks of the Staunton River, Indian Jim's Cave is a place of aboriginal occupation dating to 2000–1000 B.C. and possibly earlier. The floor of the cave preserves intact cultural layers of its various periods of occupancy. The shelter takes its name from the tradition that during the 18th century Indian Jim, Halifax County's last surviving aboriginal inhabitant, lived in the cave with his black wife. The archaeological remains here should reveal data on subsistence patterns and adaptations to seasonal changes over time by prehistoric Indians. Evidence that may shed light on local Indians' social interaction patterns also is likely preserved here. *(41–106) VLR: 03/17/81; NRHP: 08/26/82.*

MOUNTAIN ROAD HISTORIC DISTRICT, *Halifax.* Mountain Road, in the county seat of Halifax, has been noted for its handsome houses, churches, and lush landscaping for the past century. Named for White Oak Mountain, the tree-shaded road stretches

west from the courthouse square into the countryside. The road was built up slowly so that it now presents a range of buildings from the early 19th century to the present. The principal churches are St. Mark's Episcopal Church (1831), now Halifax Methodist Church (shown), and St. John's Episcopal Church (1846). Architectural styles seen in the residences include late Federal, Greek Revival, Italianate, Queen Anne, and Colonial Revival, all in a generally restrained idiom. Several of the earlier houses were designed by Dabney Cosby, Jr., son of the Jeffersonian workman Dabney Cosby, Sr. Cosby worked with his father on the courthouse, and he also built St. John's Church. *(230–78) VLR: 08/16/83; NRHP: 10/06/83.*

REDFIELD, *Oak Level vicinity.* Although antebellum Halifax County was dotted with small farm complexes, the area also saw the establishment of vast plantations with architecturally sophisticated houses. John R. Edmunds, owner of 1,110 acres on Birch Creek, was able to build an Italian Villa–style mansion with money he earned from the sale of grain to Russia in the Crimean War. The house, with its formal facade, bracketed cornice, and low wings connected by arched openings, was completed in 1857 and follows the prescription for a "small Villa in the Classical manner" promoted by Andrew Jackson Downing in *The Architecture of Country Houses* (1850). Emphasizing this formality inside is a monumental single-run central stair dominating the entrance hall. Edmunds, in addition to being a successful planter, was an advocate of reconciliation during Reconstruction. His handsomely restored house is owned by his descendants. *(41–47) VLR: 07/18/78; NRHP: 09/20/78.*

REEDY CREEK ARCHAEOLOGICAL SITE, *Reedy Creek, South Boston.* The Reedy Creek site preserves evidence of Late Archaic (2000–1000 B.C.) occupation and was the location of an Indian village between A.D. 900 and 1400. During the latter period the settlement apparently evolved from a hamlet to a concentrated, possibly palisaded village. The good state of preservation of the site's seeds, nuts, and animal bones enhances the understanding of the Indian dietary ways in the Dan River drainage. In 1975 a limited salvage excavation by the Library of Virginia archaeologist revealed post molds, house patterns, and substantial quantities of floral and faunal remains. Shown are two of the numerous Late Archaic soapstone bowl fragments found here. *(130–03) VLR: 02/15/77; NRHP: 04/26/78.*

SEATON, *Halifax vicinity.* This Gothic Revival cottage, set off by its scalloped dormer bargeboards and the crenellated parapet of its small front porch, was the creation of the Halifax master builder Josiah Dabbs. Seaton was completed in 1857 for William M. Howerton, son of tobacco entrepreneur Philip Howerton. The house illustrates the popularity of the Gothic Revival style among the planter class just before the Civil War. A two-story wing was added in 1887. At the same time the parlor was remodeled with the installation of an early Jardine pipe organ salvaged from a local church and here framed by an ornate Moorish-style wooden screen. On the grounds are remnants of 19th-century romantic landscaping as well as several early outbuildings, including a large 1887 carriage house. Seaton remains the home of Howerton descendants and preserves many early decorations such as carpeting, curtains, and furnishings. *(41–50) VLR: 03/18/80; NRHP: 05/19/80.*

SOUTH BOSTON HISTORIC DISTRICT, *South Boston.* South Boston's historic district retains many tangible reminders of the community's industrial, commercial, and residential development from after the Civil War to the 1930s. The town began as a railroad depot in 1854, and by the early 1900s it had become the country's second-largest bright-leaf tobacco market. Spread through the downtown is a wealth of tobacco warehouses and factories along with commercial buildings associated with South Boston's golden age of tobacco trading. The visual quality of the district's residential area was described in Wirt Johnson Carrington's *A History of Halifax County* (1924): "The streets are bordered with beautiful homes, large and small, old and new; some with extensive grounds ornamented with shrubs and flowers, others with greensward and forest trees, decorative plots of beauty everywhere, each vying with the other in attractiveness." *(130–06) VLR: 07/15/86; NRHP: 09/26/86.*

TAROVER, *River Road.* Tarover is one of the several architecturally distinguished houses commissioned by the Bruce family. It was built in 1855–56 for Thomas Bruce, son of James Coles Bruce for whom the nearby Greek Revival mansion Berry Hill was built. Both Berry Hill and the Gothic-style Staunton Hill, home of James Coles Bruce's half brother Charles, were designed by their architect and friend John E. Johnson. It thus is presumed that Tarover is also a Johnson design. With its projecting porch and delicate oriel lighting the chamber above, the house is based on a Gothic villa scheme published in A. J. Downing's *The Architecture of Country Houses* (1850), a work formerly in the Berry Hill library. The house lost some of its original picturesque character around the turn of the century when its icicle-like bargeboards were removed. Tarover remained in the Bruce family until 1891. *(41–53) VLR: 07/18/78; NRHP: 09/20/78.*

WILEY'S TAVERN ARCHAEOLOGICAL SITE, *Danripple vicinity.* The 18th-century Wiley's Tavern served alternately as the headquarters of British general Lord Cornwallis and his American counterpart, Gen. Nathanael Greene, during the decisive military stratagem known as the retreat to the Dan River. The tavern was built ca. 1771 for William Wiley. Constructed of log, the small, rude structure was typical of the establishments sprinkled throughout the farther reaches of Virginia in the late colonial period. The photograph shows it ca. 1924; the building eventually collapsed in the 1950s. Archaeological excavation of the tavern site should reveal architectural and artifactual data helpful to understanding rural life in Halifax County during the Revolutionary period. It may also yield data on the construction and operation of a backcountry tavern, as well as information on colonial trade on a major north-south thoroughfare. *(41–39) VLR: 07/31/80.*

CITY OF HAMPTON

Named for Hampton Creek, earlier called the Southampton River in honor of the earl of Southampton, Hampton was settled in 1610. It was formally established in 1680, incorporated as a town in 1849, and became a city in 1908. In 1952 it was merged with Elizabeth City County and the town of Phoebus, both of which thereby became extinct.

ABERDEEN GARDENS HISTORIC DISTRICT. Aberdeen Gardens was established as a New Deal planned community by and for the Afro-American workers of Newport News and Hampton. Begun in 1934 and finished by 1937, the 440-acre development, the only Resettlement Administration community for blacks in Virginia, consisted of 158 single-family homes along with a school and a commercial center, all surrounded by a greenbelt for subsistence and truck farming. The project, initiated by Hampton Institute and funded by the U.S. Department of Interior's Division of Subsistence Homesteads, was supervised by Howard University architect Hilyard R. Robinson. Though equipped with modern conveniences, the simple brick houses were intended to echo the local vernacular style. The project received national attention when visited by Eleanor Roosevelt in 1938. Although expanded in the 1940s and 1950s, the neighborhood preserves its original orderly character and remains a symbol of Afro-American pride. *(114–146) VLR: 03/10/94; NRHP: 05/26/94.*

BUCKROE BEACH CAROUSEL, *602 Settlers Landing Road.* This colorful example of American popular art is a rare surviving hand-carved wooden carousel, kept intact and working for nearly seventy years. The Philadelphia Toboggan Company of Germantown, Pa., built the carousel, originally designated "Philadelphia Toboggan Company Number 50." Commissioned by the Newport News and Hampton Railway, Gas and Electric Company, the carousel was a centerpiece of the Buckroe Beach Amusement Park and carried its first riders in May 1920. Thirty-eight oil paintings, eighteen beveled mirrors, forty-eight hand-carved horses, two hand-carved, upholstered wood chariots, and a Bruder band organ embellished the work. Master carvers Frank Caretta and Daniel C. Muller produced the horses and chariots. In 1988 the carousel was restored by R&F Designs in Bristol, Conn., and reassembled in a new pavilion on the waterfront of downtown Hampton. It resumed its cheerful operation on June 30, 1991. *(114–111) VLR: 02/28/92; NRHP: 10/27/92.*

CHESTERVILLE ARCHAEOLOGICAL SITE, *Langley Air Force Base.* Chesterville was part of a tract patented in 1619 by John Leyden. It was purchased in 1692 by Thomas Wythe, a burgess for Elizabeth City County. Wythe's great-grandson George Wythe, a signer of the Declaration of Independence and first professor of law at the College of William and Mary, is believed to have been born here. Wythe inherited the plantation in 1755 and made it a country home while maintaining his main residence in Williamsburg, in the well-known house bearing his name on Palace Green. In 1771 Wythe began construction of a new house at Chesterville that stood until destroyed by fire in 1911. A photograph shows that it had a gable-end front with an arcaded first floor. Chesterville was sold by Wythe in 1802. The property was acquired by the National Aeronautics and Space Administration in 1950. *(114–98) VLR: 06/20/72; NRHP: 08/14/73.*

REUBEN CLARK HOUSE (WILLOW DELL), *125 South Willard Avenue.* Built near the causeway to Fort Monroe, the Reuben Clark house is one of the oldest residences in this venerable city. It was completed in 1854 for steamboat captain Reuben Clark. The house escaped the burning that destroyed virtually all of Hampton's downtown buildings in the Civil War. Its proximity to Fort Monroe lent it protection, and its abundant well received heavy use from the Federal troops at the fort because the fort's water was considered less pure. With its low roof and long veranda, Captain Clark's house reflects the popularity of the Italian Villa style deemed preferable for southern houses by architectural theorist Andrew Jackson Downing. The trellis-like posts of the veranda are an imaginative variation. The house was expanded early in this century, but its original character was not compromised. *(114–50) VLR: 05/15/84; NRHP: 08/16/84.*

EIGHT-FOOT HIGH-SPEED TUNNEL, *NASA Langley Research Center.* Using concrete, the material of choice for projects funded by the Public Works Administration, the National Advisory Committee for Aeronautics completed this pioneering 8-foot high-speed tunnel in 1936. The most vibration-free wind tunnel yet experienced, it became the premier facility for testing high-speed, high-performance aircraft. Here the 16,000-horsepower electric-motor fan produced an airstream flowing at nearly the speed of sound (Mach 0.9). It was the first high-speed tunnel capable of testing large models and actual airplane sections. America's high-performance aircraft of World War II were perfected here, and critical research also led to the development of supersonic aircraft. In 1950 the slotted-throat test section was installed, enabling the initial tests that led to Richard Whitcomb's discovery of the transonic arc rule. The facility, now obsolete, serves as office and storage space. *(114–139) VLR: 02/18/86; NHL: 10/03/85.*

FORT MONROE HISTORIC DISTRICT, *Old Point Comfort.* Constructed in 1819–34 to guard Hampton Roads, the vast moated Fort Monroe is among the nation's most ambitious works of early military architecture. It was designed by Gen. Simon Bernard, a military engineer under Napoleon before becoming head of the U.S. Board of Engineers, in charge of construction of coastal defenses. During the Civil War the fort was a staging area for Union military and naval expeditions. The fort witnessed the epic fight between the ironclads *Monitor* and *Virginia,* and many area slaves found refuge here. Former Confederate president Jefferson Davis was imprisoned here from 1865 to 1867. Still an active military post, Fort Monroe is now headquarters of the Continental Army Command. The landmark designation applies not only to the fortifications but to the wide array of army buildings both within and without the fort. *(114–02) VLR: 09/09/69 (EXPANDED 10/16/84); NRHP: 10/15/66; NHL: 12/19/60.*

FORT WOOL, *off Old Point Comfort.* Originally known as Fort Calhoun, this forbidding island defense work was begun in 1819, along with Fort Monroe opposite, to protect the entrance to Hampton Roads harbor. Robert E. Lee, then an army engineer, supervised its completion in the 1830s. Its name was changed to Fort Wool in 1862 in honor of Maj. Gen. John Wool, commandant of fortifications at Hampton Roads. From Fort Wool, President Lincoln watched the embarkation of Union troops to seize Norfolk. Abandoned in 1886, the fort was reactivated and expanded during both world wars so that it now possesses a variety of military engineering works. Conspicuous among them are the sinister World War II watchtowers. The fort was abandoned once again in 1953, with ownership reverting to the Commonwealth. In 1985 the island was deeded by the state to the city of Hampton, which has opened it to limited visitation. *(114–41) VLR: 11/05/68; NRHP: 11/25/69.*

FULL-SCALE WIND TUNNEL, *NASA Langley Research Center.* Also known by the dimensions of the tunnel throat, the 30-by-60-foot wind tunnel—440 feet long by 230 feet wide by 95 feet tall—has exposed external structure and smooth tunnel interiors. By the 1920s engineers of the National Advisory Committee for Aeronautics (NACA) knew that certain research and testing could only be explored with full-scale stationary models or actual aircraft in flight-speed wind conditions. Completed in 1931, tests here proved the air-drag penalties of exposed engines and protruding struts, wires, wheels, and rivet heads. Before and during World War II, high-performance military aircraft were streamlined here to provide superior machines that contributed to America's victory. Now obsolete, the facility is currently used by Old Dominion University for graduate research projects to improve the design of aircraft, automobiles, and trucks. *(114–142) VLR: 02/18/86; NHL: 10/03/85.*

HAMPTON NATIONAL CEMETERY, *Cemetery Road at Marshall Avenue.* The toll of wounded and sick wrought by the Civil War necessitated the establishment of military hospitals, one of which was the Hampton Military Hospital at Fort Monroe. The high death rate at these hospitals required burial ground. The land set aside for the use of the Hampton hospital became the nucleus of the present-day Hampton National Cemetery, officially founded in 1866. After the war soldiers' remains were brought here for burial from military posts throughout eastern Virginia. The cemetery has since been expanded and now incorporates twenty-seven acres. In addition to U.S. soldiers, the cemetery also has graves of 272 Confederates and of World War II prisoners of war, both German and Italian. Officially closed in 1994, the cemetery now holds over 25,000 burials including eight Medal of Honor recipients. *(114–148) VLR: 10/18/95; NRHP: 02/26/96.*

HAMPTON UNIVERSITY (FORMERLY HAMPTON INSTITUTE), *East Queen and Tyler streets.* This famous institution was founded in 1868 through the efforts of Gen. Samuel Chapman Armstrong, local agent of the Freedmen's Bureau, to train the many former slaves who had gathered in the area. Though begun with only fifteen students and two teachers, the institute prospered and was chartered as the Hampton Normal and Industrial Institute in 1870. By 1874 it was embellished with its modified Châteauesque main building, Virginia Hall, designed by Richard Morris Hunt and built by the students. Hunt also designed the plainer Academic Hall, completed in 1882. The Romanesque Revival chapel with its bell tower, designed by J. C. Cady, was opened in 1886. Also on the grounds is the Mansion House, an early 19th-century plantation dwelling now the home of Hampton's president. Wigwam, an 1878 dwelling, housed Indian students. Booker T. Washington was a Hampton alumnus. *(114–06) VLR: 09/09/69; NRHP: 11/12/69; NHL: 05/30/74.*

HERBERT HOUSE, *Manna Road.* Erected ca. 1753 on Armstrong Point facing Hampton Creek and the harbor, the Herbert house is the oldest dwelling in the city of Hampton. Until 1808 it remained in the Herbert family for whom it was built. One of its owners, Capt. Thomas Herbert, served in the Virginia navy during the Revolution. Because it was a plantation house and outside the town proper, the Herbert house was spared the burning that destroyed most of Hampton during the Civil War. The structure remains a sophisticated example of colonial Georgian style, exhibiting the careful proportions and fine brickwork typical of Virginia's more substantial mid-18th-century houses. Unoccupied for several decades, the house suffers from alterations made during the last century. Surrounding modern housing has almost completely hidden this rare landmark. *(114–04) VLR: 11/16/71; NRHP: 02/23/72.*

LUNAR LANDING RESEARCH FACILITY, *NASA Langley Research Center.* This simulator facility, constructed in 1965, was used by Apollo astronauts to practice final descent and touchdown for moon landings. The airy structure, 400 feet long by 230 feet high, is a steel gantry that straddled a simulated moonscape. Suspended within this framework was the full-size, retro-rocket-controlled Lunar Excursion Module Simulator (LEMS). Lunar gravity was achieved by traveling cables supporting five-sixths of the LEMS's earth weight. The remaining one-sixth pull (lunar gravity) allowed the astronaut to "descend" to the surface. Here, on dark nights, with an artificial sun, Neil Armstrong—the first man on the moon—trained for the 1969 lunar expedition. Asked what it was like to land on the moon, Armstrong replied, "Like Langley." The LEMS is on exhibit at the Virginia Air and Space Center in Hampton, while the gantry has been adapted for other types of research. *(114–140) VLR: 02/18/86; NHL: 10/03/85.*

LITTLE ENGLAND CHAPEL, *4100 Kecoughtan Road.* The diminutive Little England Chapel is a monument to the role of blacks in helping members of their own race achieve a better quality of life and a stronger sense of community through education and spiritual growth. Completed in 1879 as a missionary chapel, the building first served a variety of uses. Hampton Institute students regularly offered Sunday school lessons to the Newtown youth, continuing this practice here until the 1930s. The Newtown Improvement and Civic Club also held meetings here. Additional programs of worship, singing, and concerts were undertaken, and by 1890 the chapel had become known for its sewing club. The Newtown Improvement and Civic Club acquired the property in 1954 and restored the building in 1990–93 for a historical, community, and nondenominational religious center celebrating the area's Afro-American culture. *(114–40) VLR: 06/16/81; NRHP: 07/08/82.*

OLD POINT COMFORT LIGHTHOUSE, *Fenwick Road, Fort Monroe.* A temporary light to guide ships into Hampton Roads existed at Old Point Comfort as early as 1774. Recognizing the necessity of a navigation guide at this site, the Virginia General Assembly in 1798 conveyed the point to the federal government for the purpose of establishing a permanent light. The present tapered polygonal structure was completed in 1802, seventeen years before the construction of Fort Monroe began. Built of sandstone ashlar painted white, the tiny structure has been in regular use since its completion, functioning as a round-the-clock navigation aid. The lighthouse, along with Fort Monroe, was maintained under Federal authority during the Civil War. Next door is the lightkeeper's residence, a simple Queen Anne structure built ca. 1890, which housed the keeper until 1973 when the light was automated. *(114–21) VLR: 06/20/72; NRHP: 03/01/73.*

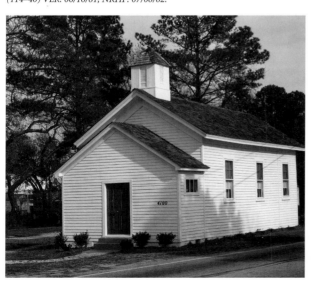

RENDEZVOUS DOCKING SIMULATOR, *NASA Langley Research Center.* One of the most significant ground-based artifacts in space exploration history, this facility enabled NASA's Gemini and Apollo astronauts to practice space rendezvous procedures that they had to master before journeying to the moon. Built in 1963, it consists of a full-scale mock spacecraft suspended by a highly maneuverable cable and gimbal system attached to an overhead carriage. By docking with a target, astronauts gained realistic training that closely approximated space operations. In 1969, when the actual lunar module lifted from the surface of the moon and caught up to the waiting Apollo command module in lunar orbit, docking was absolutely crucial for the return to earth. This simulator therefore was vital in making possible the round trip to the moon. With some adaptive reuse of components, most of the facility is preserved in place at the NASA hangar in Hampton. *(114–141) VLR: 02/18/86; NHL: 10/03/85.*

ST. JOHN'S EPISCOPAL CHURCH, *100 West Queen Street.* Completed in 1728 by builder Henry Cary, Jr., St. John's is the fourth building to serve Elizabeth City Parish, the oldest active parish of the Anglican communion in America. The church itself is the oldest building in Hampton. Its Latin-cross plan, a form usually reserved for important churches, indicated the high status of the parish. St. John's suffered considerably from the wars that plagued the area. The church was damaged during the bombardment of Hampton in 1775. In the War of 1812 British troops ransacked the building and used it for a barracks. It was renovated in 1830 and reconsecrated as St. John's Church. Retreating Confederates burned the church along with the town in 1861, leaving only the fine Flemish bond brick walls standing. Rebuilt within the walls after the war, the church was given a handsome Victorian interior. *(114–01) VLR: 12/02/69; NRHP: 02/26/70.*

WILLIAM H. TRUSTY HOUSE, *76 West County Street.* The stylish late Victorian house built in 1897 for William H. Trusty (1862–1902) stands as a reminder of the new sense of political, social, and economic freedom enjoyed by Virginia blacks in the decades following emancipation. Born of freed parents in 1862 in Prince George County, Trusty rose from humble origins to become a successful businessman and city leader. In 1901 he was elected to the city council of the newly formed town of Phoebus, thus becoming one of the first blacks to be so elected in a Virginia municipality. Trusty's home, set off by its fancy porches and projections, was built by P. A. Fuller of Fuller and Morgan and was the most expensive new house in the neighborhood. Through the efforts of Hampton preservationist Mrs. Sandidge ("Sis") Evans, the house was rescued from the threat of urban renewal in 1976 and restored for residential use. *(114–108) VLR: 02/26/79; NRHP: 06/22/79.*

VARIABLE DENSITY TUNNEL, *NASA Langley Research Center.* Called the VDT, this facility is considered the most significant of NASA's ground-based historic properties. Spurred by the European supremacy in aircraft design, a 1915 congressional bill established the National Advisory Committee for Aeronautics (NACA) and its laboratory in Hampton (1917). The United States began to surpass European technology with the VDT in 1921. It was a closed-flow wind tunnel inside a large pressure tank of riveted and welded three-inch-thick steel plates. This permitted scale-model tests at up to twenty times atmospheric pressure, which corresponded to full-scale aircraft conditions. Data obtained here led to the development of American military and commercial aircraft that has dominated the world's airways ever since. Obsolete and gutted by fire, the exterior vessel has been relocated, preserved, and interpreted in a permanent exhibit at the NASA Center in Hampton. *(114–143) VLR: 02/18/86; NHL: 10/03/85.*

VICTORIA BOULEVARD HISTORIC DISTRICT. Victoria Boulevard and adjacent streets were laid out in 1888 by local entrepreneur James S. Darling as a complement to his newly constructed electric railway, the first on the peninsula. Essentially built out by 1920, the neighborhood early became one of Hampton's most fashionable residential areas, one made up primarily of spacious, freestanding houses occupied by business leaders and professionals. The first houses made use of the Queen Anne style, but the later dwellings are assertive examples of the Colonial Revival, a reflection of Hampton's position as the nation's oldest English-speaking community. A variety of American Foursquare houses are part of the last wave of construction here. Despite the diversity of forms, the area is unified by a homogeneity of scale and materials. Nearly every house is skirted by a hospitable front porch, used as living rooms during Hampton's warm evenings. *(114–112) VLR: 08/21/84; VLR: 10/04/84.*

HANOVER COUNTY

Straddling the line between the Tidewater and the Piedmont regions, Hanover County was named for King George I, who at the time of his accession was elector of Hannover in Germany. The county was formed from New Kent County in 1720. Its county seat is Hanover Court House.

ASHLAND HISTORIC DISTRICT. With its exceptional collection of ornamental freestanding frame dwellings and a compact business core, all set among hundreds of trees, the Ashland Historic District is an engaging example of a turn-of-the-century railroad and streetcar suburb. Defining the district's spine are the tracks of the Richmond, Fredericksburg, and Potomac Railroad and the parallel Center Street, on either side of which is a full range of late 19th- and early 20th-century styles: Italianate, Eastlake, Queen Anne, and Colonial Revival. Also along the tracks is the small but sophisticated Ashland depot. The commercial area is an assemblage of "Main Street" brick structures of the 1920s. With the addition of the Randolph-Macon College quadrangle, the district illustrates the important role that both the railroad and the college have played in Ashland's development. A strong sense of community pride has served to maintain Ashland's historic flavor. *(116–01) VLR: 03/16/82; NRHP: 02/11/83.*

BEAVERDAM DEPOT, *Beaverdam.* One of Virginia's earliest surviving railroad stations, the Beaverdam depot was built in 1866 to replace a makeshift depot destroyed by Union forces on May 9, 1864, which in turn had replaced an 1862 depot destroyed in a Union raid of February 1864. The original ca. 1840 depot was likewise destroyed in a Union raid on Beaverdam on July 20, 1862. The present depot was one of several rebuilt by the Virginia Central Railroad on the sites of depots lost to war. Not long after completion of this brick facility, the Virginia Central Railroad Co. was purchased by the Chesapeake and Ohio Railway, which emerged in the 1880s as one of the state's dominant lines. Although no longer in use, Beaverdam's depot is remarkably well preserved. Both of its waiting rooms have beaded-board walls and ceilings. The office retains shelving and switching mechanisms. The long, low structure also has baggage and freight rooms. *(42–81) VLR: 04/19/88; NRHP: 11/08/88.*

CEDAR CREEK MEETING HOUSE ARCHAEOLOGICAL SITE, *Negro Foot vicinity.* A wooded knoll blanketed with periwinkle now marks the place where the Cedar Creek Meeting of the Society of Friends worshiped from 1721 until 1894. Over that period the property embraced at least three different meetinghouses. Also here is a burial ground where many of the congregation now lie in unmarked graves, such anonymity being characteristic of the Quaker faith. The second meetinghouse, built ca. 1768, was replaced by a third structure, completed by 1799. A schoolhouse was erected at the same time. The last meetinghouse, a brick structure, either a replacement or an expansion of the 1799 structure, was destroyed in a forest fire in 1904. Archaeological testing has revealed features relating to the 1799 meetinghouse. Further investigation could unearth important data on the religious and educational facilities of an enduring and influential organization of dissenters. *(42–121) VLR: 07/15/86.*

CLOVER LEA, *Old Church vicinity.* Clover Lea's broad lawns and old trees combine with the porticoed house to present an idealized picture of an antebellum plantation residence. Although the structure is not large compared to the Greek Revival houses of the Deep South, its tall square pillars, high-ceilinged rooms, and handsome woodwork give it the stately air inherent in the Grecian mode. The use of a portico on the facade is a departure from the Richmond region practice of placing the portico on the rear or garden elevation. The house was built for George Washington Bassett who with his wife, Betty Burnet Lewis Bassett, moved into their completed home in September 1844 and here eventually raised eleven children. The property remained in the Bassett family until the end of the 19th century. During the Civil War, Clover Lea was raided by Union cavalry seeking Gen. J. E. B. Stuart. *(42–47) VLR: 10/17/78; NRHP: 02/01/79.*

COLD HARBOR NATIONAL CEMETERY, *Route 156, Mechanicsville vicinity.* Established on April 30, 1866, the Cold Harbor National Cemetery contains 2,099 interments, including 1,313 unknown Union dead from the Civil War. A Medal of Honor recipient, Sgt. Maj. Augustus Barry, 16th U.S. Infantry, is also buried here; he was the cemetery superintendent when he died in 1871. Most of the soldiers were killed in the campaigns of 1862 and 1864 around Richmond. Many died during or soon after the battles of Mechanicsville, Gaines's Mill, Savage's Station, and Cold Harbor. After the war the U.S. dead were gathered from the sites of their hasty battlefield burials and reinterred in this and other national cemeteries. Confederate soldiers likewise were reinterred in such burial grounds as Hollywood Cemetery in Richmond. The Cold Harbor cemetery includes a Second Empire–style superintendent's house built in 1870 from a design by Quartermaster General Montgomery C. Meigs. *(42–136) VLR: 4/28/95; NRHP: 8/10/95.*

DEWBERRY, *Coatsville vicinity.* The Palladian concept of breaking up the massing of a country house gained popularity in England in the early 1700s and spread to Virginia through published designs by James Gibbs, Robert Morris, and other British architects. Following the precedent of Virginia Palladian-style houses such as Blandfield or Battersea, the five-part Dewberry is a late expression of this form. The stately structure was built in 1833 for the Rev. John Cooke, rector of Fork Church, who was instrumental in having nearby Trinity Church built. Such an expansive house was normally beyond the means of a cleric, but Cooke was married to a propertied widow. The design was given added presence by the use of three-part windows. Cooke's expertise in gardening is shown in the remnants of his large formal garden behind the house. Dewberry has been owned by the Dixon family since 1921. *(42–07) VLR: 03/20/96; NRHP: 05/31/96.*

FORK CHURCH, *Ashland vicinity.* Fork Church was erected ca. 1737 as the second Lower Church of St. Martin's Parish. Typical of Virginia's rectangular colonial churches, Fork Church has a front and a side entrance and a simple gable roof. Like many churches built in the first half of the 18th century, the walls are laid in Flemish bond with glazed headers. The segmental-arch windows are also characteristic of the early 18th century. Fork Church is one of Virginia's few colonial churches not to have been vandalized by Northern troops during the Civil War. It thus retains many early fittings, including its rear gallery, portions of the original pews, and an early holy table. Also surviving is an 1834 pipe organ. Patrick Henry, Dolley Madison, and Thomas Nelson Page were all regular worshipers here. *(42–12) VLR: 12/02/69; NRHP: 02/26/70.*

HANOVER COUNTY COURTHOUSE, *Hanover Court House.* Hanover County's courthouse survives as the archetypal example of colonial Virginia's arcaded court structures, of which only six remain. Each of these buildings has refined brickwork and an arcade or arcades topped by a tall hipped roof. The Hanover courthouse was erected ca. 1737–42 and has been in continuous use since. In 1763 its courtroom was the scene of Patrick Henry's first well-known case, the Parson's Cause, in which he attacked the misrule of the king and the greed of the Anglican clergy. The building was also the site of a 1774 gathering to address grievances in anticipation of the Virginia convention when the colonists voiced their support for the Bostonians' "tea party" actions. The courthouse has undergone several renovations, leaving little of the original interior fabric. The exterior, however, continues to convey the simple dignity inherent in colonial Virginia's public architecture. *(42–16) VLR: 11/05/68; NRHP: 10/01/69; NHL: 11/07/73.*

HANOVER COURT HOUSE HISTORIC DISTRICT. This county-seat village retains the essential ingredients of a rural Virginia courthouse settlement. The principal element is the arcaded courthouse of ca. 1737–42, a major monument of Virginia's colonial public architecture. On its surrounding green is the 1835 stone jail and a brick clerk's office of the same period. Across the road is the Hanover Tavern, a rambling late 18th-century hostelry, probably the largest and best-preserved of Virginia's early courthouse taverns. Until recent years the tavern had long been the home of the well-known Barksdale Theatre. It is now restored for exhibition and special events. A late addition to the complex is the 1942 Pamunkey Regional Library, an articulate Colonial Revival structure. Hanover Court House witnessed much Civil War activity. It was here that J. E. B. Stuart was commissioned a major general in the Confederate cavalry. *(42–86) VLR: 07/06/71; NRHP: 09/22/71; BHR EASEMENT (HANOVER TAVERN).*

HANOVER MEETING HOUSE ARCHAEOLOGICAL SITE (POLEGREEN CHURCH), *Rural Point vicinity.* The 1740s Polegreen reading house and the adjacent 1750s church were the base from which Pastor Samuel Davies carried the widespread social and spiritual movement of the Great Awakening throughout much of the South. Polegreen was Davies's first church, and here he stirred the popular disaffection that led to the Parson's Cause and related social, literary, and legal confrontations between New Side Presbyterians and the Anglican establishment. The sermons Davies delivered at Polegreen had a profound effect on the political disposition and oratory of Patrick Henry. The church was destroyed on June 1, 1864, during early stages of the battle of Cold Harbor. The site is now maintained by the Historic Polegreen Church Foundation, which sponsored an archaeological investigation in 1990 when the sites of the church and reading house were identified. *(42–480) VLR: 06/19/91; NRHP: 09/04/91.*

HANOVER TOWN ARCHAEOLOGICAL SITE, *Studley vicinity.* The 18th-century port village of Hanover Town grew up beside tobacco warehouses on the uppermost part of the Pamunkey River. The village site was patented in 1672 by Col. John Page, and the first warehouse began operation in 1730. The community was formally established in 1762 by the House of Burgesses through the efforts of Mann Page II of Rosewell, who had inherited much of John Page's property. Hanover Town was raided by Lord Cornwallis's army during the Revolution and declined after the war when the silting of the river inhibited commerce. By the mid–19th century it had almost completely disappeared; shown are the foundations of Page's warehouse. The village site holds potential archaeological information relating to the structures and layout of a colonial port town. *(42–97) VLR: 06/18/74; NRHP: 09/17/74.*

PATRICK HENRY'S BIRTHPLACE ARCHAEOLOGICAL SITE, *Studley vicinity.* Documentary research has confirmed the oral tradition that this site, near a later house in eastern Hanover County, is that of the Studley farmhouse in which Revolutionary orator Patrick Henry was born in 1736. Scientific excavation of the site could yield new insights into the early life of the noted patriot, who lived here until he was fourteen. The plantation dwelling house also was occupied by burgess and magistrate John Syme, cartographer John Henry (Patrick Henry's father), and Judge Peter Lyon, a member of Virginia's first Court of Appeals. The site is now owned by the Association for the Preservation of Virginia Antiquities and is planned for development into a memorial park honoring Henry. *(42–114) VLR: 03/17/81; NRHP: 08/02/82.*

HICKORY HILL, *Hanover Court House vicinity.* This extensive Hanover County plantation has been the property of the Wickham family since 1820 when Robert Carter of Shirley left 1,717 acres to his daughter and son-in-law Anne Butler Carter and William Fanning Wickham of Richmond. The Wickhams' son, Williams Carter Wickham of Hickory Hill, was a Confederate general and legislator and later served as president of the Chesapeake and Ohio Railway. The original house, completed by 1827, burned in 1875 and was replaced by the present brick house, erected in a form reminiscent of the antebellum period. An 1857 brick wing survived, however, as well as an important collection of antebellum outbuildings and farm buildings, including a Gothic Revival library. The spacious grounds are a remarkable example of antebellum landscaping, containing a romantic-style park with outstanding specimen trees, a geometric boxwood garden, and a tree-box walk of unusual height. *(42–100) VLR: 09/17/74; NRHP: 11/21/74.*

IMMANUEL EPISCOPAL CHURCH, *Old Church vicinity.* Although the Gothic Revival style never completely dominated America's architectural scene as did the Greek Revival, the Gothic nonetheless permeated many aspects of the built environment, especially ecclesiastical works. This was especially so with the Episcopal church, which wanted to acknowledge its medieval roots and its relation to the magnifi-

cent creations of the Age of Religion. Many 19th-century American Episcopal churches thus displayed references to the lofty Gothic grandeur. A small country church such as Immanuel Church could find itself decked out with pinnacles, pointed windows, and buttresses echoing buildings of long ago and far away. As originally built in 1853, Immanuel was a plain rectangular structure. It acquired its Gothic character in an 1881 remodeling which included the facade with its stepped parapet, finials, and "rose" window. One of the state's most picturesque churches, Immanuel serves an active parish. *(42–125) VLR: 12/06/95; NRHP: 05/23/96.*

LAUREL MEADOW, *Mechanicsville vicinity.* Laurel Meadow's dwelling house is a model example of the eastern Virginia vernacular farmhouse of the first half of the 19th century. Its dormered gable roof, hall-parlor plan, and asymmetrical facade are all features associated with the building type, one that developed in the late 17th century. The construction date is unknown, but the house probably was fairly new in 1821 when the Oliver family occupied the property. It was acquired by George K. Hundley in 1860. In 1862 it was used as a campground respectively by both Union and Confederate troops. Hundley family tradition holds that Gen. Stonewall Jackson spent a wakeful night here writing dispatches. Additional fighting occurred nearby in 1864. Although it has passed through various owners, the house remains little changed and preserves several outbuildings. *(42–244) VLR: 04/28/95; NRHP: 07/07/95.*

MARLBOURNE, *Old Church vicinity.* Edmund Ruffin, the pioneering agronomist and ardent secessionist, made his Hanover County plantation a laboratory for his agricultural theories. By showing that exhausted soils could be revitalized with the application of marl, scientific crop rotation, and other advanced farming methods, he contributed to a renaissance of agriculture in the South. Violently opposed to any political interference from the North, he symbolized his dedication to the Confederate cause by firing one of the first shots on Fort Sumter. Although sacked by Union troops, Ruffin's substantial frame house at Marlbourne, built ca. 1845, survived without significant damage and still overlooks the broad, fertile bottomlands of his splendid farm, owned and operated by his descendants. Ruffin, who committed suicide over distress at the Confederate defeat, lies buried in the family cemetery. *(42–20) VLR: 09/09/69; NRHP: 10/15/66; NHL: 07/19/64.*

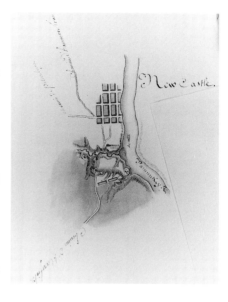

NEWCASTLE TOWN ARCHAEOLOGICAL SITE, *Old Church vicinity.* Newcastle was a colonial port town established by the General Assembly on a forty-acre tract on the Pamunkey River owned by William Meriwether. In 1739 its fifty-two lots, along with six lots reserved for warehouses, were surveyed by John Henry, father of Patrick Henry. On May 2, 1775, at the summons of Patrick Henry, the Hanover volunteers met at Newcastle to protest Governor Dunmore's removal of the colony's gunpowder from Williamsburg. Considerable military activity took place in the vicinity in 1781. Baron von Closen, aide-de-camp to Rochambeau, visited the town at that time and described it as "situated rather pleasantly on the banks of the Pamunkey." A French army cartographer drew the map shown. The silting of the river in the early 19th century led to Newcastle's decline and eventual disappearance, making the site valuable today for archaeological investigation. *(42–101) VLR: 12/16/75.*

OAKLAND, *Montpelier vicinity.* Oakland was the birthplace and childhood home of Virginia author Thomas Nelson Page (1853–1922). On this plantation Page absorbed the atmosphere and legends of Virginia that gave realism to his somewhat idealistic novels and short stories about the Old South. Among his most popular works is the children's book *Two Little Confederates.* His major novel, *Red Rock,* depicts the southern view of Reconstruction. The original house, built by the Nelson family in 1812, was a typical Virginia vernacular dormered dwelling, enlarged several times. Nelson described it in *Two Little Confederates* as "not a handsome place" and having "as many wings as Ezekiel." It burned in 1898, but Page had it immediately rebuilt in similar form on the original foundations. In addition to his literary activities, Page served with distinction as U.S. ambassador to Italy. Oakland is still owned by the Page family. *(42–24) VLR: 02/19/74; NRHP: 07/30/74.*

OAKLEY HILL, *Mechanicsville vicinity.* Built ca. 1839 by the Sydnor family, Oakley Hill's residence is representative of the numerous simple wood-frame houses that served the masters of the many small postcolonial plantations in the counties around Richmond. Most of these dwellings were situated inland, near creeks and springs, and contrasted in their simplicity with the mansions along the tidal rivers. Typically, Oakley Hill has little architectural pretension but achieves dignity by its placement at the end of a long cedar-lined avenue. It was expanded just before the Civil War when a full second story was added. The conservative character illustrates the persistence of vernacular patterns, particularly the I-house form, in rural Virginia. On the grounds is a rare two-unit servants' house and an early smokehouse. The property was spared the Civil War action that decimated much of this rural neighborhood. *(42–137) VLR: 03/10/94; NRHP: 05/19/94; BHR EASEMENT.*

PINE SLASH, *Studley vicinity.* Pine Slash was the first home of Patrick Henry and his bride, Sarah Shelton Henry. Her family gave them a manor house and 316 acres on the occasion of their marriage. The house was almost immediately destroyed by fire, and the couple moved into a cottage on the place that henceforth has been known as the "Honeymoon Cottage." This ca. 1750 structure may be a unique survival of a rare form of colonial vernacular construction. Both exterior and interior walls are built of heavy vertical planks. The planks are sheathed with weatherboard outside but are exposed inside, their joints covered with battens. Another interesting interior feature is the simple stair with its faceted newel pendant. The cottage was enlarged ca. 1800 but has escaped modernization. Nearby is a ca. 1830 gambrel-roof farmhouse built for the Jones family. *(42–25) VLR: 12/09/86; NRHP: 11/19/87; BHR EASEMENT.*

RANDOLPH-MACON COLLEGE COMPLEX, *College Avenue, Ashland.* Randolph-Macon College, chartered in 1830, is the oldest Methodist-related college in the United States still in operation. At the southwest corner of its 85-acre campus are the three buildings of its historic core, the first brick buildings constructed after the institution's move to Ashland from Boydton in 1868. The Italianate Washington and Franklin Hall is the school's oldest building.

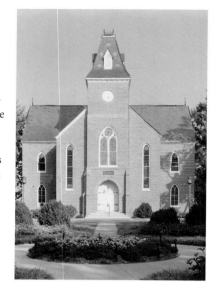

Designed by B. F. Price of Alexandria and completed in 1872, it long stood in deteriorated condition but underwent an extensive restoration in the 1980s. Pace Lecture Hall (1876), also in the Italianate style, was the school's principal academic building. It is currently undergoing extensive renovation. The 1879 Gothic Revival Duncan Memorial Chapel (shown) was designed by Richmond architect William West. Set in a tree-studded lawn, the group forms a nostalgic image of a small late Victorian collegiate complex. *(166–02) VLR: 04/17/79; NRHP: 06/19/79.*

RURAL PLAINS, *Rural Point vicinity.* One of the oldest dwellings in Hanover County, the gambrel-roofed house at Rural Plains is an important example of a substantial, nonacademic Tidewater farmhouse of the mid–18th century. It is distinguished by its large scale, Flemish bond brickwork, and curious porch chamber above the entrance, a very early, if not original, feature. The property has been the home of the Shelton family since 1670. An 18th-century owner, John Shelton, who was also proprietor of Hanover Tavern, was the father of Sarah Shelton Henry, Patrick Henry's first wife. Most of the original woodwork was removed during 19th-century remodelings. The property was the scene of Civil War action during the battle of Totopotomoy Creek. Union general Winfield S. Hancock made his headquarters here, forcing the Shelton family to live in the basement. *(42–29) VLR: 03/18/75; NRHP: 06/05/75; BHR EASEMENT.*

ST. PAUL'S EPISCOPAL CHURCH, *Hanover Court House.* The wooden St. Paul's Church, in a tree-shaded churchyard off busy U.S. 301, exemplifies a rural American interpretation of the glories of the Gothic style. Hundreds of such churches were hammered together throughout the country in the 19th century, and all have undeniable character. St. Paul's demonstrates how basic lumber—mainly simple boards— could be used with ingenuity to give architectural effect, seen here primarily in the decorative surfaces of the tower. Like the outside, the interior remains little altered with a vaulted ceiling of bent wood. The chancel and sanctuary retain their original wooden fittings ornamented with trefoils and quatrefoils. The church was built in 1895 to replace an 1845 church on the site that burned. Adjacent is a cemetery established in the 1840s. *(42–87) VLR: 03/10/94; NRHP: 05/19/94.*

SCOTCHTOWN, *Negro Foot vicinity.* Patrick Henry, the Revolutionary orator, made his home at this Hanover County plantation from 1771 to 1778, when he was active in shaping the course of events leading to Independence. Henry was living here when he was elected in 1776 as Virginia's first nonroyal governor. The barnlike house was built ca. 1719 as the country residence of Charles Chiswell of Williamsburg. Dolley Payne, later the wife of James Madison, lived here as a child. Scotchtown is probably the largest one-story colonial house in Virginia, with eight rooms and a center passage all on one floor. The otherwise plain exterior is given visual interest by the use of a jerkinhead roof. Scotchtown was rescued from deterioration in 1958 when it was acquired by the Hanover Branch of the Association for the Preservation of Virginia Antiquities. The carefully restored property is now a museum. *(42–30) VLR: 09/09/69; NRHP: 10/15/66; NHL: 12/21/65.*

SLASH CHURCH, *Ashcake vicinity.* This weatherboarded structure was erected in 1729–32 by Thomas Pinchback and Edward Chambers, Jr., as the Upper Church of the Anglican St. Paul's Parish. The building survives as the best-preserved wooden colonial church in the state, the only one to escape enlargement. Typical of up-country ecclesiastical structures, the building is a simple rectangle with a gable roof and front and side entrances. Its roof framing employs an early king-post truss system. Next to the swampy woods whence it derives its present name, the church claims among its early worshipers Patrick Henry, Dolley Madison, and Henry Clay, all sometime residents of the area. The church fell into disuse after the disestablishment and eventually was taken over by the Methodists and the Disciples of Christ. The latter denomination has used the church exclusively since 1842. *(42–33) VLR: 08/15/72; NRHP: 09/22/72.*

SPRINGFIELD, *Coatsville vicinity.* Springfield's brick dwelling house, a standard two-story Federal residence, was built in 1820 for Lucy Grymes Nelson, widow of Thomas Nelson, Jr., a signer of the Declaration of Independence and governor of Virginia. Though Mrs. Nelson was of the most patrician of Virginia families, her house is surprisingly unpretentious. Her lofty status, however, made Springfield a place of social importance, one served by thirty-seven slaves. Except for the replacement of some first-floor woodwork with Greek Revival trim and one-story additions built on the side and rear in 1970, the house has been little changed. In front of the house is a circle of very old English boxwood with a large tree box in the center, said to be a remnant of a garden planted by Mrs. Nelson. Behind the house is an original frame kitchen-laundry outbuilding and a frame smokehouse. *(42–428) VLR: 06/15/94; NRHP: 08/16/94.*

SYCAMORE TAVERN, *Montpelier*. The simple dignity of Virginia's traditional rural buildings is well depicted in this country tavern with its dormers and engaged front porch, the latter a feature typical of early taverns. The construction date is unknown, but it was first recorded as a tavern in 1804 when it was serving as the fourth stagecoach stop on the Old Mountain Road, a historic route between Richmond and Charlottesville. In the mid–19th century it was known as Shelburn's Tavern after its preacher-innkeeper the Rev. Silas Shelburn. In this century author Thomas Nelson Page, a Hanover County native, founded a library here in memory of his second wife. Although the building is owned by the county, the Florence L. Page Memorial Library continues to be funded by a trust established by Page and now specializes in local history and genealogy. *(42–85) VLR: 08/15/72; NRHP: 07/24/74.*

TRINITY CHURCH, *Beaverdam vicinity*. A rare example of a country Episcopal church untouched by the ecclesiological reforms of the late 19th century, Trinity Church was constructed in 1830 by William and Milton Green, local builders. Following the low-church Episcopal tradition, the interior focused on a center pulpit rather than an altar. This arrangement was given distinction here by the use of a semicircular communion railing enclosing the curved rostrum and a curved holy table. Beyond the railing is a curved ring of communion benches. Another rare survival is a sign in the gallery which reads: "FIRST THREE PEWS ON THIS SIDE, FOR SERVANTS." Trinity has always been a part of St. Martin's Parish, which was formed in 1726. The congregation merged with Fork Church in the 1960s. The parish holds an annual service here each Trinity Sunday. *(42–38) VLR: 02/20/90; NRHP: 12/27/90.*

TOTOMOI, *Rural Point vicinity*. Named for Totopotomoy, husband of the queen of the Pamunkey Indians, who was slain in 1656 in a battle nearby, Totomoi is an undisturbed plantation complex in the midst of a rapidly developing area of Hanover County. The centerpiece is a ca. 1795 frame dwelling house which preserves its original side porches with their scalloped eaves, as well as an unusual two-level entrance porch. The rear is dominated by a pair of chimney stacks connected by pent closets. Nearly all of the house's original fabric, inside and out, survives. Complementing the scene are early outbuildings, an informal park, a family cemetery, and a formal garden. The complex as a whole evokes a memorable picture of rural life in old Virginia. The property was granted to Thomas Tinsley in 1689 and is still owned by his descendants. *(42–39) VLR: 02/17/76; NRHP: 12/12/76; BHR EASEMENT.*

WILLIAMSVILLE, *Studley vicinity*. One of the grandest Federal houses in Hanover County, Williamsville was begun in 1794 for George William Pollard who succeeded his father as county clerk. Pollard's precise business methods earned him the nickname "Billy Particular." Pollard family papers document that the house was constructed by Benjamin Ellett. The handsomely proportioned structure has been little changed over the past two centuries, retaining its finely executed detailing inside and out, including mantels with Adamesque ornaments. Because the house enjoyed a commanding view from its position on one of the highest elevations in the area, it became a choice location for military operations in both 1862 and 1864. At varying times Union generals Grant, Hooker, and Meade made Williamsville their headquarters. The house escaped damage from the occupation. Williamsville was restored after its purchase in 1964 by Mr. and Mrs. Robert Woodrow Cabaniss, noted preservationists. *(42–27) VLR: 04/16/85; NRHP: 11/18/85.*

CITY OF HARRISONBURG

The county seat of Rockingham County, Harrisonburg was named for Thomas Harrison, who donated land for the town site. It was established in 1780 and incorporated as a town in 1849. Harrisonburg became a city in 1916.

THOMAS HARRISON HOUSE, *30 West Bruce Street.* The modern city of Harrisonburg grew up around this modest stone house erected for Thomas Harrison ca. 1750. Harrison laid out the town that was to bear his name on fifty acres of his holdings and was also instrumental in having Harrisonburg established in 1780 as the Rockingham county seat. The first courts were held in his home. Bishop Francis Asbury, pioneer leader of the Methodist Episcopal church, often visited Harrison and conducted some of the county's first Methodist services in the house. The first annual Methodist conference west of the Blue Ridge Mountains was held here in 1794. The Harrison house is an example of the Shenandoah Valley's earliest form of stone vernacular architecture. Its window architraves are cut from solid walnut timbers. The house remained in the Harrison family until 1870 and is now an office. *(115–08)* VLR: 06/19/73; NRHP: 07/26/73.

ANTHONY HOCKMAN HOUSE, *Market and Broad streets.* Anthony Hockman, one of Harrisonburg's local builders, designed and built this elaborately ornamented Italianate residence for himself in 1871. An excellent example of the architecturally spirited late Victorian dwellings of prosperous small towns, the house incorporates a traditional symmetrical plan with fancy ornament inside and out. Its lacy sawn trim is typical of Harrisonburg houses in the last decades of the century, reflecting the town's growing awareness of architectural fashion. Hockman set his house apart from more standard dwellings by using a multiwindowed cupola with an eye-catching concave pyramidal roof. A highlight of the interior is the elaborate stenciled decorations on the dining room ceiling. *(115–23)* VLR: 01/20/81; NRHP: 07/08/82.

JOSHUA WILTON HOUSE, *412 South Main Street.* Harrisonburg's Joshua Wilton house is among the Shenandoah Valley's more vigorous examples of Victorian domestic architecture. The house also represents the late 19th-century practice of businessmen erecting proud, self-assertive, often extravagantly embellished dwellings along principal streets to serve as statements of their wealth and position. Joshua Wilton came to Harrisonburg from Canada in 1865 and quickly became one of the town's mercantile and civic leaders. His fancy house, showing Gothic, Italianate, and Queen Anne influences, was built ca. 1888 and clearly illustrates how such residences lent prestige to their owners while giving embellishment to the town. The building received rough-and-tumble use as a fraternity house for a number of years but is now a handsomely restored bed-and-breakfast inn. *(115–20) VLR: 10/17/78; NRHP: 05/24/79.*

ROCKINGHAM COUNTY COURTHOUSE, *Court Square.* One of nearly 200 buildings designed by Staunton architect T. J. Collins, the Rockingham County Courthouse reveals his mastery of the fashionable Richardsonian Romanesque and Renaissance Revival styles of the late 19th century. The building was constructed by the Washington, D.C., firm of W. E. Spiers between 1896 and 1897 and is the fifth courthouse to stand on the site since the county was formed from Augusta in 1778. The courthouse, one of Virginia's grandest of the period, reflects Rockingham County's late 19th-century prosperity. Collins even outfitted the second floor with an auditorium for public entertainments. With its lively elevations and lofty clock tower, all faced with rough-hewn sandstone ashlar, the courthouse remains Harrisonburg's most prominent architectural landmark. *(115–02) VLR: 07/20/82; NRHP: 09/16/82.*

HENRICO COUNTY

Located at the fall line of the James River, Henrico County was named for Henry, Prince of Wales, eldest son of King James I. It was one of the eight original shires established by 1634. The county seat is a modern government complex in Richmond's western suburbs.

FLOOD MARKER, *Curles Neck.* The disastrous flood of May 27, 1771, when "all the great Rivers of this county were swept by Inundations Never before experienced, Which changed the face of nature," is commemorated on this stone obelisk in the woods of eastern Henrico County. The flood was 18th-century Virginia's worst natural disaster. The monument, erected that same year by Ryland Randolph on a bank above the James River bottomlands, was intended as a memorial to his parents, Richard and Jane Bolling Randolph. The flood so impressed Randolph that he had the monument inscribed with a description of the disaster, partially quoted above. The obelisk is an unusually large and impressive example of a colonial memorial piece. Its capstone was lost through Civil War damage. *(43–23) VLR: 07/07/70; NRHP: 09/22/71.*

FORT HARRISON NATIONAL CEMETERY, *8620 Varina Road.* Taking its name from the nearby Confederate fortification, part of the Richmond defenses, Fort Harrison National Cemetery was established in May 1866. Of the 1,522 total interments, the majority of which are known and unknown Civil War dead, most were killed in the fighting around Richmond in 1864. One, Pvt. George A. Buchanan, of the 148th New York Infantry, fell on September 29, 1864, while attacking a Confederate battery at Fort Harrison and was awarded the Medal of Honor posthumously. Four others died while prisoners of war. Many buried in the cemetery were soldiers of the U.S. Colored Troops. The Second Empire–style superintendent's lodge was built in 1871 from a design by Quartermaster General Montgomery C. Meigs. The largest monument in the cemetery is a seacoast artillery tube set in a concrete base. *(43–134) VLR: 04/28/95; NRHP: 08/10/95.*

GLENDALE NATIONAL CEMETERY, *Route 156, Providence Forge vicinity.* Glendale National Cemetery, established on July 14, 1866, contains 2,000 casketed remains of U.S. soldiers, most of whom were killed during the closing hours of the Seven Days' campaign. The campaign included the battles of Glendale, White Oak Swamp, and Malvern Hill, which occurred June 30–July 1, 1862. After the war the soldiers' remains were collected from their shallow battlefield graves and reinterred both here and at other cemeteries. Quartermaster General Montgomery C. Meigs designed the superintendent's quarters, or lodge, in the Second Empire style; it was constructed in 1874. *(43–753); VLR: 10/18/95; NRHP: 02/26/96.*

LAUREL INDUSTRIAL SCHOOL HISTORIC DISTRICT, *Hungary Road.* The Progressive Era's spirit of reform is tangibly memorialized in the surviving buildings of the Laurel Industrial School. The Prison Association of Virginia, a group of private citizens seeking to reform the treatment of juvenile offenders, established this institution in 1892 as a model boys' reformatory. Privately owned and administered, the school received state appropriations until the Commonwealth took control in 1920. The complex was sold to private owners when its functions were moved to Goochland County in 1932. In its heyday about 300 boys were housed here, attending classes and working in the shops or on the farm. The principal surviving structure of this high-minded effort is the 1896 Main Building, a Romanesque-style work recently rehabilitated for new use. Also remaining are the infirmary, the administration building, and the superintendent's house, all relatively modest structures. The farmland has succumbed to modern development. *(43–292) VLR: 10/15/85; NRHP: 06/12/87.*

MALVERN HILL, *Varina vicinity.* Malvern Hill is marked by the foundations and a small section of wall of a late 17th-century manor house built for Thomas Cocke (d. 1697), sheriff of Henrico County and a member of the House of Burgesses. The house was destroyed by fire in 1905, but its exterior appearance is known through photographs. It apparently began as a brick-ended frame house. The chimneys later were incorporated in a cruciform-plan brick house. Malvern Hill figured in three wars. Lafayette encamped here in July and August 1781, and the Virginia militia made camp here in the War of 1812. The bloody Civil War battle of Malvern Hill took place nearby during the Peninsula campaign. Some 5,500 Confederates fell on the hill's slopes on July 1, 1862. The house served as a Union headquarters. *(43–08) VLR: 05/13/69; NRHP: 11/17/69.*

MANKIN MANSION, *4300 Oakleys Lane.* This singular complex was the creation of Edward Thurston Mankin, owner of E. T. Mankin, Inc., a brick-manufacturing company. Constructed in 1924, the house, along with a landscaped garden defined by brick walks, walls, garden structures, and a profusion of brick details, presents a comprehensive essay in brick construction techniques. Both the sprawling house and ancillary structures display Mankin's idiosyncratic interpretation of the Georgian Revival style, while the brickwork throughout the complex exhibits samples of Mankin's bricks. Mankin's brick factory was established in 1903 on a site south of the house and operated until his death in 1951. The company supplied bricks for many Richmond buildings as well as for Colonial Williamsburg projects. The kilns were demolished in the 1960s, but the house and grounds remain unchanged. *(43–68) VLR: 08/18/93; NRHP: 10/14/93.*

MEADOW FARM, *Glen Allen vicinity.* Meadow Farm figured in the 1800 insurrection instigated by the slave Gabriel. Gabriel's goal was to have an army of slaves capture Richmond. Mosby Sheppard of Meadow Farm was warned of the pending action by family slaves and notified Governor James Monroe, who halted the revolt before it began. News of the would-be insurrection spread fear and demand for repression throughout the South, resulting in the execution of Gabriel and some thirty-five other slaves associated with the plot. The two slaves who warned Sheppard were given their freedom. The present house, begun in 1810, is a standard medium-size vernacular dwelling of the period and replaced the Sheppard house standing at the time of the insurrection. Meadow Farm was given to Henrico County by a Sheppard descendant and is now exhibited as a museum of the region's early rural life. *(43–31) VLR: 05/21/74; NRHP: 08/13/74.*

VIRGINIA RANDOLPH COTTAGE, *2200 Mountain Road.* This brick cottage honors a black woman who gained national repute as an educator. In 1908 Henrico County instructor Virginia Estell Randolph (1874–1958) was appointed the nation's first Jeanes supervising industrial teacher. The Jeanes supervisor was the concept of a wealthy Philadelphian, Anna T. Jeanes, who established a fund to employ black supervisors for vocational training in the South. The program became institutionalized under the Negro Rural School Fund and spread throughout the southern states and eventually abroad. Virginia Randolph thus became a model for thousands of teacher supervisors. Throughout her career she maintained an interest in Mountain Road School where she first worked in the 1890s. The school was reestablished as the Virginia Randolph Education Center in 1969, and the 1937 cottage where she taught home economics and kept an office is now a museum honoring the distinguished educator, who is buried in front. *(43–43) VLR: 03/18/75; NHL: 12/02/74.*

RICHMOND NATIONAL BATTLEFIELD PARK, *eastern Henrico County, also in Hanover County and Richmond.* In order to protect their capital from Union invasion, Confederate forces constructed an extensive system of earthworks around Richmond. These were put to the test in the Peninsula campaign of 1862 when Union general George B. McClellan advanced to the city but ultimately was outfought by Gen. Robert E. Lee during the Seven Days' campaign. Heavy action again took place east of Richmond in May–June 1864, when Gen. Ulysses Grant moved south from Spotsylvania and confronted Lee at Cold Harbor where the Union army was beaten back with heavy losses. Today the network of battlefields and fortifications extending from north of Richmond to the James River, and including the site of Chimborazo Hospital in Richmond, is exhibited as a historical park by the National Park Service. *(43–33) VLR: 01/16/73; NRHP: 10/15/66.*

RICHMOND NATIONAL CEMETERY, *1701 Williamsburg Road.* Some 9,200 interments, including 5,706 unknown Union soldiers and one unknown Confederate soldier, have taken place in Richmond National Cemetery since it was established on September 1, 1866. The Union dead were gathered after the war from the battlefields of Seven Pines and Cold Harbor, among others, from Hollywood and Oakwood cemeteries, and from the prisoner-of-war graveyard on Belle Isle in the James River. The remains of the lone Confederate soldier now buried here were discovered early in 1978 at the Beaver Dam Creek battlefield in Hanover County and reinterred on April 7, 1978. The 1870 Second Empire superintendent's lodge was designed by Quartermaster General Montgomery C. Meigs. *(43–126) VLR: 08/28/95; NRHP: 10/26/95.*

SEVEN PINES NATIONAL CEMETERY, *400 East Williamsburg Road.* Although the Seven Pines National Cemetery is located on the 1862 battlefield of the same name, most of the nearly 1,400 Union soldiers buried here were moved from graves at Savage's Station and other locations within a four-mile radius of the cemetery. The cemetery was established on June 27, 1866; the frame superintendent's lodge built that year was replaced in 1874 by a Second Empire–style lodge designed by Quartermaster General Montgomery C. Meigs. Seven Pines National Cemetery preserves part of the battlefield on which Gen. Robert E. Lee took command of the Army of Northern Virginia on June 1, 1862. *(43–755) VLR: 08/28/95; NRHP: 10/26/95.*

structure was erected in the late 18th century by Miles Selden, the county clerk and local politician. During Selden's tenure Tree Hill was known for its racetrack; Lafayette attended a well-publicized horse race here in 1824. The property passed to Selden's son-in-law William Roane, a U.S. congressman and senator. At Tree Hill on April 3, 1865, Richmond mayor Joseph Mayo surrendered the Confederate capital to Maj. Gen. Godfrey Weitzel, commander of the Union army in front of Richmond. The plantation maintains a scenic rural edge for Richmond's east end. *(43–32) VLR: 05/21/74; NRHP: 10/17/74.*

VARINA PLANTATION, *Varina Road.* Settled during the early 17th century, Varina plantation was the site of the Henrico Parish glebe, established before 1640. The first Henrico County courthouse was built at Varina before 1666. The Rev. James Blair, who later became the first rector of the College of William and Mary, lived at Varina between 1685 and 1694 when he was minister at Varina Parish. During the 1720s Thomas Randolph of Tuckahoe purchased land at Varina, and his son Thomas Mann Randolph developed the property into a prosperous plantation. In 1828 Thomas Mann Randolph, Jr., sold the plantation to Pleasant Aiken of Petersburg, whose son Albert M. Aiken built the present brick dwelling just before the Civil War. Aiken's Landing became one of two major points in the South where prisoners of war were exchanged. A persistent legend linking Varina with John Rolfe and Pocahontas arose in the mid–19th century. *(43–20) VLR: 09/21/76; NRHP: 04/29/77.*

TREE HILL, *Osborne Turnpike.* On a commanding bluff overlooking the bottomlands of the James River with a panoramic view of the Richmond skyline to the west, this imposing frame house with its surrounding outbuildings was the home of two prominent Henrico County families, the Seldens and the Roanes. The original portion of the much-evolved

WALKERTON, *Mountain Road, Glen Allen vicinity.* A massive but plain brick structure, Walkerton was built in 1825 as a tavern serving travelers along Mountain Road, once a major artery between Richmond and the western Piedmont. Stagecoaches stopped here regularly before the Civil War; as late as 1908 a large carriage shed and stable accommodating twenty horses stood in the backyard. The building takes its name from John Walker, who undertook the construction of the present building and died just as it was completed. The property was acquired in 1828 by John B. White, a licensed tavern keeper. The swinging, hinged partition on the second floor is a feature frequently found in early taverns. When opened it created a large room for dancing and receptions. The tavern's last private owner, S. Douglas Fleet, undertook an extensive restoration of the building in the 1980s. The property is now owned by Henrico County. *(43–19) VLR: 10/16/84; NRHP: 12/06/84.*

WOODSIDE, *South Gaskins Road.* Originally part of Tuckahoe plantation, Woodside was a farm tract purchased from the Randolph family in 1800 by John Wickham, builder of Richmond's Wickham-Valentine house, now the Valentine Museum. Wickham's son Littleton Waller Tazewell Wickham built the present Greek Revival villa in 1858 as a rural retreat. On the basis of an original paint contract, the design of the house is attributed to Albert L. West, the most noted of Richmond's mid-19th-century native architects. The dwelling is significant for its unusual massing and floor plan, as well as its sophisticated interior and exterior detailing. Much of the building's original decorative painting is intact, including rare fragments of exterior stuccoing painted to resemble cut stone. The house and its park are surrounded by woods from which the place takes its name. *(43–12) VLR: (02/20/73); NRHP: 07/24/73; BHR EASEMENT.*

HENRY COUNTY

Named for Patrick Henry, first governor of the Virginia Commonwealth, this southern Piedmont county was formed from Pittsylvania County in 1776. Its county seat is Martinsville.

BEAVER CREEK PLANTATION, *Figsboro Road, Martinsville vicinity.* This spread-out wooden mansion stands on property that was part of Beaver Creek plantation where Col. George Hairston built a brick residence in 1776. The colonial dwelling burned in 1839 and was replaced with the core of the present frame house by Hairston's son Marshall Hairston. The new structure followed a standard two-story, five-bay format used by many of Virginia's well-to-do landed families in the early 19th century. Its interior is trimmed with straightforward Greek Revival woodwork. Wings, a portico, and a veranda were added around 1900. The Hairston family was one of the state's largest landholders and accumulated great wealth as tobacco planters. At a time when most tobacco farmers owned around 100 acres, George Hairston by 1826 owned 143,000 acres. In 1900 the family still controlled some 60,000 acres. Beaver Creek plantation, their core holding, formerly included about 1,200 acres. *(44–01) VLR: 04/16/85; NRHP: 05/09/85.*

BELLEVIEW, *Ridgeway vicinity.* A handsome specimen of provincial Georgian architecture, Belleview was built in the late 18th century for John Redd, a pioneer settler who served as a member of the county court and participated during the Revolution in several frontier actions against the crown's Loyalist and Indian supporters. The property descended in the family to Kennon C. Whittle (died 1967), member of the Virginia Supreme Court of Appeals. In the hilly reaches of the county, the dwelling remains true to its name in enjoying a splendid view across the undulating countryside. Sheltering the center bay is a naive though graceful two-level Ionic portico. The house was restored by its present owner in 1984. *(44–02) VLR: 05/21/74; NRHP: 06/10/74.*

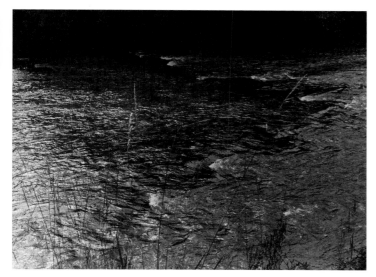

MARTINSVILLE FISH DAM, *Smith River, Martinsville vicinity.* The Martinsville fish dam is one of the few such aboriginal fish traps of its type remaining in the state. The structure consists of stones piled in the bed of the river to form a low V-shaped wall or dam extending from bank to bank with the apex of the V pointing downstream. The dam originally was probably a foot or more high. The apex of the V was left open, and a basket was held there to trap fish as they swam with the current and were funneled into the basket. The dam is partially exposed when the river is low and is in a good state of preservation. It likely was associated with an Indian village site nearby on the south bank of the river. Half of the dam is now owned by the Archeological Society of Virginia. *(44–86) VLR: 09/18/73; NRHP: 01/21/74.*

STONELEIGH, *Stanleytown.* Built 1929–31 after the plans of Leland McBroom of the Des Moines, Iowa, firm of Tinsley and McBroom, Stoneleigh is an impressive example of the Tudor Revival style. It was commissioned by industrialist Thomas B. Stanley, later governor of Virginia. The Tudor Revival, an outgrowth of the English Arts and Crafts movement, enjoyed popularity in America in the 1920s and 1930s. The construction of this meticuously crafted house coincided with the end of Stanley's active career as a furniture manufacturer and the beginning of his long political association with the state Democratic party that led to the governorship in 1954. Stoneleigh's extensive gardens, designed by E. S. Draper of North Carolina and later reworked by Charles F. Gillette of Richmond, were the inspiration of Mrs. Stanley, née Anne Pocahontas Bassett. *(44–87) VLR: 03/16/82; NRHP: 11/24/82.*

HIGHLAND COUNTY

Named for its mountainous terrain, Highland County was formed from Pendleton County (now in West Virginia) and Bath County in 1847. Its county seat is Monterey.

MCCLUNG FARM HISTORIC DISTRICT, *Clover Creek.* Far from modern bustle, the scenic mountains and valleys of Highland County maintain, perhaps best, the serenity of 19th-century rural Virginia. The several components of the Mc-Clung farm, situated along the Bullpasture River, capture this image in a single scene. This historic homestead has remained in the same family since William McClung purchased the farm in 1838. The brick farmhouse, architecturally akin to contemporary dwellings in adjacent Augusta County, was built by McClung in 1844. Essentially unchanged, its interior preserves boldly detailed mantels and original graining. Nearby stands a collection of wood-frame farm buildings erected around the end of the 19th century. A short distance from the complex is the quaint 1880s Clover Creek Presbyterian Church built on land donated by the McClung family. Members of the family are buried in the church cemetery. *(45–11) VLR: 08/21/90; NRHP: 01/25/91.*

MONTEREY HOTEL (HIGHLAND INN), *Main Street, Monterey.* Built in 1904, this reminder of a bygone era is Monterey's signature landmark. From the mid–19th century through the early 20th century, western Virginia was known for its numerous resort hotels offering a salubrious climate for visitors seeking to escape the summer heat and unwholesome airs of the seaboard cities. A more hurried lifestyle, easier long-distance travel, and air-conditioning resulted in the demise of nearly all of these hostelries, making the Monterey Hotel a rare survival. The hotel's first owner was S. W. Crummett of Staunton, who commissioned the Eustler brothers of Grottoes to construct the building for $6,000. Its dominant feature is the inviting wraparound Eastlake gallery with its lacy spindle friezes. Early guests include Harvey Firestone and Henry Ford. The restored hotel now hosts visitors under the name Highland Inn. *(262–04) VLR: 10/16/73; NRHP: 01/18/74.*

CITY OF HOPEWELL

A community at the junction of the Appomattox and James rivers was established in 1613 as Bermuda City and was later known as City Point. The adjacent Hopewell industrial community was incorporated as a city in 1916 and enlarged by the annexation of City Point in 1923.

APPOMATTOX MANOR, *Cedar Lane and Pecan Avenue.* Occupying the tip of City Point, at the confluence of the James and Appomattox rivers, Appomattox Manor is one of the oldest extant estates in America. It was patented by Francis Eppes in 1635 and remained in the Eppes family until 1979. The house was built ca. 1763 and subsequently expanded. The outbuildings date from the 19th century. British soldiers under Gen. Benedict Arnold marched through the property during the Revolution. From June 1864 until April 1865, it was the headquarters of Gen. Ulysses S. Grant. From his tent and later from his cabin, Grant directed the far-flung Union armies during the final ten months of the Civil War. President Abraham Lincoln visited Appomattox Manor in 1864 and 1865, meeting with Grant in the drawing room. The property is now part of the City Point unit of the Petersburg National Battlefield. *(116–01) VLR: 11/05/68; NRHP: 10/01/79.*

CITY POINT HISTORIC DISTRICT. A settlement was established at City Point as early as 1613. First called Bermuda City, the village was renamed Charles City Point, and eventually City Point. It was incorporated in 1826 and annexed to Hopewell in 1923. The community remained small throughout the 18th and 19th centuries. The weight of history descended on City Point in 1864 when Gen. Ulysses S. Grant made it his base of operations. Thousands of Union soldiers disembarked here, and numerous wharves, warehouses, depots, and tents were quickly put up. A Catholic chapel (shown) survives from the period. President Abraham Lincoln visited City Point to observe the progress of the war. The community once again became a sleepy port village after the conflict and remained so until the DuPont Co. munitions plant was established nearby in 1913. Today, City Point is a tree-shaded residential neighborhood, with 18th- and 19th-century buildings scattered among architecturally harmonious later ones. *(116–06) VLR: 09/19/78; NRHP: 10/15/79.*

CITY POINT NATIONAL CEMETERY, *Tenth Avenue and Davis Street.* Established in July 1866, the City Point National Cemetery occupies part of the site of the great Union supply depot created in June 1864 for the army besieging Petersburg and Richmond. During the last year of the Civil War, U.S. soldiers who died in City Point hospitals were buried here, and after the war reinterments occurred from grave sites in Charles City and Chesterfield counties. Also reburied in the cemetery were the remains of twenty Confederate and Union soldiers discovered in and around Hopewell in the 1950s and 1980s. Altogether there are 5,156 interments of Civil War soldiers and sailors, of which 118 are Confederates. The superintendent's lodge dates from 1928. *(116–08) VLR: 04/28/95; NRHP: 08/10/95.*

WESTON MANOR, *Weston Lane and Twenty-first Avenue.* This Georgian plantation house stood almost unknown until the mid-1970s when it was donated by Raymond Broyhill to the Historic Hopewell Foundation. The house is on land acquired by William and Christine Eppes Gilliam in the late 18th century and probably was erected for them in the 1780s. The frame structure follows the formal rectangular format of mid-18th-century Virginia plantation dwellings and is notable for preserving nearly all of its original fabric, including molded weatherboards, window sash, and interior woodwork. The house was shelled by a Northern gunboat in the Civil War and photographed by Mathew Brady during its occupation by Northern troops. The surrounding farmlands have been developed, but the house preserves a pleasant setting on terraced banks overlooking the Appomattox River. Weston Manor is now a local museum and cultural center. *(116–02) VLR: 11/16/71; NRHP: 04/13/72.*

ISLE OF WIGHT COUNTY

Named for the Isle of Wight off England's south coast, this county on the south shore of the James River was first called Warrosquyoake and was one of the eight original shires formed by 1634. It was given its present name in 1637. The county seat is Isle of Wight Court House.

BASSES CHOICE ARCHAEOLOGICAL DISTRICT, *Mogarts Beach vicinity.* At the confluence of the James and Pagan rivers, the Basses Choice Archaeological District reflects a nearly continuous span of human occupation from ca. 4000 B.C. through the 19th century. Prehistoric site types range from small, temporary Archaic and Woodland camps to larger, more sedentary Woodland communities. Historic-period occupation includes portions of three Virginia Company settlements, two of which suffered heavily in the 1622 Indian attack. Archaeological excavation of the sites should yield new information on the material culture and architecture of Virginia's earliest English settlers. The site takes its name from Nathaniel Basse, who patented land here in 1622. The property was occupied by the Wilson family in the early 19th century and by the Blackwell family during the Civil War. *(46–94) VLR: 04/19/83; NRHP: 07/28/83.*

BOYKIN'S TAVERN, *Isle of Wight Court House.* Standing next to the courthouse, Boykin's Tavern illustrates the functional relationship such early hostelries had with rural county-seat complexes. The tavern's original core was constructed around 1780 as a residence for Francis Boykin, a Revolutionary officer, county clerk, and justice of the county court. In 1800 Boykin gave land for the relocation of the county seat from Smithfield in return for permission to erect the new county buildings here. After Boykin's death in 1804, his son Francis Marshall Boykin enlarged the tavern by raising it to two full stories and adding the gambrel-roof wing. The portico probably was also added at this time. Despite further changes made ca. 1900, the tavern retains exceptionally fine 18th-century paneling in two of its rooms. Now owned by the county, the building has long been unoccupied but is scheduled for renovation. *(46–28) VLR: 05/21/74; NRHP: 06/19/74; BHR EASEMENT.*

FORT BOYKIN, *Mogarts Beach vicinity.* Situated on a bluff overlooking the James River, this earthwork fortification was constructed by the Confederate army between June 1861 and May 1862 as part of the system for blocking Union access to Richmond by river. The fort was captured by Federal troops shortly after its completion and has remained essentially intact. Archaeological testing has revealed intact subsurface features that could add to the information on military activities in the fort as well as explain camp life and material culture from the Civil War period. The earthwork is part of the Fort Boykin Historical Park maintained by the Isle of Wight Public Recreational Facilities Authority. *(46–95) VLR: 06/18/85; NRHP: 08/01/85.*

FOUR SQUARE, *Smithfield vicinity.* One of southeastern Virginia's best collections of domestic outbuildings and early farm buildings is preserved on this Isle of Wight plantation. The two-story, L-shaped house was built in 1807 for the Woodley family on land they had owned since the late 17th century. Its generous proportions and robust interior woodwork make the house representative of the region's more prosperous early 19th-century homesteads. The domestic outbuildings consist of a cookhouse, dairy, smokehouse, and slave house. The farm buildings include an early granary of log construction. The archaeological sites of a number of other subsidiary buildings remain scattered among the standing structures. A family member once described Four Square in its heyday, when all of its early buildings were standing, as being "like a busy village." *(46–26) VLR: 04/17/79; NRHP: 07/26/79.*

JOSEPH JORDAN HOUSE (DEWS PLANTATION), *Raynor vicinity.* Built for the planter Joseph Jordan, this small brick-ended farmhouse with its distinctive architectural detailing typifies the moderate-sized southeastern Virginia plantation house of the late 18th century. It belongs to a group of architecturally related houses in the Blackwater River area that represent the first flush of prosperity for the middling planters who settled here. A singular feature of these houses is the long shed dormer that lights the top floor, used instead of the more standard dormers. The later additions on the house, the outbuildings, and the 150-acre tract complete the picture of a typical 19th-century farmstead of the region. The property has been known variously as Jordan's or Boykin's Quarter, the Hattie Barlow Moody farm, or Dews Plantation. *(46–82) VLR: 02/26/79; NRHP: 06/22/79.*

OLD ISLE OF WIGHT COURTHOUSE, *Main and Mason streets, Smithfield.* The former Isle of Wight courthouse is one of Virginia's six remaining arcaded colonial court structures. It was completed, along with the clerk's office and jail, in 1752, following the relocation of the county seat from Glebe Farm to Smithfield. Built by William Rand, it is notable among its contemporaries for having a curved apse with conical roof, following the precedent of the curved apses on the first Capitol in Williamsburg. The courthouse was converted to a residence after the transfer of the county seat from Smithfield in 1802. Its arcade was blocked up and its roof changed from a hip to a gable. In 1938 the building was acquired by the Isle of Wight Branch of the Association for the Preservation of Virginia Antiquities, which restored its mid-18th-century appearance in 1959–62. It is now a visitors' center. *(300–02) VLR: 06/02/70; NRHP: 09/15/70.*

POPLAR HILL, *Smithfield vicinity.* A little-altered example of Tidewater Virginia vernacular architecture, Poplar Hill was built ca. 1793 for John Stott, a native of Scotland who came to Virginia with two brothers, settling in Isle of Wight County. Though built for a Scotsman, the house shows no hint of any specifically Scottish character. It is, rather, a standard hall-parlor frame dwelling with dormers and end chimneys, a house type preferred by the region's middling planters. A noteworthy original feature is the stenciled decoration on three of the stair risers. Stott was an enterprising individual. He purchased nearby Wrenn's Mill, and by his death in 1814, he owned 700 acres along with livestock, slaves, a brandy still, and $1,350 in cash. Poplar Hill has been passed down through the same family to the present day. *(46–96) VLR: 06/27/95; NRHP: 08/18/95.*

ST. LUKE'S CHURCH, *Benns Church.* This time-honored house of worship, originally known as Newport Parish Church, is America's purest expression of authentic Gothic architecture. Although simple in design, its buttressed walls, lancet side windows, and traceried east window have for more than three centuries formed one of the New World's most direct links with the architecture of the Middle Ages. The construction date is controversial. Most likely it was built with its tower near the end of the 17th century when the colonists began to undertake more substantial architectural works. St. Luke's fell into disrepair after the disestablishment and was more or less ruinous for most of the 19th century. A series of repairs, begun in 1894, culminated in a thorough and meticulous restoration completed in 1957. No longer a parish church, St. Luke's is an official historic shrine of the Episcopal Diocese of Southern Virginia. *(46–24) VLR: 09/09/69; NRHP: 10/15/66; NHL: 10/09/60.*

WILLIAM SCOTT FARMSTEAD, *Windsor vicinity.* Preserving the continuity and sense of place so strongly associated with Tidewater Virginia, the William Scott farmstead centers on a brick plantation house where many generations have left their mark. The dwelling's core, constructed in finely crafted Flemish bond with glazed headers, was likely built sometime after 1740 by William Scott. It apparently was enlarged to a two-story structure in the late 18th century by Scott's son, also named William Scott. The house has had subsequent modifications and additions but maintains a venerable 18th-century character. The interior retains early paneled doors and sections of paneled trim. In the basement is an original cooking fireplace. Around the house is an important collection of little-altered early 19th-century ancillary structures, among which are a quarters building, kitchen, smokehouse, and barn-stable. *(46–86) VLR: 04/17/90; NRHP: 01/25/91.*

SMITHFIELD HISTORIC DISTRICT. On the banks of the Pagan River, this compact community survives as perhaps the most intact of Virginia's colonial seaports. World-famous for the Smithfield hams produced here commercially for over two centuries, the quiet little town has escaped significant modernization. Smithfield was founded in 1749 on the plantation of Arthur Smith and was incorporated in 1752. With a population of a little over 1,000, the district has approximately fifty buildings of exceptional architectural interest. A rich sampling includes the 1752 courthouse; the late 18th-century Todd house, home of the town's earliest meat-packers; The Grove, a formal Federal house; and the lavish Queen Anne–style P. D. Gwaltney, Jr., house, home of a modern meatpacking family. The Colonial Revival Boykin house is the largest of the many fine residences lining tree-arched Church Street. Numerous lesser buildings of various types contribute to the town's historic ambience. *(300–87) VLR: 02/20/73; NRHP: 07/02/73.*

WOLFTRAP FARM, *Smithfield vicinity.* An architectural curiosity, this vernacular farmhouse survives as Virginia's only known example of an early dwelling with a double tier of dormer windows. Another such house, Bewdley in Lancaster County, was destroyed by fire in 1917. Unlike Bewdley, Wolftrap has its two rows of dormers on only one roof slope, giving the house an asymmetrical profile. Multiple tiers of dormers are common in central Europe but rare in Britain; hence, this roof treatment was not widely used by settlers of English descent. In Virginia rows of dormers were sometimes employed on large industrial buildings, especially urban mills, but almost never on houses. Wolftrap was erected for the Jones family in the second decade of the 19th century. Although in need of repair, the house has escaped significant alterations. *(46–70) VLR: 09/17/74; NRHP: 10/15/74.*

JAMES CITY COUNTY

Bordered by the James and York rivers, James City County was named for King James I. Established by 1634, the county was one of Virginia's eight original shires. Parts of New Kent and York counties were added later. Its county seat is Williamsburg.

CARTER'S GROVE, *Williamsburg vicinity.* This famous exemplar of colonial Virginia's plantation architecture was built 1750–55 for Carter Burwell, grandson of Robert ("King") Carter. David Minitree, a bricklayer, and James Wheatley, a house carpenter, were the principal builders. The interior woodwork, considered some of the most handsome of the colonial period, was executed in part by Richard Baylis, an English joiner. Carter's Grove stood essentially unaltered until 1928 when its owners engaged architect W. Duncan Lee to restore and enlarge the house. The roof was heightened, dormers were added, and the dependencies were enlarged and connected to the main house. The Colonial Williamsburg Foundation acquired the property in the 1960s and now exhibits it. The extensive garden was reconstructed in the 1970s after detailed archaeological investigations. The excavations uncovered the site of Wolstenholme Town, an early 17th-century settlement now exhibited in conjunction with an interpretive museum. *(47–01) VLR: 09/09/69; NRHP: 11/12/69; NHL: 04/15/70.*

CHICKAHOMINY SHIPYARD ARCHAEOLOGICAL SITE, *Toano vicinity.* In 1776 the Virginia Committee of Safety decided to establish a small navy for the protection of the colony during the Revolutionary War. Master shipbuilder John Herbert was employed to examine the James River and its tributaries for sites suitable for a shipyard. The site selected was on the Chickahominy, sixteen miles west of Williamsburg. The ships *Thetis* and *Jefferson* were constructed here, as were numerous other vessels. Many Virginia naval craft were also repaired and outfitted here. Activity ceased in 1781 when the British seized and burned the shipyard. The site consists of both submerged and dryland components and is the state's only known essentially intact archaeological site of its type. A modern fish house stands near the site of the colonial ships' ways, and foundations of associated buildings are in nearby fields. *(47–78) VLR: 02/26/79; NRHP: 06/28/79.*

CROAKER LANDING ARCHAEOLOGICAL SITE,
Croaker vicinity. This riverside site incorporates a well-preserved stratified midden deposit containing evidence of Indian habitation through the Woodland period (ca. 1000 B.C.–A.D. 1600). Located on the rich tidal flat–marsh environment of the York River, the site is known to contain projectile points, ceramics, and faunal remains in a stratified context. These diagnostic artifacts can more precisely define Indian chronologies for Virginia's coastal plain. The faunal remains can document changes over time in human adaptation to the region's natural environment. Identified as a small campsite culturally associated with larger village sites across the York River, the site in its deepest level contains examples of some of the earliest pottery types made in Tidewater Virginia, dating from ca. 1200 to 800 B.C. *(47–93) VLR: 03/17/87; NRHP: 05/14/87.*

GOVERNOR'S LAND ARCHAEOLOGICAL DISTRICT, *Jamestown vicinity.* The Virginia Company of London instructions to incoming Governor Sir George Yeardley specified that 3,000 acres immediately upstream from Jamestown Island be set aside for the use of the incumbent governor and his successors. As a subsidiary community of Jamestown, the capital, this land was one of the nation's first suburbs. The Governor's Land included Argall's Town, a small settlement established in 1617 and occupied continuously throughout the colonial period. Some twenty 17th-century sites were identified through an extensive survey conducted by the Virginia Department of Historic Resources in the 1970s. Excavations revealed many significant artifacts, shedding new light upon Virginia's material culture during the first decades of settlement. The artifacts include pieces of English armor as well as an unusual 17th-century three-bowled tobacco pipe. *(47–82) VLR: 07/17/73; NRHP: 09/21/73.*

GREEN SPRING ARCHAEOLOGICAL SITE, *Williamsburg vicinity.* Named for a natural spring on the property, Green Spring was patented by 1643 by Governor Sir William Berkeley. He constructed a substantial brick dwelling here in 1645 and developed the property into a manorial estate. During the English Civil War, Berkeley resigned his office and withdrew to Green Spring. He became governor again following the Restoration. The mansion later sustained massive damage during Bacon's Rebellion and was largely rebuilt by Berkeley's widow. Through her marriage to Philip Ludwell, Green Spring passed into the Ludwell family who owned it over the next century. Architect Benjamin Henry Latrobe recorded the mansion's appearance in a 1796 watercolor drawing. William Ludwell Lee subsequently replaced the mansion with a new house which burned in the 19th century. Only the brick shell of a colonial outbuilding remains. The Green Spring site is now part of the Colonial National Historical Park. *(47–06) VLR: 03/19/97; NRHP: 12/29/78.*

HICKORY NECK CHURCH, *Toano vicinity.* This tiny brick building is the remaining part of the Lower Church of Blisland Parish, one of the Virginia colony's more important rural churches. The original portion, a large nave, was begun in 1734 and completed in 1736. Its builders, John Moore and Lewis Deloney, both worked on Williamsburg's Bruton Parish Church. A north transept was added in 1773–74. Following the disestablishment, the nave of the then-abandoned church was dismantled, and the north transept was extended to create the present structure, which was put into service as a local school. The name Hickory Neck, used since the mid–18th century, was retained for the school. In 1907 the building was reconsecrated as an Episcopal church. Today the timeworn structure stands as evidence of the difficulties suffered by Anglican churches in the early 19th century. *(47–08) VLR: 11/09/72; NRHP: 07/02/73.*

JAMESTOWN NATIONAL HISTORIC SITE, *Jamestown Island.* Jamestown is the site of the first permanent English settlement in America, founded in 1607. The first meeting of the Virginia House of Burgesses, held here in 1619, signaled the beginning of representative legislative government in the New World. That same year America's first blacks arrived in Virginia. Jamestown was torched in 1676 by Nathaniel Bacon's followers. The town was partially rebuilt, but the capital was moved to Williamsburg in 1699. By the late 19th century, the only structures on the island were the 17th-century Jamestown Church tower, Confederate earthworks, and the ruins of the 18th-century Ambler house. The Association for the Preservation of Virginia Antiquities acquired a portion of the island in 1893. Jamestown Island is today preserved and exhibited by both the APVA and the National Park Service. Recent archaeological investigations by the APVA have revealed the site of the Jamestown fort. *(47–09) VLR: 10/18/83; NRHP: 10/15/66.*

KINGSMILL PLANTATION ARCHAEOLOGICAL DISTRICT, *Williamsburg vicinity.* This large tract along the James River boasts a series of colonial archaeological sites excavated by state archaeologists between 1972 and 1976 under the sponsorship of Anheuser Busch, Inc. The principal site (shown), marked by a pair of brick dependencies, is of the ca. 1736 mansion of Lewis Burwell. Excavations showed the house to have had a formal plan, an elaborate paved forecourt, terraced gardens, and numerous outbuildings. Burwell's Landing nearby contains an 18th-century warehouse and tavern site, as well as Revolutionary War and Civil War fortifications. In addition, three 17th-century sites provided information on material culture in the early colonial period. These and various other sites have been preserved and incorporated into the landscaping scheme of Kingsmill on the James, a residential community developed by Busch Properties, Inc. *(47–10) VLR: 03/21/72; NRHP: 04/26/72.*

PASPAHEGH ARCHAEOLOGICAL SITE, *Jamestown vicinity.* Identified on John Smith's map of 1612, Paspahegh was one of the thirty districts of the Powhatan chiefdom. Its 17th-century inhabitants were among the first Indians to establish contact with the Jamestown settlers. The earliest cultural evidence at the site dates from the Paleo-Indian period (ca. 9500–8000 B.C.). Other intact deposits may help archaeologists learn about the cultural development of the Native Americans from the Middle Woodland (ca. 500 B.C.–A.D. 900) and Late Woodland and contact (ca. A.D. 900–1646) periods. The site may also provide information about the Native American–European relations during the early colonial period. Archaeological discoveries at the site include post molds associated with longhouse patterns, human burials, ceramics, stone tools, copper and shell ornaments, and textiles. *(47–98) VLR: 04/21/93; NRHP: 06/26/93; BHR EASEMENT.*

PINEWOODS, *Norge vicinity.* Pinewoods, also known as the Warburton house, is a modest plantation dwelling of the pre-Georgian period, one of the few remaining in the greater Williamsburg area. The house was set apart from most of its vanished contemporaries by its brick construction, which was employed only rarely for rural houses in the early colonial period. The architectural forms and details of the house suggest that it was erected in the first decade of the 18th century. The house was gutted by fire in the early part of this century, but the Flemish bond brick walls and the decorative T-shaped chimney stacks survived. Owned by the Warburton family throughout its history, Pinewoods has been rebuilt within its walls for use as a hunting lodge. *(47–14) VLR: 10/06/70; NRHP: 11/12/71.*

POWHATAN, *Williamsburg vicinity.* Richard Taliaferro, called a "most skillful architect" by Thomas Lee in 1749, lived at Powhatan from 1755, when he turned his Williamsburg house over to his son-in-law George Wythe, until his death in 1775. The construction date of Powhatan is uncertain; Taliaferro may designed the house for himself and his bride, Elizabeth Eggleston Taliaferro, on land she inherited. Marked by finely crafted glazed-header Flemish bond and massive T-shaped chimney stacks, Powhatan is a classic essay in early Georgian design. The interior was destroyed by fire during the Civil War but was rebuilt shortly afterward. The house was restored closer to its original appearance in 1948 when the later gable roof was replaced with the present hipped roof. Now the centerpiece of a modern housing development, Powhatan's axial approach and immediate setting of ancient oaks have been sensitively maintained. *(47–16) VLR: 07/07/70; NRHP: 09/15/70.*

RIVERVIEW, *124 Riverview Plantation Drive, Williamsburg vicinity.* As its name implies, this antebellum dwelling enjoys panoramic views of the York River. Built in the 1850s on or near

an 18th-century site, the frame structure with its I-house plan and paired windows has architectural interest not because of its antiquity but because of its comparatively late date. In its configuration, plan, and details, it is little different from Virginia plantation houses dating a century earlier. It began as a side-passage house but was enlarged to its symmetrical form within the decade. Its original owner was Albert Hankins whose forebears had owned the land since the mid–18th century. The one-story wings were added in 1913 by Louis C. Phillips. Phillips's brother-in-law, Governor John Garland Pollard, spent much time at Riverview. The house, recently restored, is now within a development on a five-acre tract. *(47–25) VLR: 06/19/96; NRHP: 12/06/96.*

STONE HOUSE ARCHAEOLOGICAL SITE, *Toano vicinity.* The Stone House, called by James Galt Williamson in 1838 "one of the most antique buildings in the country," has been the subject of local lore for over two centuries. Built of stone in an isolated location and in difficult topography, the structure has been claimed to be everything from a stronghold associated with Nathaniel Bacon's rebellion to the storehouse for Blackbeard's plunder. The building had fallen into ruin by the time of Edmund Ruffin's visit in 1841. A sketch of the ruin (shown) appeared in Henry Howe's *Historical Collections of Virginia* (1845). Parts of its walls survived into this century. A 1972 survey by the Virginia Department of Historic Resources identified the foundations, which are of uncut sandstone 2 feet thick. More extensive archaeological investigation might solve the mystery of this intriguing structure. *(47–36) VLR: 02/20/73; NRHP: 08/14/73.*

TUTTER'S (TUTTEY'S) NECK ARCHAEOLOGICAL SITE, *Williamsburg vicinity.* Originally called Tuttey's Neck, this property was included in a 1637 patent to Humphrey Higginson and later came into the hands of Thomas Pettus of Littletown. By 1704 Tuttey's Neck was owned by Frederick Jones whose wine bottle seal was found on the site during archaeological excavations. The plantation was acquired by the Brays and eventually incorporated into Kingsmill plantation. A simple colonial manor house stood upon the property until it was destroyed in the last quarter of the 18th century. Archaeological test excavations conducted by Ivor Noël Hume in 1960 and 1961 revealed evidence of a 42-by-19-foot frame house (see conjectural rendering). Complete excavation of the Tutter's Neck homesite likely would increase knowledge of the cultural traditions and architecture of gentry-class colonial Virginians in the vicinity of the colonial capital. *(47–33) VLR: 12/02/69.*

WINDSOR CASTLE, *Toano vicinity.* Though conjuring up images of battlements and pageantry, Windsor Castle is, unlike its famous namesake, a typical example of the Virginia vernacular. The oldest part began as a side-passage, double-pile house built in the third quarter of the 18th century. It was expanded in the early 1800s into a center-passage dwelling. The exterior is highlighted by its four exterior end chimneys, the oldest of which has two sets of weatherings and a T-shaped stack, a chimney type in use in Virginia since the 17th century. The interior has a mixture of 18th- and 19th-century trim. In the oldest section is an original built-in walnut corner cupboard. The property is one of the few 18th-century farmsteads on the Lower Peninsula to have remained in continuous agricultural use and to have been held by a succession of related owners. *(47–21) VLR: 07/21/87; NRHP: 12/14/87.*

KING AND QUEEN COUNTY

Formed from New Kent County in 1691, King and Queen County was named for King William III and Queen Mary II, who were called to the English throne in 1688. The county seat is King and Queen Court House.

BEWDLEY, *St. Stephen's Church vicinity.* On a high bank above the Mattaponi River, this 1760s L-shaped brick house is a proficient work of Tidewater colonial architecture. It was probably built by William Tunstall, son of Richard Tunstall, clerk of the court, on the site of an earlier house owned by Obadiah and Elizabeth Marriott. The interior stood unfinished when the house was offered for sale in 1767. A *Virginia Gazette* advertisement of that year described it as "a new brick house . . . which may be finished at small expense." The partitions and ceiling joists all date from the original construction. The relatively simple woodwork, including the stairs, mainly dates from the early 1800s when Bewdley was owned by the Roys. Subsequent interior modifications were made by the Latanes in the 1870s, the Fleets in the 1920s, and the Smiths in the 1950s. *(49–04) VLR: 07/18/78; NRHP: 11/16/78.*

FARMINGTON, *St. Stephen's Church vicinity.* The original portion of this substantial frame house was built between 1795 and 1798 by Josiah Ryland, member of one of the area's landed families. His son, John N. Ryland, substantially enlarged and remodeled the house in the Italianate style in 1859–60, leaving little trace of the former appearance. The remodeling is well documented in Ryland's letters to his wife. Ryland had a highly diversified farming operation at Farmington, maintaining 900 acres in cultivation. In 1864 Union troops under Gen. Philip Sheridan ransacked the house and made off with livestock and foodstuffs. The property left the Ryland family in 1909 but was purchased by John N. Ryland's grandson in 1928 and has remained in the family to the present. On the property are several early outbuildings including a weaving house and a rare antebellum Tidewater braced-frame barn. The house underwent extensive restoration in 1993. *(49–23) VLR: 01/15/95; NRHP: 03/17/95.*

FORT MATTAPONY (RYEFIELD) ARCHAEOLOGICAL SITE, *Walkerton vicinity.* Surviving at Locust Grove, a plantation owned by the Walker family since 1665, are the remains of Fort Mattapony, a small military complex built by the Virginia government in 1679. The archaeological site of a wooden storehouse was identified during a 1981 survey by the Department of Historic Resources. It was within this area that a brass cannon fragment (shown) was discovered in the 1930s and later established by the National Park Service to date from between 1650 and 1750. The fort was constructed and manned not only for protection against Indian incursion but perhaps as a reaction to Bacon's Rebellion. It was one of four such forts ordered for the headwaters of the colony's four major rivers. The fort was abandoned in 1682. Nearby is the late 17th-century site of Ryefield, the home of Col. Thomas Walker. *(49–185) VLR: 04/20/94; NRHP: 08/19/94.*

HOLLY HILL, *Aylett vicinity.* Named for its wooded promontory, this Mattaponi River plantation was established in 1784 by Moore Fauntleroy from land that was formerly part of Ring's Neck, a property owned in the late 17th century by Joseph Ring, clerk of York County. The present house, a stately work, was built in the second decade of the 19th century for Fauntleroy's son, Samuel Griffin Fauntleroy. In form and details the L-shaped house varies little on the exterior from dwellings erected in the region over a half century earlier, thus illustrating eastern Virginia's architectural continuity and conservatism. Like its predecessors, Holly Hill has a symmetrical five-bay facade, relatively unadorned brick walls, and a hipped roof with modillion cornice. The interior preserves its original restrained Federal woodwork. The estate remained in the Fauntleroy family until 1946. *(49–33) VLR: 06/19/73; NRHP: 07/24/73.*

HILLSBOROUGH, *Walkerton vicinity.* This imposing colonial house preserves a timeless setting in the midst of cultivated fields along the banks of the Mattaponi River. Hillsborough has special architectural interest by being the only known frame house of the period to combine masonry end walls with a hipped roof. Brick-ended houses are common in the Chesapeake region but are rarely found west of the York River. The interior preserves much of its original paneled woodwork including a Georgian stair. The outstanding parlor paneling, however, was removed in the 1930s and is now in Mount Cuba, a Delaware mansion. A rare survival at Hillsborough is the colonial store building, constructed of thin, Dutch-type bricks. The main house was most likely built for Col. Humphrey Hill, who is recorded as owning the property in 1752. The plantation remains the home of Hill family descendants. *(49–31) VLR: 03/02/71; NRHP 09/22/71.*

MATTAPONI CHURCH, *Cumnor vicinity.* Mattaponi Church is an impressive example of a cruciform church, a plan reserved for colonial Virginia's larger, more important Anglican churches. Typical of such buildings, the walls are laid in Flemish bond with glazed headers, and the entrances are framed with pedimented frontispieces of gauged and molded brick. A church, designated Lower Church, St. Stephen's Parish, was built here ca. 1674, when the parish was formed from Stratton Major Parish. The present church was built ca. 1730–34. The names or initials inscribed on three bricks are probably those of masons. Abandoned by the Anglicans after the Revolution, the church was taken over by Baptists in 1803, who still occupy it. Fire destroyed the original interior in 1922, but the building was repaired and returned to use. The four original altarpiece tablets were saved and reinstalled. Three colonial grave slabs remain in the churchyard. *(49–43) VLR: 09/19/72; NRHP: 03/20/73.*

NEWTOWN HISTORIC DISTRICT, *Newtown and immediate vicinity.* Newtown originated in the late colonial period as a crossroads settlement on the Great Post Road that ran from Williamsburg to Philadelphia. Supporting a long succession of private schools, Newtown prospered in the antebellum period as the county's largest post village. During the Civil War it was the scene of troop maneuvers by both sides. Newtown's former prosperity is reflected in its collection of a half-dozen Federal-period frame houses, all substantial two-story structures on high brick basements. One of the houses served as the Newtown Female Institute from 1854 to the Civil War. At the crossroads is the Lee Boulware house, which later became the home of Dr. Thomas Bates who cared for Confederate sick and wounded. Although now devoid of commercial activity, Newtown preserves its quiet 19th-century flavor. *(49–145) VLR: 03/17/81; NRHP: 10/29/82.*

UPPER CHURCH, STRATTON MAJOR PARISH, *Shanghai vicinity.* The artistry of the colonial mason is well demonstrated in this former Anglican church. The otherwise simple building is accented by walls of Flemish bond with glazed headers, gauged-brick arches, rubbed-brick corners, and molded-brick doorways. A triangular pediment is employed on the south doorway; the west entrance, disfigured by a modern addition, has a segmental pediment. Upper Church was built between 1724 and 1729 and is the only colonial church of its parish to survive. The building was abandoned by the Anglicans in 1768. A Methodist congregation was present here in 1789 and subsequently coexisted with Baptists until the Baptists withdrew in 1842. The church burned in the mid-1840s but was rebuilt within the original walls. The Methodists gained full control in 1869. It is now identified by its Methodist congregation as Old Church. The colonial-style sashes were installed in 1989. *(49–50) VLR: 10/17/72; NRHP: 04/02/73.*

KING GEORGE COUNTY

Named in honor of King George I, this Northern Neck county was formed from Richmond County in 1720.
Part of Westmoreland County was added later. The county seat is King George.

BELLE GROVE, *Port Conway.* Belle Grove belongs to a group of sophisticated late 18th-century dwellings in the Port Royal region that feature wide elliptical arches on the interior and distinctive projecting entrance halls. It was built in 1792 by John Hipkins for his only child, Fannie, wife of William Bernard. Its design is attributed to Richard and Yelverton Stern, who built a similar house for Hipkins at Gay Mont in Caroline County. Carolinus Turner, who bought Belle Grove in 1839, modified the interior and added the porticoes and terminal wings. The land front is set off by visually striking undulating porches. During the mid–18th century the property was owned by the Conway family, and in 1751, in a long-vanished house here, Eleanor Rose Conway Madison gave birth to James Madison, fourth president of the United States. Belle Grove is currently undergoing extensive restoration. *(48–27) VLR: 09/19/72; NRHP: 04/11/73.*

CLEYDAEL, *Weedonville vicinity.* This unpretentious frame dwelling was built in 1859 as a summer retreat for Dr. Richard H. Stuart. In locating his house away from the Potomac River, Stuart was persuaded that an inland site on high ground would offer a more healthful respite from muggy Tidewater summers. Extra ventilation was provided by Cleydael's T-shaped floor plan. Dr. Stuart moved his family to Cleydael for the duration of the Civil War, trusting it would be safe from Union aggression. Gen. Robert E. Lee sent his two daughters to stay with their cousins at Cleydael when his family was forced to leave Arlington. Following his assassination of Abraham Lincoln, John Wilkes Booth, with compatriots, sought medical aid here from Dr. Stuart at Cleydael. Stuart, aware of the assassination, was suspicious and refused his visitors assistance and shelter, dispatching them after giving them dinner. *(48–41) VLR: 07/15/86; NRHP: 12/18/86. BHR EASEMENT.*

EAGLE'S NEST, *Caledon Natural Area vicinity.* On a ridge overlooking the Potomac River, Eagle's Nest is the ancestral home of the Fitzhugh family. The property is the core of a 17th-century plantation that originally exceeded 54,000 acres. The present house was severely damaged by fire in the late 18th century and was extensively repaired and subsequently enlarged. The regular lines of the exterior disguise an unusual floor plan, which features two end stair halls connected by a central transverse hall. Many of the alterations were made in the 19th century when the property was owned by the Grymes family. On the grounds is an early garden and a family cemetery. Original outbuildings include two dovecotes and a smokehouse with a tilted false plate, a construction feature characteristic of early vernacular structures. *(48–44) VLR: 12/12/89; NRHP: 10/29/92.*

LAMB'S CREEK CHURCH, *Graves Corner vicinity.* Employing a rectangular plan, hipped roof, and side entrance, Lamb's Creek Church is a classic example of a rural colonial Anglican church. The church was built in 1769–77 to serve Brunswick Parish. Its elegant proportions, precise brickwork, and gauged-brick doorways illustrate an achievement of sophistication with minimal ornamentation. Because of its similarity to the 1769 Payne's Church, Fairfax County (destroyed), the design of Lamb's Creek Church is attributed to the colonial architect John Ariss, or "Ayres" (as noted in church records), the documented designer of Payne's. Union troops used the church as a stable during the Civil War, destroying most of the original woodwork and furnishings. Restored to service by the Episcopalians in 1908, the church at present is inactive, being used only for an annual memorial service. The parish still possesses a rare Vinegar edition Bible (1716) and a 1662 missal. *(48–10) VLR: 08/15/72; NRHP: 09/22/72.*

EMMANUEL EPISCOPAL CHURCH, *Port Conway.* This tiny but visually memorable house of worship is part of Virginia's small but interesting collection of Gothic Revival country churches. Completed in 1860 and attributed on its stylistic basis to the Baltimore architectural partnership of Niernsee and Neilson, the church has an architectural presence despite its diminutive size. Contrasting with the Gothic nave is the Italianate tower, enriched with a bold bracketed cornice and concave pyramidal cap, similar to Martin's Brandon Church in Prince George County. Although damaged during the Civil War, the church retains its original gallery and a Henry Erben pipe organ dating to the third quarter of the 19th century. The still active church is the only remnant of the village of Port Conway and is a familiar landmark to motorists crossing the Rappahannock River at Port Royal along U.S. 301. *(48–07) VLR: 10/14/86; NRHP: 01/07/87.*

MARMION, *Osso vicinity.* Marmion was the seat of the Fitzhughs, a leading colonial landed family. The present house probably was built in the second quarter of the 18th century for John Fitzhugh or his son Philip. Although the house appears plain and unrefined, its parlor paneling, now displayed in the Metropolitan Museum of Art, comprised one of America's most elegant colonial rooms. The remaining interiors are simpler and more typical of the period. The stack of the south chimney boasts Virginia's only known example of all glazed-header brickwork. The original outbuildings, forming a quadrangle around the house, include a kitchen, plantation store, dairy, and smokehouse. Marmion was sold by the Fitzhughs ca. 1785 to George Lewis, son of Fielding Lewis of Kenmore. It was owned by Lewis descendants until 1977 and has since undergone careful restoration. *(48–12) VLR: 12/02/69; NRHP: 02/26/70.*

NANZATICO, *Welcome vicinity.* The architectural formality that could be achieved in a relatively small wooden house is demonstrated at Nanzatico, a plantation dwelling on the banks of the Rappahannock River. The house is traditionally dated ca. 1770, when the land was owned by the Carter family; however, its architectural detailing suggests a date after 1780, following Thomas Turner's purchase of the property. As built, Nanzatico was a near twin to Belle Grove upstream (before the latter's ca. 1839 alterations), which also has an engaged Ionic portico and projecting entrance hall with an interior elliptical arch. Richard and Yelverton Stern, builders of another similar house at Gay Mont, Caroline County (since burned), may have constructed both Belle Grove and Nanzatico. Unlike the others, Nanzatico survives almost unchanged. Many of the woodwork details appear to follow illustrations in Abraham Swan's *A Collection of Designs in Architecture,* an 18th-century English design book. *(48–15) VLR: 05/13/69; NRHP: 11/12/69; BHR EASEMENT.*

NANZATTICO INDIAN TOWN ARCHAEOLOGICAL SITE, *Welcome vicinity.* In a field to the east of the Nanzatico plantation house is the site of a village occupied by the Nanzattico Indians. The village, which was established in prehistoric times, was one of the largest and most important Indian settlements on the Rappahannock in the early 17th century. It likely was similar to the village shown in Theodore de Bry's engraving in Thomas Harriot, *A Briefe and True Report of the New Found Land of Virginia* (1590). The name is a corruption of Nantaughtacund, a tribal name originally identified by Capt. John Smith. Although partial examination of the site has already uncovered significant artifacts from the Townsend and Potomac Creek components, complete archaeological investigation could provide important information on Indian life before and during the early contact period. *(48–84) VLR: 09/19/72.*

OFFICE HALL, *Office Hall.* The two picturesque outbuildings at this busy highway intersection are the remnants of an extensive 18th-century farmstead that was the birthplace and childhood home of William ("Extra Billy") Smith (1797–1887), U.S. congressman, Confederate general, and twice governor of Virginia. Built ca. 1805–20, the kitchen is one of the very few one-room-plan, two-story brick plantation kitchens recorded in Virginia. It exhibits several unusual features including formal Federal-style detailing, an odd hierarchy of brickwork patterns, and a second-story room originally accessible only by an exterior stair. At various points in its history the kitchen served as servants' lodgings and as a private school. The contemporary smokehouse has an unusual roof structure featuring false joists and outriggers. Both buildings remain remarkably unaltered and illustrate the broad repertoire of the vernacular Virginia builder. *(48–16) VLR: 08/21/90; NRHP: 01/24/91.*

ST. PAUL'S EPISCOPAL CHURCH, *Owens.* Preserving its rural setting, St. Paul's is one of two remaining Virginia colonial churches with a true Greek-cross plan and two tiers of windows. It was constructed in 1766 and is the third church to serve its parish. The simplicity of its exterior, relieved only by its fine brickwork and modillion cornice, makes the building more akin architecturally to English dissenter chapels of the period than to the richer Georgian churches of the colony. Although the church fell derelict after the disestablishment, it was renovated as a school by 1813 and was returned to the Episcopalians by 1830. As a result of this unsettled period, the present woodwork, both inside and out, is mostly 19th century. The communion service of 1721 and a 1762 Bible are treasured possessions of the parish. *(48–21) VLR: 01/16/73; NRHP: 05/25/73.*

WOODLAWN HISTORIC AND ARCHAEOLOGICAL DISTRICT, *Port Conway vicinity.* This district encompasses Woodlawn plantation, assembled in the early 18th century by Col. Thomas Turner. The earliest portion of the present house, the east wing, was built for the Turners ca. 1790. The main part, built around 1841, continued the traditional rectangular, hipped-roof format of the area's larger colonial dwellings. Adjacent to the house are two outbuildings and a slave house. Intact elements of the antebellum plantation landscape are the field system, the farm road network, a drainage ditch network, and various outbuilding sites. Also on the plantation is an important series of Indian archaeological sites including what may be a palisaded enclosure within a more broadly distributed village along the Rappahannock. Many of the artifacts relate to the early 17th century when various groups of the Powhatan chiefdom were migrating west, distancing themselves from the European settlements. *(48–26) VLR: 10/16/90; NRHP: 01/03/91; BHR EASEMENT.*

KING WILLIAM COUNTY

Formed from King and Queen County in 1701, this rural Tidewater county bordered by the Pamunkey and Mattaponi rivers was named for King William III. Its county seat is King William Court House.

BURLINGTON, *Aylett vicinity.* Burlington, a 700-acre plantation on the Mattaponi River, has been the property of the Gwathmey family since Owen Gwathmey II acquired the land in the mid–18th century. The tract is dominated by a small plateau providing panoramic views of surrounding countryside. On the plateau is an interesting two-part residence, the main portion of which is a stuccoed Classical Revival dwelling erected in 1842 by Dr. William Gwathmey. The rear wing is a section of a colonial frame dwelling built by the Burwell family. The wing has an original Georgian stair and other colonial woodwork. In the vicinity of the house is a 19th-century boxwood garden, an early smokehouse, the Gwathmey family cemetery, and an early barn that served as the original meetinghouse for Beulah Baptist Church. The Burlington lands probably were originally occupied by Mattaponi Indians. *(50–10) VLR: 03/15/77; NRHP: 01/30/78; BHR EASEMENT.*

CHELSEA, *West Point vicinity.* Chelsea's plantation house merits recognition as one of Virginia's foremost works of colonial architecture. Set off by outstanding brickwork, the two-story front section is a demonstration of grandeur on a restrained scale. The principal first-floor rooms are fully paneled. The stair passage, decorated with fluted pilasters, is one of Virginia's only rooms paneled in walnut. A long-held tradition holds that the house was built in 1709 by Augustine Moore. The architectural character, however, suggests the possibility that it was built for his son, Bernard Moore, after he inherited the plantation in 1742. The gambrel-roof wing was likely added before 1766. Complementing the house are several early outbuildings and an isolated setting on the Mattaponi River. From this plantation Governor Alexander Spotswood and his "Knights of the Golden Horseshoe" embarked on their pioneering expedition across the Blue Ridge in 1716. *(50–12) VLR: 09/09/69; NRHP: 11/12/69.*

CHERICOKE, *King William Court House vicinity.* This Pamunkey River plantation has been the property of the Braxton family and their descendants since the mid–18th century. It was first owned by George Braxton (died 1757), who left it to his son Carter Braxton, signer of the Declaration of Independence. Carter Braxton built a large house at Chericoke in 1770, one reputedly bigger than his substantial dwelling at nearby Elsing Green. This house burned five years later, but its undisturbed site is likely of archaeological interest. Braxton is thought to lie buried nearby in an unmarked grave. The present plantation dwelling, erected in 1828 for Charles Hill Carter Braxton, grandson of the signer, is characteristic of homes of prosperous Virginia planters of the Federal period. Similar to contemporary Richmond houses, it has a simple entrance front and a porticoed garden or river front. *(50–13) VLR: 04/18/78; NRHP: 09/08/80.*

ELSING GREEN, *Lanesville vicinity.* One of the state's most impressive Tidewater plantations, Elsing Green is marked by a prodigious U-shaped house, a grand expression of colonial Virginia's formal architecture. Stretched along the Pamunkey River, the plantation was owned in the 17th century by Col. William Dandridge. The property was purchased ca. 1753 by Carter Braxton, a signer of the Declaration of Independence, who probably built the main house. The house burned in the early 19th century, but its brick walls survived unmarred. Rebuilt within the walls, the house was long the home of the Gregory family. In the 1930s, during the ownership of Mr. and Mrs. Beverley D. Causey, architect Edward F. Sinnott restored the original roof pitch and installed 18th-century-style woodwork. Edgar Rivers Lafferty, Jr., who purchased Elsing Green in 1949, developed the plantation into a model farm and wildlife preserve. *(50–22) VLR: 05/13/69; NRHP: 11/12/69; NHL: 11/11/71; BHR EASEMENT.*

HORN QUARTER, *Hanover Court House vicinity.* Richly ornamented and impeccably crafted, Horn Quarter has few peers among the Commonwealth's Federal-period residences. Its pedimented portico and generous scale combine with refined Adamesque detailing to produce a composition of assured competence. The house was built in 1829–30 for George Taylor, son of agrarian reformer John Taylor of Caroline County. It has architectural parallels to a group of Federal mansions that includes Hampstead in New Kent County, Magnolia Grange in Chesterfield County, and Upper Brandon in Prince George County, all likely sharing common artisans who used Asher Benjamin's *American Builder's Companion* (1806) as a source for details. The cynosure of the interior is a spiral stair ascending from basement to attic. Notable as well are the plasterwork ceiling medallions and cornices. The house has formally arranged outbuildings and remnants of terraced gardens. *(50–32) VLR: 03/18/80; NRHP: 06/09/80.*

KING WILLIAM COUNTY COURT-HOUSE, *King William Court House.* King William County's courthouse is the best preserved of Virginia's eleven colonial court buildings. Erected in the second quarter of the 18th century, the T-shaped structure is regarded as the nation's oldest courthouse in

continuous use. Precedent for its arcaded front is the arcade connecting the wings of the first Capitol in Williamsburg. Such arcades were traditional public gathering places. Lending additional character is the Flemish bond brickwork with glazed headers and rubbed-brick arches and corners. The courthouse grounds are surrounded by a 19th-century brick wall built to keep out wandering livestock. Most of Virginia's early colonial courthouses were located near the geographic center of their counties, unrelated to any town. King William's courthouse followed this pattern and still preserves its rural setting. *(50–38) VLR: 11/05/68; NRHP: 10/01/69.*

MANGOHICK CHURCH, *Mangohick.* This simple but dignified colonial church was built ca. 1730–32 as a chapel of ease for St. Margaret's Parish but soon became the upper church of St. David's Parish. Although no less well crafted, such chapels were nearly always considerably plainer than their parent churches, relying mainly on fine brickwork and careful proportions for aesthetic effect. William Byrd II of Westover passed by Mangohick in 1732 and noted it as the "New Brick Church" in his journal of the "Progress to the Mines." The church was abandoned after the disestablishment and later became a free church, available for use by any denomination. Since the late 19th century it has been the home of a black Baptist congregation. The interior preserves its original gallery. The colonial-style window sashes were installed in 1980. *(50–41) VLR: 08/15/72; NRHP: 12/05/72.*

MOUNT COLUMBIA, *Manquin vicinity.* Mount Columbia is situated on one of the highest points in King William County, property that originally was part of the vast landholding of the College of William and Mary. The two-part dwelling illustrates the refinement of architectural taste that occurred in the area in the early 1800s. The older section, a simple single-cell house erected for Gideon Bosher in the 1790s, typifies the homes of the period's moderate inland planters. The sophisticated Federal-style front section, built in the 1830s for Bosher's son William, reflects the gentry's increasing tendency to display prosperity in a more stylish manner. The general appearance of the later section may have been influenced by Virginia's Executive Mansion. William Bosher's brother John, a carpenter, and his neighbor Christopher Tompkins, a master builder, were both involved in the building of the mansion. *(50–49) VLR: 04/19/88; NRHP: 01/19/89; BHR EASEMENT.*

PAMUNKEY INDIAN RESERVATION ARCHAEOLOGICAL DISTRICT, *Lanesville vicinity.* Over 7,000 years of aboriginal occupation on this 1,700-acre, marsh-rimmed Pamunkey River peninsula give this tract unique archaeological interest. A survey undertaken in 1979 by archaeologists of the Virginia Department of Historic Resources and Virginia Commonwealth University identified fifteen sites ranging from the Middle Archaic period (5000–3000 B.C.) to the postsettlement era. The Pamunkey tribe was first identified by Europeans when Capt. John Smith explored the upper reaches of the York River in 1607. Today the reservation sustains about seventy inhabitants, representing a continuity of many centuries. Further archaeological research could trace the cultural evolution and adaptation of the Pamunkey tribe from the time of contact with European civilization through subsequent phases of Virginia history. The Tribal Cultural Center (shown), its design inspired by the round-roofed Indian houses shown in early engravings, displays Pamunkey artifacts and crafts. *(50–34) VLR: 10/21/80; NRHP: 09/16/82.*

ST. JOHN'S EPISCOPAL CHURCH, *Rose Garden vicinity.* An outstanding example of the colonial mason's craft, St. John's Church was completed ca. 1734 and enlarged to its present T-shape before 1765. Its parish, St. John's, was one of the few colonial parishes named in honor of a saint. During the 1770s the church's eloquent and popular rector, the Rev. Henry Skyren, drew large crowds to his services. Among the regular worshipers here was Carter Braxton, signer of the Declaration of Independence. St. John's fell into disuse after the disestablishment. It was for a time occupied by Baptist and Methodists, but today it is once again an Episcopal parish church, undergoing a long-term restoration. The building is noted for its sparkling Flemish bond brickwork and its molded-brick pedimented doorways. The principal colonial-era interior features are the north and west galleries. *(50–61) VLR: 10/17/72; NRHP: 04/24/73.*

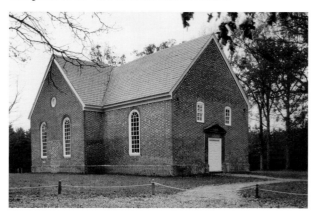

SEVEN SPRINGS, *Enfield.* This compact colonial dwelling boasts a unique square plan with a center chimney. Despite its small size, the house is comparable in its craftsmanship and detailing to many more architecturally ambitious plantation mansions. The construction date is undocumented, but the house likely was built for Capt. George Dabney before his death in 1729. Although Seven Springs was remodeled in the early 19th century, some important original features, such as the walnut stair, paneled doors, and rare foliated hinges, remain intact. Distinguishing exterior features are the jerkinhead roof, the glazed-brick raking courses, and the gauged-brick jack arches. Its snug outline makes Seven Springs one of the state's most fetching works of colonial architecture, an all-too-rare example of the tidy charm that architects of the Colonial Revival aspired to instill in their works. *(50–64) VLR: 12/21/76; NRHP: 05/06/80.*

SWEET HALL, *Sweet Hall vicinity.* Sweet Hall is the sole surviving Virginia house with upper-cruck roof framing and is one of only two known cruck-roof houses in the country. Crucks—massive curved timbers providing wall and roof support—were used for English vernacular buildings from the medieval period into the 17th century. The use of crucks was rare in Virginia and was essentially abandoned by the mid–18th century. Its singular roof framing notwithstanding, Sweet Hall, with its T-plan, symmetrical facade, elaborate T-shaped chimney stacks, and hall-parlor plan, is one of the state's finest pre-Georgian manor houses. It likely was erected in the first or second decade of the 18th century for Thomas Claiborne (1680–1723), grandson of Secretary of the Colony William Claiborne. Sweet Hall preserves a quiet remoteness on the banks of the Pamunkey, overlooking broad stretches of marsh. *(50–67) VLR: 02/15/77; NRHP: 11/07/77.*

WEST POINT HISTORIC DISTRICT. Strategically situated where the Pamunkey and Mattaponi rivers join to form the York River, West Point was originally the site of an Indian village and later a colonial plantation. Development of a town here was spurred when the peninsula was selected as the terminus of the Richmond and York River Railroad, completed in 1861. The railroad and fledgling community were heavily damaged by Union forces during the Civil War, but the railroad was rebuilt by 1869. West Point became a thriving commercial port and resort in the late 1800s. Laid out in a regular grid with half-acre lots, the historic district today is composed primarily of late 19th- and early 20th-century dwellings in a variety of simplified styles. A small commercial area is situated along Main Street, the center street. Minimal development in the past half century has preserved the town's quiet historic flavor. *(325–02) VLR: 03/20/96; NRHP: 10/03/96.*

WINDSOR SHADES, *Sweet Hall vicinity.* Windsor Shades, sometimes known as Waterville, is a little-altered colonial planter's house. Although built of wood and employing a gambrel roof, the house has much of the refinement found in the larger houses of the period. A visually arresting feature is the massive east chimney structure, incorporating two stacks and five fireplaces, one of which is an unusually large basement kitchen fireplace. The chimney structure also contains two closets, each with a window. A fine Georgian stair graces the center

passage. The parlor is embellished with a Georgian chimneypiece and paneled wainscoting. With the loss of county records, the early history of Windsor Shades remains veiled. The house may have been built ca. 1750 by Augustine Claiborne. The property was later owned by the Ruffins and then the Chamberlayne family. *(50–70) VLR: 12/21/76; NRHP: 05/22/78.*

WYOMING, *Etna Mills vicinity.* This two-story, five-bay frame house was built ca. 1800 for the Hoomes family. While maintaining the traditional Georgian flavor of earlier decades, Wyoming is considerably larger in both exterior dimensions and room sizes than other Tidewater houses of the same style, and it may be the largest traditional center-passage plantation dwelling in eastern Virginia. The house was part of a wave of construction of residential architecture that took place in the Virginia countryside following the Revolution, a building boom that resulted in the remodeling or replacement of the majority of the small, often rude colonial farmhouses of the Tidewater region. Like many of these post-Revolutionary structures, Wyoming's interior is embellished with paneled chimneypieces and wainscoting. Its name may allude to the Revolutionary battle of Wyoming Valley, Pa., or to the Indian word for "plain." *(50–75) VLR: 09/18/79; NRHP: 02/08/80.*

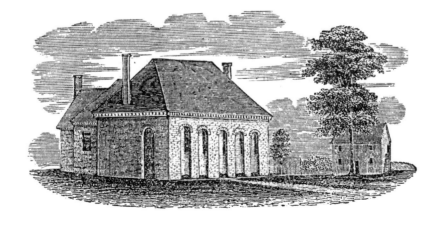

LANCASTER COUNTY

Probably named for the English shire, Lancaster County was formed from Northumberland and York counties in 1651. The county occupies the southern tip of the Northern Neck. Its county seat is Lancaster Court House.

BELLE ISLE, *Litwalton vicinity.* The formal, symmetrical arrangement of buildings and gardens of the great Tidewater colonial seats is present on a reduced scale at Belle Isle, a Rappahannock River plantation named for a marshy island formerly part of the property. The complex includes a compact Georgian manor house flanked by two perpendicularly placed dependencies. The grounds preserve original terraces for formal gardens. The complex was probably built for Thomas Bertrand Griffin after his marriage to Judith Burwell of Carter's Grove in 1766. One-story wings were added around 1790 during the ownership of Rawleigh Downman. Sections of the interior paneling were removed in the 1920s and later were acquired by the Henry Francis du Pont Winterthur Museum. The complex was restored in the 1940s by architectural historian Thomas T. Waterman. The curtilage remains private property, but the balance of the plantation is now Belle Isle State Park. *(51–01) VLR: 03/02/71; NRHP: 02/06/73.*

CHRIST CHURCH, *Irvington vicinity.* Enhanced by its quiet rural setting, Christ Church is without peer among Virginia's colonial churches in the quality of its architecture and state of preservation. The cruciform structure was commissioned by Robert ("King") Carter, the most prosperous and influential of Virginia's colonial planters. Completed by 1735, the exterior is set off by its beautiful brickwork, especially the molded-brick doorways, the nation's finest examples of their type. The tall arched windows, with their original sash, are accented by sandstone keystones, imposts, and sills, as well as by gauged-brick voussoirs. The original interior fittings include the paneled box pews, triple-decker pulpit, and walnut altarpiece. In the churchyard are the richly carved tombs of Carter and his two wives. Still a functioning Episcopal church, the property is maintained by the Foundation for Historic Christ Church. *(51–04) VLR: 09/09/69; NRHP: 10/15/66; NHL: 05/30/61; BHR EASEMENT.*

COROTOMAN ARCHAEOLOGICAL SITE, *Weems vicinity.* An extensive archaeological excavation conducted by the Department of Historic Resources in 1978 revealed the form and size of the mansion of Robert ("King") Carter, colonial Virginia's richest and most powerful planter. Carter began building the house in 1720 and lived here until it burned in 1729. The excavation uncovered the foundations of what must have been the most impressive and richly appointed house of the period: a 40-by-90-foot two-story structure with corner towers connected by a long veranda. Archaeological evidence confirms that the central passage was paved with marble and that the fireplaces had marble trim and were lined with delft tiles. The thousands of artifacts, including fragments of tankards, storage vessels, porcelain teacups, and wine bottles, as well as buckles, clasps, and hardware, help to reconstruct the lifestyle of one of the great figures of America's colonial era. *(51–34) VLR: 12/02/69; NRHP: 09/15/70; BHR EASEMENT.*

FOX HILL, *Lively vicinity.* Historically named Farmville and renamed Fox Hill by a recent owner for David Fox, the 17th-century proprietor of the property, this Northern Neck planta-tion is dominated by an L-shaped Federal dwelling placed amid broad level fields. The severely formal house, with its five-bay facade and hipped roof, echoes the Georgian style of the preceding generation and is set off by its tidy Flemish bond brickwork and molded-brick cornices. Inside is restrained but well-crafted Federal trim. Complementing the house is a two-story kitchen of the same formal character. It and a brick smokehouse are remnants of an early complex of five outbuildings. The property may also contain the archaeological site of David Fox's manor house. The plantation was acquired in 1793 by Richard Selden II, who is believed to have built the present house in 1803 or possibly later. *(51–09) VLR: 04/18/78; NRHP: 11/17/78.*

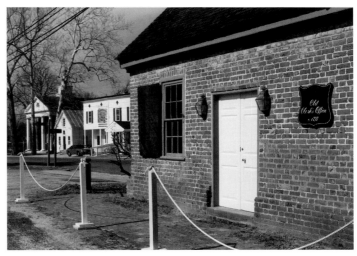

LANCASTER COURT HOUSE HISTORIC DISTRICT. The tiny community of Lancaster Court House is one of the least disturbed of eastern Virginia's rural courthouse villages. The district's principal element is the 1861 brick courthouse, built by Edward O. Robinson. Its Tuscan portico was added in 1937. The courthouse complex includes the former jail and old clerk's office, both dating from the 18th century. Near the latter is an 1872 Confederate memorial, believed to be the first such monument erected in Virginia. A ca. 1800 tavern, mid-19th-century post office, a Carpenter's Gothic church, turn-of-the-century store, and several detached 19th- and early 20th-century dwellings complete the linear village. Nearly free of modern intrusions, the district maintains a harmony of scale, color, texture, and materials, all within a larger agrarian setting. The county seat was established at this location in 1740. *(51–81) VLR: 01/18/83; NRHP: 08/11/83.*

LOCUSTVILLE, *Ottoman vicinity.* The persistent influence of standard Georgian forms on the mid-19th-century farmhouses of eastern Virginia is demonstrated at Locustville, which acquired its present appearance ca. 1855 either through a remodeling or a replacement of an earlier house. With its five-bay facade and gable roof, Locustville has the formality of colonial plantation houses. Relieving the plain exterior is a handsome Greek Revival dwarf portico sheltering the entrance. Locustville was the home of John A. Rogers whose account book shows that local builder F. A. Pierce was employed to work on the house. Pierce's name and the date 1855 are inscribed on the back wing. Rogers kept twenty-three slaves to work his considerable acreage, land that he was forced to sell off in small parcels following the Civil War. The house has undergone few alterations and retains most of its simple Greek Revival woodwork. *(51–50) VLR: 08/17/94; NRHP: 10/21/94.*

MILLENBECK ARCHAEOLOGICAL SITES, *Millenbeck.* The area around the present settlement of Millenbeck on the Corotoman River, a tributary of the Rappahannock, contains several colonial archaeological sites. A fort, known as the fort at Ball's Point, was established here around the time of Bacon's Rebellion, and traces of it are believed to remain. The site of the late 17th-century family home of Hannah Ball, great-grandmother of George Washington, is near the fort location. The

archaeological remains of a later Ball mansion, as well as those of another colonial-era house, are also among the historic resources here. The early date of the fortification and the residences of Washington's ancestors give this complex particular archaeological interest. Limited salvage excavation of the area was undertaken in 1971 under the sponsorship of the Mary Ball Memorial Museum and Library. Brick foundations exposed at that time have since been covered over. *(51–29) VLR: 12/02/69.*

POP CASTLE, *White Stone vicinity.* On the shores of the Rappahannock, this substantial weatherboarded house was built in 1855 for James Gresham and his wife, Ann Armstrong Gresham, on the foundations of a 1780s dwelling. The earliest section of the architecturally conservative structure employs the single-pile, center-passage form favored by landed families since colonial times. The several additions reflect the fact that the house at one time accommodated two separate households. The property was the site of the Wright's Ferry terminus as early as 1702 and thus may preserve archaeological resources related to that activity. The origin of the plantation's colorful name is uncertain. It may allude to action that took place here during the War of 1812, although the earliest use of the name appears in 1851. Pop Castle was again the focus of war activity in 1861 when a Union gunboat bombarded the house, inflicting considerable damage. *(51–75) VLR: 12/13/88; NRHP: 06/16/89.*

VERVILLE, *Merry Point vicinity.* This visually engaging brick plantation house is one of a handful of colonial buildings remaining in Lancaster County. While its form is typical of the 18th-century Chesapeake area, early records indicate that Verville was always considered a superlative example of local domestic architecture. The house is the only standing structure on a plantation that once had many outbuildings and agricultural buildings. It was built in the 1740s by James Gordon, a Scotch-Irish immigrant. Both he and his son, James Gordon, Jr., were influential merchants, planters, and public officials. During the early 19th century Verville was the home of Ellyson Currie, a justice of the Virginia General Court, who added the wings. Verville's interior has some finely detailed Federal interior woodwork, including mantels based on designs in Owen Biddle's *Young Carpenter's Assistant* (1805). The house has since been expanded with several architecturally compatible additions. *(51–26) VLR: 12/09/86; NRHP: 04/24/87.*

ST. MARY'S WHITECHAPEL, *Lively vicinity.* The vicissitudes suffered by Virginia's Anglican churches are expressed in the fabric of this colonial house of worship, named for the London suburb that was the place of origin of some of its first communicants. A church apparently existed here as early as 1669. This was replaced in 1739–41 with a cruciform structure possibly incorporating parts of the older church. The building was abandoned after the disestablishment but was reoccupied in 1832. A much-diminished congregation removed the deteriorated nave and chancel and used their bricks to fill the voids between the transepts. Though its 18th-century form has been significantly altered, the building's remaining portions are reminders of its parish's former importance. Preserved on the interior are two sets of altar tablets dating from 1702 and 1718. St. Mary's was the parish church of the family of Mary Ball, mother of George Washington. *(51–22) VLR: 09/09/69; NRHP: 11/12/69.*

LEE COUNTY

Lee County was named for Henry ("Light-Horse Harry") Lee, governor of Virginia from 1791 to 1794. Occupying the extreme southwestern tip of the state, Lee County was formed from Russell County in 1792, with part of Scott County added later. Its county seat is Jonesville.

CUMBERLAND GAP HISTORIC DISTRICT. Cumberland Gap, at the extreme western tip of the state, for centuries was the principal route through the Allegheny Mountains to the west and south. Witnessing the movement of peoples from aboriginal Indians to modern man, the gap played an important role in western expansion. Following Dr. Thomas Walker's discovery of the gap in 1750, pioneers ventured through it seeking fertile lands and good hunting in Kentucky, Tennessee, and beyond. Trailblazers such as Daniel Boone finally established a safe route known as the Wilderness Road. During the 1790s as many as a hundred settlers a day journeyed through the gap to a new life. Cumberland Gap was strongly fortified by both sides during the Civil War but saw little action. Remains of fortifications survive along the scenic trace. The district includes the Virginia sections of the Cumberland Gap National Historical Park.
(52–17) VLR: 10/18/83; NRHP: 10/15/66.

DICKINSON-MILBOURN HOUSE, *Jonesville.* Completed in 1848 for Benjamin Dickinson, a prosperous landowner, this imposing Federal-style house is among the few early brick dwellings in Lee County. In 1851 the property was acquired by Andrew Milbourn from Dickinson's heirs. On January 3, 1864, during the battle of Jonesville, Union troops used the house and its outbuildings for protection from Confederate attack. Much of the fighting as well as the subsequent Federal surrender took place on the property, although the house was not seriously damaged and probably served as a hospital after the battle. The two-story, center-passage dwelling is unusually sophisticated for the region and has survived with few alterations, retaining much of its original interior trim. A 19th-century brick smokehouse remains on the property. Later owners of the property were Capt. Henry Joslyn, Milbourn's son-in-law, and M. B. Wygal, grandfather of the present owner.
(245–04) VLR: 06/16/93; NRHP: 08/12/93.

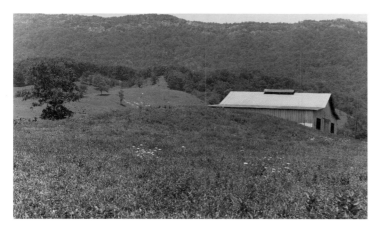

ELY MOUND ARCHAEOLOGICAL SITE, *Rose Hill vicinity.* Dating to the Late Woodland–Mississippian period (ca. A.D. 1200–1650), the Ely Mound archaeological site is the only clearly identified substructure or town-house mound in Virginia. As such, the mound and associated occupation areas should supply much information on the development of increasingly complex societies in southwestern Virginia during the Late Woodland–Mississippian period and the interactions of those societies with the more complex societal groups in what are now North Carolina and Tennessee. The Ely Mound is also significant in the history of American archaeological studies. Lucian Carr's excavations here in the 1870s led him to reject emphatically the "lost race" hypothesis for Mound Builders in eastern North America, a popular theory among 19th-century American archaeologists. *(52–18) VLR: 04/19/83; NRHP: 07/28/83.*

JONESVILLE METHODIST CAMPGROUND, *Jonesville vicinity.* A surge of evangelical fervor in the early 19th century resulted in the establishment throughout the country of campgrounds to hold summer religious revival meetings. Spacious, shedlike auditoriums were built to shelter the large numbers attending the services. A particularly early example of this building type is found at Jonesville in the southwestern tip of the state. Surrounded by a wide lawn used for campsites, the 1827–28 structure was built on land established by the Methodist Episcopal church of Lee County as a religious campground in 1810. The building has a long gable roof supported on massive oak timbers and side panels that can be raised for ventilation. It has been in continuous use since its completion. *(52–07) VLR: 07/17/73; NRHP: 05/16/74.*

CITY OF LEXINGTON

This collegiate community and county seat of Rockbridge County probably was named for Lexington, Mass., where the first battle of the Revolution was fought. The town was established in 1778 and incorporated in 1874. It became a city in 1965.

ALEXANDER-WITHROW HOUSE, *Main and West Washington streets.* An enduring landmark in the heart of Lexington's downtown, the Alexander-Withrow house is set apart from its neighbors by its corner chimneys and diaper-patterned brickwork. Corner chimneys are a peculiarity of several early Rockbridge County houses, while diapering is found but rarely in the Shenandoah Valley. The house was completed by 1790 for William Alexander to serve as his store and residence. Originally the house was covered by a gable roof, which must have looked odd with corner chimneys. It received its present stone-lined shop fronts and low roof with heavy Italianate cornice when Main Street was lowered in the 1850s. After years of neglect, the restoration of the exterior was undertaken in 1969 by the Historic Lexington Foundation. This singular element in the city's historic fabric has been a popular inn for the last quarter century. *(117–01) VLR: 01/05/71; NRHP: 07/02/71.*

COL ALTO, *Nelson Street and Spotswood Drive.* One of several large early residences surrounding downtown Lexington, Col Alto was completed in 1827 for James McDowell, governor of Virginia from 1847 to 1849. The design of the Classical Revival structure is attributed to Samuel McDowell Reid, an amateur architect who was McDowell's cousin. Typical of the region's early high-style houses, Col Alto employs generously scaled classical detailing set off by fine brickwork. In 1898 Col Alto was purchased by Henry St. George Tucker, dean of the Washington and Lee University Law School and later acting president. Tucker also served in Congress from 1921 to 1932. Tucker's daughter, Rosa Tucker Mason, who acquired Col Alto in 1932, commissioned the New York architect William Lawrence Bottomley to design a striking Palladian-style veranda. Mason also commissioned landscape architect Rose Greely to design the grounds. The property is now part of an inn complex. *(117–03) VLR: 09/20/88; NRHP: 11/19/90.*

STONEWALL JACKSON HOUSE, *8 East Washington Street.*
From 1859 to 1861 this early 19th-century dwelling near the
county courthouse was home to Confederate general Thomas
J. ("Stonewall") Jackson and his wife. It was built for Cornelius
Dorman in 1801 as a typical Valley I-house. The facade was altered and a stone addition was erected before Jackson bought
it. In 1906 the house was sold to the United Daughters of the
Confederacy and incorporated into the Stonewall Jackson
Memorial Hospital, with the front being completely remodeled
in a Classical Revival style. In the 1970s the Historic Lexington
Foundation, with architect Milton L. Grigg, undertook the
restoration of the house to its appearance during Jackson's
tenure, even reproducing the mid-19th-century facade with its
shifted openings. The house is now a museum honoring the
life of one of the most brilliant military tacticians in history.
(117–09) VLR: 09/19/72; NRHP: 04/24/73.

LEE CHAPEL, *Washington and Lee University.* Robert E. Lee,
the president of what was then Washington College, was in-

strumental in having the school chapel constructed in 1867. Although the design of the simple neo-Norman-style building
has long been attributed to Lee, documentation has established
that the building is the work of Col. Thomas Hoomes
Williamson, professor of civil and military engineering at the
Virginia Military Institute. Williamson, however, apparently
worked closely with Lee in formulating the design. The body of
the former Confederate commander lay in state in the chapel
in 1870 and was later interred in a family crypt established here.
In 1883 a rear extension designed by J. Crawford Neilson was
completed to house Virginia sculptor Edward V. Valentine's re-
cumbent statue of Lee. Lee's office in the chapel basement has
been carefully preserved as he left it. *(117–19) VLR: 09/09/69; NRHP:
10/15/66; NHL: 12/19/60.*

LEXINGTON HISTORIC DISTRICT. Nestled in the
Rockbridge County countryside, this well-known community
boasts a rich history and outstanding architectural variety.
Building types range from Shenandoah Valley vernacular forms
through sophisticated examples of Romantic Revivalism. Lending luster are works by the nationally prominent architects
Thomas U. Walter, Alexander Jackson Davis, and Bertram
Grosvenor Goodhue. The town was authorized in 1778 and was
a prospering county seat by the 1790s. Growth was stimulated
by the establishment of Washington and Lee University and the
Virginia Military Institute. Their adjoining campuses constitute one of America's celebrated architectural assemblages.
Scattered through the shady residential areas is a delightful mix
of dwelling types. Prominent representatives are the Federal
Reid-White house of 1821 and the Presbyterian manse, an archetypal Gothic Revival villa. The district is now protected by
historic zoning with the commercial area having undergone extensive rehabilitation spearheaded by the Historic Lexington
Foundation. *(117–27) VLR: 03/02/71; NRHP: 06/26/72.*

LEXINGTON PRESBYTERIAN CHURCH, *Main and Nelson streets.* The 19th-century Philadelphia architect Thomas U. Walter provided the design for this chaste but architecturally powerful Greek Revival church, the purest examples of its style in the community. Samuel McDowell Reid, clerk of the county court and an amateur architect, was instrumental in having Walter commissioned for the job, which was completed in 1845. Although Walter worked in a number of historic styles, his mastery of the Grecian mode is evident both here and in several other Greek Revival churches designed by him for Virginia congregations. This Lexington house of worship, a Doric temple capped by a belfry and spire, demonstrates how the simplest classical forms could be adapted for Christian purposes, particularly the lean liturgy of the Presbyterians. Despite later modifications and additions, the original architectural character remains strongly evident. *(117–12) VLR: 05/16/78; NRHP: 05/24/79.*

MULBERRY HILL, *U.S. Route 60 West.* The much-evolved Mulberry Hill, one of the several historic houses atop the hills around Lexington, illustrates changes in local architectural taste over a hundred-year period. The house grew from a one-story, double-pile core to a two-story, gable-roof dwelling, and finally to a hipped-roofed mansion. Its regionalized Georgian woodwork and plasterwork are some of the finest in the area. Apparently situated on the site of the 1777 residence of William Graham, the original section was begun ca. 1797 for Andrew Reid, the first Rockbridge County clerk. It was enlarged in the mid–19th century for his son Samuel McDowell Reid and was given its present appearance ca. 1903 by local architect William C. McDowell after it was sold to Elinor Jackson Junkin Latane. Mulberry Hill's early 20th-century garden frames a view of House Mountain, a well-known natural landmark. *(117–10) VLR: 06/15/82; NRHP: 09/09/82; BHR EASEMENT.*

STONO, *Institute Hill (VMI campus).* Erected in 1818 by entrepreneur and builder John Jordan as his own residence, Stono is noteworthy for its use of the three-part Palladian scheme favored for a number of early 19th-century Virginia houses. Though its proportions and details are somewhat exaggerated, the layout and columned portico reflect Jordan's exposure to the architecture of Thomas Jefferson, who was especially fond of these elements. Jordan made bricks for Monticello in 1805. With his partner Samuel Darst, he also designed and built the porticoed Washington Hall at Washington and Lee University, as well as other buildings in the Lexington area. He placed Stono in a commanding position above the Maury River, immediately east of the property where Virginia Military Institute was later established. Stono now serves as an official guesthouse for VMI. *(117–16) VLR: 12/17/74; NRHP: 04/01/75.*

VIRGINIA MILITARY INSTITUTE BARRACKS, *Virginia Military Institute.* Philip St. George Cocke, member of the Virginia Military Institute Board of Visitors, wished to make the newly established state military academy a great southern polytechnic institute housed in a prominent architectural complex. He was instrumental in having the renowned architect Alexander Jackson Davis commissioned to design the physical plant. From 1848 to 1861 Davis provided six castellated Gothic-style buildings, forming one of the nation's first Gothic Revival campus complexes and a prototype for numerous other military schools. The dominant element of the group is the Barracks, a prodigious, fortresslike structure with corner towers, crenellated parapets, and a galleried inner quadrangle. The building was burned by Union forces in 1864 but was rebuilt to Davis's design in 1867–68. The structure has since been extended, but the east elevation, the main front, preserves much of the original romanticism of Davis's design. *(117–07) VLR: 09/09/69; NRHP: 10/15/66; NHL: 12/21/65.*

VIRGINIA MILITARY INSTITUTE HISTORIC DISTRICT. Organized in 1839, Virginia Military Institute is the nation's earliest state-supported military school and has supplied the country with many outstanding military leaders, most prominently General of the Army George C. Marshall. The campus consists of some twenty-five major buildings united by a castellated Gothic Revival style. The focal point, The Barracks, is a much-evolved complex originally designed by Alexander Jackson Davis. Davis also designed Gothic Revival faculty houses lining the Parade Ground, of which the Gilham house (1852) and the Superintendent's Quarters (1860) survive. In the 1910s architect Bertram Grosvenor Goodhue was commissioned to design Jackson Memorial Hall and additional faculty houses. The original Gothic character established by Davis has been carefully maintained in these and later works. Lending variety is a scattering of 19th-century and later dwellings including the Gothic Revival Pendleton-Coles cottage (shown) where General Marshall was married. *(117–17) VLR: 09/09/69; NHL: 05/30/74.*

WASHINGTON AND LEE UNIVERSITY HISTORIC DISTRICT. The historic heart of Washington and Lee University is an architecturally harmonious complex of buildings forming one of the nation's most dignified and beautiful campuses. The central element, the Colonnade, gives the impression a single design concept. It is, in reality, the product of a building program extending over 150 years. The first buildings, erected in 1803 for what was then Washington College, have disappeared. The classical theme of the complex was established by the oldest existing building, the temple-form Washington Hall completed in 1824. Its builder-architects, John Jordan and Samuel Darst, here transformed the prevailing Roman Revival style into a sturdy regional idiom. Washington Hall was flanked by Payne Hall in 1831 and by Robinson Hall in 1842. Two pairs of porticoed faculty residences also were added in 1842. Stylistically contrasting elements are the distinctive President's House of 1868 and the Lee Chapel of 1866–67. *(117–22) VLR: 10/06/70; NRHP: 12/18/70; NHL: 11/11/71.*

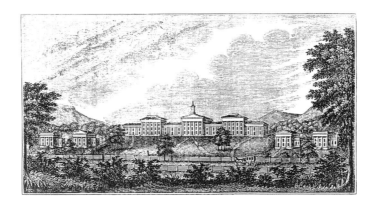

LOUDOUN COUNTY

This northern Virginia county, formed from Fairfax County in 1757, was named for John Campbell, fourth earl of Loudoun, who was commander of British forces in North America during the early part of the French and Indian War and governor of Virginia in 1756–59. Its county seat is Leesburg.

ALDIE MILL HISTORIC DISTRICT, *Aldie.* Charles Fenton Mercer, military officer, legislator, and advocate of the colonization of blacks, settled here in 1804. He named his property for Aldie Castle, his Scottish ancestral home. The large merchant mill, constructed in 1807 by Mercer's partner William Cooke, survives as one of the best-outfitted early mills in the state. The three-part complex includes what was a plaster mill at one end and a store at the other. The mill's twin overshot Fitz wheels, installed in 1900, are a unique surviving pair in Virginia. Overlooking the mill is a large Federal house, built by Mercer in 1810 as his residence. Behind the mill is the miller's house. Completing the grouping is an early stone bridge across Little River. The mill operated into the 1970s when it was donated to the Virginia Outdoors Foundation, which has since undertaken an extensive restoration. *(53–114) VLR: 06/02/70; NRHP: 09/15/70.*

BALL'S BLUFF BATTLEFIELD AND NATIONAL CEMETERY, *Leesburg vicinity.* Ball's Bluff Battlefield and National Cemetery are poignant reminders of a disastrous Union defeat in the first year of the Civil War. On October 21, 1861, a Union force commanded by Col. Edward D. Baker, a senator from Oregon and a friend of President Lincoln, crossed the Potomac River and scaled Ball's Bluff on the Virginia shore, determined to capture Leesburg. Quickly surrounded by Confederates, Baker was killed and his men were stampeded over the bluff. Many drowned, and their bodies washed ashore downstream in Washington. Two months later Congress established its Joint Committee on the Conduct of the War to investigate the defeat. The Ball's Bluff National Cemetery, the nation's smallest military cemetery, was established in December 1865 as the burial place of fifty-four Union casualties of the battle. *(53–307) VLR: 10/16/84; NHL: 04/27/84.*

BELMONT, *Leesburg vicinity.* This superlative five-part Federal plantation house, erected 1799–1802, was the home of Ludwell Lee, son of Richard Henry Lee, signer of the Declaration of Independence. The house ranks in quality with the five-part mansions of Washington, Baltimore, and Annapolis, as well as Woodlawn in Fairfax County. No name, however, has been associated with its design. Ludwell Lee served as aide-de-camp to Lafayette in the campaign of 1781. Failing in politics, he spent his days as a planter and host at Belmont, entertaining Lafayette in 1825. Later owners of the estate include Mr. and Mrs. Edward B. McLean, Washington socialites, and Patrick J. Hurley, secretary of war in the Hoover administration. Belmont was purchased by the IBM Corporation in 1969 but was never used. Since sold, the property is scheduled for conversion to a country club. *(53–106) VLR: 09/21/76; NRHP: 02/08/80.*

BENTON, *Leithtown vicinity.* Benton's dwelling house and outbuildings were the nucleus of a prosperous antebellum northern Virginia plantation. The surviving complex includes a formal brick residence built 1831–33, complete with dependencies and a rare early brick barn. Although the house is architecturally conservative, the high quality of the construction reflects the skill of its builder and first owner, William Benton. Benton was an expert brickmaker and mason who served as the foreman for the building of Oak Hill, James Monroe's Loudoun County home. He is credited with making bricks for most of the early brick houses in the Middleburg area and with supervising their construction. Except for a remodeling of the north front and some of the interior after 1908 when it was purchased by Mr. and Mrs. Daniel Sands, the house has changed little since it was completed. *(53–107) VLR: 05/17/83; NRHP: 06/14/84.*

BLUEMONT HISTORIC DISTRICT. This settlement on the slope of the Blue Ridge Mountains was first known as Snickers Gap, after the Snickers family. By 1824 it was incorporated as Snickersville, prospering from its location on a trade route between the Shenandoah Valley and ports on the Potomac. Snickersville was the scene of Civil War skirmishes as both armies vied for control of the Shenandoah Valley. After the war it declined as a commercial center until the railroad came in 1900. In order to promote the community as a mountain resort, managers of the Washington and Old Dominion Railroad succeeded in changing the town's name to Bluemont, and the effort did attract Washington residents for summer vacations. Although most structures date from the turn of the century, a number of earlier stone and log structures remain as reminders of the town's importance as a 19th-century trade center. *(404–12) VLR: 01/17/84; NRHP: 02/23/84.*

BROAD RUN BRIDGE AND TOLLHOUSE, *Sterling Park vicinity.* The stone-arched Broad Run Bridge was destroyed by tropical storm Agnes in 1972. The storm, however, spared the accompanying stone tollhouse, possibly the state's only extant bridge tollhouse of the period. The bridge and tollhouse were part of the Leesburg Turnpike system incorporated in 1809 to connect Leesburg with Alexandria. Construction of the project went slowly; the bridge was not completed until 1820. Tolls ceased to be collected during the Civil War, and the bridge was abandoned in 1949 for a larger one to accommodate modern State Route 7 immediately adjacent. At the west end of the ruined bridge, of which only the abutments now remain, the tollhouse currently serves as a private residence. *(53–110) VLR: 12/02/69; NRHP: 04/17/70.*

CARLHEIM (PAXTON HOUSE), *Leesburg.* Carlheim is a large Victorian country house dating from the 1870s, a period when few important dwellings were erected in Virginia because of the economic deprivation resulting from the Civil War. The thirty-two-room stone house, combining the Italian Villa style with the Second Empire mode, was designed by Henry C. Dudley of New York for Charles R. Paxton, a Pennsylvania industrialist. The interior is well appointed with stone mantels, plasterwork ceiling medallions, and a grand staircase. To assure comfort, the house was equipped with central heating, hot and cold running water, and carbide gas lighting. The mansard roof atop the tower was destroyed by lightning in recent years. Among the outbuildings is a peacock house. Known currently as the Paxton Child Development Center, the property is now a preschool and day-care center. *(53–380) VLR: 10/16/79; NRHP: 12/28/79.*

CATOCTIN CREEK BRIDGE, *Route 662, Waterford vicinity.* A typical example of Pratt truss construction, this 150-foot, single-span bridge was once numbered among scores of similar structures but is now one of the last through-truss metal bridges in northern Virginia. Department of Transportation records state that it was constructed in 1925 by the Variety Iron Works of Cleveland, Ohio. It was originally located on Route 7 spanning Goose Creek in Loudoun County. The bridge was dismantled and moved to its present location around 1932 where it now serves a tree-shaded, unpaved country lane bordered by well-tended estates. *(53–131) VLR: 01/15/74; NRHP: 06/25/74.*

CATOCTIN RURAL HISTORIC DISTRICT. Extending from the outskirts of Leesburg north to the Potomac River along historic Route 15, with Catoctin Mountain forming its western border, this 25,000-acre rural district is a varied pastoral landscape of forested hillsides, undulating pastures, and winding roads. Scattered through its farmland is a broad range of 18th-, 19th-, and early 20th-century rural architecture. The district includes several large estates with grand houses such as Selma but is also sprinkled with vernacular farmhouses and farm buildings. Small crossroad settlements contain schools, churches, and commercial structures. From its earliest settlement by Tidewater planters through the establishment of large dairy farms and grazing farms in this century, the fertile area has been important to Loudoun County's agricultural economy. The district also preserves four historic ferry crossings. Though still possessing a strongly agrarian character, the district is threatened with suburban development. *(53–12) VLR: 12/13/88.*

CLAPHAM'S FERRY, *Lucketts vicinity.* Clapham's Ferry has been the site of a Potomac River ferry crossing since 1757 when the General Assembly awarded Josias Clapham permission to operate a public ferry here offering access to Maryland. The property was owned by the Clapham family until 1820 when they sold it to William Hawling. The ferry operated until the Civil War. Archaeological features of ferry-related structures likely remain at river's edge. The existing stone dwelling, presently encased in later extensions, probably was built in the early 19th century during the later Clapham or Hawling tenure. It apparently served as the residence of the ferry operator as well as the nucleus of a farm operation. Adjacent are a log meat house and a log kitchen. Nearby is a bank barn, one of the county's largest, a 1930s rebuilding of an earlier one struck by lightning. *(53–71) VLR: 3/19/97; NRHP: 09/04/97.*

CLEREMONT FARM, *Upperville vicinity.* The inimitable organic quality of historic farmsteads is well exhibited at Cleremont, a picturesque grouping in the famed countryside of the Upperville area. The property was purchased in 1761 by William Rust of Westmoreland County, who presumably built the original simple stone cottage shortly afterward. The earliest part of the present main dwelling house, a two-bay stone structure, was built by Rust's son George around 1820. It was soon expanded by a three-bay log and frame section. A two-story log wing was added in the 1870s, and smaller wings came later. Since stuccoed, the exterior gives no hint of its mixed materials. On the grounds is a stone kitchen outbuilding. Most of the original farm buildings were burned during the Civil War. The present appearance of the house dates from a 1940 renovation, reputedly by architect William B. Dew of Middleburg. *(53–1038)* *VLR: 06/19/96; NRHP: 01/25/97.*

DODONA MANOR, *217 Edwards Ferry Road, Leesburg.* General of the Army George Catlett Marshall made his home at this gracious Federal house from 1941 until his death in 1959. He named it for the mythical Greek forest of Dodona. During these years Marshall rose from a respected army officer to one of the 20th century's most influential figures. As army chief of staff from 1939 to 1945, he directed the nation's military effort. He later served as secretary of state and secretary of defense. He is best remembered for developing the 1947 European Recovery Program, known as the Marshall Plan, which launched the restoration of Europe's economy. Marshall's Leesburg retreat was built in the 1820s and later expanded. Other than establishing an extensive garden, Marshall made few changes here. The property is being developed by the George C. Marshall International Center into a museum honoring this American hero. *(253–09) VLR: 12/04/96; NHL: 06/19/96; BHR EASEMENT.*

DOUGLASS HIGH SCHOOL (DOUGLASS SCHOOL), *East Market Street, Leesburg.* Douglass High School symbolizes the quiet tenacity and sense of purpose maintained by Loudoun County's black citizens in their determination to secure a high standard of secondary education for their children. The school stands on land purchased by the blacks and presented to the county school board in 1940. Though the building was paid for with public funds, the black community raised money for furnishings, laboratory equipment, and band instruments. Named for Frederick Douglass, a former slave and prominent abolitionist, the school operated as the county's first and only black high school from its opening in 1941 until 1968 when segregated education was ended. The building today houses an alternative school, serving students with special needs. *(253–70) VLR: 10/09/91; NRHP: 09/24/92.*

EBENEZER BAPTIST CHURCHES, *Bloomfield.* This gentle ensemble in the pastoral landscape of southern Loudoun County has richly varied associations. Baptists had a meetinghouse at this location as early as 1769. The existing stone meetinghouse was likely built ca. 1806 when the minutes of the newly constituted Ebenezer Church meeting discussed "finishing the Meeting House." The new Ebenezer Baptist Church, a country Greek Revival work, was built ca. 1855 to accommodate the New School Baptists, who broke off from the Old School Baptists and constructed their own building next to the old one. The Civil War disrupted the activities of both churches, causing services to be canceled for three years. Around 1876 local artist Lucien Whiting Powell, who gained a national reputation as an artist, decorated the interior of the new church with folk-like trompe l'oeil decorations. Both churches are today owned and maintained by the Ebenezer Cemetery Company. *(53–140) VLR: 03/10/94; NRHP: 06/03/94.*

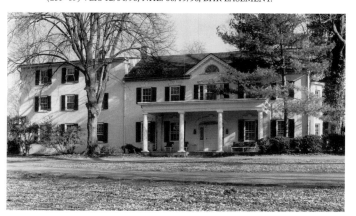

FARMER'S DELIGHT, *Leithtown.* Farmer's Delight was part of an 18th-century tract for which George Washington and Lord Fairfax once served as trustees. The estate boasts a mansion patterned after Tidewater Georgian plantation houses. One of the county's oldest brick dwellings, it was built ca. 1791 for Joseph Lane who served in the General Assembly and was a lieutenant colonel in the army during the Whiskey Rebellion of 1794. The Flemish bond brickwork is highlighted by a belt course and gauged-brick jack arches. The interior preserves Federal woodwork typical of the region. From 1856 until 1919 Farmer's Delight was owned by the Leith family. It later was acquired by horseman Henry J. Frost, Jr., who added the wings. In 1948 the estate was purchased by George C. McGhee, former ambassador to Turkey and Germany, who developed an extensive garden and arboretum here designed by landscape architects Boris Timchenko of Washington and Meade Palmer of Warrenton. *(53–121) VLR: 04/17/73; NRHP: 07/02/73; BHR EASEMENT.*

FLEETWOOD FARM, *Arcola vicinity.* Originally called Peggy's Green, Fleetwood Farm was the home of William Ellzey from 1761 until his death in 1795. A lawyer and businessman, Ellzey also participated in the Revolution by signing the 1774 Loudoun County Resolves for Independence. The date of the house is uncertain; it likely was built by Ellzey after his purchase of the property, although it has been claimed that it was built by the Rev. Charles Green, the previous owner. The house originally was a basic side-passage dwelling sheathed in weatherboards. The interior details, however, particularly the stair balustrade and parlor paneling, exhibit parallels to Tidewater Georgian design. The house was stuccoed during the course of alterations undertaken around 1940. A wing was added to the east end in 1984, balancing an early wing opposite. Near the house are an early fieldstone springhouse and smokehouse. *(53–629) VLR: 12/12/89; NRHP: 02/01/91.*

GLEBE OF SHELBURNE PARISH, *Lincoln vicinity.* Nestled in the shadow of Mount Gilead, in the pastoral landscape of the Goose Creek Historic District, the former glebe house of Shelburne Parish is one of the state's handful of extant colonial glebe houses and perhaps the only one for which original specifications survive. It is also the only remaining glebe house in northern Virginia. It was begun on the 465-acre glebe in 1773 by the builder Appolis Cooper. Its first occupant was the Rev. David Griffith who left in 1776 to become a chaplain in the Continental army. Unlike most other glebes, Shelburne Glebe was not relinquished immediately after the disestablishment of the Anglican church but was held defiantly by its parish for thirty-eight years. Although extensively remodeled and enlarged after its sale to private owners in 1840, its colonial brick walls attest to the house's early origins. *(53–186) VLR: 11/19/74; NRHP: 04/01/75; BHR EASEMENT.*

GOOSE CREEK HISTORIC DISTRICT. The Goose Creek Historic District is a scenically cohesive rural area of some 10,000 acres in central Loudoun County that sustained Virginia's largest concentration of Quaker settlers. The English Friends who came into the area from Pennsylvania, Maryland, and New Jersey beginning in the 1730s gave their community a distinctive cast that is still reflected in the region's small farms, many of which are yet defined by their 18th-century land patents. Worked without slave labor, Quaker farms were limited in size to what could be run by a family unit. The district, which centers on the village of Lincoln, preserves a rich collection of 18th-, 19th-, and 20th-century rural vernacular architecture, much of it incorporating the superb stone masonry peculiar to Quaker settlers. Though threatened by creeping suburbanization, it retains a high degree of unspoiled pastoral beauty. *(53–02) VLR: 07/21/81; NRHP: 11/14/82.*

GOOSE CREEK MEETINGHOUSES, *Lincoln.* This group of three buildings in the village of Lincoln illustrates the continuity of the Quaker tradition in northern Virginia. The 1765 stone meetinghouse (shown), now a residence, is the state's second-oldest Friends' meetinghouse. Its successor, an 1817 brick structure across the road, remains in regular use by its meeting. This latter building originally had two stories, but after windstorm damage in 1944, it was rebuilt as a one-story building. On the meetinghouse grounds is the Oak Dale School, an 1815 one-room brick structure, now used for First Day school. Also nearby is the Quaker burying ground. The Goose Creek Meeting was organized ca. 1750 under the leadership of Jacob Janney of Bucks County, Pa. The group first met in a log building erected at the place in the woods where Janney's wife Hannah held regular private devotions. *(53–305) VLR: 01/15/74; NRHP: 07/24/74.*

GOOSE CREEK STONE BRIDGE, *Atoka vicinity.* The Goose Creek Stone Bridge is the longest remaining stone turnpike bridge in Virginia. The exact construction date of the massive four-span, 212-foot structure has not been determined, but it may have been built as early as 1801–3. The bridge accommodated the extension of the Ashby's Gap Turnpike from the then western end of the Little River Turnpike at Aldie through Ashby's Gap to the Shenandoah River. The earliest documented reference appears in the 1820 report of the Board of Public Works, which mentions the collecting of tolls on the Goose Creek Bridge. The bridge was the scene of Civil War action between Gen. J. E. B. Stuart and Union forces under Gen. Alfred Pleasonton. The bridge was bypassed by the realignment of U.S. Route 50 in 1957. Its custodianship was given to the Fauquier and Loudoun Garden Club in 1975, which has since maintained it. *(53–156) VLR: 05/21/74; NRHP: 10/09/74.*

HILLCREST (EDWARD NICHOLS HOUSE), *330 West Market Street, Leesburg.* This finely appointed residence was built in 1899 for Edward Nichols, a local lawyer and businessman. Designed by Washington architect Lemuel Norris, the dwelling combines elements of both the Queen Anne and Colonial Revival styles. The original architectural drawings and specifications attest to the architect's talent, high standards of quality, and attention to detail. Norris made reference to the area's Federal style with his use of splayed stone lintels and keystones. The interior has dignified but restrained Georgian Revival woodwork, including delicately ornamented plasterwork ceilings. The house survives in an excellent state of preservation, having escaped any significant alteration. The property also includes a laundry, storage shed, gazebo, and a carriage house with a water storage tower. *(253–63) VLR: 10/20/87; NRHP: 12/04/87.*

HILLSBORO HISTORIC DISTRICT. Extending along State Route 9, Hillsboro preserves the image of a typical 19th-century linear community of northern Virginia. The village grew along a minor trade artery connecting Leesburg with Charles Town (now West Virginia) during the early 19th century. Its residents provided economic and social services to farmers of the vicinity, and the town retains its rural setting, surrounded by the scenically beautiful countryside for which western Loudoun County is noted. The architectural fabric consists mainly of two-story, gable-roof stone residences, illustrating the influence of Pennsylvania vernacular building types on northern Virginia. Victorian porch and bay window additions indicate that residents remained current with architectural fashions. *(236–40) VLR: 09/19/78; NRHP: 05/07/79.*

INSTITUTE FARM, *Aldie vicinity.* The Loudoun County Agricultural Institute and Chemical Academy erected this large but plain building ca. 1854 for its Institute Farm, the first agricultural school in the Commonwealth and one of the first schools of scientific agronomy in the United States. The institute was a precursor of the agricultural colleges that would be established under federal auspices with the passage of the Morrill Act in 1862. From the late 18th century, Loudoun's citizens had pioneered in agricultural experimentation, and the school's founders included a number of larger landholders and agriculturalists. Despite its pioneering aspirations, the school failed to thrive and closed in 1860. Since 1916 it has been the headquarters of the National Beagle Club of America. Facing the Institute building is a series of rustic log cabins built to house the club's members during the annual beagle field trials. *(53–139) VLR: 03/17/81; NRHP: 07/08/82; BHR EASEMENT.*

JANELIA, *Ashburn vicinity.* This capacious mansion was completed in 1936 for correspondent and author Robert S. Pickens and his wife, Vinton L. Pickens, artist and civic leader. It was designed by Philip H. Smith of Smith and Walker of Boston and is significant as one of Virginia's latest representatives of the country house ideal fostered in England and spread to America in the late 19th century. The place has the essential ingredients of a proper country estate: sprawling manor house, service building, formal gardens, and scenic vistas. With irregular massing and complex hipped roof, the house is a blend of the Normandy Manor style popular in the 1920s and the Modernist tenets of the 1930s. Though recently converted to executive offices, the house remains a document of the lifestyle of the affluent just before World War II. *(53–84); VLR: 06/17/86; NRHP: 03/20/87; BHR EASEMENT.*

LEESBURG HISTORIC DISTRICT. Established in 1758, the original sixty-acre portion of Leesburg, laid off around Nicholas Minor's tavern, is a gently evolved Piedmont county seat with a varied assemblage of domestic, commercial, and governmental buildings built during three centuries. Preserving a nostalgic small-town character, the district is centered around a parklike court square containing the 1895 Loudoun County Courthouse (shown) and a porticoed Greek Revival academy building, now used for county offices. Lending distinction is a collection of regional vernacular architecture, including shops, town houses, and three early taverns. A scattering of Victorian structures contrasts with these plainer buildings. Leesburg was first known as Georgetown, after George II, but its name was changed to honor Francis Lightfoot Lee, signer of the Declaration of Independence, who owned property nearby. The district's thirty-six blocks are in an irregular grid of largely tree-lined streets. *(253–35) VLR: 12/02/69; NRHP: 02/26/70.*

LUCKETTS SCHOOL, *Lucketts.* A relic of simpler times, this little-altered elementary school is the principal landmark of Lucketts, a farming community steadily witnessing suburban encroachment. Built in 1913, the weatherboarded structure originally had four classrooms with no electricity or indoor plumbing. Although lacking modern utilities, the building was not without architectural dignity. With its regular facade and belfry, its design conformed to those published in architectural plan books of the early 1900s. The building was expanded in 1919 and again in 1929 when an auditorium wing was added. The interior retains many early fittings including wooden wainscoting, embossed metal ceilings, slate blackboards, and a flexible wooden room divider. The school closed in 1972. A focus of local preservation interests, the building was converted to a community center. Since 1981 it has been operated by the Loudoun County Department of Parks, Recreation, and Community Services. *(53–287) VLR: 08/18/93; NRHP: 10/14/93.*

MIDDLEBURG HISTORIC DISTRICT. The physical and psychological heart of northern Virginia's hunt country, Middleburg is a compact and fastidious village retaining the qualities of its early years. Founded in 1787 by Leven Powell, a Revolutionary War officer and regional Federalist leader, the town developed as a coach stop and relay station on Ashby's Gap Turnpike, becoming by midcentury a commercial center for lower Loudoun and upper Fauquier counties. The town saw frequent Civil War cavalry action and won a reputation for fierce Confederate loyalty, but afterward it declined in fortune and population. By the second decade of the 20th century, it assumed a new identity as a social and equestrian center. With its tree-lined streets, brick sidewalks, and harmonious scale, the town has a diverse collection of late 18th- to early 20th-century architectural styles highlighted by early stone and brick structures. *(259–162) VLR: 12/15/81; NRHP: 10/29/82.*

MORVEN PARK, *Leesburg vicinity.* Morven Park is best known as the home of Westmoreland Davis, governor of Virginia from 1918 to 1922. From the time he acquired the property in 1903, Davis set a standard for grand-scale living and made Morven Park a model dairy farm. His sprawling mansion has had a complicated evolution. It incorporates a 1780s farmhouse, first owned by Wilson Cary Selden. Judge Thomas Swann acquired the place in 1808 and added the Doric portico and dependencies in the 1830s. In 1858 Swann's son, Thomas Swann, Jr., later governor of Maryland, engaged Baltimore architect Edmund George Lind to remodel the house into a grandiose composition calling for four Italianate towers. The main tower was omitted, and the tops of the other four towers were later removed. In 1955 Governor Davis's widow established the Westmoreland Davis Foundation, and Morven Park was opened to the public as a museum, cultural center, and equestrian institute. *(53–87) VLR: 11/19/74; NRHP: 02/18/75.*

MUCH HADDAM, *Middleburg.* Situated at the western edge of Middleburg, on land originally owned by Leven Powell, founder of Middleburg, Much Haddam exemplifies northern Virginia's early 19th-century vernacular architecture. With its five-bay facade and two stories over a high basement, the house was a type favored by many of the region's more prosperous farmers. It probably was erected in 1820 by Richard Cochran adjacent to his own home, Capitol Hill. Much of the original simple Federal woodwork is preserved within, including a delicate Federal stair. The house originally had a log section behind the rear ell. Long missing, this was replaced with an early log structure found in the countryside. On the grounds is a rare two-story kitchen outbuilding, one of the state's few examples with a square plan. Embellishing the hillside site is a storybook old-fashioned garden. *(259–164) VLR: 04/17/90; NRHP: 12/28/90; BHR EASEMENT.*

OAK HILL, *Aldie vicinity.* James Monroe began construction of his Loudoun County mansion between 1820 and 1823 and lived here following his presidency until 1830, the year before he died. For its design, Monroe sought ideas from both Thomas Jefferson and James Hoban, architect of the White House. The house was constructed by the local builder William Benton. Its dominant architectural feature is the unusual pentastyle portico. Oak Hill was visited by Lafayette in 1825 during his tour of America, and it was here that Monroe worked on the drafting of the Monroe Doctrine. The estate passed out of the family after Monroe's death. The house was increased in size in 1922 by the enlargement of its wings and the addition of terminal porticoes during the ownership of Mr. and Mrs. Frank C. Littleton. Still a private residence, this historic seat is a fitting monument to the last of the "Virginia Dynasty" of presidents. *(53–90) VLR: 09/09/69; NRHP: 10/15/66; NHL: 12/19/60.*

OATLANDS, *Leesburg vicinity.* Begun in 1804 and embellished over the next two decades, this monumental mansion, along with its numerous outbuildings and extensive gardens, forms one of the nation's most elaborate Federal estates. The complex was developed by George Carter, one of the scions of prominent Tidewater families who migrated to northern Virginia after the Revolution. Carter developed the mansion's design from illustrations in William Chambers's *A Treatise on Civil Architecture* (1786). With its stuccoed walls, demioctagonal wings, parapeted roof, and a portico of slender Corinthian columns added by Carter in 1827, the house has a special lightness and elegance. The airy rooms with their intricate Federal ornamentation complement the exterior. Oatlands remained in the Carter family until 1897. In 1903 it was acquired by William Corcoran Eustis, grandson of banker and philanthropist William Wilson Corcoran. The estate was donated to the National Trust for Historic Preservation in 1965. *(53–93) VLR: 09/09/69; NRHP: 11/12/69; NHL: 11/11/71.*

OATLANDS HISTORIC DISTRICT. This rural district incorporates the Oatlands estate and several associated historic properties. At the southern end, along Goose Creek, is the site of Oatlands Mills, a milling complex established by George Carter of Oatlands in the early 19th century. The large mill was destroyed in 1905, leaving today only a small ruin and extensive archaeological remains. Surviving from the village of Oatlands nearby are several houses and the Episcopal Church of Our Savior (shown), a simple brick structure erected in 1878. A later parish hall stands next to it. At the northern end of the district, on U.S. Route 15, is the Mountain Gap School, the county's last operating one-room school when it closed in 1953. Most of the property in the historic district is protected by preservation easements or is owned by the National Trust for Historic Preservation. *(53–446) VLR: 02/19/74; NRHP: 05/03/74.*

OLD STONE CHURCH ARCHAEOLOGICAL SITE, *Cornwall Street, Leesburg.* In the heart of Leesburg, this site contains the archaeological remains of the earliest Methodist meetinghouse in Virginia. Constructed between 1766 and 1770 and rebuilt in 1785, the church stood until 1902. The surviving colonial churches and church sites in Virginia consist mostly of Anglican examples, with few that represent the dissenting congregations of Quakers, Baptists, Presbyterians, and Methodists. Having been in continuous use between the 1760s and 1902, the Leesburg site is likely to contain artifacts relating both to the congregation and to the structure itself. The Old Stone Church was also the first Methodist-owned property in the United States and was the location of the sixth American conference of Methodists in 1778 (the first such conference in Virginia). The site is an official National Historic Shrine of the United Methodist Church. *(253–67) VLR: 04/19/88; NRHP: 09/07/89.*

RED FOX INN, *Middleburg.* One of the Virginia hunt country's best-known landmarks, the Red Fox Inn occupies a site used for a tavern since the 18th century. Rawleigh Chinn, who originally owned the land on which Middleburg developed, reputedly built a tavern near this intersection in 1728. The present stone building may incorporate earlier fabric but was mostly constructed in 1830 for Nobel Beveridge, who stated in a newspaper advertisement that year: "A new House of Entertainment has been built . . . with all the rooms comfortable and well-furnished. The subscriber's bar is well-appointed with choice liquors." Beveridge's tavern since has been remodeled and enlarged several times. Its present appearance, largely dating from a 1940s renovation by local architect William B. Dew, is designed to attract its clientele with an old-fashioned ambience. The tavern has since become an area institution and remains a fashionable venue for lodging and repast. *(259–18) VLR: 03/19/97; NRHP: 11/13/97.*

RICH BOTTOM FARM, *Purcellville vicinity.* With a lazy pond reflecting the informal manor house and its long front porch, Rich Bottom preserves a scene of quietude and old-fashioned ways. The earliest part of the house, a fieldstone structure, was built in 1780 for Samuel Purcell, a grain farmer and millowner. It was soon enlarged with a stone section of equal size and further expanded in 1820 with a three-bay brick section. Three of the rooms in the stone portion have exposed ceiling joists with beaded edges. Except for 19th-century additions to the porch, the house has changed little since the 1820s. Adding to the picture of domesticity are two early stone outbuildings, a springhouse and a smokehouse. The property remained in the Purcell family until the 1940s. The nearby village that grew up around the store operated by Samuel Purcell's offspring was named Purcellville in 1852. *(53–422) VLR: 12/04/96; NRHP: 02/21/97.*

ROCKLAND, *White's Ferry vicinity.* Rockland takes its name from the limestone outcroppings permeating the 600-acre farm. Gen. George Rust, a Loudoun County gentleman, replaced deteriorating wooden structures with this imposing brick mansion in 1822. Of large scale and with boldly detailed woodwork, the house is one of the finest of several important Federal plantation dwellings in the area. The property was later inherited by Gen. Rust's son, Col. Armistead T. M. Rust, an 1842 West Point graduate who served with the 19th Virginia Infantry during the Civil War. His death in 1887 left his second wife, Ida Lee, with fourteen children and an encumbered estate. Exuding tremendous energy and business acumen, she repaid the debt and educated her youngest children. With regained prosperity, her son Edwin enlarged Rockland around 1908. The estate remains owned by Rust family descendants. *(53–96) VLR: 03/17/87; NRHP: 05/14/87.*

ROKEBY, *Gleedsville Road.* Built in 1757 by Charles Binns II, first clerk of the circuit court of Loudoun County, Rokeby is the place where the Articles of Confederation, the Declaration of Independence, and the Constitution were stored for safekeeping in 1814 during the British occupation of Washington. The hallowed documents were kept in a still-intact vaulted room in the cellar. Rokeby is the largest and most formal colonial house in the region. Much of its original Georgian character was changed in 1836 when, in the course of an extensive renovation by its owner, Benjamin Shreve, Jr., the clipped gables were removed, the windows were remodeled, and the interior trim was replaced. The house was enlarged in 1886 with an extensive rear addition and was returned somewhat to its early appearance during a 1958 restoration. *(53–97) VLR: 05/20/75; NRHP: 05/30/76.*

ROSE HILL FARM, *Atoka vicinity.* This spacious Federal vernacular farmhouse was built in 1820 for Amos Denham who operated the house as a tavern serving travelers along Ashby's Gap Turnpike. Thomas Glascock, a large landowner, purchased the farm in 1853 and made extensive improvements including adding a cast-iron veranda said to have been shipped from  New Orleans. Glascock also built a large stone granary. During the Civil War, Confederate ranger Col. John S. Mosby was a frequent dinner guest at Rose Hill. The house served as an observation point for Gen. J. E. B. Stuart in 1863. Union troops burned Glascock's barns in 1864. Despite the Civil War action, Rose Hill preserves, in addition to the granary, a stone slave quarters now attached to the house, an octagonal icehouse, a three-story brick slave quarters, and an early stone bridge. It remains a working farm owned by Glascock descendants. *(53–01) VLR: 06/15/94; NRHP: 08/25/94.*

SUNNYSIDE, *Hamilton vicinity.* The Quaker ethic of simplicity is evident in the original section of this much-expanded farmhouse. This core, a three-bay, hall-parlor dwelling constructed of local fieldstone, is characteristic of the Federal vernacular favored by these diligent and peaceable farmers. Isaac Nichols, son of Quaker settlers who migrated from Philadelphia, apparently had the house built ca. 1815 for his son William. William died before inheriting the property; thus it passed to his son William, Jr., who added the stone outbuildings in the 1820s. William Nichols, Jr., moved to Ohio in 1836 following a daughter who married outside of the Friends meeting. A frame addition was erected ca. 1855–60 by the McCray family. The original section acquired a projecting bay ca. 1890, which was remodeled ca. 1910. Other additions have made this once-simple house an interesting amalgamation of vernacular forms. *(53–304) VLR: 06/15/94; NRHP: 08/16/94.*

TAYLORSTOWN HISTORIC DISTRICT. A steady supply of waterpower and the surrounding fertile farms of the Quaker settlers made Taylorstown an ideal site for milling operations. The first mill was established here in the 1730s by Richard Brown, whose stone house, Hunting Hill, survives in the tiny hamlet. The present stone mill (shown) was erected by Thomas Taylor ca. 1784. Also in the district is an 18th-century stone cottage known as Foxton, an example of Loudoun County's early vernacular architecture. The other buildings include an early 19th-century store building, a rusticated concrete store of 1904, and two late Victorian dwellings. Free from modern intrusions save for a new concrete bridge across Catoctin Creek, Taylorstown has been a sleepy crossroads since milling operations ceased in 1958. The mill, one of the few remaining in a county once noted for its many mills, is now a private residence. *(53–603) VLR: 12/21/76; NRHP: 01/30/78.*

WATERFORD HISTORIC DISTRICT. Nestled in the countryside of Loudoun County's northern tip, Waterford developed as a Quaker milling community. The village traces its origins to ca. 1733 when Amos Janney and other Friends arrived from Pennsylvania and established a mill complex here. By the 1830s Waterford was a flourishing community of some seventy houses with a tannery, chairmaker, and boot manufacturer, along with shops and a tavern. Commerce declined by the early 20th century, leaving Waterford a remarkably preserved hamlet free of modern intrusions. Its quiet shady streets remain lined with examples of regional vernacular styles, both freestanding and attached, in a variety of materials including brick, stone, and log. A mid-19th-century mill stands at the north edge of town. Aggressive preservation efforts by the Waterford Foundation since the 1940s have maintained the town's unique character. Some sixty properties are protected by preservation easements. *(401–123) VLR: 05/13/69; NRHP: 06/03/69; NHL: 04/15/70.*

WAVERLY, *604 South King Street, Leesburg.* Built ca. 1890 as the retirement home of Robert T. Hempstone, a Baltimore businessman, Waverly displays the prosperity of its original owner. At a time when the economy of Loudoun County still suffered from the devastating effects of the Civil War, large dwellings such as Waverly were built primarily by individuals who had acquired their wealth elsewhere. A finely appointed example of a late Victorian residence incorporating features of both the Queen Anne and Colonial Revival styles, the house was built by the Leesburg firm of John Norris and Sons, probably using a scheme published in one of the many architectural design catalogs of the period. Waverly stood in shabby condition for many years but was restored in the 1980s and again in 1995, after a major fire, as the centerpiece of an office development known as Waverly Park Corporate Center. *(253–48) VLR: 05/18/82; NRHP: 02/10/83.*

WELBOURNE, *Upperville vicinity.* Set in the heart of Loudoun County's hunt country, Welbourne is a patrician homestead expanded in stages over a century and a half to meet the tastes and needs of seven generations of the same family. John Peyton Dulany purchased the nucleus of the present house, an 18th-century stone dwelling, in 1833 and enlarged it into a five-bay structure. The house was further enlarged in the 1840s with one-story wings with demioctagonal ends. Additional embellishment came in the 1850s with Italianate porticoes on the facade and rear ell. A two-story south wing rounded out the house in the 1870s. Each part of the house retains an individual character. Located on the parklike grounds is an early formal garden and an extensive collection of outbuildings. Filled with an accumulation of family possessions, Welbourne offers a keenly felt continuity with the past. *(53–120) VLR: 07/06/71; NRHP: 02/23/72; BHR EASEMENT.*

WOODBURN, *Leesburg vicinity.* This Loudoun County estate contains an impressive Federal farmhouse and an important collection of ancillary structures illustrating the evolution of a northern Virginia farm over several decades. The property was patented in the mid–18th century by George Nixson, who put up the oldest buildings, including the log "patent" house—a dwelling required for the receipt of a land grant. Nixson also built the stone and frame gristmill in 1777 and the stone miller's house in 1787. Nixson's son George, or possibly his grandson, began the main house around 1820. The unusually large scale of the house, including its extensive rear wing, earned it the name "Dr. Nixson's Folly." Contemporary with the house is the springhouse and an impressive fine brick barn, complete with an arcaded ground level and brick lattice vents. A recent owner of Woodburn was the ballet dancer Rudolph Nureyev. *(53–105) VLR: 09/21/76; NRHP: 12/12/76.*

LOUISA COUNTY

Located in the heart of the Virginia Piedmont, this rural county was named in honor of Princess Louisa, a daughter of King George II. It was formed from Hanover County in 1742. The county seat is Louisa.

ANDERSON-FOSTER HOUSE, *Holly Grove vicinity.* This side-passage country cottage documents the continuity of Virginia's vernacular style over a century-long span. Appearing little different from a house dating at least seventy-five years earlier, the Anderson-Foster house was actually built in 1856, long after more stylish locales and clients had abandoned the regional idiom. The first owner of the dwelling was Dr. James B. Anderson, a country physician who bowed somewhat to contemporary taste by installing simple Greek Revival trim in a building that is otherwise almost completely lacking in academic architectural influence. The house has been restored and added to in recent years. *(54–181) VLR: 07/18/78; NRHP: 11/17/78.*

BOSWELL'S TAVERN, *Boswell's Tavern.* A landmark for travelers since Nicholas Johnson built its earliest section ca. 1735, this weatherboarded structure on the edge of the Green Springs Historic District is one of the state's time-honored rural taverns. The tavern was purchased in 1761 by Johnson's brother-in-law, John Boswell, who served as proprietor until his death in 1788. It served as a headquarters for the marquis de Lafayette in 1781. British colonel Banastre Tarleton captured colonial troops here during his attempt to seize Thomas Jefferson. The marquis de Chastellux referred to the Boswells' hospitality in his *Travels in North America in the Years 1780, 1781, and 1782.* The tavern is divided into two sections: a public area containing two large public rooms, a warming room, stair hall, and bar area and the innkeeper's wing with a winding corner stair leading to sleeping quarters. The landmark building is now a private residence. *(54–07) VLR: 11/05/68; NRHP: 11/25/69.*

CUCKOO, *Cuckoo.* Built ca. 1819 for Henry Pendleton, this stately old homestead stands near the site of the 18th-century Cuckoo Tavern, from which the patriot Jack Jouett began his legendary ride to warn Thomas Jefferson and General Assembly members of impending British capture. The Pendleton family was prominent in local and state affairs; several members became well-known physicians. On the grounds are two doctor's office outbuildings, one 18th century and one 19th century. The two-story brick dwelling is an interesting blend of original Federal-style details and early 20th-century Colonial Revival renovations. The interior preserves several early Federal mantels. An unusual feature is the rounded pent closet with its demiconical roof, also an original feature. Dr. Eugene Pendleton renovated the house in 1910, replacing a Victorian-era porch with the present classical portico. The property remains in the ownership of Pendleton descendants. *(54–16) VLR: 04/20/94; NRHP: 08/19/94.*

GRASSDALE, *Boswell's Tavern vicinity.* This brick dwelling, embellished with a festive bracketed cornice and veranda, is one of Virginia's very few fully developed Italianate country houses built before the Civil War. Such houses are relatively common in northern states, but Virginia's economic and political uncertainty, as well as conservative tendencies, inhibited the construction of plantation houses in the period's prevailing taste. Grassdale was completed in 1861 for James Maury Morris, Jr., and is an important architectural component of the Green Springs Historic District. The house shows the influence of the numerous designs for rural seats appearing in popular architectural pattern books of the period. Handsomely maintained and little-altered, Grassdale is situated to take advantage of a view across broad, gently sloping pastures. Immediately around the house is a park of towering oak trees. *(54–32) VLR: 02/20/73; NRHP: 07/02/73.*

GREEN SPRINGS, *Poindexter vicinity.* Overlooking the verdant farmland of the Green Springs area, near the springs whence the plantation derives its name, the Green Springs house is the area's best example of the formal vernacular dwelling of the late 18th century. The tall two-story frame house, accented by its slender exterior end chimneys, shows the influence of Virginia's academic Georgian style. Its double-pile floor plan is interesting for combining a hall-parlor with a center-passage scheme. The two front entrances reflect the former plan type, and the stair chamber between the two rear rooms reflects the latter plan type. The three surviving outbuildings near the house add to the picture of a rural domestic group of the period. Green Springs was built in 1772 for Col. Richard O. Morris, whose family settled and developed this section of Louisa County. *(54–57) VLR: 05/16/72; NRHP: 06/30/72.*

GREEN SPRINGS HISTORIC DISTRICT. From the earliest days of settlement in the Piedmont, the Green Springs area has been known for its exceptional fertility, prosperity, and beauty. Its farms, buildings, and families represent many generations of agricultural, architectural, and social history. Contrasted with the surrounding hilly land with its thin soil and scrub woodlands, this 14,000-acre bowl, a geological formation that defines Green Springs, is composed of lush, rolling pastures. First settled in the 1720s by Tidewater families, the area takes its name from a mineral spring that served as a spa during the late 18th century. Two families in particular built a number of plantation houses here. The Morrises built or extended Green Springs, Sylvania, Hawkwood, and Grassdale. The Watson family places include Ionia, Bracketts (shown), and Westend. These and numerous other buildings form an assemblage of rural architecture of outstanding variety and quality embellishing this gently civilized countryside. *(54–111) VLR: 02/20/73; NRHP: 03/07/73; NHL: 05/30/74.*

HAWKWOOD, *Zion Crossroads vicinity.* Until it was gutted by fire in 1982, Hawkwood was the best-remaining example of the Italian Villa–style houses designed by New York architect Alexander Jackson Davis. Completed in 1855, the house was built for Richard Overton Morris, a wealthy planter who promoted scientific agricultural methods to restore Virginia's depressed economy. While much of Davis's architecture was inspired by Greek and Gothic forms, he also was a popularizer of the Italian Villa style fostered in America by his collaborator Andrew Jackson Downing. Downing wrote that with its shading eaves, verandas, and picturesque massing, the villa style was most appropriate for country houses in the South. A hallmark of the style, demonstrated in Hawkwood, is the square tower. Hawkwood's walls and tower were spared in the fire and have since been stabilized and reroofed. Complete restoration of the house is contemplated. *(54–36) VLR: 09/01/70; NRHP: 09/17/70.*

JERDONE CASTLE, *Bumpass vicinity.* The oldest section of Jerdone Castle was built ca. 1745 by Francis Jerdone who immigrated to Louisa County from Scotland in 1740. In addition to expanding his original landholdings and building a residence, Jerdone operated stores, mills, and a forge. The later main section of the house was built in 1858 for Francis Jerdone's descendant Sarah Jerdone Coleman and her husband, Gen. Clayton Coleman. The structure's generous size is emphasized by an Italianate bracketed cornice and cupola. In 1879 the estate was purchased by Frank T. Glasgow of Richmond, father of the author Ellen Glasgow. Ellen Glasgow spent her childhood summers at Jerdone Castle, which she later said greatly influenced her writing. In the fourth chapter of *The Woman Within,* entitled "I Become a Writer," Miss Glasgow describes lying in the meadow at Jerdone Castle and coming to the realization that writing was to be her future. *(54–45) VLR: 08/21/84; NRHP: 10/04/84.*

IONIA, *Poindexter vicinity.* Ionia's dwelling house, with its symmetrical facade, hall-parlor plan, shed-roof porch, weatherboarded walls, and narrow dormers, illustrates the rational simplicity of the colonial Virginia farmhouse, a simplicity not based on economic necessity. Despite its small size and ordinary materials, the house has the architectural dignity inherent in many vernacular buildings of the period. Built in the early 1770s for Maj. James Watson, it is one of the oldest residences in the Green Springs area. Expanded at least four times by different generations of the family, the house retains its self-effacing aspect. Several early domestic outbuildings, including a large early barn, add interest to this venerable homestead. *(54–43) VLR: 05/16/72; NRHP: 06/30/72.*

LOUISA COUNTY COURTHOUSE, *Louisa.* The monumental Louisa County Courthouse is a symbol of the civic pride that permeated many rural counties across America in the late 19th and early 20th centuries. For many such counties the courthouse was the county's only significant work of architecture. The porticoed structure was built in 1905 and is the third courthouse associated with the site, replacing

a courthouse of 1818. Its architect, D. Wiley Anderson of Richmond, specialized in monumental classical designs and gave the building prominence through the use of a large octagonal dome. Typical of Anderson's works, the courthouse has an exaggerated verticality, emphasized by unusually slender Ionic columns. Other buildings in the complex include the old jail, now a county museum, and the R. Earl Ogg Memorial Building, formerly a bank and now seat of the general district court. *(54–81) VLR: 04/17/90; NRHP: 12/28/90.*

PROVIDENCE PRESBYTERIAN CHURCH, *Gum Spring vicinity.* Providence Church is one of Virginia's few remaining wood-frame colonial churches and is among the first churches to be built in the central part of the state by the Presbyterians. The congregation was organized ca. 1747 under the aegis of Samuel Morris, an early dissenter; the church was put up that same year. The first minister was the Rev. Samuel Davies, the pulpit orator and founder of the Hanover Presbytery. Davies remained at Providence until 1759, when he left to assume the presidency of the College of New Jersey (later Princeton University). The severely plain weatherboarded building, in a clearing at the end of a wooded lane, has a typical early meetinghouse arrangement with side and end entrances and an original gallery extending around three sides of the interior. The English evangelist George Whitefield preached here ca. 1755. *(54–61) VLR: 01/16/73; NRHP: 04/13/73.*

WESTEND, *Boswell's Tavern vicinity.* Thomas Jefferson's vision of a prosperous agrarian republic with landowners occupying modest but sophisticated classical villas is given tangible expression at Westend, one of the landmarks of the Green Springs Historic District. Employing the Palladian format of a porticoed center section with one-story wings, a design admired by Jefferson, the house was completed in 1849 for Susan Dabney Morris Watson, widow of Dr. James Watson of the neighboring plantation Bracketts. The contractor was James Magruder. The academic correctness of the classical details is probably due to Malcolm F. Crawford, a master carpenter who became literate in the Roman orders while employed at the University of Virginia. Both wings were originally fronted by orangeries, one of which remains. The house and its formally positioned outbuildings are the nucleus of a 600-acre farm still owned by Watson descendants. *(54–73) VLR: 09/01/70; NRHP: 09/17/70; BHR EASEMENT.*

LUNENBURG COUNTY

Named for Lüneburg, one of the German possessions of Great Britain's Hanoverian kings, this Southside county was formed from Brunswick County in 1745. Its county seat is Lunenburg Court House.

FLAT ROCK, *Kenbridge vicinity.* Flat Rock's interestingly evolved plantation house is a study in local vernacular building traditions. The oldest part was erected in the late 18th century for James Hooper using a two-story, side-passage format. The Chambers family added an east room just before 1820. In 1855 Flat Rock became the property of Robert S. Bagley during whose tenure a second story was put on the east room and one-story wings were added, making a relatively large, formal house out of a formerly unpretentious one. A stylish note of this later enlargement is the unusual hexagonal chimney stacks placed atop the older chimneys. The early interior woodwork is almost completely intact and reflects the various changes. On the grounds are a rare plank smokehouse and a large, granite-lined ice pit. Carefully restored in recent years, Flat Rock is owned by Robert Bagley's descendants. *(55–03) VLR: 12/19/78; NRHP: 05/21/79.*

JONES FARM, *Kenbridge vicinity.* The soil of eastern Lunenburg County is particularly suited for tobacco. The landscape of tobacco cultivation and production is preserved in the Jones farm, an agricultural unit assembled in the 1840s by L. C. Jones. Jones completed the present country Greek Revival dwelling by 1846. Like a number of other old Southside houses, it began as a smaller two-story structure, which became a wing attached by an enclosed hyphen after the main house was constructed. The latter preserves its original beaded and molded weatherboards as well as its mantels, stair, and other interior trim. Typical of a tobacco farm, the land is dotted with structures, including five tobacco barns and supporting outbuildings. The changed status of the labor force after the Civil War is reflected by the three ca. 1900 tenant houses. The farm is still owned by Jones's family. *(55–182) VLR: 06/19/96; NRHP: 09/27/96.*

LUNENBURG COURT HOUSE HISTORIC DISTRICT.
This rural Southside county seat, still barely more than a cross-roads, is dominated by its dignified Roman Revival courthouse, one of the group of public buildings reflecting the influence of Thomas Jefferson's strict classicism in antebellum Virginia. The commission appointed to supervise the project directed that the building be modeled after the newly completed courthouse in Charlotte County, designed by Jefferson himself. Builders William A. Howard and Dabney Cosby, Sr., admirably carried out their task, completing the academically correct design in 1827. Here the stately Roman Doric order was employed rather than the more usual Tuscan. The exterior stairs were added in 1850 when the interior was divided into two levels. An original apsidal end was later encased in an extension. Surrounded by farmland, the tiny settlement presents a memorable picture with the gleaming courthouse portico looming above the sprinkling of 19th-century structures. *(55–105) VLR: 03/02/71; NRHP: 02/23/72.*

VICTORIA HIGH SCHOOL, *Victoria.* Until the 20th century, most of Virginia's rural and small-town public schools were surprisingly primitive. Victoria's first public school, erected in 1895, was a one-room log building. It was replaced in 1902 by a one-room frame building. Only in 1912 did the town acquire an up-to-date facility for its high school: a two-story brick structure. By the 1920s population growth necessitated an additional building, and a new high school was completed in 1922 next to the old one. The new school was described as having "large and well lighted rooms with steam heat, water, and electric light," amenities not altogether common in the region. The high school was enlarged and remodeled in 1928 at which time the portico was added. Closed in 1966, the building was spared threatened demolition in 1993 and has since been rehabilitated by the Victoria High School Preservation Foundation for alternative use. *(317–12) VLR: 10/18/95; NRHP: 01/22/96.*

CITY OF LYNCHBURG

Named for John Lynch, owner of the original town site, this industrial and business center, located along the James River between Bedford and Campbell counties, was established in 1786 and was incorporated as a town in 1805. It became a city in 1852.

ACADEMY OF MUSIC, *522–526 Main Street.* Lynchburg's Academy of Music was built as a vaudeville theater and opera house, one of the few surviving in Virginia. Completed in 1905, it was designed by the local firm of Frye and Chesterman, which embellished Lynchburg with many of its best buildings. The theater burned in 1911 but was rebuilt within its walls under the direction of architect C. K. Howell, with Lynchburg's J. M. B. Lewis as associate. The present facade is a sophisticated essay in the neoclassical style recalling 18th-century English Palladianism. The elegant interior is enriched with plasterwork decorations and a colorful painted ceiling of clouds, muses, and cherubs. In its heyday the academy boasted Sarah Bernhardt, Pavlova, and Paderewski among its performers. Vacant for some forty years, the theater is scheduled for renovation. *(118–01) VLR: 11/05/68; NRHP: 06/11/69.*

ALLIED ARTS BUILDING, *Eighth and Church streets.* A symbol of progressive modernity, Lynchburg's Allied Arts Building is a conspicuous expression of the Art Deco Skyscraper style that dominated tall buildings in the 1920s and 1930s. Designed by Lynchburg architects Stanhope Johnson and Raymond O. Brannan and completed in 1931, the strongly vertical composition recalls the visionary skyscraper renderings of Hugh Ferriss. For Johnson, who worked primarily in the Colonial Revival style, the design marked a break with the past and an effort to put his city in the forefront of contemporary design. The steel-frame structure is clad in a combination of buff brick and locally quarried greenstone. Effective use of these materials visually divides the building into three major components: base, office shaft, and capital. Still a dominant element of Lynchburg's skyline, the Allied Arts Building continues to provide professional office space. *(118–110) VLR: 04/16/85; NRHP: 12/19/85.*

THE AVIARY, *Miller Park, 402 Grove Street.* An adaptation of the Queen Anne style, this pagodalike building is the state's earliest known municipal aviary and is an example of the civic amenities resulting from turn-of-the-century private philanthropy. Designed by Frye and Chesterman of Lynchburg and opened in Miller Park in 1902, the aviary was the gift of Randolph Guggenheimer, a Lynchburg native who became a New York businessman. The aviary is also an expression of the nationwide enthusiasm for zoological parks and gardens in metropolitan areas that prevailed in the late 19th and early 20th centuries. Here originally were housed cages containing monkeys, alligators, cockatoos, doves, parrots, and canaries. The interior was remodeled in 1931 when it was converted to a library. Since 1975 it has been leased by the city to the Lynchburg Council of Garden Clubs for a garden center. *(118–155) VLR: 04/15/80; NRHP: 07/30/80.*

BRAGASSA TOY STORE, *Twelfth and Court streets.* Opened for business in 1876, Lynchburg's first toy and confectionery store was operated here by the Bragassa family. The building is itself a little-altered example of the simple Italianate commercial architecture that once defined so many American downtowns. Italians by birth, the Bragassas were associated with the toy and candy business as early as 1858. In 1871 Francisco Bragassa purchased part of the Lynchburg Female Seminary property and built the present building in 1875. Family tradition holds that the shop front had the first plate-glass windows in Lynchburg. Mrs. Bragassa's candies were famous throughout the city, and the store was a popular gathering place for neighborhood children. Owned by the Bragassas until 1987, the building, a nostalgic link with simpler times, is now headquarters for the Lynchburg Historical Foundation. *(118–176) VLR: 08/21/90; NRHP: 01/11/91.*

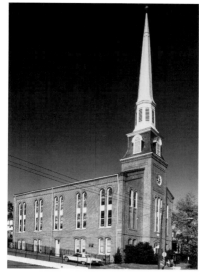

COURT STREET BAPTIST CHURCH, *Court and Sixth streets.* Court Street Baptist Church is the mother church of Lynchburg's black Baptists and the most conspicuous landmark of the city's Afro-American heritage. When completed in 1880, it was the city's largest church, and its spire dominated the skyline. The congregation was organized in 1843 when black Baptists separated from the parent First Baptist Church. The building was designed by a local white architect, Robert C. Burkholder, but was built exclusively with black labor. Although its location in a fashionable white neighborhood, near the First Baptist Church, caused considerable controversy, the completed church was praised by the local press, which wrote: "With its tall and symmetrical spire pointing silently but unmistakably heavenward, it stands an almost imperishable monument to the vigor, enterprise and religious zeal of the society to which it belongs." The steeple, damaged in a 1993 storm and subsequently removed, has been rebuilt. *(118–156) VLR: 06/16/81; NRHP: 07/08/82.*

DANIEL'S HILL HISTORIC DISTRICT. This downtown residential neighborhood, on a ridge above the James River, holds a variety of 19th-century styles and house types. Concentrated building activity began in the 1840s after the subdivision of the Cabell-Daniel family plantation whose mansion, Point of Honor, forms the neighborhood's focal point. Cabell Street (shown), the district's main street, is lined with a progression of mid- and late 19th-century mansions, all solid examples of their respective styles. Particularly interesting is the Y-shaped dwelling at Cabell and B streets, built in 1875 by architect Robert C. Burkholder for himself. More typical is the 1853–54 Greek Revival Dabney-Scott-Adams house at 405 Cabell Street. Another Greek Revival landmark is Rivermont, a frame mansion. Contrasting with these showy dwellings are the vernacular workers' houses scattered along the back streets. Protected by historic zoning, the district is undergoing slow rehabilitation. *(118–198) VLR: 12/14/82; NRHP: 02/24/83.*

DIAMOND HILL HISTORIC DISTRICT.

Immediately south of the downtown, Diamond Hill was once one of Lynchburg's most prestigious residential neighborhoods. Its development began in the 1820s, and it enjoyed its greatest prosperity at the turn of the century. The latter period was marked by the construction of numerous large residences, ranging from speculative rental units to stately architect-designed houses usually in either the Queen Anne or Georgian Revival style. The family homes of businessmen and civic and political leaders were clustered along Washington, Clay, Pearl, and Madison streets, with Washington Street (shown) the most prestigious address. Especially interesting is the Queen Anne–style residence at 1314 Clay Street designed by architect J. M. B. Lewis for himself. After a significant decline Diamond Hill in recent years has experienced considerable restoration activity. *(118–60) VLR: 05/15/79; NRHP: 10/01/79.*

FIRST BAPTIST CHURCH, *Court and Eleventh streets.*

This vigorous composition, with its many gables highlighted by a needle spire, is perhaps Virginia's best representative of the High Victorian Gothic style, a richly ornamented interpretation of the Gothic mode inspired by the writings of John Ruskin. Its architect was John R. Thomas, who practiced first in Rochester and later in New York City. Thomas also designed the well-known Brooks Hall at the University of Virginia. Construction of the church began in 1884; in 1928 the architecturally compatible Sunday school wing, designed by Stanhope Johnson, was added. One of the building's highlights is its richly colored, locally manufactured Victorian stained glass. Commissioned for a well-to-do and influential congregation, the church was the product of an era of growth and prosperity in Lynchburg. The spire was blown down during a 1993 storm but has since been rebuilt. *(118–25) VLR: 04/21/81; NRHP: 09/09/82.*

FEDERAL HILL HISTORIC DISTRICT.

One of the earliest and most distinctive of several neighborhoods situated on Lynchburg's several hills, Federal Hill has served primarily as a residential area favored by merchants and civic leaders. Spread through the district's dozen blocks is an assemblage of freestanding dwellings in architectural styles popular from the early 1800s through the early 1900s. Most significant are the neighborhood's early Federal houses, which include some of the oldest and finest dwellings in the city, among them the ca. 1816 Roane-Rodes house on Harrison Street and the 1817 Norvell-Otey house built on Federal Street for banker William Norvell. Several other early Federal houses, including the Micajah Davis and the Gordon houses (shown), both built before 1819, are scattered along Jackson Street. The area was incorporated into Lynchburg through annexations in 1814 and 1819. *(118–56) VLR: 05/20/80; NRHP: 09/17/80.*

GARLAND HILL HISTORIC DISTRICT.

Named for Samuel Garland, Sr., a local lawyer who was among the area's first residents, Garland Hill is perhaps the best preserved of the prosperous neighborhoods that sprang up on Lynchburg's hills during the 19th century. The hill, subdivided into approximately ten blocks in 1845, built up slowly, so that it now has a rich mixture of freestanding houses representing styles in vogue from the 1840s to World War I. The grandest dwellings line Madison Street. At its eastern end are two large Queen Anne residences: the 1897 Frank P. Christian house and the 1898 George P. Watkins house (shown), both designed by Edward G. Frye. The most singular structure is the huge Ambrose H. Burroughs house of 1900, a castlelike dwelling designed by J. M. B. Lewis. Because there are no through streets, an air of quiet dignity still pervades the district. *(118–26) VLR: 08/15/72; NRHP: 09/07/72.*

CARTER GLASS HOUSE, *605 Clay Street.* This skillful rendition of the Federal style was the home of the statesman Carter Glass from 1907 to 1923, the period in which he exerted great influence on the nation's political and economic life. In addition to serving as Woodrow Wilson's secretary of the treasury, Glass also served as chairman of the House Committee of Banking and Currency and was for many years a U.S. senator. He is best remembered for drafting the legislation establishing the Federal Reserve System, still the guiding institution of the American banking structure. Glass's home was built in 1827 for John Wills, who may have been its architect. The house survives in its original condition except for the present roof, cornice, and dormers, all added by Glass before moving to his country home Montview. It now houses parish offices for St. Paul's Episcopal Church next door. *(118–06) VLR: 02/15/77; NHL: 12/08/76.*

JAMES RIVER AND KANAWHA CANAL SITES. Included in this complex are the surviving elements of the canal system through Lynchburg: the Lower Basin and Ninth Street Bridge (shown), the Blackwater Creek Aqueduct, and the Waterworks Dam, the James River Dam, and the Guard Locks at the lower end of Daniel's Island. The James River and Kanawha Canal was one of 19th-century America's major transportation arteries. Lynchburg was the terminus of the "First Grand Division," which extended 146.5 miles from Richmond. Opened in 1840, this section was the only one of the three divisions ever completed. The canal enjoyed its greatest prosperity during the 1850s and spurred Lynchburg's development as a leading commercial and industrial center. In 1880 the newly organized Richmond and Alleghany Railway Co. acquired the canal company's property and laid tracks over much of the system. The canal's Lynchburg remnants are important relics of a great engineering achievement. *(118–209) VLR: 12/11/84.*

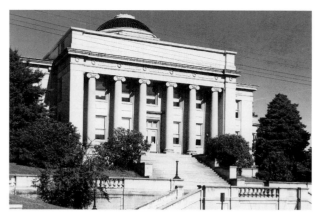

JONES MEMORIAL LIBRARY, *434 Rivermont Avenue.* The Jones Memorial Library is Lynchburg's finest example of the American Renaissance, an architectural and artistic movement that dominated American public and institutional buildings in the early 20th century. Designed by the local firm of Frye and Chesterman, the library was given by Mary Frances Watt Jones as a memorial to her husband, George Morgan Jones, a Lynchburg industrialist, merchant, and financier. Opened in 1908, the stately domed structure, with its monumental facade of Ionic columns, is an expression of the philanthropy and cultural development that followed Lynchburg's growth at the end of the 19th century. The series of steps and terraces, constructed in 1924, was designed by Boston landscape architect Bremer Pond. The collections have since been moved to the Lynchburg Public Library, and the building now serves as an educational center named the Patrick Henry Institute. *(118–153) VLR: 07/31/80; NRHP: 10/30/80.*

KENTUCKY HOTEL, *900 Fifth Street.* An anchor to the past on a busy commercial artery, the Kentucky Hotel is one of three surviving early Lynchburg ordinaries. The original three-bay section was probably built ca. 1800 and was likely expanded to its present five-bay form shortly before James Mallory obtained a license to sell liquor here in 1816. It was one of sixteen Lynchburg inns and taverns licensed that year, when the bustling town was described by Thomas Jefferson as "the most rising place in the United States." Mallory sold the property in 1826 to Jacob Feazel at which time it was called the Kentucky Hotel. The building passed through many owners until the 1980s when it was rescued from the lowest point of its fortune and carefully restored. Although it had been neglected for many years, the building remarkably retained nearly all of its simple early 19th-century woodwork. *(118–177) VLR: 06/17/86; NRHP: 12/11/86; BHR EASEMENT.*

LOCUST GROVE, *Boonsboro vicinity.* This visually appealing farmhouse began as a modest side-passage dwelling for the Cobbs family, possibly in the 18th century. It was enlarged to its present center-passage plan in the early 19th century and included an octagonal room. The story of the Cobbses, a well-to-do and respected gentry family, is a story shared by rural Virginia families in the mid–19th century who faced the specter of declining land productivity along with the trials of the Civil War and Reconstruction. Their fortune dwindled as tobacco planting sapped their soil. The family was bankrupt by 1877 but managed to hold onto the property into the 1910s. In 1932 Locust Grove was purchased by John Capron, an amateur historian who in the antiquarian spirit of the times restored the house in the Colonial Revival taste but preserved original Federal trim. *(118–219) VLR: 06/19/91; NRHP: 12/17/92.*

LOWER BASIN HISTORIC DISTRICT. A once colorful area spread along Lynchburg's James River waterfront, the Lower Basin defined the city's historic wholesale and industrial center. Beginning as Lynch's Ferry in the 1750s and emerging as an important canal and railroad transportation center a century later, Lynchburg maintained its role as a leading manufacturing and marketing center well into the 20th century. The Lower Basin area takes its name from an expanded portion of the James River and Kanawha Canal, which linked the city to eastern markets. Canal traffic and the arrival of the Virginia and Tennessee Railroad in 1849 resulted in increased commercial activity in the Lower Basin. It was during the early 20th century that most of the commercial warehouses, factories, and jobbing houses were built. The district's multistory brick structures are an important display of historic commercial architecture. *(118–211) VLR: 10/14/86; NRHP: 04/24/87.*

SAMUEL MILLER HOUSE, *1433 Nelson Drive.* Tobacconist, merchant, and railroad investor Samuel Miller (1792–1869) rose from poverty to become one of the wealthiest men in the antebellum South. A recluse, he resided in this prosaic ca. 1826 frame house on the outskirts of Lynchburg and quietly amassed his fortune. During the battle of Lynchburg (June 1864), a cavalry skirmish took place here, and Union troops pillaged Miller's home. Upon entering, they encountered an elderly, bedridden, but defiant Samuel Miller, who had successfully hidden his financial papers. Considered a miser during his lifetime but a generous philanthropist after death, Miller bequeathed both funds and land to the city of Lynchburg. His educational endowments today help support the University of Virginia and two institutions that bear his name: the Miller School of Albemarle and the Miller Home of Lynchburg for girls. *(118–223) VLR: 09/15/92; NRHP: 11/12/92.*

MILLER-CLAYTOR HOUSE, *Riverside Park at Miller-Claytor Lane.* The Miller-Claytor house, erected in 1791 for tavern keeper John Miller, is Lynchburg's only remaining 18th-century town house. It originally stood at Eighth and Church streets downtown but was moved by the Lynchburg Historical Society to its present location at the entrance to Riverside Park in 1936, during Lynchburg's sesquicentennial. Serving as a historic exhibit, the two-story frame structure is an intriguing example of urban vernacular architecture. The several exterior doors of its two-room plan suggest that part of the house may have been intended for commercial use. Rebuilt under the direction of Lynchburg architect Stanhope Johnson, the dwelling's orientation and garden size at the new location were carefully selected to approximate its original setting. The garden was designed by Charles F. Gillette. The property is now owned by the Lynchburg Historical Foundation. *(118–12) VLR: 10/21/75; NRHP: 05/06/76.*

MONTVIEW, *Liberty University, Candler's Mountain Road.* This expansive Dutch Colonial country house served as the rural retreat of Carter Glass from 1923 until his death in 1946. A foremost public figure of the 20th century, Glass is chiefly remembered for his sponsorship of the Glass-Owen Act of 1913, which established the Federal Reserve banking system. Glass built Montview while serving in the U.S. Senate. It was at Montview that he wrote many of his speeches defending the Federal Reserve System and completed a book on the subject, *An Adventure in Constructive Finance.* Despite membership in the Democratic party, Glass opposed much of President Roosevelt's New Deal policy. He later supported Roosevelt's war efforts and, as chairman of the Senate Appropriations Committee, helped pass measures to pay for military activity. Glass's funeral was held at Montview. The house is now the office of the president of Liberty University. *(118–210) VLR: 12/09/86; NRHP: 06/05/87.*

JOSEPH NICHOLS TAVERN (WESTERN HOTEL), *Fifth and Madison streets.* Joseph Nichols built this Federal tavern on Lynchburg's busy Fifth Street in 1815 to replace his previous establishment, which had been destroyed by fire. Although its original facade was oriented to Madison Street, the forthright brick structure has long been a familiar landmark on Fifth Street, for many years the western entrance to the city. This location was the inspiration for a later designation, the Western Hotel, by which the building was known for over a century. A rear wing was added in the 1830s. One of Lynchburg's earliest surviving commercial structures, the tavern stood derelict for many years but was rehabilitated in 1975 by the Lynchburg Restoration and Housing Corporation, a local nonprofit organization. *(118–20) VLR: 06/18/74; NRHP: 07/22/74.*

OLD CITY CEMETERY, *Fourth and Monroe streets.* This public burying ground in the heart of the city was opened in 1806 on land donated by John Lynch, founder of Lynchburg. First known as the Methodist Cemetery, it was bounded by a brick wall in 1827. The cemetery is perhaps best remembered for its Civil War associations. Cadets from the Virginia Military Institute used the cemetery as a campground. Lynchburg served as a major hospital center during the conflict, and over 2,000 soldiers who succumbed from wounds or disease were buried here. Located among their grave markers is an 1868 obelisk to the Confederate dead and a domed speaker's stand. The arched entryway of Lynchburg greenstone, designed by Lynchburg architect Preston Craighill and erected in 1926, leads to the Confederate section. A re-creation of the "pest house," one of Lynchburg's Civil War hospitals, stands just outside the wall. *(118–27) VLR: 09/19/72; NRHP: 04/02/73.*

OLD LYNCHBURG COURTHOUSE, *Ninth and Court streets.* Lynchburg's temple-form former courthouse has been a dominant feature of the city's skyline since its completion in 1855. It was designed by William S. Ellison, who came to Lynchburg as a division engineer with the Virginia and Tennessee Railroad. The Doric portico with its paired columns is inspired by that of a Greek ruin, first illustrated in James Stuart and Nicholas Revett's *Antiquities of Athens* (begun 1762). Although the portico and other details are based on published illustrations, Ellison's design, employing implied side porticoes and a dome topped by a belfry, is a strikingly original composition. The building is dramatically located at the top of Monument Terrace, a steep flight of terraced steps constructed in 1925 as the city's war memorial. Following the removal of court functions, the courthouse was restored in the 1970s as Lynchburg's history museum. *(118–02) VLR: 04/18/72; NRHP: 05/19/72.*

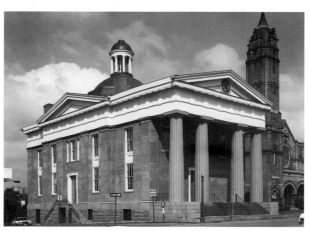

POINT OF HONOR, *112 Cabell Street.* On the prow of Daniel's Hill overlooking the downtown, Point of Honor ranks with the Commonwealth's most articulate works of Federal architecture. Originally serving a 900-acre plantation, the house was built ca. 1815 for Dr. George Cabell. Distinguished by its polygonal projections and beautifully executed interior woodwork, the house is one of several fine Piedmont houses erected for the Cabell family. Its designer is not known, but many of its details are adapted from illustrations in Owen Biddle's *The Young Carpenter's Assistant* as well as design books by William Pain. Point of Honor was remodeled in the Italianate style in the mid–19th century, but most of its original embellishments, save for the front porch, survived. It was acquired by the city in 1928 and received hard use as a neighborhood center until 1968 when the Historic Lynchburg Foundation undertook its restoration as a museum. *(118–14) VLR: 12/02/69; NRHP: 02/26/70.*

ROSEDALE, *Graves Mill Road.* Rosedale encompasses several related structures of significance in the development of the Bedford and Campbell County section of Piedmont Virginia. The oldest structure, the Christopher Johnson cottage, was built ca. 1767 and is one of the area's few remaining houses associated with the Quaker migration from eastern Virginia. Its interior has a noteworthy Federal mantel. The adjacent mansion, built ca. 1836 for Gen. Odin Clay, first president of the Virginia and Tennessee Railroad, is one of the earliest houses in the area to display Greek Revival details inspired by illustrations in Asher Benjamin's *Practical House Carpenter* (1830). It was enlarged with a rear wing in 1902 and a side wing in the 1920s. With the nearby remains of an 18th-century mill, numerous subsidiary farm buildings, and its hilly terrain, the Rosedale property is a rural enclave amid suburban development. *(118–201) VLR: 10/19/82; NRHP: 07/07/83.*

RANDOLPH-MACON WOMAN'S COLLEGE MAIN HALL, *2500 Rivermont Avenue.* Founded in 1891 under the original Randolph-Macon College charter of 1830, Randolph-Macon Woman's College was the first college for women admitted to membership in the Southern Association of Colleges and Secondary Schools. Main Hall, erected in stages over a nine-year period beginning in 1891, remains the architectural highlight of the institution. The huge structure appears as a range of connected buildings, stretched along a ridge at the head of a tree-dotted campus. It was designed by the Washington, D.C., architect William M. Poindexter and is the state's most ambitious and probably most sophisticated example of the late 19th-century Queen Anne style. Poindexter's use of red brick, white trim, towers, turrets, classical detailing, and a multiplicity of window types closely relates the building to the best of contemporary Queen Anne structures in Great Britain. *(118–149) VLR: 02/26/79; NRHP: 06/19/79.*

ST. PAUL'S EPISCOPAL CHURCH, *Seventh and Clay streets.* This robust composition, serving Lynchburg's oldest Episcopal congregation, is Virginia's finest ecclesiastical example of the Romanesque Revival fostered by Boston architect H. H. Richardson. Typical of the style, St. Paul's features a solid outline and rugged textured stonework. The church, built in 1889–95, was designed by Frank Miles Day of Philadelphia, who is remembered for his partner-

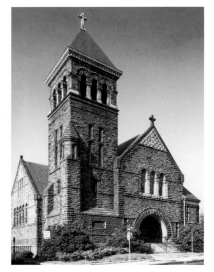

ship with Charles Z. Klauder and their neo-Gothic collegiate buildings at Princeton and other universities. The belfry was added in 1912 and departs slightly from Day's design. The lofty interior is defined by massive Romanesque arches supporting an exposed-timber roof and is lit with several contemporary stained-glass windows portraying biblical scenes. The church is one of several architecturally imposing churches in the neighborhood that together create a lively skyline for downtown Lynchburg. *(118–196) VLR: 04/21/81; NRHP: 09/09/82.*

ST. PAUL'S VESTRY HOUSE, *308 Seventh Street.* Built ca. 1850 for St. Paul's Episcopal Church, which had just completed a new church at this steep hillside location, this discreet little building has enjoyed a tradition of community service. Although later called the "Old Rectory," the building was never a parish residence but instead provided meeting space for the vestry, the parish governing body. It served thusly until 1871 when it was given over to Sunday school classes. The building fell vacant in 1895 with the completion of a new church a few blocks away. In 1903, however, it became the meeting room of the Woman's Club of Lynchburg. Like similar clubs, the Woman's Club was part of a national movement to help ladies become better educated and more active in civic affairs. The club moved in 1916; the building has since served a variety of uses. *(118–78) VLR: 12/04/96; NRHP: 02/21/97.*

SOUTH RIVER QUAKER MEETING HOUSE, *5810 Fort Avenue.* Quakers settled in the area of present-day Lynchburg in the mid–18th century and built their first meetinghouse in 1757. The present meetinghouse, completed in 1798, is the third on the site. Originally known as the South River Friends' Meeting House, the building was typical of the sturdy, plain structures favored by the Quakers, being constructed of local fieldstone with an almost domestic appearance. It lost most of its congregation to westward migration in the 1830s. The building stood as an abandoned ruin from the 1850s until 1904 when its stone walls were restored and it was reroofed for use by the Presbyterians. Buried in the adjacent Quaker cemetery ("God's Acre") are John Lynch, Lynchburg's founder, and his mother, Sarah Clark Lynch, one of the original Quaker settlers. The building is currently maintained by the Quaker Memorial Presbyterian Church. *(118–15) VLR: 05/20/75; NRHP: 08/28/75.*

SANDUSKY, *Sandusky Drive.* This brick farmhouse, formerly on the outskirts of the city but now within a suburban neighborhood, was built ca. 1808 for Charles Johnston, who named it after the Ohio Indian camp where he was once held prisoner. The two-story structure, with its regular five-bay facade, Doric cornice, and interior arched recesses, was one of the area's first houses to display the details and refinement of high-style Federal architecture. The front porch is a later addition but may be similar to an original one. In 1864, during the battle of Lynchburg, Sandusky served as headquarters for Union general David Hunter. Two of Hunter's staff at Sandusky were future presidents Rutherford B. Hayes and William McKinley. Hunter had been a West Point classmate of Confederate major George C. Hutter, who owned Sandusky at the time of the Union occupation. *(118–17) VLR: 02/16/82; NRHP: 07/26/82.*

ANNE SPENCER HOUSE, *1313 Pierce Street.* During her long and active life, Anne Spencer (1882–1975) was recognized as a lyric poet of considerable talent. Given the climate of the times, it was a remarkable feat for a black woman to win recognition from her intellectual peers. Through quiet dedication to her craft and causes, she gained respect not only as a writer but as a humanitarian. Although she was a foe of bigotry, her poems dwell more on the universal themes

of love, beauty, truth, nature, and the human spirit. Among the many visitors to her Lynchburg home were W. E. B. Du Bois, Langston Hughes, Martin Luther King, Jr., and Thurgood Marshall. Mrs. Spencer's commodious but unpretentious Queen Anne–style house of 1903 remains unchanged since her death, preserved by the Friends of Anne Spencer Memorial Foundation, Inc. In the garden is Edankraal, a one-room cottage where she wrote and thought. *(118–61) VLR: 09/21/76; NRHP: 12/06/76.*

VIRGINIA EPISCOPAL SCHOOL, *400 VES Road.* Virginia Episcopal School is symbolic of the many dedicated efforts of religious institutions at the turn of the century to improve the availability of quality secondary education and to foster Christian principles. The school was founded in 1916 by the Rev. Robert Carter Jett who was particularly concerned about western Virginia's lack of adequate schools for boys of moderate means, especially sons of clergy. Jett had the foresight to realize that much of the success of a religious preparatory school depended on superior facilities. He thus engaged the prominent Washington architect Frederick H. Brooke to design a cohesive, well-appointed complex. Brooke's dignified Georgian Revival scheme, including classroom and dormitory structures, a chapel, and gymnasium, was largely realized. One of the school's leading original benefactors was Lady Astor, née Nancy Langhorne of Albemarle County. *(118–224) VLR: 06/17/92; NRHP: 10/28/92.*

J. W. WOOD BUILDING, *23–27 Ninth Street.* Dating from ca. 1853, the J. W. Wood Building is the largest and best preserved of the small number of antebellum commercial structures remaining in Lynchburg. Its cast-iron storefront is the city's sole surviving example of its type. The manufacturer of the storefront is unknown, but it possibly was made in Richmond, which was a center of cast-iron production. Noteworthy elements of the storefront are the Corinthian pilaster capitals and the foliated ornaments in the pilaster shafts. The Italianate structure is also one of the few visual reminders of the city's bustling commercial activity of the 1850s, the decade in which Lynchburg was declared by the U.S. Census to be the country's second-richest city on a per capita basis. *(118–09) VLR: 05/18/82; NRHP: 02/17/83.*

JOHN MARSHALL WARWICK HOUSE, *720 Court Street.* Prominently placed atop the ridge overlooking downtown Lynchburg, this square brick house is among Virginia's most handsomely appointed Federal-period urban residences. Highlighting the facade is the pair of panels with husk swags and bows, one of the state's few instances of this type of high-style decoration. Panels of fine Adamesque ornaments are also found inside along with carved doorframes and original King of Prussia marble mantels. The house was built in 1826 for John Marshall Warwick, a tobacconist and mayor of the city. The Warwick house was also the childhood home of John Warwick Daniel, Civil War hero, U.S. senator, and orator. The house was modified in the Victorian period when the sawn-work front porch and the Gothic Revival doorcase were added. Changes inside include two Rococo Revival marble mantels and the present Italianate stair. *(118–19) VLR: 12/06/95; NRHP: 12/06/96.*

MADISON COUNTY

In the hills of the Piedmont, against the Blue Ridge Mountains, Madison County was formed from Culpeper County in 1792 and was named for James Madison, who then represented the area in Congress. The county seat is Madison.

BIG MEADOWS ARCHAEOLOGICAL SITE, *Big Meadows, Shenandoah National Park.* The Big Meadows site, one of the most intensively investigated sites in the Shenandoah National Park, has revealed Indian habitation here occurring between ca. 2500 B.C. and A.D. 800. Yielding the park's oldest example of prehistoric art and possibly evidence of a dwelling, the site also has produced large quantities of locally and regionally imported raw materials, indicating the extent to which its prehistoric occupants exploited a large and varied territory on a seasonal basis. The population peak of the site was reached in Late Archaic–Early Woodland times and contrasts with subsequent sparse use of the region by Late Woodland peoples (ca. A.D. 800–1600). *(56–56) VLR: 09/16/82; NRHP: 12/13/85.*

BRAMPTON, *Woodberry Forest vicinity.* The Greek Revival style permeated nearly every corner of antebellum America. No structure, however remote, was safe from being adorned as an ancient temple with columns and entablatures. Such predilection for classical trappings gripped John Hancock Lee and his wife, Frances Madison Willis Lee, niece of James Madison, when they commissioned a residence for their farm originally called Buena Vista. Constructed ca. 1843 by a yet-unidentified builder, their home was embellished with a tetrastyle portico with exaggerated Ionic capitals. The portico originally had no pediment but was topped by a simple blocking course. Around 1900 the house was remodeled with the addition of a gable roof, giving the portico a steep pediment. A cross gable and rear addition were part of the remodeling. During the Civil War, Brampton, as it later came to be called, served as an observation point for Gen. J. E. B. Stuart. *(56–01) VLR: 10/15/85; NRHP: 12/12/85.*

CAMP HOOVER, *Shenandoah National Park, Graves Mill vicinity.* A little-known presidential retreat, Camp Hoover is at the Rapidan River headwaters, high in the Blue Ridge Mountains. The rustic complex was developed between 1929 and 1932 as a "summer White House" by President Herbert Hoover and First Lady Lou Henry Hoover on a 164-acre parcel owned by them. Here the president sought recreation and spiritual renewal. He also used the camp for working vacations, stating: "I have discovered that even the work of government can be improved by leisurely discussions of its problems out under the trees where no bells or callers jar one's thoughts." Among Hoover's guests here were Ramsay MacDonald, Charles Lindbergh, and Thomas Edison. The Hoovers deeded the camp to the Commonwealth in 1932; it later was transferred to the National Park Service. The camp is now undergoing a restoration scheduled for completion in the year 2002. *(56–62) VLR: 02/16/88; NHL: 06/07/88.*

GEORGE T. CORBIN CABIN, *Shenandoah National Park, Nethers vicinity.* A humble dwelling high in the Blue Ridge Mountains, the Corbin cabin is one of the few remaining intact log houses in the Shenandoah National Park, a single vestige of a vanished community. It is situated in Nicholson Hollow, a narrow valley settled as early as the late 18th century. The livelihood of these mountaineers depended on grazing, apple growing, distilling, poultry raising, and other agricultural pursuits. Utterly simple, the cabin is typical of the more modest homes of hollow settlements. Using traditional forms and construction techniques, the cabin was built ca. 1921 by George T. Corbin. It originally had a single room with a loft. Corbin added a kitchen and was building a lean-to when he was evicted in 1938 for the creation of the Shenandoah National Park. Since 1954 the cabin has been used as a hikers' shelter. *(56–61) VLR: 09/20/88; NRHP: 01/13/89.*

CLIFF KILL ARCHAEOLOGICAL SITE, *Big Meadows vicinity, Shenandoah National Park.* This site on the crest of the Blue Ridge, in the Shenandoah National Park, is Virginia's only known example of a prehistoric cliff kill site. Despite the absence of faunal remains, analysis of the lithic assemblage supports the interpretation of the site as a kill site dating from the mainly Middle to Late Archaic periods (ca. 4000–1500 B.C.) with a Late Woodland component. The prehistoric inhabitants mortally wounded game by driving it over the edge of the cliff, a sheer drop on the eastern edge of Big Meadows. Studies on the relationship between the Cliff Kill site and other Archaic-period sites on Big Meadows will allow for increased understanding of settlement and subsistence patterns in the Blue Ridge Mountain region. *(56–59) VLR: 09/16/82; NRHP: 12/13/85.*

GENTLE ARCHAEOLOGICAL SITE, *Fishers Gap vicinity, Shenandoah National Park.* One of the largest Woodland-period archaeological sites in the Shenandoah National Park, the Gentle site near the crest of the Blue Ridge poses significant questions concerning its relationship to Late Woodland sites in the Piedmont and the interaction of inhabitants of the two regions along this "cultural frontier" in the Woodland period. By raising the question of the identity of the Blue Ridge as a frontier zone in Late Woodland times, the site might also provide evidence of a link with early European settlement of the mountains. *(56–58) VLR: 09/16/82; NRHP: 12/13/85.*

GREENWAY, *Madison Mills.* Built ca. 1780 for Francis Madison, a younger brother of President James Madison, Greenway is a traditional vernacular building type commonly used in Piedmont Virginia from the mid–18th to the mid–19th century. The original core, a single-pile, hall-parlor dwelling, is interesting confirmation that acceptance of such indigenous forms extended even to members of influential families such as the Madisons. The facade formerly had side-by-side entrances, one for each room. These were replaced in the early 20th century by a single entrance sheltered by the gable-roofed porch. A rear wing, added ca. 1790, preserves a fine original mantel with pilasters and paneled frieze. Greenway has been a working farm since the 18th century and includes several farm buildings. Ownership has passed to descendants of a stepson of Francis Madison's daughter Catherine. *(56–20) VLR: 09/20/88; NRHP: 11/16/88.*

HEBRON LUTHERAN CHURCH, *Madison vicinity.* Dating from 1740, this simple cruciform church, set in the pastoral landscape of Madison County, is America's oldest house of worship in continuous use by Lutherans. The congregation was formed by 1725 by German families, some of whom came to Virginia in 1717 to work at Germanna, Lieutenant Governor Alexander Spotswood's frontier mining community. They built their church in what was essentially thinly settled backcountry. The building was enlarged ca. 1800, at which time Hebron's celebrated pipe organ, crafted by David Tannenburg of Lititz, Pa., was installed. The interior has been remodeled several times. An interesting Victorian adornment is the elaborate frescoed ceilings painted by the Italian-born artist Joseph Oddenino. *(56–06) VLR: 03/02/71; NRHP: 07/02/71.*

MADISON COUNTY COURTHOUSE, *Madison.* Master builders William B. Phillips and Malcolm F. Crawford embellished central Virginia with a series of dignified courthouses in Thomas Jefferson's Roman Revival idiom, learned while working at the University of Virginia. The Madison courthouse, completed in 1830 with the assistance of Richard Boulware, survives as perhaps the most potent example of these builders' architectural skills. Prominent Jeffersonian devices employed here are the monumental Tuscan entablature and pediment with its lunette window. The arcaded ground floor, a holdover from colonial courthouses, is given a more classical, hence Jeffersonian, quality with the use of keystones and impost courses making them similar in appearance to Jefferson's arcades on the university's ranges. The beautiful brickwork, with its even-color Flemish bond and precise jointing, is characteristic of Phillips's craftsmanship. *(256–02) VLR: 05/13/69; NRHP: 11/12/69.*

MADISON COUNTY COURTHOUSE HISTORIC DISTRICT. The village of Madison has served as the county seat and commercial hub of Madison County since its formation from Culpeper County in 1793. The settlement was formally established as a post office town in 1801, several years after the erection of the county's first courthouse, clerk's office, and jail. The district's most prominent building is the 1830 Jeffersonian-style courthouse. A key element of the courthouse complex is the ca. 1832 tavern (shown), a large brick structure with stepped parapets. A principal historic residence is the Greek Revival house occupied by Confederate major general James Lawson Kemper, who later served as governor. In addition to its early and mid-19th-century structures, the district also has a late 19th-century commercial core along with several decorative Victorian residences. The town's quiet village ambience has been enhanced by the bypassing of U.S. Route 29. *(256–04) VLR: 05/15/84; NRHP: 08/16/84.*

THE RESIDENCE, *Woodberry Forest School.* This compact plantation house was built ca. 1793 for William Madison, member of the Virginia House of Delegates for seven consecutive terms and brother of President James Madison. In 1793 Thomas Jefferson was asked by James Madison to supply plans for a house for his brother. James Madison later wrote to Jefferson saying that William had adopted the plans. No Jefferson drawings have been positively identified as the Madison design, but the correspondence authenticates the Jefferson connection. The original, unacademic two-column portico suggests, however, that Jefferson was not involved in the execution. In 1870 the property was purchased by Robert Walker, who remodeled the house in 1884. It was here that Walker founded Woodberry Forest School, naming it after the Madison plantation. The house was renamed The Residence and became the headmaster's home. *(56–55) VLR: 02/26/79; NRHP: 06/19/79.*

ROBERTSON MOUNTAIN ARCHAEOLOGICAL SITE, *Robertson Mountain, Shenandoah National Park.* One of the few sites in the Shenandoah National Park to provide clear evidence of stratified cultural deposits, Robertson Mountain was occupied by Native Americans for the entire span of the Archaic period (8000–1000 B.C.), making it a valuable record of cultural and environmental changes in the Blue Ridge. Scientific excavation of the elevated site may provide information on food-gathering activities in the highland zone. In one of the most botanically unaltered sections of the park, the site is a reminder of the habitat in which mountain dwellers flourished for thousands of years. *(56–57) VLR: 09/16/82; NRHP: 12/13/85.*

CITY OF MANASSAS

The county seat of Prince William County began in 1852 as Manassas Junction, the intersection of the Manassas Gap Railroad and the Orange and Alexandria Railroad. It was incorporated as the town of Manassas in 1874 and became a city in 1975.

CANNON BRANCH FORT, *Manassas Municipal Airport vicinity.* Cannon Branch Fort, also known as the Wakeman site, includes the archaeological remains of a Civil War–era fortification for which there is no documentation in the historic record. The most likely hypothesis is that the fort was constructed by Union forces late in the war (1863–64) in order to defend Northern supply lines along the Orange and Alexandria Railroad. During this period Confederate forces under Col. John Singleton Mosby were constantly raiding these lines. The site, now on a wooded knoll above Cannon Branch, is one of only two remaining fortifications within the present-day limits of Manassas. Archaeological investigation is likely to provide more definitive information on the enigmatic site. *(155–5001) VLR: 03/20/96.*

LIBERIA, *8700 Centerville Road.* This Federal-style farmhouse was used as a headquarters by both Confederate and Union forces during the Civil War. Gen. P. G. T. Beauregard occupied it in 1861 during the first battle of Manassas. A year later, when Maj. Gen. Irvin McDowell set up Union headquarters at Liberia, President Abraham Lincoln along with Secretary of War Edwin M. Stanton held council with McDowell here on June 19, 1862. The house was built in 1825 for William Weir, whose wife, Harriet Bladen Mitchell Weir, inherited the property from her Carter ancestors. During the late 19th century, Liberia was owned by Robert Portner, an inventor and businessman. The house preserves most of its handsome original woodwork. Surrounded by modern development, this Civil War landmark is owned by the city of Manassas and is part of the Manassas Museum System. *(155–01) VLR: 12/18/79; NRHP: 03/20/80.*

MANASSAS HISTORIC DISTRICT. Incorporated as a town in 1873, Manassas sprang from a vital but war-torn railroad junction to become the transportation, commercial, and governmental hub of Prince William County. The junction of the Orange and Alexandria Railroad with the Manassas Gap Railroad in the 1850s made the adjacent area a natural candidate for settlement. In 1892 the county seat was moved from Brentsville to Manassas, an event which resulted in the construction of the Romanesque-style courthouse in 1894. County-seat status accelerated growth of both the commercial and residential area. The broad variety of turn-of-the-century houses served both county officials and railroad workers. An anchor of the district is the 1914 railroad station. Today the district maintains the image of an old-fashioned American town, a district intact and thriving but ringed by suburban sprawl. *(155–16) VLR: 02/16/88; NRHP: 06/29/88.*

MANASSAS INDUSTRIAL SCHOOL FOR COLORED YOUTH (JENNIE DEAN MEMORIAL SITE), *1906 Prince William Street.* The Manassas Industrial School was established in 1893 by Jennie Dean, a former slave who believed in the value of vocational education for Afro-American youth. Through her fund-raising efforts, Jennie Dean persuaded Emily Howland, Frances Hackley, and Andrew Carnegie to donate funds for buildings that were named in their honor. The school operated as a private residential institution until 1938 when it became a public regional high school for blacks. After the construction of a modern facility building in 1958–59, the former

industrial school buildings were demolished. The site, which now contains a memorial to the school and its founder, holds potential archaeological evidence that may lead to greater understanding of this pioneering institution. The memorial is part of the Manassas Museum System, opened to the public in 1995. *(155–10) VLR: 04/20/94; NRHP: 08/01/94.*

MAYFIELD FORTIFICATION SITE, *Quarry Road, Manassas.* This Civil War feature is the only earthwork remaining of the eleven constructed by the Confederates to guard the Orange and Alexandria Railroad at Manassas Junction (now the city of Manassas). Put up by slave laborers and local troops under Col. George H. Terrett, the fort was begun in May 1861 and completed the following month. Confederate soldiers occupied the earthwork until March 1862, and Union troops held it from August 1862 to November 1864. The Mayfield site is now owned by the city. Archaeological investigation may yield data relating to the periods of occupation by Confederate and then Union troops as well as the fort's relationship to other, now-vanished area forts. *(155–5002) VLR: 12/13/88; NRHP: 08/08/89.*

CITY OF MANASSAS PARK

The largely residential community of Manassas Park was established in 1955 as an outgrowth of the town of Manassas. It was incorporated as a town in 1957 and became a city in 1975.

CONNER HOUSE, *Conner Elementary School grounds.* The Conner house achieved significance in the Civil War first as Confederate headquarters for Gen. Joseph E. Johnston from July to November 1861 and then as a hospital for the wounded of the second battle of Manassas. One of the few remaining antebellum residences in the growing Manassas region, the plain stone house was built ca. 1820, probably as an overseer's house, and later extended. Using the local dark brown sandstone, it survives as an example of an indigenous vernacular dwelling type. During the first half of the 20th century, the property was owned by the Conner family, proprietors of one of Prince William County's major dairy farms. The city of Manassas Park has undertaken a long-term restoration of the house as a civic amenity. *(152–01) VLR: 01/20/81; NRHP: 10/06/81.*

CITY OF MARTINSVILLE

Established in 1791, Martinsville, the county seat of Henry County, was named for Joseph Martin, an early settler and Revolutionary War soldier who represented the area in the General Assembly. It became a city in 1928.

JOHN WADDEY CARTER HOUSE, *324 East Church Street.* Built in 1896, during a period of architectural gusto nationwide, the John Waddey Carter house is a textbook example of the American Queen Anne style. With its sawn ornaments, shingled surfaces, and spindle friezes, the house, known locally as "The Gray Lady," displays the virtuosity of the Victorian carpenter. A dominant characteristic of this country's interpretation of what began as an English revival of vernacular forms is the variety of porches, features that enhanced sociability during America's warm summers. The interior features large pocket doors, a stained-glass window, and handsome brass hardware. The house was built in 1896 by local attorney and later city mayor John Waddey Carter for his bride. It remained in the family until 1987 when it was purchased by Rives S. Brown who restored the house and opened it to the public in 1989. *(120–35) VLR: 09/20/88; NRHP: 11/03/88.*

LITTLE POST OFFICE, *207 Starling Avenue.* A tiny but finely detailed building, the Little Post Office is associated with an important period in U.S. Postal Service history: the ascendancy of the star route mail delivery system during the late 19th century. The system developed as a consequence of railroad expansion, and star routes—so named for the custom of designating the routes with asterisks in postal records—served rural post offices away from rail lines. The scheme brought postal delivery to the entire nation. Star route couriers were engaged by contract speculators who obtained rights to routes from the government. John B. Anglin, a remarkably successful contract speculator, had this building erected in 1893 to aid him in supervising his star route contracts, which at one point numbered over 500 and were spread through ten states. Anglin sold the property in 1917. The building is now a private office. *(120–47) VLR: 12/04/96; NRHP: 02/21/97.*

SCUFFLE HILL, *311 East Church Street.* Regarded as Martinsville's most impressive house, Scuffle Hill was originally built in 1905–6 for Benjamin F. Stevens, a former executive of the Liggett & Myers tobacco company. Stevens shared the house with his son-in-law and daughter, Mr. and Mrs. Pannill F. Rucker. Rucker was himself a well-to-do local tobacco manufacturer. The twenty-room mansion, originally called Oak Hill, burned in 1917. The surviving walls were incorporated by the Ruckers into the present house, a grand Georgian Revival work with fine interior appointments. Later occupants have included furniture executive Rives S. Brown and textile magnate Walter L. Pannill, who renamed the place Scuffle Hill. Since 1959 the house has been the Christ Episcopal Church parish house. Though no architect's name has been associated with Scuffle Hill, the house remains an imposing local symbol of business success. *(120–06) VLR: 12/04/96; NRHP: 02/21/97.*

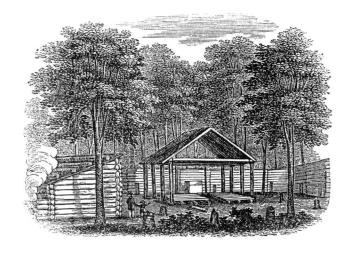

MATHEWS COUNTY

At the eastern tip of Virginia's Middle Peninsula, Mathews County was named for Thomas Mathews, Speaker of the Virginia House of Delegates. It was formed from Gloucester County in 1790. The county seat is Mathews.

FORT CRICKET HILL, *Cricket Hill.* This simple, worn earthwork is the tangible remnant of the event that marked the end of the last vestige of British rule in the Virginia colony. In July 1776 Virginia troops commanded by Gen. Andrew Lewis took up position here to keep in check the camp set up by Lord Dunmore, Virginia's last royal governor, across Milford Haven inlet on Gwynn's Island. Lewis's batteries opened fire on the British on July 8, forcing Dunmore to abandon his position and sail with his fleet for England. Only a small section of the original earthwork remains, preserved in front of a yacht-storage facility. *(57–14) VLR: 12/02/69; NRHP: 06/15/70.*

HESSE, *Cobbs Creek vicinity.* Named for the German land-graviate, Hesse was the seat of the Armisteads, a colonial family whose members, by virtue of their marriages, were progenitors or relatives of nearly every leading landed family in Virginia. Archaeological investigation has revealed the foundations of the original colonial house, which burned in 1798. It was replaced soon afterward by the present brick structure, erected a few feet away. The situation of both houses was likely chosen because of the impressive view of Godfrey Bay at the mouth of the Piankatank River. The present house, with its formal five-bay facades and paneled woodwork, illustrates the persistence of traditional Georgian forms in Virginia's eastern counties during the Federal period. The house was meticulously restored in the late 1970s at which time the gambrel-roofed wings were added. *(57–07) VLR: 11/20/73; NRHP: 02/12/74.*

MATHEWS COUNTY COURTHOUSE SQUARE, *Mathews.* Mathews County's cluster of small-scale brick government buildings is a well-integrated complex dating from the third decade of the 19th century. The nucleus of the group, the T-shaped brick courthouse, was erected ca. 1830 to replace what was probably a frame courthouse. Its pediment employs a three-part lunette with intersecting tracery, a feature found in Mathews County buildings attributed to local builder Richard Billups. Included on the grassy square are the old sheriff's office, built near the same time as the courthouse, and the 1827 clerk's office. The tiny jail, now a furnace building, was constructed in the mid–19th century. Also on the square are the 1930s former public library and a 1950s colonial-style county office building. A monument to the county's Confederate dead stands next to the courthouse. *(57–22) VLR: 12/21/76; NRHP: 08/18/77.*

METHODIST TABERNACLE, *Mathews vicinity.* The Methodists were among the first and most enthusiastic supporters of revivals—special religious events frequently held outdoors and designed to renew and intensify faith. All through the 19th century, revivals grew less spontaneous and more routine and institutionalized. Erected in 1922, Mathews County's tabernacle is one of the state's few remaining examples of the permanent shelters required as revivals became regularly scheduled occasions. The airy structure is essentially a pavilion and preserves most of its original accoutrements, including speaker's platform, choir tiers, and mourners' bench. Well-maintained, the structure is still used for its original purpose. The tabernacle is built on the site of an earlier and smaller Methodist tabernacle established in 1879. During the Civil War there was a brush arbor here where ladies would gather to pray for sons and husbands in the service of the Confederacy. *(57–30) VLR: 04/15/75; NRHP: 05/21/75.*

MILFORD (BILLUPS HOUSE), *Moon.* At the head of Billups Creek amid the marshy flats of Mathews County, Milford is typical of dwellings erected by Tidewater Virginia's middling gentry in the late 18th century. Characteristically, the wood-frame house has a plain but pleasingly proportioned exterior. Inside are an impressive paneled parlor chimney wall and a fine Georgian stair. The house stands on property that has remained in the ownership of the Billups family since the 17th century. It is likely that the present house was erected for John Billups or his son, John Billups, Jr., between 1774 and 1784. Except for the modern shingle siding and a 20th-century wing, the house survives without significant alteration. *(57–23) VLR: 05/17/77; NRHP: 03/26/80.*

NEW POINT COMFORT LIGHTHOUSE, *Bavon vicinity.* The New Point Comfort peninsula has served as a point of reference for navigators since the 17th century and has been known by its present name since before 1690. Because of the threat to navigation caused by the point and its shoals, Congress appropriated funds in 1801 for the construction of a permanent lighthouse. Built by Mathews County resident Elzy Burroughs, the lighthouse was completed in 1805. Similar to the Old Point Comfort lighthouse at Fort Monroe, the gently tapered structure of whitewashed sandstone ashlar was in use until 1963 when a new light was constructed on piers to the south. The original lighthouse has been transferred by the Coast Guard to Mathews County to be preserved as a historic landmark and as a day reference for passing boats. Changes in currents have separated the lighthouse from the mainland, leaving it on a tiny island. *(57–64) VLR: 06/20/72; NRHP: 03/01/73.*

POPLAR GROVE MILL AND HOUSE, *Mathews vicinity.*
Poplar Grove Mill is the only surviving tide mill in Virginia.
Tidal power, along with wind power, was harnessed by necessity in the low-lying coastal regions where ordinary waterpower did not exist. The present mill replaced a colonial mill burned during the Civil War. The mill operated until 1912 and has since been restored. Across the mill's lagoon is the multisectioned Poplar Grove house, the earliest portion of which probably was built in the late 18th century, possibly for the Williams family. The central portion was constructed in the Federal period, probably after 1799 when the property was acquired by John Patterson. It has the individualized details associated with local builder Richard Billups. Patterson's granddaughter, the nurse Capt. Sally Tompkins, the only woman to be commissioned an officer in the Confederate army, was born at Poplar Grove in 1833. *(57–08) VLR: 05/13/69; NRHP: 11/12/69.*

MECKLENBURG COUNTY

Formed from Lunenburg County in 1764, this Southside county was named in honor of Charlotte of Mecklenburg-Strelitz, consort of King George III. The county seat is Boydton.

THE BOYD TAVERN, *Washington Street, Boydton.* The core of this tavern was erected ca. 1785 by Alexander Boyd, Sr., an area businessman and founder of Boydton. The hostelry thrived, and its presence greatly influenced the selection of Boydton as the Mecklenburg County seat. The popular establishment evolved over the next decades into a rambling frame structure of thirty-five rooms highlighted with fancy sawnwork detailing. The ornamentation was the work of the regional builder-architect Jacob W. Holt, who made such enrichments his hallmark. The tavern closed in the late 19th century and was converted into a boarding school and subsequently into apartments. To save the building from neglect, the Boyd Family Memorial Foundation purchased the property in 1974. In 1988 the tavern was deeded to the Boyd Tavern Foundation, whose goal is to restore the tavern to its original use. *(173–01) VLR: 02/17/76; NRHP: 09/29/76.*

CEDAR GROVE ARCHAEOLOGICAL SITE, *Cedar Grove vicinity.* Used for tobacco agriculture for 100 years, from the 1840s to the 1940s, Cedar Grove is an antebellum farmstead site preserving archaeological data relating to rural life of the region. The site is situated on the top of a ridge extending into the John H. Kerr Reservoir, its lowlands having been inundated following acquisition of the property by the federal government. The main house is represented by a 35-foot-square fieldstone pier foundation, a stone and brick cellar divided by a load-bearing wall, and two brick chimney falls. Nearby, within the curtilage, are the sites of a well, a double-flue tobacco barn, ordering rooms, and various outbuildings. Large oaks, ornamental vegetation, piles of fieldstone, and an old road trace are also present on the site. *(58–5004) VLR: 06/19/96.*

ELM HILL, *Elm Hill State Game Management Area, Castle Heights vicinity.* Elm Hill is one of the Roanoke River basin's early plantation houses. Although unoccupied and in deteriorated condition, the T-shaped house preserves nearly all of its original fabric including bold provincial Federal woodwork. Elm Hill was built ca. 1800 as the residence of Peyton Skipwith, although title to the property was held by his father, Sir Peyton Skipwith, Bart., of Prestwould. Elm Hill remained the property of the Skipwiths into the late 19th century. Owned in recent years by the Virginia Commission of Game and Inland Fisheries, title to the house and a small surrounding parcel has been transferred to the Historical Society of Mecklenburg, which is undertaking a long-term restoration. The house overlooks Lake Gaston and the John H. Kerr Dam. *(58–66) VLR 05/15/79; NRHP: 07/27/79; BHR EASEMENT.*

ELM HILL
ARCHAEOLOGICAL SITE,
Elm Hill State Game Management Area, Castle Heights vicinity. In a bottomland field of the Elm Hill plantation, the Elm Hill site preserves stratified deposits dating from the Late Archaic through Late Woodland periods (2500 B.C.–A.D. 1600). Scientific study of these deposits would contribute significantly to the limited data currently available about this portion of the Roanoke River. Late Archaic projectile points and flakage have been discovered in the lowest test level of the site. Multiple Woodland-period occupations are denoted in pit features, hearths, and human burials. These features have both dense concentrations of ceramic artifacts and well-preserved animal bones and shellfish remains. The Elm Hill site may be the last intact stratified bottomland site in the area since other potential sites have been inundated by Buggs Island Lake and Lake Gaston. *(58–84) VLR: 11/15/83; NRHP: 03/14/85.*

EUREKA, *Baskerville vicinity.* Jacob W. Holt (1811–1880), a regional architect and builder, erected this Italian Villa–style house for the Baskervill family in 1854–59. Holt began his career in Warren County, N.C., and was active in Mecklenburg County in the mid-1850s. Typical of Holt's work, Eureka is lavishly ornamented with scrollwork brackets, heavy moldings, and other fancy wooden ornaments. The model for the exterior is "Design 31" of William H. Ranlett's *The Architect* (1847–49), a popular architectural pattern book. Holt accented the design by adding a tower. The house was first owned and occupied by Dr. Robert D. Baskervill and remained the property of his descendants until 1974 when the house and surrounding acreage were purchased by Mr. and Mrs. William E. Blalock, who have since restored the place. The lofty interior retains nearly all its original woodwork including a spiral stair and doors with original painted graining. *(58–10) VLR: 07/19/77; NRHP: 09/17/80.*

GARRETT WOODS ARCHAEO-LOGICAL COMPLEXES NOS. 1, 2, AND 3, *Clarksville vicinity.* The undisturbed sites of three adjacent tobacco farmsteads form the Garrett Woods complex, part of the assemblage of archaeological resources in the John H. Kerr Reservoir area. Complex no. 1, occupied from the early 1800s until purchased by the federal government in the 1940s, is composed of the sites of the Garrett house, a well, four tobacco barns, one shed, and two unidentified structures. Complex no. 2, dating from the late 1800s to the 1900s, has a large L-shaped domestic structure remnant and sites of various outbuildings and farm buildings. The third grouping, occupied from the late 1800s until the 1940s and representative of a small-scale tobacco farm, preserves sites of a house, two tobacco barns, and fence lines. Also present is a family cemetery. Scientific investigation here could piece together a picture of regional agrarian culture spanning a century and a half. *(58–5001, 5002, 5003) VLR: 06/19/96.*

IVY HILL PLANTATION ARCHAEOLOGICAL SITE,
Ivy Hill vicinity. The seat of Samuel Tarry who died in 1757, the
Ivy Hill site holds the archaeological remains of a plantation
mansion, associated outbuildings, a still, well, and large family
cemetery. Research indicates that the land probably belonged
to the Tarry family from the initial grant through its 1940s acquisition for the John H. Kerr Reservoir. The complex shares
the fieldstone foundation and brick chimney construction seen
in area buildings. The four chimney falls indicate that the main
house measured 70 by 60 feet. A brick-lined cellar remains intact. Other sites include those of roadbeds, fence lines, and two
tobacco barns. The cemetery contains at least 128 burials, both
marked and unmarked. Eleven graves are marked with Tarry
and related names. Further investigation here could reveal information relating to exceptionally early gentry life in one of
the colony's farthest corners. *(58–88) VLR: 06/19/96.*

LONG GRASS, *Eppes Fork.* Long Grass, farmed since the early 1800s by generations of the Tarry family, ranks among Mecklenburg County's finest historic plantation complexes. The
original section of the much-evolved H-plan house probably
dates to the early 19th century and began as a compact hall-
parlor structure. George Tarry enlarged the house in 1840 with
a two-story Greek Revival wing, giving his home a formal front
section. The addition is attributed to the prolific regional
builder-architect Jacob W. Holt. In the 1850s Tarry expanded
the original section with a second story and a large Victorian
porch. The existing farm buildings were erected at the turn of
the century during the ownership of George B. Tarry. Early
outbuildings remaining in the curtilage include a log schoolhouse, kitchen-laundry, smokehouse, and an icehouse. Nearby
stand a log tenant house and a tobacco packhouse. *(58–185) VLR:
04/28/95; NRHP: 07/21/95.*

MECKLENBURG COUNTY COURTHOUSE, *Washington
Street, Boydton.* Of Virginia's courthouses influenced by the architecture of Thomas Jefferson, none has a more elegant formality than Mecklenburg's courthouse of 1838–42. It is the only
temple-form building of the group employing a Roman Ionic
order and having a hexastyle portico. With its brick walls now
painted white, the building has a striking resemblance to Jefferson's Virginia State Capitol, both using similar Ionic capitals.
The courthouse was built by the area master builder William A.
Howard, who also built the Cumberland courthouse and
helped build the Lunenburg courthouse. Boydton was established as the county seat in 1811. The county outgrew its first
structure and in 1838 voted to erect the present building. Also
on the tree-shaded court square is the clerk's office and a Confederate monument. *(173–06) VLR: 06/17/75; NRHP: 07/17/75.*

NEWMAN POINT ARCHAEOLOGICAL SITE, *Boydton
vicinity.* Fieldstone foundations, well remnants, and chimney
bases of various structures mark the arrangement of a grange
occupied from the mid-1700s into the 1800s, now situated on a
peninsula of the John H. Kerr Reservoir. One domestic structure, partially eroding into the reservoir, is marked by two brick
chimney bases. Within the central area is a dressed-stone foundation of a barn. Nearby a brick-lined cellar and two chimney
falls remain from a mid-1700s domestic structure, one of the region's earliest identified domestic sites. Scattered about it are
four brick and stone chimney bases probably of outbuildings.
The artifact frequency and diversity at Newman Point are adequate to address questions of social status and frontier market
access. The complex is on John H. Kerr Reservoir property,
managed by the Army Corps of Engineers. *(58–5007) VLR: 06/19/96.*

OCCONEECHEE PLANTATION ARCHAEOLOGICAL COMPLEX, *Occoneechee State Park.* The site of a 19th-century tobacco plantation, Occoneechee contains four archaeological areas: the central plantation house, slave quarters, a barn, and the overseer's house, which together formed a functioning farmstead into the 20th century. The fieldstone foundations and brick chimney ruins indicate a high potential for preservation of subsurface trash pits and related features. The house, shown in an old photograph to have been a huge two-story mansion, was constructed in 1839 by William Townes and was the focus of a 3,000-acre plantation. The house survived the Civil War but burned in 1898, forcing relocation of the then resident-owners, Capt. Dempsey Graves Crudup and family. Within the mansion area are indications of a kitchen, servants' quarters, stables, smokehouse, icehouse, and well. Traces of formal gardens also remain. *(58–91) VLR: 06/19/96.*

PRESTWOULD, *Clarksville vicinity.* Sir Peyton Skipwith, the only Virginia-born baronet, moved to his Roanoke River lands after he married Jean Miller, his second wife, in 1788. In 1795 he completed his large Georgian mansion, the nucleus of a 10,000-acre plantation. Built of dressed sandstone, Sir Peyton's house, with its French scenic wallpapers and fine furnishings, is a memorable expression of the elegant lifestyle maintained by Virginia's gentry in the remote countryside. The formal garden, laid out by Lady Skipwith, is one of the state's most thoroughly documented historic gardens. On the grounds is an unusually complete collection of outbuildings including an octagonal garden pavilion and a rare 18th-century slave house. Prestwould was owned by Skipwith descendants until 1914. In 1963 the house and forty-six acres were acquired by the Prestwould Foundation, which exhibits the property and is engaged in long-term restoration of the plantation's many components. *(58–45) VLR: 11/05/68; NRHP: 10/01/69.*

RED FOX FARM, *Skipwith vicinity.* The various buildings on this Mecklenburg County farm survive as a tangible illustration of the bright-leaf tobacco–curing process pioneered here. Throughout the 19th and 20th centuries, tobacco has been the principal cash crop for Southside Virginia, enabling the region's farmers to sustain themselves following the Civil War and Reconstruction. The industry was spurred by the development of a profitable method of producing flue-cured bright-leaf tobacco by Robert M. Jeffreys at Red Fox Farm in the 1880s. Bright-leaf tobacco was used principally for cigarettes, and once Jeffreys's method was implemented, the demand for it increased significantly over the dark tobacco used for chewing. Along with the main house, the buildings connected with this enterprise include five log tobacco barns, a packhouse, strip house, smokehouse, log cabins, and a farm store, or commissary. *(58–131) VLR: 04/21/93; NRHP: 06/10/93.*

CLARK ROYSTER HOUSE, *300 Rose Hill Avenue, Clarksville.* This prim transitional Federal–Greek Revival dwelling was built ca. 1840 for Clark Royster, founder of Clarksville. Royster established the town at the site of a ferry landing he operated on the south side of the Roanoke River. The town grew rapidly and was incorporated by the General Assembly in 1821. Growth no doubt was spurred by Royster's tobacco warehouse. The volume of business passing through Royster's warehouse and one other here secured Clarksville as one of the largest tobacco inspection towns in the state. Situated on the town's highest point, the house originally was part of a large farm which Royster inherited from his father. Though architecturally restrained, the house has fine Flemish bond brickwork and carefully detailed original woodwork, all exhibiting the handiwork of the skilled craftsmen available here during the antebellum period. *(192–70) VLR: 06/19/96; NRHP: 12/16/96.*

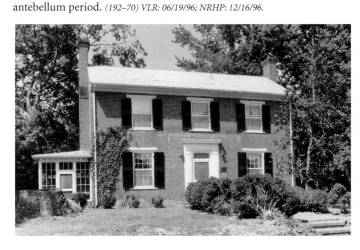

**RUDD BRANCH RIDGE ARCHAEOLOGICAL COM-
PLEXES 1–2 AND 3–4,** *Boydton vicinity.* These four archaeological complexes within the John H. Kerr Reservoir area contain the undisturbed remains of adjacent tobacco farms. The
time period extends from the late 1800s to the 1940s when the
tracts were purchased by the federal government for the reservoir. The two house sites are surrounded by an extensive array
of ornamental vegetation including boxwood, privet, flower
bulbs, grapevines, cedar, periwinkle, rose bushes, ivy, magnolia,
and fruit trees. Associated with complexes 1 and 2 are the stone
foundations of outbuildings, tobacco barns, and a tobacco ordering room. Complexes 3 and 4 likewise have sites of outbuildings and farm buildings, including tobacco barns and a tobacco
ordering room. The study of these sites and the related landscape could reveal insight into the broad patterns of tobacco
culture in the southern Piedmont. *(58–5005, 5006) VLR: 06/19/96.*

SHADOW LAWN, *27
North Main Street, Chase
City.* A regionalized expression of the Italianate style,
Shadow Lawn evolved in tan-
dem with the town's transformation from the cross-
roads village of Christians-
ville into a thriving colony of
northern immigrants after
the Civil War, renamed
Chase City. The house began
ca. 1834 as the home of
Richard Puryear, a landowner and proprietor of a local
tavern. An extensive remodeling was undertaken in 1869–70 for
George Endly, the cofounder of Chase City, who moved here
from Pennsylvania in 1868. The project is attributed to Jacob W.
Holt, a Virginia-born architect-builder who worked in both
North Carolina and Virginia, creating a distinctive body of
structures in a boldly ornamented Italianate style. In 1902 Shadow Lawn became part of the Mecklenburg Mineral Springs Hotel complex. The hotel burned in 1909. The house is now a private residence. *(58–130) VLR: 12/15/81; NRHP: 10/19/82.*

SUNNYSIDE, *104 Shiney Rock Road, Clarksville.* Virginia's
Southside plantation houses are either formal works of architecture such as Prestwould and Berry Hill or houses that started modestly and evolved to meet subsequent needs. Among the
latter type is Sunnyside, a multisectioned homestead, the earliest part of which was built in 1833 for Samuel and Eliza Hester
on property inherited from Eliza's father, Robert Greenwood.
To their simple three-bay, side-passage dwelling an I-house section was added following Tucker Carrington's acquisition of
the place in 1836. Carrington was a local politician and businessman, as well as a developer of Clarksville. In the 1850s the
I-house section was enlarged with one-story wings, possibly
executed by area builder Jacob W. Holt. After the Civil War,
Carrington's four unmarried daughters opened a school for
young ladies at Sunnyside, which operated until 1908. The
house is currently undergoing restoration. *(192–02) VLR: 06/19/96;
NRHP: 12/06/96.*

MIDDLESEX COUNTY

Formed from Lancaster County about 1669, Middlesex County, on the Rappahannock River side of Virginia's Middle Peninsula, was named for the extinct English shire that bordered London. Its county seat is Saluda.

CHRIST CHURCH, *Christchurch.* The present and second church of the Christ Church Parish was completed in the 1720s. Alexander Graves served as its mason and John Hipkins, Sr., as its carpenter. Among its patrons were the Wormeleys of Rosegill. Although of modest size, the church had a richly appointed interior and a chancel screen. The building was abandoned after the disestablishment and fell into ruin; only its Flemish bond walls survived. The parish was revived in 1840, and the church was restored to use in 1843. In 1921 Christchurch School, a boys' preparatory school, was established nearby. The church since has served as both the school chapel and the local Episcopal parish church. The interior was restored in the 1980s under the direction of architect James Scott Rawlings. The churchyard contains an outstanding collection of colonial tombstones, the most impressive ones marking the graves of Wormeley family members. *(59–02) VLR: 03/21/72; NRHP: 11/03/72.*

DEER CHASE, *Healys vicinity.* With its brick construction, jerkinhead roof, and center-passage plan, Deer Chase typifies the medium-size colonial plantation house of Virginia's Tidewater region. Although modest in appearance, the house is generously proportioned compared to the rude wooden cottages that housed most colonial farmers. Capt. Oswald Cary was granted 460 acres on the Piankatank River in 1685; the present house was likely built several decades later by a descendant of Cary. Fire gutted the interior in the early 19th century; the present woodwork dates from the rebuilding. The repairs also resulted in the number of bays on the facade being changed from five to three. An 1885 plat shows as many as seventeen outbuildings and farm buildings, as well as a formal garden. Of these, a frame schoolhouse and the foundations of an office remain. Deer Chase preserves its isolated rural setting. *(59–17) VLR: 06/19/73; NRHP: 08/14/73.*

HEWICK, *Urbanna vicinity.* Hewick was the 18th-century seat of the Robinson family. Although long believed to have been constructed in two sections, the house most likely was built as a unit in the mid–18th century for the planter Christopher Robinson III (1705–1768), grandson of Christopher Robinson I, colonial councillor and secretary of state, who probably occupied an earlier house on the property. In its original form the house was only one story high with a clipped-gable roof. The roof was changed to a gambrel roof in the early 19th century. Around 1849 the front section was raised to two full stories with a low gable roof. These various alterations illustrate the region's changing needs and tastes in house forms. The house is set in a broad, level yard flanked by fields and is approached by a long, tree-lined lane. *(59–06) VLR: 07/18/78; NRHP: 11/17/78.*

LANSDOWNE, *Virginia Street, Urbanna.* This mid-18th-century T-shaped mansion in the center of Urbanna was built as a secondary residence for Ralph Wormeley III of nearby Rosegill. Although not well known, the house ranks with Virginia's finest examples of Georgian architecture. The front section is the earliest; the large rear wing was added probably within five years. The interior was altered in the early 20th century with the relocation of the stair and other changes, but a large quantity of original paneling survives and is an exceptional demonstration of colonial design and craftsmanship. Preserved in the attic is a rare section of mid-18th-century wood-shingle roofing. In 1791 Lansdowne became the home of Arthur Lee, diplomat and governmental figure. At Lee's death the next year, Lansdowne was inherited by his brothers Richard Henry Lee and Francis Lightfoot Lee, signers of the Declaration of Independence. *(316–03) VLR: 09/17/74; NRHP: 11/08/74.*

LOWER CHAPEL, *Hartfield vicinity.* Lower Chapel is one of two chapels ordered in 1710, along with the main parish church, to serve Middlesex County's Christ Church Parish. The other chapel does not survive. Lower Chapel, begun in 1714, was so named because it was located in the lower part of the parish. As a secondary structure, the building was architecturally spare, having plain English bond walls instead of Flemish bond, with no rubbed or otherwise decorated brickwork. It achieves visual distinction, however, through the use of a steep clipped-gable roof. Completed in 1717, the chapel served the parish until it was abandoned following the disestablishment. The building was acquired by the Methodists in 1857 and has since been used by that denomination, with the designation Lower Church. *(59–07) VLR: 10/17/72; NRHP: 04/24/73.*

MIDDLESEX COUNTY COURTHOUSE, *Saluda.* Conspicuously placed at a well-traveled intersection in the village of Saluda, the 1852 courthouse is a late example of the temple-form, arcaded-front court structures erected by many Virginia counties in the first half of the 19th century. Beginning with the 1704 Capitol in Williamsburg, the arcade has been a traditional architectural feature of Virginia public buildings. The county seat was moved from Urbanna to Saluda in 1849, and John P. Hill was commissioned to erect the present courthouse. The building has since been enlarged, but its original section, still serving its original function, is clearly evident. *(59–08) VLR: 04/18/78; NRHP: 11/21/78.*

OLD MIDDLESEX COUNTY COURTHOUSE (MIDDLESEX COUNTY WOMAN'S CLUB), *Virginia Street, Urbanna.* Although much altered from its original, and probably very simple, appearance, the former courthouse of Middlesex County is one of Virginia's rare colonial court structures. A courthouse was ordered for Urbanna in 1685, but local arguments over ferry access to the county seat prevented any construction until 1748. During the Revolution the local Committee of Safety met here to try local gentry for suspected loyalty to the crown. In 1849 the Middlesex justices moved the county seat to the more accessible settlement of Saluda. The former courthouse was then remodeled in the Gothic style and used as interdenominational chapel. During the Civil War the building served as a barracks for Confederate troops. From 1920 to 1948 it housed an Episcopal congregation, after which it was deconsecrated and deeded to the Middlesex County Woman's Club, which it continues to serve. *(316–02) VLR: 06/15/76; NRHP: 11/21/76.*

ROSEGILL, *Urbanna vicinity.* One of Virginia's most historic estates, Rosegill was established in 1649 by Ralph Wormeley I. Sir Henry Chicheley, deputy governor of the colony, married Wormeley's widow and made his home at Rosegill. Ralph Wormeley II (1650–1700), holder of several public positions including that of president of the governor's council, made the plantation an elaborate family seat consisting of some twenty buildings. Lord Howard of Effingham, a colonial governor in the late 17th century, used Rosegill as a summer home. The present complex, consisting of four brick buildings, most likely was erected during the tenure of Ralph Wormeley IV (1715–1790). The main house evolved from a small brick dwelling into a large U-shaped structure covered by a gambrel roof. In the 1850s the extending wings were removed and the second story was added. The likely concentration of many 17th-century building sites makes the plantation of paramount archaeological significance. *(59–09) VLR: 02/10/73; NRHP: 11/27/73.*

OLD TOBACCO WAREHOUSE, *Virginia Street, Urbanna.* Dating from the 1760s, this simple storehouse, built for the factor James Mills, is a rare example of a colonial commercial structure run by a resident factor of a British company. At such an establishment, tobacco, instead of being consigned directly to England, was sold to the factor, who sent it abroad as trade for English goods to be bought by the local planters. Mills and his employers were Scottish, as were many of the merchants active in Virginia's early tobacco trade. After serving various uses, the building was purchased by the Association for the Preservation of Virginia Antiquities in 1938 and restored to its colonial appearance in the 1960s. Long used as the town library, the building was acquired by the town of Urbanna in 1997 for conversion to a visitors' center. *(316–04) VLR: 04/18/72; NRHP: 11/07/72; BHR EASEMENT.*

URBANNA HISTORIC DISTRICT. This colonial port town was established in 1680 and evolved gradually over the succeeding three centuries. It served as a tobacco port in the 18th century and was

a mercantile and commercial fishing center in the 19th century. By the 20th century it had become a summer resort and was known for its oyster-packing plants. Formerly the county seat, Urbanna contains one of Virginia's eleven surviving colonial courthouse buildings. Its principal architectural landmark is Lansdowne, a colonial mansion in the heart of the town. Reflecting its history as a tobacco port is the Old Tobacco Warehouse, picturesquely situated on the lane leading to the waterfront. Opposite the warehouse is Sandwich (shown), an early brick dwelling traditionally thought to have been the customshouse. Mingled among these early structures is a mix of 19th- and 20th-century houses, churches, and commercial buildings maintaining the small-town character. *(316–09) VLR: 08/21/90; NRHP: 02/07/91.*

WILTON, *Stampers vicinity.* Completed in 1763 by Col. William Churchill, clerk of the county court for nearly three decades, this finely crafted structure is one of Tidewater Virginia's most sophisticated colonial plantation houses. Notable features include its T-plan, Flemish bond brickwork, Georgian stair, paneled woodwork, and gambrel roof. The parlor paneling, with its chimneypiece framed by fluted pilasters on pedestals, is some of the finest in the state. The brickwork in the gables indicates the house was intended to have A-shaped gables, but the original roof framing suggests that the roof shape was changed during construction. Also, the recent discovery that the front section formerly had a staircase lends credence to the tradition that the house is the result of evolution. The rear wing has had a gambrel roof since its inception with its end hipped rather than gabled. *(59–10) VLR: 10/17/78; NRHP: 02/01/79.*

WORMELEY-MONTAGUE COTTAGE, *Virginia Street, Urbanna.* The Wormeley-Montague cottage is the simplest of the few early houses remaining in this once-active colonial port. It stands on a lot originally owned by the Wormeley family of Rosegill, and it is assumed that they erected the building ca. 1747 to house either an employee or a tenant. It was later owned by Arthur Lee of nearby Lansdowne. The small house, with its side-hall plan, gabled dormers, and steep roof, is a typical example of Tidewater Virginia vernacular architecture. The asymmetrical chimney, with its tiled weatherings, is a fine specimen of 18th-century masonry. The interior is simple and likely never had much decoration. Early fabric, some of which dates from the Federal period, includes several raised-panel doors and a double-beaded chairboard. An enclosed straight-run stair ascends from back to front. Rescued from threatened demolition, the house was restored in 1976 by preservationist Robert L. Montague III. *(316–06) VLR: 12/20/77; NRHP: 05/23/80.*

MONTGOMERY COUNTY

Named for Gen. Richard Montgomery, who was killed in the American assault on Quebec in 1775, this Southwest Virginia county was formed in 1776 from the former Fincastle County. Parts of Botetourt and Pulaski counties were added later. The county seat is Christiansburg.

ALLEGHANY SPRINGS SPRINGHOUSE, *Alleghany Springs.* This unforgettable structure is without parallel in Virginia as an example of rustic work. Rustic architecture and furniture, most frequently associated with the Adirondack camps of the late 19th century, employed untrimmed limbs, branches, and vines to give buildings and objects a naturalistic, "of-the-forest" look. The two-tiered springhouse, a large octagonal pavilion, is supported on rough cedar posts with complex intertwined knots of rhododendron branches and roots forming brackets, railings, and even "vaulted" ceilings. Sheltered within is a marble counter for serving springwater. Established in 1853, Alleghany Springs was one of Virginia's most popular spas until the main hotel burned in 1904. In one season following the Civil War, the springs hosted nine former Confederate generals. Now surrounded by modern houses, the fantastic springhouse, built ca. 1890, is the principal reminder of this once-popular place. *(60–476) VLR: 06/20/89; NRHP: 11/13/89.*

AMISS-PALMER HOUSE, *Mountain View Drive, Blacksburg.* Edwin J. Amiss built this brick mansion around 1856 on an elevated hillock which then commanded the road into Blacksburg. Amiss, a merchant and landowner, assembled several tracts, including a 125-acre parcel where the house was erected. The finely appointed dwelling boasts a Flemish bond facade, an entrance portico with paired Ionic columns, and marble mantels within. On the grounds are three early outbuildings: a brick kitchen, a log cottage probably for slaves, and a log meat house. The place was purchased in 1880 by W. H. Palmer, Amiss's son-in-law, who added a deck-on-hip roof over the original lower roof. The farm was developed in the mid–20th century, reducing the land around the house to a three-acre yard. Despite the loss of its rural setting, the house remains one of Blacksburg's principal antebellum landmarks. *(150–14) VLR: 06/20/89; NRHP: 11/13/89.*

BARNETT HOUSE (BIG SPRING), *Elliston.* The large brick residence built in 1808 for David Barnett originally was a dignified Federal residence, one of several in the narrow valley that also contains Fotheringay and the Madison farm. As completed, it was a five-bay I-house with a one-story ell. In 1907 the farm was purchased by Capt. "Black" Barger of nearby Walnut Grove for his daughter and her husband, O. N. Moomaw. Moomaw took advantage of the Big Spring on the property and built a series of lakes to raise watercress. It was a successful venture; Moomaw's cress eventually graced the salads of fine restaurants and ocean liners. In 1910 Moomaw undertook a remodeling that transformed the house into a Colonial Revival mansion. The alterations were confined mainly to the exterior and included the Doric portico and veranda, the deep eaves, and the pedimented dormers. *(60–440) VLR: 06/20/89; NRHP: 11/13/89.*

WILLIAM BARNETT HOUSE, *Alleghany Springs vicinity.* Distinguished by its two-tiered gallery extending across a remarkably long facade, the William Barnett house is an amalgamation of additions built around a log core. The two-story log section is of undetermined age; local tradition places it as early as 1813. A 1937 WPA inventory claims it dates from 1850, the year the property was purchased by the Barnett family. Regardless of its age, the house is interesting as a demonstration of the regional practice, seen especially in towns, of extending a building parallel to its road frontage. The house may have been increased in size as many as five times but is unified by its continuous gable roof and the late 19th-century sawn-work railing. With three early outbuildings, the Barnett house preserves considerable information on the way a homeplace evolved in the idiom of an area's vernacular tradition. *(60–472); VLR: 06/20/89; NRHP: 11/13/89.*

BIG SPRING BAPTIST CHURCH, *Elliston.* A landmark of Montgomery County's black religious community, the Big Spring Baptist Church was organized with the support of Capt. Charles S. Schaeffer, founder of the Christiansburg Industrial Institute, a training school for former slaves. Schaeffer, an agent of the Freedmen's Bureau, was a northern Quaker educator who came to the area after the Civil War to equip blacks to deal with freedom. While engaged in his educational activities, Schaeffer also found time to organize several black Baptist congregations including Elliston's Big Spring Baptist Church. Completed in 1880, the church, later renamed the First Baptist Church, was built by Joseph Pepper. With its front tower and Gothic windows, the building is a more ambitious structure than the usual country church, symbolizing the rapid transition of the area's blacks from chattel property to responsible citizens. The church continues to serve its congregation. *(60–435) VLR: 06/20/89; NRHP: 11/13/89.*

BISHOP HOUSE, *Graysontown.* Perched on the edge of a steep bluff, high above the Little River and the village of Graysontown, the Bishop house is a dwelling of immediate and unique appeal. The setting, compact scale, and quaint architecture combine to make a memorable picture of late 19th-century individualism and domesticity. The dominant design element is the fanciful Eastlake front porch with its turned posts, pendants, balusters, and spindles. This is echoed on the rear with a two-tiered porch overlooking the river valley. Inside, the house is trimmed with unpainted pine woodwork accented with details in walnut. The house, probably built in the 1870s, was originally the home of Dr. William Bishop, a Civil War veteran. Local tradition holds that Dr. Bishop played bugle calls from this hill every Sunday evening. *(60–107) VLR: 06/20/89; NRHP: 11/13/89.*

BLACKSBURG HISTORIC DISTRICT. Blacksburg's downtown incorporates a varied collection of historic structures chronicling the town's evolution from 1798, when it was laid out by its namesake William Black on a sixteen-square grid, into the present century. The town is unusual for the region because it became a successful community without being a county seat. Although it originally flourished by serving the area's prosperous farming community, Blacksburg's steady growth and affluence were assured when Virginia Polytechnic Institute was established here in 1872. Blacksburg has since comfortably accommodated its role as a classic college town. The large number of university students and employees has maintained the Main Street commercial area as a remarkably cohesive core for a town its size. The parallel Church Street (shown) is aptly named for its splendid progression of churches. Sprinkled through the district is an impressive range of house types, from log structures to bungalows. *(150–108) VLR: 06/20/89; NRHP: 01/31/91.*

BOWYER-TROLLINGER FARM, *Childress vicinity.* Logs were the most available and hence the preferred building material for early Montgomery County farmhouses. Built ca. 1825 for Thomas Bowyer as a single-pen log structure, the core of the Bowyer-Trollinger house is one of fewer than ten log dwellings in the county employing this once-standard form. Typically, the house was soon expanded with a second log pen. A ca. 1880 addition transformed the house into a center-passage dwelling. The weatherboarding and the Colonial Revival front porch give the exterior a conventional look. Thomas Bowyer was known for his fine horses and maintained a racetrack on the place. Little changed since the turn of the century, the farm's historic character is reinforced by the survival of several late 19th-century outbuildings and farm structures. The complex is set in a small valley of unspoiled pastoral scenery. *(60–84) VLR: 06/20/89; NRHP: 02/01/91.*

POMPEY CALLAWAY HOUSE, *Elliston.* This 1910 house in the historically black section of Elliston is the individual architectural expression of a former slave, Pompey Callaway, working with traditional forms and building practices. Callaway was born in Franklin County. His origins apparently had a strong impression on him, for his Elliston home is said to have been modeled after the residence of his former master, which explains why this early 20th-century house has the appearance of a dwelling normally dating from the antebellum period. The I-house plan and the entrance with sidelights and transom could easily be mistaken for a mid-19th-century work. Not only did Callaway undertake the construction, he made his own bricks, molding them and firing them in a kiln nearby. The house took many years to complete because Callaway, a railway station worker, was forced to confine his labor to weekends. *(60–434) VLR: 06/20/89; NRHP: 11/13/89.*

CAMBRIA DEPOT, *630 Depot Street, Christiansburg.* The architecturally delightful Cambria Depot is a small-town celebration of early rail travel. The Virginia and Tennessee Railroad reached Christiansburg in 1854, and a depot, built in the present-day suburb of Cambria, was opened in 1857. Union troops burned the depot in 1864; its replacement, the present depot, was part of the railroad restoration program instigated by the rail company's new president, William Mahone. The Italianate style chosen for the depot was popular for railroad structures of the time. In *Country Seats* (1865), author Henry Holley stated that the easily constructed Italian style was "appropriate for stations in rural settings." The depot was converted to a freight station in 1906 when a new station was built nearby. The building was sold into private ownership and restored for adaptive reuse in the 1980s. It remains one of the oldest depots in the state. *(60–62) VLR: 04/16/85; NRHP: 12/12/85.*

CAMBRIA HISTORIC DISTRICT, *Christiansburg.* Cambria's development began in the early 1850s after the laying of the Virginia and Tennessee Railroad tracks a mile north of Christiansburg. The settlement that sprang up around the depot functioned as a "port" for Christiansburg and enabled area farmers and manufacturers to reach distant markets. Cambria developed its own identity by the late 19th century, when several still-extant commercial buildings were constructed near the tracks. Among these are the Surface-Lee Block, built for a wholesale grocery business, and the former Dew Drop Inn, a little-altered commercial building that housed the county's first hospital. Up the hill from the tracks is a scattering of early 20th-century residences and commercial buildings including the Cambria Hardware Company building, constructed of rusticated concrete blocks. Although a 1947 fire destroyed many commercial buildings, the district still evokes a flavor of old-time small-town commercialism. *(154–48) VLR: 06/20/89; NRHP: 01/10/91.*

CHRISTIANSBURG POST OFFICE, *East Main and North Franklin streets, Christiansburg.* The hundreds of well-designed, well-crafted post offices built across the United States during the Great Depression symbolized the government's effort to instill civic pride and to restore confidence in federal institutions. These buildings, both great and small, frequently were the chief architectural works in their respective communities and set standards for other buildings. Begun in 1936, the Christiansburg Post Office, a neat and sophisticated work despite its diminutive size, is an excellent demonstration of the federal presence in a country town. The modified Georgian work, like many others in the program, was designed by Louis A. Simon, chief architect of the U.S. Postal Service. A lobby mural by Paul DeTroot, depicting local events of the French and Indian and Revolutionary wars, is typical of the accomplished public art sponsored by the Works Progress Administration. *(154–27) VLR: 06/20/89; NRHP: 02/01/91.*

JAMES CHARLTON FARM, *Radford vicinity.* The house built ca. 1810 for James Charlton carries an aura of great age. Charlton, proprietor of 1,500 acres and a slave owner, employed log construction for what is a unique surviving example in Montgomery County of a double-pile log house devoid of a center passage. Such a room arrangement suggests a Germanic influence which may stem from the fact that Charlton was a native of Pennsylvania's Lancaster County. The double-pile plan is reflected in the pair of stone end chimneys (the rooms opposite have no heat source). Like many early log houses, this one was sheathed in weatherboards, and sections of early beaded weatherboarding remain. The exterior underwent remodeling in the mid–19th century when it received its bracketed cornice and scalloped bargeboards. The stone chimney of an original kitchen remains along with several later outbuildings. *(60–137) VLR: 06/20/89; NRHP: 11/13/89.*

CHRISTIANSBURG PRESBYTERIAN CHURCH, *107 West Main Street, Christiansburg.* The Christiansburg Presbyterian Church is one of a related group of Greek Revival churches concentrated in and around the Roanoke Valley. Common features of these buildings are the temple form, usually with a portico *in antis;* meticulous brickwork; and a square belfry framed with paired pilasters and topped by a steeple. The architectural details mostly are adapted from builders' pattern books, particu-

larly those of Asher Benjamin who popularized the Greek Revival style for local builders. The church was erected in 1853 by James E. Crush of Fincastle, who was assisted by the brothers Samuel M. and James W. Hickok. In contrast to the many mundane small-town churches of the period, Christiansburg Presbyterian displays remarkable inventiveness in the simplification of its classical details. Presbyterians came to Montgomery County in the late 18th century; the Christiansburg congregation was organized in 1827. *(154–03) VLR: 06/21/77; NRHP: 01/30/78.*

CROCKETT SPRINGS COTTAGE, *Alleghany Springs vicinity.* A relic of an era when western Virginia's many mineral springs were the destination of hundreds seeking relief from aches and other ailments, as well as for the pleasures of leisurely social intercourse, the Crockett Springs Cottage is the only remaining historic structure of a once-popular place. Crockett Springs, one of Montgomery County's several spas, opened in 1889 under the ownership of the newly founded Virginia Arsenic Bromide and Lithia Springs Company. It claimed its waters were an effective treatment for maladies ranging from eczema to insomnia. The two-unit building was originally among several that framed a rambling wooden hotel. It was equipped with the inevitable front porch, a venue for relaxing and enjoying the mountain air. Crockett Springs was the county's last operating spa when it closed in 1939. The cabin is now part of a religious campground. *(60–487) VLR: 06/20/89; NRHP: 11/13/89.*

CURRIE HOUSE, *1105 Highland Circle, Blacksburg.* The Currie house stands as a highly proficient and personal expression of 1960s Modernism, an architectural style influenced by the International Style of earlier decades. A rare instance where the architect was his own client, the house was designed in 1960 by Leonard J. Currie, head of the Virginia Polytechnic Institute School of Architecture, for his own residence. Currie was a student and former colleague of both Walter Gropius and Marcel Breuer, leading proponents of the International Style. He incorporated into his design their penchant for strong horizontality and large glass areas. Competed in 1961, the house won American Institute of Architecture awards in 1962 and 1982. Currie departed somewhat from his mentors' industrial character by using a spreading hipped roof, a feature reminiscent of the works of Frank Lloyd Wright. Currie sold the house in 1966 to its present owner. *(150–19) VLR: 04/20/94; NRHP: 09/14/94.*

CROMER HOUSE (HOGAN FARM), *Childress vicinity.* The log house is one of America's icons. Taking advantage of a seemingly endless supply of timber, hundreds of log dwellings were erected throughout the Appalachian region. While many survive, a log house still evokes a certain reverence. The Cromer house, a single-pen, rectangular log dwelling, is among the best preserved of Montgomery County's most prevalent type of log house. Though log construction was used by the earliest settlers, this example was likely built in the early 19th century. The house is interesting for having its log construction exposed both inside and out and for having exposed beaded ceiling joists and ceiling boards inside. By the mid–19th century, logs were considered a pedestrian material and normally were hidden behind sheathing or plaster. After standing unoccupied for several decades, the Cromer house is undergoing long-term restoration. *(60–121) VLR: 06/20/89; NRHP: 11/13/89.*

EARHART FARM, *Ellett vicinity.* This farmstead was established by the locally prominent Earhart family. The property was among the holdings of George Earhart (born ca. 1773), and the complex was probably built around 1856 by Earhart for his son Henry (born ca. 1838) as he came of age. Land tax records show that the tract acquired improvements valued at $2,000 in that year. The center-passage frame dwelling has an element of sophistication with the use of a pilastered and paneled wall under the porch, a treatment similar to that at Solitude on the Virginia Polytechnic Institute campus. Purely vernacular, however, is the log kitchen nearby (shown), an important example of a domestic outbuilding of the period. Perched on a slope, the kitchen has a limestone foundation forming a storage cellar. The exposed logs preserve early mud and wood chinking and traces of exterior whitewash. *(60–380) VLR: 06/20/89; NRHP: 11/13/89.*

GEORGE EARHART HOUSE, *Ellett vicinity.* A reminder of the persistence of traditional dwelling forms, this brick I-house was built ca. 1840 for George Earhart's residence on his 537-acre farm on the North Fork of the Roanoke River. The I-house was popular among the more temperate and frugal farming families of the antebellum period. Its attractive simplicity was not based on economic necessity but on doctrines that held no place for stylistic trappings. Here the chief embellishments are the molded-brick cornices, which were originally developed as fireproof alternatives to wooden cornices but became a regional decorative motif. Although the I-house was a widely popular form, only a handful of brick examples remain in the county. George Earhart lived here until his death in 1880. From the late 1880s to 1902 the property was used by Montgomery County as a "Poor-House Farm." It is now in private ownership. *(60–300) VLR: 06/20/89; NRHP: 11/13/89.*

EAST MAIN STREET HISTORIC DISTRICT, *Christiansburg.* Up the hill from the once-bustling commercial core of this county seat, the East Main Street residential area preserves an air of genteel decorum, one appropriate for this fashionable old quarter. The shady neighborhood is marked principally by freestanding houses from the turn of the century onward, although two early dwellings, the antebellum Barnett-Montague house and the log Lane-Moore house, provide historic perspective. The former, an early 19th-century hall-parlor house, has a log kitchen wing. Other dwellings include typical small-town examples of the Queen Anne, Colonial Revival, and Foursquare styles. Pepper Street is lined with brick bungalows. Accenting the district are three institutional buildings: the Christiansburg Municipal Building, the former Christiansburg High School, and the former Christiansburg Elementary School, the latter two dating from the early 20th century. *(154–01) VLR: 06/20/89; NRHP: 01/10/91.*

EDGEMONT CHRISTIAN CHURCH, *Mud Pike Road, Christiansburg vicinity.* Built in 1883, the Edgemont Christian Church was organized in the mid-1800s by Cephas Shelburne, who moved to Montgomery County in 1843 and served as an elder in the Cypress Grove Christian Church in Snowville. The congregation first worshiped in a log building that also served as a schoolhouse and stood on the site of the present church building, property purchased in 1856. Dr. Chester Bullard, famous leader of the Christian Church (Disciples of Christ) in Southwest Virginia, preached at the dedication service here. Although Edgemont Church reflects the simplicity of this basically congregational denomination, the building was given more architectural treatment than usual. The otherwise straightforward structure is set off by its segmental arched windows, pedimented gable end, and pilastered corners. The church continues in regular use. *(60–139) VLR: 06/20/89; NRHP: 11/13/89.*

EVANS HOUSE, *Prices Fork vicinity.* The I-house, a center-passage dwelling, was the most popular of the mid-19th-century house types in Montgomery County. The Evans house is an interesting variation in that it has an irregular five-bay facade rather than the more standard symmetrical three-bay format. It is also one of the few examples constructed of brick. The brickwork employs a functional, though not usual, six-course American bond and has a molded-brick cornice, a detail commonly found on vernacular brick houses in the Shenandoah Valley and Southwest Virginia. Ignoring any influence from contemporary architectural fashions, the house was built ca. 1860 shortly after the farm was presented by Adam Wall to his daughter Ellen and her husband, George R. Evans. The Eastlake porch and present window sash were added ca. 1900. *(60–223) VLR: 06/20/89; NRHP: 11/13/89.*

FORT VAUSE ARCHAEOLOGICAL SITE, *Shawsville.* A simple palisaded fort was established here in the mid–18th century. The fort was attacked by Indians in June 1756, and a relief party led by Maj. Andrew Lewis arrived too late to save most of its occupants. The fort was quickly rebuilt by Capt. Peter Hogg and probably was a composite earth and palisade structure. George Washington inspected Fort Vause in October 1756. Archaeological test excavations undertaken in 1968 identified the location and general size of the second fort as well as evidence of its predecessor. More extensive examination may provide data on living conditions along Virginia's frontier during the mid– to late 18th century. *(60–17) VLR: 12/02/69; BHR EASEMENT.*

FOTHERINGAY, *Shawsville vicinity.* Fotheringay was the home of George Hancock (1754–1820), a colonel in the Virginia Line during the Revolutionary War and aide-de-camp to Count Casimir Pulaski. He later served in both the Virginia House of Delegates and the U.S. Congress. Hancock's daughter Julia was married to the explorer William Clark. Dramatically placed against a steep mountain, Hancock's house, built ca. 1815, is an elegant expression of the Federal style for what was a distant area. The ornate interior woodwork is highlighted by chimneypieces and doorways decorated with motifs copied from design books by the English architect William Pain. The delicately carved work exhibits the high quality of the area's post-Revolutionary craftsmanship. As originally built, the house lacked the two bays south of the portico, resulting in an unbalanced look. An architecturally compatible wing added in the 1950s made the facade symmetrical. *(60–05) VLR: 05/13/69; NRHP: 11/17/69.*

NEALY GORDON FARM, *Bush Harbor vicinity.* The farmsteads of the Appalachian uplands are characterized by the frontier rusticity inherent in the use of logs, the most available and easily worked material. The Nealy Gordon farm is among the county's more complete of such complexes, which were crafted by the people who would use them. Demonstrating the perpetuation of vernacular forms, the residence, a square, single-pen log house, was built by Nealy Gordon in the last years of the 19th century and is one of a handful of square-plan log houses left in the county. The vernacular tradition was continued when a frame addition was built ca. 1900, giving the house the popular saddlebag plan. The most prominent structure in the important assemblage of contemporary farm buildings is a barn (shown) constructed of untrimmed saddle-notched logs. Other structures include a meat house, a smaller log barn, and a corncrib. *(60–392) VLR: 06/20/89; NRHP: 11/13/89.*

JOHN GRAYSON HOUSE (GRAYSON), *Graysontown vicinity.* The I-house, a two-story, gable-roof dwelling with a center passage and end chimneys, marked a revolution in early 19th-century American housing. The form brought an order and dignity to vernacular dwellings and became a prevalent element of the landscape, especially in Virginia. The John Grayson house is regarded as one of the county's most pristine examples of the type. Here the otherwise plain form acquired a stateliness through the use of a two-level pedimented portico. With its rear ell, the house has a total of ten rooms. The wainscot, mantels, and floors are original. The recently restored house, renamed Grayson by its owners, was built ca. 1850 for John Grayson, a member of a family of millers who established the settlement of Graysontown in 1847. *(60–118) VLR: 06/20/89; NRHP: 11/13/89.*

GRAYSON-GRAVELY HOUSE, *Graysontown.* Occupying the edge of a steeply sloped rise in Graysontown, this festive Victorian house is a surprisingly bold architectural statement for a somnolent hamlet. Particularly striking is the idiosyncratic treatment of the porch gable and second-floor window hoods, which are gaily decked out with patterned shingles, scrolled brackets, turned finials, and lacy sawn facias. Distinctive as well is the three-level side tower with its sawn-work railing. The house was built ca. 1881 for Ephraim C. Grayson, member of the village's local founding family. It was sold in 1889 to J. H. H. Gravely who moved the house to its present site from farther up the hill. Local tradition has it that the house received its decorative flourishes at the behest of Mrs. Gravely after the move. Much of the material may have been produced in the local Grayson family sawmill. *(60–177) VLR: 06/20/89; NRHP: 11/13/89.*

GRAYSONTOWN METHODIST CHURCH, *Graysontown.* The importance of spiritual nourishment in rural America is manifest in the plethora of small wooden churches dotting the nation's villages and countryside. These churches, especially those erected in the earnest decades of the late 19th century, are endowed with an austere dignity reflecting the demeanor of the mainly Protestant denominations they served. The 1896 Graysontown Methodist Church, with its plain rectangular sanctuary enlivened by "American Gothic" windows, typifies the country-church aesthetic. It achieves heightened presence, however, with its shingled vestibule and bracketed tower. At its dedication service the church was called "truly a light house and soul saving station." Built by Brother Cook and other members of the congregation, it was constructed using mainly donated materials. Declining membership led the Methodist Conference to close the church in 1976. The building was then purchased by local citizens, and now it functions as an interdenominational church. *(60–109) VLR: 06/20/89; NRHP: 11/13/89.*

GUERRANT HOUSE, *Pilot.* The principal building in the easily missed crossroads of Pilot, the Guerrant house was erected sometime after 1870 on or near the site of the Pilot House, an antebellum hostelry. The dwelling was built on property owned by William C. Guerrant, an entrepreneur who in 1870 was paying taxes on over 11,000 acres. Local lore suggests that the house was intended to serve some hotel function, a notion supported by the fact that the floor plan was arranged so that only one internal door connected the front half of the house with the rear, each section having its own staircase. Whatever its intended function, the dwelling, with its hipped roof, columned porch, and regular facade, is one of the most prominent late 19th-century houses in the county to be influenced by the Colonial Revival style, a style that was to dominate the architecture of succeeding decades. *(60–07) VLR: 06/20/89; NRHP: 11/13/89.*

THOMAS HALL HOUSE (CATALPA HALL FARM), *Childress vicinity.* Unlike many other societies, where tradition and social status rigidly dictate architectural norms, Americans have felt little restraint in deciding for themselves the appearance of their homes. Those who have eschewed standard models have given us interesting expressions of individual taste. Thomas Hall's house of 1882 illustrates one person's attempt to make a standard house form stand apart from the uninspired vernacular of the neighborhood. Here Hall, perhaps belatedly influenced by pattern-book fashion, applied board-and-batten siding to a traditional I-house. He also gave his residence a distinct if austere monumentality by using a two-story portico with paired square columns. The result is an odd though effective composition, unparalleled in the region. The slate roof adds a further touch of "class" to this eye-catching naive work. *(60–82) VLR: 06/20/89; NRHP: 11/13/89.*

HORNBARGER STORE, *Vicker's Switch.* An image of the innocent days of turn-of-the-century small-town America is captured in this toylike store building, one of two remaining commercial buildings in the tiny railroad community of Vicker's Switch. It was built in 1910–11 by Edward Hornbarger and is somewhat old-fashioned for its date, being embellished with a bracketed cornice both at the roofline and above the large windowed shop front. Like many such structures, the upper floor was given over to residential use; here it is reached by a porch on the east side. Since cessation of its function as a store, the center of the shop front has been modified for conversion into a garage door. The modification did not affect the main shop windows and the large clerestory. The residential upper-floor area is still occupied. *(60–153) VLR: 06/20/89; NRHP: 11/13/89.*

HOWARD-BELL-FEATHER HOUSE, *Riner vicinity.* On a hillside above Elliott Creek, the Howard-Bell-Feather house is Montgomery County's only early 19th-century stone house. Though stone is readily available, for no apparent reason other than the fact that stone is more difficult to handle than brick or wood, the county never developed a strong tradition of stone construction. Stone buildings in Southwest Virginia are generally associated with German settlers, but there is no evidence that the builder here was ethnic German. The severely plain vernacular house was probably built ca. 1810 for William Howard. The original three-room plan was changed when a partition was removed, although some simple early trim remains. An early owner, the Rev. John Bell (died 1833), along with members of the Feather family, lies buried in a family cemetery. The property is still owned by Feather family descendants. *(60–24) VLR: 06/20/89; NRHP: 11/13/89.*

KEISTER HOUSE, *607 Giles Road, Blacksburg.* Now part of Blacksburg, the Keister house is one of Montgomery County's only examples of a hall-parlor dwelling of brick construction. The original house on the property was a log structure built soon after 1800. The brick house was constructed in the 1830s and was connected to the log house by a corridor. Tax records show that John Keister owned the property in 1840; the place remained in the Keister family until a 1935 foreclosure. The log section was demolished and the corridor incorporated in an addition after the foreclosure sale. Despite the loss of the earlier dwelling, the brick section remains without significant alteration. The four-bay Flemish bond facade has a molded-brick cornice. The first-floor rooms have Federal mantels with sunbursts and reeded end blocks. Early graining survives on some of the woodwork. *(150–5014) VLR: 06/20/89; NRHP: 11/13/89.*

KENTLAND FARM HISTORIC AND ARCHAEOLOGICAL DISTRICT, *Whitethorn.* James Randal Kent (1792–1867) assembled this plantation in the early 19th century and by 1860 had holdings of 6,000 acres worked by 123 slaves. Kent completed his immense plantation house in 1835. One of the area's most ambitious early dwellings, the brick mansion has sophisticated Federal detailing including important carved mantels. The prehistoric archaeological resources of Kentland include the sites of a Late Woodland–period village and camp sites. The district also incorporates Buchanans Bottom, one of the earliest patented tracts on the New River drainage (1750), as well as a portion of Adam Harmon's ford, the southern terminus of the mid-18th-century Shenandoah Valley Indian Road. Also in the district are several late 19th- and early 20th-century farm buildings and the 19th-century Kent-Cowan Mill. The property is now owned and managed by Virginia Tech. *(60–202) VLR: 04/17/91; NRHP: 07/03/91.*

MICHAEL KINZER HOUSE, *Blacksburg vicinity.* While many of Montgomery County's antebellum houses show the influence of contemporary architectural fashion, the majority were vernacular structures of uncompromising simplicity. Among the latter is Michael Kinzer's ca. 1845 brick house, a solidly functional dwelling devoid of the decorative devices purveyed by many architectural pattern books. A locally popular vernacular form, the house has a four-bay, two-room format with each of the two first-floor rooms entered by its own door. The primary decorative motif is the molded-brick cornice, a common feature of western Virginia's folk housing. Near the house is the archaeological site of the temporary brick kiln where the brick used in the house was fired. Though it was common practice to make brick on site, this is one of the only kiln sites in the region to have been studied. *(150–5024) VLR: 06/20/89; NRHP: 11/13/89.*

LAFAYETTE HISTORIC DISTRICT, *Lafayette.* This level area at the confluence of the north and south forks of the Roanoke River has been occupied since the mid–18th century. A Presbyterian meetinghouse was here before 1769 but did not prosper. The spot attracted attention in the 1820s because of its potential for becoming a commercial hub serviced by riverine traffic. The town was officially established in 1828 and laid out on six blocks. By 1835 it was a busy place, having forty-three houses, a large mill, tavern, shops, a shoe factory, and a tanyard. The extant Methodist church (shown), a simple brick meetinghouse, was erected in 1848 on the public square. Growth halted in 1846 when Lafayette was bypassed by the Southwestern Turnpike. Today the tiny village has about a half-dozen antebellum structures amid a scattering of later ones. Though a dormant settlement, off the beaten path, the village maintains its historic character. *(60–418) VLR: 06/20/89; NRHP: 01/10/91.*

FRANK LAWRENCE HOUSE, *Pilot vicinity.* The ability of mail-order companies to bring stylish, well-crafted houses to the American countryside is clearly demonstrated in the Frank Lawrence house, a commodious multigabled Colonial Revival residence in sparsely populated southern Montgomery County. The house was built around 1918 using a model from a Sears, Roebuck and Company catalog. Most of its elements were shipped by railroad. The Sears catalog describes the model as a "large modern residence with a large front porch with Colonial columns." Interior details included with it were "colonnaded openings between hall and living room; built-in bookcases with leaded glass doors in living room; china closet in dining room; and semi-open stairs." The house, model C215, was offered from 1911 to 1917 and was priced at $1,561. The Frank Lawrence house is the only dwelling in Montgomery County positively identified as a mail-order structure. *(60–03) VLR: 06/20/89; NRHP: 11/13/89.*

LINKOUS-KIPPS HOUSE, *Blacksburg vicinity.* The weatherboarding on this L-shaped farmhouse masks one of the county's most substantial log dwellings. The oldest section, the east wing, is said to have been built by Henry Linkous, Sr., following his purchase of the property in 1799. The west wing, also log, was likely added by Henry Linkous, Jr., after he inherited the farm in 1822. The house was substantially improved in the 1850s when a stair was inserted in what was formerly an open passage. Despite the antebellum modernizations, the interior preserves many early finishes, including exposed ceiling joists, unpainted floorboards, and exposed log wall surfaces. The log walls of the east-wing parlor retain a coating of rags and whitewash. Weatherboarding may have been applied in the 1850s, although most of the present siding is early 20th century. The present owner, a member of the Linkous family, has undertaken a careful restoration. *(150–5020) VLR: 06/20/89; NRHP: 11/13/89.*

MADISON FARM HISTORIC AND ARCHAEOLOGICAL DISTRICT, *Shawsville vicinity.* Among the numerous historic resources in the narrow valley of the South Fork of the Roanoke River is the Madison farm, established by William Madison and his wife, Elizabeth Preston Madison, on a part of the property acquired by his father, John Madison, ca. 1766. Madison or his wife, daughter of William Preston, built the two-story, hall-parlor house in the late 18th century. Though altered and expanded through several generations, the house, still owned by descendants, remains endowed with an aura of antiquity. Adjacent are several early outbuildings including a log meat house, a log corncrib, and a slave house. James Madison, another son of John Madison, was the first bishop of the Episcopal Diocese of Virginia. The farm has a series of important archaeological sites including sites of outbuildings and a Late Woodland–period (ca. A.D. 800–1600) Indian village site known as the Marye site. *(60–565) VLR: 06/20/89; NRHP: 01/25/91.*

JOSEPH MCDONALD FARM, *Prices Fork vicinity.* Maintaining an image of a simpler time, this farmstead preserves the county's finest collection of early vernacular outbuildings. The dwelling, one of the county's oldest hall-parlor log houses, is a residence type favored by the region's earliest settlers. It was built ca. 1800 by Joseph McDonald on property he purchased in 1763. McDonald was an enterprising individual who, in addition to farming, operated a powder mill, gristmills, a tannery, and a blacksmith shop. Joseph McDonald was also a religious man and held camp meetings here. Although expanded and changed by generations of McDonalds, the house's log core is intact. The complex includes a log kitchen, log springhouse, log corncrib, and frame barn. Still owned by the McDonald family, the house has recently been rehabilitated. *(60–235) VLR: 06/20/89; NRHP: 02/01/91.*

MILLER SOUTHSIDE HISTORIC DISTRICT, *Blacksburg.* These shady residential streets present a model image of a wholesome small-town neighborhood of the first half of the 20th century. The houses, though unpretentious, are comfortable, well built, and well designed. With an abundance of lawn and trees, they make the perfect setting for nurturing the American family ideal. Individuality is preserved through some half-dozen stylistic idioms including Dutch Colonial, Tudor Revival, Georgian Revival, Bungalow, and Foursquare. The grid-plan blocks comprise two contiguous additions. The first was a 1913 development by the Southside Land Company. The second, the Miller Addition, was laid out in 1919. An openness and cohesion were achieved with a 20-foot setback and minimum construction value. Virginia Tech architectural professor Clinton Harriman Cowgill helped set the architectural tone in the 1930s by designing some ten houses, all variations of the Colonial and Tudor revivals. *(150–109) VLR: 06/20/89; NRHP: 01/11/91.*

MONTGOMERY PRIMITIVE BAPTIST CHURCH, *Merrimac.* Erected in 1922, this severely plain church reflects the extreme simplicity of the religious tenets of this branch of Baptists. The Primitive Baptists grew out of an early 19th-century reaction against missionary and tract activities. Believing that changes compromised the basic spiritual simplicity of Calvinist principles, they withdrew from the mainline Baptist church and identified themselves as Primitive Baptists. Their liturgy was the simplest possible, and thus their services required only fundamental shelter. Primitive Baptists were a strong force in Montgomery County until the 20th century. The earliest churches either have disappeared or have been replaced by modern structures. The Montgomery Primitive Baptist Church is the county's oldest and stands essentially unaltered from its original form. The interior is sheathed in unpainted tongue-and-groove boards. Plain wooden pews fill the space, and a pair of wood stoves provide heat. *(60–175) VLR: 06/20/89; NRHP: 11/13/89.*

NORTH FORK VALLEY RURAL HISTORIC DISTRICT. The North Fork Valley of the Roanoke River extends for approximately nine miles from the Roanoke County line to Lusters Gate. The exceptionally scenic area preserves an agrarian landscape of historic significance spanning the years from 1746 to the 1940s. The tangible relics of agricultural practices include fields, fence lines, barns, and other farm structures. Farm buildings of the early 20th century make up the majority of the resources. The domestic buildings cover a broad range of vernacular and high-style house types, mostly dating from the early 19th century on. Log structures are common. The I-house, either brick or frame, was a popular house form. Many of the early houses preserve outbuildings such as smokehouses, offices, and springhouses, usually placed adjacent to vegetable gardens. A focal point of the district is the frame McDonalds Mill (shown), erected in the 1850s. *(60–574) VLR: 06/20/89; NRHP: 02/01/91.*

THE OAKS, *311 East Main Street, Christiansburg.* A classic example of a Queen Anne residence, The Oaks was originally the home of William H. Pierce, a local insurance executive and landowner. Pierce had the house built in 1893, and here he and his wife raised six children. He died in 1949, and his widow continued to live here until her death in 1968. This seventy-five-year occupancy by the original owners accounts for the remarkably unaltered state of the house. The large but homey residence has the requisite elements of an American Queen Anne dwelling: complex roofline, corner tower, shingled and weatherboarded sheathing, and hospitable wraparound porch. The porch is a uniquely American feature of this essentially British style. Decorative pseudo-half-timbering ornaments the gables. The interior preserves original woodwork including a Jacobean-style stair. The immaculately maintained structure is now a bed-and-breakfast inn. *(154–01–05) VLR: 04/20/94; NRHP: 07/15/94.*

OLD CHRISTIANSBURG INDUSTRIAL INSTITUTE AND SCHAEFFER MEMORIAL BAPTIST CHURCH, *High Street, Christiansburg.* On a promontory above the town of Christiansburg, the Old Christiansburg Institute (Hill School) and the Schaeffer Memorial Baptist Church, both built in 1885, are monuments in the social, educational, and religious history of Montgomery County's black community. Through the early efforts of Capt. Charles S. Schaeffer, an agent of the Freedmen's Bureau and later an ordained Baptist pastor, formal instruction was begun for the area's blacks in 1866, five years before the public school system was established. Technical, academic, and religious training were emphasized during Schaeffer's thirty-year affiliation. In 1895 the school was reorganized under the direction of Booker T. Washington, who instituted a much-expanded curriculum. The church, with its 1888 frame annex, remains in active use. Industrial training continued at the Hill School until 1953. Since 1967 the school building has served as a community center. *(154–5004) VLR: 05/16/78; NRHP: 04/06/79.*

PHILLIPS-RONALD HOUSE (FIVE CHIMNEYS), *Washington and Draper streets, Blacksburg.* This Blacksburg landmark was built ca. 1852 for John R. Phillips, a merchant and physician who also was a director of the Olin and Preston Institute, a forerunner of the Virginia Polytechnic Institute. Phillips experienced financial difficulties and sold the house, which he apparently never occupied, in 1853 to Nicholas M. Ronald, a merchant and banker. In 1986 the property was purchased by the town of Blacksburg, which today uses the house for offices and meeting rooms. The house is one of the region's few antebellum dwellings to employ a one-story, double-pile format. For many years it has been known popularly as Five Chimneys for the conspicuous quintet of chimneys that project from its side walls. The late Victorian porch was added shortly after 1891 when the place was sold by the Ronald family to O. C. Peters. *(150–15) VLR: 06/20/89; NRHP: 11/13/89.*

PHLEGAR BUILDING, *2 South Franklin Street, Christiansburg.* The Phlegar Building, long a familiar fixture on Christiansburg's public square, appears at first observation as an example of a late 19th-century small-town office building. It actually incorporates remnants of the early 19th-century Montgomery County clerk's office, originally a two-room, one-story building with a Flemish bond facade, sections of which remain visible. When a new courthouse was built in 1834, the clerk's functions were accommodated elsewhere, and the building was rented out for law offices. In 1897 it was purchased by Archer A. Phlegar who added the upper stories, the two-level Eastlake gallery, and a large rear wing. The attic story was left unfinished; its windows merely ventilated the space. The property was reacquired by the county in recent decades, and the building currently houses county offices. *(154–07) VLR: 06/20/89; NRHP: 11/13/89.*

PIEDMONT CAMP MEETING GROUNDS, *Piedmont.*
The Piedmont campgrounds had their origin in 1873 when a Methodist chapel was established here. This occurred at a time when the Methodist denomination began a nationwide movement focusing on the doctrine of holiness or sanctification. The movement later led to a split in the church, resulting in the eventual establishment of the Pentecostal denomination. The Piedmont Methodists held a tent revival at the chapel in 1910, but the Pentecostal element of the group was forced to set up their own camp meeting across the road. An annual camp meeting has been held here ever since, with permanent cottages erected in the 1930s and 1940s. An open-sided tabernacle was built in 1939. The Methodist chapel and camp were eventually incorporated into the complex. The campgrounds provide a tangible link with 19th-century spiritual fervor and show evidence of the strong influence of religion on rural life. *(60–500) VLR: 06/20/89; NRHP: 01/10/91.*

PRESTON HOUSE, *U.S. Route 11/460, Christiansburg vicinity.* The connoisseurship of America's roadside eccentricities is ever-growing as appreciation for American individualism increases. Seekers of the bizarre have been rewarded for several decades with the spectacle of William Preston's remarkable work of self-expression prominently located on U.S. Route 11/460. A do-it-yourself fairyland bungalow, Preston's handiwork, begun in 1942, literally was his dream house. As Preston explained to his sister, "One night I had a dream of this house, so I built it just like the dream." The result is a conglomeration of towers, porches, gables, and sawn ornament, all with a gaudy color scheme. Although some of the ornaments, particularly the latticework, have been lost, they are well documented with photographs and could be returned, restoring this landmark of folk aesthetic to its full intensity. *(60–270) VLR: 06/20/89.*

PRICES FORK HISTORIC DISTRICT, *Prices Fork.*
Prices Fork evolved in the mid–19th century on lands owned by the Price family. The stringtown settlement developed on the old Pepper's Ferry Road at a fork with the Brown's Ferry Road. Although a sprinkling of buildings existed by the Civil War, the linear village's present buildings date from the 1870s or later. The principal historic structures today are the 1871 James Bain Price house and the adjacent store building. Nearby are the Prices Fork Methodist Church and the former St. Mark's Lutheran Church (shown), now in residential use. Both are simple wooden country churches. The district's western end is marked by a store and house built by another member of the Price family. Numerous large trees formerly gave visual cohesion to the scattered buildings. The historic ambience recently has been severely compromised by road widening and other highway "improvements." *(60–224) VLR: 06/20/89; NRHP: 01/10/91.*

REED FARM (BLANKENSHIP FARM), *Ellett vicinity.*
The Reed farm complex was established in the early 20th century by H. Cephus Reed. The residence is a conventional foursquare dwelling. Highly unconventional, however, is the fourteen-sided barn Reed built in 1929. The visually striking structure, covered by a spreading faceted roof, was inspired by agricultural writings of the period that espoused the economy of round or polygonal barns. Such barns, it was claimed, were more practical than rectangular barns because less distance between workstations was involved for barn workers, and such structures required fewer materials and took less time to build. Though a reaction to rectangular barns, round and polygonal barns never really caught on. Despite its shape, the Reed barn uses two traditional features, an interior center aisle and an attached concrete silo. *(60–386) VLR: 06/20/89; NRHP: 11/13/89.*

RIFE HOUSE, *Shawsville vicinity.* Proudly placed in plain view of travelers along U.S. Highway 11/460, the historic way to the West, this large frame house was built ca. 1905 for K. M. Rife, a recent arrival to the area from the coalfields of western Virginia. Rife used his new home as a display of his affluence. Little altered over the past ninety years, the house is one of the county's few textbook examples of the Queen Anne style. Developed in late 19th-century England, the Queen Anne style was a revival of 17th- and early 18th-century vernacular forms. It was given a distinctly American flavor here with the use of weatherboarded walls and a wraparound front porch. The general appearance was likely based on illustrations published in house catalogs. The materials and decorative details probably were purchased by suppliers in Roanoke, then experiencing a building boom. *(60–443) VLR: 06/20/89; NRHP: 11/13/89.*

RINER HISTORIC DISTRICT, *Riner.* Riner began before the Civil War as a spontaneous, unplanned crossroads settlement serving the surrounding farming community. First known as Five Forks for its situation at the junction of five roads, the hamlet offered mercantile, religious, and milling services to the neighboring folk. Riner thrived after the mid-1850s construction of the Christiansburg and Floyd Turnpike through the village. By the 1870s it boasted a store, meetinghouse, school, lumberyard, tanyard, hotel, shoe factory, barrel factory, blacksmith shop, and tobacco factory. Since bypassed by progress, Riner today is a somnolent relic of a bygone era. The heart of the historic area is marked by buildings either empty or no longer serving their original function, among them the 1908 Methodist Episcopal church, the 1913 former Bank of Riner; the mid-19th-century Jonathan Hall house-store, and the ca. 1910 Surface Mill. *(60–44) VLR: 06/20/89; NRHP: 01/10/91.*

SHAWSVILLE HISTORIC DISTRICT, *Shawsville.* This tiny settlement began in the 1850s as a rail stop for nearby Allegheny Springs. It took its name from Charles B. Shaw, principal engineer for Virginia during whose term the Southwest Turnpike was built through the nascent town. From the 1870s into the 1920s, Shawsville developed slowly but steadily, acquiring along a short stretch of turnpike a commercial main street of shops, a general store, dwellings, and a church, all in the vernacular of small-town America. The most architecturally prestigious structure, the classical-style Bank of Shawsville, was built in 1910. Growth essentially ceased in the 1930s when through traffic was rerouted to the new Lee Highway to the south. Commerce received another blow in the 1970s when the depot closed and later burned. The town's remaining fabric, now largely idle, is an interesting though plaintive vestige of a community that was. *(60–456) VLR: 06/20/89; NRHP: 01/10/91.*

SMITHFIELD, *Blacksburg.* Smithfield was the home of William Preston (1729–1783), Revolutionary officer, surveyor, and member of the House of Burgesses, who was instrumental in opening up much of the region to settlement. His L-shaped frame residence, built in the mid-1770s, is an expression of architectural sophistication on the edge of the late 18th-century backcountry. Similar in design to a prosperous Tidewater Virginia plantation house, Smithfield has the generous scale and careful detailing typical of the colonial Virginia idiom, even boasting a stylish Chinese lattice stair railing. Preston's son James Patton Preston and a grandson, John Buchanan Floyd, both of whom served as governors of Virginia, were born at Smithfield. The house was acquired by the Association for the Preservation of Virginia Antiquities in 1959 and subsequently restored. It is a museum of the Preston family and their role in the life of early Southwest Virginia. *(150–5017) VLR: 11/05/68; NRHP: 11/17/69.*

SOLITUDE, *Virginia Tech campus, Blacksburg.* In a placid corner of the busy campus of Virginia Polytechnic Institute and State University, next to the "Duck Pond," Solitude is a much-evolved old homestead. It grew from a two-story log core probably erected ca. 1801 by James Patton Preston on land purchased from the heirs of Caspar Barger. A log wing was added in 1834, and in 1859 Preston's son, Robert Preston, remodeled the house, adding a frame wing. The veranda and provincial Greek Revival trim were added then also. With its two log outbuildings and interior woodwork of various periods, the complex is a textbook of early architectural details and construction techniques. In 1872 the property was purchased by the Virginia Agricultural and Mechanical College, the forerunner of Virginia Tech, to serve as the school's research farm. Solitude now houses an Appalachian studies center. *(150–100–3) VLR: 06/21/88; NRHP: 05/05/89.*

SOUTH FRANKLIN STREET HISTORIC DISTRICT, *Christiansburg.* South Franklin Street was platted in the 1790s and was gradually built up over the next century. Today the historic section preserves a predictable mix of residential types with two individually significant dwellings. The mid-19th-century Miller house, a frame I-house fronted by square columns, was the home of Charles Edie Miller, cousin of the noted folk artist Lewis Miller who visited here and drew many scenes of life in the town and surrounding area. Unique is the dwelling known as The Huts (shown), designed in 1919 by Mrs. William A. Rice who had lived in Rhodesia with her husband, a tobacco executive. Upon settling in Christiansburg, Mrs. Rice determined to build a house reminiscent of the native round huts she had known in Africa. The Huts is apparently the only Virginia house whose design is unquestionably inspired by African precedent. *(154–10) VLR: 06/20/89; NRHP: 01/10/91.*

SURFACE HOUSE, *High Street, Christiansburg.* Ornament was a hallmark of late 19th-century architecture throughout the Western world. From the simplest dwelling to the grandest public work, architectural decoration was considered essential for dignity of appearance. Even in a small mountain community such as Christiansburg, a cottage could find itself decked out in wooden finery, most likely produced by a local woodworking company. Christiansburg's Surface house, on one of the community's highest hills, is a simple one-story abode, but one made elegant and charming through the judicious use of ornament. Here turned posts, bracketed cornice, and sawn lintels give character to an otherwise unassertive work. A rare example for Montgomery County of an ornamented cottage, the house was built ca. 1870 for Frank Surface and remained in the Surface family until 1979 when it was sold to its present owners who carefully restored it. *(154–43) VLR: 06/20/89; NRHP: 11/13/89.*

THOMAS-CONNER HOUSE, *104 Draper Road, Blacksburg.*
A handsome and well-maintained Italianate residence, the
Thomas-Conner house was built in the 1870s for William
Thomas. It later was inherited by the Conner family who
owned it for many years. Although the house employs the fashionable Italianate detailing of the 1870s, including round-arch
windows and a deep bracketed cornice, the two-story, double-
pile, center-passage format is a traditional residential formula
used in the area over preceding decades. The restrained Italianate style echoes that used in the earliest buildings of Virginia
Tech and may have shared common builders. The house stands
prominently on one of the largest lots in the central town center, signaling the fact that this area had high social status. In recent times the house has been acquired by the town and sensitively adapted for office use. *(150–05) VLR: 06/20/89.*

**TRINITY UNITED
METHODIST
CHURCH,** *Ellett.* The
country church tradi-
tionally has been an es-
sential component of the
peaceful, ordered lifestyle
of the American farmer.
A rural landscape devoid
of these structures, how-
ever modest, would be
incomplete. Ellett's Trinity United Methodist
Church, a plain nave-
plan brick church, is
characteristic of the
many such buildings that
served agrarian commu-
nities. It is set apart from the usual area churches by the use of
a corner tower with a belfry and steeple lending the church an
audible as well as a visual presence in the neighborhood. The
congregation was organized in 1856 on property donated by the
locally prominent Earhart family. The original church fell into
disrepair and was replaced by the present building in 1908–10,
reusing the bricks from the old church. Dedicated in 1913, the
church has been in regular use since and has preserved its simple original interior. *(60–383) VLR: 06/20/89; NRHP: 11/13/89.*

VIRGINIA RAILWAY UNDERPASS, *Route 723, Ellett
vicinity.* This 15-foot-long underpass is an early demonstration
of the use of reinforced concrete rather than stone for arched
bridge construction. By 1900 zealous proponents of more economical, easily formed concrete ensured the material's pre-
dominance for construction of highway bridges and short railway spans. The railway underpasses in Montgomery County
are some of the earliest concrete works in the region and the
only ones in the state to employ a horseshoe form. Why this
particular profile was restricted to this area has not been determined, although with its wider footings this shape probably
was stronger than a straight-sided arch. Additional support for
this span was provided by angled concrete abutments on both
sides. The underpass was built by the Bates and Rogers Construction Co. and completed in 1906. The arch now supports
tracks of the Norfolk Southern system. *(60–573) VLR: 06/20/89;
NRHP: 11/13/89.*

ADAM WALL HOUSE, *Prices Fork vicinity.* Solidity and permanence are conveyed in the massive logs of this old homestead, one of the county's largest early log houses. The two-
story, hall-parlor dwelling was built in 1797–98. It originally
had a German-style center chimney which was removed in a
later alteration. As with most log houses, the logs were hidden
by beaded weatherboarding. Though altered in the mid– and
late 19th century and further modified in recent years, the
house retains much early fabric including Federal mantels and
wide-board wainscoting. It is today the residence for a dairy
farm, owned and operated by the Wall family, who have owned
the property over the past two centuries. While each generation
has left its mark, the house is permeated with an aura of antiquity, a monument to family continuity. *(60–233) VLR: 06/20/89;
NRHP: 11/13/89.*

WALNUT GROVE FARM HISTORIC DISTRICT,
Shawsville vicinity. An example of a prosperous early 20th-century livestock and dairy farm, Walnut Grove was developed by Capt. David Harvey Barger following his purchase of the property in 1890. Barger, who made a fortune in railroads and coal mining, retired to his native Montgomery County to become a gentleman farmer. He built Walnut Grove's porticoed Georgian Revival mansion in 1910 on the site of an earlier house. Structures added to accommodate his farm operation include a dairy-smokehouse, a farm office, a farm manager's house, and two frame barns. Away from the main complex is a visually appealing stuccoed mill (shown) used at one time to produce graham flour, the ingredient of graham crackers, developed as an early health food. The mill, an early 20th-century structure, may incorporate earlier fabric. A mid-19th-century log house is also part of the district. *(60–452) VLR: 06/20/89; NRHP: 01/10/91.*

WALNUT SPRING, *Kanodes Mill vicinity.* Nestled in a vale of well-tended pastures along Toms Creek, Walnut Spring belongs to an important group of Greek Revival farmhouses erected by Montgomery County's antebellum landed families. It stands on land purchased in 1850 by James Randal Kent of Kentland for his daughter Mary Louisa, fiancée of Dr. James Hervey Otey of Bedford. Family history relates that Kent sketched the house plan on the ground with his walking stick. The plan disappointed his daughter who had expected a grander residence. A memo in Major Kent's papers documents the dwelling's craftsmen, costs, and materials. The house was completed in 1855, in time for the Oteys' wedding day, and remains in the hands of their descendants. Except for an 1875 rear addition, the house has been little changed and remains, with its outbuildings, a synthesis of traditional house forms and pattern-book Greek Revival detailing. *(60–243) VLR: 06/20/89; NRHP: 11/13/89.*

WHITETHORN, *Blacksburg vicinity.* The Preston family has left an unrivaled legacy of noteworthy houses scattered through Southwest Virginia. This prosperous and influential clan has been responsible for such landmarks as Smithfield, Solitude, Herondon, and Abingdon's Gen. Francis Preston house, now the Martha Washington Inn. Maintaining the tradition, James Francis Preston, grandson of William Preston of Smithfield, around the time of his marriage in 1855 built a splendid Italianate mansion on his farm Whitethorn, originally part of Smithfield. With its grand scale and fine detailing, the house was in the forefront of contemporary architectural fashion, rivaling prestigious Italianate houses in Richmond or Petersburg. Preston served in both the Mexican War and Civil War. He died of illness in 1862. Though bordered by suburban development, Whitethorn remains a working farm. The L-shaped house is maintained in impeccable condition. *(150–5021) VLR: 06/20/89; NRHP: 11/13/89.*

YELLOW SULPHUR SPRINGS, *Blacksburg vicinity.* Developed in the early 19th century, Yellow Sulphur Springs afforded its patrons the usual middle-class leisure-time and therapeutic pursuits of the mid-Victorian-era mountain resorts. Before the Civil War, the spa was enjoyed by individuals who soon were to make history: Edmund Ruffin, Jubal Early, and P. G. T. Beauregard. Despite the loss of a later main hotel building and several cottages, the original early 19th-century hotel structure with its mid-19th-century galleried facade survives. Also remaining amid a grove of venerable oaks are three cottage rows and an early bowling alley, making the group one of the state's most complete early spa complexes. A visual accent is the polygonal gazebo sheltering the spring. Most of the cottages are now rented as apartments. The hotel building, long in a neglected state, has been restored in recent years. *(60–13) VLR: 09/20/77; NRHP: 09/20/79.*

NELSON COUNTY

In the foothills of Virginia's Piedmont, Nelson County, formed in 1807 from Amherst County, was named in honor of Thomas Nelson, Jr., governor of Virginia from June to November 1781. The county seat is Lovingston.

MIDWAY MILL, *Warminster vicinity.* So named because of its situation on the James River midway between Richmond and Lynchburg, this massive stone structure was built in 1787 for William H. Cabell, governor of Virginia from 1805 to 1808. According to tradition, the mill was constructed by Italian shipbuilders stranded in Virginia after the cancellation of a ship construction project. During the mid–19th century the mill became a prominent landmark for travelers on the adjacent James River and Kanawha Canal. The canal traffic prompted the establishment of a small settlement here to serve the passengers and boatmen. Midway Mill remained in operation until ca. 1925. Although one of Virginia's finest historic mills, the deteriorating structure has stood vacant and unmaintained for the past several decades. Dismantling of the mill began in early 1999. *(62–23) VLR: 01/16/73; NRHP: 04/11/73.*

BON AIRE, *Warminster vicinity.* Bon Aire, built ca. 1812 by Dr. George Cabell, Jr., is a three-part country house inspired by Palladian forms popularized in 18th-century English pattern books such as Robert Morris's *Select Architecture* (1755). The dwelling's designer has not been identified, but the tripartite organization of the floor plan and many details relate Bon Aire to Point of Honor in Lynchburg, built for Dr. Cabell's cousin, Dr. George Cabell. Placed on a steep slope above the James River and constructed in native materials of red brick and whitewashed wood trim, Bon Aire exemplifies the process by which Virginia builders manipulated the scale, plan, details, and materials of English prototypes to conform to local conditions. The present portico and dormers are 20th-century additions. Bon Aire is one of several architecturally distinguished houses in the vicinity built by members of the Cabell family. *(62–89) VLR: 04/15/80; NRHP: 07/30/80.*

MONTEZUMA, *Norwood vicinity.* Erected ca. 1790, Montezuma is a singular example of Piedmont Federal architecture. Its impressive scale, unusual floor plan, fine woodwork, and Roman Revival dwarf portico set it apart from the more standard gentry houses of the period and region. The inflated proportions result in exceptionally tall windows. Montezuma was built for William Cabell, Jr., a son of the immigrant William Cabell who settled in the area in the second quarter of the 18th century. The Cabells built nearly a dozen architecturally distinguished houses in what became Nelson County; Montezuma, Bon Aire, and Soldier's Joy are among those that remain. Thomas Jefferson was a friend of the family and may have had an influence on the design of Montezuma. The combination of a Chinese lattice railing with a classical portico is a distinctly Jeffersonian touch. *(62–10) VLR: 04/15/80; NRHP: 07/30/80.*

NELSON COUNTY COURTHOUSE, *Lovingston.* The tradition of applying arcades to public buildings can be traced to the arcaded ground floors of English Renaissance town halls. This tradition was maintained with the arcades of the first Williamsburg Capitol and several colonial courthouses. Nelson County's court structure of 1809 illustrates the persistence of this motif, in this case grafted onto a regionally interpreted temple-form building, a form widely used for Virginia courthouses in the first half of the 19th century, of which the Fairfax County Courthouse is the prototype. The Nelson County Courthouse was built by George Varnum according to plans submitted by Sheldon Crostwait, one of the justices, and is the only courthouse to have five arches rather than the standard four. It has been in continuous use since completion, and though enlarged and modified over the years, it is one of Virginia's best-preserved historic court structures. *(62–09) VLR: 04/17/73; NRHP: 05/17/73.*

OAK RIDGE RAILROAD OVERPASS, *Route 653, Shipman vicinity.* Spanning the tracks of the Southern Railway system, now owned by the Norfolk Southern Corporation, this metal-truss bridge is an excellently preserved representative of the many graceful metal structures that have efficiently guided vehicular traffic across obstacles since their development in the late 19th century. The bridge employs the popular single-span Pratt through truss, 100 feet in length, with two wooden-beam approach spans, each 19 feet long. It was manufactured by the Keystone Bridge Company in 1882 and has remained in continuous service since its installation. The Oak Ridge Overpass is the state's best example of its type. *(62–85) VLR: 11/15/77; NRHP: 04/15/78.*

RIVER BLUFF, *Wintergreen vicinity.* On a steep bank of the South Fork of the Rockfish River, in the shadow of the Blue Ridge Mountains, this brick farmhouse began in 1785 as a side-passage, one-room house for Nathaniel Clarke. It was made into a three-part dwelling by the addition of wings ca. 1810, during the ownership of Thomas Goodwin. One of the wings has a rare diaper-pattern decoration on the chimney. Through its transformation from a small rectangular structure to a would-be stylish, if simplified, Palladian type, River Bluff illustrates how dwellers of Virginia's remoter regions traded their rustic image for one more socially acceptable. Despite this effort, the asymmetry of the fenestration lends the composition an engaging provinciality. The house has been carefully restored by its present owner; its scenic setting has changed little since the 19th century. *(62–88) VLR: 05/20/80; NRHP: 07/30/80.*

SOLDIER'S JOY, *Wingina vicinity.* One of several substantial and well-fashioned Cabell family houses in the Piedmont region, Soldier's Joy was built in 1783–85 and enlarged in 1806. Samuel Jordan Cabell, for whom the house was built, was a Revolutionary War officer and served as the Republican congressman of the district from 1795 to 1803. Although its early 19th-century wings were later reduced in size, Soldier's Joy today remains one of the most ambitious of the Cabells' building efforts. The late Georgian dwelling with its pedimented roof has stately proportions and decorous interior detailing, much of which was added when the house was enlarged. Lending additional interest is extensive documentation, including the detailed contract of the builder, James Robards. The woodwork of the dismantled ballroom wing, executed by James Oldham, is now displayed in the Cincinnati Art Museum. *(62–15) VLR: 04/15/80; NRHP: 11/28/80.*

SWANNANOA, *Afton vicinity.* Richmond businessman and philanthropist Maj. James H. Dooley built this palatial mountaintop villa as a summer home for himself and his wife, Sallie May Dooley. Inspired by the Villa Medici in Rome, the mansion, completed in 1913, was designed by Noland and Baskervill of Richmond. The exterior is faced in Georgia marble, while the interior is richly appointed with the finest materials and decorations. An outstanding interior feature is a huge Tiffany Studios stained-glass window on the stair landing said to depict Mrs. Dooley in the gardens. Each of the principal rooms has a distinct architectural character, from the Louis XVI music room to the Turkish office. Completing the image of a Gilded Age estate is an Italian-style terraced garden. From 1949 to 1998 Swannanoa housed the University of Science and Philosophy, a cultural and religious institution founded by American sculptor Walter Russell and his wife Lao. *(62–22) VLR: 04/28/69; NRHP: 10/01/69.*

WOODSON'S MILL, *Lowesville.* A mill was first erected here in 1794 by Guilford Campbell. It was largely rebuilt around 1845 by the Fulcher family. Further alterations were made after the Civil War by Nathan Taliaferro. For over a century the mill remained an important feature of the countryside, providing essential service to a small agricultural community. In 1900 Dr. Julian B. Woodson, a local physician, orchardist, and state legislator, purchased the mill and added patent roller mills alongside the existing millstones, producing fine white flour that was shipped throughout the region. For the first half of the 20th century, Woodson's Mill not only was a gristmill but operated as a cider press, ice plant, blacksmith shop, and sawmill. Restored in 1983, this remarkably intact example of a water-powered, post-and-beam gristmill is again in regular operation and has become a tourist attraction. *(62–93) VLR: 10/21/92; NRHP: 12/17/92.*

❧ NEW KENT COUNTY

Most likely named for the English shire of Kent, this largely wooded Tidewater county east of Richmond was formed from York County in 1654. Its county seat is New Kent.

CEDAR GROVE, *Providence Forge vicinity.* This inland New Kent farm was acquired in 1789 by Robert Christian, who represented the county in the General Assembly. The present house, erected for Christian ca. 1810 as an addition to an 18th-century farmhouse, is a rural adaptation of the Richmond town house. Like its urban counterparts, the house has a side-passage plan, and its facade employs Flemish bond brickwork and a modillion cornice. Also like many Richmond town houses, Cedar Grove had stuccoed lintels, but they have been filled in with modern brickwork. Christian's daughter Letitia, born at Cedar Grove in the earlier house, was the first wife of President John Tyler. She died in the White House in 1842 and was buried in the Cedar Grove cemetery. The original frame section was replaced by the present wing in 1916. *(63–36) VLR: 10/16/79; NRHP: 12/28/79.*

CRISS CROSS, *New Kent vicinity.* Virginia's few surviving Stuart-period houses generally follow traditional English vernacular forms of earlier decades and show little classical influence. Criss Cross, an engaging small manor house in rural New Kent County, reveals this phenomenon most clearly. Named for its cross-shaped plan, the story-and-a-half house, erected ca. 1690 for George Poindexter, is dominated by a two-story projection containing the entrance and chamber above. A ca. 1790 rear wing may have replaced an original stair tower that would have made the house cross-shaped originally. Irregularities in the brickwork tell of other alterations. Inside are rare exposed framing members and decorative details. Illustrating the persistence of traditional forms in remote areas is the decidedly postmedieval quality of both the scroll carving on the post supporting a large summer beam and the paneling of the entrance vestibule doors. *(63–06) VLR: 01/16/73; NRHP: 05/11/73.*

EMMAUS BAPTIST CHURCH, *Providence Forge vicinity.* The continuity of this Tidewater Baptist congregation is embodied in its country Greek Revival church, a plain but well-crafted expression of the dignity and moral authority of proven forms. The congregation was formed in Charles City County in 1776 and prospered in the Second Great Awakening, a movement that spurred the growth of America's Protestant denominations. Expanding membership of the Emmaus congregation led to the construction of the present building in 1849 to replace a frame meetinghouse. William Clopton, a lay preacher from 1804 to 1816, was the first of three generations of Cloptons to serve the church and inspire its growth. Membership peaked at 516 in 1860 and included both blacks and whites. Little changed since its construction, the church is marked by its two entrances opening onto the two aisles inside, an arrangement typical of country Protestant churches. *(63–11) VLR: 04/21/93; NRHP: 06/10/93.*

FOSTER'S CASTLE, *Tunstall vicinity.* Joseph Foster, a native of Newport, England, was the first owner of this T-shaped manor house built close to the Pamunkey River. Although the loss of New Kent's early records inhibits precise dating, the house probably was constructed between 1685 and 1690 when Foster represented New Kent in the House of Burgesses. Foster's Castle shares with nearby Criss Cross and Bacon's Castle in Surry County the distinction of being Virginia's only remaining Stuart-period manor houses fronted by enclosed porches with chambers above, a feature typical of postmedieval English houses. Most of Foster's Castle's original interior was replaced in the early 19th century, and the one-story walls on the main body of the house were raised to two stories in 1873. Despite these changes, the surviving wall sections constitute a significant document of Virginia's oldest architecture. *(63–03) VLR: 01/16/73; NRHP: 04/11/73.*

HAMPSTEAD, *Tunstall vicinity.* The full drama of the Federal style is played out in this strongly architectural mansion, one of the state's most ambitious and accomplished works of the period. All features of the house—the delicate classical detailing, the monumental proportions, and the beautiful masonry and joinery—exude superior quality. Dominating the interior is a flying circular stair winding from basement to attic and separated from the hall by a screen of columns. Hampstead's designer has not been identified, but the house has many parallels to works by John Holden Greene of Providence, R.I. As in several of Greene's buildings, much of Hampstead's detailing follows illustrations in Asher Benjamin's *American Builder's Companion* (1806). Hampstead was built ca. 1825 for the planter Conrade Webb. Webb attended Brown University and could well have sought assistance from Providence's leading architect to carry out such a singular undertaking. *(63–13) VLR: 10/06/70; NRHP: 12/18/70.*

MARL HILL, *Talleysville vicinity.* Marl Hill is named for its deposits of marl, a clayey substance containing calcium carbonate used to fertilize soil deficient in lime. The fields surrounding the house were once the scene of marl mining. The property was settled before 1700 by Thomas Jackson who in that year sold an acre of land for the construction of nearby St. Peter's Church. The earlier and smaller part of the present house was built in the third quarter of the 18th century by the Crump family. It is characteristic of the compact but well-built dwellings occupied by the more socially elite landowners of the period, a contrast to the makeshift hovels of the poorer classes. To this was added the larger side-passage section in 1825, a typical example of country Federal architecture. The original portion has an unusual series of aligned paneled closet doors on the second floor. *(63–19) VLR: 12/12/89; NRHP: 12/21/90.*

MOYSONEC ARCHAEOLOGICAL SITE, *Lanexa vicinity.*
During his exploration of the Chickahominy River in 1607,
Capt. John Smith observed the Indian village of Moysonec, sited, as he noted, "where a better seat for a town cannot be desired." The exact site of this Late Woodland–period village was
identified in the course of a 1967–71 survey of the region conducted by the College of William and Mary Department of Anthropology. Artifacts revealed evidence of Indian occupancy
from as early as the Archaic period, or 7000–6000 B.C. Shown
are fragments of knotted net–impressed ceramics of the Middle Woodland period (500 B.C.–A.D. 900) found here. The
undisturbed village site provides an opportunity for further
study of aboriginal Virginians at the time of contact with European civilization and could furnish information on the house
forms, tools, diets, and physical conditions of the village inhabitants. *(63–77) VLR: 12/17/74; NRHP: 06/20/75.*

OLIVET PRESBYTERIAN CHURCH, *Providence Forge
vicinity.* Tucked deep in the New Kent woods, Olivet Church
shows the effectiveness of the Greek Revival style in its most elementary form. The otherwise spartan wooden church is in a
temple form and is fronted by a simple Doric portico. Its unchanged interior preserves doors and pews decorated with
their original mahogany and bird's-eye maple graining. The
pulpit is set off by marbleized steps. Presbyterians came to New
Kent County in the mid–18th century. By 1800 a congregation
was meeting in the colonial St. Peter's Church, by then abandoned by the Anglicans. In 1857 the Presbyterians decided to
erect their own church nearby, calling it Mount Olivet and later
merely Olivet. The congregation relocated in Providence Forge
in 1934 but preserves Olivet for annual memorial services.
(63–105) VLR: 07/19/77; NRHP: 01/26/78.

ST. PETER'S EPISCOPAL CHURCH, *Talleysville vicinity.*
St. Peter's is one of America's most engaging works of colonial
architecture. The main body was constructed in 1701–3 by
William Hughes, carpenter, and Cornelius Hall, bricklayer, and
employs the simple rectangular plan characteristic of Virginia's
earliest Anglican churches. The influence of the Jacobean
baroque style is evident in its restored curvilinear gables. The
tower, with its sparkling glazed-header Flemish bond, was
added in 1739–41 by William Walker and has baroque vestiges
in the molded-brick cornices, massive corner pilasters, and
four pedestals topped by crude stuccoed urns, one of which is a
chimney. The interior suffered the loss of most of the original
fabric in the course of its nearly three-century history but was
carefully reconstructed in 1964–65 in a restoration directed by
Harden de Valson Pratt. St. Peter's was the parish church of
Martha Washington during her youth. *(63–27) VLR: 11/05/68;
NRHP: 10/01/69.*

CITY OF NEWPORT NEWS

The name of this port city probably commemorates Capt. Christopher Newport, who made five voyages to Virginia between 1607 and 1619. The town was established in 1880 and incorporated as a city in 1896. It was greatly expanded in 1958 when consolidated with the city of Warwick, formerly Warwick County.

BOLDRUP PLANTATION ARCHAEOLOGICAL SITE, *Moyer Road.* Now a modern residential development, Boldrup plantation was associated with several of Virginia's most august 17th-century names. The property was patented by William Claiborne in 1626 and was later the home of Elizabeth Piercy Stephens, who in 1638 married Governor Sir John Harvey. It then reverted to Samuel Stephens, second governor of Albemarle (North Carolina). At Stephens's death in 1669, Boldrup passed to his widow, Frances Culpeper Stephens, who in 1670 married Governor Sir William Berkeley. The Berkeleys sold Boldrup in 1671 to Lt. Col. William Cole, a colonial secretary of state. Cole's 1691 armorial grave slab and those of his second and third wives are the only visible objects remaining on site. They lie in the front yard of a house on Patrick Lane. Other sites, including that of a pit house, were salvaged by Virginia Department of Historic Resources archaeologists in the 1980s. *(121–05) VLR: 09/15/81; NRHP: 09/16/82.*

DAM NO. 1 BATTLEFIELD SITE, *13560 Jefferson Avenue.* The battle of Dam No. 1, on April 16, 1862, marked the occasion of the only Union infantry attack against Confederate defenses during the monthlong siege of the Warwick-Yorktown line (the 2d Peninsula defense line). Union forces under Maj. Gen. George McClellan undertook to seize a reported weak point in Maj. Gen. John Bankhead Magruder's fortifications. The dam was one of three dams built by Magruder to enhance the ability of two earlier tide-mill dams to inundate lands to inhibit a Union advance. Poor communication among Union units left the advancing Union troops vulnerable. A Confederate counterattack drove the forces back, thus preventing a Union push to the west, to Richmond. Today the battlefield and its extensive network of earthworks are part of Newport News Park, developed around the modern dammed-up section of the Warwick River, now the city reservoir. *(121–60) VLR: 06/27/95; NRHP: 08/04/95.*

FIRST DENBIGH PARISH CHURCH ARCHAEOLOGICAL SITE, *Walters Road.* The site of the first Denbigh Parish Church is the earliest datable ecclesiastical site within the former Warwick County, now the city of Newport News. Constructed before 1635 and taking its name from the nearby Denbigh plantation, the church served the inhabitants of what was the upper portion of Elizabeth City Corporation, later Warwick County, in the earliest days of the colony. The church foundations, located and identified in a test square by archaeologists of the Virginia Department of Historic Resources, make up one of the few nondomestic 17th-century archaeological sites within a rapidly urbanizing area. Complete excavation could shed new light on the character of the nation's earliest church architecture. *(121–37) VLR: 09/15/81; NRHP: 09/07/82.*

FORT CRAFFORD ARCHAEOLOGICAL SITE, *Fort Eustis.* On Mulberry Island Point, this site derives its name from Carter Crafford, who acquired the land in 1749. A fortification was built here during the Revolution to oppose British reinforcement of Yorktown. Fort Crafford was built in early 1862 as a covering work to enhance the Mulberry Island anchor of the Confederate Warwick-Yorktown line (2d Peninsula defense line). The fort played a role in Maj. Gen. John Bankhead Magruder's defense, which delayed the Northern advance long enough to give the Confederates time to assemble a force to defend Richmond. The well-preserved pentagonal earthwork consists of an inner wall 20 feet high and covers over seven acres. Within the fort area are the foundations of Carter Crafford's house, demolished in 1924, as well as the Crafford graveyard and a slave graveyard. Also here are the sites of three magazines and two bombproof shelters. *(121–27) VLR: 10/16/73; NRHP: 05/17/74.*

HILTON VILLAGE HISTORIC DISTRICT. This eighteen-block neighborhood containing dwellings, a public square, a commercial row, and land for schools, parks, and churches, was one of the nation's first planned communities financed with U.S. government funds. The village was created to offset the critical shortage of housing for employees of the Newport News Shipbuilding and Dry Dock Co. in World War I. The company, along with the U.S. Shipping Board, chose a tract along the James River accessible to the shipyard by trolley. The project architect was Francis Y. Joannes; Vincent Hubbard provided landscape design. A modified English cottage style was chosen for the architectural theme. Houses varied in size for different income levels; included were detached houses, double houses, and row houses. Some eighty years later, Hilton Village remains a wholesome, tidy community and is one of the most popular addresses in Newport News. *(121–09) VLR: 11/05/68; NRHP: 06/23/69.*

HOTEL WARWICK, *25th Street and West Avenue.* Designed by Norfolk architect J. Kevan Peebles and conspicuously situated across the square from Victory Arch overlooking Hampton Roads, the Hotel Warwick was the first fireproof highrise hotel in Newport News. The hotel is the city's principal example of the eclectic commercial style of the 1920s and 1930s, combining features of the Art Deco and Tudor Revival styles. It was erected by the Old Dominion Land Co. in 1928 as an expansion of an earlier hotel of the same name, destroyed by fire in 1963.

During World War II the hotel was used to quarter military personnel assigned to work at the nearby shipyards, especially the Newport News Shipbuilding and Drydock Co. A striking feature of the lobby is an entrance doorway surmounted by a crenellated partition of dark-stained oak. The building was renovated in 1995 as housing for low-income residents. *(121–40) VLR: 08/21/84; NRHP: 10/04/84.*

MATTHEW JONES HOUSE, *Fort Eustis.* The main body of this T-shaped colonial dwelling, with its superb glazed-header Flemish bond brickwork, probably was built in 1727 for Matthew Jones, whose name and date are on inscribed bricks. The projecting entrance, a holdover from 17th-century house types, is one of the state's four remaining examples of this feature. The chimneys, with their great sloping haunches and divided stacks, survive from an earlier dwelling, probably frame. In 1893 the original interior trim was removed, and the sides were raised to two full stories. Despite these changes, the house is an important architectural document, illustrating the transition from the postmedieval vernacular to the Georgian style. Now within the Fort Eustis Military Reservation, the exterior is accessible to public visitation. The house underwent thorough stabilization and repair in 1992–93. *(121–06) VLR: 11/05/68; NRHP: 06/11/69.*

LEE HALL, *Route 238, Lee Hall.* Lee Hall, the stately Italianate plantation house built ca. 1850 for Richard Decatur Lee, is said to have been financed by a bumper crop of tobacco. Lee was placed in charge of the area's civil defense at the start of the Civil War. The mansion was used as the headquarters of Maj. Gen. John Bankhead Magruder, CSA, during the Warwick-Yorktown phase of the Peninsula campaign of April–May 1862. An earthen fort in the yard, used to launch a Confederate hot-air balloon on April 17, 1862, is a relic of the military occupation. Lee's support of the Confederate cause brought him financial ruin and the forced sale of the plantation in 1866. The village started in the 1880s at the nearby rail crossing took its name from the house. Lee Hall and the fort have been acquired by the city of Newport News for heritage tourism. *(121–16) VLR: 08/15/72; NRHP: 12/05/72; BHR EASEMENT.*

MATHEWS MANOR (DENBIGH PLANTATION ARCHAEOLOGICAL SITE), *Lukas Creek Road.* Much has been learned of Virginia's early domestic life from the archaeological work of Ivor Noël Hume of the Colonial Williamsburg Foundation. Among the sites excavated by him in the 1960s is that of the first Mathews Manor house, a postmedieval house built ca. 1626 for Capt. Samuel Mathews. The house, which had a center chimney and projecting porch, burned and was replaced by a smaller house in the 1650s. Mathews returned to England in 1653, so the latter dwelling was probably constructed by his son Samuel Mathews, Jr., who served as governor of the colony under the English Commonwealth from 1656 to 1660. Also within the registered area is the site of an 18th-century Digges family plantation house and several 17th-century industrial sites. The manor house foundations have been capped and are preserved within a small park of a residential neighborhood. *(121–08) VLR: 12/02/69; NRHP: 02/16/70.*

THE NEWSOME HOUSE, *2803 Oak Avenue.* This fanciful Queen Anne–style residence was the home of Joseph Thomas Newsome and his family. Newsome (1869–1942) was one of Newport News's most respected black civic leaders. A graduate of Howard University Law School, he became one of the first black lawyers to practice before the Virginia Supreme Court of Appeals. An effective advocate of civil rights, Newsome is also remembered for his many and varied community efforts. He

organized the Colored Voters League of Warwick County and was editor (1926–40) of the *Newport News Star,* the city's black newspaper. At the time of his death, Newsome was commissioner of chancery and a member of the Newport News Citizens Defense Policy Committee. Newsome purchased his Oak Avenue residence in 1906. The property is now owned the city of Newport News and operated as the Newsome House Museum and Cultural Center. *(121–52) VLR: 12/12/89; NRHP: 12/19/90.*

NORTH END HISTORIC DISTRICT. This tightly developed twenty-two-block residential district, paralleling the James River northwest of downtown, evolved in three major phases between 1900 and 1935. The 1881 extension of the Chesapeake and Ohio tracks to the deepwater terminal and the founding of the Newport News Shipbuilding and Dry Dock Co. in 1886 spurred a need for housing. The area was subsequently laid out by the Old Dominion Land Co. In the early period, 1900–1910, both shipyard managers and skilled workmen resided here. The more affluent built architecturally distinguished houses along Huntington Avenue overlooking the James. Many more dwellings were erected for the swelling population during World War I. Prominent residents have included shipyard presidents Homer L. Ferguson and Walter A. Post, who also was the city's first mayor; Samuel R. Buxton and Phillip A. Hiden, later mayors of Newport News; and Saxon W. Holt, Virginia lieutenant governor 1938–40. *(121–43) VLR: 06/17/86; NRHP: 08/28/86.*

OAKLAND FARM ARCHAEOLOGICAL SITES, *U.S. Route 60 at Enterprise Drive.* The Oakland Farm sites include three significant and distinct archaeological sites within a tract of land now being developed as the Oakland Industrial Park. Surviving intact are the archaeological remains of prehistoric occupation dating to the Early to Middle Woodland periods. Historic sites are the Queen Hith plantation, occupied by the Harwood family from the 1630s until after the Revolutionary War, and a Confederate earthwork (shown), the eastern terminus of fortifications constructed by Maj. Gen. John Bankhead Magruder before the 1862 Peninsula campaign. The fortification is a massive square earthen redoubt measuring 220 feet on each side. Thomas Harwood, who patented the property in 1632, named it Queen Hith; *hith* is an Old English word for river landing. The sites are preserved by the city of Newport News. *(121–41) VLR: 09/16/82; NRHP: 02/24/83; BHR EASEMENT (MAGRUDER REDOUBT).*

RICHNECK PLANTATION ARCHAEOLOGICAL SITE, *Richneck Drive.* Richneck was an early seat of the Cary family. The original dwelling, a cruciform house, was likely built in the late 17th century for Miles Cary, Jr. (1655–1709), who held several colonial offices including the rectorship of the College of William and Mary. His grandson, Wilson Miles Cary, was among the Revolutionaries who met in Williamsburg's Raleigh Tavern to sign the "Association of 1774." The house burned in 1865. A Cary descendant visited Richneck in 1868 and reported: "The mansion was a pile of ruins, though from the remains of the walls still standing, I could estimate its former extent. It was a long-fronted, two-storied brick building with the usual outhouses and must have been very commodious." The graves of Miles Cary, Jr., and his first wife, Mary Milner Cary, remain on what are now the grounds of a public school. *(121–28) VLR: 02/17/76; NRHP: 07/08/77.*

RIVERSIDE APARTMENTS, *4500–4600 Washington Avenue.* The Riverside Apartments were begun in 1918 by the Emergency Fleet Corporation, an agency of the U.S. Shipping Board, to alleviate the housing shortage created by the great increase of workers at the Newport News Shipbuilding and Dry Dock Co. during World War I. The project architect was Francis Y. Joannes, who also designed the houses for Hilton Village nearby. Consisting originally of four blocks, each employing the New York City open-stair tenement form, the apartments incorporated the very latest in construction techniques and fittings for fire safety, light, ventilation, health, and convenience. The complex, with its easy accessibility to the shipyard and city center, filled an important need in America's war production effort. Two of the original four apartment blocks have been demolished. The remaining two have been renovated by private developers for upgraded urban housing. *(121–39) VLR: 01/18/83; NRHP: 07/28/83.*

USS *CUMBERLAND* MARITIME ARCHAEOLOGICAL SITE, *James River bottom off downtown Newport News.* The mid-19th-century shipwreck offshore from Newport News is believed to be that of the USS *Cumberland,* sunk March 8, 1862. The *Cumberland,* a full-rigged sailing sloop, was launched in 1842 in Boston. It was part of the Union blockade of the James River when the ironclad *Virginia* entered Hampton Roads. The *Cumberland* was the first ship taken on by the *Virginia,* which fired on it at close range and then rammed it. The *Cumberland* sank within an hour. Military artifacts salvaged by archaeologists confirm that the wreck is a naval one. More extensive archaeological investigation should yield valuable data on Civil War naval architecture and artifacts. The engagement with the *Cumberland* symbolically ended the era of wooden warships. Shown is a view of the *Cumberland* under attack published in *Battles and Leaders of the Civil War* (1887–88). *(121–42) VLR: 10/19/82.*

WARWICK COUNTY COURTHOUSES, *14421 Old Courthouse Way, Denbigh.* Surrounded by sprawling suburban development, the former county-seat settlement at Denbigh preserves the two historic courthouses of the now-extinct Warwick County. The 1810 courthouse is a small T-shaped brick structure fronted by a carefully articulated Doric portico. The building was converted to the clerk's office when the 1884 courthouse was built nearby and now serves as a visitors' center. The 1884 courthouse was built in conjunction with the completion of the Chesapeake and Ohio Railroad to Newport News. An excellent example of High Victorian Italianate, it has the tall windows, bracket cornice, and cupola that are hallmarks of the style. The courthouse served the county until 1958 when Warwick County (by then an independent city) was consolidated with Newport News. The building now houses the Denbigh Community Center. On the grounds is a 1909 Confederate monument. *(121–01) VLR: 02/16/88; NRHP: 11/03/88.*

CITY OF NORFOLK

Established in 1680, Virginia's leading port derives its name from the English shire. Norfolk was created a borough by royal charter in 1736. It became a city in 1845.

ALLMAND-ARCHER HOUSE, *327 Duke Street.* A rare surviving example of Norfolk's Federal-era housing is the unassuming but finely appointed Duke Street dwelling erected in the 1790s for Matthew Hervey, a local merchant. The Greek Revival entry and heavy window lintels were added in a mid-19th-century remodeling. Contrasting with the restrained exterior is the impressive open-well stair inside, which ascends from the first floor to the attic. Other original Federal trim remains in the principal rooms. The house became the property of Harrison Allmand in 1802 and passed through marriage to the Archer family, who owned it until the 1970s when it was acquired by the Historic Norfolk Foundation. In 1993 the property was purchased by the Grand Temple Daughters of I.B.P.O.E. of the World. It is now the home of the order's Emma V. Kelly Memorial Library. *(122–01) VLR: 11/03/70; NRHP: 09/22/71; BHR EASEMENT.*

ATTUCKS THEATRE, *1010 Church Street.* A landmark of Afro-American popular culture, the Attucks Theatre is one of the country's few remaining theaters to have been financed, designed, and built exclusively by blacks. Located in Huntersville, Norfolk's historic though largely rebuilt black neighborhood, the theater was erected in 1919 after the designs of Harvey N. Johnson, one of the state's few black architects practicing at the time. The theater is named for Crispus Attucks, a black man killed in the Boston Massacre who thereby became the first casualty of the American Revolution. The theater retains its original fire curtain, painted with a scene of Attucks's death by Lee Lash Studios of New York. During its heyday many of New York's leading black road shows played here. Now owned by the Norfolk Redevelopment and Housing Authority, the Attucks is undergoing restoration as a performing arts theater. *(122–74) VLR: 07/21/81; NRHP: 09/16/82.*

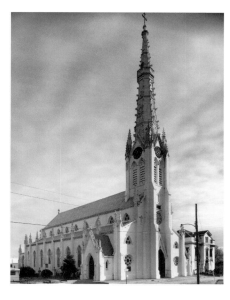

BASILICA OF ST. MARY OF THE IMMACULATE CONCEPTION (FORMERLY ST. MARY'S ROMAN CATHOLIC CHURCH), *232 Chapel Street.* Dominated by its richly decorated spire, this gleaming stuccoed church is the state's most elaborate expression of the Early Gothic Revival. Erected in 1858–59, it replaced an earlier church destroyed by fire and serves the Tidewater region's founding Catholic parish. Although the architect remains to be documented, the design is clearly from the hand of an individual of superior talent, possibly a Baltimore architect. With its rounded apse, the church has a decidedly French character. No less rich than the exterior is the lofty vaulted interior, which, though rearranged in recent years, contains a profusion of Victorian stained glass and ornamentation. Noteworthy also is its 1858 pipe organ by Richard M. Ferris and Levi U. Stuart of New York. St. Mary's serves a predominately Afro-American congregation; it became a minor basilica in 1991. *(122–24) VLR: 02/21/78; NRHP: 05/25/79.*

BOUSH-TAZEWELL HOUSE, *6225 Powhatan Avenue.* This timber-frame late Georgian house, built 1779–83, was the first significant dwelling erected in the old borough of Norfolk after the city burned in 1776. John Boush, grandson of Norfolk's first mayor and himself a mayor of the city, commissioned shipwrights to construct the house as a wedding present for his bride, Anne Waller Boush. In 1820 the house was acquired by Littleton Waller Tazewell, who held many public offices including U.S. senator and Virginia governor. Among Tazewell's visitors here were Lafayette, Andrew Jackson, Henry Clay, and John Tyler. The house was enlarged in the mid–19th century with two-story Greek Revival wings. In 1898 it was moved to its present site to prevent demolition for commercial development. Handsomely restored, the exterior is set off by its graceful two-tier portico added in 1791; the interior possesses much of its original Federal woodwork. *(122–02) VLR: 02/19/74; NRHP 07/18/74.*

CHRIST AND ST. LUKE'S EPISCOPAL CHURCH, *560 West Olney Road.* Its traceried windows, elaborate detailing, pinnacled tower, and interior carvings combine to make Christ and St. Luke's Church one of the state's purest expressions of the Late Gothic Revival, an architectural movement fostered by the Boston architect Ralph Adams Cram. As are many other churches of the movement, this example is a skillful adaptation of the English Perpendicular style. A dominant interior feature is the carved reredos containing statues of dignitaries of the Episcopal church. The congregation traces its ancestry to the Elizabeth River Parish, whose first church dated from 1637. Erected as Christ Church in 1909–10, the present edifice is effectively placed at the head of Smith's Creek in Norfolk's Ghent neighborhood. Its architects, Watson and Huckle of Philadelphia, were experts in the scholarly interpretation of medieval English styles so popular with affluent early 20th-century congregations. *(122–75) VLR: 03/20/79; NRHP: 06/18/79.*

DOWNTOWN NORFOLK HISTORIC DISTRICT. Occupying the oldest continuously settled area of Virginia's leading port, this commercial quarter is closely associated with events and developments of Norfolk's rail, banking, maritime, and naval activities. Within its irregular colonial street pattern is an important mix of late 19th- and early 20th-century commercial architecture, built on the sites of earlier structures. The building styles range from simple commercial vernacular to the grandest classicism. Prominent East Coast architects whose work is represented here include Ammi B. Young (U.S. Customs House, 1859), Charles E. Cassell (Citizens Bank Building, 1897), and J. Kevan Peebles (Lynnhaven Hotel, 1906). The rows of narrow brick storefronts on Granby Street, the principal commercial thoroughfare, constitute a cohesive early commercial streetscape. Since 1977 the district has been a conservation project administered by the Norfolk Redevelopment and Housing Authority, which has encouraged the recycling of its area's older structures. *(122–265) VLR: 12/09/86; NRHP: 03/20/87.*

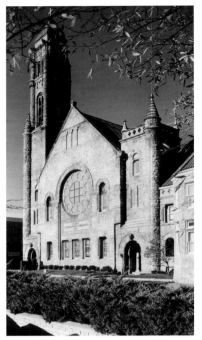

EPWORTH UNITED METHODIST CHURCH, *124 West Freemason Street.* A richly architectural church in a city renowned for its fine collection of downtown churches, Epworth United Methodist Church is the work of two Norfolk architects: James Edwin Ruthven Carpenter and J. Kevan Peebles. The congregation began in 1850; the present church was completed in 1896 on what was then the fashionable West Freemason Street. The rugged but colorful Romanesque style employed here shows the influence of H. H. Richardson's famous Trinity Church in Boston, a work that popularized the Romanesque Revival nationwide. The gray granite of the rough-faced random ashlar is set off by yellow sandstone trim. A fine collection of original stained glass enlivens the domed interior. The sanctuary's remarkable original painted decorations, which made the space one of Virginia's supreme examples of Victorian decor, have since been covered over. *(122–178) VLR: 03/20/96; NRHP: 08/21/97.*

FIRST CALVARY BAPTIST CHURCH, *813 Henry Street.* The religious zeal of Norfolk's growing black community at the turn of this century was manifested in the grandiose churches erected by the various denominations. Conspicuous among these is First Calvary Baptist Church, a monumental Georgian Revival edifice of red brick with white terra-cotta ornamentation. Dedicated in 1916, the church was designed by Mitchell & Wilcox of Norfolk. The congregation was organized in 1880 with only four members and eventually grew to more than fifteen hundred. Under the leadership of Dr. Percy J. Wallace, pastor from 1908 to 1922, First Calvary became one of the most influential black churches in the country. Dr. Wallace was instrumental in having the new church built and in getting the debt paid in only two years, a remarkable accomplishment for a congregation composed not of wealthy people but of laborers, maids, cooks, laundry workers, and small shopkeepers. *(122–73) VLR: 06/17/87; NRHP: 10/15/87.*

FIRST BAPTIST CHURCH, *418 East Bute Street.* One of Norfolk's major architectural landmarks, First Baptist is the mother church of the city's black Baptists. Norfolk's Baptists organized in 1800 and included both blacks and whites. The free blacks split off by 1830 when they built a church on Bute Street. The present church, built in 1906 on the site of the 1830 church, was designed by Tennessee architect Reuben H. Hunt. The pink granite Romanesque Revival work is among the state's most vigorous representatives of its style. Hunt's practice centered on southern ecclesiastical buildings and included Court Street Baptist Church in Portsmouth. His Norfolk church, with its grandiose scale and solid detailing, symbolized the growing economic strength of Norfolk's black community at the end of the 19th century and the importance of religious institutions to urban southern blacks. *(122–40) VLR: 04/19/83; NRHP: 07/21/83.*

FORT NORFOLK, *803 Front Street.* A fortification guarding Norfolk's harbor was established by local citizens at this site during the Revolutionary War. Recognizing its strategic location, the federal government purchased the site in 1795. In 1809 the government erected  the fort's most prominent feature, the massive walls with their great rounded bastion. Within these walls is a complex of military structures ranging in date from the early 19th to the 20th century, all approached through a picturesque gatehouse. In 1862 both the fort and the city fell to Federal forces, but the fort saw no significant action. This important example of early military architecture is owned by the U.S. Army Corps of Engineers. Today most of it is licensed to the Norfolk Historical Society, which is renovating much of the complex for exhibition and office space. *(122–07) VLR: 12/16/75; NRHP: 10/29/76.*

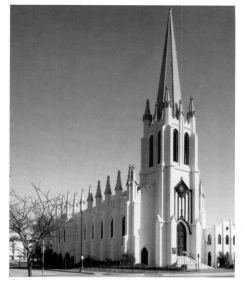

FREEMASON STREET BAPTIST CHURCH, *Freemason and Bank streets.* Philadelphia architect Thomas U. Walter designed this pinnacled downtown landmark for Norfolk's leading Baptist congregation. A complete contrast to the nearby Greek Revival Norfolk Academy building, also designed by Walter, the lofty church, completed in 1858, is a deftly handled representative of Walter's essays in the Gothic mode. With its mixture of wood, stucco, stone, and metal, all painted to resemble masonry, the church typifies the Early Gothic Revival's emphasis on dramatic effect at the expense of truth in materials. The church's steeple, with its Gabriel's horn weathervane, was somewhat modified in design after it was blown down in 1879. Urban renewal demolitions in the 1960s removed the church's surrounding historic neighborhood; however, the area is currently the scene of significant rebuilding. Freemason Street Baptist Church continues to serve an active congregation. *(122–08) VLR: 04/06/71; NRHP: 09/27/71.*

GHENT HISTORIC DISTRICT. The decades between 1890 and 1930 were a time of intensive land speculation. A positive result of this was a large number of planned suburban neighborhoods. Offering airy, attractive alternatives to dense older neighborhoods, these suburbs incorporated popular planning theories of the day. Norfolk's Ghent neighborhood, built along the Y-shaped Smith's Creek, with its concentric, tree-lined streets and landscaped open spaces, combines elements of the City Beautiful landscaping school with Beaux Arts planning concepts. The neighborhood was laid out by John Graham, a Philadelphia civil engineer. Between 1890 and 1905 it witnessed construction of a splendid range of middle- and upper-class houses in the Queen Anne, Colonial Revival, and Shingle styles. Except for demolitions along Olney Road, the district has suffered few changes. Still one of Norfolk's most fashionable addresses, Ghent was the city's first planned suburb to offer water, sewer, and gas lines. *(122–61) VLR: 06/19/79; NRHP: 07/04/80.*

WALTER E. HOFFMAN COURTHOUSE (FORMERLY THE U.S. POST OFFICE AND COURTHOUSE), *600 Granby Street.* Designed by Norfolk architect Benjamin F. Mitchell and completed in 1934, the Walter E. Hoffman Courthouse is a leading federal work in the monumental Art Deco style. The design follows the trend of the 1930s for federal architecture to serve as an assertive symbol of democratic ideals and the strength of government institutions. Like many federal projects of the depression era, the building blends stylized classical forms with the Art Deco format to create a stylish monumental character inside and out. Consistent with its dignified exterior is the main lobby, a grand hall ornamented with colorful stone veneers, metalwork details, and a richly decorated ceiling. The building was renovated and renamed in 1983 to accommodate the U.S. district court, at which time the post office function was removed. *(122–58) VLR: 10/18/83; NRHP: 10/10/84.*

JAMESTOWN EXPOSITION BUILDINGS, *U.S. Naval Base, Sewell's Point.* The seventeen remaining buildings of the 1907 Jamestown Exposition form a unique collection of early exposition pavilions. Erected for the celebration of the tricentennial of the founding of the first permanent English settlement in the New World, the complex originally contained twenty state pavilions, a history pavilion, an auditorium, and other

structures. Among those remaining are the Pennsylvania pavilion, a copy of Independence Hall; the Maryland pavilion, a copy of Homewood; and the Ohio pavilion, a copy of Adena. Unable to agree on what historic building to copy for Virginia, the Commonwealth built a standard Colonial Revival mansion. The complex was purchased by the federal government in 1917, and the site was made into a naval base and naval air station. Most of the pavilions have since been converted to officers' quarters, and today they are known collectively as Admiral's Row. *(122–54) VLR: 02/18/75; NRHP: 10/20/75.*

KENMURE, *420 W. Bute Street.* Kenmure is one of Norfolk's handful of surviving antebellum urban mansions. It was built for William Wilson Lamb, mayor of Norfolk during the Civil War, who is credited with preserving the city's historic silver mace by hiding it in the house. After Lamb's death in 1874, the house became the home of his son, William Lamb, hero of the Confederate stand at Fort Fisher, N.C. The younger Lamb also helped restore Norfolk's financial fortunes by working tirelessly to promote the city's revival as a port and a center of the cotton trade with Great Britain. The solidly proportioned house began as a two-story residence in 1845 and received an extra story around 1855. Its original waterfront setting made the house a conspicuous landmark of the West Freemason Street neighborhood. *(122–16)* VLR: 12/08/87; NRHP: 06/01/88; BHR EASEMENT.

LAFAYETTE GRAMMAR AND HIGH SCHOOL, *3109 Tidewater Drive.* Lafayette School exhibits the architectural quality that characterized Virginia's public schools at the beginning of the 20th century. The state constitution of 1902 provided for increased funding for public education and facilities, and handsome public school buildings became objects of civic pride throughout the state. Completed in 1906, the original portion of the school was designed by Vance Hebard and was the largest school in the former Norfolk County system at the time. The exterior was rendered in a robust Colonial Revival style, possibly influenced by Virginia colonial mansions. The building was enlarged in 1910 by the addition of a high school wing designed by the firm of Leigh and Diehl. The school became part of the Norfolk city system when the area was annexed in 1923. Phased out of use in the 1970s, the building has been given a new life through conversion into apartments. *(122–43)* VLR: 12/14/82; NRHP: 02/10/83.

MACARTHUR MEMORIAL, *421 City Hall Avenue.* This monumental Classical Revival public building, dominated by its portico and columned dome, was erected in 1846–50 as a city hall shortly after Norfolk became an independent city. It was designed by the nationally prominent architect Thomas U. Walter of Philadelphia; local architect William R. Singleton was also involved with the project. The building served as the city hall until 1913 when the city offices were relocated and the building became exclusively a courthouse. Here, on May 10, 1862, Norfolk mayor William Wilson Lamb surrendered the city to Union forces. In 1960 the city offered the structure as a memorial and tomb for General of the Army Douglas MacArthur, whose mother was born in Norfolk. The body of World War II's allied supreme commander in the Southwest Pacific was interred under the dome in 1964. The building also houses a museum containing MacArthur's papers and memorabilia. *(122–19)* VLR: 11/16/71; NRHP: 03/16/72.

MONTICELLO ARCADE, *Monticello Avenue between City Hall Avenue and Plume Street.* Although the form developed earlier, shopping arcades became de rigueur for cities both in Europe and the United States in the late 19th century. Nearly always highly ornamented and employing large amounts of glass, these arcades provided handsome settings for fashionable shops. Designed by the Norfolk firm of Neff and Thompson and opened in 1908, the Monticello Arcade is one of only two such arcades remaining in the state. Its developer was Percy S. Stephenson. Providing grand entrances are heroic colonnades with Beaux Arts ornamentation of polychromed terra-cotta. The lofty interior has two tiers of shops above the ground floor, all flooded in daylight through a glass ceiling. Much of the arcade's original character was hidden for many years behind tawdry later shop fronts, but a 1980s restoration has returned the building's former suave elegance. *(122–66)* VLR: 04/15/75; NRHP: 05/21/75.

MOSES MYERS HOUSE, *Freemason and Bank streets.* One of Virginia's finest examples of Federal architecture, this splendid town house was completed ca. 1792 for Moses Myers, a New York merchant who settled in Norfolk after the Revolution. Myers, the first Jew to take up permanent residence in Norfolk, held several important mercantile and public offices including president of the common council and collector of customs. Along with the Taylor-Whittle house, the Myers house illustrates the sophisticated lifestyle enjoyed in this port city in the early 19th century. Contrasting with its restrained exterior are the rich Adam-style interior decorations including ceilings, mantels, and cornices embellished with intricate composition ornaments. Members of the Myers family occupied the house until the 1930s. The house along with most of its original furnishings is now exhibited by the Chrysler Museum. *(122–17) VLR: 12/02/69; NRHP: 02/16/70.*

OLD NORFOLK ACADEMY BUILDING (HAMPTON ROADS CHAMBER OF COMMERCE), *420 Bank Street.* This leading example of the state's Greek Revival style was built to house the Norfolk Academy, a prestigious boys' school whose origins are traced to 1728 when the local authorities set aside land for the academy. The school received its present name in 1787 and was chartered by the General Assembly in 1804. The cornerstone of the present building was laid in 1840. Its architect was Thomas U. Walter of Philadelphia, famed as the designer of the dome of the U.S. Capitol. Walter was also architect of the nearby Freemason Street Baptist Church. The academy vacated the building in 1915, and in 1919 it was converted to the juvenile and domestic relations court. In 1971 the familiar downtown landmark was restored to house the Norfolk Chamber of Commerce, now the Hampton Roads Chamber of Commerce. *(122–18) VLR: 09/09/69; NRHP: 11/12/69.*

OLD NORFOLK CITY HALL, *235 East Plume Street.* Old Norfolk City Hall, with its fine stonework, classical decoration, and grand formality, is a skillful rendition of the stately neo-Palladian Revival that was popular at the end of the 19th century, especially in Great Britain. Designed in 1898 as the U.S. Post Office and Courts Building by the Baltimore firm of Wyatt and Nolting, the building illustrates the high standard of architectural civility found in works commissioned by the federal government in this period. Converted into a city hall in 1937 but abandoned in the 1960s with the construction of a modern city hall, the building has since been sensitively restored for private offices. An exceptional feature of the interior is the large central court surrounded by splendidly ornamented arcades. *(122–82) VLR: 07/21/81; NRHP 10/29/81.*

POPLAR HALL, *400 Stuart Circle.* An outstanding and little-known Georgian mansion, Poplar Hall was erected in the 1760s on the banks of Broad Creek. Its original owner was Thurmer Hoggard, a planter and ship's carpenter who developed a private shipyard in the site. With its symmetrical land and water facades, Flemish bond brickwork, and paneled woodwork, the house represents the ideal of a prosperous colonial residence. The name derives from a row of Lombardy poplar trees planted in the 1790s along the water's edge, some of the first of the species in America. The property remained in the Hoggard family until 1952 when the house and twelve acres were purchased by Mr. and Mrs. William Baker Copeland. The last vestiges of Poplar Hall's parklike setting were eradicated in 1985 when all but the house lot was sold for residential development. *(122–45) VLR: 03/19/97; NRHP: 11/07/97.*

ST. JOHN'S AFRICAN METHODIST EPISCOPAL CHURCH, *539–545 East Bute Street.* The completion of St. John's A.M.E. Church in 1888 symbolized the beginning of a period of ascendancy for Norfolk's black congregations. The church was the first of a series of architecturally assertive black churches to adorn the city. Its architect, Charles E. Cassell, was one of Norfolk's most respected architects. Cassell's design is a red brick interpretation of the Romanesque Revival style popularized by architect H. H. Richardson. Lending power to the interior are an enormous stained-glass window and a hammer-beam ceiling. St. John's congregation began in 1840 as a mission for slaves. It obtained its independence in 1863 during the Union occupation and joined the A.M.E. connection in 1864. Five bishops were consecrated here in 1908 during the Twenty-third Quadrennial Session of the A.M.E. church. *(122–211) VLR: 10/14/86; NRHP: 12/04/86; BHR EASEMENT.*

ST. PAUL'S EPISCOPAL CHURCH, *201 St. Paul's Boulevard.* This time-honored church, constructed in 1739, is the third house of worship to serve the Elizabeth River Parish and the oldest building in the city of Norfolk. Originally known as Elizabeth River Parish Church, it is believed to stand on the site of a 1641 chapel. Its burying ground, in use from the 1680s until 1836, is a peaceful, shady corner of downtown Norfolk to this day. The building was gutted by fire during the Revolutionary War when the entire city was burned. It was restored within its Flemish bond brick walls and returned to active use in 1786. Congregational divisiveness caused its abandonment to the Baptists in 1805. In 1832 it was reoccupied by Episcopalians and given its present name; it has remained in active use ever since. The bell tower was added in 1901; the present colonial-style interior is the product of a 1913 restoration. *(122–25) VLR: 03/02/71; NRHP: 07/02/71.*

TAYLOR-WHITTLE HOUSE, *225 West Freemason Street.* The prosperity of the Atlantic coast port cities in the post-Revolutionary period is reflected in the fine Federal town houses erected by merchants and civic leaders. Norfolk once boasted many such dwellings but preserves only a handful. Among them, the Taylor-Whittle house is comparable to the finest Federal houses in any of the ports, displaying refined proportions and detailing on its exterior and handsome ornamentation inside. The house was built ca. 1791 for either the merchant George Purdie or Norfolk mayor John Cowper. It was purchased in 1802 by Richard Taylor, an importer from England. A later occupant, Taylor's son-in-law, Richard Lucien Page, accompanied Commodore Perry to Japan and later organized Virginia's Confederate navy. The house was left to the Historic Norfolk Foundation in 1972. It is now owned by the city and leased for an association headquarters. *(122–21) VLR: 11/03/70; NRHP: 09/22/71.*

U.S. CUSTOMS HOUSE, *101 East Main Street.* Ammi B. Young (1798–1874), supervising architect of the U.S. Treasury Department, provided designs for some seventy customshouses and other government buildings throughout the country. All were solid, literate works and established a high standard for federal government architecture. Befitting Norfolk's status as a major port, Young's Norfolk customshouse ranks among his most ambitious schemes. For it he departed from his usual Tuscan Palazzo format in favor of a richly classical design with overtones of 18th-century Anglo-Palladianism. The dominant element is the carefully articulated Corinthian portico. Completed in 1859, the building remains free from significant alteration. With its granite walls and iron structural columns, the Customs House is an early essay in fireproof construction and still serves its original function. *(122–32) VLR: 12/02/69; NRHP: 04/17/70.*

VIRGINIA BANK AND TRUST COMPANY BUILDING (AUSLEW GALLERY), *101 Granby Street*. Erected in 1909 as the Virginia Bank and Trust Company headquarters, this "Temple of Finance" is one of Virginia's foremost works of the American Renaissance tradition. The monumentality of these solid and often huge edifices displayed commercial strength and reassured clients of their soundness. The Norfolk work was designed by two firms: Wyatt and Nolting of Baltimore, the principals, and Taylor and Hepburn of Norfolk. With its grandiose scale and giant order, the general form follows McKim, Mead and White's design for the Knickerbocker Trust and Safe Deposit Co. in New York, a work that inspired many other bank designs. The building still maintains a powerful presence amid its modern high-rise neighbors. Known as the Auslew Gallery from 1982 to 1992, it has recently been renovated to house the Virginia Club. *(122–78) VLR: 01/17/84; NRHP: 02/23/84.*

WEST FREEMASON STREET HISTORIC DISTRICT. The compact neighborhood near the Elizabeth River that includes West Freemason, Bute, Duke, Botetourt, Dunmore, and Yarmouth streets was one of the first neighborhoods outside the colonial limits of Norfolk. From the 18th century through the early 20th century, it was the city's most prestigious residential address and thus contains noteworthy examples of many styles popular during those 120 years. Key landmarks are the Federal-period Taylor-Whittle house, the Greek Revival Lamb and Camp-Hubard houses, and the Colonial Revival Roper house. Although the district has suffered some losses, it was spared the leveling that destroyed several downtown neighborhoods in the 1960s. The quiet dignity of old Norfolk is still keenly felt on the tree-shaded, stone-paved western end of West Freemason Street. *(122–60) VLR: 12/21/71; NRHP: 11/07/72.*

WELLS THEATRE, *Tazewell Street and Monticello Avenue*. Designed by the New York firm of E. C. Horne and Sons and opened in 1913, the Wells Theatre is both a celebration of early 20th-century popular culture and an outstanding example of Beaux Arts theater architecture. Part of the southern vaudeville chain operated by Jacob and Otto Wells, it was described at its opening as the chain's "most pretentious playhouse." The building displays all the lavishness associated with theaters of the period: sculptures, ornate light fixtures, stained glass, murals, and heavily encrusted plasterwork, all of which survive in a good state of preservation. Converted to a motion picture theater in the 1920s, the Wells eventually degenerated to showing X-rated films. In 1979 it was acquired and subsequently restored by the Virginia Stage Company for use as a playhouse. It is now owned by the city of Norfolk. *(122–67) VLR: 03/18/80; NRHP: 05/19/80.*

WILLOUGHBY-BAYLOR HOUSE, *601 East Freemason Street*. This architecturally restrained town house is representative of the many middle-class side-passage dwellings built following Norfolk's destruction during the Revolution. It was erected by William Willoughby soon after he purchased the lot in 1794. Willoughby, a local merchant and contractor, was also a descendant of Thomas Willoughby, original owner of the land on which Norfolk was established in 1682. Dr. Baynham Baylor, who married Willoughby's granddaughter in 1845, probably added the Doric columned porch and other Greek Revival touches then. In 1964 the house was spared the demolitions that swept away much of its neighborhood through purchase by the Historic Norfolk Foundation. The foundation restored the house as a museum illustrating the taste of Norfolk's middle-income families, a contrast to the more elegant Moses Myers house. Stewardship of the Willoughby-Baylor house was transferred to the Chrysler Museum in 1969. *(122–33) VLR: 04/06/71; NRHP: 09/22/71.*

NORTHAMPTON COUNTY

Probably named for the English shire, Northampton County originally included Virginia's entire Eastern Shore peninsula. First called Accomack, it was one of the eight original shires established by 1634. The name was changed to Northampton in 1643; the present Accomack County separated from it about 1663. Its county seat is Eastville.

BROWNSVILLE, *Nassawadox vicinity.* On a remote edge of the Eastern Shore's broad oceanside marshes is this surprisingly urbane Federal residence, built in 1806 for John Upshur. Upshur's ancestor John Browne, from whom the property derives its name, patented the land here in 1652. In 1809 Upshur added a long wooden wing to accommodate visiting relatives. The side-passage brick house is one of several Eastern Shore Federal houses boasting design, construction, and detailing of highest quality. A novel interior feature is the unusually wide arch supporting the stair. Also noteworthy are the fine woodwork and the Adamesque composition ornaments on the mantels. The property remained in the hands of Upshur's descendants until 1978 when it was acquired and restored by the Nature Conservancy as an operations center for its Eastern Shore barrier islands conservation program. *(65–03) VLR: 12/02/69; NRHP: 02/26/70.*

CAPE CHARLES HISTORIC DISTRICT. Cape Charles was laid out in 1883–84 at the southern terminus of the New York, Philadelphia, and Norfolk Railroad. The town owes its existence to its harbor, which, after dredging, enabled the railroad company to transport loaded cars by barge across the Chesapeake Bay to Norfolk. The town developed quickly and became the largest community on Virginia's Eastern Shore at the turn of the century. Its buildings were constructed on a twenty-seven-block grid dominated by a central park from which four landscaped streets extended. The remarkably intact architectural fabric ranges from small vernacular workers' housing of the 1880s to early 20th-century architect-designed commercial, residential, and municipal buildings. The preservation of the historic character was prompted by the cessation of freight and passenger ferries across the bay in the 1950s. Development was arrested, and the town became frozen in time. *(65–166) VLR: 08/15/89; NRHP: 01/03/91.*

CUSTIS TOMBS, *Capeville vicinity.* The monument marking the grave of John Custis IV is one of Virginia's most ambitious examples of colonial funerary art. The elaborately carved pyramidal-topped marble block is decorated with the Custis family coat-of-arms, a drapery-framed inscription, and a human skull motif. It was executed around 1750 by William Colley of Fenn Church Street, London, whose name and address are on the tomb. Also in the cemetery is the limestone slab of John Custis (1630–1696). The tombs are located near the site of Arlington, the Custis family seat. John Custis IV's great-grandson George Washington Parke Custis named his Fairfax County plantation, now Arlington National Cemetery, after his Eastern Shore ancestral home. The cemetery is maintained by the Northampton County Branch of the Association for the Preservation of Virginia Antiquities. *(65–66) VLR: 11/05/68; NRHP: 04/17/70.*

EYRE HALL, *Cheriton vicinity.* Eyre Hall's buildings and grounds present what is perhaps the most complete picture of gentry plantation life on the Eastern Shore of Virginia. The plantation was patented in 1662 by Thomas Eyre II. The massive gambrel-roof house was erected ca. 1760 for Littleton Eyre who acquired the land from his father. This section was built as an addition to a ca. 1735 dwelling, now incorporated in a two-story wing. The interior is embellished with superb woodwork consisting of paneled walls and pilaster-framed chimney breasts. A set of ca. 1816 French scenic wallpaper by Dufour, "Les Rives de Bosphore," decorates the hall. On the grounds are original outbuildings and a family cemetery with a series of table tombs. The early formal garden is among the state's most intact examples of its type. The plantation remains the property of Thomas Eyre's descendants. *(65–08) VLR: 09/09/69; NRHP: 11/12/69; BHR EASEMENT.*

GLEBE OF HUNGARS PARISH, *Bridgetown vicinity.* Virginia's colonial glebe houses normally served as residences for parish parsons and usually exhibited the same care in design, execution, and detailing found in the churches themselves. The Hungars Parish glebe house, with its glazed-header brickwork and interior paneling, well illustrates this high level of quality and is one of the least changed of the state's colonial glebe houses. It probably dates soon after 1745, the year in which the General Assembly authorized the building of glebe houses. As a result of the disestablishment of the Anglican church following the Revolution, the Commonwealth ordered the house to be sold by the parish. The vestry protested, and the dispute dragged on until the state took title in 1859. The property was sold into private ownership in 1870. The house was restored in the 1970s after standing empty for some thirty years. *(65–33) VLR: 12/02/69; NRHP: 02/26/70.*

GRAPELAND, *Wardtown.* Grapeland belongs to the Eastern Shore's important group of architecturally sophisticated Federal houses that includes Brownsville, Kerr Place, and Wharton Place among others. The distinguishing features of these houses are precise Flemish bond brickwork, refined proportions, and rich Federal detailing, inside and out. Set at the head of terraces leading down to Occohannock Creek, the house was erected for Edward W. Addison between 1825 and 1830. In addition to its highly refined woodwork, the interior preserves outstanding examples of original painted wood graining and marbling. Grapeland stood derelict for many years but underwent a long-term restoration in the late 1970s. A rare early 19th-century barn remains on the grounds. An 18th-century frame kitchen wing, formerly attached to the house and relocated elsewhere on the property in 1920, was returned to its original position in 1997. *(65–35) VLR: 06/21/77; NRHP: 05/06/80; BHR EASEMENT.*

HUNGARS CHURCH, *Bridgetown.* Begun in 1742 and completed by 1751, Hungars Episcopal Church is one of two remaining colonial churches on Virginia's Eastern Shore. As originally built, it was over 90 feet in length, making it the longest Anglican parish church in the colony and a testament to the importance of its parish. It was abandoned following the disestablishment of the Anglican church but was restored to use in 1819. Declared unsafe in 1850, its west wall and first bay were taken down, shortening the building's length to 74 feet. The church nevertheless remains a prime work of colonial ecclesiastical architecture. Finely executed gauged-brick arches with the rare addition of keystones highlight the windows. The 19th-century repairs included the installation of the intersecting window tracery. The church has a timeless setting in a grove of pine trees. *(65–12) VLR: 07/07/70; NRHP: 10/15/70.*

KENDALL GROVE, *Eastville vicinity.* Kendall Grove takes its name from George Kendall who in 1784 left the property to his fiancée, Margaret Eyre of Eyre Hall. In 1786 Miss Eyre married George Parker, member of a distinguished Eastern Shore family, who served in the Virginia Convention of 1788 and later was a judge on the Virginia General Court. The present house, built for the Parkers around 1813, is one of the Shore's important group of architecturally sophisticated Federal plantation houses. The exterior is marked by a pedimented central pavilion and modillion cornices. Inside are plaster cornices, reeded doorframes, paneled wainscoting, and Federal mantels, all illustrating how Eastern Shore gentry adapted urban fashions for high-style country residences. A long, low passage, or "colonnade," connecting the house to the kitchen is a feature indigenous to the region. Adjacent to the colonnade is a row of three original pyramidal-roof outbuildings. *(65–60) VLR: 10/21/80; NRHP: 06/21/82.*

NORTHAMPTON COUNTY COURTHOUSE SQUARE HISTORIC DISTRICT, *Eastville.* The assemblage of buildings on and around Eastville's court square includes the 1899 courthouse by Bartholomew F. Smith, the 1731 courthouse and clerk's office (shown), and an early 19th-century debtors' prison. The latter three buildings, maintained as museums by the Northampton County Branch of the Association for the Preservation of Virginia Antiquities, form an early court complex symbolic of the Eastern Shore's long history. The 1731 courthouse, built by John Marshall, was moved to its present location in 1913 in order to make room for a Confederate monument; the front wall was rebuilt in the process. Also here is a row of small attorneys' offices and the ca. 1800 Eastville Inn, a rambling frame courthouse tavern with several additions. Eastville has been the county seat since 1690. The county has the nation's oldest continuously kept English county records. *(214–07) VLR: 11/16/71; NRHP: 04/13/72.*

OAK GROVE, *Eastville vicinity.* Oak Grove's plantation house is situated in a commanding position at the tip of a peninsula with a sweeping vista of the Chesapeake Bay. Built in several stages, the oldest section is the gambrel-roof core that dates from the mid–18th century when the place was owned by John Haggoman. Additions made in 1811, 1840, and the 1940s give the house the evolutionary quality typical of the region, where the various generations of owners are reflected in the fabric of their dwellings. Original woodwork remains in each of the three early sections, including a paneled chimneypiece in the colonial part and intricately detailed Federal trim in the 1811 section. Oak Grove's 18th-century-style garden, designed by Richmond landscape architect Charles F. Gillette, was laid out in 1942. Among the early outbuildings are a smokehouse and an office, both of frame construction. *(65–19) VLR: 12/09/92; NRHP: 02/04/93; BHR EASEMENT.*

PEAR VALLEY, *Machipongo vicinity.* This early cottage is a textbook of early vernacular design and displays the refinement that the colonial housewright could give to small dwellings. Lending the house both dignity and stability is the brick end with its glazed headers forming decorative chevrons. The massive pyramidal chimney with its long tiled weatherings is typical of the Eastern Shore's earliest vernacular buildings. The interior retains its chamfered plate and chamfered ceiling joists, and the roof framing has the rare treatment of exposed rafter ends pegged into the plate. Pear Valley was long thought to be of 17th-century origin, but recent dendrochronology study indicates that it was built ca. 1740. Archaeological investigation has shown that the house, formerly considered to be an original one-room cottage, is the surviving end of a two-room structure and had a brick chimney opposite the existing chimney. *(65–52) VLR: 05/13/69; NRHP: 11/12/69.*

STRATTON MANOR, *Cape Charles vicinity.* Benjamin Stratton, member of a Northampton County family that had owned this land since 1636, constructed this finely crafted house about 1764, according to dated chimney bricks. Perhaps built on the site of an earlier Stratton family dwelling, the house exemplifies the 18th-century vernacular architecture typical of Virginia's Eastern Shore. Features associated with the regional form are frame construction with Flemish bond brick ends, chevron patterns in the gables (here obscured by paint), exterior chimneys with steeply sloping weatherings, and paneled chimney walls inside. In addition to tending his land, Stratton was a chairmaker, making the house interesting as an artisan's dwelling of the Revolutionary era. Stratton's home preserves its rural setting amid the flat fields of the Eastern Shore farmland. *(65–24) VLR: 09/16/80; NRHP: 11/28/80.*

SOMERS HOUSE, *Jamesville vicinity.* During the colonial period the Eastern Shore builders gave architectural quality and fine detailing not only to their larger works but to smaller ones as well. An excellent illustration of this phenomenon is the tiny Somers house, now standing abandoned and deteriorating in a field on Northampton County's Occohannock Neck. The glazed-header Flemish bond brickwork, careful proportions, and a refined interior paneled wall give this otherwise simple house all the dignity of a grand colonial mansion. The house dates after 1727, the year in which Thomas Smith gave the land to his grandson Leaven Smith, for whom the house was built. The Somers family owned it in the late 19th century. *(65–23) VLR: 12/02/69; NRHP: 02/26/70.*

VAUCLUSE, *Bridgetown vicinity.* Named for a region of southern France, Vaucluse was long the seat of the Eastern Shore's prominent Upshur family. It is believed that the brick-ended section of the present house was built for Littleton Upshur ca. 1784. His son Abel Parker Upshur (1791–1844), who was born at Vaucluse, expanded the house to approximately its present size in 1829, making it one of the county's grandest plantation dwellings. He served President John Tyler as secretary of the navy. In 1843 he was appointed secretary of state and was responsible for negotiating the treaty annexing Texas. His promising career ended abruptly in 1844 when a cannon aboard the USS *Princeton* accidentally exploded, killing Upshur and other officials. In the 1970s the plantation was subdivided for a housing development, but the waterfront setting of the house has been maintained. *(65–28) VLR: 12/02/69; NRHP: 09/15/70.*

WESTERHOUSE HOUSE, *Bridgetown vicinity.* An exceptionally rare example of Stuart-period southern vernacular architecture, this hall-parlor dwelling was built ca. 1700 and marks the first generation of structures in the area employing permanent construction. The house follows the precedent of the compact postmedieval cottages of England's West Country and Highlands. Characteristic features are the one-story elevation, steep gable roof, two-room plan, uneven arrangement of the openings, and the massive pyramidal exterior end chimney. No influence of the bookish classicism that was to mark the Georgian style is evident. William Westerhouse, a New England merchant, purchased the original 200-acre tract in 1661. The house was built either by his son Adrian or grandson William II. The house stood in a state of advanced deterioration until 1982 when it underwent renovation and received a new rear wing and dormers. *(65–30) VLR: 09/17/74; NRHP: 11/19/74.*

WINONA, *Bridgetown vicinity.* Winona is one of only two pre-Georgian houses in America to preserve Jacobean diagonally set chimney stacks. Like the other example, Bacon's Castle in Surry County, Winona employs three stacks above a massive, exterior end chimney breast. Such chimneys were a popular form on both vernacular and sophisticated buildings in Jacobean England but were used only rarely in the New World, probably because they were difficult to construct and were fashionable at a time when few permanent buildings were being erected here. Remnants of foundations projecting from the west end of the house suggest that Winona may originally have been a symmetrical building. The construction date has not been precisely determined, but it probably was built after 1681, the year Mathew Patrick acquired a reversionary interest in the property. The house is situated at the mouth of Hungars Creek, facing the Chesapeake Bay. *(65–32) VLR: 11/05/68; NRHP: 10/01/69.*

NORTHUMBERLAND COUNTY

At the tip of the Northern Neck, Northumberland County probably was named for the English shire. It was formed ca. 1645 from the district of Chickacoan, the 17th-century name of the area between the Potomac and the Rappahannock rivers. The county seat is Heathsville.

THE ANCHORAGE, *Ball Neck.* On property formerly known as Roadview, the earliest section of this two-part house was built in the second or third quarter of the 18th century, probably for Abraham Shears, grandson of the property's original patentee. The three-bay, gambrel-roof structure is typical of the many vernacular colonial dwellings once spread through the Northern Neck, of which only a handful remain. A defining feature is the massive double-shouldered brick chimney. The house was remodeled around 1800, when Federal mantels and other then-fashionable trim were added. In 1856 William C. Kent enlarged the house with a two-story wing in a country Greek Revival idiom. On the grounds are an 18th-century corn-crib and a family cemetery dating from the Kent family ownership. The house is situated on Mill Creek, a tidal tributary of the Chesapeake Bay. *(66–40) VLR: 01/15/95; NRHP: 03/17/95.*

CLAUGHTON-WRIGHT HOUSE, *Lewisetta vicinity.* The two-room-plan Claughton-Wright house is a rare surviving example of a diminutive dwelling type that was once a common element of the Tidewater Virginia landscape. Nearly all such small, well-built, and expensively finished dwellings of prosperous but unpretentious planters either have disappeared or have been engulfed in later enlargements. The house was constructed ca. 1787 by William Claughton, owner of some 422 acres and an officer in the local militia. Claughton's daughter Kitty and her husband, James Wright, remodeled the interior ca. 1827. Little changed since then, many of the 18th- and early 19th-century details survive. A striking feature is the massive brick chimney with its glazed-header Flemish bond and tiled weatherings. The house long stood abandoned but is currently undergoing a careful restoration. The archaeological sites of various outbuildings likely remain nearby. *(66–28) VLR: 03/19/97; NRHP: 05/23/97.*

COAN BAPTIST CHURCH, *Coan Stage vicinity.* A well-articulated work of country Classical Revival architecture, the Coan Baptist Church was built in 1846 to serve the growing congregation of what was originally Wicomico Baptist Church, formed in 1804. The congregation's new church reflects the Baptist revival that swept Tidewater Virginia in the mid–19th century. Under the leadership of Pastor Jeremiah Bell Jeter, the congregation grew dramatically, and it was during his tenure that the Rappahannock Association built its first campground in 1832. When completed, Coan Baptist Church, with its 70-foot sanctuary, was the Northern Neck's largest church. Its construction was a cooperative effort, with many members of the congregation helping to build it. The total cost was $900, a substantial sum in the 1840s. A conspicuous feature of the little-altered interior is the U-shaped gallery, which likely accommodated the church's nearly 200 black members. *(66–86) VLR: 01/15/95; NRHP: 03/17/95.*

HEATHSVILLE HISTORIC DISTRICT. Heathsville has served as the county seat of Northumberland County since it was established in 1681 as Northumberland Court House. Though today it is little more than a crossroads village, the present town was laid out according to a plan prepared in 1798 by the architect Benjamin Henry Latrobe. A broad range of early architecture is found in the district's 100 contributing buildings, most of it vernacular in character. Several, however, exhibit influences of academic styles. The present courthouse, a modified Queen Anne–style building, was designed by Bartholomew F. Smith and erected in 1900–1901. In front is the 1873 Confederate monument. Behind the courthouse is Rice's Hotel, the core of which is the 18th-century courthouse tavern. Nearby are an 1844 jail and an antebellum Methodist church. A small commercial core is adjacent to the court square. Maintaining the community's historic rural context are five antebellum plantation complexes. *(66–101) VLR: 12/11/91; NRHP: 02/26/92.*

DITCHLEY, *Kilmarnock vicinity.* The Ditchley tract was patented in 1651 by Richard Lee, progenitor of the Lee family of Virginia. The present mansion, begun ca. 1762 by Kendall Lee, a great-grandson of Richard Lee, is classic colonial Georgian architecture. The house has the handsome brickwork, hipped roof, and geometric proportions characteristic of Virginia's finest plantation houses. The interior preserves much original woodwork including a noteworthy Georgian stair. In 1792 the Lee family sold Ditchley to James Ball, kinsman of Mary Ball Washington, mother of George Washington. The property remained in the Ball family throughout the 19th century. In 1932 Ditchley was purchased by Mr. and Mrs. Alfred I. duPont of Wilmington, Del. Jessie Dew Ball duPont (1884–1970) was related to the Balls of Ditchley. After her husband's death, Mrs. duPont, who used Ditchley as a retreat, became one of America's most generous philanthropists, personally making grants to several hundred institutions. *(66–04) VLR: 04/22/92; NRHP: 09/24/92.*

HOLLEY GRADED SCHOOL, *Lottsburg.* Holley Graded School represents the dedicated work of a small black community that, despite economic hardship and the deterrence of segregation, erected a schoolhouse which was remarkably well appointed for its time and the people it served. It was begun ca. 1914 to replace a smaller schoolhouse erected during the Reconstruction era. It stands on property purchased shortly after the Civil War by Sallie Holley (1818–1893) of New York State, for whom the school was later named. An ardent abolitionist, Holley followed the example of her friend Emily Howland and established a school for former slaves in Northumberland County in 1869. The present school was primitive compared to the commodious facilities for white children, but it was a point of pride in that it was achieved entirely through private efforts of the black community. It now houses the county Adult Literacy Program. *(66–112) VLR: 04/18/89; NRHP: 12/19/90.*

HOWLAND CHAPEL SCHOOL, *Howland.* Howland Chapel School, the county's oldest schoolhouse, is a poignant reminder of the various efforts of idealistic northerners to assist with the education of the children of Virginia's former slaves. The simple building was erected in 1867 under the sponsorship of New York educator, reformer, and philanthropist Emily Howland (1827–1929), who came to Northumberland County at the close of the Civil War. She purchased land for blacks to farm and taught school in a small log structure. Her classes were so popular that the present, more substantial structure, designed to serve also as a chapel, was soon erected. Miss Howland returned to the North in 1870 but supported the school financially for the next fifty years. The school continued until 1958; the building now serves as a museum, community center, and adult education facility. *(66–110) VLR: 06/20/89; NRHP: 01/25/91.*

HURSTVILLE, *Ball Neck.* Contrasting with the stately brick dwellings of colonial Virginia's leading landed families, Hurstville represents the type of dwelling favored by the lesser gentry of the period. The property is part of a 1651 grant to John Waddy. The present house most likely was built soon after 1776 when the land was acquired by Thomas Hurst. The dwelling is noteworthy for its rare four-room plan and its large south chimney, an excellent example of 18th-century Virginia brickwork. In addition to the glazed-header Flemish bond, the chimney features the infrequently employed device of tumbled courses. In 1940 Hurstville was purchased by the noted philanthropist Jessie Ball duPont, who had the house restored as a residence for her sisters. Scenically located on a tidal creek with a view of the Chesapeake Bay, Hurstville preserves its 18th-century riparian ambience. *(66–35) VLR: 04/22/92; NRHP: 09/24/92.*

KIRKLAND GROVE, *Heathsville vicinity.* Named for the local Baptist preacher Dr. William Heath Kirk, who was active in the area from 1845 to 1884, Kirkland Grove is one of the state's few remaining 19th-century religious campgrounds. It is set apart from other religious meeting sites by its massive tabernacle, along with its preacher's "tent," or dwelling, and a campers' "tent." William Dandridge Cockrell designed and built the all-wood tabernacle in 1892. A local craftsman, Cockrell is reported to have designed the tabernacle to specifications from the Old Testament. Annual camp meetings held each August attracted large crowds of people who filled the tabernacle's 101 benches and stayed in the 42 cottages that once stood on the campground. Kirkland Grove is the only campground in the region that continues to hold regular yearly revivals. *(66–89) VLR: 12/11/91; NRHP: 10/15/92.*

REEDVILLE HISTORIC DISTRICT. Reedville, a maritime village on a narrow peninsula at the end of the Northern Neck, arose after the Civil War through the development of the menhaden industry by Elijah Reed. Menhaden, small bony fish, were especially abundant in summer and replaced the whale as America's primary source of fish oil. Reed established the first menhaden factory here in 1875, and by 1885 there were fifteen menhaden factories at Reedville. The village preserves a number of modest 1870s frame dwellings erected after New England prototypes by the Reed family for factory workmen and relatives. Reedville's impressive larger houses reflect the village's prosperity in its heyday at the turn of the century. Dominating the scene is an unusually fine and well-preserved collection of late Victorian and early 20th-century residences built for local industrialists, sea captains, and merchants, including Elijah Reed. *(66–83) VLR: 06/19/84; NRHP: 08/16/84.*

RICE'S HOTEL (HUGHLETT'S TAVERN), *Heathsville.*
Standing behind the courthouse, Rice's Hotel has been a key element in this county-seat complex since the late 18th century, offering food, drink, and lodging to visitors. The building, originally known as Hughlett's Tavern for its proprietor John Hughlett, began ca. 1790 as a two-room-plan building. It evolved to its present 110-foot length with its two-level gallery through additions occurring in the 1830s, 1880s, and 1920s. The tavern was purchased by John Rice in 1866 and was operated as Rice's Hotel until 1920 when converted into apartments. In 1990 Cecelia Fallin Rice donated the property to the Northumberland County Historical Society, which currently is restoring the building for a museum and special events. A 1991 investigation of the grounds revealed numerous associated archaeological features including walkways, post holes, and trash pits, along with 13,000 artifacts. *(66–09) VLR: 04/22/92; NRHP: 10/15/92; AMENDED FOR ARCHEOLOGICAL COMPONENT 12/08/93.*

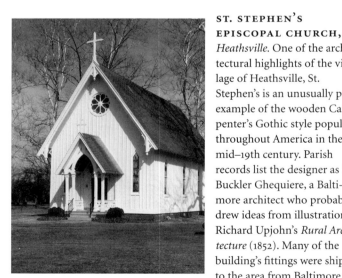

ST. STEPHEN'S EPISCOPAL CHURCH, *Heathsville.* One of the architectural highlights of the village of Heathsville, St. Stephen's is an unusually pure example of the wooden Carpenter's Gothic style popular throughout America in the mid–19th century. Parish records list the designer as T. Buckler Ghequiere, a Baltimore architect who probably drew ideas from illustrations in Richard Upjohn's *Rural Architecture* (1852). Many of the building's fittings were shipped to the area from Baltimore. Consecrated in 1881, a full generation after the Gothic style had reached its zenith in other parts of the country, the building is evidence of rural Virginia's slowly evolved architectural taste. St. Stephen's Parish was originally formed in 1698 and was reactivated in 1824 as part of the reawakening of the Episcopal church in Virginia after the disestablishment. *(66–27) VLR: 09/18/79; NRHP: 12/28/79.*

SHALANGO, *Sandy Point vicinity.* On the Great Wicomico River in the northeastern part of the county, Shalango is one of the largest antebellum plantation houses in Northumberland County. Maintaining an air of untouched antiquity, the house was erected in 1855–56 for planter John Hopkins Coles and is still owned by his descendants. Like its several contemporaries in the region, the single-pile dwelling has a straightforward conservatism, employing the five-bay, gable-roof, center-passage format in use in eastern Virginia since the colonial period. The interior, however, has more stylish Greek Revival and Italianate style detailing. Especially noteworthy is the three-story, open-well stair, one of the most impressive of its type in the region. John Hopkins Coles served in the Virginia cavalry during the Civil War and later was a county magistrate. *(66–88) VLR: 04/15/86; NRHP: 11/06/86.*

SHILOH SCHOOL, *Rehoboth Church vicinity, Ball Neck.* Recalling a bygone era of American education, Shiloh School is a rare example of an unaltered one-room school building. Such diminutive structures once dotted the American countryside, providing sound, basic education to rural children. Most of the remaining ones of this quickly disappearing building type have been converted to homes or stand abandoned; Shiloh was used for farm storage since the last classes were held here in 1929. The building was erected in 1906. The well-known philanthropist Jessie Ball (later duPont) taught here in 1906 and 1907. A great believer in the power of learning, Mrs. duPont gave a large portion of her considerable wealth to educational purposes through the Jessie Ball duPont Religious, Charitable, and Educational Fund. In 1987 the property was donated to Northumberland Preservation, Inc., which undertook the restoration of the school as a community amenity. *(66–34) VLR: 06/19/91; NRHP: 01/22/92.*

SPRINGFIELD, *Heathsville.* Springfield is a Federal house dominating a level tract of land on the edge of Heathsville. Erected in 1828 by merchant William Harding, the house was enlarged and enriched by him in 1850, so that it now presents a blend of two different styles forming one of the more impressive 19th-century houses on the Northern Neck. The stylistic contrast can be seen particularly on the interior where rich Greek Revival ceiling medallions add interest to the otherwise restrained Federal rooms. The main block of the house is framed by unusual stepped parapets on wings added in the 1850 remodeling. The present configuration of the portico with its cast-iron railing is also a product of the remodeling. On the grounds are an early office, a dairy, and a servant's house. The gardens originally were embellished with a boxwood maze. *(66–11) VLR: 09/18/79; NRHP: 12/28/79.*

SUNNYSIDE, *Heathsville.* Sunnyside represents the successful mid-19th-century farmstead complex typical of Virginia's Northern Neck. The I-house form and Federal-style woodwork of the dwelling house are common characteristics of gentry domiciles of the region. Sunnyside, however, is set apart because of its substantially unaltered state. The facade, with its columned porch and iron railings, remains unchanged from an 1883 published photograph. Adding to the scene is the collection of early outbuildings, including a kitchen which predates the house. While documentary evidence is complicated and contradictory, it is ultimately clear that the house was built and enlarged with a two-story wing for Royston Betts between 1834 and 1841. Although no longer attached to a farm, the house, outbuildings, and immediate grounds have been carefully preserved by its present owners since they purchased it in 1979. *(66–55) VLR: 10/18/95; NRHP: 05/23/96.*

VERSAILLES, *Burgess.* A tall weatherboarded I-house fronted by a two-tier portico, Versailles is one of several surviving manifestations of a domestic form that gained popularity on the Northern Neck in antebellum times. Ambitiously named for one of the world's most palatial residences, the Northern Neck Versailles does at least share with its Gallic antecedent a certain stateliness. The house was completed in 1857 for Samuel Benedict Burgess, a farmer, gristmill operator, justice of the peace, and pillar of the local Methodist church. Burgess also served a term in the Virginia House of Delegates. Like the outside, the interior of Burgess's Versailles has no-nonsense Greek Revival trim. Little changed since Burgess's occupancy, the house stands as a conspicuous historic point of interest on one of the Northern Neck's principal highways. The boxwood in front of the house are the remnants of an early garden. *(66–96) VLR: 12/04/96; NRHP: 02/27/97.*

WHEATLAND, *Lottsburg vicinity.* Wheatland was built in 1840 as the centerpiece of a 1,300-acre plantation. One of the Northern Neck's most sophisticated antebellum houses, Wheatland was originally the home of Dr. William Hopkins Harding, a wealthy physician and planter who served in the General Assembly. Except for wings added in 1848, the dwelling is little changed and exudes a stately air with its regular five-bay facades and nearly identical two-tiered Doric porticoes on the land and river fronts. Inside is bold, provincial Federal and Greek Revival–style woodwork as well as a finely detailed Greek Revival parlor ceiling medallion echoing a design in Asher Benjamin's *The Practice of Architecture* (1833). The house is set off by four symmetrically arranged original outbuildings linked by a series of early walkways. A tree-lined driveway leads across level fields to the entrance. *(66–13) VLR: 04/15/86; NRHP: 11/15/88.*

NOTTOWAY COUNTY

Nottoway County, in the heart of Southside Virginia, was formed from Amelia County in 1788 and was named for the Nadowa Indian tribe living here during the early 17th century. The county seat is Nottoway Court House.

BLACKSTONE HISTORIC DISTRICT. A full range of small-town American building types is present in the historic commercial and residential quarters of this Southside community. The town grew up around Schwartz Tavern, a late 18th-century landmark. Concentrated building did not occur until after 1881 with the formation of the Norfolk and Western Railway system, which established the community as a shipping point. The town, formerly named Black's and White's, was incorporated with its new name, Blackstone, in 1888 and became a leading tobacco market. The commercial area preserves a rich display of early 1900s facades, many faced with decorative sheet metal. The large residential neighborhood south and west of the commercial area was developed after 1900 by the Blackstone Land and Improvement Co. and contains a broad range of Queen Anne and Colonial Revival dwellings along with four churches and the 1922 Georgian Revival former Blackstone College of Girls. *(142–07) VLR: 02/20/90; NRHP: 01/25/91.*

BURKE'S TAVERN, *Burkeville vicinity.* This simple vernacular hostelry is a reminder of a flourishing period in the area, when taverns were the scene of much local socializing and political activity. Located at a rural crossroads on the Nottoway–Prince Edward County line, the tavern fostered a tiny settlement which took the name Burke's Tavern and included an extant antebellum store across the road. Although a tavern had existed at the site since the mid–18th century, the present structure was erected ca. 1827 for Samuel Burke, a militia colonel, Whig politician, and local entrepreneur. Thomas A. Smythe, the last Union general mortally wounded in the Civil War, died in the tavern on April 9, 1865. *(67–47) VLR: 06/17/75; NRHP: 07/17/75.*

LITTLE MOUNTAIN PICTOGRAPHS SITE, *Blackstone vicinity.* Adorning a rugged rockface, these pictographs belong to a class of archaeological resources whose rarity makes them significant at the national level. The pictographs feature a single human handprint, a possible "sun glyph," and a solitary "turkey-foot." All are painted in red ocher and probably date to the Late Woodland period (ca. A.D. 900–1600). Though very elementary, the pictographs reflect Native American artistic and symbolic expression rarely occurring in eastern America as painted images. The presumed ritualistic or ceremonial function of the site at such an isolated and dramatic setting further provides important insight into a poorly understood aspect of regional settlement patterns. *(67–107) VLR: 08/21/90; NRHP: 02/15/91.*

NOTTOWAY COUNTY COURTHOUSE, *Nottoway Court House.* Nottoway County's Roman Revival courthouse is the physical heart of its tiny county-seat village. Like many of Virginia's antebellum courthouses, this remarkably sophisticated and visually satisfying work shows the influence of Thomas Jefferson's architecture on the state's public buildings. The courthouse was completed in 1843 on the site of the 1798 courthouse that it replaced. Its builder was Branch H. Ellington who incorporated devices favored by Jefferson such as the three-part Palladian scheme, Tuscan portico, triple-hung sash, and carefully crafted Flemish bond brickwork. The marble sills and lintels add an element of special refinement. Union soldiers bivouacked here on April 5, 1865, during which time many county records were destroyed. The courthouse, however, especially the exterior, remains remarkably well preserved. *(67–04) VLR: 07/17/73; NRHP: 08/13/73.*

OAKRIDGE, *Blackstone vicinity.* This weatherboarded country Georgian structure is a typical and well-preserved example of a residence of a prosperous planter of Virginia's southern Piedmont. It was built ca. 1800 for Burwell Smith, a Southside landowner who, in contrast to his substantial and well-finished house, was described by one writer as "a particularly parsimonious and illiterate man." Although the generously proportioned house appears to have been built in two sections, the one-story wing is part of the original construction. The main rooms are ornamented with paneled wainscoting and paneled chimneypieces framed by fluted pilasters. A special interior feature is the Chinese lattice stair railing, a stylish device sometimes found in finer Federal houses in southern Virginia. *(67–14) VLR: 03/15/77; NRHP: 01/30/78.*

SCHWARTZ TAVERN, *111 Tavern Street, Blackstone.* Ninety-nine feet in length, this rambling historic tavern, erected in three sections, is Blackstone's oldest building. The construction date of each section is uncertain, but in 1790 the property on which the tavern stands was deeded to John Schwartz, who had been granted a license to operate an ordinary here in 1789. Tradition has it that the town derives its name from his last name, which is German for "black." Although it stood in neglected condition for many years, the tavern preserves a remarkable amount of early fabric including beaded weatherboards, original window sashes, and Federal mantels. In 1977 the Anderson family donated the tavern and its large lot to the community. The building subsequently underwent a thorough restoration under the sponsorship of the Schwartz Tavern Authority. This venerable landmark now serves as a museum and a venue for special events. *(142–01) VLR: 06/18/74; NRHP: 06/28/74.*

ORANGE COUNTY

Formed from Spotsylvania County in 1734, this pastoral Piedmont county probably was named for William IV, prince of Orange-Nassau, who married Princess Anne, eldest daughter of King George II, that same year. Its county seat is Orange.

BALLARD-MARSHALL HOUSE, *158 East Main Street, Orange.* Lending a sense of continuity and place to the town of Orange, the Ballard-Marshall house demonstrates the pervasiveness of the Classical Revival tradition in the Virginia Piedmont. Set off by its pedimented roof, classical trim, and systematic proportions, the house was built in 1832 for Garland Ballard, a local merchant. The builders are not known, but the use of finely crafted Flemish bond and informed detailing suggests a connection with local projects constructed by craftsmen formerly employed by Thomas Jefferson. During the mid–19th century the house was owned by the locally prominent Taylor family. In 1882 it became the home of Fielding Lewis Marshall, the local superintendent of public education and grandson of Chief Justice John Marshall. The property remained in Marshall family ownership until 1962. Rescued from neglect in 1986, the house has been rehabilitated for apartments. *(275–01)*
VLR: 06/21/88; NRHP: 10/27/88.

BARBOURSVILLE, *Barboursville.* Until it burned on Christmas Day, 1884, James Barbour's home at Barboursville stood essentially as completed ca. 1822 from designs supplied by Barbour's friend Thomas Jefferson. Jefferson's drawings called for a dwelling with a recessed portico on the north front and a three-part bay sheltered by a portico on the south front, with dome above—a scheme resembling Jefferson's Monticello. The dome, however, was not built. Even in its ruinous state, the house presents a romantic image of the Jeffersonian ideal, a compact but architecturally sophisticated classical villa in a carefully contrived landscape setting. The great grassy oval in front of the house was originally a racetrack. James Barbour (1775–1842), a statesman and diplomat, held many public offices, including governor of Virginia, secretary of war, and minister to Great Britain. The stabilized ruins are now the centerpiece of one of Virginia's first large-scale wineries. *(68–02)*
VLR: 09/09/69; NRHP: 11/12/69.

BERRY HILL, *Orange.* On a tree-shaded hill overlooking the town of Orange, Berry Hill is a Jeffersonian-style house attributed to William B. Phillips and Malcolm F. Crawford, master builders employed by Thomas Jefferson during the construction of the University of Virginia. The house originally had an open portico above the arcaded ground floor and thus closely resembled Pavilion VII at the university. The portico was walled in soon after the house was completed in 1824 for Reynolds Chapman, the county clerk. The two-story wing, however, is part of the original construction. Even in its altered form, the house is one of the most successful adaptations of the Jeffersonian idiom for a private residence. Although Phillips and Crawford have not been documented as having worked at Berry Hill, they were known to Chapman and were building Jeffersonian-style structures in the area at the time. *(68–04) VLR: 02/19/80; NRHP: 05/07/80.*

BLOOMSBURY, *Orange vicinity.* Bloomsbury was established sometime after 1720 by Col. James Taylor, Sr., one of the area's earliest landowners and ancestor of both presidents James Madison and Zachary Taylor. The date of the original section is undocumented, but it may have been built as early as 1722 for James Taylor II. Though its exterior is unassuming, the finely appointed interior has a unique floor plan and an unusual staircase. According to family tradition, the wide stair landing, with its decorative turned-baluster railing, formed a musicians' gallery. The house was doubled in size by a plain two-story addition around 1800. Bloomsbury is unusually well preserved and retains a scenic rural setting of broad fields and wooded hills. On the grounds are a 19th-century smokehouse, an 18th-century cemetery, and vestiges of a rare early garden with terraces and a sunken area. *(68–05) VLR: 06/19/90; NRHP: 02/27/92.*

BURLINGTON, *Barboursville.* Burlington is a classic demonstration of the transmission of sophisticated architectural design to rural buildings through the medium of publication. This stately plantation house is embellished with Greek-style decorations copied with precision from illustrations in Asher Benjamin's pattern book *The Practical House Carpenter* (1830), a work that profoundly influenced American building. It was Benjamin's handsome plates and straightforward instructions that made the grandeur of Attica accessible to the nation's nethermost regions. Burlington was constructed in 1851 by master carpenter George H. Stockdon for James Barbour Newman, nephew of Governor James Barbour. Most of the labor was provided by blacks, both free and slave. The fluted Ionic columns, doorway, window frames, mantels, and moldings are all faithfully interpreted Benjamin designs. An exception is the Chinese lattice balcony railing, a detail popularized in the area by Thomas Jefferson. Essentially unchanged, Burlington retains its gentle rural setting. *(68–07) VLR: 10/20/93; NRHP: 01/11/94; BHR EASEMENTS.*

"ENCHANTED CASTLE" AT GERMANNA ARCHAEO-LOGICAL SITE, *Germanna Bridge.* Following his term as the colony's lieutenant governor, Alexander Spotswood resided at his Spotsylvania (later Orange) County estate where in the 1720s he erected a brick and stone mansion with outbuildings and ter-

raced gardens overlooking the Rapidan River. His plantation formed part of the Germanna community, first established in 1714 as Fort Germanna, where German immigrants prospected for minerals, including iron ores, for Spotswood's Tubal Furnace. After Spotswood's death in 1740, the house was abandoned and later burned. The site remained undisturbed until 1977 when Virginia Department of Historic Resources archaeologists confirmed its location. Excavations in 1984 revealed its general configuration, which conforms to William Byrd's 1732 description of an "enchanted castle." These remnants of one of the colony's foremost plantation dwellings and gardens are now owned by the Commonwealth and managed by Mary Washington College. *(68–43) VLR: 06/21/77; NRHP: 08/24/78.*

EXCHANGE HOTEL, *400 South Main Street, Gordonsville.* This Gordonsville landmark is a forerunner of the large railroad hotels that played an important role in the transportation history of late 19th- and early 20th-century America. The galleried structure was built in 1860 for Richard F. Omohundro next to an important railroad junction. It served as a popular stopping place for travelers until the outbreak of hostilities when, because of its strategic location, it became part of the Gordonsville Receiving Hospital, admitting more than 23,000 sick and wounded in less than a year. The scene of untold agony and death, the building survived the conflict. It again became a hotel after the war and enjoyed a fine reputation until the 1940s when it went into decline. Historic Gordonsville, Inc., acquired and restored the building in the 1970s. It now serves as the Exchange Hotel Civil War Museum. *(225–08) VLR: 07/17/73; NRHP: 08/14/73.*

FRASCATI, *Somerset vicinity.* Frascati, built 1821–23 for Supreme Court justice and statesman Philip Pendleton Barbour, is one of the architectural monuments of the Piedmont. With its detailed specifications surviving, the house is also among the region's best-documented 19th-century dwellings. The monumental structure was designed and built by John M. Perry of Albemarle County, who was one of the master builders employed by Thomas Jefferson both at Monticello and the University of Virginia. Its Tuscan portico and academic classical detailing show a strong Jeffersonian influence. The plan and general outline, however, follow the more conventional Georgian schemes of that day. In the parlor are an outstanding plasterwork ceiling medallion and entablature, the latter copied from a design in Asher Benjamin's *American Builder's Companion* (1806). Surviving on the grounds are an original kitchen outbuilding and remnants of extensive original gardens. *(68–14) VLR: 09/16/80; NRHP: 06/28/82.*

GORDONSVILLE HISTORIC DISTRICT. The assemblage of 19th- and early 20th-century residential, commercial, and church buildings forming this Piedmont community reflects the vicissitudes of a Virginia railroad town. Named for Nathaniel Gordon, a late 18th-century tavern keeper here, the hamlet exploded into a thriving transportation hub in the 1840s and early 1850s with the arrival of two railroads and two major turnpikes. Gordonsville's growth, which reached its peak after the Civil War, ended suddenly with completion in the early 1880s of a north-south railroad corridor bypassing the town to the west. The district centers on a three-quarter-mile stretch of Main Street leading south past tree-shaded 19th-century residences and churches to the Chesapeake and Ohio Railway overpass. The solid row of brick commercial structures forming the town's business district was built up after fires in 1916 and 1920. *(225–30) VLR: 08/16/83; NRHP: 10/13/83.*

GREENWOOD, *Greenwood Road, Orange vicinity.* The core building of this immaculately maintained ensemble is a dignified but understated frame I-house erected ca. 1820 on property deeded in 1818 by Thomas Macon to his daughter Lucy, wife of Reuben Conway. The Macons and Conways were both locally prominent landed families and were kinsmen of James Madison who resided at nearby Montpelier. Although enlarged in 1850 with the addition of a two-story wing, and later with a modern kitchen and garage, the original portion of the house is little changed. Its interior preserves simple late Federal trim. One early outbuilding stands amid a cluster of later but architecturally compatible structures. Like many historic dwellings in Orange County, Greenwood was carefully sited to take advantage of a panoramic view of the Blue Ridge Mountains. The 111 acres remaining with the property preserve the integrity of Greenwood's rural setting. *(68–52) VLR: 10/21/92; NRHP: 12/17/92; BHR EASEMENT.*

HAMPSTEAD FARM ARCHAEOLOGICAL DISTRICT, *Somerset vicinity.* Hampstead Farm presents a unique opportunity to study nearly all the periods of human occupation of Virginia's northern Piedmont. The district is spread across 780 acres of beautiful rolling hills and bottomland along the south side of the Rapidan River. Indian remains representing cultures from the Paleo-Indian, Archaic, and Woodland periods are found at forty-six identified sites. Testing on three bottomland sites has revealed buried deposits of Indian material. Evidence of historic occupation is found on three additional sites. A section of road built by Robert Beverley in the 1730s to span his Octonia tract is clearly visible (shown). An 18th-century house site, the home of Benjamin Johnson, a captain in the Revolutionary army and father-in-law of Governor James Barbour, offers further potential for archaeological data. Three gun emplacements and a communication ditch are relics of Civil War activity. *(68–182) VLR: 05/15/84; NRHP: 08/16/84.*

HARE FOREST, *Trimmers Crossing.* Recent research has shown that this Orange County homestead, formerly believed to have been built ca. 1812 for Dr. Francis Dade, was actually erected for John S. Terrill in 1833–40. The dwelling employs a Federal vernacular idiom consistent with several other architecturally conservative buildings in the county including Bloomfield (ca. 1840), the Holladay house (ca. 1830), and the Sparks Brothers building (ca. 1829). The plain single-pile structure has an asymmetrical Flemish bond facade here given a touch of style with its flared stuccoed lintels and raised keystones. The interior preserves simple Federal woodwork. Today the house, with later additions, sits amid handsome landscaped grounds, the centerpiece of a fastidiously maintained horse farm. *(68–124) VLR: 04/17/91; NRHP: 01/28/92.*

MADISON-BARBOUR RURAL HISTORIC DISTRICT. Encompassing roughly forty square miles of Piedmont countryside, this rural historic district is one of Virginia's most intact cultural landscapes. The rolling, semimountainous terrain is broken periodically by broad stretches of fields and pastureland. A web of 18th- and 19th-century roadways offers expansive views of unspoiled pastoral scenery. For more than two and a half centuries the area's gentry have exhibited their wealth by erecting some of the state's most impressive country houses. Sprinkled through the region are several 19th-century hamlets including Tibbstown, Barboursville, and Somerset. The district's name refers to the area's two most prominent landowning families, the Madisons and the Barbours, who were responsible for its two nationally significant plantation complexes—Montpelier and Barboursville. The district also contains more than 200 contributing dwellings in various national styles and vernacular forms reflecting a broad socioeconomic spectrum. *(68–304) VLR: 07/21/87; NRHP: 01/17/91.*

MAYHURST, *Orange vicinity.* The vibrancy that American architects gave to the Italian Villa style is no better shown than in Mayhurst, described by architectural historian William B. O'Neal as "a delicious Victorian fantasy." The architect has not been recorded; however, its stylistic similarity to Camden in Caroline County has led to its attribution to Norris G. Starkweather of Baltimore. The designer might also have been Charles Haskins of Haskins and Alexander of Washington, D.C., who designed the Italian Villa–style Orange County Courthouse. The tall structure, decked out with a bracketed cornice, rusticated wood siding, and a cupola terminating in a scroll-ornamented finial, illustrates the mid-19th-century taste for the exotic. The house was commissioned by Col. John Willis, a great-nephew of James Madison, and was begun in 1859. Restored in recent years as an inn, Mayhurst retains its parklike setting. *(68–25) VLR: 09/09/69; NRHP: 11/12/69.*

MONTPELIER, *Montpelier Station.* Montpelier, the lifelong home of James Madison, "Father of the Constitution" and fourth president of the United States, was also home to three generations of the Madison family from 1723 to 1844. The mansion core was built by Madison's father ca. 1760. With advice of his friend Thomas Jefferson, Madison enlarged the house, adding the Tuscan portico ca. 1797. Additional changes were made ca. 1809 by James Dinsmore and John Neilson, master builders working for Jefferson. A domed garden temple was also built on the property. The house was further enlarged ca. 1900 by William duPont. Today it remains the nucleus of an 2,700-acre estate containing farmlands, forests, formal gardens, 135 buildings, and a steeplechase course. Madison and his wife Dolley lie buried in the family cemetery on the property. Montpelier is owned and exhibited by the National Trust for Historic Preservation. *(68–30) VLR: 09/09/69; NRHP: 10/15/66; NHL: 12/19/60.*

ORANGE SPRINGS, *Danton vicinity.* Developed around a sulphur spring, Orange Springs was one of Virginia's few early spas east of the Blue Ridge. The therapeutic quality of its waters was noted as early as 1793 when James Madison, Sr., father of the president, wrote that after bathing in and drinking the water, his wife was "restored to her former state of health." In 1792 James Coleman applied for a license to operate a tavern "at the healing springs." The existing house was built ca. 1793 as the main building of Coleman's tavern complex. It was soon converted to a house of entertainment with a dining room and "dancing room." The spa complex eventually included a series of visitors' cabins and operated until around 1850. President James Madison was one of its patrons. Since the spa's closing, the old main building has served as a farm residence. *(68–66) VLR: 06/19/90; NRHP: 02/27/92.*

ORANGE COUNTY COURT-HOUSE, *North Main Street and Madison Road, Orange.* The Orange County Courthouse marks a radical departure from the traditional classical-style Virginia courthouse, illustrating public acceptance of exotic taste in late antebellum times. Designed by Charles Haskins of the Washington firm of Haskins and Alexander and erected in 1858–59, the building has all of the major characteristics of the Italian Villa style: deep bracketed cornices, shallow-hipped roofs, and square tower. The work is Orange County's fourth court structure built specifically as such. It replaced an existing courthouse that was taken down as the result of railroad construction. The arcaded openings on the first floor were filled in ca. 1948. The courthouse is complemented by its clerk's office, jail, and Confederate monument. *(275–03) VLR: 09/18/79; NRHP: 12/28/79.*

ROCKLANDS, *Gordonsville vicinity.* Occupying a long, narrow valley west of Gordonsville, Rocklands boasts a porticoed Georgian Revival mansion set amid spacious grounds and unusually scenic fields and pastures that once saw considerable Civil War activity. The mansion was erected in 1905–7 for Thomas Atkinson of Richmond on the site of a mid-19th-century residence of Richard Barton Haxall of the Richmond milling family. Its architect has not been determined, but William Lawrence Bottomley was responsible for an extensive remodeling undertaken in the 1930s at which time the high basement was removed and the house lowered in order to give it a more direct relationship with the landscape. Bottomley also designed service buildings based on those at Upper Bremo in Fluvanna County. The work was undertaken for Mrs. Doris K. Neale, who also commissioned landscape architect Umberto Innocenti to design the formal gardens. *(68–181) VLR: 07/20/82; NRHP: 09/23/82; BHR EASEMENT.*

ST. THOMAS'S EPISCOPAL CHURCH,

119 Caroline Street, Orange. This expression of Classical Revivalism is the successor to the original church of St. Thomas's Parish, demolished after the disestablishment. Erected in 1833–34, the church originally lacked its Tuscan portico *in antis.* This feature probably was added in 1853 when the church was remodeled and enlarged. The alteration of the windows into pointed Gothic windows was made between 1890 and 1895. The builders of the church have not been documented, but they may have been William B. Phillips and Malcolm F. Crawford who worked for Jefferson at the University of Virginia and later built finely crafted Classical Revival works in the central Piedmont. During the Civil War, St. Thomas's served as a Confederate hospital after the battles of Cedar Mountain, Chancellorsville, the Wilderness, and Spotsylvania Court House. *(275–08) VLR: 02/17/76; NRHP 12/06/76.*

SOMERSET CHRISTIAN CHURCH,

Somerset. An unaltered example of a mid-19th-century country church, this diminutive building was erected ca. 1857 to serve a small but active community of the Christian denomination in the rural neighborhood of Somerset. With its bracketed cornice and porch echoing the Italian Villa influence, the prominently sited church is a stylistic departure from the Greek Revival and Gothic modes that characterized most Virginia country churches of the period. The interior retains its original furnishings, including its pews, still decorated with painted wood graining. Maintained by a dedicated congregation, the church now holds regular Sunday services following a period of sporadic use. *(68–80) VLR: 09/19/78; NRHP: 02/01/79.*

TETLEY, *Somerset vicinity.* Beautifully situated in the pastoral landscape of Orange County, a county renowned for its country estates, Tetley in antebellum times was a 1,500-acre plantation owned by William Smith. Smith was a captain in the Virginia militia and became one of the county's larger landowners. His brick mansion, built around 1843, was a finely appointed structure exhibiting influences of both the Federal and Greek Revival styles. Its similarity to area houses designed by master builder William A. Jennings favors an attribution. Smith died in 1856 leaving among his possessions fifty-eight slaves valued at over $100,000. The plantation was purchased by Charles Stoven who renamed it Tetley after a family home in England. Changes were made to both the house and gardens when the estate was purchased by the Eriksen family in 1944. On the grounds are an original octagonal icehouse, a kitchen outbuilding, and two slave houses. *(68–106) VLR: 12/11/90; NRHP: 02/05/91.*

WADDELL MEMORIAL PRESBYTERIAN CHURCH,

Rapidan. Named in honor of James Waddell, Orange County's blind preacher, this country church is Virginia's finest specimen of Carpenter's Gothic architecture. A forest of spires sprouts from the nave, transepts, and vestry of the board-and-batten structure. All of the details are formed from milled boards reduced by sawing to the desired shapes and then nailed together. Built in 1874, the church was designed by J. B. Danforth, an amateur architect who also was chief clerk at Richmond's Mutual Assurance Society. A tracing of Danforth's drawings by the Richmond carpenter-architect John Gibson, who presumably worked on the building, is in the possession of the church. The design called for a steeple, which was deleted from the finished work. The church is romantically sited on a hill overlooking the Rapidan River and broad stretches of countryside. *(68–54) VLR: 06/17/75; NRHP: 08/28/75.*

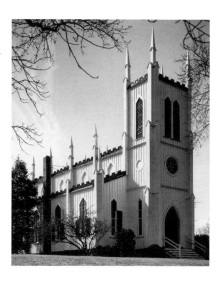

WILLOW GROVE, *Madison Mills vicinity.* Built in the late 18th century for Joseph Clark, the original frame residence at Willow Grove was substantially enlarged in 1848 by the addition of a brick wing and a unifying Tuscan portico. The remodeling was done for Clark's son William, who inherited Willow Grove in 1839. The resulting structure stands as an example of the influence of Thomas Jefferson's Classical Revival style on the country homes of Piedmont Virginia. The portico is accented by the distinctly Jeffersonian touch of Chinese lattice railings. The house is enhanced by its pastoral setting and collection of outbuildings. Later the homestead of the Shackelford family, the house and outbuildings are now used as a country inn. *(68–49) VLR: 11/21/78; NRHP: 05/07/79.*

WOOD PARK, *Rapidan vicinity.* The original section of this patrician homestead was built ca. 1799 for Baldwin Taliaferro. The weatherboarded structure is hugged by brick end chimneys and topped by a hipped roof with a distinctive pedimented cross gable. The property was purchased in 1849 by Col. George Willis. Colonel Willis and his wife, Sallie Innes Smith Willis, were well connected in Virginia society. Their prosperity is evidenced in the ballroom wing added by them in the 1850s. A contrast to the original Federal block, the wing exhibits exotic overtones in the Gothic and Moorish wooden filigree details of its veranda. The walls of the ballroom were once decorated with trompe l'oeil paintings, but these have been covered. Wood Park remains in Willis family ownership. *(68–55) VLR: 06/19/96.*

PAGE COUNTY

Between the Blue Ridge and Massanutten mountain ranges, Page County was most likely named for John Page, Revolutionary patriot, congressman, and governor of Virginia from 1802 to 1805. It was formed from Rockingham and Shenandoah counties in 1831. Its county seat is Luray.

AVENTINE HALL, *143 South Court Street, Luray.* Named for one of the seven hills of Rome, this gaily decorated Greek Revival house, with its ornaments and surfaces executed in wood, was built in 1852 for Peter Bock Borst, local Commonwealth's attorney and a founder of the Shenandoah Valley Railroad. The slender proportions and large windows are more characteristic of the Greek Revival of the North than that of Virginia. Also setting the house apart are its column capitals in the Tower of the Winds order, elaborate Doric entablature, pilastered cupola, and rich interior detailing. Borst, originally from New York State, was responsible for the design and had it executed by his carpenter, a Mr. O'Neale. The house became the principal building of Luray College when it was established in 1925. It remained college property until 1937 when it was moved to its present site from its original location west of town. *(159–01) VLR: 12/02/69; NRHP: 02/26/70.*

JOHN BEAVER HOUSE, *Salem vicinity.* A rare decorative design of lozenges formed of glazed headers in the facade brickwork sets off this Valley farmhouse. Built 1825–26 for John Beaver, the two-story dwelling combines architectural elements from both Continental and Anglo-American vernacular building traditions. The decorative brickwork, double entry, and four-bay facade are related to German house forms. The hall-parlor plan and plain Federal woodwork are more standard eastern Virginia features. John Beaver's wife, Nancy Strickler Beaver, was a descendant of Abraham Strickler, one of the Shenandoah Valley's first settlers. A two-story ell with two-level galleries was added in the late 19th century. The house long stood neglected but has been handsomely restored in recent years. A contemporary two-story smokehouse and a one-story washhouse survive on the grounds. *(69–120) VLR: 03/20/79; NRHP: 06/22/79.*

CATHERINE FURNACE, *Newport vicinity.* A relic of western Virginia's once-important iron industry, the Catherine Furnace was constructed in 1836 in the tapered square shape typical of iron furnaces of the period. The furnace produced high-quality pig iron used for shells in both the Mexican and Civil wars. It went out of blast in 1887 and stood abandoned until its purchase in this century by the federal government as part of what is now the George Washington and Jefferson National Forests. The structure is maintained today by the U.S. Department of Agriculture Forest Service as one of Virginia's best examples of a formerly prevalent industrial form. *(69–130) VLR: 07/17/73; NRHP: 01/21/74.*

FORT EGYPT, *Hamburg vicinity.* Fort Egypt, a massive, full-dovetailed log house near the Shenandoah River, is one of the earliest and most complete of a small group of houses erected in the Massanutten region by Pennsylvania settlers of both German and Swiss descent. Dating from the mid–18th century, the house was the homestead of the Strickler and Stover families and is still in the ownership of Strickler descendants. Its interior spaces were organized for work, storage, and family life throughout the agricultural year. Typical of such dwellings, it has a vaulted cooling cellar, or *Gewölbekeller.* The first floor, arranged around a massive center chimney, follows a standard Continental vernacular form. The interior also preserves much original woodwork and hardware, including vertical board partitions and a variety of door types. The original gable roof was replaced in the 19th century by the present low hipped roof. *(69–01) VLR: 02/26/79; NRHP: 06/18/79.*

FORT PHILIP LONG, *Alma vicinity.* Exuding an air of great age, this snug dwelling is among the rare surviving early Shenandoah Valley stone houses erected by Virginia's German settlers. Placed on the edge of a bank, a German practice, the simple structure is dominated on its uphill side by a massive exterior end chimney. The house is unusual in having two cellar levels, the lower of which has a tunnel leading to a well located 100 yards away. The date of the house is not known, but it likely was constructed in the late 18th century for Philip Long II, grandson of Philip Long who settled here in 1737. Also on the property is a Greek Revival brick farmhouse built in 1856 for Isaac Long, Jr. Its parlor has its original Victorian decorations, including walls painted to imitate molded plaster and ceilings painted to resemble intricate foliated plasterwork. *(69–02) VLR: 11/21/72; NRHP: 04/11/73.*

FORT STOVER, *Luray vicinity.* Built ca. 1769 for the Stover family, this two-story stone house is part of Page County's collection of early German-style dwellings. Remarkably well preserved, Fort Stover retains early woodwork with what may be original paint. As in a number of these houses, the architecture shows the influence of Anglo-American models, particularly in the use of end chimneys instead of the more purely German center chimney. Despite this, the house employs the traditional German three-room floor plan, known as the *Flurküchenhaus* plan because of the location of the kitchen, or *Küche,* in the main part of the house. Another Germanic feature is the vaulted cellar room associated with vernacular houses of the Rhineland and used for food storage. The defensive appearance of these cellar vaults has led to the mistaken notion that houses with such rooms were built as forts. *(69–05) VLR: 11/15/77; NRHP: 05/22/78.*

MASSANUTTON HEIGHTS, *Salem vicinity.* Built ca. 1820 for John R. and Elizabeth Strickler Burner, Massanutton Heights is a Valley farmstead offering an informative picture of the material culture of the region's German-American families. The plain exterior masks gaily painted interior wall decorations. With the character of folk art, the parlor embellishments include stenciled floral borders imitating printed border papers. In place of a cornice are painted drapery swags with fringe and tassels. The dado is painted to resemble paneled wainscoting. Woodwork in other areas is painted to imitate tiger maple. The artist has not been identified, but family tradition holds that some of the earliest decoration was executed by an itinerant Italian artist, and that the later drapery swags are by a Stickler family member. The property derives its name from its site above Massanutton Old Fields, a former settlement. Several early farm buildings remain. *(69–123) VLR: 02/17/76; NRHP: 07/30/76.*

HEISTON-STRICKLER HOUSE, *Luray vicinity.* On a bank above the south fork of the Shenandoah River, the Heiston-Strickler house, also known as the Old Stone House, is among the best preserved of Page County's Germanic dwellings. The unadorned structure was built ca. 1790 either for Jacob Heiston or his son Abraham and is owned by their descendants. The three-room floor plan, vaulted cellar, two-bay facade, and hillside setting are all attributes inherited from Central European prototypes and introduced by settlers of Germanic origin moving from Pennsylvania. Evidence of English influence is shown in the use of common-rafter framing and end chimneys rather than principal-purlin framing and a center chimney, the latter features being more characteristic of German houses. The house underwent alterations in the early 19th century, but the original plan is evident, and much of its original plain woodwork survives. *(69–17) VLR: 04/18/78; NRHP: 11/16/78.*

JEREMEY'S RUN ARCHAEOLOGICAL SITE, *Shenandoah National Park.* The location of the Jeremey's Run site immediately south of a complex of springs and marsh, within several rich ecological zones, probably drew prehistoric peoples to this spot for millennia. The relatively confined habitable area contains a concentration of lithic debris (fragments of stone projectile points, tools, and other artifacts) from the Middle Archaic through the Late Woodland periods (ca. 5000 B.C.–A.D. 1600), making the site important for understanding prehistoric life in the Shenandoah Valley. The site is one of several scattered through this section of the Blue Ridge Mountain chain where significant evidence of prehistoric occupation has been identified. *(69–202) VLR: 09/16/82; NRHP: 12/13/85.*

MAUCK'S MEETING HOUSE (MILL CREEK MEETING HOUSE), *Hamburg.* The Mauck's Meeting House congregation was organized ca. 1772 by John Koontz and consisted of both Mennonites and Baptists, dissenters who played an influential role in the early society of the Shenandoah Valley. The earliest mention of the building was recorded in 1798. The plain log structure was erected on land owned by Daniel Mauck. In 1807 Mauck's son Joseph deeded the property to the "Sundry persons . . . friends of religion and good order" who had been using it. The Mennonites eventually quit the area, leaving the Baptists in control. The congregation also consisted of black slaves and "free men of color." Although used principally by Baptists, the church was maintained for use by all Christians and attracted preachers of various denominations. The venerable landmark is maintained today as a historic shrine and meeting place by the Page County Heritage Association. *(69–06) VLR: 12/16/75; NRHP: 06/18/76.*

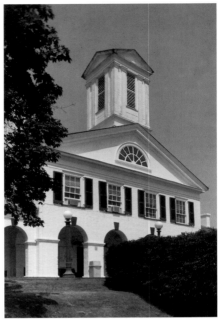

PAGE COUNTY COURTHOUSE, *116 South Court Street, Luray.* The Page County Courthouse, atop one of the highest points in Luray, was designed and constructed by William B. Phillips, mason, and Malcolm F. Crawford, carpenter, master builders formerly employed by Thomas Jefferson at the University of Virginia. Completed by 1834, the temple-form building, with its Tuscan pediment and entablature, shows the influence of the third president's distinctive classical style. Although the ground-floor arcade was also a feature favored by Jefferson, the arcade was a traditional element of Virginia courthouses since the colonial period. Here the Page County commissioners directed that the arcade be carried into the one-story wings. The pedimented belfry with its paired pilasters is also an original feature. The building's center section is very similar to that of the Madison County Courthouse, another Phillips and Crawford project. *(159–04) VLR: 01/16/73; NRHP: 06/25/73.*

ISAAC SPITLER HOMEPLACE, *Leaksville vicinity.* This complex of structures is the core of an early German farmstead reflecting the building traditions and cultural values of the Shenandoah Valley's German settlers. An outstanding historic resource here is an exceptionally rare Switzer barn, one of the few to have survived the Union barn burnings of 1864. The barn's log core, along with stone remains of a log house, the ruins of a stone outbuilding, and other outbuildings, were likely built between 1740 and 1753 by John Spitler, a stonemason and the original settler here. The large brick farmhouse was constructed in 1825 for Spitler's grandson, Isaac Spitler, and expanded in 1857. Incorporating traditional German-style features such as an asymmetrical floor plan and two front entrances, the house served as a place of worship for local German Baptist Brethren. Spitler's descendants resided here until 1934. The house was sympathetically renovated in 1990. *(69–07) VLR: 03/19/97; NRHP: 05/23/97.*

STEVENS COTTAGE, *210 Maryland Avenue, Shenandoah.* Blending Queen Anne and Bungalow influences, this architecturally refined structure was completed in 1891 to serve as the office of the newly organized Shenandoah Land and Improvement Company. It was designed by William M. Poindexter of Washington, D.C., who also was the architect of Randolph-Macon Woman's College in Lynchburg and the old Virginia State Library on Capitol Square in Richmond. Like numerous Valley communities, Shenandoah experienced the 1890s land boom that accompanied the construction of the Norfolk and Western Railroad. Anticipating growth from industrial development, land companies were formed to attract residents and investors. Shenandoah's boom was short-lived. In 1902 the office was sold to Mary and Edna Stevens. The building was acquired in 1968 by the Page County Heritage Association and is now a local history museum. *(69–94) VLR: 12/16/75; NRHP: 07/14/78.*

THE WHITE HOUSE, *Hamburg vicinity.* This austere structure was erected ca. 1760 by Pastor Martin Kauffman II and takes its name from its whitewashed stucco covering. Kauffman founded the Mennonite Baptist Church and held meetings in his house. He later removed himself from the Baptists in a disagreement over their pro-military stand and in 1793 formed the Separatist Independent Baptist Church. Kauffman's house began as a two-story, Germanic-type *Flurküchenhaus,* or three-room-plan house with a center chimney. Other features of the house type found here are a vaulted cooling cellar and a two-level storage loft. The interior finish of the White House was remodeled in the Federal style, and it retains the striking woodwork with original painted surfaces from that alteration. The unoccupied house has a rural setting in the shadow of Massanutten Mountain. *(69–12) VLR: 11/15/77.*

PATRICK COUNTY

Named for the Revolutionary patriot Patrick Henry, this county at the southern end of Virginia's section of the Blue Ridge Mountains was formed in 1790 from Henry County. Its county seat is Stuart.

AURORA, *Penns Store.* Also known as the "Pink House," Aurora is rendered in the Italian Villa style popularized by architectural theorist Andrew Jackson Downing. Employing a low hipped roof with central gable and long veranda, the exterior resembles Design XXVII, "A small Country House for the Southern States," in Downing's *Architecture of Country Houses* (1850). Downing wrote that this design "affords, in its broadly projecting roof and long extended veranda, that ample shade, so indispensable to all dwellings in a southern climate." Aurora's veranda was executed in decorative cast iron, a departure from the more normal practice of using wood. The house was built around 1853 for Thomas Jefferson Penn, a prominent farmer, merchant, and tobacconist. Penn's son, Frank Reid Penn, founded F. R. & G. Penn Co., which was eventually acquired by tobacco magnate James Duke and incorporated into the American Tobacco Company. *(70–11) VLR: 08/21/90; NRHP: 02/04/91.*

BOB WHITE COVERED BRIDGE, *Woolwine vicinity.* Covered bridges are a distinctly American building form. Hundreds of these structures formerly adorned rural byways across the country. Most have disappeared, but those that remain excite an intensity of sentiment given few other types of structures. Covered bridges are a rarity in Virginia; Patrick County has two of the handful remaining. Later than most, this bridge was constructed in 1920–21 under the direction of Walter Weaver, whose family assisted in the endeavor. The bridge is an 80-foot span of heavy oak timber framing. The exterior is covered in board and batten, while the interior has diagonal sheathing. Now in county ownership, the bridge no longer serves vehicular traffic and is kept as an object of interest beside a modern crossing. *(70–27) VLR: 04/17/73; NRHP: 05/22/73.*

COCKRAM MILL, *Meadows of Dan vicinity.* Nestled in the shadow of the Blue Ridge Mountains, Cockram Mill is one of Virginia's few operating historic mills. It was erected ca. 1885 by Jesse Blackard who used driving power from the headwaters of the Dan River to produce cornmeal, grits, buckwheat flour, livestock feed, wooden boxes, and lumber. Built with mass production in mind, the mill was unique within the local Appalachian area by virtue of having two turbine wheels instead of the usual overshot wheel. The mill introduced to the area such innovative processes as the ability to clean and shell grain. The business was purchased by W. A. Cockram in 1921. During the 1930s Cockram Mill was also the area's first and only private facility to produce electricity for sale. The mill fell into disuse in the 1970s but was restored to working order in 1984. *(70–06) VLR: 10/16/90; NRHP: 12/06/90.*

PATRICK COUNTY COURTHOUSE, *Main and Blue Ridge streets, Stuart.* The principal landmark of the village of Stuart, the Patrick County Courthouse has served as the focal point of its southern Piedmont county for over 150 years. The dignified albeit provincial edifice is an example of the tripartite Roman Revival public buildings whose designs were inspired by the works of Thomas Jefferson and the master builders who worked under him. It was commissioned in 1819 but not erected until 1822. Abram Staples, a local contractor who had served on the building committee, was responsible for both the design and construction. The exterior is dominated by a pedimented Tuscan portico reached by a tall flight of stairs. Staples's design likely influenced that of the neighboring Henry County Courthouse of 1824, which was similar in appearance before an extensive remodeling in 1929. *(307–01) VLR: 09/17/74; NRHP 12/27/74.*

REYNOLDS HOMESTEAD, *Critz vicinity.* Richard Joshua Reynolds (1850–1918), who founded the R. J. Reynolds Tobacco Company in 1875, was born one of sixteen children at this Patrick County homestead. The plain Greek Revival house was begun in 1843 for Reynolds's father, Hardin William Reynolds, and was later enlarged. The house is typical of the dwellings erected for the area's midlevel antebellum gentry. R. J. Reynolds is regarded as the father of the modern tobacco industry, which helped bring about the economic rehabilitation of the South after the Civil War. Originally called Rock Spring, the 700-acre plantation is now maintained as a continuing education and research center by Virginia Tech. The house and outbuildings have been restored for exhibition. *(70–05) VLR: 11/03/70; NRHP: 09/22/71; NHL: 12/22/77.*

JACK'S CREEK COVERED BRIDGE, *Woolwine vicinity.* One of the most elementary of the state's few remaining covered bridges, Jack's Creek Bridge presents a nostalgic image of rural America. Like the nearby Bob White Covered Bridge, the Jack's Creek Bridge was designed by the local carpenter Walter Weaver. Charlie Vaughan served as the builder. The 48-foot span was completed in 1914 and employs heavy oak framing covered with board-and-batten sheathing. A space just below the eaves was left open for light and ventilation. The bridge is preserved as a landmark under county ownership but is no longer in use, being paralleled by a modern bridge. *(70–02) VLR: 04/17/73; NRHP: 05/22/73.*

CITY OF PETERSBURG

Petersburg began in 1645 as a garrison and fur-trading post known as Fort Henry. The present name, dating from 1733, honors Peter Jones, who accompanied William Byrd II on expeditions to the Virginia backcountry. Petersburg was established in 1748. It was incorporated as a city in 1850.

APPOMATTOX IRON WORKS, *20–28 Old Street.* This complex of some nine functionally related structures forms one of the country's most complete physical records of an early iron foundry. The buildings are part of a block of Federal-period commercial-residential structures lining Old Street in the heart of the city. Although the principal buildings were not originally intended for industrial use, iron was worked here as early as 1812. The Appomattox Foundry Company, as it was first called in 1876, began at 33 Old Street but moved to its present location in 1896. The foundry building was erected in 1897. The foundry business continued until 1946, and the machine shop operated until 1952. The mill and supply store closed down in 1972, leaving an undisturbed collection of archives, patterns, molds, tools, machines, and other associated objects. Now owned by the Center for Industrial Preservation, the property is being developed for retail and museum use. *(123–87) VLR: 04/20/76; NRHP: 08/11/76.*

BATTERSEA, *793 Appomattox Street.* With its sectional massing Battersea displays, perhaps best, the Anglo-Palladian influence on Virginia's finer colonial plantation houses. The elegant but compact house was built in 1768 for John Banister, a Revolutionary delegate, congressman, and framer of the Articles of Confederation. Remodeled more than once, the three-part windows and much trim, both inside and out, are early 19th-century changes. The elaborate Chinese lattice stair, however, based on a published design by the English architect William Halfpenny, is original and is the finest example of its type in the state. The center block at one time had a two-level portico, of which parts of the lower tier remain. Despite the development of much of the plantation's former acreage, the house preserves a rural setting along the Appomattox River. Battersea is owned and exhibited by the city of Petersburg. *(123–59) VLR: 05/13/69; NRHP: 11/12/69.*

BLANDFORD CEMETERY, *319 South Crater Road*. One of Virginia's most important historic cemeteries, Blandford reflects the long history of Petersburg and surrounding counties. Centered around the colonial Blandford Church, where burials date from 1702, the cemetery is now the third largest in Virginia after Arlington and Hollywood. Two Virginia governors, a Revolutionary War British general, three Confederate generals, and 30,000 Confederate dead are buried here. Its collection of decorative fences and gates, in both cast and wrought iron, is the finest in the state. Much of the ironwork was produced by unknown artisans, but some can be traced to firms such as Barnes in Richmond, Wickersham in New York, and Wood and Perot in Philadelphia. The gravestones are a collection of sculpture in sandstone, slate, marble, and granite. The wide variety of monuments traces changing attitudes toward death and mourning. Flowers, angels, and lilies are the favorite Victorian symbols here. *(123–110) VLR: 04/22/92; NRHP: 10/15/92.*

BLANDFORD CHURCH, *319 South Crater Road*. Petersburg's oldest building, Blandford Church was built by Thomas Ravenscroft in 1734–37 as the principal church of Bristol Parish. Its north wing and the brick wall surrounding the original burying ground were added between 1752 and 1770 by Col. Richard Bland, undertaker. The church was largely abandoned after a new church was built on Courthouse Hill in 1802. It fell into ruins, but its Flemish bond brick walls survived relatively unharmed. Around the ruins was developed Blandford Cemetery, a large municipal graveyard. In 1901 the city council authorized the Petersburg Ladies' Memorial Association to restore the building as a monument to the Confederate dead. As part of the restoration, the association commissioned Louis Comfort Tiffany to design stained-glass windows for each state of the Confederacy. This collection of Tiffany glass, including a special window donated by Tiffany, is one of Virginia's artistic treasures. *(123–39) VLR: 04/18/72; NRHP: 05/31/72.*

CENTRE HILL, *Centre Hill Court*. One of Virginia's largest and most richly appointed historic houses, Centre Hill symbolizes the prosperity and sophistication enjoyed by antebellum Petersburg. It was completed in 1823 for Robert Bolling, who amassed a fortune in Petersburg real estate, tobacco inspections, and industry. It was made even more elaborate in the 1840s and 1850s when the present veranda and east wing were added and the interior trim was augmented and elaborated. Following the siege of Petersburg, the house was commandeered for Union headquarters by Gen. G. L. Hartsuff, who was visited here by President Abraham Lincoln on April 7, 1865. Centre Hill remained a Bolling home until 1900 when it was purchased by Charles Hall Davis, who further embellished the interior, adding the Federal Revival stair. President William Howard Taft was a guest at Centre Hill in 1901. The restored mansion is now a city-owned museum. *(123–57) VLR: 11/21/72; NRHP: 12/27/72.*

CENTRE HILL HISTORIC DISTRICT. In one of Petersburg's four original wards, the Centre Hill Historic District is an architecturally distinctive enclave of residential buildings surrounded on all sides by commercial, industrial, and municipal development. The district takes its name from Robert Bolling's 1823 mansion, a noted Petersburg landmark. Centre Hill's grounds were sold by Charles Hall Davis in 1910 to the Centre Hill Development Corporation. The setting of the stately Bolling residence was thus radically changed. Between 1914 and 1923 the estate's front lawn was transformed into a tightly knit residential development, called Centre Hill Court, a visually lively collection of primarily Bungalow-Craftsman–style houses. The houses contrast with the great Federal mansion and reflect the early 20th-century interest in creating small planned neighborhoods. The district also includes a collection of earlier dwellings east of Centre Hill Court. *(123–25) VLR: 10/15/85; NRHP: 06/13/86.*

CITY MARKET (FARMERS' MARKET), *9 Old Street.* Orson Squire Fowler's treatise *A Home for All* (1848) extolling the advantages of octagonal buildings resulted not only in the construction of numerous octagonal houses but in the erection of other eight-sided structures, including Petersburg's 1879 farmers' market, originally called the Farm Market Center. The focus of the city's colorful commercial area, the building is the fourth to be located on the site, the first one having been erected after the town market was established here in the 1790s. The present building was designed and built by Bernard J. Black, a Baltimore builder-designer who came to Petersburg in the 1850s. It is notable both for its shape and for its decorative cast-iron brackets supporting the canopy and projecting market shed. Although the exterior stalls still accommodate farmers, the interior has been converted into a restaurant. *(123–50) VLR: 11/05/68; NRHP: 06/11/69.*

EXCHANGE BUILDING, *15–19 West Bank Street.* This splendid Greek Revival building was completed in 1841 to house the Exchange, the city's commodities auction house. Records show that the construction was supervised by a "Mr. Berrien" of New York, probably James Berrien (or Berrian), a New York architect. Calvin Pollard corresponded with Berrien on the project; hence it is speculated that Pollard may have been involved with the design, as he was architect for the Petersburg Courthouse and the first St. Paul's Church. As originally constructed, the Exchange stood on an open ground floor where the products were displayed and traded. Auctions and public meetings took place in the domed hall above. The building was converted into a police court in this century, and the ground level was closed in. Restored by the city in the mid-1970s, it is now the Siege Museum, interpreting Petersburg's Civil War years. *(123–51) VLR: 11/05/68; NRHP: 06/11/69; NHL: 11/11/71.*

FARMERS' BANK, *19 Bollingbrook Street.* The Farmers' Bank of Virginia, incorporated in 1812, opened its Petersburg branch that same year. The bank completed the present three-story Federal structure to replace its earlier office destroyed by fire in 1815. As was customary, well-appointed living quarters were provided on the upper floors for the bank's executive officer. These rooms preserve their intricately decorated mantels and doorways, features typical of Petersburg's finer Federal structures. The banking area on the first floor retains its original vault. The branch continued in operation through the Civil War but was forced to liquidate its assets in 1866 by an act of the General Assembly that affected all state banks. The building then passed through numerous owners and served various functions until the 1960s when it was conveyed to the Association for the Preservation of Virginia Antiquities and subsequently restored as a banking museum. *(123–67) VLR: 01/18/72; NRHP: 04/13/72.*

FOLLY CASTLE HISTORIC DISTRICT. This residential neighborhood centered along West Washington Street, and including three blocks of Hinton Street as well as sections of Perry and Guarantee streets, contains an important and varied assemblage of late 18th- and 19th-century houses. Once one of the city's leading neighborhoods, it takes its name from Folly Castle, a wood-frame Georgian mansion with later modifications erected in 1763 for Peter Jones, whose progenitor and namesake was the source for the name of Petersburg. Another residence, the 1858 McIlwaine-Friend house, at 404 West Washington Street, served as Maj. Gen. George E. Pickett's Confederate headquarters from 1863 to 1864. An outstanding early frame house is the ca. 1813 Joel Hammon house at 26 Perry Street. Dominant architectural styles are Greek Revival, Italianate, and Colonial Revival. Two prominent structures are the Gothic Revival Second Presbyterian Church and the neoclassical old Petersburg High School constructed in 1917–18. *(123–96) VLR: 02/26/79 (EXPANDED 06/19/91); NRHP: 07/16/80.*

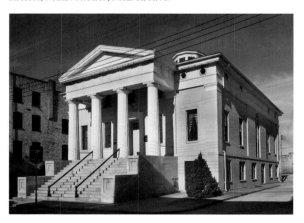

NATHANIEL FRIEND HOUSE, *27–29 Bollingbrook Street.* Nathaniel Friend, Jr., an import-export merchant and former mayor of the city, had this imposing example of Petersburg's Federal architecture built in 1815–16. Standing across Cockade Alley from the Farmers' Bank, the Friend house is in the heart of Petersburg's historic commercial area. Although the enormous dwelling has been vacant for many years and has had its first floor altered, the excellent Federal woodwork of the upper floors remains largely intact. After several private attempts at restoration failed, the property was acquired for preservation by the city, which has since undertaken basic structural stabilization. It awaits purchase by an owner committed to returning the house to its former dignity. Despite its neglected state, Nathaniel Friend's mansion remains a pivotal historic and architectural resource for the Petersburg community. *(123–66) VLR: 04/20/76; NRHP: 08/11/76; BHR EASEMENT.*

MCILWAINE HOUSE, *Old Market Square.* The rich quality of Petersburg's Federal architecture is elegantly displayed in the 1815 McIlwaine house, originally the home of George Jones, one of the city's mayors. Relatively conventional on the outside, its interior is enriched with woodwork employing the intricate elaboration characteristic of the city's older buildings. The parlor chimneypiece, with its flanking arched recesses, is a testament to the city's Federal-period craftsmanship. From 1831 to 1878 the house was the home of Archibald Graham McIlwaine, an industrialist and financier. In the early 1970s road construction required the house to be moved from South Market Street to its present site. The building was donated to the Association for the Preservation of Virginia Antiquities, which undertook the move and a partial restoration. It was purchased by the city of Petersburg in 1984 for use as a museum and visitors' center. *(123–11) VLR: 06/19/73; NRHP: 07/16/73.*

WILLIAM MCKENNEY HOUSE, *250 South Sycamore Street.* Overlooking Poplar Lawn Park, the William McKenney house is Petersburg's most extravagant example of the Queen Anne style. Designed by Maj. Harrison Waite, the city's leading architect of the time, the twenty-three-room mansion was completed in 1890. The finely articulated facade is dominated by a three-story circular tower with a conical roof. Inside is a rich display of Victorian artistry: elaborately carved woodwork in oak, cherry, and mahogany; a built-in china press and sideboard; and ten fireplaces, six of which are decorated with Italian tiles. Many of the original plumbing fixtures and combination gas and electric light fixtures remain. Commissioned by William McKenney, a Petersburg attorney, the house was later owned by David Dunlop III, a tobacco manufacturer. William Totty, a luggage manufacturer, also once lived here. A recent restoration has returned the dwelling's former splendor. *(123–102) VLR: 12/12/89; NRHP: 12/06/90.*

PETERSBURG CITY HALL, *129–141 North Union Street.* This granite edifice is part of the large number of customshouses designed by Ammi B. Young, supervising architect of the U.S. Treasury Department. Although each design differed, each was a deft statement in the then popular Renaissance Revival mode. With this effort the Treasury Department was attempting to set a high standard for federal buildings. Young's Petersburg Customs House, now the city hall, was erected in 1856–59 and followed his formula of fireproof construction, dignified proportions, lean ornamentation, and granite masonry. The building was the city's Confederate headquarters in the Civil War, and the raising of the American flag from its rooftop on April 3, 1865, signaled the end of the siege of Petersburg, one of the longest battles of the war. The building was expanded by three bays ca. 1900, and in 1938 it was acquired by the city for its present use. *(123–35) VLR: 04/18/78; NRHP: 11/16/78.*

PETERSBURG COURT-HOUSE, *Court House Avenue.* One of the Commonwealth's most beautiful public buildings, the Petersburg Courthouse is a testament to the talents of its architect, Calvin Pollard of New York. Completed in 1840, this masterpiece of the Greek Revival employs the Tower of the Winds order in both its tall portico and its elaborate octagonal cupola. The cupola, topped by a clock which is surmounted by a statue of Justice, was used as a sighting mark by Union artillery during the Civil War siege of the city. The courthouse's exterior survives largely unchanged; the interior has undergone considerable remodeling but preserves an impressive coffered domed ceiling in the courtroom. The building still houses the city's courts and remains a dominant architectural element of Petersburg's skyline. *(123–45) VLR: 04/17/73; NRHP: 05/14/73.*

PETERSBURG COURTHOUSE HISTORIC DISTRICT. Incorporating portions of some nine blocks in the heart of Petersburg, this district centers around the 1840 courthouse, which dominates the downtown skyline. Along its streets is a tight assemblage of urban architecture including public and institutional structures as well as commercial and residential buildings in various styles ranging in date from 1815 to the 1940s. An especially fine collection of commercial buildings lines North Sycamore Street, the city's main street. Individually significant landmarks in the district are the Tabb Street Presbyterian Church, St. Paul's Episcopal Church, and the former U.S. Customs House, now the city hall. The area was the target of Union bombardment during the 1864–65 nine-month siege of Petersburg. Physical damage was minimal, but the city never regained its role as one of the state's leading urban centers. The district's commercial stability, however, was sustained by Petersburg's tobacco industry. *(123–103) VLR: 08/21/90; NRHP: 12/21/90.*

PETERSBURG NATIONAL BATTLEFIELD *(also in Dinwiddie County, Prince George County, and Hopewell).* This national park consists of a vast network of fortifications and entrenchments constructed by both Union and Confederate armies during the siege of Petersburg from June 1864 to April 1865. The earthworks meander for twenty-seven miles along the outskirts of the city. Prominent among these scars of war is the Crater, a large depression created on July 30, 1864, when the Union army tunneled under Confederate lines and breached them by setting off a huge charge of explosives at the end of the tunnel. A quick response by Confederate brigadier general William Mahone plugged the gap. The long siege and Grant's maneuver around the Confederate right flank forced Lee to abandon his lines on April 2, 1865, and retreat west, giving up the capital of Richmond as well. The siege of Petersburg was the first instance of modern trench warfare. *(123–71) VLR: 10/18/83; NRHP: 10/15/66.*

PETERSBURG OLD TOWN HISTORIC DISTRICT. Occupying the lower part of the central business district and the High Street and Grove Avenue residential areas, this large district incorporates approximately 250 buildings on 190 acres. One of Virginia's oldest communities, Petersburg began as a fur-trading post in the mid–17th century. The district possesses a diversity of residential, commercial, and industrial architecture, mostly of the 19th and early 20th centuries. Of special interest is the stylistically varied progression of 18th- and 19th-century houses lining High Street. A group of early workers' cottages is clustered in the southwest portion of the area. Railroad buildings, factories, tobacco warehouses, an ironworks, and a variety of mercantile buildings are in the low areas near the Appomattox River. Although it has suffered fires, Civil War bombardment, commercial redevelopment, and a devastating tornado, the district perseveres as one of Virginia's richest assemblages of historic buildings. *(123–97) VLR: 11/20/79; NRHP: 07/04/80.*

POPLAR LAWN HISTORIC DISTRICT. The Poplar Lawn Historic District began as a fashionable 19th-century neighborhood developed around a two-block public park originally known as Poplar Lawn and now called Central Park. The park was set aside as a public open space in the first decade of the 19th century. In 1846 it was acquired by the city and transformed into a romantically landscaped common in the style of Andrew Jackson Downing. The park has been the scene of many public gatherings and military exercises. Through the 19th century many houses were erected in the adjacent eleven blocks, most of them set in shady yards. Though the park itself has lost much of its early ornamental character, it has seen some restoration. The neighborhood has retained its genteel air, and many of its houses have been rehabilitated. Architectural highlights are the Federal-period Zimmer house and the Georgian Revival Trinity United Methodist Church. *(123–94) VLR: 02/26/79; NRHP: 05/23/80.*

ST. PAUL'S EPISCOPAL CHURCH, *102 North Union Street.* St. Paul's congregation, successor to the colonial Bristol Parish, built its second downtown church in the 1830s. This burned in 1854, necessitating the construction of the present building, dedicated May 19, 1857, by Bishop William Meade. Dominated by its broached steeple, this chaste Gothic Revival work with neo-Norman influences was designed by the Baltimore firm of Niernsee and Neilson, which also supervised its construction. The partners John R. Niernsee and J. Crawford Neilson were leading designers of the period and provided works throughout Maryland and the South. Unlike the richly detailed contemporary northern churches built under the influence of the English Ecclesiological Society, St. Paul's is a much freer interpretation of the Gothic style. Gen. Robert E. Lee worshiped here during the siege of Petersburg and attended the 1867 wedding of his son Rooney to Mary Tabb Bolling here. *(123–41) VLR: 04/15/86; NRHP: 05/30/86.*

SECOND PRESBYTERIAN CHURCH, *419 West Washington Street.* Second Presbyterian Church was begun in 1861, in the opening months of the Civil War, when construction in Virginia had all but ceased. Its design is credited to the Rev. Theodorick Pryor, the church's pastor. The exterior, a typical work of mid-19th-century Gothic Revival, originally had a spire above its crenellated belfry, but it was toppled by a storm in 1862. The present spire was erected in 1984. A Union shell hit the church during a service in 1865 but failed to explode. The main glory of the church is the interior, which has some of the richest Gothic-style plasterwork in the state. Its focal point is the rostrum emphasized by a massive central pulpit and a ribbed-vaulted apse crowned by an ogival arch. *(123–42) VLR: 12/12/89; NRHP: 01/14/91.*

SOUTH MARKET STREET HISTORIC DISTRICT. This compact district incorporates a significant assortment of buildings dating from 1840 to 1905, when this street was one of the city's premier residential areas. The high-style Greek Revival and Italianate dwellings lining the two-block-long district housed some of Petersburg's economic, social, and political elite. Most of the structures display high standards of craftsmanship and are set off by ancillary features such as cast-iron fences, tiled walks, and granite curbs. A highlight is the Norman-style former South Market Street Methodist Church, completed in 1860. Several original outbuildings survive, including carriage houses and kitchens. Although demolitions have robbed the neighborhood of important structures, a cohesion is tenaciously maintained. The principal historic landmark is the Thomas Wallace house, site of President Abraham Lincoln's last meeting with Gen. Ulysses S. Grant. *(123–108) VLR: 06/19/91; NRHP: 04/22/92.*

STRAWBERRY HILL, 235 *Hinton Street.* As built for William Barksdale in 1792, Strawberry Hill followed a tripartite Palladian form, consisting of a two-story center section flanked by one-story wings. William Haxall, who purchased the house in 1800, enlarged it in 1815–16 by raising the wings to two stories. Despite this change, the house retains its rich early appointments, including a delicately carved pedimented doorway approached by marble steps with scrolled wrought-iron railings. The drawing room woodwork is noteworthy for the shell-carved niches flanking a paneled chimneypiece with broken pediment. The house underwent significant alterations in the 1880s when it was partitioned into three separate residences, and the entrance was placed off center. The disfiguring changes were removed during a long-term restoration which has returned the house to its former position as one of Petersburg's finest late Georgian residences. *(123–86) VLR: 11/19/74; NRHP: 12/23/74.*

TABB STREET PRESBYTERIAN CHURCH, 21 *West Tabb Street.* Philadelphia architect Thomas U. Walter gave Virginia a powerful interpretation of the Grecian mode with his 1843 Tabb Street Presbyterian Church. Walter, who is remembered chiefly for designing the dome of the U.S. Capitol, was perhaps most adept with the Greek orders, as evidenced in the church's Doric portico and its interior apse. The hexastyle portico is based on the Theseion, an ancient Greek temple in Athens. The apse is fronted by a colonnade in a freely adapted Tower of the Winds order, creating one of the more dramatic spaces of its type in the country. An original square belfry with a tapered spire was removed in 1938. The present church is the third to serve the congregation since its organization in 1813. *(123–43) VLR: 02/21/78; NRHP: 05/31/79.*

THOMAS WALLACE HOUSE, *South Market and Brown streets.* Thomas Wallace, a merchant and lawyer, had this Italianate mansion erected in 1855 on Market Street, then the principal artery of a fashionable quarter. The finely built structure followed the pattern of Virginia antebellum urban houses by having a two-level portico on the rear. The house was further embellished by a deep bracketed cornice, pressed-brick veneer, and cast-iron window cornices. During the Civil War the house served

briefly as the headquarters of Gen. Ulysses S. Grant. On April 3, 1865, Grant met here with President Abraham Lincoln to discuss the final strategy of the Civil War. It was Lincoln's last meeting with his commanding general. Though shabby from years of vacancy, the house is now undergoing a long-term renovation. The classical veranda with its curved projection is a later embellishment. *(123–31) VLR: 04/15/75; NRHP: 05/02/75; BHR EASEMENT.*

WASHINGTON STREET UNITED METHODIST CHURCH, 14–24 *East Washington Street.* Erected in 1842, the Washington Street United Methodist Church was for many years the state's leading church of its denomination. Here was held the first General Conference of the Methodist Episcopal Church South in 1846, an outgrowth of the schism that developed among Methodists over abolition. The church was also the scene of the first consecration of bishops of the Methodist Church South. During the Civil War the building served as a Confederate hospital. Two major alterations have given the building an extraordinary presence. A full Doric portico was applied to the original portico *in antis* in 1890, and in 1923 the flanking wings, each with its own Doric portico, were added. The wings were designed by Richmond architect Frederick A. Bishop. *(123–44) VLR: 06/17/80; NRHP: 11/24/80.*

PITTSYLVANIA COUNTY

The largest of Virginia's counties, Pittsylvania, near the center of the state's southern border, was named for the English statesman William Pitt, first earl of Chatham. It was formed from Halifax County in 1766. The county seat is Chatham.

BERRY HILL, *Berry Hill vicinity.* At the North Carolina border, Berry Hill is a remarkably complete Southside plantation grouping with a sprawling, much-evolved dwelling house and some twenty outbuildings. This unusually high number of support structures preserves a rare image of the complexity of these large agricultural units, run essentially as industries. Most of the farm structures are log, while the outbuildings, including the kitchen-laundry, dairy, and smokehouse, are wood frame, illustrating an architectural hierarchy sometimes employed in secondary structures. The present form of the main house is the result of accommodating the nine generations of the Perkins-Wilson-Hairston-Sims family who have owned the property since the 1760s. The oldest section, possibly 18th century, began as a plain three-bay structure. The house is now a jumble of wings, chimneys, porches, and roofs, the latest section dating from around 1910. *(71–06) VLR: 02/15/77; NRHP: 05/06/80.*

BILL'S DINER, *1 Depot Street, Chatham.* More recently known as "A Streetcar Named Desire," this engaging example of 20th-century Americana, formerly Bill's Diner, began life in the mid–1920s as a functioning streetcar in Reidsville, N.C. Bill Fretwell of Chatham took advantage of the elimination of streetcars in favor of buses there by purchasing this single-truck trolley car in 1937. He housed his already successful food-stand business in his newly acquired streetcar where he had both sit-down and curb service. For over forty years Fretwell operated the business that reputedly was Chatham's first establishment to serve hot dogs. Though presently closed, the diner still preserves its tight kitchen space and four table-booth units. Such "ready-made" establishments, now a fast-disappearing aspect of roadside America, exemplify the entrepreneurial spirit of the Great Depression. *(187–14) VLR: 06/19/96; NRHP: 12/16/96.*

BURNETT'S DINER, *19 South Main Street, Chatham.* The mid-1920s Danville Car No. 66 ended its transportation duties in 1938 when that city began converting to bus service. Salvaged from the scrappers, the trolley car was converted into a diner by the resourceful Burnett brothers, Henry, Frank, and Jessie. The Burnetts started their business in Chatham shortly after Bill's Diner, also a reused streetcar, opened nearby. A double-truck Perley A. Thomas car, built in High Point, N.C., Burnett's has a relatively roomy interior where a custom-built curved-end counter provides patron comfort. Food preparation origi-nally centered around a wood-burning stove. The stove was later augmented by a stainless-steel grill behind the counter. A recent restoration revealed the varnished tongue-and-groove wood-paneled ceiling. The roof-mounted neon-lit clock was cleaned and repaired. Burnett's is, at present, Virginia's last op-erating streetcar diner. *(187–13) VLR: 06/19/96; NRHP: 12/16/96.*

DAN'S HILL, *Danville vicinity.* The main residence of this Dan River plantation is one of the several stately brick dwellings erected during the early 19th century, the region's period of as-cendancy. The formal five-bay structure was built ca. 1833 for Robert Wilson, a Pittsylvania County planter. Its similarity to another Pittsylvania County house, Oak Hill, designed and built by James Dejarnett, an area master builder, has led to the attri-bution of Dan's Hill to Dejarnett. In contrast to its relatively plain exterior, the interior of Dan's Hill is finely trimmed with Federal woodwork, marble mantels, and ornamental plaster-work ceilings. The several contemporary outbuildings include an octagonal summerhouse and a brick greenhouse, both rela-tively scarce examples of their respective types. The setting is enhanced by formal gardens retaining their 19th-century layout of walks and beds. *(71–11) VLR: 10/17/78; NRHP: 05/30/79.*

LEESVILLE DAM ARCHAEOLOGICAL SITE, *Leesville vicinity.* This prehistoric site along the Roanoke River contains well-preserved archaeological material dating from the Late Woodland period. The site is characterized by high integrity of cultural features including middens, bone and seed remains, pottery shards, stone artifacts, and human remains, all of which could provide decisive data for studies of regional settle-ment patterns, subsistence material culture, and demography. The site is also the least-disturbed village site of its period along this portion of the Roanoke River. Further study could contribute significantly to knowledge of Dan River cultural in-teraction across the Virginia and North Carolina Piedmont. The site's importance has been verified with surface collection and shovel tests, but full-scale excavation has not occurred. *(71–108) VLR: 02/21/89; NRHP: 11/02/89.*

LITTLE CHERRYSTONE, *Chatham vicinity.* Named for nearby Little Cherrystone Creek, this Pittsylvania County farm has a dwelling with two distinct and contrasting sections of ex-ceptional regional importance. Its one-story frame wing was probably standing before Thomas Hill Wooding acquired the property in 1790. This section, a rare example of the area's 18th-century vernacular architecture, has partly collapsed through neglect. To this small house Wooding added in the early 19th century a two-story brick section, a finely detailed provincial interpretation of the Federal style with Flemish bond walls and stuccoed lintels and keystones. The interior woodwork is some of the most interesting in the region, consisting of intricately carved mantels, wainscoting, and cornices. Some of the wood-work retains highly elaborate early marbleizing and other forms of fancy painting. Although less deteriorated, the brick section also is in want of repair and maintenance. *(71–36) VLR: 09/09/69; NRHP: 11/12/69.*

MOUNTAIN VIEW, *Tightsqueeze vicinity.* Virginia's southern Piedmont experienced significant agricultural prosperity between 1800 and the Civil War. Evidence of its wealth can be seen in a group of large houses that formed the nuclei of vast plantations. While a few are stylish Greek and Gothic Revival works, most are in a relatively restrained late Federal style, with symmetrical facades and refined interior trim. Mountain View, built ca. 1842 for Thomas Smith Jones, is typical of these conservative dwellings. It is possibly a work by James Dejarnett, a regional builder. The double parlors are noteworthy for their plasterwork ceilings, glazed cupboards, and Greek Revival mantels. On the grounds is an early formal garden and landscaped park, features typical of such estates. Completing the picture of a flourishing plantation are several formally placed outbuildings, including an overseer's office, a schoolhouse, and a kitchen. A large slave graveyard is also on the property. *(71–25) VLR: 06/19/79; NRHP: 09/10/79.*

OLD CLERK'S OFFICE, *Chatham.* Completed in 1812 to serve the 1783 Pittsylvania courthouse, the former clerk's office is the oldest public building in Chatham. Built to be the chief repository of the county's official records, it served from 1813 to 1852 under the charges of William Tunstall, Jr., and his son William H. Tunstall, who succeeded him as clerk in 1836. The simple brick structure lost its originally intended function in 1853 with the construction of the present courthouse, which accommodated a new clerk's office. A demolished one-room addition of 1833 was reconstructed when the building was restored by the Pittsylvania County Historical Society in 1987–89. The building is now used as the society's museum and meeting place. *(187–02) VLR: 10/20/81; NRHP: 07/08/82.*

PITTSYLVANIA COUNTY COURTHOUSE, *Chatham.* This antebellum courthouse stands as a landmark to the Afro-American struggle for civil rights in the post–Civil War era. Judge J. D. Coles's attempt in 1878 to exclude blacks from jury duty here led to the Supreme Court case of *Ex parte Virginia.* The court's ruling held that Judge Coles's action violated the Civil Rights Act of 1875 and the equal protection clause of the Fourteenth Amendment of the U.S. Constitution. The case marked one of the few victories for blacks in federal courts in the generation after 1865. The courthouse was completed in 1853 by L. A. Shumaker, a regional master builder. The T-shaped structure on its high basement was modeled after the Campbell County Courthouse. Of particular interest is the courtroom with its ornate plasterwork embellishments, a room little changed from the time of Judge Coles's misguided action. *(187–07) VLR: 06/16/81; NRHP: 10/29/81; NHL: 05/04/87.*

WINDSOR, *Cascade vicinity.* Completed in 1862 for Samuel Pannill Wilson, an ardent secessionist who raised troops for the Confederacy, Windsor's Italianate mansion and collection of outbuildings form the last of the elaborate antebellum plantation complexes built in Pittsylvania County by generations of rich planters and entrepreneurs. The layout follows patterns established in the colonial period, incorporating a formal, symmetrical residence, architecturally sophisticated outbuildings, geometric gardens, and prominent siting. Of particular interest are Windsor's Victorian interior appointments, which include original gasoliers, Brussels carpeting, and plasterwork ceiling medallions. One facade is embellished with a cast-iron veranda. Family tradition maintains that the Civil War prevented the erection of a similar veranda ordered for opposite side. The parts of this veranda remain in their original packing cases here. *(71–35) VLR: 04/15/80; NRHP: 07/30/80.*

YATES TAVERN, *Gretna vicinity.* A key landmark of Virginia's vernacular architecture, Yates Tavern illustrates the translation of the 17th-century Tidewater hall-parlor house form into 19th-century upland building forms. Its two-room plan, exterior end chimney, and corner stair are features common to both regions in both periods. Particularly interesting is the eight-inch jetty, or overhang, at the second-floor level, a detail common in early New England but unique in Virginia. The jetty probably resulted from an early remodeling which placed a full second story upon the existing framing of a box cornice. The construction date is uncertain, but a court order of 1788 mentioning "Yates's Old House" may refer to the present building. Samuel Yates bought a license in 1818 "to keep a house of public entertainment where he now resides." The tavern was restored by Pittsylvania County as a Bicentennial project. *(71–60)*
VLR: 11/19/74; NRHP: 12/19/74.

CITY OF PORTSMOUTH

One of several port cities lining Hampton Roads harbor, Portsmouth was established in 1752 and named by its founder, William Crawford, for the English naval port. It was incorporated as a town in 1836 and as a city in 1858.

CEDAR GROVE CEMETERY, *301 Fort Lane.* A veritable museum of funerary art, Cedar Grove Cemetery is one of Virginia's early municipal burial grounds. By the early 19th century such public places of interment had become essential for urban areas. Churchyards were filling up, and private urban burials caused sanitation problems. Private burials became legally forbidden in 1832, the same year that Cedar Grove Cemetery was established. Public cemeteries became objects of local pride and were embellished with fine monuments. Many echoed contemporary architectural fashion; thus Greek, Egyptian, Gothic, and Renaissance styles are evident here. Monument types include mausoleums, Celtic crosses, obelisks, and angel statues. Symbolic motifs such as wreathes, torches, and anchors abound. Local history is told with the prominent individuals buried here, among whom are John L. Porter, designer of the ironclad *Virginia,* and George W. Grice, first mayor of the independent city of Portsmouth. *(124–58) VLR: 06/19/91; NRHP: 10/15/92.*

COMMODORE THEATRE, *421 High Street.* The Commodore Theatre, named for Commodore James Barron, was opened in 1945 by Portsmouth native William Stanley Wilder who owned of a chain of theaters in the Tidewater area. It was designed by Baltimore architect John J. Zink who produced a classic example of the streamlined Art Deco style. Building materials normally were not available for private commercial undertakings during World War II, but Wilder was able to procure what he needed because the theater would offer entertainment to the area's large population of military personnel. The Commodore is especially significant for preserving many of its original Art Deco appointments, including the marquee, ticket booth, ticket-taker's stand, and various architectural ornaments. Impressive Art Deco murals on the auditorium walls were reproduced when the theater underwent a meticulous restoration in 1987–89. The Commodore now serves as a motion-picture dinner theater. *(124–101) VLR: 12/04/96; NRHP: 02/27/97.*

**CONFEDERATE MONU-
MENT,** *Court and High
streets.* Portsmouth's Confederate monument, designed
by Charles E. Cassell, is one
of Virginia's most ambitious
Confederate memorials. It
consists of an obelisk on a
rusticated base guarded by
four statues representing the
branches of the Confederate
military. Unlike most monuments, the statues are not
generic figures but were
modeled after local residents.
Photographs of the models
were displayed in a shop
window, and citizens voted their choice of poses with an oblig-
atory contribution to the memorial fund. The monument was
completed in 1893, seventeen years after the cornerstone was
laid. It is one of only three monuments honoring the Confederate sailor. The sailor here faces east toward the route of CSS
Virginia from Portsmouth to her famous engagement with USS
Monitor. The monument graces the Four Corners intersection
platted by Portsmouth's founder William Crawford in 1752.
(124–183) VLR: 12/04/96; NRHP: 09/04/97.

CRADOCK HISTORIC DISTRICT. Cradock was laid out
in 1918 as a model community to accommodate the influx of
workers to the Norfolk Naval Shipyard during World War I. It
was sponsored by the U.S. Housing Corporation with architectural design by George B. Post and Sons of New York. Its name
honored British rear admiral Sir Christopher Cradock, whose
fleet was sunk by the Germans in 1914. The layout followed the
form of an anchor, the focal point being Afton Park, the town
square, which is highlighted with a bandstand. Some 759 single-family dwellings were built in cottagelike styles, varied in
shape to prevent monotony. Schools, recreational land, churches, and commercial areas were provided. Cradock remains
largely a working-class neighborhood; a strong community
pride has preserved its identity for more than seventy-five
years. *(124–37) VLR: 05/21/74; NRHP: 06/20/74.*

DRYDOCK NUMBER ONE, *Norfolk Naval Shipyard.* Constructed of large blocks of Massachusetts granite with sides
built up in a series of giant tiers, this impressive engineering
work is one of the first two drydocks erected by the U.S. government. Begun in 1827 and completed in 1834, it remains in
regular use at the Norfolk Naval Shipyard, the nation's oldest
shipyard, established in 1767. Here the Confederate navy rebuilt
the frigate *Merrimack,* which was renamed the *Virginia* and became the world's first battle-tested ironclad ship. The overall
length of the drydock is 319½ feet. It remains as built except for
the replacement of its caisson. *(124–29) VLR: 12/02/69; NRHP:
02/26/70; NHL: 11/11/71.*

**LIGHTSHIP NO.
101,** *London Slip, Elizabeth River. Lightship No.
101,* now known as
Portsmouth, is one of the
country's small number
of preserved historic
lightships. Essential
partners with lighthous-
es as aids to navigation,
lightships date from 1820
when *Lightship No. 1* was
commissioned to mark
the entrance to the Elizabeth River and the Nor-
folk Naval Shipyard.
Built in 1916 by Pusey
and Jones at Wilming-
ton, Del., *Lightship No.
101* was one of a pair of

vessels and was originally known as *Cape Charles.* It served on
at least five stations, guiding vessels into the Chesapeake Bay,
Delaware Bay, and within Nantucket Bay. The ship has undergone only minor modernization and maintains remarkable integrity for a vessel so long in service. Retired in 1960, *Lightship
No. 101* is now owned by the Portsmouth Museum System. A
conspicuous landmark along the historic waterfront, this relic
of navigation is a popular public attraction. *(124–102) VLR:
03/19/97; NHL: 05/05/89.*

OLD PORTSMOUTH COURTHOUSE, *Court and High streets.* Portsmouth's former courthouse, the pivotal landmark of the city's Four Corners at the intersection of Court and High streets, was built in 1846 as the Norfolk County Courthouse. It continued in that capacity until 1960 when the county was incorporated as the city of Chesapeake and the seat of government was moved to Great Bridge. The building served as the Portsmouth Courthouse into the next decade when its functions were transferred to a modern facility. The Greek Revival building, with a lean Doric portico above a high basement, was designed by Portsmouth native William R. Singleton and was described after its completion as "a beautiful structure, highly ornamental to the town." The courthouse is now a cultural center with its exterior restored to its original appearance, including the reconstruction of its long-vanished cupola. *(124–06) VLR: 04/07/70; NRHP: 04/29/70.*

PARK VIEW HISTORIC DISTRICT. The grid-plan Park View neighborhood was laid out between 1888 and 1892 as one of the first residential neighborhoods outside Portsmouth's original 18th-century core. Its development was facilitated by the extension of the electric trolley line to the Portsmouth Naval Hospital. Park View took its name from the hospital's park, a popular public amenity. Many of its early residents were affiliated with the hospital. Most of the houses were built in the two decades following Park View's annexation in 1894. The district's 310 structures form a cohesive but interestingly varied mix of styles. The majority are wood and are graced by front porches that served as summer living rooms and lent a sociable atmosphere to the streets. The district boasts numerous architecturally lively Queen Anne houses replete with towers, gables, and varied surface materials. Park View is now protected by local historic zoning. *(124–55) VLR: 08/21/84; NRHP: 10/04/84.*

PORT NORFOLK HISTORIC DISTRICT. Port Norfolk exemplifies late 19th-century efforts to accommodate the growing demand for uncrowded neighborhoods conveniently located near shops, recreational areas, churches, and places of employment. Bordered on the north by the Elizabeth River, Port Norfolk began as a planned suburb consisting mostly of freestanding wooden houses. Building types range from elaborate Queen Anne piles to the ever-popular bungalows. The area served successively as the glebe of Portsmouth Parish and Trinity Church, a strategic landing point in the British capture of Portsmouth and Norfolk during the Revolution, a farm, and finally a mixed-used community. Beginning in 1890, with the formation of the Port Norfolk Land Company, and continuing to ca. 1920, the community grew to its present form consisting of streets of healthful and attractive housing for employees of nearby railroad and shipping facilities. The area remains a cohesive, well-maintained neighborhood. *(124–51) VLR: 08/16/83; NRHP: 09/30/83.*

PORTSMOUTH NAVAL HOSPITAL, *Naval Regional Medical Center, Hospital Point.* Originally known as the Norfolk Naval Hospital, this famous facility was an outgrowth of the 1798 congressional act creating the Marine Hospital Service. Fort Nelson, a Revolutionary defense work guarding the Norfolk harbor, was chosen as the hospital site in 1826. The architect, John Haviland of Philadelphia, produced a preeminent work of Greek Revival institutional architecture. The decastyle Doric portico, finished in what Haviland described as "chisel-dressed Virginia freestone," is a masterpiece of monumentality. Unique are the narrow frieze windows forming the triglyphs. The shallow dome capping the operating room was added during a 1907 expansion. The hospital has had a distinguished record of service, treating naval casualties of every American conflict since its opening. Now flanked by modern hospital facilities, Haviland's original structure is undergoing a rehabilitation. *(124–36) VLR: 11/16/71; NRHP: 04/13/72.*

PORTSMOUTH OLDE TOWNE HISTORIC DISTRICT.
The historic core of Portsmouth occupies over twenty blocks in the northeastern corner of the city, overlooking the busy Elizabeth River. Preserved in the grid-plan area is a fine assemblage of late 18th- and 19th-century urban buildings, comprising the only large early townscape remaining in the Hampton Roads area. A local idiom is the district's tall, narrow Federal and Greek Revival town houses, most with side-hall plans, basements fully above ground, and entrances reached by long flights of wooden steps. Interspersed are Victorian dwellings with fancy exterior woodwork and porches. Portsmouth was founded in 1752 by Col. William Crawford who named it in honor of the English naval city. Unlike Norfolk, Portsmouth was spared the torch during the Revolution. The preservation of the district was advanced by the 1968 Olde Towne Conservation Project, Virginia's first federally assisted urban conservation effort. *(124–34) VLR: 06/02/70; NRHP: 09/08/70.*

QUARTERS A, B, AND C, NORFOLK NAVAL SHIPYARD, *Lincoln and Third streets.* These three tall houses, located behind a high brick wall on the edge of the Norfolk Naval Shipyard, were erected between 1837 and 1842 to serve as residences for the shipyard's commanding officers. Many of their details, mostly in a Greek Revival idiom, follow designs illustrated in the architectural pattern books of Asher Benjamin. The three houses survived the 1861 burning of the shipyard by evacuating Union forces and a burning the next year by departing Confederates. Well maintained, they still house the shipyard's ranking officers, with Quarters A, the largest of the three, traditionally serving as the commandant's house. The installation continues as the U.S. Navy's principal East Coast shipyard. *(124–16) VLR: 11/19/74; NRHP: 12/19/74.*

PYTHIAN CASTLE, *610–612 Court Street.* This three-story brick and stone building, with its visually arresting facade, is one of the best surviving examples of Romanesque Revival architecture in Portsmouth. Designed by local architect and builder Edward Overman, Pythian Castle was built in 1897–98. Typical of the period's fraternal lodges, the exotic edifice housed the meetings of the Knights of Pythias, a secret organization. It and similar fraternal societies were normally the patrons of such stylistically conspicuous late 19th-century buildings, usually the most elaborate structures in their communities. The "Castle" currently houses the Portsmouth Regional Office of the Virginia Department of Historic Resources. *(124–46) VLR: 07/31/80; NRHP: 10/30/80; BHR EASEMENT.*

SEABOARD COAST-LINE BUILDING, *1 High Street.* A dominant landmark of the Portsmouth waterfront, this curved-front structure has long been a symbol of the link between rail and sea commerce in Hampton Roads. Erected in 1894–95 and enlarged in 1914, the building served as the northern terminus and headquarters of the Seaboard Air Line Railroad. This railroad transported to Portsmouth

much of the South's cotton crop for shipment abroad. It also serviced the West Virginia coalfields, the steel mills of Alabama, and the fruit and produce groves of Florida. The Seaboard Air Line later merged with the Atlantic Coast Line Railroad. The offices of the resulting Seaboard Coastline Company were moved to Richmond in 1955, and the rail network eventually became part of the CSX system. The building was donated to the city in 1958 and housed municipal offices until 1980. It subsequently underwent a certified rehabilitation for mixed use. *(124–53) VLR: 08/13/85; NRHP: 10/10/85.*

TRINITY EPISCOPAL CHURCH, *High and Court streets.*
Trinity Church was built between 1828 and 1830 on the site of
the parish's original 1762 church. The congregation of the first
church dwindled after the disestablishment of the Anglican
church but was revived in 1820 under the leadership of the Rev.
John H. Wingfield. When it was attempted to enlarge the colonial church, the structure was found to be so decayed that the
building was pulled down save for one wall that is believed to
be incorporated in the present structure. During the Civil War,
Trinity was used as a Confederate hospital. The formerly simple Federal-style building has been remodeled and redecorated
many times and contains six Tiffany stained-glass windows.
The tower, an important architectural landmark for
Portsmouth's historic Four Corners, the principal downtown
intersection, was added in 1893. Trinity's churchyard contains
gravestones dating as early as 1763. *(124–28) VLR: 04/17/73; NRHP:
05/14/73.*

TRUXTUN HISTORIC DISTRICT. Truxtun was the country's first wartime government housing project constructed exclusively for blacks. Named for Thomas Truxtun, an early naval
hero, the forty-two-acre neighborhood of some 250 houses was
developed in 1918 to accommodate the growing workforce at
the Norfolk Naval Shipyard. Truxtun exhibits the high planning standards of the U.S. Housing Corporation, the federal
agency that financed and built the community as a model village. The residential streets are characterized by closely spaced
dwellings with varied roof forms so arranged that a repeated
pattern is barely discernible. Unlike the generally primitive
conditions endured by most urban blacks, Truxtun's houses
boasted indoor plumbing and electric lights. The principal architect was Rossell Edward Mitchell of Norfolk, with H. P.
Kelsey serving as chief planner. Though it has undergone moderate alterations, Truxtun retains much of its original character
and is still a black neighborhood. *(124–47) VLR: 04/15/80; NRHP:
09/16/82.*

POWHATAN COUNTY

Honoring Virginia's early 17th-century Indian chieftain, this upper James River county was formed from Cumberland County in 1777, with part of Chesterfield County added later. The county seat is Powhatan Court House.

BEAUMONT, *Michaux vicinity.* A handsome example of a Federal-period upper James River plantation house, Beaumont has been cut off from public access since 1937 when the property became a boys' reform school now known as Beaumont Learning Center, a high-security unit of the Virginia Department of Corrections. The house, originally the core of a 1,500-acre tract, was built in 1811 for William Walthall, one of Powhatan County's wealthiest landowners, who married Sally Michaux of a local Huguenot family. Following the traditional Virginia format, the two-story dwelling was embellished with a modillion cornice and a handsome pedimented doorway. A brick rear wing was added in 1840. Despite many years of institutional use, the house preserves early weatherboarding and sash, an early portico, and finely detailed regional Federal interior trim. In recent years the house has stood unoccupied, receiving minimal maintenance. *(72–95) VLR: 06/17/86; NRHP: 04/02/87.*

BELMEAD, *Powhatan Court House vicinity.* New York architect Alexander Jackson Davis designed this grand romantic mansion for Philip St. George Cocke in 1845. Although its pinnacles and other decorative elements have been removed, the house remains one of the country's preeminent examples of a Gothic Revival villa. Cocke served as a president of the Virginia Agricultural Society and was a board member of the Virginia Military Institute where he was instrumental in having Davis design the new complex. In 1893 Belmead was purchased by Mr. and Mrs. Edward de Vaux Morrell of Philadelphia, who founded here in 1895 St. Emma's Industrial and Agricultural School for black male youth. Renamed St. Emma Military Academy in 1945, the school closed in 1972. Belmead remains the property of the Sisters of the Blessed Sacrament, a Philadelphia corporation. The house is currently unused. *(72–49) VLR: 05/13/69; NRHP: 11/12/69.*

BELNEMUS, *Powhatan Court House vicinity.* The three-part Palladian scheme used in the Federal period throughout Virginia gave to rural houses an architectural formality and sophistication that is well illustrated in Belnemus. The house was erected between 1783 and 1799 for James Clarke, a Powhatan County inventor and politician, on land purchased from William Mayo. It received its present porch, siding, and rear addition around the turn of the century when it was owned by the Valentine family. Adding interest to the exterior is the curious finial at the apex of the pyramidal roof. The highlight of the interior is the late Georgian hall woodwork, which consists of an elegantly detailed pedimented chimneypiece and matching cupboard opposite. Both elements have full-height Doric pilasters supporting Doric entablatures. Several early outbuildings, including a mid-19th-century tobacco barn, remain on the grounds. *(72–02) VLR: 09/19/78; NRHP: 04/20/79.*

BLENHEIM, *Ballsville vicinity.* Snugly set in the Powhatan County countryside, this genteel homestead is among the region's earliest dwellings, situated on land patented in 1730 by the 18th-century surveyor William Mayo. The original portion began as a simple hall-parlor cottage constructed in the second half of the 18th century by Mayo's son John, a member of the House of Burgesses. This core was expanded by Mayo's grandson, William, and subsequent owners, into a rambling, U-shaped family seat. Lending visual character to the exterior are the shed dormers, a regional architectural idiom. Much of the present interior woodwork is country Federal and Greek Revival, dating from the first half of the 19th century. The younger William Mayo was a member of the first Cumberland County Court and served in the Virginia House of Delegates in 1777–81 and 1783–85. *(72–03) VLR: 07/15/86; NRHP: 12/11/86.*

EMMANUEL EPISCOPAL CHURCH, *Powhatan Court House vicinity.* A storybook country church, Emmanuel stands on land donated to Southam Parish in 1846 by Philip St. George Cocke, master of Powhatan County's great plantation, Belmead. Cocke worked with Thomas Ludwell Hobson of Brooklyn, also in Powhatan County, in having the church's bricks made at both Belmead and Brooklyn. Cocke's use of the architect Alexander Jackson Davis for the design of Belmead has led to speculation that Davis may also have designed Emmanuel Church. Though it employs the Gothic Revival style for which Davis is noted, the church probably was designed by Cocke himself. Whoever was responsible, the architecture has attracted many admirers. Bishop John Johns, who consecrated Emmanuel in 1847, wrote that it was "highly credible to the good taste and liberality of those by whom it has been erected." *(72–13) VLR: 12/12/89; NRHP: 12/27/90.*

FRENCH'S TAVERN, *Ballsville vicinity.* This rural landmark is of the few extant early taverns formerly scattered along the Old Buckingham Road connecting Richmond to Lynchburg. Though expanded and altered, it preserves much historic flavor and fabric. The original core was built between 1730 and 1734, soon after the large surrounding tract was patented by Col. Francis Eppes. The property eventually came into the possession of Thomas Jefferson through his marriage to Eppes's granddaughter Martha Wayles. Later converted to a store and ordinary, the building was purchased in 1807 by Hugh French who operated the popular tavern until 1847. Exceptional interior features include a Chinese lattice stair railing and fancy grained and marbleized woodwork. A typical tavern feature is the large "swingwall," a movable partition separating the center hall from the east parlor which could be hooked to the ceiling to create a large entertainment space. *(72–105) VLR: 12/13/88; NRHP: 04/21/89.*

HUGUENOT MEMORIAL CHAPEL AND MONUMENT, *Huguenot Springs vicinity.* This simple country chapel, erected in 1895, was the fourth church to serve the Episcopal King William Parish. The parish was part of a tract designated in 1700 as a religious haven for Huguenots—French Protestant refugees. The chapel incorporates structural members believed to have been reused from the 1730 Huguenot church. It is also thought that its large summer beam was salvaged from the 1710 Huguenot church at Manakintowne. The granite monument nearby was erected in 1937 by the Huguenot Society of the Founders of Manakin in the Colony of Virginia. The two structures are maintained by the Huguenot Society as tangible memorials to colonial America's largest Huguenot settlement. In 1954 the chapel was moved approximately 200 feet to make way for a new Episcopal church. It was again moved a short distance in 1985 to its present location on property owned by the Huguenot Society. *(72–93) VLR: 06/17/87; NRHP: 03/23/88.*

KESWICK, *Huguenot Trail, Midlothian vicinity.* Keswick is situated on part of a 1,500-acre land grant made to Charles Clarke in the early 1700s. Clarke had married Marianne Salle, member of one of the area's original Huguenot families. The present plantation house, an H-shaped dwelling, was built ca. 1800 by Maj. John Clarke (1766–1844), one of Charles and Marianne Clarke's four sons and founder of the Bellona Arsenal.

Echoing the H-shaped Tuckahoe directly across the James River, the house survives with few modifications and preserves finely detailed woodwork. On the grounds is a collection of brick outbuildings among which is an enigmatic circular structure with a conical roof and central chimney. The complex has much to show about the physical layout and social organization of a Virginia plantation. With its riverside setting and broad level fields, Keswick remains a working farm, preserving a gentle agrarian ambience. *(72–45) VLR: 11/19/74; NRHP: 12/19/74.*

NORWOOD, *Fine Creek Mills vicinity.* Norwood is among the most imposing of the postcolonial plantation houses lining the upper James River. The hipped-roofed Georgian center portion was built in the late 18th century for Thomas Harris. The Harris family sold the property, then called Greenyard, in 1834 to Robert Beverley Randolph, who, with his father-in-law, Harry Heth, operated the nearby Midlothian coal mines. In 1835 Randolph added the two-story wings and Ionic porches and installed elaborate provincial Adam-style woodwork. Enriched with paterae, colonnettes, and pineapples, the woodwork is apparently by the same artisans as the nearly identical woodwork in Castlewood in Chesterfield Court House. It is assumed that the property was renamed Norwood at this time. Randolph also built the complex of mid-19th-century brick farm buildings. The patrician residence is now the home of the Kennon family, descendants of Robert Beverley Randolph. *(72–48) VLR: 03/18/75; NRHP: 05/19/80.*

PAXTON, *Genito.* Paxton is an intact early 19th-century plantation complex. The dwelling house, a formal brick structure which may incorporate fabric dating from 1776, makes use of the traditional Virginia plan of a central passage with a single room on either side but also has an original east wing, probably built as a doctor's office. The handsome fanlight doorway is embellished with a carved floral spray. The original outbuildings include a brick smokehouse, two small frame cottages or offices, and a brick and frame icehouse. The complex was completed in its present form in 1819–23 for Ennion Skelton, a prosperous country physician. Dr. Skelton was also a partner in the Genito Mill, one of the county's main gristmills. His son, Dr. John G. Skelton, who inherited the property in 1849, became a leading physician in the Richmond medical community. The Skelton family burial ground is on the property. *(72–34) VLR: 12/12/89; NRHP: 12/28/90; BHR EASEMENT.*

POWHATAN COURT HOUSE HISTORIC DISTRICT, *Powhatan Court House.* Laid out in 1777, this compact district focuses on the diminutive 1849 courthouse, a masterpiece of Greek Revival design by Alexander Jackson Davis of New York. Davis's association with this rural county resulted from the pa-

tronage of Philip St. George Cocke, who commissioned Davis to design his Gothic Revival mansion, Belmead. Cocke was also instrumental in having Davis design the Gothic buildings for the Virginia Military Institute. As a commissioner for the new courthouse, he obtained the Doric temple design from Davis for $30. The builder was Lewis Johnson of Hanover County. Other early buildings on the court square are the 1797 former clerk's office and the ca. 1826 jail. Beside the square is the late 18th-century double-galleried Courthouse Tavern, one of the state's best-preserved county-seat hostelries. *(72–79) VLR: 12/02/69; NRHP: 02/16/70.*

ST. LUKE'S EPISCOPAL CHURCH, *Fine Creek Mills.* Throughout the 19th century Virginia's Episcopalians, though few in number, constituted much of the state's landed gentry. As a result, country Episcopal churches tended to be quite small but are noteworthy for their architectural finesse. A particularly comely example is the tiny St. Luke's Church, completed in 1844. Executed with beautiful brickwork and Classical Revival detailing, the building is a testament to William Henry Harrison, an Englishmen and veteran of the battle of Waterloo, who settled in Powhatan County in 1827. The church was built on land owned by Harrison who supervised all phases of the church's construction, even the making of its bricks. When the church was consecrated in 1845, Bishop John Johns praised its beauty though he lamented its small size. A chancel was added in 1890 and a sacristy and a vestry room in 1915. St. Luke's continues to serve descendants of original members. *(72–38) VLR: 10/18/88; NRHP: 03/20/89.*

PRINCE EDWARD COUNTY

Formed from Amelia County in 1753, this rural south-central Virginia county was named in honor of Prince Edward Augustus, a son of Frederick Louis, Prince of Wales, and a younger brother of King George III. Its county seat is Farmville.

BRIERY CHURCH, *Briery vicinity.* In an isolated woodland setting, this multigabled wooden church is a singular expression of the mid-19th-century Gothic Revival. With its verticality emphasized by board-and-batten siding, sharp gables, and narrow lancet windows, the building displays the individualism inherent in many of the architectural endeavors of rural America. Its Presbyterian congregation was organized in 1755; the present building, erected in 1856, is the third on the site. The exaggerated design is attributed to the Rev. Robert Lewis Dabney, a theologian and amateur architect who served the congregation as a supply minister from 1856 to 1858. Dabney at the time was a professor at the nearby Union Theological Seminary, then part of Hampden-Sydney College. Briery Church survives without alteration, preserving all of its original interior appointments including pews, pulpit, and "vaulted" pine ceiling. *(73–38) VLR: 05/13/69; NRHP: 11/17/69.*

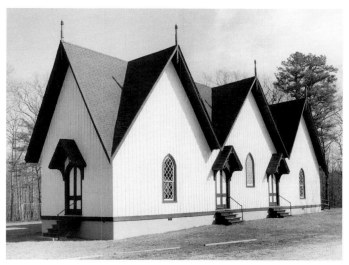

BUFFALO PRESBYTERIAN CHURCH, *Pamplin vicinity.* The very essence of a simple country church, Buffalo Presbyterian houses a congregation formed in 1739. The present building was erected sometime after the original church burned in 1785. Its plain lines were dictated by the austerity of Calvinist religious practices rather than by economic necessity. The interior preserves its early wood floors, plank ceiling, paneled box pews, and wood-burning stoves. The sanctuary formerly possessed a rear gallery reserved for free blacks and slaves, accessible by exterior stairs, since removed, on either side of the building. The entrance vestibule was added in 1931. During antebellum times Buffalo Church was closely associated with Hampden-Sydney College and Union Theological Seminary. John Holt Rice, founder of the seminary, regularly preached here in the 1820s, and Joseph R. Wilson, father of President Woodrow Wilson, was a visiting minister while on the college faculty. *(73–28) VLR: 04/28/95; NRHP: 04/07/95.*

DEBTORS' PRISON, *Worsham.* The present-day settlement of Worsham was founded in 1745 and served as the county seat until 1872 when the court moved to Farmville. The 1855 former clerk's office and the solid little structure authorized in 1786 to serve as the "Gaol for Debtors" are the tiny community's only remaining public buildings. Constructed by Richard Bigg using square-hewn logs for its walls and closely set squared logs for both floor and ceiling, the jail was built with security in mind. Debtors generally were jailed separate from criminals. The jailing of debtors was abandoned in the early 19th century, and by 1820 the jail had been converted to a residence. The building was acquired in 1950 by the Association for the Preservation of Virginia Antiquities, which restored it and deeded it to Prince Edward County in 1976. *(73–07) VLR: 08/15/72; NRHP: 09/22/72.*

FALKLAND, *Redd Shop vicinity.* One of the earliest remaining houses in Prince Edward County, Falkland was built in the last quarter of the 18th century for Francis Watkins, Sr., a longtime county clerk and trustee of Hampden-Sydney College. The four-bay, hall-parlor dwelling is a little-altered vernacular house of a type found throughout the upper South from the Virginia Piedmont westward. Falkland is an unusually large example, with generous scale and original one-story wings of unequal lengths. The house also possesses an interesting store of original woodwork, most of which is a provincial interpretation of late colonial trim. Francis Watkins, Jr., who inherited Falkland, was himself a county magistrate and captain of the local militia. Upon his move to Alabama in 1820, Watkins sold Falkland to his brother-in-law James Wood, a tobacco manufacturer who also was a Hampden-Sydney trustee. *(73–39) VLR: 03/20/79; NRHP: 06/22/79.*

FARMVILLE HISTORIC DISTRICT. Established in 1798, this central Virginia community was laid out in an irregular grid pattern and grew by steady accretion. Its commercial, residential, and industrial sections preserve an instructive assemblage of historic buildings. Main Street, the primary commercial corridor, is dominated by the 1939 Prince Edward County Courthouse and blocks of late 19th- and early 20th-century brick commercial buildings. The district's northern section contains an impressive grouping of large turn-of-the-century warehouses (shown), reflecting the importance of the tobacco industry to Farmville's economy. Three residential neighborhoods—the western High Street corridor, the area bounded by High, Beech, Randolph, and Grove streets, and First and Second avenues—hold a variety of dwellings, churches, and schools, illustrating changing architectural tastes over 150 years. These quiet, shady streets are particularly rich both in restrained antebellum brick dwellings and more architecturally assertive Victorian and Colonial Revival residences. *(144–27) VLR: 04/18/89; NRHP: 10/30/89.*

HAMPDEN-SYDNEY COLLEGE HISTORIC DISTRICT, *Hampden-Sydney.* Named for John Hampden and Algernon Sydney, 17th-century champions of English liberty, this prestigious rural Presbyterian college has operated continuously since 1776. The campus is distinguished by an important collection of collegiate structures dating from the first half of the 19th century. The earliest is Cushing Hall (shown), a four-story dormitory begun in 1822. Aligned with it across a vale are buildings erected by designer-contractor Dabney Cosby, Sr., to serve Union Theological Seminary, an associated institution (later moved to Richmond). These include two brick residences, Penshurst (1830) and Middlecourt (1829), and between them Venable Hall (1824–31), a large brick structure with a central pavilion and cupola. A primary landmark is the Greek Revival College Church, built ca. 1860 to the design of the preacher-architect Robert Lewis Dabney, who used Italianate motifs for Westmerton (1856), his own residence here. *(73–58) VLR: 12/02/69; NRHP: 02/26/70.*

LONGWOOD HOUSE, *Longwood Avenue, Farmville.* Longwood House, a Farmville area landmark, illustrates the evolution of a simple Federal farmhouse into one of the county's finest antebellum mansions. The massive wood-frame structure began as a compact dwelling built for Nathaniel E. Venable in 1815 soon after a fire destroyed an earlier house. After his rise to prominence as a state delegate and senator, Venable had his residence enlarged and refashioned in the Greek Revival style. The house has survived without significant alterations to the present, retaining its early porch, siding, and interior woodwork. Since 1929, when the State Teachers College at Farmville acquired the property as a rural student retreat, Longwood House has become the identifying symbol of the college community, giving its name to the institution in 1949. It now serves as the official home of its president. *(144–25) VLR: 10/18/83; NRHP: 03/08/84.*

ROBERT RUSSA MOTON HIGH SCHOOL, *South Main Street and Griffin Boulevard.* This innocent-looking school building was an object of national attention in Virginia's school desegregation crisis of the 1950s. The school was the scene of a strike begun on April 23, 1951, by students of the then all-black institution to protest their inadequate and unequal educational facilities. The strike led to the court case *Davis v. County School Board of Prince Edward County,* which was combined with others before the U.S. Supreme Court as *Brown v. Board of Education.* That case was the basis for the landmark decision that struck down the "separate but equal" doctrine governing public education. The decision gave birth to Virginia's massive resistance movement during which Prince Edward County closed its schools until 1964 rather than desegregate. Studies are under way for developing the school building into a civil rights museum. *(114–53) VLR: 03/19/97; NRHP: 10/24/95; NHL: 08/05/98.*

OLD PRINCE EDWARD COUNTY CLERK'S OFFICE, *Worsham.* The former clerk's office of Prince Edward County, the third to serve the county, is a relic of the period when the tiny settlement of Worsham was the county seat, formerly known as Prince Edward Court House. The last courthouse here was built in 1832. It was for this structure that the clerk's office was erected in 1855 by the builders Guthrey and Thaxton. The small but refined building is a relatively late expression of the Classical Revival and illustrates the style's persistence in rural areas. The courthouse was demolished after the county seat was moved to Farmville in 1872, and the clerk's office became a dormitory for Prince Edward Academy. It later housed a public school and eventually was converted to a residence. It was reacquired by the county in 1977 and is currently undergoing restoration. *(73–03) VLR: 06/19/79; NRHP: 09/10/79; BHR EASEMENT.*

PRINCE GEORGE COUNTY

Named for Prince George of Denmark, husband of Queen Anne, this Tidewater county was formed from Charles City County in 1702. Its county seat is Prince George.

BRANDON, *Burrowsville vicinity.* The influence of English interpretations of the villa designs of Andrea Palladio is effectively demonstrated in Brandon, one of America's most admired works of colonial architecture. Plate III of Robert Morris's *Select Architecture* (1755), an English pattern book of Palladian-style designs, provided the direct inspiration for the distinctive seven-part composition. Brandon was built ca. 1765 by Nathaniel Harrison II for his son Benjamin. The first stories of Brandon's terminal wings are earlier structures; second stories were added to fit the novel scheme. The hall was remodeled in the early 19th century when the present arcade and stair were installed. Brandon remained in the Harrison family until 1926 when it was purchased by Mr. and Mrs. Robert W. Daniel, who carefully restored the house and its formal gardens. The property's name comes from Martin's Brandon, an early 17th-century patent here. *(74–02) VLR: 09/09/69; NRHP: 11/17/69; NHL: 04/15/70.*

BRANDON CHURCH, *Burrowsville.* The fourth church of one of the Commonwealth's oldest Episcopal parishes, Brandon Church is an expression of the ecclesiastical architectural taste at the time of the revival of the Episcopal church in Virginia in the mid–19th century. Although its architect has not been documented, the Tuscan-style building, with its pink stuccoed walls and corner tower, resembles the Italianate designs of the Baltimore firm of Niernsee and Neilson. The church was consecrated in 1857 and stands across the road from the site of the parish's 18th-century church. The choir loft preserves the church's 1873 Henry Erben pipe organ. A chalice and paten, given in 1656, are believed to be the nation's oldest communion service in continuous possession of the original parish. The parish was established in 1655 and was named for Martin's Brandon, land patented by John Martin in 1618. *(74–03) VLR: 07/31/80; NRHP: 10/31/80.*

EVERGREEN, *Hopewell vicinity.* This James River plantation was established by the Ruffin family in the mid–18th century. The present house was erected ca. 1807–8 by George Ruffin, probably on the site of the original Ruffin home. With its symmetrical five-bay facade articulated by pilaster strips, the stuccoed house carries the formal image enjoyed by the Tidewater's upper-class planters. Insurance records note that the house was originally roofed with slate rather than the usual wood shingles, an indication of superior quality. One of George Ruffin's sons was Edmund Ruffin III, the southern agriculturalist and ardent secessionist. Another son, George H. Ruffin, conveyed the plantation in 1832 to his half sister's husband, Harrison H. Cocke, a Confederate naval captain who commanded the James River defenses. The house later fell into decay and was used as a barn. Its interior was extensively rebuilt in the 1930s. *(74–05) VLR: 05/15/79; NRHP: 07/24/79.*

HATCH ARCHAEOLOGICAL SITE, *Garysville vicinity.* On Powell Creek, two miles inland from the James River, the Hatch site contains archaeological remains dating from at least 8000 B.C. through the 17th century. Deep stratified deposits, a large number of Indian storage pits, hearths, human and dog burials, intact floor surfaces of living spaces, and numerous post molds offer a rare glimpse into various periods of Indian life extending into the period of European contact. The 105 dog burials form the largest concentration of such burials found in eastern North America. The site was part of the Weyanoke district of the Powhatan chiefdom, and a small number of features probably date from the contact period. Colonial post holes of possibly four structures and the remains of trenches document early European efforts at colonization. The area was likely included in land patented by Cheney Boyce in 1637. *(74–47) VLR: 02/21/89; NRHP: 11/06/89.*

FLOWERDEW HUNDRED ARCHAEOLOGICAL DISTRICT, *Garysville vicinity.* Flowerdew Hundred was among the earliest English settlements in the New World. The tract was granted in 1618 to Governor George Yeardley, who named it in honor of his wife, née Temperance Flowerdew. It was here, on Windmill Point, that America's first windmill was built ca. 1621, a fact commemorated by a 17th-century-style windmill constructed in the 1970s. The settlement survived the Indian attack of 1622 and was occupied through the 18th century. The area was developed into a plantation after its purchase by the Willcox family in 1804. The property was the scene of an extensive archaeological investigation from 1971 to 1995 by the Flowerdew Hundred Foundation. The many sites include a complex of early 17th-century structures as well as evidence of Indian occupation dating from 9000 B.C. The windmill and an archaeological museum are open to the public. *(74–06) VLR: 05/20/75; NRHP: 08/01/75.*

MERCHANT'S HOPE CHURCH, *Hopewell vicinity.* Expressing the plainness of low-church Anglican worship, this well-known colonial church is devoid of religious symbols but achieves architectural dignity from its Flemish bond brickwork, modillion cornice, and graceful splaying of its gable roof. Although most of its original interior features were lost during the Civil War, its early sash windows, gallery, stone pavers, and roof framing have survived. Claims have been made that the church dates from 1657. A building of that date could well have served the original Jordan's Parish, established in 1655, but nothing of the present building exhibits a definite 17th-century architectural character; its form and details are more typical of early and mid-18th-century Virginia churches. Merchant's Hope suffered neglect during the 19th century and was often served by clergymen from nearby parishes. Restoration begun in the 1960s has restored the original configuration of the interior. *(74–09) VLR: 11/05/68; NRHP: 10/08/69.*

UPPER BRANDON, *Burrowsville vicinity.* The architecture of Upper Brandon places this grand mansion among an important set of sophisticated Virginia Federal houses crafted by accomplished but yet unidentified builders making use of Asher Benjamin's *American Builder's Companion* (1806). These include Hampstead, Horn Quarter, and Magnolia Grange among others, all of which have related detailing. Upper Brandon's center section was erected in 1825 for William Byrd Harrison, son of Benjamin Harrison III of adjacent Lower Brandon (or Brandon). Harrison, an advocate of improved agricultural practices, contributed articles to Edmund Ruffin's *Farmers' Register.* The house was enlarged with two-story wings in 1859. The plantation was part of a 1616 grant to John Martin and has been continuously farmed since the mid–17th century. In 1984 the 2,138-acre property was purchased by the James River Corporation, which restored the house for a corporate retreat center. Protected by easements, the plantation was sold in 1998. *(74–27) VLR: 03/20/96.*

PRINCE WILLIAM COUNTY

Named for William Augustus, duke of Cumberland and third son of King George II, this northern Virginia county was formed from Stafford and King George counties in 1730. Its county seat is Manassas.

BEL AIR, *Minnieville vicinity.* This ca. 1740 brick farmhouse was originally the home of the Ewell family. Mason Locke Weems (1759–1825), clergyman, first biographer of George Washington, and inventor of the popular Washington story of the hatchet and cherry tree, married into the Ewell family and lived at Bel Air from 1809 until his death. Parson Weems lies buried in the family cemetery here. With its robust but somewhat casual proportions and massive south chimney, the house is a provincial interpretation of the Georgian style. Its interior retains ambitious and unusual woodwork, including a removable paneled partition between the passage and drawing room. In the partition are original casement windows for lighting the passage. Other noteworthy features are the Georgian stair and the parlor chimneypiece with its crosseted overmantel. Like many other colonial houses in northern Virginia, Bel Air has a fieldstone foundation. *(76–01) VLR: 12/02/69; NRHP: 02/26/70; BHR EASEMENT.*

BEN LOMOND, *Sudley Manor Drive, Manassas vicinity.* Built in 1837 by Benjamin Tasker Chinn, a grandson of Robert ("Councillor") Carter, Ben Lomond is one of the only remaining plantation houses in an area which once exhibited such fine country residences as Portici, Pittsylvania, Hazel Plain, Mountain View, Elmwood, Sudley, and Woodland. Constructed of native fieldstone, the house follows the single-pile, five-bay-facade format typical of its time and place. Its interior retains bold original woodwork. Ben Lomond was used as a hospital during the Civil War battles of first and second Manassas, which were fought nearby. Because its surroundings have succumbed to intense commercial and residential development, Ben Lomond remains a cogent reminder of the region's former agricultural character and Civil War history. The property is preserved as a public amenity by the Prince William County Park Authority. *(76–04) VLR: 05/20/80; NRHP: 07/30/80.*

BEVERLEY MILL, *Broad Run.* In Thoroughfare Gap, in full view of motorists traveling on nearby Interstate Highway 66, Beverley Mill is a landmark of the region's traditional stone construction as well as its milling industry. The bottom three stories of the towering structure belonged to a mill operated by John Chapman built before 1759, the year the mill was cited as a boundary marker between Prince William and Fauquier counties. The upper two stories were added in the 1850s, making the building one of the tallest gristmills remaining in the state. It is claimed that the mill supplied meal to troops in five wars, from the French and Indian War through the Civil War. With improved machinery, Beverley Mill was grinding approximately 100,000 bushels of grain annually as late as the 1940s. The mill burned in 1998, but the walls remain standing. *(76–02) VLR: 11/01/71; NRHP: 02/23/73.*

BRENTSVILLE COURTHOUSE (OLD PRINCE WILLIAM COUNTY COURTHOUSE), *Brentsville.* The Brentsville Courthouse is the fourth courthouse to serve Prince William County. It was built in 1820–22 along with the adjacent jail following the decision to move the county seat from Dumfries to this more centralized location. The public function of the plain country Federal structure is signaled by its octagonal belfry. The county abandoned the building after Union occupation of the area in 1862. County records strewn across the courthouse floor to a depth of 2 feet were nearly all lost. The complex was reoccupied following the war and functioned until the county seat was moved to Manassas in 1893. The building was converted to a school and later a public meeting place. It and the jail became the charge of the Prince William County Park Authority in 1974. The complex is now leased to the Prince William County Historical Commission. *(76–21) VLR: 12/13/88; NRHP: 08/18/89.*

BRENTSVILLE HISTORIC DISTRICT, *Brentsville.* Brentsville was established in 1822 as a planned community for a new Prince William county seat. In 1820 the county justices determined that this site was convenient to more of the county's population than the existing county seat at Dumfries. The town was laid off in a grid of twenty-one squares with seventy lots, most never built on. Growth all but ceased when the county seat was moved to Manassas in 1893. The tiny settlement today contains thirty-three historic structures and sites, including three churches, eleven houses, and various outbuildings. The visual highlight of the village is the 1822 brick courthouse, the county's fourth. It and the adjacent jail are now a county historic site. Of architectural interest is the 1847 Greek Revival Hatcher's Memorial Baptist Church, originally an Episcopal church, constructed of local dark red sandstone. Most of the houses are late 19th-century vernacular types. *(76–338) VLR: 02/20/90; NRHP: 12/21/90.*

BUCKLAND HISTORIC DISTRICT. This tiny village bravely holds its own against the roar of constant traffic on U.S. Route 29, which bisects the historic community. Buckland nonetheless is an especially picturesque example of the many mill-oriented settlements once scattered through the Virginia Piedmont. Chartered in 1798, Buckland was the first inland town established in Prince William County. It was an important wagon stop on the main east-west road between Alexandria and the territory beyond the Blue Ridge. The present turn-of-the century gristmill is believed to be the third mill on this site. The water for the millrace was fed by Broad Run, which flows by immediately to the north. Also included in the district is an early 19th-century tavern and a small mid-19th-century church. These buildings, in addition to several residential dwellings, sustain the village's historic character. *(76–313) 12/08/87; NRHP: 06/17/88.*

COCKPIT POINT CONFEDERATE BATTERY, *Cockpit Point Road, Cherry Hill vicinity.* Located atop a 70-foot cliff overlooking the Potomac River, the Civil War features here consist of four individual batteries forming the best preserved of several Confederate fortifications associated with the Southern blockade of Washington, D.C. Brig. Gen. Isaac Trimble, CSA, probably built the battery in the fall of 1861. On November 14, 1861, a sailing schooner loaded with firewood tried to slip past Cockpit Point. The batteries fired on it, and three rounds found their mark. The sailors dropped anchor and then swam for the Maryland shore. A dozen Confederates rowed out and set the schooner afire, but soon afterward a group of Massachusetts soldiers extinguished the blaze and towed the ship to safety. The Confederate guns then dueled Union cannon on the Maryland shore, killing only a Northern pig and mule. *(76–302) VLR: 12/13/88.*

DAVIS-BEARD HOUSE, *Bristow.* Situated at the intersection of Bristow Road and the Southern Railroad tracks, this rambling Victorian structure is a rare surviving example of a 19th-century combination dwelling and general store. It stands on the brownstone foundations of a house built by Thomas Davis around 1856 and apparently destroyed during the 1863 battle of Bristoe Station. It was replaced soon after the war by a new house called Glee Hall, a simple dwelling that was expanded around 1878. In 1891 Robert Davis added the shop-fronted section and operated a general store, hardware store, and lumber business on the premises. A post office wing was added in 1920. Sold by the Davis family in 1961, the building has served as an antiques shop and dwelling since 1966 and remains the village of Bristow's principal historic anchor. Most of the early interior appointments of the store section remain in place. *(76–245) VLR: 12/13/88; NRHP: 11/08/89.*

ECW ARCHITECTURE AT PRINCE WILLIAM FOREST PARK, *Triangle vicinity.* Representative of the 1930s New Deal efforts to provide recreational facilities for urban, low-income groups and families in the form of organized camping facilities, Prince William Forest Park is significant for its several complexes of rustic architecture set in natural landscaping with careful layouts. The park is historically important as one of six recreational demonstration areas (RDAs) established in Virginia, and the fourth largest in the nation. The project was carried out by Civilian Conservation Corps (CCC) and Works Progress Administration (WPA) laborers from 1935 to 1942. Both the CCC and the WPA were outgrowths of President Franklin Roosevelt's Emergency Conservation Work (ECW) Act of 1933. Remaining in the park's four original camp complexes—Goodwill, Mawavi, Orenda, and Pleasant—are over 150 CCC-built rustic-style structures, including cottages, crafts lodges, dining halls, and various support structures. *(76–131, 135, 136, 146) VLR: 09/20/88; NRHP: 06/12/89.*

EFFINGHAM, *Aden vicinity.* Effingham is one of several large tobacco plantations established during the 18th century in the fertile area of southern Prince William County. The original owner was William Alexander of King George County, great-grandson of John Alexander for whom the city of Alexandria was named.

William Alexander served as a member of the Prince William Committee of Safety and was a lieutenant colonel in the county militia. He purchased the Effingham property in 1777 and presumably built the house soon after. A Tidewater-style plantation house, the frame structure has a double-pile, center-passage plan with exterior chimneys connected by pent closets. The interior has sections of early trim and paneling. The several early outbuildings include a rare stone blacksmith shop, a smokehouse, and a slave quarters. Terraces of an extensive early formal garden descend from the south elevation. *(76–06) VLR: 12/13/88; NRHP: 11/09/89.*

FREESTONE POINT CONFEDERATE BATTERY, *Leesylvania State Park.* For five months, from October 1861 to March 1862, the Confederate military succeeded in blockading the Potomac River, the Union army's main riverine supply route to and from Washington, D.C. This created an embarrassing situation for Union politicians and military leaders. At the mouth of Neabsco Creek, Freestone Point Battery, constructed in September 1861, was the most northern of the blockade's gun emplacements. The battery is situated on a bluff 95 feet above the Potomac. It consists of four individual gun emplacements. The battery apparently was abandoned when the three other batteries in the blockade network were built up to sufficient strength. The rest of the batteries were abandoned after March 1862 when the Confederate army withdrew south. The earthwork today is maintained as a historic feature of Leesylvania State Park. *(76–264) VLR: 02/21/89; NRHP: 08/18/89.*

GREENWICH PRESBYTERIAN CHURCH, *9510 Burwell Road, Greenwich.* Built in 1858, this country Gothic church is accented by its rustic Gothic porches and lych-gate. The land on which the church stands was donated by Charles Green, an English cotton merchant from Savannah who built a dwelling at The Lawn nearby. During the Civil War, when Union troops attempted to seize the church for a hospital, Green objected, claiming that a clause in the deed provided that the land would revert to him if its religious use ceased, thereby making it English property. The church was thus the only one in the county not damaged by Union forces. One of Col. John S. Mosby's Confederate rangers, Bradford Smith Hoskins, is buried in the church cemetery. Wounded nearby in 1863, Hoskins was brought by Green to The Lawn where he died. *(76–175) VLR: 12/13/88; NRHP: 08/18/89.*

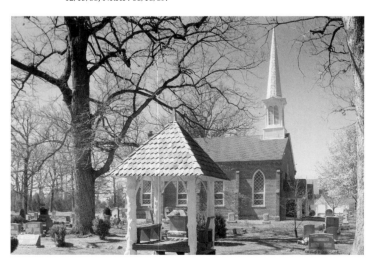

THE LAWN, *Greenwich.* Named for its immaculately maintained greensward, The Lawn was established in 1855 as a country home for the English-born Savannah cotton merchant Charles Green after his marriage to Greenwich native Lucy Ireland Hunton. He built here a fanciful complex of Carpenter's Gothic structures. Green's Savannah residence, the famous Green-Meldrim house, is also Gothic Revival. The Greenwich buildings appeared quite foreign to the area. One Civil War visitor described the house as "the strangest in Virginia." The property served as a Union camp in 1864. Green was imprisoned, accused of being a Confederate spy. The noted French author Julian Green, grandson of Charles Green, visited The Lawn in his youth and used it as the setting for his novel *Maud.* The main house burned in 1924 and was replaced with a Tudor Revival work completed in 1926, designed by A. B. Mullett and Co. of Washington. *(76–178) VLR: 12/13/88; NRHP: 10/30/89.*

LEESYLVANIA ARCHAEOLOGICAL SITE, *Leesylvania State Park, Dumfries vicinity.* The Leesylvania site is located on a small ridge overlooking the Potomac River in Leesylvania State Park. Field investigations by Virginia Department of Historic Resources archaeologists documented the presence of cultural features dating to the second half of the 18th century. The Leesylvania plantation stood on land inherited and developed by Henry Lee II. The children of Lee and his wife, Lucy Grymes Lee, who grew up here, included such notables as Light-Horse Harry Lee, Charles Lee, Richard Bland Lee, and Edmund Jennings Lee. Evidence at what are likely the foundations of the manor house indicates that the house burned late in the 18th century, after the deaths of Henry Lee II and his wife. The site is now a feature of the state park. The Lee family occupancy is commemorated by a small monument at the foot of the ridge. *(76–45) VLR: 06/19/84; NRHP: 09/13/84.*

LOCUST BOTTOM, *Hickory Grove vicinity.* The prosperity of early 19th-century Prince William County is reflected in the number of substantial, albeit relatively plain, plantation houses erected by the landed gentry. Moor Green, Liberia, Ben Lomond, Locust Bottom, and others show a certain kinship in the use of the I-house form, spare exterior elaboration, and restrained interior Federal trim. Locust Bottom departs from the norm by having a four-bay rather than a five-bay facade. James Green, owner of 610 acres, twenty slaves, and fourteen horses, had the main part of the house built around 1819. It was attached to a modest frame dwelling built in 1810 soon after Green purchased the farm. Although still the nucleus of a large farm, the house stands unrestored. Surrounding it are remnants of a large boxwood garden. A collection of farm buildings complements the agrarian landscape. *(76–88) VLR: 12/13/88; NRHP: 02/11/91.*

LOUISIANA BRIGADE WINTER CAMP ARCHAEO-LOGICAL SITE, *Manassas Park vicinity.* The Louisiana Brigade Winter Camp, also known as Camp Carondelet, served during 1861–62 as the winter quarters for the 6th, 7th, 8th, and 9th Confederate infantry regiments, the 1st Louisiana Battalion Infantry (Major Wheat's Special Battalion), and Bowyer's Virginia Artillery. Intact features include more than twenty-five hut sites (low, rectangular, earthen mounds with remnants of collapsed chimneys), road traces, rifle pits, a bottle dump, and an additional fifty features thought to be hut sites. In March 1862 the log huts were burned by the soldiers before withdrawing to the Rappahannock River. At first called "wharf rats from New Orleans," the Louisiana military units displayed a fierce fighting style in the first battle of Manassas. Thereafter, the Louisiana soldiers were considered heroes and were commonly referred to as the "Tigers." The campsite is owned by the city of Manassas Park. *(76–35) VLR: 08/15/89; NRHP: 11/16/89.*

MANASSAS NATIONAL BATTLEFIELD PARK, *Groveton.* The 300-acre tract bordered by Bull Run was the scene of two Confederate victories. The first battle of Manassas, fought July 21, 1861, was the opening engagement of the Civil War and pitted Union brigadier general Irvin McDowell's unseasoned troops against ill-trained but spirited Confederates under Brig. Gen. P. G. T. Beauregard. The Union attack was repulsed by Confederates inspired by Gen. Thomas J. Jackson and his Virginians, who stood against the enemy like a "stone wall," earning Jackson his famous epithet. Second Manassas, fought on August 28–30, 1862, cleared the way for Gen. Robert E. Lee's first invasion of the North. Surviving landmarks include the Dogan house, a Union snipers' nest in 1862; the Stone House (shown), a Union field hospital during both battles; and the stone bridge, blown up in 1861 but reconstructed in the 1880s. The battlefield is a unit of the National Park Service. *(76–271) VLR: 01/16/73; NRHP: 10/15/66.*

MITCHELL'S FORD ENTRENCHMENTS, *Old Centerville Road, Manassas Park.* As the Union army approached Manassas Junction from Washington, D.C., in July 1861, Mitchell's Ford was one of several Bull Run crossings defended by the Confederates. U.S. Brig. Gen. Daniel Tyler's brigade tried to cross at nearby Blackburn's Ford on July 18 but was repulsed. Confederate artillery in the Mitchell's Ford entrenchment withdrew when Union artillery fired on it. On July 21 Brig. Gen. Milledge L. Bonham's brigade was stationed at Mitchell's Ford when the first battle of Manassas began. Both Confederate commanders Brig. Gen. P. G. T. Beauregard and Brig. Gen. Joseph E. Johnston were so convinced that the principal Union attack would come across Mitchell's Ford that they waited on a nearby hill for an hour after the battle started to the west. The Mitchell's Ford earthworks are among the few remaining entrenchments in the area. *(76–40) VLR: 12/13/88; NRHP: 08/08/89.*

MOOR GREEN, *Brentsville vicinity.* Moor Green, erected ca. 1800–1810 for Howson Hooe, is part of an interesting group of architecturally restrained two-story, five-bay plantation houses built in Prince William County during the Federal period. It was taxed at $4,000 in 1820, a relatively high valuation for a dwelling at that time. In addition to its precise brickwork and sophisticated but simple interior woodwork, the house is distinguished by its banded American bond side and rear walls and its flounder-roofed rear ell, part of the original construction. The molded-brick cornice is also a detail common to the area's Federal houses. Moor Green stood empty and vandalized during the 1980s but was carefully restored in recent years. Although its farmlands have been developed, the house maintains a protected setting overlooking landscaped grounds. *(76–14) VLR: 07/18/78; NRHP: 11/16/78.*

NOKESVILLE METAL-TRUSS BRIDGE, *Aden Road, Nokesville.* The mass-produced metal-truss bridges of the late 19th century were a remarkable technical innovation which made rural travel safer and led to the replacement of the majority of the earlier wooden covered bridges. Although sturdy and easily maintained, most of these graceful structures are too narrow to meet today's safety standards and are in turn being supplanted by wider concrete bridges. Among the state's best surviving examples of metal-truss bridges is the Nokesville Bridge, manufactured in 1882 by the Keystone Bridge Company of Pittsburgh, a pioneer in metal-truss technology. The Nokesville Bridge consists of a single-span Pratt through truss employing wrought-iron members. It was erected to cross a line of the Southern Railroad and is the property of the Norfolk Southern Corporation. *(76–81) VLR: 11/15/77; NRHP: 04/15/78.*

MOUNT ATLAS, *Waterfall vicinity.* On a knoll commanding panoramic views, Mount Atlas is one of the more interesting examples of late Georgian domestic architecture in Prince William County. The house was built in 1795 by Peter B. Whiting and later sold to Charles B. Carter, son of Charles Carter of Shirley, Charles City County. Its three-bay facade is decorated with a modillion cornice. A striking interior feature is the parlor chimneypiece with its flanking pilasters, a marked contrast to the relatively simple woodwork elsewhere in the house. The overmantel panel is decorated with a painting titled *Maiden in Prayer,* a ca. 1830–40 portrait of a young lady. The work of an itinerant artist, the painting is a rare example of folk portraiture being used for architectural decoration. Now surrounded by modern housing, Mount Atlas presently stands unoccupied and unmaintained. *(76–15) VLR: 12/13/88; NRHP: 10/30/89.*

OCCOQUAN HISTORIC DISTRICT. The site of a tobacco warehouse as early as 1736, Occoquan grew as the focus of the commercial and manufacturing activities of John Ballendine, who erected an iron furnace, forge, and sawmills at the falls of the Occoquan River before 1759. After the Revolution the settlement emerged as a flour-manufacturing center boasting one of the nation's first gristmills employing the laborsaving inventions of Oliver Evans. Although silting of the river reduced Occoquan's shipping activity, the

town continued as a commercial and industrial center into the 1920s. The district contains a medley of late 19th- and early 20th-century vernacular residential and commercial architecture. Surviving from earlier periods are Rockledge, the ca. 1760 mansion of John Ballendine; the Mill House, a ca. 1800 structure thought to have been an office for the Occoquan Flour Mill; and the Hammil Hotel, whose core dates from the early 19th century. *(272–12) VLR: 08/16/83; NRHP: 10/06/83.*

ORANGE AND ALEXANDRIA RAILROAD BRIDGE PIERS, *Southern Railway Line at Bull Run, Manassas Park vicinity.* The remains of this historic Civil War–era crossing of the former Orange and Alexandria Railroad consist of two tapering piers of rough-faced ashlar sandstone on the banks of Bull Run. The Orange and Alexandria Railroad Company was chartered in 1848. During the Civil War several major battles, including first and second Manassas, Brandy Station, and Bristoe Station, were fought alongside this important rail line. The Confederate army encamped at Orange Court House during the winter of 1863–64 to make use of the railroad as a supply line. Between 1861 and 1865 the bridge was destroyed and rebuilt at least seven times, using these piers. In 1861 and 1864, respectively, a Confederate and a Union solder carved the names of their regiments into the piers' soft sandstone. A modern railroad bridge now stands alongside the piers. *(76–238) VLR: 12/13/88; NRHP: 08/08/89.*

PARK GATE, *Nokesville vicinity.* Foremost among Prince William County's historic dwellings is Park Gate, a visually engaging colonial plantation house. Loss of county records precludes establishing a precise construction date; however, architectural form and details suggest a mid-18th-century origin. With its engaged front porch, steep gable roof, and hall-parlor plan, the house is representative of a vernacular house type once spread through the Potomac River valley in both Virginia and Maryland. Among Park Gate's early owners was Col. Thomas Lee, son of Richard Henry Lee, signer of the Declaration of Independence. Colonel Lee married Mildred Washington, niece of George Washington. Following her death in childbirth, he married Eliza Ashton Brent, daughter of Daniel Carroll Brent. The interior was remodeled around 1830 when original woodwork was replaced with Greek Revival trim. Despite this change, the excellently maintained house preserves an aura of great age. *(76–18) VLR: 09/20/88; NRHP: 04/03/87.*

PILGRIM'S REST, *King's Crossroads vicinity.* Overlooking what is yet a rural landscape in this rapidly developing region, Pilgrim's Rest is a reminder of the rich heritage of 18th-century architecture remaining in Prince William County. The house was built ca. 1790 for Henry Dade Hooe around the time of his marriage to Jane Fitzhugh. Particularly noteworthy is the massive chimney structure, consisting of two exterior stacks joined by two levels of pent closets. Such chimneys were indigenous features of the county's Federal-period houses, but only a handful remain. The body of the house is a typical side-passage frame dwelling. The exterior flush-board siding, installed in a 1955 restoration, is a replacement of deteriorated original siding. The interior preserves much original woodwork including paneled mantels and wainscoting. An unusual aspect of the plan is the concealed stair rising between walls rather than in the passage. *(76–19) VLR: 12/13/88; NRHP: 10/30/89; BHR EASEMENT.*

RIPPON LODGE, *Woodbridge vicinity.* Richard Blackburn, colonial entrepreneur and public servant, built the core of this small plantation dwelling in the second quarter of the 18th century on a tract which he named after his native Rippon (Ripon), England. Among his many pursuits Blackburn was a building contractor and is said to have designed and built Rippon Lodge himself. Carefully sited on a hill with a view down Neabsco Creek to the Potomac, the house has acquired architectural character with its numerous later additions, which include a columned veranda. The interior preserves much original fabric, including two fully paneled rooms. Blackburn's son Thomas was active in the Revolutionary effort and entertained George Washington at Rippon Lodge on several occasions. The architect Benjamin Henry Latrobe also visited here in 1796 and made a sketch of the house showing a now-vanished companion structure. *(76–23) VLR: 01/05/71; NRHP: 07/02/71; BHR EASEMENT.*

ROCKLEDGE, *Telegraph Road, Occoquan.* Built of stone taken from a nearby quarry, this ca. 1760 elongated Georgian mansion was the home of John Ballendine, who established a foundry and milling operation immediately down the hill in the village of Occoquan. Ballendine situated his house on a ledge to overlook the falls of the Occoquan River as well as his enterprises. Although undocumented, the house is said to have been designed by William Buckland. Later owners of Rockledge include Ballendine's business partner, James Semple, and Nathaniel Ellicott, member of one of the nation's foremost Quaker milling families. Ellicott was also the founder of the Maryland milling town Ellicott City. The house stood abandoned for many years but was restored in the 1970s. Subsequently burned by arsonists, the house has since been re-restored, resuming its place as the community's principal historic landmark. *(272–01) VLR: 06/19/73; NRHP: 06/25/73.*

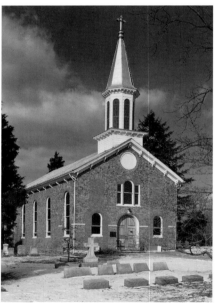

ST. PAUL'S EPISCOPAL CHURCH, *Haymarket.* Haymarket's Episcopal church was built in 1801 as a district courthouse for the counties of Fairfax, Fauquier, Loudoun, and Prince William. Like other early 19th-century Virginia courthouses, it originally had an arcaded entrance. The district court was accommodated here until 1807 when changes in the court system resulted in the eventual sale of the building and its conversion to an academy. It was first used as an Episcopal church in 1822 and was consecrated by Bishop William Meade in 1834. Near both the first and second battles of Manassas, it was used as a hospital by both sides at different times. In November 1862 Union troops converted the building to a stable and then burned it. The congregation rebuilt within the original walls in 1867, at which time the arcade was closed up for the narthex and the belfry and bracketed cornice were added. *(233–02) VLR: 12/17/74; NRHP: 01/20/75.*

SIGNAL HILL, *Signal Hill Road, Manassas Park vicinity.* Signal Hill, or the Wilcoxen Signal Station, was used by Confederate forces in the first battle of Manassas and later by Union forces. The heavily fortified station was sited to command an excellent view of the Manassas railroad junction and the Bull Run Mountains. Its commander, Edward Porter Alexander, was chief signal officer of Gen. Beauregard's army and a student of the inventor of the semaphore signaling system. On the morning of July 21, 1861, Alexander spotted Union troops attempting a movement around the Confederate flank, some eight miles away. With a semaphore he quickly signaled a station close to Col. Nathan G. Evans, "Look out on your left; you are turned." Evans hurriedly redeployed his forces, blocking the Federal advance while he awaited reinforcements. This episode marked the first use of semaphore signaling in combat. *(76–16) VLR: 12/13/88; NRHP: 08/08/89.*

WEEMS-BOTTS HOUSE, *Dumfries.* Parson Mason Locke Weems built the earliest portion of this structure ca. 1798 as a bookshop and temporary lodging after he retired from the Episcopal ministry. Weems, author of numerous moral tracts and lives of prominent Americans, was convinced that small, cheap books with uplifting messages would be an effective tool for enlightening the public. Here he wrote his pamphlet *The Life and Memorable Actions of George Washington . . .* , the first biography of Washington, containing the cherry-tree legend. Weems sold the building in 1802 to Benjamin Botts, one of the lawyers who defended Aaron Burr in his trial for treason. Botts used the building as his office until his death in the 1811 Richmond Theatre fire. The building received its two-story wing in the mid–19th century when it became a residence. Restored by Historic Dumfries, Virginia, Inc., it is now a museum. *(212–10) VLR: 04/15/75; NRHP: 05/12/75.*

THE WHITE HOUSE, *Brentsville.* Standing opposite the former county courthouse at Brentsville, the White House is an important component of this historic village. Named for its whitewashed walls, the house was built ca. 1822, the year the county seat was moved from Dumfries to Brentsville. It was originally the home of Jane Williams, widow of John Williams who had served as the county clerk from 1795 until his death in 1813. Mrs. Williams's brother, Philip D. Dowe, succeeded Williams as clerk and also moved to Brentsville upon relocation of the county seat. Mrs. Williams relinquished the house to her son John Williams, Jr., when he became clerk in 1832. Serving members of the local elite, the two-story, five-bay house was a fine dwelling for its time and place. It was used as a private school following the Civil War and was restored in 1941 after standing empty for a decade. *(76–31) VLR: 12/13/88; NRHP: 10/30/89.*

WILLIAMS'S ORDINARY, *U.S. Route 1, Dumfries.* This stately Georgian mansion is Virginia's only surviving colonial building employing header-bond brickwork. Header bond was popular for finer-quality 18th-century buildings in England and is found on several mansions in Annapolis, Md., but it was rarely used elsewhere in the colonies. It is likely that the building is the work of Maryland masons. The formality of its design is emphasized by its five-bay facade, hipped roof, stone quoins, keystone lintels, and rusticated doorway. The building has long been a prominent landmark of old King's Highway, now the busy U.S. Route 1. Its early history is obscure, but it probably was constructed in the 1760s and may originally have been a merchant's house. George Williams was the proprietor of an ordinary here as early as 1788. *(212–01) VLR: 05/13/69; NRHP: 11/17/69.*

PULASKI COUNTY

Formed in 1839 from Montgomery and Wythe counties, this Southwest Virginia county was named for Count Casimir Pulaski, the Polish patriot who served in the American army during the Revolutionary War. The county seat is Pulaski.

BACK CREEK FARM, *Dublin vicinity.* Back Creek Farm is a product of Southwest Virginia's second generation of settlement. Nestled at the foot of Cloyd's Mountain, the farm was established by Joseph Cloyd, whose pioneer parents were killed by Indians. The present house, a stately provincial Georgian mansion with finely carved woodwork, was built in the early 19th century on what Cloyd described as "the sun shiny ridge." The outbuildings, including a brick dairy and a two-story kitchen, are unusually large and well crafted. The antebellum stone barn, a Pennsylvania type, is one of the few stone barns to have been built in Southwest Virginia. War struck the farm in May 1864 when the battle of Cloyd's Mountain was fought here. The house served as both a hospital and headquarters for Union general George Crook, under whose command were captains and future presidents Rutherford B. Hayes and William McKinley. *(77–02) VLR: 02/18/75; NRHP: 05/21/75.*

BELLE-HAMPTON, *Highland vicinity.* Originally known as Hayfield, Belle-Hampton was the home of agricultural and industrial promoter James Hoge Tyler, who served as governor of Virginia 1898–1902. The property was settled in the 18th century by Tyler's ancestors. The original part of the present house, a substantial brick dwelling, was built in 1826 for Tyler's grandfather, James Hoge, Jr., from whom Tyler inherited the property. Although active in politics, Tyler made a considerable fortune through exploitation of a coal seam on the family homeplace. The mining profits enabled Tyler in 1879 to front the house with a large Italianate-style extension topped with a bold bracketed cornice. The resulting dwelling is an interesting juxtaposition of two architectural traditions. Renamed Belle-Hampton by Tyler, the property is owned by his descendants. Among the outbuildings is a commissary built to serve the mining enterprise. *(77–03) VLR: 04/18/89; NRHP: 11/13/89.*

DALTON THEATRE BUILDING, *Washington Avenue, Pulaski.* Designed by James C. Lombard and Co. of Washington, D.C., and opened in 1921, the Dalton Theatre followed the prototype theater design of Louis Sullivan's Auditorium Theatre in Chicago, in which the theater section is fronted by an office building. Its original owner was the firm of Dalton Brothers and Richardson. The plain, businesslike exterior contrasted with rich plasterwork decorations of the theater interior, which collapsed in a flood over a decade ago. The original tenants of the shop fronts were a bank and a drugstore; offices and apartments occupied the upper two floors. The theater had one of the largest stage areas on the rail line between Richmond and Tennessee and accommodated vaudeville performances in its heyday. Vaudeville shows ended by the 1930s, but the theater continued to exhibit films until the mid-1960s. *(125–02) VLR: 11/15/77; NRHP: 05/07/79.*

DUBLIN HISTORIC DISTRICT. The town of Dublin came into being in 1854 when the Virginia and Tennessee Railroad established a depot where the rail line crossed the Giles and Pulaski Turnpike. The settlement became a center of commerce and transportation. As such, it served as a Confederate army supply link during the Civil War, over which the 1864 battle of Cloyd's Mountain was fought. The district's earliest buildings date to the mid–19th century, but the majority were built following the Civil War into the 1920s with its heyday occurring in the early 1900s. Today a community of some 2,000, Dublin preserves an unhurried, small-town quality with a mix of unassertive commercial and residential architecture. The houses are generally freestanding single-family structures in shady yards. A principal landmark is the 1913 Norfolk and Western Railway depot, a low wooden building marking the heart of the district. *(210–04) VLR: 06/17/92; NRHP: 10/15/92.*

JOHN HOGE HOUSE, *Belspring vicinity.* A relic of the early settlement of Pulaski County's uplands, the John Hoge house is one of the region's very few dated log structures. The date 1800 is carved into an original stone chimney. The first owner of the house is not known; however, in 1812 the property was purchased by John Hoge, a slave-owning planter whose ancestors came to the area in the mid–18th century. In its original form the house was a two-story hall-parlor dwelling with two stone chimneys. The V-notched logs were covered at an early date with beaded weatherboarding, sections of which survive. The house was altered and enlarged in the third quarter of the 19th century with a two-story frame wing concealing the early dwelling within. Despite the changes, the core structure holds exceptional antiquarian interest. *(77–154) VLR: 04/19/88; NRHP: 08/25/88.*

INGLES FERRY, *Radford vicinity.* Ingles Ferry was started by William Ingles in 1762 when he obtained a license to operate a ferryboat across the New River. Ingles was assisted by his brother-in-law John Draper. Over the ferry moved many of the settlers taking up land in Kentucky and Tennessee; the boat ran day and night with tolls amounting to over a thousand dollars a month. The Ingles Ferry Tavern, erected in 1772 on the Pulaski side of the river, became a popular social center for the travelers. Andrew Jackson and George Rogers Clark were among its patrons. The ferry was eventually replaced by a bridge which was burned in the Civil War. The ferry was again put into operation and continued until 1948. The 1840 ferry-house burned in 1967. The log and frame tavern (shown) has been renovated, and the crossing remains undisturbed by modern intrusions. *(77–13) VLR: 05/13/69; NRHP: 11/25/69.*

NEWBERN HISTORIC DISTRICT. This mile-long linear village preserves the early image of the region's 19th-century turnpike towns. Newbern was laid out in 1809 by Adam Hance with twenty-nine lots along the Wilderness Road. Purchasers were required to build a house within two years "at least 16 feet square, 1½ stories high of hewn logs with a stone or brick chimney." The principal house types—the two-story rectangular log house and the two-story frame house, both sheathed in weatherboards—conform to these standards. These well-finished log buildings make the district representative not of a frontier settlement but of a second-generation village. Newbern became the county seat in 1837. The courthouse burned in 1893, and the county seat subsequently was removed to Pulaski, a more promising site on the railroad. Newbern since then has been a quiet residential community unmarred by modern development. *(77–22) VLR: 02/18/75; NRHP: 06/04/79.*

PULASKI COMMERCIAL HISTORIC DISTRICT. Spurred by the construction of the Norfolk and Western Railway line, Pulaski's downtown served as the late 19th-century industrial and commercial center of the county. As with most of the manufacturing centers that sprang up along the railroad, prosperity declined significantly after the economic panic of 1893. The relocation of the county seat to Pulaski in 1895, however, spurred the town's dominance in the region. Growth through the first decades of the 20th century was gradual, and the town's generously scaled plat of 1888 filled in slowly. The district today retains the context and fabric of a turn-of-the-century boomtown. It comprises most of Pulaski's commercial center and consists of some one hundred buildings including commercial structures, industrial buildings, multifamily dwellings, two railroad depots, a church, the courthouse, the former high school, and the town park. *(125–05) VLR: 12/17/85; NRHP: 03/13/86.*

PULASKI COUNTY COURTHOUSE, *Main Street, Pulaski.* The rugged Pulaski County Courthouse, the dominant landmark in the town of Pulaski, is one of the state's few large public buildings reflecting the Romanesque style of the noted architect H. H. Richardson. The firm of W. Chamberlin and Co. of Knoxville, Tenn., designed the building, employing stone quarried from nearby Peak Creek. In contrast to the smaller courthouses of eastern and central Virginia, the Pulaski courthouse echoes the showy structures built in county seats of midwestern states at the end of the century, serving as symbols of local pride and prosperity. Its construction grew out of a controversy concerning the location of the county seat at Newbern, Dublin, or Pulaski which was settled by the highest state court in Richmond in favor of Pulaski. Completed in 1896, the courthouse was gutted by fire in 1989 but was restored and reopened three years later. *(125–01) VLR: 09/15/81; NRHP: 07/08/82.*

PULASKI RESIDENTIAL HISTORIC DISTRICT. Pulaski's historic residential district was platted along with the town's commercial areas in 1884 and 1888 by the Pulaski Land and Improvement Company. The spacious neighborhood developed gradually and was not fully built out for several decades. By 1913 it had some 100 houses, and today it has over 350 houses. Accommodating both factory workers and factory managers, the fabric of the district is a graphic illustration of America's craving for individual identity. Eschewing the uniformity that has characterized workers' housing in many other countries, this neighborhood has remarkable diversity. Drawing from perhaps a dozen different stylistic influences, the houses vary in size, shape, and use of materials, all built over hardly more than a half century. Architectural highlights are provided by the district's eight churches. *(125–06) VLR: 02/16/88; NRHP: 08/11/88.*

PULASKI SOUTH RESIDENTIAL AND INDUSTRIAL HISTORIC DISTRICT. This irregularly shaped district takes in most of the south side of the town of Pulaski. The area was the location of the majority of the town's businesses and residences in 1886 when Pulaski, formerly known as Martin's Tank, was incorporated. A leading contributor to the community's growth was the Bertha Zinc and Mineral Co. The company's workers' houses, commissary, and office occupy the district's west end. A contrast to the usual detached frame workers' houses is the Bertha Company's two-story, six-unit residential structure (shown) on State Street. By 1900 the district had acquired an unusually fine collection of Queen Anne residences, most of them embellished with fancy wooden porches with sawn-work or turned ornaments. The closing of several industries before or during the depression slowed growth and facilitated the preservation of the neighborhood's early 20th-century character. *(125–08) VLR: 08/21/91; NRHP: 10/29/91.*

SNOWVILLE CHRISTIAN CHURCH, *Snowville.* Though architecturally noteworthy as an elegantly simple expression of country Greek Revival design, this church is best known for its association with Chester Bullard (1809–1893), a charismatic religious leader. Born in Massachusetts, Bullard came to the area at age seventeen and settled in Snowville, a manufacturing village founded by his brother-in-law Asiel Snow. He became influenced by the local religious revivals and developed an individual interpretation of Scripture, subsequently founding a number of churches. His followers were known as Bullardites. In 1840 he united his churches with the Disciples of Christ, or Christians. The Snowville church was organized by Bullard as New Salem Church in 1836–37. The present church was built in 1864 on the site of a previous building, on land originally belonging to Bullard. *(77–06) VLR: 12/09/86; NRHP: 04/02/87.*

SNOWVILLE HISTORIC DISTRICT. This tiny community on the banks of the Little River, in the scenic eastern section of Pulaski County, was founded in the 1820s by Asiel Snow, an emigrant from New England. By the 1850s the village had become a small manufacturing center with industries that utilized locally produced raw materials such as iron ore, lumber, and wool. An early progressive school and the county's first newspaper, public library, and Masonic temple were initiated in Snowville. The industrial and commercial activity have all but disappeared, leaving Snowville a sleepy, tree-embowered rural settlement of mostly late 19th- and early 20th-century structures. The principal landmarks of the linear district are the Snowville Christian Church and the distinctive Masonic temple (shown). With few contemporary intrusions, Snowville retains the sense of 19th-century isolation that characterized many pre-railroad villages. *(77–48) VLR: 12/17/85; NRHP: 01/07/87.*

CITY OF RADFORD

Radford has had many names including Lovely Mount, English Ferry, Ingles's Ferry, and Central Depot. It was established as Central City in 1885 and incorporated in 1887. In 1890 the name was changed to Radford in honor of local citizen John Blair Radford. Radford became a city in 1892.

HARVEY HOUSE, *706 Harvey Street.* This demonstration of shingled walls binding curved and angled volumes is a powerful expression of the American Queen Anne style. The house was built in 1891–92 during the industrial boom when Radford was laid out by the Radford Land Improvement Company. It was originally the residence of J. K. Dimmick, the company's general manager. Although its designer is undocumented, the able Philadelphia architect Frank Miles Day was credited with a house in Radford in the *Builder's, Decorator's, and Woodworker's Guide* (August 1890). Day specialized in the Queen Anne style; thus it is safe to speculate that the Harvey house was his Radford commission. The panic of 1893 ended the land boom, and Dimmick left town. In 1906 the house was purchased by Lewis Harvey, in whose family it has remained to the present. The interior preserves richly detailed woodwork and many original finishes, all carefully preserved. *(126–01) VLR: 04/20/76; NRHP: 07/30/76.*

INGLES BOTTOM ARCHAEOLOGICAL SITES, *Ingleside.* The tract of floodplain along the New River in southwest Radford incorporates a variety of sites of human occupation from 8000 B.C. to the present. Prehistoric sites range from the Archaic through the Woodland periods. The area takes its name from the Ingles family, who settled 400 acres here about 1762. Test excavations have revealed the site of a log house—the home of William Ingles and his wife, Mary Draper Ingles, known for her dramatic escape from Indian captivity in the 1750s. The family operated a ferry here which served the many settlers traveling through Southwest Virginia to western lands. Other resources associated with the Ingles family include a stable and a family cemetery. Ingleside, a late 18th-century dwelling, the home of William Ingles's son John, is also located here. The property remains in the ownership of Ingles descendants. *(126–04) VLR: 06/15/76; NRHP: 12/05/78.*

LA RIVIERE, *5 Ingles Street.* With its wraparound veranda and crenellated tower, La Riviere displays the curious mix of modern domesticity with romantic historicism that characterizes American's Queen Anne style. It was designed by William Ingles for himself. Ingles, a member of a locally distinguished family, had a successful career as a civil engineer, designing railroad structures in several states. He also was a Radford businessman and civic leader. His prosperity enabled him to build a finely appointed mansion overlooking the New River, but the house burned the night before he and his wife were to move in. The present house, completed in 1892, was built on the foundations of the original one. Typical of the Queen Anne style, La Riviere combines many forms and materials. The rich interior, dominated by a grand stair rising in the tower, remains almost untouched. The property is still owned by Ingles family members. *(126–08) VLR: 06/15/94; NRHP: 08/16/94.*

RAPPAHANNOCK COUNTY

Scenically situated against the Blue Ridge Mountains, this sparsely populated county was named for the Rappahannock River, which forms its northern border. It was formed from Culpeper County in 1833. The county seat is Washington.

BEN VENUE, *Ben Venue.* Dominating a hilltop with broad views of the Blue Ridge Mountains, Ben Venue, well known for its row of brick slave houses, is one of the region's more complete antebellum plantation complexes. The two-story brick house was completed in 1846 for William V. Fletcher and is attributed to James Leake Powers, a local builder. Its parapet gables, corbeled shoulders, and chimneys oddly placed against the front wall lend the house architectural distinction. The three brick slave houses, lining a ridge in a field to the south, are among the several stylistically related outbuildings. Like the main house, the slave houses have parapet gables and corbeled shoulders. Their placement and detailing suggest that they were intended as picturesque features of a scenic view. Slave quarters rarely are found in the Piedmont uplands; no others in the state possess such architectural refinement. *(78–03) VLR: 10/16/79; NRHP: 12/28/79.*

CALEDONIA FARM, *Flint Hill vicinity.* The rich scenery of Rappahannock County provides a matchless setting for this early homestead. A farm has existed here since the 18th century. The present house was erected in 1812, after the 1805 purchase of the property by John Dearing, an officer in the Fauquier County militia during the Revolution. The symmetrical Federal dwelling has an indigenous quality, with its walls constructed of native fieldstone. Dearing and his family maintained a gentry lifestyle here, owning more than twenty slaves and nine horses. Typical of upper-class farmhouses, the household was served by an outdoor kitchen, which, though now connected to the main house by a sheltered passageway, is the only remaining early outbuilding. The house stood derelict for some fifteen years and was restored in 1963–64. Interior modifications were made, but much original woodwork, including Federal mantels, remains. *(78–64) VLR: 06/19/90; NRHP: 12/28/90; BHR EASEMENT.*

JOHN W. MILLER HOUSE, *Slate Mills vicinity.* The John W. Miller house is a prominent landmark in the undulating landscape of southern Rappahannock County. It was built in 1842–43 using the conventional I-house format. A remodeling in 1880–81 resulted in its lacy Italianate sawn-work porch, central bay window, and bracketed cornice. The facade was extended one bay to the east around 1900. From 1844 to 1871 John W. Miller, for whom the house was built, owned and operated the nearby Slate Mills, an industrial complex where he maintained a merchant mill, sawmill, and plaster mill. In addition to the house, the curtilage includes a detached kitchen–servants' quarters, an icehouse, a ca. 1925 barn, and the Miller cemetery. The property remained in the Miller family until 1956. After a period of neglect, the house was restored in the late 1980s. *(78–161) VLR: 04/17/90; NRHP: 01/03/91.*

MONTPELIER, *Sperryville vicinity.* The core of this sprawling porticoed mansion was built in the mid–18th century by Francis Thornton as a residence for his son William. The Thornton family settled here ca. 1740, obtaining a grant for thousands of acres, including the F. T. (Francis Thornton) Valley. On a hill with views down the F. T. Valley, the original farmhouse was enlarged with end wings in the mid–19th cen-

tury, and the whole was united by a huge unacademic colonnade crowned by a bracketed cornice. The resulting edifice makes for an arresting, if provincial, composition with a wonderful backdrop of pastoral and mountainous scenery. Montpelier was inherited by William Thornton's son Dr. Philip Thornton and remained in the family until 1876. The house stood unoccupied in recent years but was renovated in the 1970s by James W. Fletcher, whose wife Mildred was a descendant of Francis Thornton. *(78–28) VLR: 01/16/73; NRHP: 04/11/73.*

MOUNT SALEM BAPTIST MEETING HOUSE, *Washington vicinity.* Although the Mount Salem Baptist congregation was organized in 1824, the present meetinghouse was not begun until March 1850. The congregation, which included both whites and blacks on its first membership list, flourished for many years, remaining active until World War II. The remotely located house of worship survives unaltered from its original state, exhibiting mid-19th-century Virginia's penchant for plainness in its country church architecture. The stuccoed exterior is in a simplified Federal style, and the few details of the interior show the influence of Greek Revival pattern books. Its construction was supervised by Henry Miller, a local builder. The meetinghouse closed in 1942 but was restored in 1977. Revived regular services ceased in 1989 although the church continues to be maintained by its trustees. *(78–33) VLR: 12/19/78; NRHP: 05/24/79.*

SPERRYVILLE HISTORIC DISTRICT. This upper Piedmont crossroads town has remained little changed since the 1920s. Laid out in 1820 by Francis Thornton, Jr., on a narrow level area between the Thornton River and the hills of the northern Blue Ridge, the village grew slowly until 1867 when the Smoot family of Alexandria established a tannery here. The resulting influx of workers led to the construction of many of the unadorned wooden residences still standing in Sperryville. Intermingled are postbellum houses influenced by the 19th-century Romantic Revival and a scattering of late 19th-century workers' houses. In the center of the community is an early brick and frame tavern (shown). Most of the district's buildings line U.S. Route 522 and local Route 1001. An absence of significant modern intrusions has preserved the early village image of this quiet community. *(78–93) VLR: 12/14/82; NRHP: 02/10/83.*

WASHINGTON HISTORIC DISTRICT. In the shadow of the Blue Ridge Mountains, the village of Washington is perhaps the best preserved of the Piedmont's county-seat communities. Its name honors George Washington, who platted the grid plan in 1749. The community was incorporated in 1796, at which time it received its present name. It became a county seat in 1833 when Rappahannock County was established. Although most of its buildings, both commercial and residential, follow regional vernacular patterns, the district has several architecturally prominent structures. The chief landmark, the 1833 Roman Revival courthouse, was built by Malcolm F. Crawford, who had worked at the University of Virginia. Adjacent is a cluster of mid-19th-century county structures including the clerk's office, treasurer's office, and jail. The district's main vernacular structure is the Washington House Tavern, a rambling early 19th-century building. *(322–11) VLR: 04/15/75; NRHP: 05/28/75.*

WASHINGTON MILL, *Washington.* A landmark on the eastern edge of the county-seat village of Washington, Washington Mill served as the town mill for most of the 19th century. Built ca. 1800 with subsequent additions in 1840 and 1860, the mill is an artifact of the grain and milling economy once a dominant aspect of the state's agricultural scene. The gambrel-roof structure is believed also to have served as a neutral bartering place between Union and Confederate lines during the Civil War. No longer in operation, the mill, like the majority of Virginia's historic mills, has stood vacant and untended for many years. *(78–89) VLR: 11/18/80; NRHP: 09/02/82.*

CITY OF RICHMOND

Laid out in 1737, Virginia's capital was named by William Byrd II after the Thameside borough of Richmond, England. Richmond was designated the state capital in 1779. It was incorporated as a town in 1782 and as a city in 1842. From 1861 to 1865 Richmond was the capital of the Confederate States of America.

AGECROFT HALL, *4305 Sulgrave Road.* Overlooking the James River from its parklike grounds with Elizabethan-style gardens, this half-timbered mansion is a product of the antiquarianism and Anglophilia that permeated Virginia's upper classes in the 1920s. Agecroft Hall was originally a postmedieval manor house built by John Langley near Manchester, England. By 1925 it stood neglected amid coal mines and railroads. Richmond businessman Thomas C. Williams, Jr., purchased the house and had it carefully dismantled and shipped to Richmond where it was reconstructed in modified form in Windsor Farms, a garden suburb developed by Williams. The project's architect was Henry Grant Morse of New York. Outstanding original features include the elaborately patterned black and white timbering and a splendid leaded window in the great hall. The gardens and grounds were designed by Charles F. Gillette. Agecroft Hall is now a museum owned by the Agecroft Association. *(127–223) VLR: 07/18/78; NRHP: 12/13/78.*

ALMSHOUSE, *210 Hospital Street.* Built in 1860–61 as a place of refuge for the city's white poor, the Richmond Almshouse is an impressive monument to the reform movement that originated in the antebellum period. Designed by Richmond city engineer Washington Gill, the Italianate structure replaced an older poorhouse built before 1810. Gill gave the new building a striking outline by using three pedimented pavilions. The Almshouse served during the Civil War as the first major hospital of the Confederacy and later as a temporary home for the Virginia Military Institute. The institutional use of the Almshouse eventually ceased, and the building was sold by the city for private development. It was renovated in 1984–85 to house apartments for low-income elderly residents. Included on the property is the 1908 West Building, erected to house the city's indigent blacks and also renovated for housing the elderly. *(127–353) VLR: 07/21/81 (EXPANDED 08/15/89); NRHP: 10/29/81; BHR EASEMENT.*

NATHANIEL BACON SCHOOL, *815 North Thirty-fifth Street.* Exuding the confidence of a former era, this handsome school closed in the 1980s, the victim of changed demographics and priorities. With its high ceilings, large windows, and generally imposing presence in tree-shaded grounds, the facility expressed the civic pride of the neighborhood it served. It was designed by the Richmond firm of Carneal and Johnston and opened in 1914. William L. Carneal, the firm's principal architect, designed numerous local institutional works as well as buildings for the Virginia Military Institute and Virginia Tech. Like many of the firm's works, the school displays a literacy in historic styles while being at the same time a thoroughly modern work. Originally a white elementary school, it became a black high school in 1958 and operated as the East End Junior High School from 1971 until it closed. It is scheduled for rehabilitation for housing. *(127–833) VLR: 12/11/91; NRHP: 08/24/92.*

BARRET HOUSE, *15 South Fifth Street.* This Greek Revival mansion is a vestige of the antebellum dwellings formerly spread over Richmond's hills. It was built in 1844 for William Barret, son of John Barret, a three-term mayor. Barret, a tobacconist, was regarded as the city's richest citizen at his death in 1870. In 1876 the house was rented to the vicomte de Sibour, the French consul. It was spared demolition in 1936 when purchased by Richmond architectural historian Mary Wingfield Scott and her cousin Mrs. John Bocock. Scott donated the property in 1978 to the Virginia Foundation for Architectural Education. It is now the headquarters of the Virginia Society of the American Institute of Architects. Typical of Richmond's finer antebellum houses, the rear elevation has a monumental portico. The interior preserves noteworthy Greek Revival woodwork and decorative painting. Also on the property is a carriage house with servants' quarters. *(127–29) VLR: 11/16/71; NRHP: 02/23/72; BHR EASEMENT.*

BEERS HOUSE, *1228 East Broad Street.* Sheltered by magnolia trees, this town house is the sole reminder of the former residential character of the downtown portion of Richmond's Broad Street. It also serves as an architectural link between its two nationally significant neighbors: Monumental Church and the Egyptian Building. Dating from 1839, the house was built for William Beers, a merchant tailor. Typical of antebellum Richmond town houses, it has a side-hall plan and a small columned porch sheltering its entrance. The original gable roof was removed in 1860 and replaced with a full third story topped by an Italianate cornice. Preserved without significant alteration since that time, the house is now owned by the Medical College of Virginia Foundation. *(127–356) VLR: 11/05/68; NRHP: 04/16/69.*

BELGIAN BUILDING, VIRGINIA UNION UNIVERSITY, *North Lombardy Street and Brook Road.* This singular architectural work was originally the Belgian Pavilion for the 1939 New York World's Fair. It was designed by the Belgian architects Victor Bourgeois and Leon Stijnen under the direction of Henri Van de Velde, a pioneer of the Modernist movement. It was intended to be dismantled and rebuilt in Belgium after the fair, but the outbreak of World War II led to its donation to Virginia Union University where it was reerected in 1941. The choice of Richmond stemmed from the availability of a good site and the school's need for additional facilities. Dominated by what was originally a clock tower containing a carillon, the sprawling building with its clean geometry is a monument of the 1930s International Style. Near the base of the building are sculptured murals relating to Belgium and the former Belgian Congo. *(127–173) VLR: 12/02/69; NRHP: 02/26/70.*

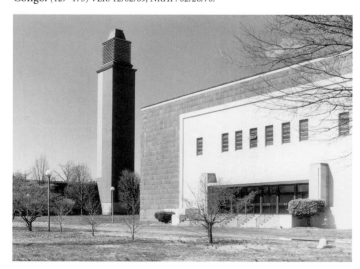

BELL TOWER, *Capitol Square.* A familiar landmark in the southwest corner of Capitol Square, the Bell Tower was built in 1824 as a guardhouse and signal tower for the Public Guard. Levi Swain, its contractor and presumably its designer, gave the otherwise plain brick structure a liveliness with the use of a blind arch on each elevation and a fanciful cupola topped by a fish weathervane. The tower's bell sounded in 1861 to warn of the approach of the Federal gunboat *Pawnee* and again in 1864 to sound the alarm for Dahlgren's raid. During the administration of Governor John N. Dalton, the tower served as the office of the Lieutenant Governor Charles S. Robb. In 1982 it was converted to a visitors' center for the Virginia Division of Tourism. Its bell still rings to call members of the General Assembly to session. *(127–121) VLR: 11/05/68; NRHP: 06/11/69.*

BELLE ISLE, *accessed via Tredegar Street.* A rugged 54-acre island in the James River rapids, Belle Isle has played a significant role in Richmond history. Capt. John Smith explored here in 1607. The first William Byrd and his heirs owned it for over 100 years. Following the opening of a nail factory in 1814, the island became a manufacturing site. During the Civil War, Belle Isle gained dubious national attention as a prisoner-of-war camp for Union soldiers. The camp's conditions rivaled those of the infamous Andersonville Prison in Georgia. After the war the Old Dominion Iron and Nail Co. continued the island's industrial activity until closing in 1972. Factory ruins survive along with granite quarry pits, the stone piers of bridges that once connected the island with the mainland, and the ruins of the 1904 Virginia Electric Power Co. generating plant. Today Belle Isle is a popular city park. *(127–455) VLR; 01/15/95; NRHP: 03/17/95.*

BLUES ARMORY, *Sixth and East Marshall streets.* The castellated Blues Armory in the heart of downtown is a memorable example of the massive urban armories erected from the 1870s to the 1920s. It was designed by the Washington, D.C., firm of Averill and Hall and was completed in 1910. The building had a ground-floor arcaded market, a large drill hall on an upper level, a rifle range, and related military facilities. Built to withstand siege, the armory was until the early 1960s the headquarters of the now disbanded Richmond Light Infantry Blues. Formed in 1789, the Blues served in every major conflict from the War of 1812 to World War II. The exterior and portions of the ground floor were restored in the 1980s as part of the Sixth Street Marketplace, an urban redevelopment project. The west side was incorporated into a vast glass-covered hall containing food courts. *(127–128) VLR: 12/16/75; NRHP: 05/17/76.*

BOULEVARD HISTORIC DISTRICT. Extending from Broad Street to Byrd Park, this divided thoroughfare is an expression of Progressive Era urbanity and a reflection of the expansive idealism of the City Beautiful movement. Although a street was here in 1817, the Boulevard did not acquire its present character until a century later. The avenue is distinguished by porticoed apartment houses built to accommodate the new fashion for large, well-appointed flats popularized in New York City. These are interspersed with porch-fronted town houses in varying harmonious styles. A setting for several institutional buildings was provided by the grounds of Robert E. Lee Camp No. 1, Confederate Soldiers' Home, on which were built the Virginia Museum of Fine Arts, the Virginia Historical Society, and the headquarters of the United Daughters of the Confederacy. These buildings, along with several churches, constitute a veritable museum of early 20th-century urban architecture. *(127–398) VLR: 02/18/86; NRHP: 09/18/86.*

BRANCH BUILDING, *1015 East Main Street.* After its destruction during the Evacuation Fire of 1865, most of Richmond's commercial area was rebuilt with structures employing cast-iron trim or full cast-iron facades, nearly all in a rich Italianate style. Of the three ironfronts remaining in the area, the Branch Building of 1866 stands as a particularly engaging representative of this American architectural fashion. Built as the headquarters of the Virginia Fire and Marine Insurance Company, the four-bay, four-story building features an intricate ground-floor loggia composed of free-standing Corinthian columns. Its current name derives from the fact that the building for many years housed the offices of the Branch Co., later Branch, Cabell & Co., a brokerage firm. *(127–196) VLR: 12/02/69; NRHP: 04/17/70.*

BRANCH HOUSE, *2501 Monument Avenue.* This prodigious mansion, commissioned in 1916 by John Kerr Branch, Jr., is the work of New York architect John Russell Pope, who also designed Richmond's Broad Street Station. Completed in 1919, the house is one of the country's finest examples of the Tudor-Jacobean style and is the only one by Pope in which the interiors, including a series of stately reception rooms, have survived. The house originally served as a setting for the collection of Renaissance art objects amassed by Branch, a Richmond stockbroker and bank president. Pope and his partner Otto R. Eggers blended their interior detailing with woodwork from 16th-century English houses. The house is a manifestation of the admiration for English styles and their upper-class associations that swept the country during the early 1900s. It was carefully restored in the 1980s for use as offices. *(127–246) VLR: 01/17/84; NRHP: 02/23/84; BHR EASEMENT.*

BROAD STREET COMMERCIAL HISTORIC DISTRICT. The ten-block stretch of Broad Street, between Fourth and Henry streets, holds one of the most important assemblages of turn-of-the-century commercial buildings in the state. The richly detailed facades are set off by the generous width of Broad Street, which originally accommodated a railroad and later the tracks for the city's trolley system. Many of the buildings are architect-designed, several by prominent out-of-state firms. A dominant form is the three-bay, two-, three-, or four-story commercial structure, generally built between 1880 and 1900. Outstanding individual landmarks are Jackson C. Gott's Masonic Temple of 1888–93 and John Eberson's 1930 Art Deco tower for the former Central National Bank. The district has traditionally been a retail area, with many jewelry and furniture stores. Overcoming eroding prosperity, a number of structures in recent years have been converted to housing and offices. *(127–375) VLR: 10/14/86; NRHP: 04/09/87.*

BROAD STREET STATION (UNION STATION OF RICHMOND, NOW SCIENCE MUSEUM OF VIRGINIA), *2500 West Broad Street.* Richmond's Broad Street Station is one of the last remaining great terminals of America's Golden Age of railroads. The competition for its design was won by New York architect John Russell Pope in 1913. Like McKim, Mead and White, Pope employed a grandly scaled, serene classicism that he later used on the Jefferson Memorial and the National Gallery of Art in Washington, D.C. Faced with Indiana limestone and dominated by a huge Tuscan colonnade and Roman dome—the first use of a dome for a major railroad station—the building was completed in 1919 for the Richmond, Fredericksburg and Potomac and the Atlantic Coast Line railroads. Acquired by the Commonwealth in 1975, the station, including the cast-iron and steel butterfly canopies and Pope's vast 100-foot-high rotunda, has been sympathetically adapted as headquarters of the Science Museum of Virginia. *(127–226) VLR: 11/16/71; NRHP: 02/23/72.*

BYRD THEATRE, *2908 West Cary Street.* Opened in 1928, the Byrd Theatre is an important representative of the many movie palaces that sprang up around the country in the 1920s. Built when lavish architectural decoration was still relatively inexpensive, these glittering confections vied with one another to attract and dazzle cinemagoers. Dazzling still, the theater was designed and built by Frederick A. Bishop of Richmond with the decoration and artwork of the unrestrained classical interior executed by the Brounet Studios of New York. The Byrd was one of the first theaters outfitted for sound motion pictures, being equipped with Vitaphone, a sound synchronization system pioneered by Bell Telephone Laboratories. Many recordings have been made on its outstanding Wurlitzer pipe organ. In regular use and meticulously maintained in its original brilliance, the Byrd is among Richmond's most popular landmarks. *(127–287) VLR: 06/21/77; NRHP: 09/24/79.*

HENRY COALTER CABELL HOUSE, *116 South Third Street.* This antebellum mansion is the sole survivor of the many large houses that once characterized Gamble's Hill, a fashionable 19th-century neighborhood. It was built in 1847 for William O. George but was rented for three decades beginning in the 1850s to Richmond lawyer Henry Coalter Cabell, with whom it has since been identified. The portico uses an order invented for American buildings by the Brooklyn architect Minard Lafever and popularized throughout the country by his architectural design book *The Beauties of Modern Architecture* (1835). The capitals, composed of Grecian elements, now have an Egyptian character here because the row of acanthus leaves originally around the lower part of each capital has been removed. The house has served as the headquarters of the Virginia Education Association since 1951. *(127–225) VLR: 11/16/71; NRHP: 12/27/72.*

JOHN B. CARY SCHOOL, *2100 Idlewood Avenue.* Named for John B. Cary, superintendent of Richmond public schools from 1886 to 1889, this castellated granite structure was designed by Charles M. Robinson, the talented supervising architect of the Richmond Board of Public Instruction from 1910 to 1929. In that capacity Robinson provided Virginia's capital with a distinguished collection of school buildings including Albert Hill School and Thomas Jefferson High School. Robinson also prepared master plans for James Madison and Radford universities and designed buildings for other state colleges. Robinson was adept in various historic styles; his choice of a castellated Gothic Revival mode for the Cary School is evidence of his versatility. Despite its historicism, the building was a thoroughly modern facility when opened in 1913. The name was changed to West End School in 1954 when it became a school for blacks. Since closed, the building is scheduled for rehabilitation for housing. *(127–824) VLR: 12/11/91; NRHP: 08/24/92.*

CATHEDRAL OF THE SACRED HEART, *Laurel Street and Floyd Avenue.* Fronted by Richmond's Monroe Park and forming the visual pivot between the city's commercial area and the residential Fan District, the Cathedral of the Sacred Heart is a glorious celebration of Roman Catholic art and architecture. The domed Renaissance Revival edifice, along

with its cloisters and bishop's residence, is the work of Joseph H. McGuire, a New York architect whose practice centered on Roman Catholic churches and institutional buildings. It was begun in 1903 and completed in 1906 with funds given by financier, promoter, and philanthropist Thomas Fortune Ryan, a Nelson County native. The cathedral's interior, the most majestic ecclesiastical space in the state, is richly embellished with Renaissance-style architectural decoration. McGuire's original drawings for the cathedral are preserved in Richmond's Valentine Museum. *(127–137) VLR: 12/15/81; NRHP: 07/08/82.*

CENTENARY METHODIST CHURCH, *411 East Grace Street.* Centenary's congregation was established in 1810. An inspirational visit from Bishop Francis Asbury in February 1812 rallied the members to complete their first building, known as the Methodist Meeting House on Shockoe Hill. The present church, erected 1841–43, was originally a simple Greek Revival work by the local builder-architects John and Samuel Freeman. It was completely remodeled in the Gothic style in 1874–76 by Richmond architect Albert L. West, who graced the facade with an imposing bell tower. Its twelve-bell carillon, known as the Talbott Chimes, first sounded on Easter Sunday, 1882. A landmark of downtown Richmond, Centenary remains the city's oldest Methodist church building and one of its chief expressions of the Gothic Revival. The interior is dominated by large Gothic arches defining the chancel and framing an elaborate organ case installed in 1965. The richly colored cathedral-glass windows date from 1908–9. *(127–321) VLR: 10/16/79; NRHP: 12/28/79.*

CHESTERMAN PLACE, *100 West Franklin Street.* This weighty urban mansion, built 1876–79 with boldly carved brownstone details, is among Richmond's most extravagant expressions of the High Victorian Italianate. The Franklin Street landmark was designed by a yet-unidentified architect for James B. Pace, a tobacconist and banker whose fortune was one of the largest in the South. The pair of three-part bays is the dominant element of the design. The richly carved staircase is a testament to the skill of Richmond woodworker B. B. Van Buren. In 1908 a local contractor, Wirt S. Chesterman, from whom the building takes its present name, purchased the property and converted it into a luxury apartment house, adding a large wing onto the rear designed by Aubrey Chesterman. The building was rehabilitated in the 1980s. *(127–607) VLR: 07/21/87.*

CENTRAL NATIONAL BANK BUILDING, *219 East Broad Street.* Built for the former Central National Bank, this office tower is Virginia's outstanding example of the Art Deco skyscraper and has long been one of Richmond's most conspicuous buildings. It was designed by New York architect John Eberson; the local firm of Carneal, Johnston and Wright served as consultants. Ground was broken in 1929, with completion the next year. In addition to its soaring exterior, the bank has a lofty vaulted banking hall, still one of the most spectacular commercial spaces in the city. Its Art Deco ornamentation includes floors of colorfully patterned terrazzo and ceilings with floral and geometric patterns. The Central National Bank was founded in 1911 when the Broad Street merchants decided to start a bank that would be convenient to their businesses. The present building was a project begun under the leadership of the bank's president, William Harry Schwarzschild. *(127–309) VLR: 04/18/78; NRHP: 09/20/79.*

CHURCH HILL NORTH HISTORIC DISTRICT. The twenty-five-block area immediately north of the St. John's Church Historic District is a remarkably intact, mostly 19th-century neighborhood. The area was laid out in the 1780s on land belonging to Col. Richard Adams. Many of its early residents were merchants or tradesmen. Employing a grid plan with relatively wide streets, the blocks are lined with tightly spaced town houses in a variety of styles. Twelve of the oldest houses are Federal-style structures built between 1810 and 1839. These and other Federal dwellings since destroyed originally had large lots, but their open spaces were filled in as the century progressed so that most blocks today display considerable architectural variety. Minimal construction since the early 1900s has preserved a cohesive historic flavor. The neighborhood went into economic decline after World War II but is now enjoying steady rehabilitation. *(127–820) VLR: 09/18/96; NRHP: 09/05/97.*

COLUMBIA, *1142 West Grace Street.* A rare surviving high-style Federal villa, Columbia was built in 1817–18 for Philip Haxall of Petersburg who moved to Richmond in 1810 to operate the Columbia Flour Mills, from which the house derives its name. The Virginia Baptist Educational Society purchased the property in 1834 and made it the main academic building of Richmond College, later the University of Richmond. Except during the Civil War when the house was a Confederate hospital and later a Union barracks, Columbia functioned for a century and a half as an educational facility. It housed the university's T. C. Williams School of Law from 1917 to 1954 and received a large wing in 1924. In 1984 Columbia was purchased by the American Historical Foundation for its headquarters. Although altered, the interior retains much important Federal-period fabric, including marble mantels, decorative plasterwork, and carved woodwork. *(127–45) VLR: 03/16/82; NRHP: 09/16/82; BHR EASEMENT.*

COMMONWEALTH CLUB HISTORIC DISTRICT. The area around West Franklin Street's 400 block holds one of Richmond's more impressive clusters of turn-of-the-century, upper-class town houses. Its focal point is the Commonwealth Club, a gentlemen's club designed in the 1890s by Carrère and Hastings of New York and one of Richmond's earliest expressions of the Colonial Revival. Although the block was once part of an unbroken progression of fine residences extending from Capitol Square to Monument Avenue, it is now a detached enclave in the midst of high-rise development. The stylistic diversity of the period is well illustrated here with houses in the Italianate, Romanesque, and Renaissance styles, all executed with harmonious scale and materials. The Commonwealth Club remains an influential social institution for the city; most of the district's houses have been rehabilitated for offices. *(127–373) VLR: 10/19/82; NRHP: 04/07/83.*

CONFEDERATE MEMORIAL CHAPEL, *2900 Grove Avenue.* The white-painted wooden Gothic-style chapel on the grounds of the Virginia Museum of Fine Arts was built in 1887 to serve the veterans of the Confederate Soldiers' Home, a large complex that then occupied much of the block. Designed by local architect M. J. Dimmock and built by Joseph Wingfield, the chapel was paid for by the veterans themselves and was dedicated to their dead comrades. The visually endearing landmark served the former "Rebs" until the last one died in 1941. Now maintained by the state, it is used for special occasions and as a visitor attraction. The windows contain a colorful variety of Victorian stained glass. *(127–224) VLR: 11/16/71; NRHP: 02/23/72.*

CROZET HOUSE, *100 East Main Street.* A familiar Main Street landmark, this dignified brick house was built ca. 1815 by Curtis Carter, a local brickmason and contractor, as his own home. The five-bay structure has more of the appearance of a prosperous farmhouse than an urban dwelling, making it exceptional among downtown Richmond's early dwellings. From 1828 to 1832 it served as the home of French-born engineer Col. Claudius Crozet. Appointed principal engineer of Virginia in 1823, Crozet mapped watercourses and planned turnpikes, railroads, canals, and tunnels. He is perhaps best remembered as engineer of the first tunnel through the Blue Ridge Mountains and as one of the founders of the Virginia Military Institute. The house was restored by architect Edward F. Sinnott in 1940 when it received its colonial-style brick doorway. Most of the original, somewhat plain interior woodwork survives. *(127–47) VLR: 11/16/71; NRHP: 02/23/72.*

DONNAN-ASHER IRON FRONT BUILDING, *1207–1211 East Main Street.* Built in 1866 as part of the reconstruction of Richmond's commercial area after the Evacuation Fire of 1865, this exuberant building has one of only three completely cast-iron facades remaining in the city. It was built for the Donnan Brothers, hardware merchants. The iron facade was popular at the time because it could provide maximum elaboration with minimal expense and construction time. Inspired by the Renaissance palaces of Venice, most of the iron facades were rendered in a rich Italianate style. The ironwork on this facade is attributed to George H. Johnson, an English architect who came to this country in 1851. The iron was produced by Hayward, Bartlett & Co. of Baltimore, which employed Johnson at the time. A 1960s shop front mars the otherwise unaltered facade. *(127–163) VLR: 12/02/69; NRHP: 02/26/70.*

EGYPTIAN BUILDING, *College and East Marshall streets.* No purer expression of the mid-19th-century Egyptian Revival exists in America than this exotic work, a masterpiece by Philadelphia architect Thomas S. Stewart. Completed in 1846, the Egyptian Building originally housed Hampden-Sydney College's medical department, which moved to Richmond in 1837. The department became an independent institution in 1854 and came under state control in 1860. In 1893 it became the Medical College of Virginia, now the Virginia Commonwealth University School of Medicine. The institution has since been expanded into a vast complex, but the Egyptian Building, one of the oldest medical education buildings in the South, remains its architectural symbol. The style alluded to Egypt's ancient medical tradition. Emphasizing the Egyptian theme is the cast-iron fence with its mummylike posts, or herm figures, and its granite piers in the shape of obelisks. *(127–87) VLR: 11/05/68; NRHP: 04/16/69; NHL: 11/11/71.*

ENGLISH VILLAGE, *3418–3450 Grove Avenue.* English Village was one of the state's earliest ventures in cooperative planned communities, a precursor of today's condominiums. Notable for its Tudor-style architecture and innovative planning and design, the U-shaped multifamily complex was designed by Richmond architect Bascomb J. Rowlett and built in 1927 by Davis Brothers, a local contracting firm. Although most cooperative housing in that period was built for workers and owned collectively, English Village was built for upper-middle-class families, with each owner holding title to his own unit. All but one of the first owners lost their titles through mortgage foreclosures in the depression. Home ownership gradually resumed, however, allowing the complex to survive as a successful entity to the present. One of its bylaws includes a restriction on exterior changes, a factor critical to the maintenance of English Village's architectural integrity. *(127–374) VLR: 08/16/83; NRHP: 09/29/83.*

EXECUTIVE MANSION, *Capitol Square.* First occupied in 1813 by Governor James Barbour, Virginia's Executive Mansion is the nation's oldest governor's mansion in continuous use. Its architect, Alexander Parris, was a native of Maine who lived briefly in Richmond and later became a leading architect in Boston. Constructed by builder Christopher Tompkins, the mansion is a skillful essay in the Federal style. During its many years of service, the mansion has accommodated such guests as Lafayette, the Prince of Wales (later King Edward VII), Marshal Foch, Winston Churchill, and Elizabeth, the queen mother. The bodies of Stonewall Jackson and tennis champion Arthur Ashe have lain in state here. Except for architect Duncan Lee's 1908 dining room addition and the creation of the ballroom after a 1926 fire, the house has been little changed. The exterior was restored during the administration of Governor Gerald L. Baliles when the balustrades and decorative panels were reconstructed. *(127–57) VLR: 11/05/68; NRHP: 06/04/69; NHL: 06/97/88.*

FAN AREA HISTORIC DISTRICT. This residential neighborhood of over a hundred city blocks is noted for its architectural cohesiveness and its association with Richmond's transformation into a modern city. Located west of the city's commercial core, the turn-of-the-century district is an outgrowth of the demand for better housing and improved services by a new, urban middle class who spurred architects, builders, and speculators to develop entire blocks of town houses. The district conveys a unity that depends not so much on consistent architectural style as on intrinsic qualities of good urban design such as uniform heights and setbacks, compatibility of texture and building materials, and consistent planting of trees. Each of the district's several thousand buildings is an essential element of the neighborhood's many visually charming block facades, all characterized by lively rooflines and a multiplicity of porch types. *(127–248) VLR: 08/13/85 (EXPANDED 04/15/86); NRHP: 09/12/85.*

FIRST NATIONAL BANK BUILDING, *823 East Main Street.* Commissioned by the Chesapeake and Ohio Railway Co., the First National Bank Building, with its elegant detailing, Corinthian columns, and lofty banking hall, is a potent example of 20th-century Neoclassical Revival architecture. Its architect was Alfred Charles Bossom, an associate with Clinton and Russell of New York. The building was completed in 1913 as the city's first high-rise building, combining monumental scale with the technological daring of steel-frame skyscraper construction. Bossom stated his approach to the design: "The building externally should look like a BANK and should call attention to itself by substantial and conservative appearance." In the heart of Richmond's financial district, the structure was long the headquarters of the state's oldest banking institution, now merged with NationsBank. The exterior appearance was altered when its Florentine-style cornice was removed. The building now houses office condominiums. *(127–381) VLR: 02/26/82; NRHP: 04/12/82.*

FOURTH BAPTIST CHURCH, *2800 P Street.* Fourth Baptist Church is a symbol of black religious strength in the Confederacy's former capital during the decades following Emancipation. The congregation began as a regular assembly of slaves in their quarters and transferred to the basement of Leigh Street Baptist Church in 1861. In 1865, under the leadership of the Rev. Scott Gwathmey, the congregation built its own church with lumber salvaged from Union barracks. This was replaced in 1875 by a simple frame church which burned in 1884 as the present church was nearing completion on a new site. Situated on the northern side of Church Hill, the present building boasts a stylish Victorian interior behind a plain but dignified Greek Revival exterior which, with its Doric portico *in muris,* was inspired by Richmond's Old First Baptist Church. The church continues to house one of the city's oldest black congregations. *(127–318) VLR: 05/15/79; NRHP: 09/07/79.*

0–100 BLOCK EAST FRANKLIN STREET HISTORIC DISTRICT. This small urban neighborhood, incorporating one block of Franklin Street and buildings on Main and Grace streets, is a cohesive assemblage of 19th-century residential architecture. The district is on lands once part of Rutherfoord's Addition, property owned by cotton and tobacco manufacturer Thomas Rutherfoord, who started selling tracts here in 1795. Although some lots were developed immediately, the existing fabric dates from the 1830s into the early 1900s. Including sophisticated examples of Greek Revival, Italianate, Queen Anne, and Georgian Revival styles, most of the houses were built as two- or three-story side-passage town houses. A conspicuous exception is the 1845–46 Kent-Valentine house, a freestanding mansion designed by Isaiah Rogers and later remodeled. The district's oldest structure is the 1836 William Allen double house on Main Street. Most of the houses have been sympathetically converted to offices, shops, or apartments. *(127–317) VLR: 10/16/79; NRHP: 02/27/80.*

200 BLOCK WEST FRANKLIN STREET HISTORIC DISTRICT. Within this one block of Franklin Street is perhaps Richmond's most diverse concentration of 19th-century domestic architecture. Except for two demolitions, the block has changed little since before World War I when it was one of the city's best addresses. The ca. 1800 Cole Diggs house, now the headquarters of the Association for the Preservation of Virginia Antiquities, is the earliest house in the group. An outstanding work of the Eastlake style is the ca. 1886 T. Seddon Bruce house, designed by M. J. Dimmock. Finally, an able example of the French Renaissance mode is the 1896 Carter-Mayo house by Carrère and Hastings. The block was rescued from threatened development in 1977 by the Historic Richmond Foundation. The district has since been expanded to include Main Street's Queen Anne Row. All of the buildings have been rehabilitated. *(127–281) VLR: 05/17/77 (EXPANDED 08/17/94); NRHP: 11/17/77; BHR EASEMENTS.*

GINTER PARK HISTORIC DISTRICT. Ginter Park, one of Richmond's first streetcar suburbs, was conceived by tobacco magnate Maj. Lewis Ginter. In the 1890s Ginter turned his attention to community planning, recognizing the need for new neighborhoods accessible to the city center by electric streetcar. Incorporating some twenty-one blocks, Ginter's grid-plan development offered large grassy yards and tree-lined streets, a fresh-air contrast to the sooty, densely packed downtown. Ginter Park was incorporated in 1912 and annexed to the city in 1914. To provide an institutional anchor, Ginter donated land for a new campus for Union Theological Seminary. By the 1930s most lots had been filled with a variety of freestanding dwellings, forming a picture of the American suburban ideal. Though Chamberlayne Avenue, the principal thoroughfare, has suffered loss of its former character, many other streets, particularly Seminary Avenue and Brook Road, retain a wholesome ambience. *(127–201) VLR: 06/17/86; NRHP: 09/22/86.*

ELLEN GLASGOW HOUSE, *1 West Main Street.* Virginia author Ellen Glasgow made her home in this Greek Revival mansion from 1887, when at age 13 she moved in with her family, until her death in 1945. Her father purchased the house from the family of local industrialist Isaac Davenport. Glasgow's many novels depicted life in the South with a realism devoid of the nostalgic sentimentality that characterized much southern writing of the period.

Elected to the American Academy of Arts and Letters in 1938, she was also awarded the Pulitzer Prize in 1942 for her last novel, *In This Our Life.* Her home, typical of the large Greek Revival houses that once lined Richmond's streets, was built in 1841 for David M. Branch, a tobacco manufacturer. Glasgow's "square gray house" was purchased by the Association for the Preservation of Virginia Antiquities in 1947. Since sold with protective covenants, it is once again a private residence. *(127–56) VLR: 01/18/72; NRHP: 05/05/72; NHL: 11/11/71.*

WILLIAM A. GRANT HOUSE, *1008 East Clay Street.* The antebellum mansion opposite the Valentine Museum is an early use of the Italianate style in Richmond. The massive scale and square proportions employed here were inspired by the Renaissance palaces of Florence. Notable features of the house include the thin-jointed pressed-brick facade, marble entrance steps, elaborately detailed porch, and cast-iron hood moldings over the windows.

Dating from 1853, the house was the home of William A. Grant, a tobacco manufacturer whose factory survives in Shockoe Valley. It was sold to the Sheltering Arms Hospital in 1882. The hospital has since moved, and the mansion is now owned by the Virginia Commonwealth University School of Medicine, which has sympathetically restored the first-floor reception rooms. The Grant house and nearby dwellings are part of a progression of distinguished houses that once formed a leading residential neighborhood. *(127–17) VLR: 11/05/68; NRHP: 04/16/69.*

2900 BLOCK GROVE AVENUE HISTORIC DISTRICT.

A departure from the tight town-house development of the surrounding neighborhood is this distinctive tree-shaded block of four freestanding houses in the 2900 block of Grove Avenue. Although the easternmost house is a more conventional turn-of-the-century dwelling with Craftsman overtones, the remaining three form a trio of highly individualized interpretations of the Queen Anne style with the flavor of suburban villas. Faced with gray granite, each house has a lively outline with angled projections and a corner tower. Although their architect remains unidentified, they are among Richmond's more interesting examples of late Victorian architecture. Adding to the block's fanciful quality are the ornamented wooden carriage houses behind the main dwellings. Both 2911 and 2915 Grove Avenue were sympathetically converted to doctors' offices in the 1980s and are now the property of the Virginia Museum of Fine Arts. *(127–238) VLR: 10/17/72; NRHP: 02/20/73.*

HANCOCK-WIRT-CASKIE HOUSE, *2 North Fifth Street.*

Benjamin Henry Latrobe's designs for Richmond houses with demioctagonal bays provided the prototype for Michael Hancock's 1809 dwelling, a surviving example of the many elegant Federal houses that once graced the city. The arcaded gallery, Flemish bond brickwork, marble trim, and interior woodwork are all of the highest quality and unite to form a distinctive composition. Much of the interior detailing is based on designs in William Pain's *Carpenter's and Joiner's Repository,* an 18th-century English design book. The house was purchased in 1816 by William Wirt, a year before he was named U.S. attorney general. It next served as the home of two Richmond mayors, Benjamin Tate and later his son Joseph, and was long the residence of Mrs. Benjamin Caskie, who died in 1941. In private ownership, the house has been undergoing a long-term, museum-quality restoration. *(127–42) VLR: 12/02/69; NRHP: 04/17/70.*

HASKER AND MARCUSE FACTORY (CHURCH HILL HOUSE), *2300 and 2400 blocks of Venable and Burton streets.*

Constructed between 1893 and 1895, the Hasker and Marcuse Factory developed the process of manufacturing polychromatic printed tobacco tins. Shipped nationwide, the firm's tins were the primary means of advertising and marketing the products of the newly consolidated tobacco companies formed in Richmond during the 1890s. Integral to this manufacturing process were the development and application of the technology of tin-printing processes, which resulted in the invention and widespread use of offset lithography. This mass production of labeled tins marked the beginnings of the modern packaging industry. The four-story brick building with its unadorned walls and large window areas is typical of the industrial architecture of the period. Renamed Church Hill House, it has been preserved through adaptation as housing for the low-income elderly. *(127–299) VLR: 04/19/83; NRHP: 08/11/83.*

HIGHLAND PARK PUBLIC SCHOOL (BROOKLAND PARK PLAZA), *1221 East Brookland Park Boulevard.*

Distinguished by its skillful massing and subtle facade, the Highland Park Public School demonstrates the talent of Charles M. Robinson, one of the state's leading designers of educational facilities. Although his works include buildings at Mary Washington College and the College of William and Mary, Robinson is best known as supervising architect to the Richmond Board of Public Instruction from 1910 to 1929, during which time he designed twenty school buildings and additions to schools. Built in 1909, Highland Park School departs from the usual Georgian and Gothic formulas by employing a Mediterranean idiom, using a spreading tile roof, stuccoed wall panels, and an Italian-style arcade. After the removal of the school functions to modern facilities, the building was rehabilitated in 1990–91 to accommodate seventy-seven apartments for the elderly and was renamed Brookland Park Plaza. *(127–355) VLR: 10/09/91; NRHP: 10/22/91.*

HOLLY LAWN, *4012 Hermitage Road.* Holly Lawn is remembered as the home of the esteemed physician Dr. Ennion G. Williams, who lived here from 1913 until his death in 1931. Under Dr. Williams's leadership as the Commonwealth's first commissioner of public health, a post to which he was appointed in 1908, Virginia's health board became one of the country's first such departments to apply scientific knowledge for the improvement of public hygiene through a system of prevention as well as cure. Built in 1901 for Andrew Bierne Blair, a Richmond insurance agent, the ambitious Queen Anne–style residence was designed by Richmond architect D. Wiley Anderson for what was then a turn-of-the-century streetcar suburb. Typical of its mode, the house has a complex roofline, irregular plan, and wraparound porch. For many years the house served as the headquarters of the Richmond Council of Garden Clubs. *(127–55) VLR: 05/18/82; NRHP: 08/26/82.*

HOLLYWOOD CEMETERY, *412 South Cherry Street.* Named for its stand of holly trees, Hollywood Cemetery was laid out in 1848 by John Notman, a Scottish architect who settled in Philadelphia and became a pioneer in the design of romantically landscaped parks and cemeteries. Hollywood follows Notman's usual format, being spread across hills and ravines, with winding, tree-shaded roadways and paths. Large landscaped cemeteries were both popular and practical in their day; they were attractive places to visit and objects of civic pride. Over the next century Hollywood became an outdoor pantheon of notable Virginians and was embellished with an outstanding collection of monuments and ornamental ironwork. Interred here are U.S. presidents James Monroe and John Tyler and Confederate president Jefferson Davis, as well as J. E. B. Stuart, John Randolph of Roanoke, and Matthew Fontaine Maury. A huge dry-laid stone pyramid marks the graves of 18,000 Confederate soldiers. *(127–221) VLR: 09/09/69; NRHP: 11/12/69.*

HOME FOR NEEDY CONFEDERATE WOMEN, *301 North Sheppard Street.* This skillfully scaled-down version of the White House was completed in 1932 to serve wives, widows, daughters, and sisters of Confederate veterans. After a fire at the previous home downtown, Mrs. Andrew Jackson Montague, wife of the governor, campaigned for a fireproof facility. Sufficient funds were obtained by 1929; the site chosen was on the grounds of R. E. Lee Camp No. 1, Confederate Soldiers' Home. The design was provided by Richmond architect Merrill C. Lee. The choice of the White House as a model is not without irony; the nation's executive mansion traditionally has been associated with domesticity, and its image offered a stately setting for these revered ladies. With eligible occupants becoming extinct in 1980s, the property was transferred to the Virginia Museum of Fine Arts in 1990 and has been restored for studios and offices. *(127–380) VLR: 04/16/85; NRHP: 11/07/85.*

HOTEL WILLIAM BYRD (WILLIAM BYRD APARTMENT HOMES), *2501 West Broad Street.* Towering above its neighbors, both residential and commercial, the eleven-story former Hotel William Byrd proclaims the growing popularity of the steel-frame, high-rise architecture in the 1920s. The hotel was built in 1925 primarily to serve the patrons of the Broad Street railroad station directly across the street. It was designed by Marcellus E. Wright, Sr., one of the city's leading architects, who embellished the exterior with a subtle, restrained classicism. When the hotel opened, the

Richmond News Leader described it as "a monument to Richmond energy, talent, and progressiveness." For many years the William Byrd and Broad Street Station formed the traveler's gateway image of Richmond. The hotel closed in the 1980s but was sensitively rehabilitated in 1996 for use as apartments for the elderly. *(127–466) VLR: 09/18/96; NRHP: 12/16/96; BHR EASEMENT.*

JACKSON WARD HISTORIC DISTRICT. Richmond at the turn of the 20th century had one of the nation's most thriving black business communities. The hub of this activity was Jackson Ward with its fraternal organizations, banks, insurance companies, and other institutions, all founded and run by blacks. The neighborhood developed before the Civil War and originally was populated primarily by citizens of German and Jewish extraction but with many free blacks. After the war Jackson Ward gradually became predominantly black. Redevelopment and expressway construction have reduced its size, but the remaining blocks place Jackson Ward among the nation's largest historic districts associated primarily with black culture. The area is dominated by three-bay, side-passage town houses in various styles. Many have locally manufactured cast-iron porches, the state's richest display of ornamental ironwork. In recent years the area has become the focus of increasing rehabilitation activity. *(127–237) VLR: 04/20/76; NRHP (07/30/76); NHL: 06/02/78.*

THE JEFFERSON HOTEL, *West Franklin and Adams streets.* The opulence of America's Gilded Age was given full expression in the hotel commissioned in the 1890s by Richmond tobacconist Maj. Lewis Ginter. Ginter engaged the New York firm of Carrère and Hastings, a leading practitioner of the Beaux Arts style, and charged it to provide the finest hostelry in the South. Completed in 1895, the Renaissance Revival masterpiece, inspired by Rome's Villa Medici, exhibits an exuberance seldom seen in commercial buildings. The magnificent interior featured a regal progression of public rooms in addition to its 342 guest rooms. A fire destroyed the south half of the building, but it was sympathetically rebuilt in 1901 by Norfolk architect J. Kevan Peebles, who replaced the original glass and iron court with the present Edwardian Baroque lobby and its grand stair. A comprehensive rehabilitation has returned this architectural and social landmark to its former magnificence. *(127–01) VLR: 11/05/68; NRHP: 06/04/69.*

JAMES RIVER AND KANAWHA CANAL HISTORIC DISTRICT. This linear district includes the canal route from the Great Ship Lock in Richmond's east end to Bosher's Dam in western Henrico County. The parent James River Company was founded in 1784 with George Washington serving as honorary president. In 1835 the James River and Kanawha Canal Company was formed from the original company to connect the James with the Kanawha River and thus provide a navigation system to the Ohio and Mississippi rivers. A series of basins, locks, and docks was built through downtown in the 1850s. The canal operated until 1880 when it was purchased by the Richmond and Alleghany Railway Company. Although much of the system has been built over, its course can yet be traced through the city. The lower locks of the Tidewater Connection have been restored by the Reynolds Metals Company, and restoration of other sections was carried out in 1997–99. *(127–171) VLR: 09/09/69; NRHP: 08/26/71.*

KENT-VALENTINE HOUSE, *12 East Franklin Street.* Merchant Horace L. Kent commissioned Boston architect Isaiah Rogers in 1844 to design this Franklin Street mansion. Most of Rogers's works have been destroyed; 12 East Franklin Street is his only known surviving residential design. The house was originally a three-bay Italianate dwelling skirted by an intricate cast-iron veranda. In 1904 Granville G. Valentine, owner of a meat-extract company, engaged the firm of Noland and Baskervill to expand the house into a five-bay composition, extending the veranda. The veranda was replaced by the present Ionic portico around 1909. The final result is a successful amalgam of antebellum and early 20th-century styles. Noland and Baskervill's Georgian Revival drawing room provides an interesting contrast to Rogers's Gothic Revival double parlors. The house was restored in the early 1970s to serve as the headquarters of the Garden Club of Virginia. *(127–112) VLR: 10/06/70; NRHP: 12/18/70; BHR EASEMENT.*

BENJAMIN WATKINS LEIGH HOUSE, *1000 East Clay Street.* John Wickham, original owner of the famous mansion across the street that later became the Valentine Museum, had this capacious four-bay town house built for his daughter Julia between 1812 and 1816. Julia Wickham Leigh and her husband, Benjamin Watkins Leigh, a Richmond lawyer who served in the U.S. Senate during the Jackson administration, were living here by 1826. The house, an unusually large dwelling for early 19th-century Richmond, was remodeled in the Italianate mode with a bracketed porch and cornice after 1851 when it was sold to Lieutenant Governor John M. Gregory. In 1932 the house was incorporated into the Sheltering Arms Hospital complex. It is now used for offices by the Virginia Commonwealth University School of Medicine. *(127–65) VLR: 11/05/68; NRHP: 04/16/69.*

LEIGH STREET BAPTIST CHURCH, *East Leigh and Twenty-fifth streets.* This Greek Revival church, one of the architectural highlights of Richmond's venerable North Church Hill neighborhood, was designed by Philadelphia architect Samuel Sloan and was completed in 1857. Sloan, in addition to his numerous commissions, was the author of *The Model Architect* (1852), a design book which had a great influence on the architecture of mid-19th-century America. The church's congregation was organized in the early 1850s by Baptist missionary Reuben Ford, and under its auspices seven other Richmond Baptist churches were started. Leigh Street Baptist is the oldest traditionally white Baptist church in the city still occupied by its congregation. Although the interior has been remodeled and the south wall hidden by a later wing, Sloan's restrained design, dominated by a hexastyle Greek Doric portico, remains a potent architectural statement. *(127–11) VLR: 11/16/71; NRHP: 03/16/72.*

LINDEN ROW, *100–114 East Franklin Street.* The British concept of connected town houses, or a terrace, is effectively interpreted in red brick and crisp white wooden trim on Linden Row, a block of architecturally unified dwellings designed by Otis Manson. Named for the linden trees that once shaded a garden on the site, the original eastern five houses were erected as a business venture by Fleming James in 1847. The block was completed in 1853 by Samuel and Alexander Rutherfoord. The simple, straightforward facades serve to set off the beautifully executed Greek Doric entrance porticoes. Linden Row was long a sought-after address, housing families, schools, and businesses. The two easternmost houses were demolished in 1922. Between 1950 and 1957 the remaining houses were purchased by Richmond preservationist Mary Wingfield Scott, who in 1980 gave Linden Row to the Historic Richmond Foundation. The row has since been restored as the Linden Row Inn. *(127–22) VLR: 07/06/71; NRHP: 11/23/71.*

LOEW'S THEATER (CARPENTER CENTER FOR THE PERFORMING ARTS), *East Grace and Sixth streets.* Designed by the legendary John Eberson and built by the Loew's Theater Corporation, Richmond's Loew's is in the front rank of 1920s movie palace architecture. With its mixture of Moorish and Spanish baroque influences, Loew's was considered the most up-to-date theater in the South when it opened on April 9, 1928. The auditorium, with churrigueresque facades and a ceiling treated to give the illusion of a starry night sky with moving clouds, gave the effect of a Spanish plaza. Such architectural theatricality was essential to the so-called atmospheric motion-picture house, where the viewer, seated in the proper atmosphere, would achieve greatest enjoyment of the film. The theater was acquired and restored in the 1980s by the Virginia Center for the Performing Arts and later renamed the Carpenter Center for the Performing Arts. *(127–324) VLR: 09/18/79; NRHP: 11/20/79.*

MAIN STREET STATION, *East Main Street at Sixteenth Street.* Completed in 1901, the Renaissance-style Main Street Station was designed by Wilson, Harris, and Richards of Philadelphia and served the Chesapeake and Ohio and the Seaboard Air Line railroads. One of Richmond's most admired landmarks, the impressive composition is dominated by its dormered roof and clock tower. Its golden Roman brick walls are richly trimmed with terra-cotta ornaments. The contrastingly airy train shed, 530 feet in length, was built by the Pencoyd Iron Works of Pencoyd, Pa., and is one of the country's last remaining gable-roof train sheds. Its wrought-iron members employ riveted construction, a technology that made skyscrapers possible. Closed in the 1970s, the station was later restored as a shopping mall. Since converted to state offices, the facility is now scheduled to be returned to use as a train station. *(127–172) VLR: 07/07/70; NRHP: 10/15/70; NHL: 12/08/76.*

JOHN MARSHALL HOUSE, *818 East Marshall Street.* John Marshall, chief justice of the U.S. Supreme Court, built this dignified Georgian house in 1790 and made it his home for forty-five years. Marshall was appointed to his high post in 1801 and held the position until his death in 1835. Although his judicial duties took him away from Richmond for months at a time, he was able to spend long periods at home, writing many of his decisions establishing the fundamental principles for constitutional interpretation. The house, one of the oldest brick dwellings in Richmond, was owned by Marshall descendants until 1907. It was rescued from threatened demolition that same year following its purchase by the city. In 1911 it was placed in the perpetual care of the Association for the Preservation of Virginia Antiquities. The restored dwelling is now a museum furnished with many of Marshall's possessions. *(127–73) VLR: 09/09/69; NRHP: 12/15/66; NHL: 12/19/60.*

MASONIC TEMPLE, *101 West Broad Street.* Richmond's Masonic Temple, designed by Baltimore architect Jackson C. Gott and erected in 1888–93, is a brick and brownstone extravaganza of the American Romanesque Revival, a style made fashionable by Boston architect H. H. Richardson. The weighty edifice, with its mass countered by a large corner tower, delicate corner bartizans, and a multiplicity of windows, was the largest building put up by Virginia Masons by that time and brought a big-city quality to Broad Street. In addition to the Masonic meeting rooms, the building accommodated a department store and cultural facilities. Its main reception room provided a grand setting for many balls, concerts, and banquets, most notably a banquet held for President Theodore Roosevelt in 1905. Abandoned by the Masons for a number of years, the building has since been restored for mixed use. *(127–296) VLR: 12/14/82; NRHP: 02/10/83.*

MASONS' HALL, *1807 East Franklin Street.* Standing aloof from the bustle of the surrounding restaurants and shops of Richmond's Shockoe Valley, Masons' Hall, completed in 1787, is the oldest Masonic hall in continuous use in the country. Edmund Randolph and John Marshall belonged to what was originally Lodge No. 13, and the marquis de Lafayette was made an honorary member when he visited the hall in

1824. The late Georgian building, capped by a jaunty cupola, was remodeled in the mid–19th century when much of its exterior trim was replaced by Greek Revival work. The remarkable interior, however, decked out in Masonic paraphernalia on all three floors, retains much original fabric. The building is now the home of Richmond Randolph Lodge No. 19. *(127–19) VLR: 01/16/73; NRHP: 07/20/73.*

MAYMONT, *1700 Hampton Street.* The eclectic tastes of the late Victorian era in architecture, interior decoration, art collecting, and gardening are lavishly displayed at Maymont, the suburban estate created by Richmond philanthropist Maj. James H. Dooley and his wife Sallie May. The combination Romanesque- and Châteauesque-style stone mansion was designed by Edgerton S. Rogers and completed in 1893. Contrasting with its somber exterior is a glittering interior where each room has its own stylistic character. The Dooleys filled the house with a singular collection of artistic objects gathered on world travels. They also developed the estate's 100 acres into a series of gardens, including an English-style park, an Italian terraced garden with fountains, a Japanese garden, and a grotto. At Mrs. Dooley's death in 1925, the estate became a city-owned museum and park. Since 1975, custodianship for this Gilded Age monument has been entrusted to the Maymont Foundation. *(127–182) VLR: 07/06/71; NRHP: 12/16/71.*

MAYO HOUSE (MAYO MEMORIAL CHURCH HOUSE), *110 West Franklin Street.* As originally built for Samuel Taylor in 1845, this Greek Revival mansion was a three-part composition consisting of a temple-form center section with one-story wings. In 1883 the house was purchased by Richmond tobacconist Peter H. Mayo, who spared no expense in remodeling the interior in the latest, most opulent taste. Mayo collected the finest cabinet woods and had them fashioned by artisans into door and window cases, stairs, mantels, and parquet floors, all in a Renaissance flavor. He also added second stories to the wings. The elaborate interior decorations were largely covered over during various modernizations after the Mayo family donated the house to the Episcopal Diocese of Virginia in 1923. Much of the interior's rich 1880s character was restored during a 1982 renovation. The house continues as a diocesan headquarters. *(127–75) VLR: 05/16/72; NRHP: 04/02/73.*

JAMES MONROE TOMB, *Hollywood Cemetery, 412 South Cherry Street.* The tomb of President James Monroe, the chief ornament of John Notman's romantically landscaped Hollywood Cemetery, is a tour de force of both Gothic Revival design and artistry in cast iron. The simple granite sarcophagus is enclosed by an iron screen surmounted by an ogee dome of openwork tracery. The scheme recalls Henry VII's tomb in Westminster Abbey, similarly enclosed but lacking a dome. The tomb was designed by Albert Lybrock, an Alsatian architect who settled in Richmond in 1852. The iron was cast by the Philadelphia firm of Wood and Perot and was assembled in 1858 by Asa Snyder, a Richmond ironworker. Monroe died and was buried in New York City in 1831. His body was moved to Richmond on the centennial of his birth in 1858, a cooperative effort by citizens of New York and Virginia. *(127–382) VLR: 03/19/97; NHL: 11/11/71.*

MONROE PARK HISTORIC DISTRICT. Monroe Park occupies land acquired by the city in 1851 to be a park for the developing western suburbs. After serving as an agricultural exposition site and a camp for Confederate troops, the property finally became a park in the 1870s. The layout is a pattern of walks radiating from an elaborate cast-iron fountain. Framing the park's north and west sides is a remarkable assemblage of buildings ranging from the 1895 Gothic Revival Grace and Holy Trinity Episcopal Church to the 1906 Renaissance Revival Cathedral of the Sacred Heart. Most conspicuous is the 1927 Islamic-style city auditorium, originally known as the Mosque. Several late 19th-century town houses and two Tudor-style apartment towers reflect the district's former residential character. The buildings, and especially their amazing collective skyline, demonstrate the eclecticism of the period, while the park is an example of late Victorian urban landscaping. *(127–383) VLR: 11/15/83; NRHP: 07/05/84.*

MONUMENT AVENUE HISTORIC DISTRICT. One of America's most splendid turn-of-the-century residential boulevards, Monument Avenue illustrates the best of Beaux Arts planning ideals and the aspirations of the City Beautiful movement. The concept of a great divided street honoring Confederate heroes coincided with the 1888 extension of Franklin Street to the proposed Lee monument. Jean Antoine Mercié's equestrian statue of Robert E. Lee, the hub of a fashionable new residential area, was unveiled in 1890. By 1907 Edward Valentine's Jefferson Davis monument and Fred Moynihan's equestrian statue of J. E. B. Stuart were completed. Frederick Sevier's equestrian statue of Stonewall Jackson at the Boulevard was unveiled in 1919; his Matthew Fontaine Maury monument was erected in 1929. The avenue's cohesive architecture, dating mainly from 1890 to 1930, consists of mansions, town houses, churches, and apartment blocks. Its architects include John Russell Pope, William Lawrence Bottomley, W. Duncan Lee, and Noland and Baskervill. *(127–174) VLR: 12/02/69 (EXPANDED 12/12/89); NRHP: 02/26/70; NHL: 12/03/97.*

MONUMENTAL CHURCH, *1224 East Broad Street.* An architectural landmark of national significance, Monumental Church was built in 1812–14 as a memorial to seventy-two people who perished in an 1811 theater fire at this site. Its architect, Robert Mills, studied under both Thomas Jefferson and Benjamin Henry Latrobe and combined elements favored by both his mentors. The octagonal form and Delorme-type dome were features admired by Jefferson. The Greek Doric order and the refined, highly personalized classical details were hallmarks of Latrobe's work. Mills's design heralded a new approach for the state's ecclesiastical architecture, treating the interior as an auditorium with the principal focus on the pulpit. Monumental Church served an Episcopal parish until 1965 when it became a chapel for the Medical College of Virginia. A long-term restoration of Mills's original design was begun in the 1970s. The building is now owned by the Historic Richmond Foundation. *(127–12) VLR: 11/05/68; NRHP: 04/16/69; NHL: 11/11/71.*

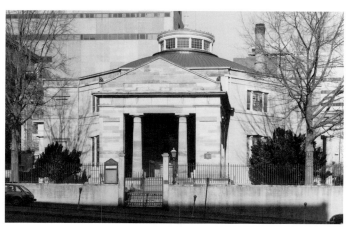

MOORE'S AUTO BODY AND PAINT SHOP, *401 West Broad Street.* This curved arcade comfortably maintains a presence among the larger-scale buildings of West Broad Street. It serves as a tangible demonstration of how visual dignity can be imparted to the most utilitarian buildings through the competent use of the architectural vocabulary of classicism. The Mediterranean-style work is the facade of an 1875 brick stable. The design was commissioned by J. Luther Moore from the firm of Lee, Smith, and VanderVoort after Moore purchased the stable in 1926. Acknowledging West Broad Street's fashionable character, the architects ingeniously gave the block an elegant corner. The building was used as an automotive service station until 1936. Since then it has offered automobile repairs by various successive firms. The present occupant has owned the property since 1976, thus maintaining a century-old tradition of servicing transportation vehicles here. *(127–834) VLR: 08/18/93; NRHP: 10/14/93.*

MORSON'S ROW, *219–223 Governor Street.* The three bow-fronted Italianate town houses forming Morson's Row were erected as rental properties in 1853 by James Marion Morson and are the last vestige of the former residential character of Capitol Square. The row is attributed to Richmond architect Albert Lybrock because Lybrock listed Morson as a client in 1854, and the houses are in the Italianate idiom Lybrock favored. Little changed inside or out, each house has an oval parlor with cherry and mahogany woodwork and heavily carved Victorian marble mantels. Beginning in 1920, 223 Governor Street was occupied for several decades by the Southern Planter Publishing Company. A. E. Peticolas, an anatomist, first rented 221 Governor Street, and it later was the home of Dr. Robert Gamble. The row is now the property of the Commonwealth, and for many years it housed the Department of Historic Resources. *(127–79) VLR: 11/05/68; NRHP: 06/11/69.*

OLD CITY HALL, *1000 East Broad Street.* Richmond's Old City Hall, one of the nation's foremost examples of the High Victorian Gothic style, was designed by the Detroit architect Elijah E. Myers, architect of five state capitols. With its fairy-tale skyline and profusion of carved ornament, the four-story building forms a dramatic backdrop for Capitol Square. Built of Richmond granite, the massive structure was completed in 1894 and at once became a symbol of the city's recovery from the Civil War and Reconstruction. It was built primarily by black laborers under the supervision of City Engineer Col. Wilfred E. Cutshaw. The interior court is an extraordinary composition of tiers of Gothic arcades and flights of stairs all in cast iron. The building was sold to the state in 1981 and is leased through the Historic Richmond Foundation to private developers who restored the building for commercial offices. *(127–03) VLR: 11/05/68; NRHP: 10/01/69; NHL: 11/11/71.*

OLD FIRST AFRICAN BAPTIST CHURCH, *301 College Street.* Built in 1876, this church housed the mother congregation of Richmond's black Baptists until its members moved to a new location in 1955. It stands on the site of the First Baptist Church of 1802, which was sold to its black members in 1841 when the white Baptists erected their new church at Broad and Twelfth streets. The original congregation included both slaves and free blacks. The 1802 building was taken down and replaced with the present structure, which, with its Doric portico *in muris,* followed the model of Thomas U. Walter's stately First Baptist Church a block away. Its interior was remodeled for offices after its acquisition by the Medical College of Virginia in 1955. Although no longer used for worship, Old First African Baptist remains a symbol of progress for Richmond's black citizens in the late 19th century. *(127–167) VLR: 11/05/68; NRHP: 04/16/69.*

OLD FIRST BAPTIST CHURCH, *East Broad and Twelfth streets.* Thomas U. Walter of Philadelphia provided the restrained but authoritative design for this Greek Revival church. Walter, best known as architect of the dome of the U.S. Capitol, designed some ten buildings for Virginia; First Baptist is his only remaining Richmond work. Construction was begun in 1839, and two years later the congregation moved in. Walter's design, dominated by a Doric portico *in muris,* had a strong influence on the city's ecclesiastical architecture; at least four Baptist churches were modeled directly after it. During the Civil War the church was used as an emergency hospital for Confederate soldiers. The congregation sold the building to the Medical College of Virginia in 1928. Threatened with demolition in the 1970s, Old First Baptist has since been sympathetically renovated by Virginia Commonwealth University School of Medicine for mixed uses. *(127–168) VLR: 11/05/68; NRHP: 04/16/69.*

OLD STONE HOUSE (POE MUSEUM), *1916 East Main Street.* This modest dwelling, beset by the workaday clatter of Shockoe Valley, is the capital's only remaining colonial-era house. Its enigmatic character has inspired much speculation, some suggesting that the house is of 17th-century origin. Recent dendrochronological study, however, indicates that the house was built ca. 1754. The uneven spacing of the openings, original hall-parlor plan, and dormered gable roof are features common to mid-18th-century vernacular houses. The earliest documented reference appears in the city land tax book for 1783, which records it as the home of Samuel Ege, a flour inspector. The property was acquired by the Association for the Preservation of Virginia Antiquities in 1911 and in 1921 became part of a museum complex commemorating Edgar Allan Poe, who spent his youth in Richmond. The museum is operated by the Poe Foundation, Inc. *(127–100) VLR: 10/16/73; NRHP: 11/14/73.*

OLD TRINITY METHODIST CHURCH (NEW LIGHT BAPTIST CHURCH), *2000 East Broad Street.* A robust essay in the Italianate style, the former Trinity Methodist Church was designed by Albert L. West, a 19th-century Richmond architect. A devout Methodist, West designed church buildings not only in Richmond but for several North Carolina cities and even Yokohama, Japan. Characterized by its stuccoed walls, tiers of arched windows, and bracketed cornice, Trinity was begun in 1859, but the Civil War delayed its completion until 1866. West's remarkably tall and slender spire was not added to the entrance tower until 1875. Damaged by Hurricane Hazel, the spire was dismantled in 1955. The church originally held the city's oldest Methodist congregation. The congregation moved to a new church in 1945 and sold the building to the New Light Baptists, a black congregation which has maintained this Church Hill landmark for the past half century. *(127–401) VLR: 12/09/86; NRHP: 04/16/87.*

OREGON HILL HISTORIC DISTRICT. On a promontory above the James, Oregon Hill encompasses an intact working-class neighborhood begun in the mid–19th century. Between 1850 and 1860 local industries and population grew until Richmond was the second largest city in the South and preeminent in industrial production. In the aftermath of the war, it was the Oregon Hill workers who gave their skills to resuscitate the devastated city and restore its industries. A tight-knit community, Oregon Hill was bound together by the common desire of its residents for a better life achieved through the work of their own hands. In the 1860s and 1870s, the expanding need for laborers in riverside industries intensified development here. Still a cohesive neighborhood, Oregon Hill is characterized by unified streetscapes of mostly simple Italianate row houses but including both antebellum and later dwellings. Fifteen houses are protected by preservation easements. *(127–362) VLR: 12/11/90; NRHP: 02/05/91.*

PACE-KING HOUSE, *205 North Nineteenth Street.* Amid a cluster of old buildings in the heart of Shockoe Valley, the Pace-King house is one of the city's last grand mansions erected before the Civil War. Its generous scale and rich detailing represent a final expression of architectural fashion before the dissolution of the Old South. The Italianate-style house and its kitchen outbuilding were completed in 1860 for Charles Hill, an auctioneer and local politician. Its cast-iron veranda is an outstanding example of the ironworker's art. From 1865 to 1881 the house was owned by tobacconist and later bank president James B. Pace. A later owner was businesswoman Jane King, who operated an ice company here. The house was rescued from dereliction in 1976 by the Association for the Preservation of Virginia Antiquities. It was later sold and handsomely restored by its present owner as offices for Scope Mechanical Contractors. *(127–229) VLR: 04/20/76; NRHP: 07/30/76.*

PLANTERS NATIONAL BANK BUILDING, *1200 East Main Street.* Originally built as the State Planters Bank, this robust brick and brownstone pile in the city's financial district is a highly original expression of the Romanesque Revival. It was designed in 1893 by Charles H. Read, Jr., who fought in the battle of New Market while a Virginia Military Institute cadet. He later studied at the University of Virginia. Read contributed several other exemplary buildings to Richmond including the Union Theological Seminary quadrangle. Among the first of the grand banks to be built in Richmond, Planters exemplifies the Romanesque qualities of permanence and fortresslike protection. Rescued in the 1980s even after demolition by the state had begun, the building was carefully restored as the headquarters of the Virginia Retirement System. The project included the construction of an architecturally harmonious office wing with parking deck attached to the east side. *(127–150) VLR: 07/20/82; NRHP: 02/10/83.*

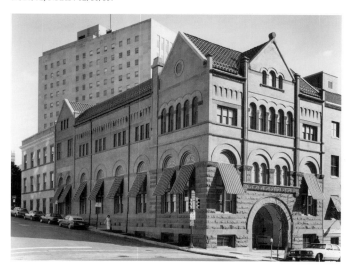

PUTNEY HOUSES, *1010–1012 East Marshall Street.* Surrounded by the stark modernity of a medical college complex, these two town houses were once part of a well-to-do residential neighborhood. Similar in their use of the Italianate style with side-hall plans, the two houses were built for Samuel Ayres in 1859. From 1862 until 1894 they were the residences of Samuel and Stephen Putney, father and son shoe manufacturers. The two-tiered cast-iron veranda on the Stephen Putney house was produced by the local Phoenix Iron Works and is the most ambitious production of domestic ironwork in a city famed for cast iron. Both houses have been restored for use as offices by the Virginia Commonwealth University School of Medicine. Fragments of painted trompe l'oeil architectural panels were discovered on the parlor walls of the Stephen Putney house during the restoration, and the scheme was faithfully reproduced. *(127–85) VLR: 11/05/68; NRHP: 06/11/69.*

REVEILLE, *4200 Cary Street Road.* This early 19th-century brick country residence was built for the Southall family on land granted in the early colonial period to the Kennon family. Its side-passage plan shows the influence of urban house types on the design of rural dwellings of the post-Revolutionary period. The house was enlarged with a wing and remodeled inside with Greek Revival woodwork ca. 1842, after its acquisition by James M. Boyd. Reveille's farmland has since been incorporated into the city and has become part of a residential area. The house was acquired by the Reveille Methodist Church in 1950 and was used first as a parsonage and later as administrative offices. Despite the loss of its rural setting, the dignified old house, now handsomely maintained as a church meeting space, stands as a reminder of the once-agrarian character of Richmond's west end. *(127–310) VLR: 10/17/78; NRHP: 02/01/79.*

RICHMOND ACADEMY OF MEDICINE, *1200 East Clay Street.* A pristine example of the Georgian Revival style, the Richmond Academy of Medicine was built in 1932 as the headquarters of an institution that traces its origins to 1820, when a group of Richmond and Manchester physicians organized the city's first medical society. The building is the physical embodiment of the unification of various factions of the area's medical profession, representing the merger of representatives of the local medical colleges and hospitals into a single professional fraternity. The Richmond architectural firm of Baskervill and Lambert planned the building to house a collection of early medical manuscripts, artworks, and medical instruments. A lecture hall and reception rooms provided space for assembly and scholarly discourse. The academy continues as an active institution, serving as a social and academic center for the area's distinguished medical community. *(127–250) VLR: 05/15/84; NRHP: 08/16/84.*

RANDOLPH SCHOOL, *300 South Randolph Street.* Randolph School is a landmark of civic pride and the desire to have first-rate public education for youth. The original portion was built in 1896. Like many late 19th-century urban public schools, the building was made an architectural showpiece. Its brick facade is embellished with pilasters and highlighted by a mansarded tower which visually dominates the neighborhood. The school was constructed to accommodate the westward expansion of Richmond's population. To meet growing demand, it was extended in 1900 and 1934. The building's original function has since been removed to more up-to-date facilities, but the structure acquired a new lease on life when it was sympathetically converted to housing in 1985. The construction of the immediately adjacent downtown expressway in the 1970s has made Randolph School a point of interest to thousands of commuters. *(127–388) VLR: 08/21/84; NRHP: 10/04/84.*

ST. ALBAN'S HALL, *300 East Main Street.* Construction of this Masonic temple, St. Alban's Hall, began two years after central Richmond burned at the end of the Civil War. Its completion marked part of the city's return to normal life. A prototype for later Masonic buildings in Richmond, the hall contained shops and a concert hall as well as Masonic meeting rooms. The commodious facility quickly became a center of postwar Richmond's social and political life. Long abandoned by the Masons, the building was sympathetically renovated for commercial use in 1982. Its tall ceilings give the building an exaggerated verticality. The stuccoed walls, pedimented windows, and rusticated corners show the influence of the Renaissance Revival or Tuscan Palazzo mode, a style popular in the North in the 1860s but rarely found in the war-ravaged South. *(127–130) VLR: 07/20/82; NRHP: 09/09/83.*

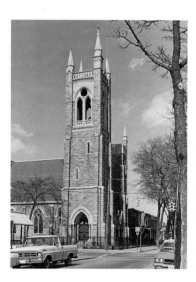

ST. ANDREW'S EPISCOPAL CHURCH COMPLEX, *Laurel and Idlewood streets.* This complex was created to serve Oregon Hill, a neighborhood populated by workers at the Tredegar Iron Works and other nearby factories. Grace Arents, a niece of tobacco magnate Maj. Lewis Ginter and heir to the Ginter fortune, was the project's sponsor. With this philanthropic gesture, Arents was following the example of Andrew Carnegie, Jane Addams, and other nationally recognized exponents of Progressive Era social conscience. Built between 1900 and 1908, the complex contains a visually dominant church designed by A. H. Ellwood of Elkhart, Ind., and a parish hall, library, and faculty residence by Noland and Baskervill of Richmond. The school building is the work of Richmond architect D. Wiley Anderson. The finely crafted stone church, one of Richmond's purest examples of the High Victorian Gothic mode, contains a splendid interior. The complex continues as a neighborhood architectural and social anchor. *(127–314) VLR: 04/17/79; NRHP: 06/22/79.*

ST. JOHN'S CHURCH HISTORIC DISTRICT. Popularly known as Church Hill, the restored neighborhood surrounding the colonial St. John's Church contains an assemblage of 19th-century domestic architecture that makes up the city's chief historic quarter. A scattering of houses was erected on Church Hill in the late 18th century, but all have disappeared. It was not until the early 19th century that building began in earnest. Growth was gradual; thus each street today presents a variety of domestic styles, all in compatible scale and materials. Because the neighborhood was primarily middle-class, its houses are restrained compared to the mansions built downtown. Church Hill's deterioration in the first half of the 20th century was checked in 1956 with the formation of the Historic Richmond Foundation, which acquired and restored many of the houses and was instrumental in having the city adopt a historic zoning ordinance in 1957. *(127–192) VLR: 06/02/70 (EXPANDED 04/17/90); NRHP: 09/15/70.*

ST. JOHN'S EPISCOPAL CHURCH, *East Broad Street at Twenty-fifth Street.* In St. John's Church on March 23, 1775, Patrick Henry delivered his "Liberty or Death" speech, sounding a clarion call for American independence before a convention of members of the Virginia General Assembly whose ranks included George Washington, Thomas Jefferson, George Mason, and Richard Henry Lee. The group met to debate

the defense of the colony from ever-increasing British oppression. The church, then the largest building in town, began as a simple rectangle, built in 1739–41 by Richard Randolph on land donated by Richmond's founder, William Byrd II. Two years before Henry's speech, an addition was made to the north side to accommodate additional seating. St. John's has been altered and enlarged several more times since its great moment in history. Buried in its picturesque old churchyard are George Wythe and Elizabeth Arnold Poe, mother of Edgar Allan Poe. *(127–13) VLR: 09/09/69; NRHP: 10/15/66; NHL: 01/20/61.*

ST. LUKE BUILDING,
900–904 St. James Street. The St. Luke Building was erected as the national headquarters of the Independent Order of St. Luke, a black benevolent society founded after the Civil War to provide guidance and financial aid to struggling freed slaves. Under the leadership of Maggie L. Walker, the pioneering black businesswoman, philanthropist, and educator, the society prospered through services that helped bridge the gap between slavery and freedom. Its many activities effectively eased the burdens of illness and death, encouraged savings and thrift, provided an outlet for inexpensive but well-made retail goods, and promoted them through its news weekly. The headquarters, the oldest black-affiliated office building in Richmond, was designed by Peter J. White and built in 1903. The building was enlarged in 1917–19 under the direction of Charles T. Russell of Virginia Union University, one of Virginia's first black architects. *(127–352) VLR: 04/21/81; NRHP: 09/16/82.*

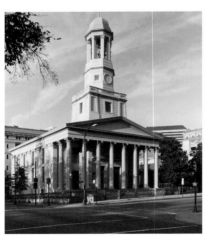

ST. PAUL'S EPISCOPAL CHURCH, *815 East Grace Street.* This finely articulated Greek Revival church was designed by Philadelphia architect Thomas S. Stewart. Completed in 1845, the temple-form building is fronted by a portico in the Greek Corinthian order, employing capitals of cast iron. A richly ornamented Greek Revival ceiling dominates the spacious interior. Except for the removal of a spire, the deepening of the apse, and the installation of stained-glass windows, several from the Tiffany Studios, the church remains little changed. Jefferson Davis, Robert E. Lee, and many Virginia governors have regularly worshiped here. It was in St. Paul's, on April 2, 1865, that President Davis received word that General Lee no longer could hold the lines at Petersburg and thus defend the capital, a message that resulted in the immediate evacuation of the Confederate government from Richmond. St. Paul's continues as one of the state's leading Episcopal parishes. *(127–14) VLR: 11/05/68; NRHP: 06/04/69.*

ST. PETER'S ROMAN CATHOLIC CHURCH, *Grace and Eighth streets.* St. Peter's was built in 1834 under the guidance of Father Timothy O'Brien and is the city's oldest Roman Catholic church. The Classical Revival building has unusually tall proportions with a facade dominated by a portico of paired Roman Doric columns. Topping the church is an octagonal belfry. Many of St. Peter's first members were Irish and Germans who helped build the James River and Kanawha Canal. Although a bishop was assigned to Richmond as early as 1829, one did not take up residence here until 1840. St. Peter's was declared the cathedral of the Diocese of Richmond the following year. Under Bishop John McGill, who came in 1850, the apse and transepts were added in 1855. St. Peter's retained cathedral status until 1906 when the Cathedral of the Sacred Heart was opened. The church continues to serve a downtown parish. *(127–15) VLR: 11/05/68; NRHP: 06/23/69.*

ST. SOPHIA HOME OF THE LITTLE SISTERS OF THE POOR (THE WARSAW), *Floyd Avenue at Harvie Street.* The former charitable hospital of the Little Sisters of the Poor is a massive and rare example for Richmond of late Victorian institutional architecture. The building is believed to incorporate the walls of Warsaw, a brick farmhouse built in 1832 as the residence of William Anderson, on whose farm a large part of the surrounding neighborhood, the present Fan District, was built. Warsaw was acquired by the Little Sisters of the Poor, a Catholic order of nuns, in 1877. Over the next two decades, it was transformed into a huge Second Empire–style building, a conspicuous symbol of ministry to the indigent in an otherwise tidy middle-class neighborhood. The nuns relocated in the late 1970s, and the complex was sold and remodeled into luxury condominiums known as The Warsaw. *(127–319) VLR: 02/19/80; NRHP: 05/07/80.*

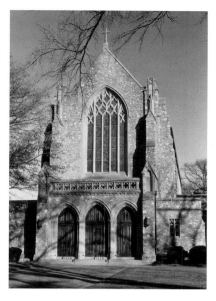

ST. STEPHEN'S EPISCOPAL CHURCH, *6004 Three Chopt Road.* Designed by Frank E. Watson of Philadelphia and initially completed in 1928, St. Stephen's illustrates in its form, materials, and ornamentation the exemplary scholarship and competence inherent in America's works of the Late Gothic Revival. Built with rubblestone walls pierced by tall, pointed windows, the long, narrow structure is an adaptation of an Early English–style parish church. Under the direction of Philip H. Frohman, architect of the Washington Cathedral, the church was lengthened one bay and received a new facade in the Decorated style in 1950. St. Stephen's thus grew in size and with stylistic variation much as its medieval models did. Among its appointments is a collection of stained-glass windows by the Willet, D'Ascenzo, and J. & R. Lamb studios. A polychromed triptych reredos, designed by Watson and executed by the woodcarvers of Oberammergau, Germany, embellishes the sanctuary. *(127–346) VLR: 01/20/81.*

SHOCKOE HILL CEMETERY, *Hospital Street at Second Street.* The rapid growth that followed Richmond's designation as the state capital quickly overwhelmed available burial space. The city recognized the need for a public cemetery and purchased a 28.5-acre parcel on Shockoe Hill. Richard Young, the city surveyor, laid out the new cemetery in 1824. Surrounded by a tall brick wall, the cemetery is subdivided by four roads and twenty-six grassy walkways. The straight roads and paths and the regular layout of plots contrast with the romantic informality that characterized many later municipal cemeteries. Shockoe is endowed with a rich collection of 19th-century funerary sculpture, with many works signed by local stonemasons. Among the 36,000 interments are Chief Justice John Marshall; engineer Claudius Crozet; Dr. William Foushee, Richmond's first mayor; and Union spy Elizabeth Van Lew. A rough granite boulder marks the graves of several hundred soldiers, both Confederate and Union. *(127–389) VLR: 04/28/95; NRHP: 07/07/95.*

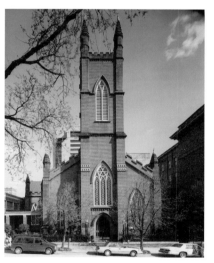

SECOND PRESBYTERIAN CHURCH, *5 North Fifth Street.* In its endeavor to build a church that would be "the most symmetrical and pleasing to an educated eye," the congregation of Second Presbyterian authorized a committee to call on the eminent Brooklyn architect Minard Lafever. A set of plans was purchased, and the church was completed in 1848. The resulting work, Virginia's only Lafever building, is a demonstration of the strength and inspirational quality of the Gothic Revival. The restrained exterior, dominated by a pinnacled tower, contrasts with the lofty interior and its magnificent hammerbeam ceiling. The church was later expanded with the addition of transepts consistent with Lafever's work. A rear chapel served as a hospital in the Civil War and was redesigned in the early 20th century by William C. Noland. The Rev. Dr. Moses Drury Hoge, a renowned 19th-century preacher, was pastor of Second Presbyterian from its founding in 1845 until his death in 1899. *(127–16) VLR: 11/16/71; NRHP: 03/29/72.*

SHOCKOE SLIP HISTORIC DISTRICT. Adjacent to Richmond's financial district, this compact quarter consists primarily of three- and four-story Italianate brick commercial structures, many with cast-iron architectural trim. The area has served as a neighborhood of warehouses, tobacco storage buildings, and wholesale outlets since the 1780s. Leveled by the Evacuation Fire of 1865, it was quickly rebuilt. The heart of the district is a trapezoidal stone-paved piazza known as Shockoe Slip, an early connection between Main Street and the James River and Kanawha Canal. Highlighting the piazza is an ornamental fountain donated as a watering spot for horses. The area declined after World War II, but steady rehabilitation since 1970 has transformed Shockoe Slip's buildings into restaurants, shops, offices, and apartments. Protected by a city historic designation, Shockoe Slip continues to play an important role in the city's business and social life. *(127–219) VLR: 11/16/71 (EXPANDED 07/20/82); NRHP: 03/29/72.*

SHOCKOE VALLEY AND TOBACCO ROW HISTORIC DISTRICT. Named for the creek that served as the western boundary of Richmond's original settlement and for the row of tobacco warehouses and factories that constitutes its industrial quarter, this brawny historic district encompasses the area of the city's earliest residential, commercial, and manufacturing activity. Covering approximately 129 acres and containing over 500 structures, the district is an eclectic jumble of building styles, types, and periods from the colonial vernacular to high-style antebellum and 20th-century industrial. The streets follow the original grid laid out by William Byrd in 1739. The heart of the district is the Seventeenth Street Market, a farmer's market in use since the late 18th century. Increasing rehabilitation activity is assuring the district a future role in the life of the city. Tobacco Row, one of the South's most impressive industrial complexes, is undergoing long-term conversion into housing. *(127–344) VLR: 07/21/81; NRHP: 02/24/83.*

SIXTH MOUNT ZION BAPTIST CHURCH, *14 West Duval Street.* The Rev. John Jasper, born a slave in Fluvanna County on July 4, 1812, organized the Sixth Mount Zion Baptist Church congregation in 1867 in a former Confederate stable on Brown's Island. A nationally celebrated preacher, Jasper was famed for the 1879 sermon "De Sun do Move," which he later delivered more than 250 times, once before the Virginia General Assembly. In 1869 the congregation moved to its present site on Duval Street in Jackson Ward. The core of the present church was begun in 1887 by George Boyd, an Afro-American builder. It was remodeled and extended by Charles T. Russell, one of the first Afro-American architects to maintain an architectural practice in Virginia. Russell employed a modified Romanesque style for the remodeling. Jasper's fame helped spare the church in 1956 from threatened demolition for the construction of the Richmond-Petersburg Turnpike (Interstate 95). *(127–472) VLR: 06/19/96; NRHP: 12/16/96.*

SPRINGFIELD SCHOOL, *608 North Twenty-sixth Street.* Built in 1913, the Springfield School was designed by the Richmond firm of Carneal and Johnston, which has provided designs for scores of public buildings during its long and active career. Faced with Richmond granite, the exterior is in a modified Gothic style similar to that used by the firm for its buildings at Virginia Tech. A two-room school was operating on this site as early as 1869. It was replaced by a brick building in 1880 that was later demolished to make room for the present school. In 1948 it was converted from a school for whites to one for black children, the first public school for blacks in the Church Hill neighborhood. At that time the name was changed to Bowler School in honor of J. Andrew Bowler, a civic leader and teacher. The school was eventually closed but in 1996–97 underwent conversion to apartments for low-income residents. *(127–832) VLR: 12/11/91; NRHP: 08/24/92.*

STEAMER COMPANY NO. 5, *200 West Marshall Street.* With its demioctagonal projections, Steamer Company No. 5 is an architectural work ingeniously adapted to an irregular site. The Italianate structure was built in 1883 to continue the firefighting and police station functions begun in 1849 in a earlier building at this intersection in the Jackson Ward neighborhood. The building's configuration and fabric illustrate the transition from horse-drawn to motorized equipment. Its name also suggests a certain archaic quality, referring to the days when steam was required to produce water pressure in vehicles. A fire-fighting tradition of 119 years at this site was ended in 1968 when a new firehouse was built nearby. The building, the best preserved of Richmond's early firehouses, was sold into private ownership in 1976 and has since been developed as the Virginia Fire and Police Museum. *(127–370) VLR: 10/19/94; NRHP: 02/08/95.*

STEARNS BLOCK, *1011 East Main Street.* The cast-iron architecture of the Stearns Block is Richmond's best surviving example of the architectural exuberance that could be achieved with an otherwise commonplace material. Constructed to replace buildings destroyed in the Evacuation Fire, this and numerous other ironfronts gave downtown Richmond a rich, dignified architecture by the quickest and least-expensive means. Inspired by Venetian Renaissance palaces, most of America's ironfronts are characterized by windows framed with delicate classical elements and a deep ornamented cornice topping the whole. The building was completed in 1869 for Richmond businessman Franklin Stearns, once Virginia's largest landowner. The ironwork was designed by architect George H. Johnson, who moved to America from England in 1851 and worked with the Baltimore foundry of Hayward, Bartlett & Co. on many of Richmond's iron facades. The four buildings were combined into a single commercial structure known as "The Ironfronts" in a 1974 renovation. *(127–23) VLR: 12/02/69; NRHP: 02/26/70.*

STONEWALL JACKSON SCHOOL, *1520 West Main Street.* The pride with which public education was once regarded is evident in this forthright Victorian structure. Originally named the West End School, it was built in 1886–87 to serve Richmond's westward expansion. The school's construction marked the end of a turbulent period in the history of the city's public education when considerable controversy surrounded the establishment of free public schooling for both races. The large scale and self-assured Italianate design made the school a prominent visual element of the neighborhood. Distinctive features are the richly detailed porticoes sheltering the principal entrances. The building served its original purpose for over eighty years and was closed when it could no longer meet modern standards. Since sold to developers, it has been sympathetically converted to office and restaurant use. A 1990 fire caused significant damage, but the building was completely restored. *(127–376) VLR: 03/20/84; NRHP: 05/03/84.*

STEWART-LEE HOUSE, *707 East Franklin Street.* This town house briefly served as the home of Robert E. Lee after the surrender at Appomattox. Almost the sole survivor of the scores of Greek Revival dwellings that once lined the streets of downtown Richmond, 707 East Franklin Street was begun in 1844 for Norman Stewart, a tobacco merchant from Rothesay, Scotland. After the outbreak of the Civil War, Stewart's nephew, John Stewart, rented the house to Gen. Custis Lee to serve as a bachelor officers' quarters. In 1864 the house was given over to Robert E. Lee's wife and daughters, left homeless after the federal government confiscated Arlington. In June 1865 Lee, seeking privacy after years of war, moved his family from here to Powhatan County. The Stewart family presented the house to the Virginia Historical Society in 1893 for its headquarters. The building is now owned by the Historic Richmond Foundation. *(127–64) VLR: 01/18/72; NRHP: 05/05/72.*

TAYLOR FARM, *4012 Walmsley Boulevard.* Surrounded by a residential development in suburban south Richmond, the Taylor farm forms a time capsule illustrating a once-typical rural homestead. Owned by the Aubrey Taylor family since 1917, the farm is a three-acre parcel, the core of a larger farmstead established shortly after the Civil War. The simple frame dwelling was built in stages beginning about 1870 for the family of blacksmith Joseph T. Williams. It features an unusual gable-fronted, two-room-plan main block with rear and side wings. Other buildings, all dating to the early 20th century, include a garage, storage shed, barn, lumber shed, and corncrib. Decorative landscape elements surrounding the house, designed by lifelong resident and amateur gardener Olin Taylor, date largely from the 1930s. They include a rock-walled flower garden, an ornamental fish pool, rubblestone retaining walls, and shingled entry gates, all amid ornamental shade trees. *(127–667) VLR: 06/19/90; NRHP: 01/24/91.*

THIRD STREET BETHEL AFRICAN METHODIST EPISCOPAL CHURCH, *616 North Third Street.* A landmark of the Jackson Ward Historic District, Third Street Bethel A.M.E. Church was built ca. 1857 to house one of Virginia's first congregations to join the African Methodist Episcopal denomination. The building is among the very few antebellum black churches remaining in the country. Richmond before the Civil War boasted a large free Afro-American population; thus an independent black congregation, while rare, was not extraordinary. To conform with pre–Civil War Virginia law, the church's first pastor, G. W. Nolley, was white. In 1867 the Virginia Conference of the African Methodist Episcopal Church was organized here. The congregation prospered, and in 1875 the exterior of the originally plain brick church was embellished with a new facade incorporating brick towers and Gothic windows. The building was further remodeled in 1914 under the direction of architect Carl Ruehrmund. *(127–274) VLR: 02/18/75; NRHP: 06/05/75.*

TREDEGAR IRON WORKS, *500 Tredegar Street.* This industrial complex was the leading ordnance foundry of the Confederacy. Tredegar maintained wartime production despite severe shortages of raw materials, skilled labor, and effective transportation. It enabled the South to sustain itself as a viable war machine for four years. Chartered in 1837 and named for the ironworks at Tredegar in Wales, Tredegar's rise to preeminence began in 1841 when Joseph Reid Anderson took over the company. Known as the "Ironmaker to the Confederacy," Anderson guided the firm through the war and to prosperity in the following decades. Tredegar eventually declined to a small local concern and left the site in 1958. The derelict complex was then acquired by Ethyl Corporation, which undertook a restoration of the complex's antebellum buildings as a civic amenity. Tredegar's principal structure is the gable-roofed gun foundry where most of the Confederate armaments were produced. *(127–186) VLR: 01/05/71; NRHP: 07/02/71; NHL: 12/22/77.*

UNION THEOLOGICAL SEMINARY QUADRANGLE, *3401 Brook Road.* Begun in 1896, the seminary complex is a collection of dark red brick High Victorian Gothic, Late Gothic Revival, and Queen Anne buildings. The ground plan and the majority of the buildings were designed by Richmond architect Charles H. Read, Jr. Later works were designed by Charles K. Bryant and Baskervill and Lambert, the latter completing the quadrangle in 1921 with Schauffler Hall, a Late Gothic Revival edifice, portions of which were incorporated into a new library erected in 1997. The whole forms a coherent expression of the dignity and style accorded academic campuses at the turn of the century. Founded in 1812 at Hampden-Sydney College as a Presbyterian theological school, the seminary relocated in Richmond in 1896 on a twelve-acre site donated by Richmond tobacconist Maj. Lewis Ginter. The seminary has since played a leading role in religious education in the South. *(127–316) VLR: 09/16/82; NRHP: 04/14/83.*

THOMAS JEFFERSON HIGH SCHOOL, *4100 West Grace Street.* A striking contrast to the spiritless architecture of today's public schools, Thomas Jefferson High School is a celebration of education, a building redolent of civic pride. The last and largest Richmond school building designed by Charles M. Robinson, supervising architect of the Richmond Board of Public Instruction, Thomas Jefferson is also his masterpiece. An Art Deco vocabulary is employed for the decoration of the elevations, which themselves have massing of classical monumentality. The detailing, particularly the sculptured busts of the central pavilion, is of the highest quality. Proclaimed to be the city's largest and most modern public school when it opened in 1930, the building was designed to accommodate 2,000 pupils and boasted a planetarium. Still an active school, Thomas Jefferson is a demonstration of the lasting benefits of a successful fusion of architectural quality and functional planning. *(127–431) VLR: 10/20/93; NRHP: 12/23/93.*

U.S. CUSTOMS HOUSE (U.S. COURTHOUSE BUILD-ING), *1000 East Main Street.* The two-story core of Richmond's former U.S. Customs House was designed by Boston architect Ammi B. Young, who as supervising architect of the U.S. Treasury Department supplied designs for numerous customshouses throughout the country. Completed in 1858 under the direction of local architect Albert Lybrock, the building was taken over by the Confederacy in 1861 to house both the treasury and the offices of President Jefferson Davis. The gray granite structure remarkably escaped damage during the Evacuation Fire of 1865. On May 13, 1867, Davis was brought here to be indicted for treason, but the indictment was dismissed in 1868. Although the building has been greatly enlarged over the years, Young's distinctive Tuscan Palazzo style has been maintained. Forming a backdrop for Capitol Square, it now houses the U.S. District Court and U.S. Court of Appeals for the Fourth Circuit. *(127–170) VLR: 11/05/68; NRHP: 06/04/69.*

VIRGINIA HOUSE, *4301 Sulgrave Road.* A handsomely crafted expression of the American Country House movement, Virginia House symbolizes the predilection of the Commonwealth's upper classes for identifying themselves with their English heritage. The estate was the creation of diplomat Alexander W. Weddell and his wife Virginia. The Tudor-style mansion is built largely of architectural elements from England's Warwick Priory, a late medieval structure later modified with distinctive Flemish gables. The Weddells purchased the ruined priory in 1925 and had portions of it shipped to Richmond where architect Henry Grant Morse incorporated them into his design for their Windsor Farms residence, completed in 1928. A Renaissance-style loggia by William Lawrence Bottomley was added in 1945. The extensive gardens, developed between 1927 and 1940, are the masterpiece of Richmond landscape architect Charles F. Gillette. The Weddells bequeathed the estate to the Virginia Historical Society, which has exhibited it since their deaths in 1948. *(127–255) VLR: 06/20/89; NRHP: 06/13/90.*

THE VIRGINIA BUILDING, *East Main and Fifth streets.* Designed by the Richmond firm of Noland and Baskervill, The Virginia was erected in 1906 as the Richmond headquarters of the Virginia State Insurance Company and stands as an individualized example of early 20th-century commercial classicism. In addition to housing the city's second-largest insurance company and other offices, the building accommodated prestige apartments, a combination of uses then unique in Richmond but one that did not catch on. Located on fashionable Fifth Street, the structure was designed to complement the neighborhood through a restrained and inventive treatment of the exterior which made use of a curved facade, rusticated brickwork, and subtle spacing of bays. In addition to offices, the building now houses facilities for the adjacent Second Presbyterian Church. *(127–215) VLR: 12/14/82; NRHP: 02/10/83.*

VIRGINIA STATE CAPITOL, *Capitol Square.* Virginia's famed Capitol was designed by Thomas Jefferson with the assistance of the French architect Charles Louis Clérisseau. Inspired by the Maison Carrée, a Roman temple in Nîmes, France, which Jefferson later visited, the building marks the beginning of America's Classical Revival movement. Begun in 1785, the Capitol became the home of the General Assembly of Virginia after the removal of the seat of government from Williamsburg. The building served as the meeting place of the Confederate Congress during the Civil War. Wings and hyphens designed by a team of architects headed by J. Kevan Peebles and William C. Noland were added in 1906 to provide larger chambers. Still in use, the Capitol is the home of the oldest legislative assembly in the Western Hemisphere. The Capitol Square grounds were laid out in the 1850s by Philadelphia landscape architect John Notman. *(127–02) VLR: 11/05/68; NRHP: 10/15/66; NHL: 12/19/60.*

VIRGINIA TRUST COMPANY BUILDING, *815 East Main Street.* Completed in 1921 as the headquarters of the Virginia Trust Company, this bank building is a salient example of the Neoclassical Revival, an architectural style of the early 20th century directly inspired by the grandiose works of ancient Rome. The white granite facade is reminiscent of a Roman triumphal arch, and the banking room is dominated by a gilded coffered ceiling heavily encrusted with classical ornamentation. The bank was designed by Alfred Charles Bossom, an Englishman who maintained a New York practice from 1903 to 1926 and then returned to Britain for a political career which culminated in 1960 by his being made a life peer. This work is perhaps the most elegant of the some half-dozen buildings Bossom designed for Richmond and is among the best-preserved bank buildings of its style and period in the state. *(127–249) VLR: 02/15/77; NRHP: 11/07/77.*

VIRGINIA UNION UNIVERSITY, *North Lombardy Street and Brook Road.* The history of Virginia Union University exemplifies the efforts to bring higher education to southern blacks following the Civil War. Because literacy among former slaves was often limited to black clergymen, seminaries and missionary societies frequently formed the kernels for black colleges. Virginia Union began in 1896 through the merger of Richmond Theological Seminary and Wayland Seminary of Washington, D.C. Further mergers have transformed the school into a leading institution dedicated to higher education primarily for blacks, though the school is now racially integrated. The main complex of Virginia Union is a late Victorian collegiate grouping in the Romanesque Revival style. The gray granite dormitories, classroom buildings, chapel, president's house, and power plant, each with its own massing and lively silhouette, were designed by Washington architect John H. Coxhead. *(127–354) VLR: 06/16/81; NRHP: 07/26/82.*

VIRGINIA WAR MEMORIAL CARILLON, *Byrd Park.* Popularly known simply as the Carillon, Virginia's War Memorial reflects the patriotic fervor of the 1920s. It was sponsored by the Commonwealth of Virginia to commemorate the "patriotism and valor of the soldiers, sailors, marines, and women from Virginia" who served in World War I. Although a commission to study a design and site was formed as early as 1922, public campaigns altered the initial proposal and delayed completion of the project until 1932. The resulting edifice, designed by the nationally prominent Ralph Adams Cram of the Boston firm of Cram and Ferguson, is a brilliant interpretation of the Italian *campanile* in Georgian classicism. As stated at the time, the style was chosen expressly because the "Commonwealth of Virginia is the great southern exponent of that noble Colonial architecture." Its bells were originally intended to ring out patriotic tunes familiar to those whom the structure memorialized. *(127–387) VLR: 08/21/84; NRHP: 10/04/84.*

MAGGIE L. WALKER HOUSE, *110 East Leigh Street.* Maggie Lena Mitchell Walker (1867–1934), daughter of a former slave, rose by her work with a black fraternal order to become the first American woman to establish and head a bank. In addition to serving as president of the St. Luke Penny Savings Bank, now the Consolidated Bank and Trust Company—the oldest black-owned bank in continuous use in the country—Mrs. Walker was active in many civic and charitable  causes. She was founder and president of the Richmond Council of Colored Women and employed her fund-raising talents to aid improved health care for blacks. In 1904 she purchased a ca. 1883 Italianate town house in Jackson Ward and later enlarged it. The house is preserved and furnished exactly as she left it and has been acquired by the National Park Service for exhibition as a National Historic Site. *(127–275) VLR: 04/15/75; NRHP: 05/12/75; NHL: 05/15/75.*

WEISIGER-CARROLL HOUSE, *2804 Bainbridge Street.* A landmark of early Manchester, a community on the south bank of the James annexed by Richmond in 1910, this raised cottage is a rare surviving example of Federal-period urban vernacular architecture. John Mayo, Manchester's leading entrepreneur, originally owned the land on which the house stands. Mayo sold the tract in 1816 to Richard Kendall Weisiger, who probably built the house sometime after that date. The property passed by marriage to John A. Carroll, an Irish Catholic who assisted in founding Manchester's Sacred Heart Catholic Church. The house served as a Confederate hospital during the Civil War, and more than 100 Confederate soldiers who died here lie buried in an adjacent cemetery. The house remains surprisingly unaltered, preserving original woodwork including an unusually sophisticated mantel. *(127–850) VLR: 03/10/94; NRHP: 05/19/94; BHR EASEMENT.*

WEST FRANKLIN STREET HISTORIC DISTRICT. An 1867 annexation brought West Franklin Street to Lombardy Street into the city limits, and grand town houses soon went up. The blocks from Monroe Park to Monument Avenue retain a colorful progression of architectural styles, including Second Empire, Italianate, Romanesque, Queen Anne, and Georgian Revival, with an underlying harmony from uniform scale and quality of design. Individually outstanding houses are the 1888 Romanesque Revival Ginter mansion (901 West Franklin), designed by Harvey L. Page for tobacco magnate Maj. Lewis Ginter, and the opulent 1906 Scott-Bocock house (909 West Franklin), by Noland and Baskervill. The district's oldest house is the Ritter-Hickock house (821 West Franklin), built ca. 1850. The most architecturally individual town house is the eclectic Millhiser house (916 West Franklin), a Romanesque–Queen Anne confection designed by William M. Poindexter. Many of the houses are now part of Virginia Commonwealth University. *(127–228) VLR: 03/21/72; NRHP: 09/14/72.*

WEST OF THE BOULEVARD HISTORIC DISTRICT. Taking its name from its eastern boundary, this extensive, primarily residential neighborhood encompasses some sixty-nine blocks and over 1,700 contributing buildings. Laid out on level fields of Henrico County farmland, the district developed rapidly from 1895 to 1943, a period of intense economic growth. The straight, tree-shaded streets are lined mainly with attached two-story brick town houses, most of which have front porches. Great variety is achieved within this formula: styles include Tudor, Craftsman, and Mediterranean, although modified Georgian predominates. Interspersed among the mostly middle-class houses are a number of distinctly Richmond three-story apartment blocks with galleried porticoes. The majority of buildings date from 1910 to 1930, when real estate corporations and building firms such as Davis Brothers, Inc., and Muhleman and Kayhoe began developing whole blocks. Several churches and schools highlight the district. *(127–742) VLR: 12/08/93; NRHP: 03/07/94.*

WHITE HOUSE OF THE CONFEDERACY, *1201 East Clay Street.* Built in 1818 for Dr. John Brockenbrough, this stately mansion served as the official residence of Confederate president Jefferson Davis from 1861 to 1865. It was seized by Union forces on April 3, 1865, visited briefly by Abraham Lincoln the following day, and held by the U.S. government until 1870 when it became a public school. In 1893 it was acquired by the Confederate Memorial Literary Society and was made into a museum of Confederate memorabilia now known as the Museum of the Confederacy. Some sources attribute the original two-story design to Robert Mills, but evidence is ambiguous. A third story and rococo-style interior details were added in 1857. The interior was gutted in 1894 when the building was made fireproof, but most original trim was saved and reinstalled. A 1980s restoration has recaptured the wartime mid-Victorian elegance of the principal rooms. *(127–115) VLR: 09/09/69: NRHP: 10/15/66; NHL: 12/19/60.*

WICKHAM-VALENTINE HOUSE (VALENTINE MU-SEUM), *1015 East Clay Street.* This nationally significant work of Federal architecture was designed by Alexander Parris with advice from Benjamin Henry Latrobe. Parris, a native of Portland, Maine, moved to Richmond ca. 1811 where he planned several houses, including this house for Richmond lawyer John Wickham. Completed in 1812, Wickham's house has an elegantly restrained neoclassical exterior. Inside is a resplendent suite of reception rooms arranged around a circular hall containing a graceful curved stair. Each room boasts remarkable long-hidden painted wall decorations carefully uncovered and conserved in a comprehensive restoration begun in the 1980s. Mann Valentine II purchased the house in 1882 and filled it with his collection of art, Indian artifacts, and historic objects. In 1892 he left the property and collections to serve as a museum of Richmond history and culture known today as the Valentine Museum and since expanded into adjacent historic buildings. *(127–20) VLR: 11/05/68; NRHP: 06/11/69; NHL: 11/11/71.*

WILTON, *South Wilton Road.* The high-style Georgian mansion built in 1750–53 for William Randolph III originally stood on a site overlooking the James River in eastern Henrico County, some fifteen miles east of its present location. Because of the threatened industrial development of its surroundings, the National Society of Colonial Dames in America purchased the house in 1933 and had it dismantled and carefully reerected on a new site overlooking the James in Richmond's west end. The accuracy of the rebuilding preserved the integrity of the house as an architectural landmark. With its regular five-bay facades and geometric proportions, Wilton is a superb essay in colonial design. Every room is fully paneled, and its main stair, with its spiral-carved balusters, shows colonial artistry and craftsmanship at their best. Wilton now serves as a museum of colonial architecture and decorative arts. *(127–141) VLR: 10/21/75; NRHP: 04/30/76.*

JOSEPH P. WINSTON HOUSE, *103 East Grace Street.* The cheerfully decorous flavor that late 19th-century affluent Americans required for their houses is exhibited in this narrow Richmond town house, a remnant of a formerly residential neighborhood. It was completed in 1874 for Joseph P. Winston, a wholesale grocer. Built at a time when elaborate architectural elements were popularized in builders' catalogs, most of the details used here, including the cornice, doors, moldings, mantels, and balusters, were stock materials

available from local distributors or manufacturers. Although these pieces were mass-produced, their quality was in keeping with the period's high standards of craftsmanship. A conspicuous feature is the cast-iron front porch, which employs patterns found in no other of Richmond's many iron porches. Also lending character is the ogee mansard roof sheathed in rounded slates. The house has been sympathetically restored for office use. *(127–222) VLR: 02/21/78; NRHP: 06/11/79.*

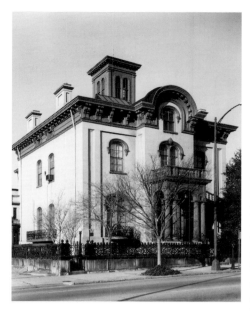

THE WOMAN'S CLUB (BOLLING HAXALL HOUSE), *211 East Franklin Street.* A foremost example of the Italian Villa style, this Franklin Street mansion was completed in 1858 for Bolling Haxall, a prosperous mill-owner and president of the Old Dominion Iron and Nail Works. The design is attributed to architect William Percival who listed Bolling Haxall as a reference. The builders were John and George Gibson. With its roof topped by a square cupola, and its front accented by some of the city's most elaborate cast-iron railings, the house is a striking downtown landmark. The stately interior is highlighted by boldly molded woodwork, a spiral stair, and carved marble mantels. The Woman's Club, founded in 1894 for the serious education of women, purchased the house in 1900 for its permanent headquarters. The club, along with the associated Bolling Haxall House Foundation, maintains the house as a community resource for a variety of cultural and educational programs. The club added an auditorium in 1915. *(127–33) VLR: 11/16/71; NRHP: 03/16/72.*

WOODWARD HOUSE, *3017 Williamsburg Avenue.* John Woodward, captain of the sloop *Rachell* and other ships operating out of the nearby port of Rocketts, occupied this wood-frame dwelling in the first two decades of the 19th century. The house is the only remaining building of the dockside neighborhood where ship captains and sailors, harbormasters and tobacco inspectors, tavern keepers and draymen, and assorted craftsmen and laborers once lived and worked. Much evolved and enlarged over the years, the house began before 1780 as a modest one-room cottage. Its present appearance was achieved by 1829 when the front two-and-a-half-story portion was added. Captain Woodward's house was spared a proposed demolition in 1974 and was acquired by the Historic Richmond Foundation. It has since been sold and restored as a private residence. *(127–119) VLR: 05/21/74; NRHP: 06/19/74.*

YWCA BUILDING, *6 North Fifth Street.* Richmond's YWCA was organized in 1887 out of concern for the welfare for the city's growing number of working women. Inspired by the Social Gospel philosophy of the Progressive Era, the Richmond YWCA was the first branch of the association in the South. The stated object of the Richmond branch was to "promote the spiritual and temporal welfare of indigent and dependent women . . . and young women as must rely on their own exertions for a livelihood." The effort produced impressive results. In 1914 the Richmond YWCA moved into a handsome new facility, a Renaissance-style structure designed by the local firm of Noland and Baskervill. Offering the city's only swimming pool exclusively for women, the building also was equipped with a gymnasium, library, cafeteria, and bedrooms. The YWCA continues as a social service organization for women and their families. *(127–300) VLR: 03/20/84; NRHP: 05/03/84.*

RICHMOND COUNTY

Along the Rappahannock River side of the Northern Neck, Richmond County was named for either the borough of Richmond in Surrey County, England, or the duke of Richmond. It was formed from the extinct Rappahannock County in 1692. Its county seat is Warsaw.

FARNHAM CHURCH, *Farnham.* Farnham Church has survived abandonment, wars, and fire. Dominating its tiny crossroads settlement, the church was built ca. 1737 to replace a mid-17th-century church. The church originally had a hipped roof covering its Latin-cross plan. Its early parishioners included the Carters of Sabine Hall and the Tayloes of Mount Airy. It was left vacant after the disestablishment and was riddled with bullets in a skirmish during the War of 1812. Federal troops used it to stable horses during the Civil War. Restored to service, it was gutted by fire in 1888 and stood a roofless ruin until it was again restored in 1922. The Flemish bond brick walls, enriched with glazed headers and rubbed-brick corners and jambs, are the only original features remaining. Their superior quality is a signal of the wealth and influence of the colonial-period parish. *(79–14) VLR: 09/19/72; NRHP: 08/14/73.*

GROVE MOUNT, *Warsaw vicinity.* Proudly placed atop a high ridge with a sweeping view of the Rappahannock River valley, this frame plantation house was built between 1780 and 1800 for Robert Mitchell and his wife, Priscilla Carter Mitchell. Mitchell was a planter, sheriff, and justice of Richmond County. His wife was a daughter of Robert ("Councillor") Carter of Nomini Hall and sister of George Carter of Oatlands. With its hipped roof and carefully proportioned five-bay facade, the exterior maintains the traditional restrained Georgian organization of colonial mansions. The opposite side departs slightly from the formula with its projecting ell. The similarity of the interior woodwork to that formerly in nearby Menokin, especially the stair railing with its diagonally set balusters, strongly suggests common joiners. On the grounds are an 18th-century dairy and remnants of an early terraced garden. *(79–50) VLR: 12/12/89; NRHP: 01/03/91; BHR EASEMENT.*

INDIAN BANKS, *Simonson.* This compact plantation house stands on land patented by Thomas Glascock in 1652. Traditionally dated to 1699, the house may have been built in 1728 for Capt. William Glascock and his wife, Esther Ball Glascock, second cousin of George Washington. Indian Banks is on the site of an Indian village visited by Capt. John Smith in 1608. The diminished proportions, tall hipped roof, and comparatively large windows give the L-shaped house a distinctly English flavor, one more Queen Anne than Georgian. The scrolled soffit of the jack arch above the main entrance, a common feature in England, is one of only two known Virginia examples. Much of the original interior woodwork disappeared, but a closed-string stair with turned balusters, a second-floor fireplace surround, several doors, and window frames with paneled window seats survive from the original construction. A one-story colonial-style wing was added in 1975. *(79–09)* VLR: 01/21/75; NRHP: 03/20/80.

LINDEN FARM, *Farnham.* The earliest portion of this vernacular farmhouse was erected ca. 1700, making it perhaps the oldest dwelling on the Northern Neck. Surviving in a remarkably good state of preservation, the house has massive asymmetrical chimney stacks, a closed-string provincial Jacobean stair, and some original riven clapboard sheathing. Its tilted false-plate framing is an early form of Virginia timber construction. Also preserved here is rare surviving evidence of a sliding casement window, a window type once common in early vernacular houses. The house was probably built for Andrew Dew, Jr. The Dew family was established in the Farnham area by 1661. The house was lengthened by an addition on the north end ca. 1725–35. Stewardship by the present owners has protected the special character of this important architectural document. *(79–10)* VLR: 09/21/76; NRHP: 04/13/77.

MENOKIN, *Warsaw vicinity.* Menokin was the home of Francis Lightfoot Lee, colonial statesman and patriot and a signer of the Declaration of Independence. Small but unusually formal with its stuccoed walls and dark stone trim, the house was commissioned in 1769 by Lee's father-in-law, John Tayloe of Mount Airy, and was presented upon completion around 1775 to Lee and his bride Rebecca as a wedding present. The original architectural drawings (unsigned) survive in the Tayloe papers at the Virginia Historical Society. The house was abandoned in the 1940s, and the woodwork was removed in the 1960s to protect it from theft. In 1995 the ruins, original woodwork, and 500 acres of the original plantation were presented by T. Edgar Omohundro to the Menokin Foundation to be used as a field school for architectural conservation and archaeological study. Plans call for the phased reconstruction of the house. *(79–11)* VLR: 11/05/68; NRHP: 10/01/69; NHL: 11/11/71; BHR EASEMENT.

MOUNT AIRY, *Warsaw vicinity.* Dramatically set on a plateau above the broad bottomlands and marshes of the Rappahannock River, this five-part neo-Palladian plantation house is the most architecturally sophisticated of Virginia's surviving colonial mansions. It was built in 1748–58 by the wealthy planter John Tayloe II to replace an earlier house. The designer is unknown, but the stone facades are adapted from a design in James Gibbs's *Book of Architecture* (1728). In 1762 Tayloe employed the architect and joiner William Buckland to finish Mount Airy's interior. Buckland's work, believed to have been exceptionally rich, was destroyed when the house burned in 1844. The interior was rebuilt in a plain Greek Revival style. The park on the land side and the garden terrace on the river side are important remnants of colonial landscaping. Various colonial outbuildings complete the plantation image. Mount Airy remains the home of the Tayloe family. *(79–13)* VLR: 09/09/69; NRHP: 10/15/66; NHL: 10/09/60; BHR EASEMENT.

RICHMOND COUNTY COURTHOUSE, *Warsaw.* Many of Virginia's colonial courthouses had arcaded fronts, but Richmond County's courthouse was built with the unusual scheme of four-bay arcades along its two sides. Each arcade was supplemented with two blind arches to give the appearance of six bays. The building dates from 1748 when Landon Carter won the commission for a new brick courthouse. The arcades were filled with windows when the building was extensively remodeled in 1877 under the direction of Baltimore architect T. Buckler Ghequiere. Ghequiere apparently admired the structure, for he published a detailed description of its original appearance in *American Architect and Building News,* June 23, 1877. The courthouse remains in use and is the town of Warsaw's principal historic landmark. Next door is the colonial clerk's office. The citizens of the county expressed their patriotic sentiments here in June 1774 when they adopted resolutions against taxation without representation. *(321–04) VLR: 08/15/72; NRHP: 12/05/72.*

SABINE HALL, *Warsaw vicinity.* Robert ("King") Carter's three sons each built a Georgian mansion on a plantation given to them by their father. Of the three, only Sabine Hall, the ca. 1738–42 home of Landon Carter, survives. Still owned by Carter's descendants, the architecturally formal mansion was endowed with the requisite geometric proportions and fine brickwork and was enriched with rusticated sandstone center bays. A ca. 1829 remodeling resulted in the present window sash, the north portico, and the lowering of the hipped roof. The wings are also later alterations, although the southeast wing incorporates an early dependency. The stately paneled hall is one of the country's finest colonial rooms. The carved walnut stair, ascending in a lateral passage, likewise is one of the finest of the period. Sabine Hall's terraced garden, which retains its original layout, is an important example of colonial-period formal landscaping. *(79–15) VLR: 05/13/69; NRHP: 11/17/71; NHL: 04/15/70; BHR EASEMENTS.*

WOODFORD, *Sharps vicinity.* Woodford is an example of 18th-century Virginia's transitional vernacular architecture, combining features of the simple cottages of early colonial times with more formal, symmetrical qualities of the Georgian style. The cottagelike aspect is emphasized by the quaint silhouette of the clipped-gable roof, a roof form popular in 18th-century Northern Neck houses. Woodford's traditional hall-parlor plan incorporates the central passage associated with Georgian plans. The otherwise formal exterior has irregularly spaced openings that reflect the unevenness of the room sizes. The house was built between 1756 and 1773 for Billington McCarty, Jr., whose family had owned the property since 1661. The stair has an unusual banister, at first appearing to have upside-down balusters but actually following sophisticated English precedents. Rare survivals are the remnants of interior clapboarding used here as a cheap but practical second-floor wall and ceiling finish. *(79–20) VLR: 07/21/81; NRHP: 02/24/83.*

CITY OF ROANOKE

Originally known as Big Lick for the salt deposits here, this Roanoke Valley community was established in 1852 and was incorporated in 1874. Its name was changed to Roanoke in 1882, and it became a city in 1884. The city was enlarged by the annexation of part of Roanoke County in 1976.

BELLE AIRE, *1320 Belle Aire Circle, S.W.* The refined proportions and correct classical detailing of this Greek Revival farmhouse illustrate the strong influence of architectural pattern books in the mid–19th century and the uses to which imaginative local craftsmen could put them. Most of the detailing was adapted from illustrations in the works of Boston architect Asher Benjamin and applied to the regional I-house form. The house was completed in 1849 for Madison Pitzer, a landowner with extensive holdings. Local builder Gustavus Sedon, who erected similar area houses, is recorded to have installed Belle Aire's windows and may have played a role in the design. A stately air is achieved with the use of a two-level Doric portico, a device reserved for more important antebellum dwellings of the Roanoke Valley. The wide corner pilasters are features common to brick Greek Revival houses in the area. *(128–52) VLR: 10/21/75; NRHP: 04/30/76.*

BOXLEY BUILDING, *416 Jefferson Street, S.W.* Roanoke's Boxley Building was built in 1921–22, in the city's "Golden Age of Municipal Progress," which occurred in the decade after World War I. The eight-story building has a granite-faced first story with beige enameled brick and terra-cotta decoration above and is topped by a deep copper cornice. It was designed by area architect Frank Stone who was in partnership with Edward G. Frye. Stone had previously worked in the firm of D. H. Burnham of Chicago, and his design reflects the influence of Chicago's pioneering tall buildings. The building was commissioned by W. W. Boxley, developer, quarry owner, railroad contractor, and mayor of Roanoke at the time of its construction. Boxley ensured the use of the finest materials available for his steel-frame structure, creating a work which is still a dominant feature of the city's skyline. *(128–47) VLR: 10/18/83; NRHP: 03/08/84.*

BUENA VISTA, *Jackson Park, Penmar Avenue, S.E.* Buena Vista was built in 1850 for George Plater Tayloe (1804–1897) who was born at Mount Airy, the Tayloes' Richmond County plantation. He moved to the Roanoke Valley after his marriage in 1830 and managed two iron furnaces. He later became a benefactor of Hollins College and a delegate to the Secession Convention of 1861. Tayloe's home typifies the region's bold though somewhat provincial Greek Revival works, which are characterized by simple white architectural elements against red brick walls. A visitor in 1862 described Buena Vista as a "spacious peace-embowered house . . . with the summer breezes stealing around its white pillars and swaying its muslin curtains." Buena Vista remained in the Tayloe family until 1937 when it was sold to the city for a park. The house now accommodates the Roanoke Regional Office of the Virginia Department of Historic Resources. *(128–01) VLR: 01/15/74; NRHP: 07/30/74.*

THE COFFEE POT, *2902 Brambleton Avenue, S.W.* An example of the architecture of roadside popular culture, sometimes referred to as "mimetic" architecture, The Coffee Pot, built in 1936, was clearly designed to attract the attention of the passing motorist. The gimmick feature of the building is the large coffeepot structure, which originally had steam emanating from its spout. Such three-dimensional signs signaled the function of the places they adorned, making them amusing, unforgettable landmarks. Ironically, though it sported a coffeepot, the building originally was designed as a teahouse and filling station. Its basic architectural character is the rustic style popularized by National Park Service facilities, here employing unhewn vertical logs. The coffeepot itself is a masonry-formed structure. The Coffee Pot eventually became a popular roadhouse where locals and travelers alike congregated for dancing and beer drinking. It continues as an entertainment venue. *(128–50) VLR: 03/20/96; NRHP: 05/31/96.*

CAMPBELL AVENUE COMPLEX, *118–128 Campbell Avenue.* An important vestige of Roanoke's first major wave of urban construction, the Campbell Avenue Complex is a row of five contiguous three-story commercial buildings erected to accommodate retail shops and offices. Built between 1892 and 1909, the structures are a reflection of many early commercial ventures and sprang up in the newly incorporated city to serve its principal industry: the Norfolk and Western Railway Co. Only two blocks from the rail yards, the solid, urbane architecture represented a change from the saloons of Salem Avenue to a more conventional business environment. The buildings are typical of the period, blending Italianate and Neoclassical Revival styles and employing bold sheet-metal cornices. Threatened with demolition in the late 1980s, four of the buildings were purchased for preservation by the city with the assistance of a state grant. The buildings have since been sold for rehabilitation. *(128–206) VLR: 08/21/90; NRHP: 01/24/91; BHR EASEMENTS.*

COLONIAL NATIONAL BANK (COLONIAL ARMS BUILDING), *202–208 South Jefferson Street, S.W.* The Colonial National Bank was erected in 1926–27 and was an important element of the development of Roanoke as a banking hub of Southwest Virginia. Twelve stories high, with granite ashlar on the first three stories and gray-enamel brick and terra-cotta decoration above, the steel-frame building was designed by the local firm of Frye and Stone. With its lean ornamentation and functional aspect, it represents the transition from the Neoclassical Revival to Modernism. Roanoke's tallest building for fifty years, the Colonial National was one of Virginia's first skyscrapers. The bank's successor sold the building in 1981 but continues to occupy the banking hall. The upper floors have since been remodeled for office rental, and the edifice has been renamed the Colonial Arms Building. *(128–44) VLR: 09/16/82; NRHP: 02/17/83.*

CRYSTAL SPRING STEAM PUMPING STATION, *Crystal Spring Park, 2016 Lake Street, S.E.* Manufactured in 1905 by the Snow Steam Pump Company of Buffalo, N.Y., the water pump at this station is believed to be the only one of its type to survive. A kinetic wonder for its time, the pump employs the Corliss method of valve control, a technical breakthrough for the period. It drew water from Roanoke's Crystal Spring until 1957, supplying the city with a reliable water source during its years of rapid growth. Recently restored, the pump, with its elaborate flywheel, pistons, and gears, is now exhibited by the city as an artifact of industrial technology. This remarkable relic of the machine age is housed in a plain industrial structure on the edge of Crystal Spring Park. *(128–39) VLR: 12/28/79; NRHP: 05/23/80.*

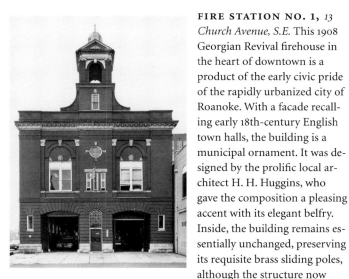

FIRE STATION NO. 1, *13 Church Avenue, S.E.* This 1908 Georgian Revival firehouse in the heart of downtown is a product of the early civic pride of the rapidly urbanized city of Roanoke. With a facade recalling early 18th-century English town halls, the building is a municipal ornament. It was designed by the prolific local architect H. H. Huggins, who gave the composition a pleasing accent with its elegant belfry. Inside, the building remains essentially unchanged, preserving its requisite brass sliding poles, although the structure now houses motorized fire engines rather than horse-drawn ones. The first floor has an elaborate pressed-metal ceiling. The upper level retains most of its early woodwork, including maple floors and natural-finish pine trim. Still in use, the firehouse illustrates a continuity of fire-fighting facilities over the past eighty years. *(128–33) VLR: 09/19/72; NRHP: 05/07/73.*

FIRST NATIONAL BANK BUILDING, *101 South Jefferson Street, S.W.* Roanoke's former First National Bank, erected in 1901, is the work of architect J. Kevan Peebles of Norfolk. Combining the most modern concepts of bank and office design with Renaissance detailing, the building demonstrates Peebles's practical training as an engineer as well as his mastery of the repertoire of revivalist styles. The First National Bank occupied the building until 1926 when it was sold to the Liberty Trust Company. In 1953 it was purchased by the People's Federal Savings and Loan Company, and in 1981 the building was bought by MFW Associates, which has renovated it for office use, preserving the columned banking hall. Although no longer serving its original function, the building remains one of the state's best-preserved Progressive Era bank buildings and is a reminder of Roanoke's historic position as a banking center. *(128–40) VLR: 02/16/82; NRHP: 06/14/82.*

GAINSBORO LIBRARY, *15 Patton Avenue, N.W.* Opened in 1942, the Gainsboro Branch of the Roanoke City Public Library provided Roanoke's Afro-American residents a facility where children and adults could pursue self-education. Designed by Eubank and Caldwell of Roanoke, the domestic-scale Tudor Revival building was the Gainsboro neighborhood's second public library. The first, housed in an Odd Fellows hall, was established in 1921. Expansion became necessary by the late 1930s, but the existing space was too small for remodeling. After debate between city fathers and black leaders, it was agreed the neighborhood should have a new, up-to-date library. Virginia Young Lee, the librarian for more than forty years, motivated children to use the library and created a special collection of Afro-American materials which is still maintained. The Gainsboro Library continues to serve as a neighborhood icon and as a cultural and educational resource for the Roanoke area. *(128–256) VLR: 09/18/96; NRHP: 12/02/96.*

HARRISON SCHOOL, *523 Harrison Street, N.W.* Completed in 1917, Roanoke's Harrison School is a monument to the pioneering efforts of Lucy Addison (1861–1937) to offer public academic secondary instruction to all children regardless of race. These efforts were all the more remarkable in view of Virginia's paucity of black public high schools during this period and the prevailing educational theory that blacks should receive vocational rather than academic instruction. The first class of Roanoke's blacks to complete four full years of high school under Miss Addison's tutelage graduated in 1924. Designed by J. H. Page, the building is a typical public school design of the period, employing a modified Georgian format. The school closed in the 1960s with the termination of segregated schools. It was renovated for residential use in the 1980s and now also houses the Harrison Museum of African American Culture. *(128–43) VLR: 05/18/82; NRHP: 09/09/82.*

HOTEL ROANOKE, *110 Shenandoah Avenue.* One of Virginia's preeminent landmarks, Hotel Roanoke is in the tradition of the great American hotels. On a hill dominating the city's downtown, the sprawling half-timbered Tudor Revival structure stands on the site of the original hotel erected in 1882 by the Norfolk and Western Railway Co., the same year the company established its headquarters in Roanoke. The present building, though architecturally unified, has had a complicated evolution. The dominant portion dates from 1938 and was designed by Knut W. Lind, a hotel specialist and partner in the New York firm of George B. Post & Sons. Attached are wings dating from 1931, 1946, and 1954. The original hotel, rebuilt in 1899 following a fire, was demolished for the present structure. The hotel closed in 1989 and was donated to Virginia Tech. After extensive restoration and the addition of a large conference center, the hotel reopened in 1995. *(128–25) VLR: 10/18/95; NRHP: 02/16/96.*

HUNTINGDON, *320 Huntington Boulevard.* This dignified example of a Federal-period gentry farmhouse was built ca. 1819 for Elisha Betts, a native of Northumberland County, who migrated to the Roanoke Valley about 1807. The house originally was the nucleus of a 500-acre working plantation and took some twenty-five years to complete. Following Betts's death in 1825, his widow, Sara Watson Betts, continued to reside here, adding handsome Greek Revival porches. The dormers, front entry, and one-story rear wing are early 20th-century additions. The house retains some of its original Federal interior woodwork. Remaining on the eight-acre tract are the Betts family cemetery and a small one-story frame outbuilding that may have been slave quarters. Now surrounded by 20th-century development, the recently restored complex is a historic anchor in a growing modern city. *(128–05) VLR: 08/21/91; NRHP: 11/08/91.*

LONE OAKS (BENJAMIN DEYERLE PLACE; ALSO WINSMERE), *1402 Grandin Road Extension, S.W.* During the mid–19th century the now largely developed Roanoke Valley was sprinkled with farms with many of the more prominent dwellings designed in a plain but imposing Greek Revival style. One to survive is Lone Oaks, built ca. 1853 by the entrepreneur Benjamin Deyerle for his own residence. Among his several businesses Deyerle operated brick kilns, and tradition has it that he made the bricks for Lone Oaks. Deyerle is also credited with building a number of similar houses in the area, although his activity as a master builder is yet to be documented. Features that Lone Oaks shares with other Roanoke Valley Greek Revival houses are the plain Doric entablature with corner pilasters, a three-bay facade, a shallow hipped roof, and an entry portico. Lone Oaks remains a private residence and preserves several original outbuildings. *(128–10) VLR: 01/16/73; NRHP: 04/11/73.*

MONTEREY, *301 Tinker Creek Lane, N.E.* An architectural anomaly for the region, this low, verandaed dwelling is more akin to the spacious mid-19th-century cottages of the Gulf Coast than the standard two-story houses of Virginia. Like many Greek Revival works throughout the state, the house has details derived from Asher Benjamin's widely popular pattern book *The Practical House Carpenter* (1830). Monterey was built in 1846 for Yelverton Oliver, a landowner. Family tradition holds that Oliver got his idea for the form while on a trip to New Orleans to race horses. Monterey is an exceptionally well-crafted building, employing precise Flemish bond brickwork and boldly molded woodwork. Distinctive features are the exterior Doric cornice and the facade's triple-hung sashes. A rear wing was added around 1870. Although within the city limits, the house retains a rural setting. *(128–35) VLR: 04/16/74; NRHP: 07/30/74.*

MOUNTAIN VIEW, *714 Thirteenth Street, S.W.* The grandiose Colonial Revival mansion erected in 1907 for Roanoke businessman and civil leader Junius Blair Fishburn was regarded by its architect H. H. Huggins as an object of great personal achievement. In a 1908 advertisement in the *Roanoke City Directory,* Huggins boldly stated: "Under my plans and direction, there has been erected in Roanoke one of the finest residences in the state of Virginia." The house was Fishburn's home until his death in 1955 when it was given to the Roanoke Department of Parks and Recreation. Rather than evoke a specific image, the "colonial" style here is freely interpreted to make a grand effect suitable for the city's leading citizen. Typical of many Colonial Revival dwellings, Mountain View has a large central portico projecting over a one-story porch. The mansion, inside and out, survives essentially untouched and is kept in an excellent state of preservation. *(128–22) VLR: 06/17/80; NRHP: 10/31/80.*

MOUNT MORIAH BAPTIST CHURCH, *3521 East Orange Avenue.* On a wooded hillside above the bustle of a commercial strip, this Afro-American religious complex consists of a plain wooden church and a half-acre cemetery with over 100 graves. Mount Moriah's members comprise one of the region's earliest black congregations, originating in a Sunday school for slaves established in the mid-1800s by Dr. Charles L. Cocke, founder of Hollins College. The group gained permission to build its first church in 1858. The present church, the congregation's third, was built in 1908. The simple building has been little changed and preserves its original furnishings. The cemetery, expanded from a former slave burial ground, is nearby along an old road trace. A source of pride for the local black community, Mount Moriah has been a spiritual reference point for its members for more than 130 years. *(128–234) VLR: 06/15/94; NRHP: 09/08/94.*

PATRICK HENRY HOTEL, *617 Jefferson Street, S.W.* A skillful application of the Georgian Revival style to a modern high-rise structure, the Patrick Henry Hotel, completed in 1925, was part of Roanoke's second major wave of construction, one that dominated the decade following World War I. Designed by New York hotel architect William Lee Stoddart, the Patrick Henry was one of the most conspicuous efforts of the local civic leader, busi-

nessman, and former mayor W. W. Boxley to bring status and a cosmopolitan atmosphere to the "Magic City." Boxley was largely responsible for engineering what is now referred to as Roanoke's "Golden Age of Municipal Progress." The hotel long enjoyed a fine reputation but declined in the 1960s. It underwent a comprehensive renovation in the early 1990s for the stated purpose of "restoring and preserving the authenticity of the Hotel Patrick Henry" to its former position as an integral part of downtown Roanoke. *(128–235) VLR: 04/17/91; NRHP: 07/03/91.*

ROANOKE CITY MARKET HISTORIC DISTRICT.
Roanoke's Market District has served as the primary market-place for the city and surrounding counties for over a century. The district comprises more than sixty structures displaying the full range of late 19th- to early 20th-century commercial styles. Its centerpiece is the City Market building on Market Square, constructed in 1922 to replace Roanoke's first market, erected in 1886. The square is framed with brick two- and three-story commercial buildings that present vistas of architectural unity and appealing scale. During recent years the area has become a target of ongoing revitalization efforts. Innovative design concepts and local historic district zoning have been combined with public and private backing for the adaptive reuse of the City Market building and for the conversion of the McGuire Building into a cultural and science center called Center in the Square. *(128–45) VLR: 09/16/82; NRHP: 04/20/83.*

ROANOKE WAREHOUSE HISTORIC DISTRICT. The Roanoke Warehouse Historic District, also known as Wholesale Row, consists of a block of five warehouses between Norfolk Avenue, S.W., and the railroad tracks, all erected between 1889 and 1902 for the storage of wholesale food in transit. Closely identified with Roanoke's emergence at the turn of the century as the wholesale capital of Southwest Virginia, the district's buildings exemplify the functional tradition of early industrial warehouse design. The brick structures have powerful rectangular lines, rows of deep-set segmental-arched windows, and iron door and window moldings. Their structural systems incorporate post-and-beam timber supports and cast-iron tie-rods. Structural systems are also expressed by the framing of the bays with brick piers. Two of the warehouses have a conspicuous outline with their stepped-gable roofs, giving them a north European flavor. *(128–46) VLR: 09/16/82; NRHP: 03/29/83.*

ROANOKE FIREHOUSE NO. 6, *1015 Jamison Avenue, S.E.*
This ingenious, if not amusing, architectural work contradicts the Modernists' tenet that form follows function. Firehouse No. 6 was built in 1911 to serve the growing Belmont neighborhood and was one of the city's first to be equipped with motorized fire engines. The design of this and three other firehouses provided by architect Homer M. Miller was influenced by concern that new firehouses be compatible with the residential character of their respective neighborhoods. No. 6 thus was disguised to look like just another house on the block, even with a front porch. The only giveaways were the wide double doors and the wider width of the center bay to accommodate the fire trucks. The station served until 1979 when replaced by a modern station; it is now used as a neighborhood center. *(128–51) VLR: 04/17/90; NRHP: 01/24/91.*

ST. ANDREW'S ROMAN CATHOLIC CHURCH, *631 Jefferson Street, N.E.* Overlooking downtown Roanoke, St. Andrew's Church is one of Virginia's foremost examples of the High Victorian Gothic, a style known for its architectural richness and historical association. With its twin spires, rounded apse, and gabled transepts, the composition follows basically French precedents. A departure from tradition is the use of the modern yellow pressed bricks, which give the building a golden hue.

Its construction was due largely to the efforts of Father John Lynch, who organized Roanoke's Roman Catholic community, then composed primarily of recently arrived railroad workers. Lynch said his first mass in the area in 1882 in a passenger car. The congregation grew rapidly, and the church, designed by William P. Ginther of Akron, Ohio, was completed in 1902. Its interior, embellished with vaulting, carving, stenciling, and stained glass, is a dazzling expression of late Victorian Catholic art. *(128–30) VLR: 10/17/72; NRHP: 05/07/73.*

SOUTHWEST HISTORIC DISTRICT. One of the state's largest and most intact early 20th-century urban residential neighborhoods, this historic district is characterized by blocks of freestanding Queen Anne, Colonial Revival, Bungalow, and American Foursquare dwellings. Developed primarily between the years 1882 and 1930, a period of tremendous growth and prosperity in the city, the area is Roanoke's most architecturally cohesive residential neighborhood, yet one with much diversity. The district has three distinct sections: Old Southwest, Mountain View, and Hurt Park. Together they grew in response to the tremendous demand for housing during Roanoke's formative years. The development addressed the needs of both workmen and community leaders, including officials of the Norfolk and Western Railroad Co. The excellent preservation of the architectural fabric has kept the area popular and has spurred much recent rehabilitation. Of the district's nearly 1,700 buildings, only around 90 are incompatible modern structures. *(128–49) VLR: 04/16/85; NRHP: 06/19/85.*

ST. JOHN'S EPISCOPAL CHURCH, *Jefferson Street and Elm Avenue.* St. John's Parish traces its origins to the 1830s when the Rev. Nicholas Hamner Cobbs of Bedford began ministering in the Roanoke Valley. With Roanoke's rapid urbanization at the end of the century, St. John's became the largest Episcopal parish in Southwest Virginia. In 1891–92 the congregation erected the present church designed by Charles M. Burns of Philadelphia with William C. Noland as resident architect. The rugged stone building is one of the region's most literate works of Late Gothic Revival and displays the scholarship and craftsmanship inherent in this architectural movement. The cynosure of the lofty interior is the rhythmic timberwork of the hammerbeam ceiling as well as the aisle clerestories. Stained-glass windows by the Tiffany and Lamb studios also highlight the space. In 1919 St. John's became the headquarters of the newly created Diocese of Southwestern Virginia. *(128–236) VLR: 06/19/91; NRHP: 08/23/91.*

ROANOKE COUNTY

Occupying the Roanoke Valley and named for the Roanoke River that flows through it, Roanoke County is the gateway to Southwest Virginia. It was formed from Botetourt County in 1838, with part of Montgomery County added later. The county seat is Salem.

DENTON MONUMENT (OLD TOMBSTONE), *Old Tombstone Cemetery, Hollins vicinity.* One of Virginia's most important works of folk art, the Denton Monument was carved sometime after 1805 by Laurence Krone, the most noted of the early 19th-century Valley German stone carvers. Krone's only signed work, the monument was designed as a memorial to the young Robert Denton and as a register of his immediate family. It takes the form of a small coffin containing a folk image of the deceased child. Germanic folk motifs along with a lengthy inscription in Latin, German, and English decorate the surfaces. The head and upper torso were originally covered by a removable stone lid which has since disappeared. Krone, a native of Central Europe, arrived in Virginia around 1800. Legend holds that the monument was an expression of Krone's gratitude for care received from the Denton family during an illness. *(80–59) VLR: 07/19/77; NRHP: 03/25/80.*

HARSHBARGER HOUSE, *316 John Richardson Road.* Samuel Harshbarger built the original stone portion of this house, one of Roanoke County's oldest dwellings, in 1797. The use of stone here is a rare reminder of a German-influenced building tradition in the area. Samuel Harshbarger came from Pennsylvania with a group of Swiss or German Brethren, known as Dunkards. The family added the brick wing around 1825. The Harshbargers are said to have been rigorous in their use of German customs and language. Their Brethren principles led them to oppose slavery. Fearing he would be unable to compete with area slaveholding farmers, Samuel's son Jacob sold his portion of the property in 1831 and moved to Indiana. His father eventually followed him, selling his land to John Jeffries in 1837. Though now surrounded by suburban development, the house enjoys a protected setting. A recent restoration has enhanced its historic character. *(80–13) VLR: 10/09/91; NRHP: 10/15/92.*

HOLLINS COLLEGE QUADRANGLE, *Hollins.* The historic core of Hollins College is a complex of brick buildings enclosing a rectangular tree-shaded lawn. The school was founded in 1837 as the Roanoke Female Seminary. Charles L. Cocke took charge in 1846 and made it a leading woman's college. Its name was changed to Hollins in 1855 to honor Mr. and Mrs. John Hollins of Lynchburg who paid for East Dormitory, the quadrangle's oldest building. Completed in 1858, the colonnaded structure is one of the region's major Greek Revival works. Main Building (shown), at the north end, was begun in 1861. Bradley Chapel, a modified Romanesque Revival building, was the school's first post–Civil War structure. The octagonal dining hall, Botetourt Hall, was completed in 1890. West Dormitory, designed by H. H. Huggins, dates from 1900. Closing in the quadrangle is the 1908 neoclassical Charles L. Cocke Library, now administrative offices, designed by Frye and Chesterman of Lynchburg. *(80–55) VLR: 05/21/74; NRHP: 11/05/74.*

ROCKBRIDGE COUNTY

Rockbridge County was named for Natural Bridge, the famous rock formation located in the county. The county was formed from Augusta and Botetourt counties in 1778. Its county seat is Lexington.

ANDERSON HOLLOW ARCHAEOLOGICAL DISTRICT, *Denmark vicinity.* Anderson Hollow contains seven prehistoric and historic archaeological sites representing the full range of hollow settlement patterns as they occurred within the ridge-and-valley region of western Virginia. In the 19th century relatively poor but independent families moved into the mountain hollows. The historic sites within Anderson Hollow, dating from 1826 to 1960, are particularly significant because of the limited knowledge of the cultural adaptations that developed in this sort of environment. Several of the sites consist of chimney bases and stone foundations probably of log houses. Archaeological investigation here should yield new information about land use over time, thus providing an opportunity to define with greater precision the various forms of agriculture and other subsistence practices within the uplands of western Virginia. *(81–407) VLR: 04/19/83; NRHP: 07/21/83.*

BROWNSBURG HISTORIC DISTRICT. Established in 1783, Brownsburg was laid out on the lands of Robert Wardlaw and Samuel McChesney along a main stage line. By 1835 the community was a hub of activity, containing about twenty dwellings, a mill, three stores, two shoe factories, three wheelwrights, two blacksmith shops, two tailors, a tanyard, a saddlery, a cabinetmaker, a carpenter, and a hatter. Brownsburg lost commercial importance after 1884 when the Valley Railroad was built several miles to the east, initiating a slide into a long decline. Now a well-preserved but somnolent residential village, Brownsburg is composed of buildings dating mostly before 1860 and the period 1870–1910. Prevalent along the tree-shaded main road is the unembellished Valley Federal style, in both frame and brick construction, though several buildings have log cores. A noteworthy individual dwelling is Sleepy Hollow, a ca. 1800 stone structure with an 1830s brick wing. *(81–121) VLR: 02/20/73; NRHP: 07/02/73.*

CEDAR HILL, *Route 608, Buena Vista vicinity.* Cedar Hill is one of a group of prosperous farms established during the 18th century in the countryside east of Lexington. The present house, a formal five-bay brick dwelling, was completed in 1821 for James Templeton. Atop a ridge adjacent to the "Great Road," a historic trace paralleling the Maury River, the house commands panoramic views of the Blue Ridge Mountains. In 1827 the property was purchased by Galbreath Hamilton, whose son, A. J. Hamilton, gained the dubious distinction of being the first cadet to desert the Virginia Military Institute. The house is significant for its well-finished and little-altered condition. The interior retains original six-paneled doors and paneled wainscoting. The mantels are embellished with Valley-style gouge-work decoration. On the property are two early log outbuildings and a stone springhouse. *(81–19) VLR: 04/20/94; NRHP: 07/15/94.*

CLIFTON, *East Lexington.* Erected ca. 1815, Clifton was originally the home of Maj. John Alexander, a veteran of the War of 1812 who served as a trustee of nearby Washington College (now Washington and Lee University) from 1812 to 1853. Alexander's widow sold Clifton to Louisville, Ky., lawyer William Preston Johnston, who was President Jefferson Davis's aide-de-camp during the Civil War. Invited by Robert E. Lee to join the Washington College faculty, Johnston served as full professor until 1872. While residing at Clifton, Johnston wrote a biography of his father, Confederate general Albert Sidney Johnston. Johnston later became the first president of Tulane University. On a hill overlooking the Maury River, the imposing house with its molded-brick cornice is a characteristic example of a gentry homestead of the region. The two-level portico, a 20th-century addition, was designed by architect Thomas W. S. Craven. *(81–288); VLR: 04/20/94; NRHP: 07/22/94.*

CHURCH HILL, *Timber Ridge.* Church Hill was first occupied in 1848 by Horatio Thompson, a minister of the nearby Timber Ridge Associated Reformed Presbyterian Church. The house is an earnest example of builder's Greek Revival; its solid mass and forthright lines reflect the Calvinistic tradition of the region. The exterior is set off by massive corner pilasters and a carefully proportioned dwarf portico. The interior, though generally plain, has trompe l'oeil painted decoration on the main stair. The property was formerly owned by the pioneering Houston family who acquired title in 1742. In a log dwelling, probably demolished to make way for the present house, Sam Houston, the Texas pioneer, was born in 1793 to Samuel and Elizabeth Houston. Tradition has it that some of the logs from the Sam Houston birthplace were incorporated in a later log structure on the property. *(81–65) VLR: 06/21/77; NRHP: 02/23/79.*

FOREST OAKS, *Natural Bridge vicinity.* This sprawling but well-appointed mansion is an interesting essay in alterations and enlargements. The original core is a side-hall Federal dwelling built ca. 1806 for Matthew Houston, member of one of the area's prominent Scotch-Irish families. It was enlarged by Houston to a five-bay structure around 1812. The enlargement included a two-story center hall with arched ceiling, the form said to have been inspired by nearby Natural Bridge. The house was transformed into a Colonial Revival mansion in 1916 through further additions and alterations by architect Curtis Walton of Cleveland, Ohio, for his adoptive mother Lilly Walton. This remodeling included two large wings, the two-story east portico, and the Greek Revival–style window lintels. The principal interior change was the installation of an elaborately trimmed neo-Jacobean stair. *(81–207) VLR: 06/19/91; NRHP: 08/23/91.*

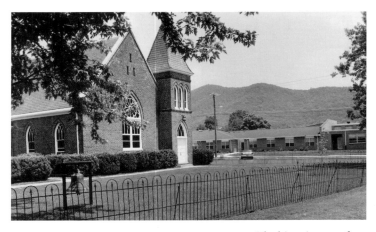

GLASGOW HISTORIC DISTRICT. The historic core of the quiet James River community of Glasgow represents a moment in time: a railroad-era boomtown preserved in the incipient stages of its ill-fated prosperity. Established in 1890, the year of the boom, Glasgow experienced dramatic growth during the first six months of its existence. Stylish commercial blocks were erected at key intersections with a scattering of smaller stores, offices, and dwellings on adjacent lots. Despite zealous promotional efforts by the principal developer, the Rockbridge Company, and its president, former governor Fitzhugh Lee, the development slowed in 1891, and in the ensuing national depression Glasgow nearly disappeared. Industrial plants were cannibalized for materials; St. John's Episcopal Church (shown), for example, was built of bricks from an abandoned factory. A modicum of activity returned by 1900, and the town has since maintained a placid existence as a small manufacturing community. *(223–03) VLR: 08/28/95; NRHP: 10/30/95.*

HAYS CREEK MILL, *Brownsburg vicinity.* Hays Creek Mill is a surviving example of the many mills that served the abundant farms of Rockbridge County in the 18th and 19th centuries. Built around 1819 by William Steele, the stone and wood-frame structure was originally smaller but was enlarged to its present configuration in the 1870s. The mill remained in operation until 1957, functioning at various times during its commercial life as a gristmill, sawmill, and fulling mill. From 1871 until the 1920s it was owned and operated by the McClung family and was known as McClung's Mill. The present owner, who acquired the property in 1974, has undertaken a program of stabilizing the long-neglected structure and uses it for a woodworking shop and storage. Most of the milling equipment was removed decades ago, but the metal overshot wheel remains. Next to the mill is a mid-19th-century miller's house. *(81–159) VLR: 06/27/95; NRHP: 08/04/95*

GOSHEN LAND COMPANY BRIDGE, *Route 746, Goshen.* This lacy metal-truss bridge, with its distinctive thirty-degree skew, was built by the Groton Bridge Company for the Goshen Land and Improvement Company in 1890 when the Shenandoah Valley was undergoing a real estate and industrial boom. The developers of Goshen naively hoped that the community would grow into the "Birmingham of America"; but the boom ended quickly, and the bridge remains one of the company's few tangible accomplishments. Supported on limestone ashlar abutments and piers, the bridge is composed of a Pratt through truss consisting of two spans with an overall length of 258 feet. Above the portal is an ornate cresting sign proudly listing the officers of the Goshen Company. The bridge was originally built to accommodate trolley tracks as well as a roadway. *(226–5001) VLR: 11/15/77; NRHP: 04/15/78.*

ZACHARIAH JOHNSTON HOUSE (STONE HOUSE), *Lexington vicinity.* On a tree-shaded knoll on the edge of Lexington, this solidly proportioned five-bay limestone house shows the influence of the Georgian architecture of eastern Virginia. As recorded on a date stone, the house was constructed for Zachariah Johnston in 1797 by John Spear, a little-known but obviously skilled builder. Johnston served as a member of the Virginia ratification convention of 1788, a presidential elector, and a member of the House of Delegates, where he was chairman of the standing committee on religion and demonstrated his strong advocacy of religious freedom. The house, which has undergone few changes, was restored in 1965–66 under the direction of Thomas W. S. Craven. A modern passageway connects the main section to the original kitchen outbuilding. The front porch, with its chamfered posts, replaced an earlier porch around 1900. *(81–168) VLR: 05/16/78; NRHP: 05/24/79.*

KENNEDY-LUNSFORD FARM, *Raphine vicinity.* Tucked into the bucolic landscape of northeastern Rockbridge County, this homey stone dwelling was built ca. 1797 for Joseph Kennedy, member of one of the early Presbyterian Scotch-Irish families of the area. Kennedy was given the property by his father, Andrew Kennedy, who established the nearby Kennedy-Wade Mill. The house is among the handful of early stone dwellings remaining in the county, houses that superseded the crude pioneer dwellings built by the first settlers. Although later modified, the house apparently originally had a hall-parlor plan. In the basement is an original cooking fireplace with an enormous wooden lintel topping its opening. The farm was purchased by William Lunsford in 1891, and it remained in the Lunsford family until 1958. The house underwent extensive restoration in 1975 after the farm's acquisition by its present owners. *(81–32) VLR: 03/20/96; NRHP: 06/07/96; BHR EASEMENT.*

KENNEDY-WADE MILL HISTORIC DISTRICT, *Wade's Mill.* This tiny settlement preserves a picture of a typical 19th-century Shenandoah Valley mill community. Nestled in the hills of western Rockbridge County, the district includes the Kennedy-Wade Mill, a miller's house, an assistant miller's house, a frame I-house, a brick farmhouse, and several early outbuildings. The mill is the only operating water-powered gristmill in the region. The miller's house (begun ca. 1850) and the assistant miller's house (ca. 1900) stand nearby, with the latter built into a bank, following a regional custom. The 1913 Charles Wade house is a two-story I-house with a full-width front porch and weatherboard siding. The district's oldest house is the McFadden house, a ca. 1793 bank-sited brick dwelling with an asymmetrical facade. Capt. Joseph Kennedy originally owned the 113-acre tract that comprises the district. *(81–33) VLR: 03/10/94; NRHP: 05/26/94.*

KENNEDY-WADE MILL, *Wade's Mill.* Of the supportive industries required by the agrarian society of 19th- and early 20th-century western Virginia, the gristmill was the most essential. The Kennedy-Wade Mill, near Brownsburg, is the only mill still in commercial operation in Rockbridge County, its machinery still powered by its Fitz overshot metal wheel. Andrew Kennedy acquired the property ca. 1760 and presumably built the stone portion of the structure. The mill burned in 1873 and was rebuilt incorporating the original stone walls. The resulting mill, with its board-and-batten superstructure and updated machinery, was acquired in 1882 by James F. Waid (Wade), whose family sold it in 1991 to the present owners. Extensively renovated the following year, the mill is a fully operational flour mill using its original millstones. *(81–33) VLR: 05/16/78; NRHP: 07/13/79.*

LEVEL LOOP, *Brownsburg vicinity.* Named for the level loop of bottomland formed by nearby Hays Creek, this genteel farmstead preserves a high-style brick dwelling built in 1819 for William Houston, a relative of the Texas pioneer and Rockbridge County native Sam Houston. The house is noted for its fine regional Federal woodwork, particularly an exceptional carved mantel in what is now the dining room. The mantel, a regional interpretation of the Adam style carved with almost bizarre gusto, is en-

riched with a central patera, thumb-nail gouge work, and fylfots (a German-style pinwheel motif). The restrained Federal character of the exterior, with its molded-brick cornice, a local idiom, illustrates the image of dignity favored by the Shenandoah Valley's rural elite in the decades following the Revolution. Several 19th-century outbuildings remain on the property, including a board-and-batten smokehouse with a small cupola. *(81–34) VLR: 06/16/93; NRHP: 08/12/93; BHR EASEMENT.*

LIBERTY HALL ACADEMY RUINS, *Lexington vicinity.*
These gaunt ruins are the remains of Liberty Hall Academy, the
predecessor of Washington and Lee University. In 1749 Augusta
Academy, the first school of consequence west of the Blue
Ridge Mountains, was founded near Greenville. The academy,
patriotically renamed Liberty Hall Academy, was relocated
twice before settling in 1792 immediately west of Lexington.
Constructed in 1793, the limestone building stood three stories
tall with a gable roof. An unusual treatment, found in at least
three Rockbridge County buildings, was the placement of the
fireplaces in the outside corners. The academy was housed here
only a short while, for the building was gutted by fire in 1803.
The school, by then known as Washington Academy, relocated
to a new site in Lexington where it evolved into the present
university, which owns and maintains the ruins. *(81–87) VLR:
12/21/76; NRHP: 08/16/77.*

WILLIAM MACKEY HOUSE, *Timber Ridge vicinity.* The
William Mackey house illustrates the transition from rude
frontier structures to solid, permanent dwellings with architectural pretensions that occurred in the Shenandoah Valley in the
late 18th century. Compared with its simple log predecessors,
the limestone-built Mackey house is a sophisticated structure
with finely crafted detailing, including a decorative classical
cornice. Except for a front porch and a rear wing, both added
around 1900, the house survives without significant alteration,
preserving nearly all of its original interior woodwork. It was
built in 1796 for William Mackey, son of the Scottish immigrant
and Rockbridge County pioneer John Mackey. The property,
situated in an exceptionally scenic section of the county, remains in the ownership of Mackey's descendants and is one of
the oldest family holdings in the region. *(81–39) VLR: 08/18/93;
NRHP: 10/29/93.*

LOCUST HILL, *Mechanicsville vicinity.* Rockbridge County's
Federal farmhouses are endowed with a robust, self-assured
quality consistent with the independent-minded Scotch-Irish
farmers who built them. Although each has its individual character, they share many common traits. Locust Hill is typical of
these with its use of fine Flemish bond, molded-brick cornice,
and I-house plan. The house was built in 1826 for John Hamilton, whose father came to America from Northern Ireland in
1771. Hamilton was an active layman in the Methodist Episcopal church and helped to organize the Wesley Chapel congregation. A 20th-century resident, Col. Samuel Millner, was a highly
regarded professor at the Virginia Military Institute for over
fifty years. Locust Hill's interior was damaged by fire in 1855,
and Greek Revival trim was subsequently installed. On the
grounds are a 19th-century log dependency and several late
19th-century farm buildings. *(81–179) VLR: 10/15/85; NRHP: 05/12/86.*

MAPLE HALL, *Timber
Ridge vicinity.* This stately
antebellum residence, a
historic reference point for
the many motorists racing
by on nearby Interstate
81/64 and U.S. Route 11,
was built in 1855 for John
Beard Gibson, a local
farmer who became suc-
cessful in milling and distilling operations. His
newly gained wealth en-
abled Gibson to build
Maple Hall, a house whose
size and appointments
surpassed those of the
homes of other gentry in
the region. Set off by its
two-tiered portico, the

boldly scaled structure reflects the influence of architectural
pattern books on local builders. Many of the Greek Revival details, specifically the first-floor mantels, were adapted from designs in Asher Benjamin's popular work *The Practical House
Carpenter* (1830). Two early outbuildings, one of brick, the other of log, remain on the grounds. The complex has been restored as a country inn. *(81–41) VLR: 02/18/86; NRHP: 01/29/87.*

MCCORMICK FARM AND WORKSHOP (WALNUT GROVE), *Steeles Tavern vicinity.* On this farm Cyrus Hall McCormick (1809–1884) developed the first effective reaper. This invention, successfully demonstrated in July 1831, revolutionized world agricultural production, for it permitted the farmer to reap with minimal effort as much grain as he could sow. McCormick patented the machine in 1834 and made improvements in the 1840s. Commercial manufacture of the reaper began at Walnut Grove. In 1847 McCormick, in partnership with his brother Leander, founded the McCormick Harvesting and Machine Company in Chicago and became one of the most successful manufacturers in America's industrial age. Walnut Grove is now owned by Virginia Tech, which operates the farm as the Shenandoah Valley Research Station. The log workshop where the first reaper was built and the adjacent log mill are exhibited to the public. *(81–73) VLR: 09/09/69; NRHP: 10/15/66; NHL: 07/19/64.*

MULBERRY GROVE, *Brownsburg vicinity.* This picture-book amalgamation of vernacular forms chronicles building customs in the farming community of northwestern Rockbridge County. The core is a simple single-cell dwelling with an upper-level chamber constructed ca. 1790 by Joseph Skeen, a Scotch-Irish settler. In 1824 Samuel Willson, a more affluent farmer, purchased Mulberry Grove and made three brick additions employing regional Federal detailing. James E. A. Gibbs, an inventor of the sewing machine, purchased the home for his daughter, Ellabell Gibbs Moore, in 1880. M. McClung Stenett, a great-grandson of Samuel Willson, acquired the property in 1926. Additions in 1937, 1965, and 1984 expanded the house to its present form. Mulberry Grove is named for the Chinese mulberry trees that Samuel Willson grew here in an attempt to raise silkworms. An early log meat house and a double-pen log barn survive on the property. *(81–14) VLR: 04/20/94; NRHP: 07/28/94.*

NATURAL BRIDGE, *Natural Bridge.* Since its discovery in the 1730s, Natural Bridge has been one of America's most recognizable icons of the wonders of nature. Its image was popularized by artists and illustrators and by a stream of illustrious visitors who waxed eloquent on its inspiring form. The bridge so captured the attention of Thomas Jefferson that he purchased it in 1774 and later wrote that he considered the bridge a public trust and would not allow it to be ignored, defaced, or masked from public view. Pictures of the bridge appeared in numerous publications, both American and foreign, and its image became a primary identifying symbol of Virginia. During the 19th century the bridge became a popular tourist destination and the focal point of a resort development. Still visited by thousands, Natural Bridge has been owned and exhibited by Natural Bridge of Virginia, Inc., since 1925. *(81–415) VLR: 03/19/97; NRHP: 11/18/97; NHL: 08/05/98.*

NEW PROVIDENCE PRESBYTERIAN CHURCH, *Brownsburg vicinity.* With its temple form and Doric portico *in antis,* this country Greek Revival church follows the format favored by Robert Lewis Dabney, a Presbyterian pastor and amateur architect. New Providence was completed in 1859 and closely resembles Dabney's 1850 Tinkling Spring Presbyterian Church in Augusta County. Because New Providence's minister, James Morrison, was Dabney's father-in-law, Dabney may well have had a direct influence on the design. Except for a large Sunday school addition, the building is little changed. The main interior feature is the engaged pulpit tabernacle, consisting of paired Doric pilasters supporting an ornamented entablature. The sanctuary also has a gallery supported on Doric columns. The New Providence congregation was organized in 1746 by the pioneering Presbyterian pastor John Blair. *(81–46) VLR: 02/21/78; NRHP: 03/26/80.*

OAK SPRING FARM (FULTZ HOUSE), *Steeles Tavern vicinity.* Oak Spring Farm takes its name from a spring once used by Indian hunting parties. The brick dwelling, a classic example of the I-house form, was built in 1826 by William Moore, Jr. A significant feature is a ca. 1860 two-story ell of horizontal-plank construction—a technique employing oak planks stacked horizontally, coated with mortar, and covered with clapboards. In 1845 Oak Spring was purchased by Uriah Fultz, member of a Pennsylvania German farming family. One of Fultz's brothers developed a nonbearded strain of wheat called "Fultz Wheat." Uriah Fultz later passed title to Oak Spring to his brother Isaac who set up a blacksmith shop here where he shod horses for the Confederate army. The farm's bank barn, one of the largest in the county, was built in 1878 on the foundations of the original barn, burned in 1864 by Union troops. *(81–48) VLR: 04/20/94; NRHP: 10/19/94.*

ROCKBRIDGE ALUM SPRINGS, *California vicinity.* Set in the mountains west of Lexington, this former resort was once one of Virginia's most noted antebellum spa complexes. In its heyday Rockbridge Alum ranked second only to the White Sulphur Springs in prestige and popularity. The mineral spring itself is at the base of a cliff and is housed in a columned pavilion topped by a statue of Hygeia. The original complex, consisting of a central hotel flanked by cottages and service buildings, has mostly disappeared. The current owner, however, a Christian youth ministry, is restoring four original buildings and the spring pavilion. In their pastoral wilderness setting, the surviving structures form a nostalgic scene of a happy and active place. The springs were originally developed by Alexander Campbell. Most of the buildings of the formerly thirty-six-building complex were erected after 1852 by John W. Frazier. *(81–86) VLR: 04/21/87; NRHP: 01/19/89.*

ROCKBRIDGE INN, *Natural Bridge vicinity.* The original core of this prominently situated tavern was built by John Galbraith in 1821–23 and was first known as Galbraith Tavern. Functioning as both a dwelling and a stagecoach stop on the busy Valley Turnpike, the finely crafted two-story brick structure was enlarged in 1841 with the addition of a large two-story frame wing. The expansive two-level galleries were added in the 1880s when the property was owned by Col. H. C. Parsons, the primary developer and promoter of the Natural Bridge. The inn served as a stopping point for stagecoaches carrying visitors to see the natural wonder. The building continued as an inn operated by George W. Parsons and his wife until the 1940s when a rerouting of the adjacent highway put it out of business. The inn's interior retains features reflecting its various remodelings. *(81–399) VLR: 04/28/95; NRHP: 04/07/95.*

TANKERSLEY TAVERN, *Lexington.* Nestled against a hillside just across the Maury River from Lexington, this visually inviting structure, with its two-level gallery, is associated with the region's early transportation system. It was built in 1835 as a tollhouse at end of the bridge carrying the Valley Turnpike into Lexington. It eventually became a combined canal ticket office, general store, post office, and tavern. The original core was constructed by Col. John Jordan, one of Rockbridge County's most active builders and entrepreneurs, whose residence, Stono, stands atop a steep hill across the river. In 1886 the property was purchased by the Tankersley family and was run as a tavern for many years, its colorful reputation enhanced by the fact that the Tankersleys manufactured and dispensed their own rye whiskey. The building has since been restored as a private residence. *(81–201) VLR: 04/21/87; NRHP: 11/03/88.*

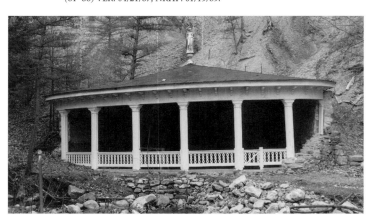

THORN HILL, *Lexington vicinity.* Thorn Hill, one of Rock-bridge County's most venerable links to the past, was built ca. 1792 for John Bowyer, a schoolteacher who settled here in 1753. Bowyer helped organize Rockbridge County in 1778. In 1782 he became a colonel in the Rockbridge County militia, and he later served as justice of the peace. He was appointed one of the first trustees of Liberty Hall Academy in 1792. Bowyer's command-ingly situated homestead is noted for its elaborate but eccentri-cally proportioned late Georgian woodwork. Its joiner was ob-viously untutored in architectural refinements but was highly skilled and possessed an entertaining sense of design. The south facade retains its delicate Federal porch; what was a two-level porch on the opposite front was replaced in the 19th century with four heavy Greek Doric columns. Several early outbuild-ings are placed to make a forecourt on the house's south side. *(81–84) VLR: 02/18/75; NRHP: 06/18/75.*

TIMBER RIDGE PRESBYTERIAN CHURCH, *Timber Ridge.* Though considerably altered and enlarged during its more than two centuries of service, this stone meetinghouse, built in 1755, is the second-oldest Presbyterian house of wor-ship in the Shenandoah Valley. The congregation was organized in 1746 by the pioneering minister John Blair and worshiped in a log structure until this building was erected. For several years after 1776, Timber Ridge supported the newly established Au-gusta Academy, later Liberty Hall Academy, the predecessor of Washington and Lee University. One of the congregation's early leaders was John Houston, great-grandfather of Sam Houston, the Texas pioneer. In keeping with Calvinist tradition, the building in its original form was probably a stern little struc-ture, devoid of prideful embellishment. The present facade, with its arcaded porch, was added in 1871. *(81–66) VLR: 09/09/69; NRHP: 11/12/69.*

VINEYARD HILL, *Buffalo Forge vicinity.* Commanding a hill over-looking Poague Run, Vineyard Hill is a vestige of Rockbridge County's earliest substantive rural housing. The rough-coursed limestone struc-ture was built ca. 1774 by Scotch-Irish settler Alexander Beggs. The house shows a Quaker influence with its three-room plan and corner staircase. An exceptional feature is the enormous cooking fireplace in the basement. The name Vineyard Hill derives from the use of the property as a vine-yard during its ownership by the Weaver family. The Weavers aspired to be winemakers and engaged a French horticulturist to establish a vineyard about 1870. The wine proved to be un-salable in the export market, and the effort was discontinued. The house was restored in the 1970s. On the property are the foundations of a springhouse and an ironworking mill. *(81–71) VLR: 12/06/95; BHR EASEMENT.*

VIRGINIA MANOR, *Natural Bridge Station vicinity.* Origi-nally known as Glengyle, Virginia Manor evolved from a sim-ple vernacular structure into a high-style country estate. It be-gan in 1800 as the two-story log home of John Fleming. In 1856 the log house became the rear wing of the two-story, five-bay frame home of Thomas Burks. In 1890 the property was sold to the Rockbridge Company, a land development company hop-ing to capitalize on the development of nearby Glasgow. The company president, Gen. Fitzhugh Lee, nephew of Robert E. Lee, set up residence at Glengyle. The development scheme failed, and in 1897 the property was purchased by Mrs. George W. Stevens, whose husband was president of the Chesapeake and Ohio Railway Co. The Stevenses transformed the property into a summer residence called Virginia Manor, further remod-eling and enlarging the house and adding various outbuildings, including a private railroad station. *(81–295) VLR: 03/17/87; NRHP: 09/10/87.*

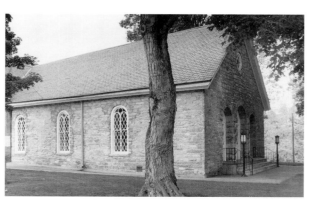

ROCKINGHAM COUNTY

Formed from Augusta County in 1778, this largely agricultural Shenandoah Valley county was named for Charles Watson-Wentworth, second marquess of Rockingham, who supported the colonists in their disputes with Great Britain. The county seat is Harrisonburg.

BAXTER HOUSE, *Edom vicinity.* Conspicuously located alongside the road between Broadway and Harrisonburg, the Baxter house displays Virginia log construction at its finest. The western half of the double-pen structure has full-dovetail corner notching. The precisely fitted logs, devoid of chinking, illustrate a building method associated with the Valley's German settlers. The quality of the construction is on a par with that usually associated with fine furniture. The eastern and earlier half has less uniformly dressed logs with regular chinking, making it typical of the log construction employed by Scotch-Irish settlers. It was built in the late 18th century for George Baxter, whose son served as one of the early presidents of Washington College in Lexington. *(82–71) VLR: 07/17/73; NRHP: 10/03/73.*

JOHN K. BEERY FARM, *Edom vicinity.* In a secluded valley in the Linville Creek area of Rockingham County, the John K. Beery complex is one of the most complete early rural homesteads in the region. The grouping, which boasts nearly a dozen farm structures, includes a stone dwelling house, well house, kitchen-washhouse, and rare stone barn with slotted ends. Beery, a descendant of Swiss immigrants who settled in Pennsylvania, established the complex over the period 1819–39. A strict Mennonite who opposed the use of churches, Beery for many years held services for the local congregation in the east wing of his house. The barn was burned in the Civil War but was rebuilt within the stone walls. Abandoned for almost two decades, the complex was carefully restored between 1974 and 1977. *(82–02) VLR: 07/17/73; NRHP: 09/19/73.*

BETHLEHEM CHURCH, *Tenth Legion.* Built in 1844–45 by the local stonemason Jeremiah Clemens, Bethlehem Church is the oldest stone church in Rockingham County and the second church of a local Quaker meeting. With its rectangular form, gabled roof, and limestone construction, the austere exterior reflects the conservative character of the Shenandoah Valley's mid-19th-century country churches. It also demonstrates the persistence of a strong local masonry tradition in the Linville and Smith Creek areas. The two-door, two-aisle arrangement was a hallmark of country meetinghouses. During the Civil War the church stood in the line of battle in the Valley campaigns and served as a hospital. The Quakers merged with the local Christian Church after the Civil War. Regular services ceased to be held in the building in 1952 when a new church was built next door. *(82–03) VLR: 12/16/80; NRHP: 06/25/85.*

BIG RUN QUARRY ARCHAEOLOGICAL SITE, *Big Run, Shenandoah National Park.* The continuity of human occupation in Virginia before European settlement is vividly apparent in this quarry site along the mountain stream Big Run. Covering about 1,400 square meters, this site has yielded huge amounts of stone debris typical of a prehistoric Native American quarry site. The site was the largest and most intensively used quarry located within the Shenandoah National Park and contrasts with other quarry sites in the sheer amount of debris present. Projectile points found here date to the Middle and Late Archaic periods (ca. 5500–100 B.C.). *(82–323) VLR: 09/16/82; NRHP: 12/13/85.*

BRIDGEWATER HISTORIC DISTRICT. Bridgewater is one of the largest and most intact of a string of towns that developed along the Shenandoah Valley's former Harrisonburg–Warm Springs Turnpike. It began as a river port for neighboring farms to float their goods downstream to Port Republic. The lots were laid out by the Dinkle family in the 1820s, and the community was formally established as a town in 1835. Bridgewater today preserves an extensive assemblage of vernacular architecture. The historic district focuses primarily on Main Street, with its rows of closely packed mid-19th-century dwellings, but it includes several early cross streets and the core of the campus of Bridgewater College, founded in 1882. Many of the buildings are cloaked with rich Victorian decoration, lending the town an air of turn-of-the-century prosperity. *(176–03) VLR: 06/19/84; NRHP: 11/01/84.*

DAYTON HISTORIC DISTRICT. Established in 1833, Dayton is among the several historic communities lining the Shenandoah Valley's former Harrisonburg–Warm Springs Turnpike. The turnpike and later the railroad serviced local enterprises. The establishment of Shenandoah Seminary (later renamed Shenandoah College and Conservatory of Music) in 1875, followed by the formation of the Ruebush-Kieffer Co. in 1878, brought Dayton special renown. One of the South's largest musical printing houses, the Ruebush-Kieffer Co. popularized the singing school and shaped-note traditions of county resident Joseph Funk. With over fifty songbooks, the Ruebush-Kieffer Co. reached a national audience. Since the company's dissolution in 1931 and the removal of the music conservatory to Winchester in 1960, Dayton has lost much of its bustle. It remains, however, the commercial center for a large community of Old Order Mennonites. Its streets, lined with rows of structures in local vernacular styles, recall Dayton's heyday. *(206–02) VLR: 06/19/84; NRHP: 08/16/84.*

GEORGE EARMAN HOUSE, *Harrisonburg vicinity.* The George Earman house is a vivid example of the creativity and sense of ornament found in the carving, joinery, and decorative painting of various early 19th-century Shenandoah Valley farmhouses. Hidden within an exceptionally plain, ca. 1822 brick I-house, this remarkable decoration reveals the persistence of the German influence after the Continental house forms had been abandoned for the more popular English-influenced models. Here local craftsmen freely interpreted Federal pattern-book motifs, carving them in the more robust German manner and integrating them with traditional local designs to create very individualized compositions. The parlor woodwork retains its original boldly colored painting scheme including marbleizing, woodgraining, and sponge-painted panels, forming an important work of Valley folk art. *(82–137) VLR: 09/15/81; NRHP: 07/08/82.*

FORT HARRISON (DANIEL HARRISON HOUSE), *Dayton.* Built ca. 1749 for Daniel Harrison, one of the area's earliest settlers, this rugged farmhouse was constructed of limestone in the plain style favored by the region's early settlers for their more substantial dwellings. During the Indian raids associated with the French and Indian War, the strong, well-positioned house served as a defense point and was locally referred to as a fort. The property remained in the Harrison family until 1821. Later owners made alterations, especially in 1856 when the rear brick section was added. It was probably then that the front windows were changed from evenly spaced openings to the present paired windows. Now restored to its mid-19th-century appearance, the venerable landmark is exhibited as a house museum by Fort Harrison, Inc., a nonprofit organization. *(206–01) VLR: 06/19/73; NRHP: 07/24/73.*

JOSEPH FUNK HOUSE, *Singers Glen.* Joseph Funk (1777–1862) was the grandson of Henry Funk, the first Mennonite bishop in America, and the son of Henry Funk, Jr., founder of the "Funkite" branch of the Mennonite church. The Funks moved to the region from Berks County, Pa., when Joseph Funk was a child. In 1847 Funk established his own press in what became the village of Singers Glen where he published his English translations of German Mennonite theological tracts and choral music. Funk also set up singing schools in the village and in other Shenandoah Valley towns and promoted the patent or shaped-note system, which was employed in his own widely used hymnal, *Harmonia Sacra.* Funk's simple weatherboarded log house in Singers Glen was built ca. 1810. Its press was located in the loom house nearby, which has since been destroyed. *(82–69) VLR: 11/19/74; NRHP: 02/24/75.*

HARNSBERGER FARM, *Shenandoah vicinity.* The Harnsberger farm complex has multiple points of interest. The oldest building is an early 19th-century log dwelling, an interesting vernacular structure showing a German influence with its three-room plan and central chimney. The main house was built in 1859–61 for George Harnsberger and his wife who acquired the property in 1849. Harnsberger was a descendant of Stephen Harnsberger, one of the Shenandoah Valley's early 18th-century Swiss-German settlers. Except for its I-house plan, the house is a stylish Italianate dwelling showing a break with the exterior plainness of the local vernacular tradition. Intact inside is the ca. 1890 decorative painting of the walls, ceilings, and mantels, including stenciling, graining, and marbleizing. The ceilings of the parlor and second-floor passage are painted with trompe l'oeil panels and medallions. *(82–132) VLR: 10/09/91; NRHP: 01/22/92.*

STEPHEN M. HARNSBERGER HOUSE, *Grottoes.* Built in 1856 as the residence of Stephen M. Harnsberger on what was originally known as Cottage Plains Farm, this singular dwelling is a Shenandoah Valley example of the octagonal building fad that spread across the nation in the mid–19th century. While the facade and shape of the house clearly reflect an awareness of the fashion popularized in Orson Squire Fowler's *A Home for All, or The Gravel Wall and Octagon Mode of Building* (1848), the interior retains the traditional arrangement of spaces in a center-passage, double-pile Georgian scheme. Instead of Fowler's recommended gravel-wall construction, the Harnsberger house is built of brick, which was originally covered with horsehair stucco. It was rerendered with the present rough stucco in 1916. Stephen M. Harnsberger was a descendant of John Harnsberger, a Swiss-German who settled near Germanna in the early 18th century. *(82–134) VLR: 01/20/81; NRHP: 07/08/82.*

INGLEWOOD, *Harrisonburg vicinity.* A leading historic farm in a region of fine farms, Inglewood occupies a commanding site just north of Harrisonburg. The property was purchased in 1818 by Robert Gray, a Harrisonburg attorney. Gray built Inglewood's residence ca. 1849–51 for his younger son Douglas on the occasion of his marriage to Isabella Pinkney, daughter of the Maryland diplomat William Pinkney. With its gable roof and regular five-bay facade, the double-pile brick house recalls the Federal dwellings of earlier decades. A full complement of outbuildings and farm buildings reinforces an air of agrarian prosperity. In 1876 Inglewood was purchased by Gen. John E. Roller, CSA, for his parents. Margaret Grattan Weaver, a granddaughter of General Roller, and her husband, James M. Weaver, purchased the estate from Lucy Cabot Roller in 1945. During a subsequent renovation remarkable antebellum folk-carved mantels from a Roller house in Harrisonburg were installed in Inglewood. *(82–51) VLR: 05/17/83; NRHP: 05/30/85.*

LINCOLN HOMESTEAD AND CEMETERY, *Broadway vicinity.* President Abraham Lincoln's great-grandfather John Lincoln moved from Pennsylvania and settled in the Linville Creek area of Rockingham County in 1768. Although John's eldest son, Abraham, grandfather of the president, migrated to Kentucky, a younger son, Jacob, remained to build the present Federal farmhouse around 1800 near the site of the original family home. The refined details and academic proportions make the house sophisticated for its time and place. The urbane exterior contrasts with the neighboring German-style farmhouses. A noteworthy feature is the handsomely detailed pedimented doorway. The property remained in the Lincoln family until 1874. The family cemetery, high on the hill behind the house, contains the graves of five generations of Lincolns, including John and Jacob Lincoln, and two of the Lincoln family slaves. *(82–14) VLR: 08/15/72; NRHP: 12/05/72.*

LINVILLE CREEK BRIDGE, *Broadway.* The Linville Creek Bridge is Virginia's only Thacher truss bridge and one of only two surviving examples of its type in the country. The Thacher truss was patented in 1883 by Edwin Thacher (1839–1920), who worked with several railroad companies and with the Louisville Bridge and Iron Co., as well as with the Keystone Bridge Co. in Pittsburgh. He patented eight bridge designs and published a series of tables for calculating bridge stress coefficients. He designed over 2,000 steel and 200 concrete bridges. The bridge was manufactured in 1898 by the Wrought Iron Bridge Company of Canton, Ohio, and remains in daily use. The Wrought Iron Bridge Company was one of the leading bridge-building firms in the nation and constructed as least nine other metal-truss bridges in the Shenandoah Valley region. *(117–5001) VLR: 11/15/77; NRHP: 04/15/78.*

MILLER-KITE HOUSE (STONEWALL JACKSON'S HEADQUARTERS), *302 East Rockingham Street, Elkton.*
Henry Miller, Jr., descendant of one of the earliest settlers west of the Blue Ridge Mountains, had this substantial and finely detailed brick house built for his residence in 1827. As noted in the contract, the dwelling's carpentry and joinery were executed by Samuel Gibbons of Rockingham County, making this one of the few houses in the area with which a specific craftsman is associated. The woodwork, especially a mantel carved with a tulip-and-vine motif, shows the influence of the German style on an otherwise non-Germanic house. Stonewall Jackson used the house as his headquarters in April 1862, beginning his famous Valley campaign from this location. In 1984 the house was donated by the Kite family to the town of Elkton. It has since been restored by the Elkton Historical Society for use as a museum. *(82–133) VLR: 10/17/78; NRHP: 02/01/79.*

PETER PAUL HOUSE, *Dayton vicinity.* This plain dwelling near the town of Dayton is one of the few Continental-type farmhouses surviving from the heavy German settlement in the Shenandoah Valley. Distinguished by its central chimney, the house is also one of the latest and most southern of these Germanic dwellings. The walls are of log construction but were stuccoed over at an early date. Nearly all of the original interior fittings, including beaded partitions, simple Federal mantels, a ladder stair, paneled door, and batten door survive despite modern alterations. The house was built by Peter Paul between 1805 and 1815 on land formerly owned by the Harrison family. Paul appears in the Rockingham County records in 1802 and was first taxed for owning land in 1807. *(82–31) VLR: 10/16/79; NRHP: 12/28/79.*

PORT REPUBLIC HISTORIC DISTRICT. On the South Fork of the Shenandoah River in eastern Rockingham County, this grid-plan village was founded in 1802 and became a booming river port. It served as the shipping point for the agricultural and industrial products of the upper Shenandoah River until the 1890s when the railroad was built east of town. The town's collection of 19th-century vernacular buildings and numerous archaeological sites preserves the story of the community's growth and decline. Port Republic gave its name to a Civil War battle, the conclusion of Stonewall Jackson's Valley campaign, fought just to the north of town. Today the community preserves an open, almost rural quality with houses and outbuildings sprinkled among large lots. The most imposing structure, the Dundore house (shown), is a 1760s log structure with a Federal-period brick section and still-later stocky Doric portico. *(82–123) VLR: 07/18/78; NRHP: 09/08/80.*

SINGERS GLEN HISTORIC DISTRICT. This idyllic village began when Joseph Funk moved here in the early 19th century and established a publishing firm for Mennonite religious tracts and choral music. The settlement that grew up around his farm was called Mountain Valley but was renamed Singers Glen in 1860 in honor of the choral publications. The publishing firm moved from Singers Glen in 1878, but the village continued to prosper as other businesses, including a carriage works, located here. The late 19th-century prosperity resulted in the construction of a number of spacious wooden houses, many of them with decorative turned- and sawn-work porches, including those built by members of the Funk family. Contrasting with these richly trimmed structures is Joseph Funk's plain little house in the center of the village. The halt of growth after World War I has preserved Singers Glen's wholesome village character. *(82–125) VLR: 12/21/76; NRHP: 01/20/78.*

SITES HOUSE, *Broadway vicinity.* Rockingham County's Linville Creek area was first populated by settlers of German origin who incorporated Continental building forms into their New World homes. Although once common, only a handful of these German-style farmhouses remain; the Sites house is a notably pure and well-preserved one. Characteristic of these houses is the stone construction, the centered chimney stack, and the sloping site location. The three-room plan is also a telltale feature of German houses, known as a *Flurküchenhaus* plan because one of the rooms, that with the largest fireplace, was the *Küche,* or kitchen. Adding interest to the house is the large amount of original woodwork, including the exposed, molded summer beam and joists and an unusual roof-framing system with molded purlins. Built ca. 1800, the house was originally the home of Christian Sites. Long vacant, it has been restored in recent years. *(82–35) VLR: 10/17/78; NRHP: 04/03/79.*

TUNKER HOUSE, *Broadway.* This plain Shenandoah Valley brick farmhouse is a relic of the early German Baptist Brethren, or Dunkers, known originally in the area as the Society of Tunkers, who opposed the use of churches and held their religious services in selected homes. The house was erected between 1802 and 1806 for Benjamin Yount, who outfitted the front portion of the first floor with hinged partitions that could be raised to accommodate religious gatherings. Yount's daughter was the wife of Peter Nead, a leading member of the Tunkers and author of *Primitive Christianity,* which served as the Brethren's first theological work in English. The Neads occupied her father's house until 1839. Although it is now a private residence, the hinged partitions of this combination church-home remain in place. *(82–25) VLR: 03/02/71; NRHP: 07/02/71.*

RUSSELL COUNTY

Formed from Washington County in 1786, this pastoral Southwest Virginia county was named for William Russell, a Clinch Valley pioneer and the member of the House of Delegates who introduced the legislation forming the county. The county seat is Lebanon.

DAUGHERTY'S CAVE AND BREEDING ARCHAEO-LOGICAL SITE, *Lebanon vicinity.* Along the banks of Big Cedar Creek near its junction with the Clinch River, these two sites contain Indian artifacts dating from 8000 B.C. to A.D. 1600. Excavations at Daugherty's Cave show deeply stratified cultural deposits containing stone projectile points and tools, ceramic potsherds, unusually well-preserved bone and skull fragments, and hearth features. The adjacent Breeding site contains a greater amount of specifically Early Archaic period (8000–6000 B.C.) remains. Future investigation of both sites should provide contrasting information on Indian lifestyles at various periods in both rockshelters and open habitats. *(83–22) VLR: 12/21/76; NRHP: 06/23/78.*

OLD RUSSELL COUNTY COURTHOUSE, *Dickensonville vicinity.* The second courthouse of Russell County is one of the earliest public buildings in Southwest Virginia. The simple stone structure was built in 1799 to replace the first courthouse, a log building destroyed by fire. It served the county until the county seat was moved to Lebanon in 1818. The courthouse was then acquired by the Dickenson family who made it the wing of a brick farmhouse. Despite its conversion to residential use, much of the building's original interior fabric was preserved. In recent years the property was again acquired by the county, and both the stone section and the brick addition have been restored as a museum. *(83–01) VLR: 06/19/73; NRHP: 07/16/73.*

SMITHFIELD, *Rosedale vicinity.* Smithfield, a 980-acre farm in the scenic countryside along Elk Garden Creek, has been the home of the Smith family for more than two centuries. It was first settled by Col. Henry Smith who came here from Stafford County in 1776. His descendant, Dr. John Taylor Smith, built the present house in 1848–50. Dr. Smith, whose medical practice covered seven counties, was one of the area's first physicians to inoculate against smallpox. His generously scaled residence, its bricks made by slaves, is one of the county's most impressive examples of antebellum architecture, ornamented inside and out with regionalized interpretations of pattern-book Greek Revival detailing. Smith's farm, in addition to its cattle and sheep, produced corn, oats, wool, butter, flax, and maple sugar. Smithfield was converted to a dairy farm in the 1940s in response to the government's encouragement of milk production for the war effort. *(83–12) VLR: 06/15/94; NRHP: 08/16/94.*

✤ CITY OF SALEM

The Roanoke county seat was laid out in 1802 and is said to have been named for Salem, N.J., home of one of the settling families. It was incorporated as a town in 1836 and became an independent city in 1968.

ACADEMY STREET SCHOOL, *Academy Street.* Completed in 1890 on the site of a private female academy, the Academy Street School was one of the first modern public schools in Southwest Virginia, an outgrowth of the state's late 19th-century educational reforms. Taking advantage of its prominent location at the head of a street, the building was given a fashionable Victorian silhouette emphasized by decorative brickwork, bracketed cornices, and entrance tower originally topped by a mansard roof. Its well-lighted, centrally heated, and spacious classrooms, arranged around an octagonal central hall, indicated an enlightened attitude toward public primary education, a contrast to the one-room wooden schoolhouses most Virginians attended at the time. The school originally was in the Roanoke County school system but later was incorporated into that of Salem. Closed in 1977, the building was sold by the city and converted into apartments. *(129–02) VLR: 01/20/81; NRHP: 10/01/81.*

DOWNTOWN SALEM HISTORIC DISTRICT. Salem's historic district embraces the core of the present-day city. Within this twenty-five-acre area is the town's original platted grid, laid out in 1802 along the Great Road by James Simpson. The town's designation as the Roanoke county seat in 1838 spurred development. The community gained prestige when Virginia Collegiate Institute, later named Roanoke College, was located here in the 1840s. Salem escaped the Civil War with minimal damage. Today the district possesses a varied concentration of buildings ranging in date from the early 1800s to the mid-1900s. It is characterized by its mixed-use commercial structures as well as churches, courthouse, post office, and library. Prosperity is reflected in the fine quality of many individual buildings. The rapid emergence of neighboring Roanoke encouraged Salem's more measured growth and the resulting preservation of its historic character. *(129–75) VLR: 03/20/96; NRHP: 06/05/96.*

EVANS HOUSE, *213 North Broad Street.* John M. Evans, farmer, Civil War veteran, businessman, and investor in Salem's land boom, built this compact Broad Street mansion in 1882. The house is a near-perfect example of the American Second Empire style, employing both a mansard roof and a reverse-curved mansard tower. Local tradition holds that the style was intended to please Evans's French bride. The bold outline and fine proportions disguise the building's relatively small size. The sophistication of the design suggests the involvement of a skilled architect. Such exuberant late Victorian houses were never common in Virginia, and many that were built have since been demolished, leaving the Evans house a significant landmark both of its style and of the boom period in western Virginia. Always maintained as a prestige address, the house is in excellent condition and survives essentially unchanged. *(129–17) VLR: 03/21/72; NRHP: 05/19/72.*

OLD ROANOKE COUNTY COURTHOUSE, *301 East Main Street.* A hometown expression of the American Renaissance, the former 1910 Roanoke County Courthouse, with its three-story Ionic portico and an eagle-topped cupola, has the classical grandeur and assertiveness inherent in the movement's most ambitious works. It was designed by H. H. Huggins, a Roanoke architect of ability and remarkable self-confidence, who regularly boasted about the quality and quantity of his output. Following its completion, the local newspaper focused attention on the courthouse clock: "It is not only highly useful in its lofty setting, but is quite ornamental. In size it is commensurate with the new courthouse itself, which adds dignity to the whole square." The courthouse was built of buff pressed brick, considered a prestige material because it complemented classical stone detailing. The building was purchased by Roanoke College in 1987; an extensive rehabilitation for academic use was completed in 1996. *(129–08) VLR: 03/17/87; NRHP: 05/14/87.*

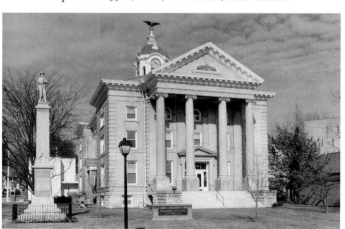

ROANOKE COLLEGE MAIN CAMPUS COMPLEX, *College Avenue.* In a tree-shaded campus in the heart of Salem, this group of academic buildings displays the evolution of the area's architectural tastes from the mid–19th century through the early 1900s. First known as Virginia Collegiate Institute, Roanoke College was founded in Augusta County in 1842 by two Lutheran pastors and was moved to Salem in 1847. That same year builders James C. and Joseph Deyerle began erecting Main Building, now the Administration Building. Originally Greek Revival, the building was remodeled in the neoclassical taste in 1903, receiving a third floor and Corinthian portico. Flanking it are Miller and Trout halls, both begun in 1856. The Gothic-style Bittle Hall was completed in 1879 as a library and is now the office of the Virginia Synod of the Evangelical Lutheran Church in America. Roanoke College continues as a leading educational institution of the region. *(129–05) VLR: 05/16/72; NRHP: 03/07/73.*

SALEM POST OFFICE, *103 East Main Street.* This pristine interpretation of the late Colonial Revival style was designed in 1917 under the supervision of Treasury Department architect Louis A. Simon. Actual construction was postponed until 1922 when a Republican appointee could become Salem's postmaster. Completed in 1923, the building is a handsome example of the federal presence in small-town America. The restraint in the scale and ornamentation of this and similar post offices was the result of new federal initiatives aimed at cutting costs of government buildings. The policy encouraged standardization and simple design, using variations on the same scheme for many communities. Officials rationalized the federal building program by relating the size and architectural embellishment of post offices to a community's population and annual postal receipts. Decommissioned in 1985, the post office was sensitively rehabilitated for doctors' offices in 1989–91. *(129–37) VLR: 04/22/92; NRHP: 09/24/92.*

SALEM PRESBYTERIAN CHURCH, *East Main and Market streets.* The inventiveness and keen aesthetic sense of America's Greek Revival architects and master builders are displayed in Salem's Presbyterian church. Its designer has not been identified; however, much of the woodwork likely was executed by Gustavus Sedon, a skillful Roanoke Valley carver and master carpenter. Many of the classical details show a reliance on popular pattern books of the period such as those by Asher Benjamin and Owen Biddle. Organized in Salem in 1831, the Presbyterians outgrew their first church and began construction of the present building in 1851. The church tower was originally topped by a spire; the present octagonal lantern dates from 1928. *(129–09) VLR: 06/18/74; NRHP: 10/15/74.*

SALEM PRESBYTERIAN PARSONAGE, *530 East Main Street.* Set in a shady lawn along Salem's main thoroughfare, this much-evolved house began in 1847 as a typical regional I-house, built by John Day, a local blacksmith. Its location on what was the Great Road was chosen so that Day could easily serve the route's many travelers. The noted artist Edward Beyer documented the early configuration of the house in an 1850s landscape of Salem, even depicting what may have been Day's blacksmith shop across the road. The Salem Presbyterian Church purchased the house in 1854 for a parsonage, making substantial additions to both front and rear during the late 19th and early 20th centuries. Elements of the original facade were reused on the new front. It continued to serve as a parsonage until 1939. A garden, designed by Virginia landscape architect Stanley Abbott, was laid out in 1946–47. *(129–14) VLR: 08/21/91; NRHP: 01/28/92.*

SOUTHWEST VIRGINIA HOLINESS ASSOCIATION CAMP MEETING, *202 and 208 East Third Street.* This camp meeting complex had its origins in the Holiness movement, a mid-19th-century offshoot of Methodism. Adherents of the movement dedicated themselves to living perfect or "holy" lives according to scriptural teaching. Critical to the movement's activities was the camp meeting, an ecstatic form of worship with deep roots in the religious life of rural America. Camp meetings usually involved several weeks of intensely emotional worship. The chief patron of the movement's Salem branch was Demetrius Bittle Strouse who had the original meeting hall or tabernacle erected in 1901. The present tabernacle, a plain wooden hall, was built in 1922; the adjacent dormitory was put up in 1928. Regular summer meetings were held here until 1993 when diminished participation prompted their cancellation. Since sold, this landmark of religious fervor is now used for a youth theater along with gospel sings and other special events. *(129–123) VLR: 10/18/95; NRHP: 01/22/96.*

WILLIAMS-BROWN HOUSE-STORE, *East Main Street.* This combination commercial and residential building is perhaps the area's last remaining example of a type once prevalent in towns along the much-traveled Great Road to Kentucky and Tennessee. It related to its street-front site by having galleries incorporated into the volume of the building and entered from the footpath through arches in the side walls. Dating from ca. 1845–52, the building was constructed and first occupied by William C. Williams, who was also one of the builders of Salem's first courthouse. It later passed to the Brown family who owned it until 1963. Threatened with demolition, the building was moved in 1987 a short distance west to a city park where it again was situated fronting the former Great Road (U.S. Route 11). It is now a museum of local history operated by the Salem Historical Society. *(129–10) VLR: 07/06/71; NRHP: 11/23/71.*

SCOTT COUNTY

This mountainous county near Virginia's southwestern tip was named for Gen. Winfield Scott, a native of Virginia, in recognition of his victories during the War of 1812. It was formed in 1814 from Lee, Russell, and Washington counties. Its county seat is Gate City.

A. P. AND SARA CARTER HOUSE, *Maces Spring.* This unassuming but commodious residence was the home of country music legend Alvin Pleasant Delaney (A. P.) Carter from 1927 until his death in 1960. From his youth, Carter maintained an abiding interest in the music of the mountain folk. He collected the region's traditional songs and performed them verbatim or reworked them in his own individual style. The same year that he purchased this house, Carter and his also musical wife, Sara, were auditioned by the Victor Talking Machine Co. Their talents were immediately recognized, and thus were planted the seeds of the nation's country music recording industry. Carter's collection of some 250 to 300 songs, ballads, lyrics, and gospel music was recorded between 1927 and 1941, simultaneously ensuring the preservation of a significant facet of American culture and launching a new one. *(84–14) VLR: 04/16/85; NRHP: 06/12/85.*

A. P. CARTER HOMEPLACE, *Maces Spring vicinity.* A. P. Carter (1891–1960), progenitor of the famous Carter family of country musicians, was born in this simple log dwelling situated alongside a footpath in Little Valley in scenic Scott County. Although Carters had lived in the area for over a hundred years, the cabin probably was erected by Carter's father, Robert, not long before A. P.'s birth. A. P. Carter was one of eight children raised here. The cabin is a representative example of the unglamorous folk housing of the region's farming families and illustrates the persistence of traditional forms. Little different from cabins built decades earlier, the homeplace is a one-room square or English cabin with an enclosed corner stair. The logs have typical half-dovetail notching. A lean-to kitchen was added later. Now used for storage, the cabin is still owned by the Carter family. *(84–07) VLR: 12/16/75; NRHP: 07/30/76.*

A. P. CARTER STORE (CARTER FAMILY MEMORIAL MUSEUM), *Maces Spring.* Trained as a carpenter, A. P. Carter, patriarch of the Carter family of musicians, built this country store with the help of his son Joe. He opened it in 1943 soon after the original Carter Family music group disbanded. A. P. continued to be involved with music during the years he operated the store, collecting, composing, and performing traditional regional music. Following his death in 1960, his daughter, Janette, used the building to perpetuate the family's music tradition, holding "Old Time Music" shows beginning in 1974. She later transformed the store into the Carter Family Memorial Museum, exhibiting much family memorabilia. Although its use has changed, the building preserves many of its original fittings and maintains the air of the simple country stores that long served rural areas. *(84–06) VLR: 04/16/85; NRHP: 06/14/85.*

MAYBELLE AND EZRA CARTER HOUSE, *Maces Spring.* Ezra Carter and his wife, Maybelle Addington Carter, members of the Carter family of musicians, moved into this house after marrying in 1926. Ezra was the brother of A. P. Carter, and Maybelle was cousin to A. P.'s wife Sara. They added the porch when the house was enlarged in 1936. After the original Carter Family performing group disbanded in 1943, Maybelle formed a group with her three daughters entitled Mother Maybelle and the Carter Sisters. The group first performed on Richmond's WRVA Old Dominion Barn Dance but soon moved to Nashville where they gained fame performing with the Grand Ole Opry. Maybelle's daughter June married singer Johnny Cash, and together they continued the family music tradition, moving more into the realm of popular country music. In 1981 the house was purchased by Johnny and June Carter Cash who continue to own it. *(84–15) VLR: 04/16/85; NRHP: 06/12/85.*

FLANARY ARCHAEOLOGICAL SITE, *Dungannon vicinity.* The Flanary archaeological site contains stratified deposits dating to the Archaic and Late Woodland periods of Indian settlement. Well-preserved Archaic period deposits (8000 to 1000 B.C.) occur rarely in the western portion of the state, and the site's Late Woodland period remains (A.D. 800–1600) overlying these deposits could provide significant data for regional studies on Indian subsistence and settlement. Shown is a ca. 1500 B.C. incised soapstone vessel fragment found here. The presence of artifacts at the site relating to the Indians of eastern Tennessee and western North Carolina is valuable in documenting the interactions of Virginia Indians with their neighbors to the south. *(84–12) VLR: 09/16/82; NRHP: 07/07/83.*

KILGORE FORT HOUSE, *Nickelsville vicinity.* Indians remained a threat to Southwest Virginia settlers well into the late 18th century. Military blockhouses were no longer deemed essential, but strongly built log dwellings were considered prudent. Robert Kilgore's stout log house of ca. 1790 represents this stage in frontier development. Both its lower and upper stories are separated into two rooms by log partitions built as strongly as the outer walls, providing the possibility of several strategic retreats. Although threatened on various occasions, the Kilgore house survived the last Indian attack. Kilgore, who lived here until his death in 1854 at the age of eighty-eight, was a Primitive Baptist preacher as well as a farmer. The house stood neglected for many years but was restored in the 1970s by the Lenowisco Planning District Commission with the assistance of other area agencies to serve as a visitor attraction for a wayside park. *(84–03) VLR: 01/18/72; NRHP: 05/19/72.*

MOUNT VERNON UNITED METHODIST CHURCH, *Maces Spring.* A laconically plain country church, Mount Vernon United Methodist in Maces Springs follows the pattern of scores of rural religious structures scattered through the Virginia hinterland. This particular church, built in 1906, gains fame for its association with the Carter Family, renowned country music performers. The church was a cornerstone in the lives of A. P. Carter and his wife Sara and their kinswoman Maybelle Carter. All three were devout Christians and active in the life of the church. Local church music was an important influence in their careers, and many of the songs they recorded were hymns and other religious pieces. A. P. Carter developed his vocal talents here as a boy singing in the church choir. The church is still attended by what is today the sixth generation of Carter family members. A. P. and Sara are both buried in the church cemetery. *(84–13) VLR: 04/16/85; NRHP: 06/12/85.*

SHENANDOAH COUNTY

Shenandoah County originally was named Dunmore in honor of Lord Dunmore, governor of Virginia at the time it was formed from Frederick County in 1772. The present name, from the river that passes through it, was substituted in 1778 as a result of antiroyalist sentiment. The county seat is Woodstock.

CAMPBELL FARM, *Lantz Mills.* On an eminence dominating the village of Lantz Mills, Campbell farm is a remarkably intact late 19th-century rural complex exuding the air of confidence and prosperity that characterized the late Victorian era. The principal feature of the grouping is a frame Queen Anne mansion with octagonal corner towers. Immediately adjacent are seven frame buildings that served the farm. The complex was built in 1888–89 for Milton C. Campbell, a local resident who married into a family of ironmasters with Canadian and Pennsylvanian connections. They purchased two Shenandoah County iron furnaces, Columbia and Liberty furnaces, after the Civil War, following other northern entrepreneurs into what they hoped would be a prosperous southern economy. The venture eventually failed, and Campbell sold the property in 1908. Despite the family's decline, the property has enjoyed subsequent owners who have kept the buildings in excellent condition. *(85–127) VLR: 04/17/90; NRHP: 08/15/90; BHR EASEMENT.*

EDINBURG MILL, *Edinburg.* The large gristmill on Stony Creek at the western end of the historic community of Edinburg is a relic of the region's early agricultural industry. The present structure was built ca. 1850 by George Grandstaff to support a mill complex developed by his father beginning in 1813. The mill was set afire during Union general Philip Sheridan's sweep of the Valley in 1864. Tradition has it, however, that the ladies of the town persuaded the Union officers to save the remaining flour supply. They and the Union soldiers then extinguished the flames, rescuing the mill and most of the contents. The machinery was modernized at the turn of the century, and milling operations continued until 1978. The mill has since been secured through acquisition for adaptive use as a restaurant. *(85–110) VLR: 06/19/79; NRHP: 09/07/79.*

FORESTVILLE MILL (ZIRKLE MILL), *Forestville.* Probably dating from the late 18th century, this gristmill on Holmans Creek at the edge of the village of Forestville was erected by Andrew Zirkle, Sr., and originally accommodated the labor-saving machinery promoted by mill theorist Oliver Evans. The mill prospered in the antebellum period under the proprietorship of Jacob Bowers, who founded the adjoining village of Forestville on portions of the original mill property in 1838. Unlike many of the region's mills, the Forestville Mill survived the Civil War intact. The tall wooden building retains a collection of early milling machinery, illustrating the technological changes that transformed Zirkle's burr mill into a roller mill by the turn of the century. Despite the changes in the milling process, the mill kept its overshot exterior wheel. It ceased commercial operation in the 1950s. *(85–122) VLR: 12/14/82; NRHP: 02/10/83.*

FORT BOWMAN, *Middletown vicinity.* Standing on an undisturbed section of the old Valley Turnpike, Fort Bowman, also known as Harmony Hall, illustrates the Pennsylvania German influence on early Shenandoah Valley architecture. Notable German characteristics are the limestone construction, the dressed ceiling joists, and the principal-purlin roof framing. The house was built ca. 1753 for George Bowman, who with his wife Mary migrated to Virginia from Pennsylvania in 1731–32. Mary Bowman was the daughter of Jost Hite, regarded as the region's first white settler. Among those buried in Fort Bowman's graveyard are George Bowman's son Isaac Bowman, who aided George Rogers Clark in the conquest of the Northwest, and Samuel Kercheval, Shenandoah Valley historian. Except for the addition of the small Greek Revival portico and a kitchen wing, the house survives little changed. *(85–04) VLR: 11/05/68; NRHP: 11/25/69.*

DR. CHRISTIAN HOCKMAN HOUSE, *Edinburg vicinity.* Dr. Christian Hockman's house, conspicuously located on U.S. Route 11, is a rare example of the Italian Villa style in the lower Shenandoah Valley. The square tower is the style's signature feature. The mass-manufactured exterior and interior woodwork is illustrative of an important change in the region's building tradition. Supplanting ornaments made by hand, the machine-made components were sold through illustrated catalogs in major towns and cities and were distributed through rural areas by the ever-widening railroad network. The Hockman house was built in 1868–70 just as rail service was opened from Baltimore to nearby Edinburg. Dr. Hockman is listed in the 1885 directory as a dentist living just north of Edinburg on the Valley Turnpike. The house stood unoccupied for several years but has since been restored and is now a bed-and-breakfast inn. *(85–76) VLR: 01/17/84; NRHP: 02/23/84.*

HUPP HOUSE, *551 North Massanutten Street, Strasburg.* The Hupp house, also known as the Hupp homestead or Frontier Fort, was likely built as early as 1755, presumably by Peter Hupp, a settler of German extraction who came to the area from Pennsylvania. The house has been the property of the Hupp family to the present. With its limestone construction, hillside site, two-room plan, and center chimney, the house has the essential features of the plain Continental-type houses erected by the region's earliest settlers. Such houses are rare and important relics of the Shenandoah Valley's ethnic German community. Considerable action took place in the vicinity of the Hupp house during the Civil War, but the house escaped unscathed. George Hupp, Jr., and his brother served under Gen. Stonewall Jackson. A masonry block wing was added to the house in 1956. Later stucco was removed from the stonework in 1995. *(85–07) VLR: 12/04/96; NRHP: 02/21/97.*

LANTZ HALL, *Woodstock.* Lantz Hall was built in 1907 as the second structure of Massanutten Military Academy, the main building of this still-active institution. Chartered in 1899, Massanutten was organized by the Virginia Classis of the Reformed Church, presently the United Church of Christ, and was one of twelve Reformed Church institutions in the country. It was designed by the Clarksville, W.Va., firm of Holmboe & Lafferty, which made use of the modified castellated Gothic style that was popular for military schools. The composition is dominated by a central tower with corner crenellated turrets. The building originally housed fifty-two boys and four teachers and contained an auditorium and gymnasium. Its patron, William C. Lantz, a founding trustee of the academy, dedicated the hall to the memory of his parents, Mr. and Mrs. George Lantz, descendants of early German settlers of Shenandoah County. *(330–05) VLR: 10/21/92; NRHP: 12/30/92.*

MEEMS BOTTOM COVERED BRIDGE, *Route 720, Mount Jackson vicinity.* Constructed in 1893–94, this 200-foot single-span structure crossing the Shenandoah River is the longest of the Commonwealth's handful of remaining covered bridges. Probably constructed by John W. V. Woods for F. H. Wisler, the bridge is approached from the east by a tree-lined axial avenue across the flat fields of Meems Bottom whence the bridge derives its name. The structural system employed is a Burr arch-truss or king-post arch system, which consists of two great wooden arches spanning the full distance between the abutments. The bridge was damaged by fire in 1976, but the structural timbers survived with only charring. The frame was repaired and strengthened and re-covered with roofing and weatherboards by the Virginia Department of Transportation, allowing the bridge to be returned to limited use. *(85–103) VLR: 04/15/75; NRHP: 06/10/75.*

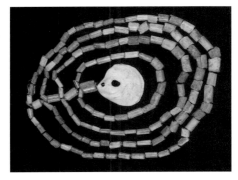

MILEY ARCHAEOLOGICAL SITE, *Maurertown vicinity.* In the Seven Bends area of the Shenandoah River, the Miley site consists of the remains of a palisaded village of the Late Woodland period (A.D. 900–1600). Approximately 15 percent of the site was excavated in 1964 under the direction of the Library of Virginia, revealing a village area over 250 feet in diameter. The remains of five circular houses of various diameters were uncovered within the two concentric palisade lines. Also discovered were evidences of food storage pits, stone-lined hearths, and graves. The remaining unexcavated areas likely hold important information on the region's Indian life. Shown are bone and shell beads found on the site. *(85–101) VLR: 04/16/74.*

MOUNT JACKSON HISTORIC DISTRICT. Established as Mount Pleasant in 1826, this community was later renamed Mount Jackson for Andrew Jackson. It prospered as a commercial, milling, and transportation center, primarily because of the routing of the Valley Turnpike through the town in the 1830s and the arrival of the Manassas Gap Railroad in 1859. Surviving from the earliest period are several log houses, a scattering of Federal-period dwellings, and the ca. 1825 Union Church. This church was one of the town's several buildings to have served as a Confederate hospital; the names of presumably convalescent soldiers and their companies survive on the interior walls. The oldest dwelling on Main Street is probably the log Stoneburner house. Most of the buildings, however, date from after the Civil War. Noteworthy among the latter are an 1872 frame mill, three Victorian Gothic brick churches, and several turn-of-the-century residences. *(265–04) VLR: 04/21/93; NRHP: 06/17/93.*

NEW MARKET BATTLEFIELD, *New Market vicinity.* Gen. John C. Breckinridge's Confederate brigades, joined by the 247-man cadet corps of the Virginia Military Institute, repulsed the Union forces at New Market on May 15, 1864, thus preserving the supply and communication lines between the Army of Northern Virginia and the Shenandoah Valley. This victory permitted Gen. Robert E. Lee to concentrate his full efforts toward halting the Union advance on Richmond. In their only engagement of the war, the VMI cadets, the eldest of them under eighteen, distinguished themselves with a gallant charge and the capture of a battery and an enemy flag. Some 160 acres of the battlefield are maintained by the Commonwealth as the New Market Battlefield Historical Park and memorialize the cadets who fought and died here. On the eastern edge of the battlefield is the restored Bushong house, used by both sides as a hospital. *(85–27) VLR: 06/02/70; NRHP: 09/15/70.*

NEW MARKET HISTORIC DISTRICT. New Market, originally called Cross Roads, is one of western Virginia's best-preserved historic linear towns. The site was selected by John Sevier, later governor of Tennessee, who established a trading post here in 1761. The village was laid out in 1785 along the Great Road—the wagon route to the south and west—and was named New Market in 1796. Settled both by Germans and Scotch-Irish, New Market prospered to become an active commercial and industrial center by the 1830s, serving travelers on the newly established Valley Turnpike. Growth ceased in the mid–19th century, however, when the town was bypassed by the railroad. Fierce fighting occurred here during the 1864 battle of New Market with townspeople turning out to treat the wounded. Lining the highway is a mixture of 19th-century brick, frame, and log structures. Several of the earlier houses employ German vernacular forms. *(269–05) VLR: 05/16/72; NRHP: 09/22/72.*

ORKNEY SPRINGS, *Orkney Springs.* In the shadow of the Allegheny Mountains, Orkney Springs presents what is perhaps the state's most complete picture of the many spa complexes that sprang up around Virginia's mineral springs in the 19th century. Orkney Springs was known as early as 1800, and a small community was established here in the 1830s. Resort development began in the 1850s. Surviving from Orkney Springs's period of greatest popularity is the 1876 Virginia House, a wooden hotel surrounded by tiers of galleries. The oldest building is the 1853 Maryland House, also highlighted by galleries. Other hotel structures and a range of cottages complete the picture of a 19th-century resort. Although most of its sister spas have succumbed to fire, abandonment, or demolition, Orkney Springs has managed to survive through use as a summer music camp and a retreat for the Episcopal Diocese of Virginia known as Shrine Mont. *(85–39) VLR: 03/18/75; NRHP: 04/22/76.*

QUICKSBURG ARCHAEOLOGICAL SITE, *Quicksburg vicinity.* Test excavations undertaken by the Library of Virginia at this site on the Shenandoah River have revealed evidence of one of the region's few palisaded Indian villages of the Late Woodland period (A.D. 900–1600). Within the village compound were found indications of circular dwellings as well as food storage pits and graves. Further investigation of the site should provide important information on Indian communal life in the lower Shenandoah Valley. *(85–102) VLR: 04/16/74.*

SHENANDOAH COUNTY COURTHOUSE, South Main and West Court streets, Woodstock.

The original section of the Shenandoah County Courthouse, erected in 1795 to replace a log courthouse, is considered to be the oldest court structure west of the Blue Ridge Mountains. The architecture of the limestone building reflects the dominance of the German settlers in the Woodstock area. Its most conspicuous feature, the hexagonal, ogee-roofed cupola, recalls the belfries of German baroque parish churches. The original form of the courthouse remains evident despite alterations and additions. A brick Greek Revival wing was added in 1840, and a handsomely ornamented Victorian clerk's office was attached in 1880. The Tuscan portico dates from 1920; its pediment echoes the pediment of the original central pavilion. A new county courthouse was built in the 1970s; the historic one now houses county offices, and the restored courtroom is used for public gatherings. *(330–02) VLR: 06/19/73; NRHP: 06/19/73.*

SHENANDOAH COUNTY FARM, Mauertown vicinity.

The 1829 almshouse at the Shenandoah County Farm is perhaps Virginia's only early county poorhouse still serving its original purpose. The two-story brick structure, with its low dormitory wings, is a comely work of local Federal-style architecture embellished with finely detailed interior woodwork. The farm was part of the colonial Beckford Parish glebe, established in 1769 and acquired by the county during the disestablishment of the Anglican church. The first almshouse was set up here in 1800 in the original glebe house. By 1829 its deteriorated condition required its replacement with the present structure. The farm was the scene of a Union bivouac the night before the 1864 battle of Toms Brook. By 1991 the place housed only seven permanent residents. The property is now administered by a nonprofit organization under lease from the county. *(85–86) VLR: 08/18/93; NRHP: 10/29/93.*

SNAPP HOUSE, Fishers Hill vicinity.

This late 18th-century log farmhouse is one of Shenandoah County's best representatives of the Continental-type central-chimney dwellings built by the area's German-speaking settlers. The Germanic tradition is evident in the hillside setting, with the original log section built over a spring. This log section has a four-room, or *Kreuzhaus*, plan and also features complex roof framing. An 1824 stone wing and the remains of a springhouse-kitchen add to the picture of early German-American life in the Shenandoah Valley. The exact construction date of the original section is unknown, although it is likely that it was built by Lawrence Snapp ca. 1750, when he arrived in the Valley from Pennsylvania. The house has been carefully restored in recent years. *(85–29) VLR: 11/21/78; NRHP: 05/07/79.*

STRASBURG HISTORIC DISTRICT.

Strasburg was an important focus of early migration in the Valley of Virginia. Founded in 1749, the town was settled exclusively by Germans, most of whom came from York County, Pa. By the early 19th century, Strasburg prospered as a flour-milling center. In the antebellum period it was associated with the manufacture of high-grade pottery. The town's strategic location on the Manassas Gap Railroad and the Valley Turnpike gave Strasburg a pivotal role in the Civil War during Gen. Stonewall Jackson's Valley campaign of 1862. Strasburg was the first town in the western part of Virginia to be served by two railroads. By 1890 it was an important industrial center and home to the region's largest printing and publishing establishments. The district exhibits a rare continuum of architectural styles, periods, and building types spanning two centuries of occupation. *(306–16) VLR: 05/15/84; NRHP: 08/16/84.*

STRASBURG MUSEUM, *East King Street, Strasburg.* The Strasburg Stone and Earthenware Manufacturing Company built this two-story structure in 1891 as a factory intended to put the Shenandoah Valley's long tradition of pottery making on a high-volume industrial basis. The project was part of the brief economic boom experienced in the 1890s with the construction of a new railway line in the eastern part of the Valley. The company quickly failed because of competition from other regions and other wares. In 1913 the building was converted into a railroad depot. The building now houses the Strasburg Museum, which maintains it as an example of industrial architecture, a relic of the Valley's short-lived venture into specialized industrial development. The building further represents a failed attempt to convert a handicraft industry into one of mass production. *(306–09) VLR: 04/17/79; NRHP: 06/19/79.*

WOODSTOCK HISTORIC DISTRICT. Woodstock's rich and varied collection of residential, commercial, and church buildings reflects the evolution of this Valley linear community over two centuries. Established in 1761, Woodstock boasts the 1795 Shenandoah County Courthouse, reputedly the oldest courthouse west of the Blue Ridge Mountains. Commercial development was spurred by the construction of the Valley Turnpike in the 1830s and the Manassas Gap Railroad in 1856. Although Woodstock witnessed troop movements, it was spared significant Civil War damage. The local economy was sustained into the 20th century by the establishment of several small industries and businesses. The historic district centers on a mile-long stretch of Main Street, the former Valley Turnpike, which is lined with closely spaced buildings, most placed directly against the street. A principal institution is the Massanutten Military Academy. *(330–15) VLR: 06/27/95; NRHP: 10/25/95.*

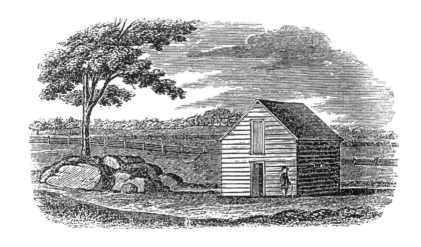

SMYTH COUNTY

In the heart of Southwest Virginia, Smyth County was named for Gen. Alexander Smyth, a congressman from western Virginia from 1817 to 1830. It was formed in 1832 from Washington and Wythe counties. The county seat is Marion.

ASPENVALE CEMETERY, *Seven Mile Ford.* This historic cemetery is noted primarily for containing the grave of Gen. William Campbell, a Virginia-born hero of the American Revolution. Campbell led his soldiers to victory over Loyalist forces at the battle of King's Mountain on October 7, 1780. Campbell later joined Lafayette in eastern Virginia, remaining with him until Campbell's death on August 22, 1781, shortly before the siege of Yorktown. The Campbell-Preston family plot in which Campbell is buried also contains the graves of his mother, widow, daughter, and son and several succeeding generations. Privately owned, the walled cemetery is above Seven Mile Ford, an early settlement on the Middle Fork of the Holston River. *(86–13) VLR: 09/16/80; NRHP: 12/05/80.*

CHILHOWIE UNITED METHODIST CHURCH, *501 Old Stage Road, Chilhowie.* When completed in 1894, this Gothic Revival church was a conspicuously high-style addition to the otherwise straightforward village of Chilhowie. Built of locally made golden-brown pressed brick, the church is distinguished by its literate use of Gothic forms, particularly its tall steeple and

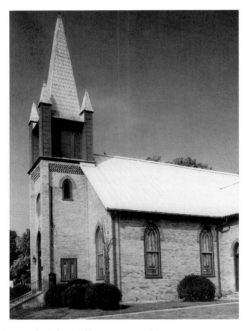

pinnacles. Such assertive, ecclesiologically correct architecture was a striking contrast to the simple country churches prevalent in the region, which usually were severely plain wooden structures. Although no architect has been associated with this church, the design is believed to have been influenced by E. J. Rutland, superintendent of the local brick factory. Born and raised in Sheerness, England, Rutland came to Chilhowie from Ohio in 1890 to manage the new brick plant. His familiarity with Victorian church architecture in England, where articulate Gothic design prevailed, likely shaped the appearance of this Methodist edifice. *(189–15) VLR: 04/17/91; NRHP: 07/03/91.*

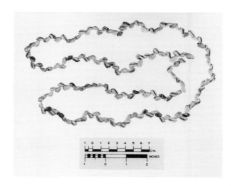

FOX FARM ARCHAEOLOGICAL SITE, *McMullin vicinity.* In the horseshoe bend of the Middle Fork of the Holston River, opposite Wassum Valley, Fox Farm preserves an Indian village site occupied between the 14th and 15th centuries in the Late Woodland period. The site holds invaluable information on the interaction and development of regional Indian groups as represented by various ceramics types. Furthermore, the presence of ornaments made with marine shells documents the participation of the site's inhabitants in regional trade networks with Indians who lived along the Atlantic coast. The site also maintains excellent conditions for preservation and provides information on structures, mortuary practices, and subsistence. Documented by the Holston Chapter of the Archeological Society of Virginia in 1973, the site was further defined by the Virginia Department of Historic Resources in 1994. *(86–11) VLR: 04/19/77; NRHP: 06/23/78.*

R. T. GREER AND CO. BUILDING, *107 Pendleton Street, Marion.* From the early 1900s until 1968, R. T. Greer and Co. was the Appalachian region's leading dealer in medicinal plant materials. The business was founded in 1904 by Riley Thomas Greer, George W. Greer, and F. P. McGuire. The company collected, dried, ground, and labeled untold numbers of roots, herbs, barks, and berries. These products were shipped to pharmaceutical houses all over the country and abroad, even to China. The Appalachian region had an abundance of herbs, and the herb business represented a way of life for area inhabitants, often providing their sole means of income. The company erected the present building in 1916 and operated the business here until 1968. The store stood empty until 1992 when its was reopened, selling local crafts and herbs and holding classes on uses of herbs. *(119–12–19) VLR: 03/19/97; NRHP: 05/23/97.*

HENDERSON BUILDING (SOUTHWESTERN STATE HOSPITAL), *East Main Street, Marion.* The Henderson Building, the main building of Southwestern State Hospital, was constructed in 1887 as part of Virginia's program to provide expanded mental health care and services to its citizens. The hospital was one of several large regional facilities. Its domed centerpiece was designed by McDonald Brothers of Louisville, Ky., and was later named for Dr. E. H. Henderson, the hospital's superintendent from 1915 until his death in 1927. The building was given an arresting visual presence by the 1930–31 addition of beautifully crafted Italian Renaissance–style galleries across the facade. Large connected wings, built in 1896 for hospital wards, were razed in 1986 and replaced with more modern patient-care facilities. The main section, however, continues to house the administrative offices. *(119–04) VLR: 02/21/89; NRHP: 12/21/90.*

HERONDON (PRESTON HOUSE), *Seven Mile Ford.* On the Middle Fork of the Holston River at Seven Mile Ford, Herondon was built in 1842 for John Montgomery Preston on land inherited by his wife, Maria Thornton Carter Preston. The property earlier had belonged to her grandfather Gen. William Campbell, Revolutionary War hero of the battle of King's Mountain. Preston built the structure as a conspicuously grand tavern, placing it on the site of an earlier log tavern. The first building had a dubious reputation, and tradition has it that Preston wanted to rid the region of its stigma by creating a clearly superior establishment. The building employed both Federal and Greek Revival elements and served travelers along the Wilderness Road until 1864 when it became a private residence for Preston's son. Union troops sacked the house that same year while on a raid toward Saltville and Abingdon. *(86–03) VLR: 09/09/69; NRHP: 11/25/69.*

HOTEL LINCOLN, *107 East Main Street. Marion.* Designed by Eubank and Caldwell of Roanoke, the Hotel Lincoln was completed in 1927 and is one of Southwest Virginia's few early 20th-century hotels to continue operation since opening. It was named for Charles Clark Lincoln, a well-to-do Marion citizen who developed the project in partnership with Dr. William M. Sclater. The hotel took advantage of the influx of travelers brought about by the construction of the Lee Highway (U.S. Route 11). Though built for a small town, Hotel Lincoln had the quality of an urban hostelry, being outfitted with a drugstore, coffee shop, beauty salon, and barbershop. Its reception rooms offered space for public and private meetings. Its guest rooms were equipped with private baths and telephones. The Georgian Revival exterior conformed to the latest architectural fashion. A recent renovation has ensured its continued service. *(119–10) VLR: 04/28/95; NRHP: 07/21/95.*

KONNAROCK TRAINING SCHOOL, *Konnarock.* Southwest Virginia's long-established Lutheran community began to expand its missionary activity in the region in the 1920s. A principal accomplishment was the Konnarock Training School, begun in 1924 by the Woman's Missionary Society of the United Lutheran Church in America. The school served simultaneously as a private boarding school and a public day school with a special focus on the cultural, spiritual, and social development of girls from underprivileged mountain families. Surviving elements of the complex include the school's main building, a 1925 rustic-style classroom-dormitory designed by Richmond architect Henry Carl Messerschmidt who clad the building with distinctive chestnut-bark shingle siding. A 1936 bungalow in similar style originally served as the school's health center. The Lutherans' Board of American Missions considered its work done in 1958 and closed the school. The complex is now owned by the USDA Forest Service. *(86–27) VLR: 03/19/97; NRHP: 06/05/97.*

LINCOLN THEATRE, *117 East Main Street, Marion.* The Lincoln Theatre is a rare relic of the exotic 1920s movie-palace fad as adapted for a small-town cinema. Built in 1929, its interior employs an unexpected Mayan-style theme for its decoration. Three-dimensional appliqués and stenciled Mayan designs of gods, animals, mythological creatures, and Mayan calligraphy embellish the walls and ceiling. Equally striking, but bearing no relation to the Mayan idiom, are six large murals depicting scenes from American and local history. The 750-seat theater was built by Charles C. Lincoln, Sr., Marion's wealthiest resident. The interior was designed by the Novelty Scenic Studios of New York City. The Lincoln originally offered first-run films and vaudeville acts and served as a regional meeting place. Closed in 1977, it was purchased in 1988 by the Lincoln Theater Foundation, which is restoring the theater for a regional cultural center. *(119–09) VLR: 10/21/92; NRHP: 12/17/92; BHR EASEMENT.*

MARION MALE ACADEMY, *343 College Street, Marion.* A landmark of local educational efforts, the Marion Male Academy was established in 1873 by local academic D. C. Miller to offer quality schooling for boys. Although the Underwood Constitution of 1869 mandated free public schools throughout Virginia, the farther reaches of the state were slow to offer public education. Private academies continued to fill the gap for several decades. For its first three years, the Marion Male Academy held classes in different locations. The brick academy building was therefore erected in 1876 through private subscription and served both elementary and high school levels. The academy operated until 1893 when the Marion Public High School was opened and D. C. Miller became the first superintendent of public schools. The academy building was auctioned in 1901 and subsequently was converted to residential use. *(119–06) VLR: 08/15/89; NRHP: 11/02/89.*

MARION RAILWAY DEPOT, *651 North Main Street, Marion.* This turn-of-the-century depot provided its area with passenger service, express freight, and telegram service for sixty-seven years. Marion was a hub of regional transportation as early as the 1840s. In 1903 the Norfolk and Western Railway Company chose Marion as a site for a new passenger and freight station and contracted with J. C. Nesbit of Harrisburg, Pa., to build the facility. The carefully detailed structure, with its spreading hipped roof and wide dormers, illustrates the high standards of design for N&W Railway facilities. Such stations usually were designed by railroad company architects. Passenger service was continued here until 1971. In 1993 the building was sold to a developer and converted to office and retail use, a project that has preserved a once-common aspect of the American scene. *(119–03) VLR: 10/19/94; NRHP: 02/08/95.*

OLD STONE TAVERN, *Atkins vicinity.* Old Stone Tavern on the Wilderness Road (now U.S. Route 11) was erected before 1815 by Frederick Cullop to accommodate travelers in the heavy westward migration through the Cumberland Gap to the West in the early 19th century. Constructed using local limestone, the tavern is one of the oldest stone buildings in Smyth County. It reflects the influence of the stone vernacular architecture of rural Pennsylvania on the settlement arteries into Kentucky and Tennessee, where similar structures can be found. Typical of early taverns, the front is sheltered by a two-level gallery which here is given a festive quality by the use of scalloped eaves. The interior preserves some early, very plain woodwork. *(86–02) VLR: 03/17/81; NRHP: 07/08/82.*

SCOTT-WALKER HOUSE, *Saltville vicinity.* The solidly built Scott-Walker house is the oldest stone farmhouse in Smyth County and an outstanding example of the region's early vernacular architecture. It was erected sometime between 1800 and 1815 for Charles Scott, a prosperous farmer and slave owner in what was then Washington County. Little changed since Scott's tenure, the house is constructed with massive walls of coursed limestone rubble. The interior has a hall-parlor plan and features exceptional decorative woodwork including cornices with punch-and-dentil work. The mantels have frieze panels decorated with scalloped borders. Taking advantage of the area's abundance of timber, the woodwork employs unpainted maple, cherry, and walnut. Original flooring and hardware, including decorative strap hinges, also remain in place. An unusual feature is the finished attic space with wide boards lining the ceiling and knee walls. The house has recently been restored. *(86–26) VLR: 03/10/94; NRHP: 05/19/94.*

ABIJAH THOMAS HOUSE, *Adwolf vicinity.* This singular brick dwelling is Virginia's most sophisticated representation of Orson Squire Fowler's advocacy of octagonal architecture that caught the imagination of Americans in the reform movement of the 1850s. In his book *A Home for All, or The Gravel Wall and Octagon Mode of Building* (1848), Fowler stated that an octagonal plan encloses one-fifth more floor area than a square of the same total length of wall and allows for more compact internal planning. Built in 1856–57 for Abijah Thomas, a Smyth County landowner and developer of mines, mills, and foundries, this house retains a variety of graining, marbleizing, and stenciling. Sections of painted ashlar on the plaster wall of one of the principal rooms may be a unique survivor in Virginia of this once-popular decorative treatment. The house has stood empty and deteriorating for many years. *(86–04) VLR: 09/16/80; NRHP: 11/28/80.*

SOUTHAMPTON COUNTY

Formed in 1749 from Isle of Wight and part of Nansemond counties, this rural southern Tidewater county was named for either the English borough of Southampton or for Henry Wriothesley, third earl of Southampton. Its county seat is Courtland.

BELMONT, *Capron vicinity.* The Nat Turner Insurrection, America's bloodiest and most notorious slave revolt, was halted at Belmont, home of Dr. Samuel Blunt, on August 23, 1831. Turner, a black slave, believed he was divinely selected to lead his people out of bondage and drew about eighty followers to go on what became a journey of murder and pillage through Southampton County. Turner was eventually captured on October 30 and hanged on November 11, 1831. The short but violent revolt so alarmed the South that a much stricter regimen was soon instituted against slaves and free blacks alike, leading to further hardening of attitudes between the North and South. Belmont's dwelling house, a typical Southside plantation residence, was built in the late 18th century for George Carey. It has a touch of elegance in the Chinese lattice railing framing the stairwell. The Blunts acquired Belmont in the early 19th century. *(87–30) VLR: 07/17/73; NRHP: 10/03/73.*

BROWN'S FERRY, *Drakes Corner vicinity.* A long-standing tradition maintains that Brown's Ferry was the birthplace of William Mahone (1826–1895), the colorful Confederate general who achieved fame during the 1864 siege of Petersburg. Known as the "Hero of the Crater," Mahone closed the gap caused when Union forces tunneled under the Confederate lines and set off a huge explosion. After the war Mahone became a railroad executive and leader of the Readjuster party and also played a significant role in improving the state's public schools. Brown's Ferry was completed by 1818 for William Hodges and was one of the largest and finest Federal dwellings built in Southampton County. Mahone's father, Fielding Mahone, purchased the property from Hodges's heirs in 1826. Generous in scale, the two-story structure has finely detailed Federal woodwork. The house is now unmaintained and in a state of collapse. *(87–120) VLR: 03/20/79; NRHP: 06/18/79.*

ELM GROVE, *Courtland vicinity.* Elm Grove is a vernacular domestic complex little changed since the 19th century and is thus valuable for illustrating the rural lifestyle of Virginia's southern Tidewater region. The farm was probably organized by the Williams family in the late 18th century. The house began as a one-room dwelling with a lean-to, an elementary domestic form widely employed even among the region's more prosperous planters well into the 19th century. It was expanded to its present, hardly insubstantial appearance by the 1820s. Its outbuildings include an early 19th-century office, an early dairy with ventilation slats, and a comparatively large saddle-notched log smokehouse containing four smoke pits. The only known multipit smokehouse in the state, this unusual outbuilding is probably contemporary with the earliest portion of the main house. *(87–103) VLR: 05/15/79; NRHP: 07/24/79.*

JERICHO (BEECHWOOD), *Beales vicinity.* Jericho is characteristic of the spacious but unostentatious houses favored by southeastern Virginia planters in the early 19th century. Like many of the region's early dwellings, it began as a one-room, one-story house and evolved into its present form through a series of additions. Family tradition dates the original core to 1730–40. Despite the changes, the Federal-period main portion gives a unified appearance with its early beaded weatherboards, modillion cornice, and handsomely detailed pedimented front porch. The property was owned in the 18th century by the Denson family and has been held by Denson family descendants to the present. Thomas Pretlow, son-in-law of Jordan Denson, made the last significant additions to the house by 1820. A more recent family member to own Beechwood was Colgate W. Darden, Jr., governor of Virginia in 1942–46 and later president of the University of Virginia. *(87–02) VLR: 09/19/78; NRHP: 02/01/79.*

ROSE HILL, *Capron vicinity.* The Rose Hill dwelling house is among the earliest and least-altered I-houses in Southampton County. Characteristic of the form, it has a passage between the two rooms of each floor. The house stands on land deeded by the Nottoway Indian tribe to John T. Blow in 1792. The comparatively late Indian tenure explains why some early deeds refer to the property as Indian Land. Contemporary records and archaeological research document continuous Indian occupancy here throughout the colonial period. As recently as the early 20th century, Indians gathered at Rose Hill for religious and cultural purposes. In 1804 Blow willed the land to his son Henry, who built the house between 1805 and 1815. Its plain Federal woodwork retains early painting, graining, and marbleizing throughout. A noteworthy structural feature is the king-post roof-framing, a heavy framing system usually restricted to colonial mansions. *(87–52) VLR: 09/18/79; NRHP: 12/31/79.*

SUNNYSIDE, *Newsoms vicinity.* This Southampton County plantation has one of southeastern Virginia's most complete groupings of domestic and farm outbuildings. The complex is scattered about an architecturally evolved main residence and includes a schoolmaster's house, dairy, tenant's house, smokehouse, kitchen, various sheds, and a peanut house which together maintain the villagelike image that dominated a traditional Virginia plantation. The house itself began as a one-room structure built ca. 1810–11 for Joseph Pope. It was remodeled and enlarged in 1847 and again in 1870 by his son Harrison who was among the county's most ambitious 19th-century planters. The porticoed front section, which combines Greek Revival and Italianate elements, is one of the region's few Reconstruction-period structures with architectural pretension. *(87–98) VLR: 10/21/81; NRHP: 07/08/82.*

SPOTSYLVANIA COUNTY

Straddling the fall line, Spotsylvania County was formed from Essex, King William, and King and Queen counties in 1720. It was named for Alexander Spotswood, lieutenant governor of Virginia from 1710 to 1722. Its county seat is Spotsylvania Court House.

ANDREWS TAVERN, *Glenora vicinity.* Andrews Tavern has served at various times as an ordinary, a school, a polling place, and a residence. The brick portion was built for Samuel Andrews soon after he reached his majority in 1815. Its fine masonry, simple but well-executed woodwork, and hall-parlor plan make it a model of the countrified Federal architecture of Piedmont Virginia. Andrews began his tavern business here when he added the frame wing ca. 1848. The building housed a U.S. post office from 1842 until 1862, then a Confederate post office until 1865. Andrews served as postmaster for both governments. It became a U.S. post office again in 1885 during the ownership of Horace Cammack. Although now a private residence, the tavern, with its complex of outbuildings, is a tangible reminder of institutions important to 19th-century rural life. *(88–136) VLR: 04/20/76; NRHP: 07/30/76.*

FAIRVIEW, *2020 Whitelake Drive, Fredericksburg vicinity.* Among the largest and finest of the various late Federal plantation houses scattered through Spotsylvania County, Fairview was built in 1837 by the entrepreneur, builder, and planter Samuel Alsop, Jr., as his own residence. The double-pile structure has an almost overwhelming scale, one tempered by carefully handled proportions. The large front porch is a mid-19th-century replacement of the original but repeats original details. The interior preserves nearly all of its fine woodwork. Originally encompassing 1,200 acres, the plantation was developed for housing in the 1970s, leaving the house with five acres. A two-story dependency with a 10-foot cooking fireplace and caretaker's quarters is the only remaining outbuilding. Alsop built numerous houses in the vicinity including Oakley (1828), Kenmore Woods (1829), Coventry (1834), Mill Brook (1836), and several Fredericksburg houses. As demonstrated at Fairview, intricately carved wooden mantels were Alsop trademarks. *(88–12) VLR: 10/20/93; NRHP: 12/30/93.*

KENMORE WOODS, *Spotsylvania Court House vicinity.* A gracefully proportioned late Federal dwelling, this country house would not be out of place among its contemporaries in downtown Fredericksburg. The polished architectural character is the handiwork of Samuel Alsop, Jr., a prominent local builder. Alsop bought the property in 1821 and built the house in 1828–29 as a gift for his son-in-law John M. Anderson and daughter Ann Eliza. Alsop's dwellings are noted for their careful detailing, and Kenmore Woods, with its intricate cornice, Federal mantels, and other ornamental interior trim, is typical of his work. Anderson advertised the property for sale in 1832, calling it a "desirable little farm" having "a beautiful two story brick building . . . well situated for a physician or lawyer." The house served as a Confederate headquarters during the 1864 battle of Spotsylvania Court House. Carefully restored in the 1940s, it stands amid handsome landscaped grounds. *(88–38) VLR: 04/21/93; NRHP: 06/24/93.*

LA VUE, *New Post vicinity.* The plain but dignified brick house at La Vue was constructed by 1848 for John F. Alsop on family property. The date is confirmed by a substantial increase in taxes that year for a new building. The house was placed on the edge of a steep hill to take advantage of views of level fields. The view was not altogether pastoral since the lines of the Richmond, Fredericksburg, and Potomac Railroad had been laid at the foot of the hill in 1837. Alsop's growing family necessitated a two-story ell in the 1850s. Little changed since then, the dwelling's clean lines and hipped roof reflect the conservative taste of the local antebellum gentry. Contrasting with the exterior simplicity are richly colored stenciled decorations on the interior. Such painted embellishments were not unusual for the period, but they rarely survive. *(88–39) VLR: 10/20/93; NRHP: 01/11/94.*

MASSAPONAX BAPTIST CHURCH, *Massaponax.* This country Greek Revival brick church was built in 1859 to serve a congregation founded in 1788. It was here, on May 21, 1864, that Gen. Ulysses S. Grant held a war council after the Union victory at the battle of Spotsylvania Court House. Soldiers removed the pews from the church and arranged them in a circle in the yard. Timothy O'Sullivan, a photographer traveling with the army, captured the scene on glass plates. The widely published photograph shows Grant with several of his generals, as well as Assistant Secretary of War Charles A. Dana. One of the outstanding photographers of the mid–19th century, O'Sullivan is known for his later images of the American West, as well as for his record of the Civil War. His unique wartime photographs show the generals and their staffs conferring, studying maps, and writing dispatches. *(88–122) VLR: 02/20/90; NRHP: 01/24/91.*

PROSPECT HILL (LITTLEPAGE INN), *Belmont vicinity.* Built in 1810–14, Prospect Hill is an architectural document frozen in time. The undisturbed condition of the massive yet restrained exterior and the plain country Federal woodwork inside make the house an excellent representative of the spacious but unpretentious center-passage dwellings favored by the period's gentry. The house was constructed by builder Spotswood Dabney Crenshaw for Waller Holladay. Holladay experimented with crop rotation and fertilization at Prospect Hill, an early effort at restoring farmlands depleted by tobacco growing. Holladay also held various local offices and served in the General Assembly. The property's historic ambience is enhanced by the survival of several early outbuildings. Still owned by the Holladay family, Prospect Hill is now an inn known as Littlepage Inn. A collection of architectural drawings in the Holladay family papers at the Virginia Historical Society appears to be preliminary studies for the house. *(88–56) VLR: 06/15/82; NRHP: 09/09/82.*

RAPIDAN DAM CANAL OF THE RAPPAHANNOCK NAVIGATION, *Chancellorsville vicinity.* The Rappahannock Navigation, which consisted of twenty dams, each with its own system of locks, is ranked by canal experts as the country's most intact example of a lock-and-dam navigation system for bateaux. The Rapidan Dam Canal with its associated locks is the system's best-preserved segment. The system was a compromise—typical in southern waterways—between an expensive continuous canal for horse-drawn boats and an inexpensive but unreliable riverbed sluice navigation for bateaux, which were poled and rowed and required no towpath. Construction of the fifty-mile project began in 1829 and was not completed until twenty years later, just as railroad competition made it useless. The Rapidan Dam Canal parallels the Rappahannock River from the mouth of the Rapidan for one and a half miles and then reenters the river through three locks. *(88–137) VLR: 06/19/73; NRHP: 07/27/73.*

ST. JULIEN, *New Post vicinity.* St. Julien was the home of Francis Taliaferro Brooke (1763–1851), who was appointed to the Virginia General Court in 1804 and later served as president of Virginia's Supreme Court of Appeals. Brooke served in the General Assembly in 1794 and 1795. In 1796 he transferred his law practice to Fredericksburg and purchased a nearby farm, which he named St. Julien. He described the dwelling that he constructed here in 1804 as a "small brick house with a shed to it." Although compact in scale, Brooke's house stands as one of the area's most refined examples of rural Federal architecture. Its two-level recessed entry capped by a pediment is an imaginative and effective facade treatment. The refinements of the building include its Flemish bond brickwork, carved stone lintels and keystones, and finely detailed interior woodwork. Among St. Julien's several early outbuildings is an early board-and-batten office. *(88–61) VLR: 03/18/75; NRHP: 06/05/75.*

SPOTSYLVANIA COURT HOUSE HISTORIC DISTRICT. Spotsylvania Court House, established on what was once the main road from Richmond to Fredericksburg, was the site of one of the most vicious and bloody struggles of the Civil War. In and around the tiny village in May 1864 the Union army suffered 18,000 casualties and the Confederates under General Lee experienced an estimated 9,000 killed or wounded, with neither side claiming a clear victory. The Tuscan-porticoed courthouse, completed in 1840 by Malcolm F. Crawford, who participated in the construction of the University of Virginia, was largely rebuilt because of heavy damage sustained during the conflict. Remaining in the village are four other buildings standing at the time of the battle: a ca. 1800 tavern, two antebellum churches, and a ca. 1840 farmhouse. Also within the district is the Confederate cemetery, located on what was the principal Confederate defense line. *(88–142) VLR: 01/18/83; NRHP: 09/08/83.*

STIRLING, *Massaponax vicinity.* In view of thousands of motorists daily racing by on Interstate Highway 95, Stirling is an anchor to the past for a region experiencing erosion of historic identity. The property is dominated by a prodigious hipped-roofed brick mansion erected in 1858–60 for John Holladay, a wealthy landowner. The house marks the end of plantation house construction in the area, an activity stopped by the Civil War. Stirling is of special interest because it has remained in the same family, retaining its original interior architectural decoration and paint finishes. The family's plantation account books document the sources of the materials used in the construction. Stirling's conservative Georgian character may have been reinforced by the fact that John Holladay was fifty-nine years old when the house was started. The curtilage preserves the original kitchen outbuilding and smokehouse and the archaeological sites of other outbuildings. *(88–66) VLR: 02/16/88; NRHP: 05/05/89; BHR EASEMENT.*

TUBAL FURNACE ARCHAEOLOGICAL SITE, *Chancellorsville vicinity.* The Tubal Furnace site holds the remains of the earliest archaeologically identified iron furnace in Virginia. Constructed ca. 1717 under the direction of Lieutenant Governor Alexander Spotswood, the furnace was operated by skilled black slaves, a pioneering use of slave labor for a technological industry. In 1732 William Byrd II visited the furnace and wrote that it was built of rough stone and that an overshot wheel, 20 feet in diameter, powered its bellows. Water was conveyed from streams by wooden pipes. The industry continued under the direction of Spotswood's descendants for two generations, with operations ceasing in the early 19th century. *(88–74) VLR: 05/18/82; NRHP: 10/19/82.*

✤ STAFFORD COUNTY

On the Potomac River, at the junction of Tidewater and northern Virginia, Stafford County was formed from Westmoreland County in 1664 and named for the English shire. Its county seat is Stafford.

ACCOKEEK IRON FURNACE ARCHAEOLOGICAL SITE, *Stafford vicinity.* The Accokeek Iron Furnace was constructed ca. 1726 on land owned by Augustine Washington, father of George Washington. Washington Sr. had a lease agreement with the Principio Company, which constructed the furnace. The industry operated until 1756. The site represents the second-oldest 18th-century blast furnace site identified in Virginia. Archaeological remains at Accokeek should preserve evidence of its store, warehouses, mill, and forge as well as workers' living quarters. Features thus identified include the furnace location, the mill wheel pit and races, a retaining wall made of slag, an extensive slag debris dump, and mine pits. Verified 18th-century industrial sites are rare in Virginia, and a thorough investigation of Accokeek could increase knowledge of early iron technology. In 1996 the site was acquired from Stafford County by Kenmore Plantation and Gardens. *(89–66) VLR: 03/20/84; NRHP: 05/15/84.*

AQUIA CHURCH, *Aquia.* This cruciform-plan church is one of the nation's outstanding examples of colonial ecclesiastical architecture. Although built to serve a rural parish, the design is endowed with urbanity and sophistication. The brick walls are highlighted by quoins and rusticated doorways crafted in stone from nearby Aquia Creek. On a wooded site used for worship as early as 1654, the present building was begun in 1751 but burned on February 17, 1754, three days before completion. It was rebuilt within the walls in 1754–57 under the direction of Mourning Richards, the original contractor, and William Copein, the mason. The interior preserves a unique three-tiered pulpit as well as the original altarpiece, west gallery, and box pews, all excellent examples of colonial joinery. The pews, however, were reduced in height in the 19th century. The church's former isolated setting has given way in recent years to suburban development. *(89–08) VLR: 05/13/69; NRHP: 11/12/69. NHL: 07/05/91.*

BELMONT, *224 Washington Street, Falmouth.* The academic painter Gari Melchers made this historic Falmouth estate his home and studio from 1916 until his death in 1932. Born in Detroit in 1860 and trained in Europe, Melchers excelled in genre pictures, religious works, portraits, and murals, drawing inspiration from many sources. His works are housed in major American museums, and his murals of allegories on peace and war decorate the Library of Congress. The Belmont house and studio, along with their furnishings and many of his pictures, were left to the state by Melchers's widow and are exhibited under the auspices of Mary Washington College as the Gari Melchers Estate and Memorial Gallery. Although it may incorporate colonial fabric, the house was mostly built after 1825, following Belmont's purchase by Joseph Ficklen, whose family owned it until Melchers bought it. The stone studio to the south of the main house was built by Melchers in 1924. *(89–22) VLR: 09/09/69; NRHP: 11/15/66; NHL: 12/21/65.*

CARLTON, *501 Melchers Drive, Falmouth.* This conspicuously placed dwelling is one of several large old houses crowning the heights around Falmouth and Fredericksburg. The exterior follows a standard Georgian format, employing a five-bay facade and hipped roof. Most of its original exterior and interior fabric survives, including a large built-in glass-door cupboard in the dining room. The stair rail is terminated at the newel with a vertical spiral or ram's horn carving. Located at the edge of a steep promontory directly overlooking Falmouth, Carlton was the home of John Short, a local merchant who had the house built ca. 1785 after his marriage to Judith Ball of Lancaster County. Adding to the historic ambience are three original outbuildings: a kitchen-laundry, dairy, and smokehouse. *(89–10) VLR: 07/17/73; NRHP: 10/03/73; BHR EASEMENT.*

CLEARVIEW, *Telegraph Road, Falmouth.* On a hilltop overlooking Falmouth and Fredericksburg, Clearview is representative of the architecture of lesser plantation dwellings of the late 18th century. Using the double-pile plan, hipped roof, and symmetrical five-bay facade, the composition varies little from that frequently employed a half century earlier. Clearview probably was built shortly after the property was acquired in 1786 by Andrew Buchanan, a major in the Caroline County militia during the Revolution. The house has received a later wing and porches but retains most of its early interior woodwork. The farm was used for a Federal gun emplacement during the battle of Fredericksburg in 1862. Some earthwork gun pits remain intact southeast of the house. *(89–12) VLR: 11/19/74; NRHP: 02/24/75.*

FALMOUTH HISTORIC DISTRICT. Laid out in 1727 at the falls of the Rappahannock, Falmouth was a prosperous port and regional trading center until 1850 when dwindling river traffic and the construction of the railroad sapped its commercial life. Although modern intrusions have replaced much of Falmouth's early fabric, enough buildings remain from its period of ascendancy to invoke Falmouth's early history. Along the waterfront are Basil Gordon's brick warehouse and an adjacent large commercial building of the early 19th century. Nearby, on Cambridge Street, is the tiny Federal-period customshouse, one of the nation's smallest. Scattered through the district is a variety of early residences including some rare examples of vernacular worker housing. The facade of the Federal-period Union Church has been preserved as a landmark. Also in the district, on the heights overlooking the town, are the landmark houses Carlton, Clearview, and Belmont. *(89–67) VLR: 12/02/69; NRHP: 02/26/70.*

FERRY FARM, *712 Kings Highway, Fredericksburg vicinity.* George Washington moved with his parents to Ferry Farm, from Little Hunting Creek, Fairfax County, in 1738, when he was six years old. Here, on the banks of the Rappahannock, he spent most of his boyhood, and here are set the legends, made famous by Parson Mason Locke Weems, of his cutting down the cherry tree and throwing a stone (in later versions a silver dollar) across the river. Washington's widowed mother remained at Ferry Farm until 1772. The one early structure on the property, a frame outbuilding, dates from the early 19th century, but the archaeological remains of earlier buildings are present. In 1996, in the wake of threatened commercial development, seventy-one acres of the original Washington property were acquired by Kenmore Plantation and Gardens, which uses the site for interpretive programs relating to George Washington's youth. *(89–16) VLR: 11/16/71; NRHP: 05/05/72.*

HARTWOOD PRESBYTERIAN CHURCH, *Hartwood.* The country Greek Revival Hartwood Presbyterian Church and its predecessor, known as the Hartwood Chapel or Yellow Chapel, were long important landmarks on the Marsh Road leading to Falmouth. Yellow Chapel and later the present church provided the only place of worship for Stafford County's Presbyterians until recent years. Members of the Irvine family, assisted by their slaves, built the Hartwood Church between 1857 and 1859. Used periodically by both sides during the Civil War, the church was the scene of Confederate general Wade Hampton's November 1862 capture of 137 men of the Third Pennsylvania Cavalry who were asleep inside the church. Caught in the crossfire of subsequent skirmishes, the church suffered considerable wartime damage. Most of the wooden elements and furnishings were burned, but the brick walls survived. In 1915 the Hartwood congregation received $800 in reparations from the U.S. Congress. *(89–82) VLR: 04/18/89; NRHP: 11/13/89.*

HUNTER'S IRON WORKS ARCHAEOLOGICAL SITE, *Falmouth vicinity.* Described as "one of the finest and most considerable iron works in North America" by the 18th-century traveler John David Schopf, Hunter's Iron Works played a vital role in the Revolutionary War. James Hunter, a Falmouth merchant, started the works around 1750. It quickly became the colony's leading producer of hardware. With the outbreak of the Revolution, Hunter devoted his full energies to supplying the Continental army, so much so that Governor Thomas Jefferson ordered special military protection for the industry. Although some of the buildings may have been in use as late as the Civil War, none survives. A survey undertaken by the Virginia Department of Historic Resources staff in 1974 located the foundations of at least five buildings and many iron artifacts (shown). Further investigation could provide valuable information on 18th-century iron manufacturing. *(89–06) VLR: 10/16/73; NRHP: 01/18/74.*

MARLBOROUGH POINT ARCHAEOLOGICAL SITE, *Indian Point vicinity.* Strategically situated at the tip of a peninsula jutting into the Potomac River at Potomac Creek, Marlborough Town was established under the Town Act of 1691 on the land of Giles Brent and served as the county seat of Stafford County. After its decline in the first quarter of the 18th century, it became the seat of John Mercer. Preserved in John Mercer's letter book is a copy of the 1691 Theodoric Bland survey of the town (shown). Archaeological investigation undertaken by the Smithsonian Institution in 1956 identified Marlborough Town's location. More extensive investigation of the town site should provide much information on the commercial life of a Potomac River port town in the first half of the 18th century. *(89–01) VLR: 12/02/69.*

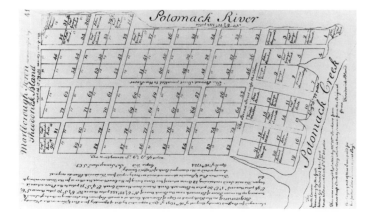

POTOMAC CREEK ARCHAEOLOGICAL SITE, *Indian Point vicinity.* This two-acre site on the peninsula formed by Accokeek and Potomac creeks includes the location of the Potomeck Indian village known as Patawomeke. Shown are samples of the decorative treatments that occur on the rims of Potomac Creek ware, dating to the Late Woodland period (A.D. 1300–1600). The village had been abandoned by the Indians before 1635 when the property was patented by Giles Brent. The site was identified through an investigation undertaken by the Smithsonian Institution in the 1930s. Threatened by modern residential development, the site was further investigated by the College of William and Mary in 1997. The remains of several palisade lines and a large ditch were encountered. The broad sample of botanical and faunal remains recovered will provide a more complete picture of the dietary habits of the occupants. *(89–02) VLR: 05/13/69; NRHP: 12/02/69.*

WHITE OAK PRIMITIVE BAPTIST CHURCH, *McCarthys Corner vicinity.* The simple rectangular plan of the White Oak Primitive Baptist Church was considered proper for a religious sect that stressed simplicity in all its activities. The Primitive Baptists' faith is based on the precept that doctrine should only originate from clear scriptural statements rather than from human interpretations. Its adherents, to this day, thus do not believe in such things as Sunday school or missionary programs. The severely plain church building, believed to have been built about 1835 or possibly earlier, reflects the conservative and nonhierarchical theology of this sect. Moreover, the fact that only modest changes have been made to the church since its construction is a testimony to the steadfast adherence of church members to their beliefs. Included on the flat one-acre lot are women's and men's outhouses and a graveyard started in 1897. *(89–76) VLR: 08/21/90; NRHP: 01/03/91.*

❧ CITY OF STAUNTON

The county seat of Augusta County most likely derives its name from Rebecca Staunton Gooch, wife of Sir William Gooch, lieutenant governor of Virginia from 1727 to 1749. Staunton was laid out in 1748 and was established as a town in 1761. It was incorporated in 1801 and became a city in 1871.

AUGUSTA COUNTY COURTHOUSE, *South Augusta and East Johnson streets.* Completed in 1901, the Augusta County Courthouse stands where all of the county's courthouses have stood since the first one was built in 1745. Its imposing architectural design is local architect T. J. Collins's interpretation of the florid classicism made popular by the American Renaissance movement. Dominated by a tall dome and Composite-order portico, the finely crafted building symbolizes the prosperity enjoyed by Staunton and Augusta County at the turn of the 20th century and remains a prominent landmark of the city's historic downtown. The exterior survives essentially unaltered, and much of the original character of the interior is intact. Several antebellum law offices remain on the compact court square. *(132–01) VLR: 06/15/82; NRHP: 10/26/82.*

BEVERLEY HISTORIC DISTRICT. The Beverley Historic District includes approximately 150 buildings in some eleven blocks of downtown Staunton. Although the area was part of the mid-18th-century settlement founded on the land of William Beverley, its principal business artery, Beverley Street, is a classic Victorian main street. This and the district's secondary streets have few detracting modern intrusions. The dome of the Augusta County Courthouse, the old YMCA clock tower, the observation tower of the Masonic building, and several church spires enliven its skyline. Nearly every phase of the region's 19th- and early 20th-century stylistic development is to be found on the narrow streets, from Federal-period shops to a Beaux Arts bank. The buildings reflect Staunton's growth from an early mill settlement to one of the Shenandoah Valley's most prosperous communities. Much of district's historic character has been restored in recent years through a facade-improvement program. *(132–24) VLR: 11/20/79; NRHP: 07/15/82.*

BREEZY HILL, *1220 North Augusta Street.* The prosperity of Staunton's boom years at the turn of the century is confidently displayed in Breezy Hill, one of the most ambitious and articulate of the large houses of the period scattered through the city. Incorporating fine materials and craftsmanship, the irregularly massed suburban villa of some thirty rooms is a knowing blend of the Queen Anne and Shingle styles—late Victorian modes favored by the nation's upper class. The exterior combines limestone, fieldstone, and shingled surfaces. The house was begun ca. 1896 for Mrs. Thomas B. Grasty and completed in 1909 after many changes by the owner during construction. It was designed by T. J. Collins, the city's leading architect for several decades. While many of its contemporaries across the country have succumbed to demolition, Breezy Hill has been successfully adapted for alternative uses. *(132–30) VLR: 02/16/82; NRHP: 07/08/82.*

CATLETT HOUSE, *303 Berkeley Place.* This striking composition, a classic example of the American interpretation of the Queen Anne style, is one of a collection of sophisticated turn-of-the-century dwellings dotting Staunton's downtown neighborhoods. Completed in 1897 for Fannie Catlett, widow of local attorney R. H. Catlett, the house incorporates all the elements associated with the mode: a mixture of surface materials, asymmetrical floor plan, corner tower, gables, classical details, and a multiplicity of window types. Lending particular interest is the lavish use of wood-shingle cladding, echoing the tile cladding of English vernacular buildings. Many of America's Queen Anne houses have been neglected or disfigured; the Catlett house, by contrast, is in an excellent state of preservation. *(132–32) VLR: 05/18/82; NRHP: 07/15/82.*

GOSPEL HILL HISTORIC DISTRICT. Occupying most of the eastern section of the hilly older quarter of Staunton, this primarily residential area contains a rich assemblage of 19th- and early 20th-century styles. The houses, mostly freestanding ones on small lots, range from simple Federal structures to mansions in the later revivalist styles, including Greek Revival, Italianate, Queen Anne, and Colonial Revival. Many of the more distinctive Colonial Revival residences were designed by the Staunton architect T. J. Collins. The district remains devoid of significant visual intrusions. Few of the streets are through ones, assuring an air of quiet dignity in many blocks. Particularly interesting architectural variety is found on East Beverley and Kalorama streets. The district is bordered on the east by the Virginia School for the Deaf and the Blind and on the west by Mary Baldwin College. *(132–35) VLR: 01/17/84; NRHP: 02/14/85.*

HILL TOP, *Mary Baldwin College campus.* Erected for Benjamin H. Brady, this ca. 1815 mansion is dominated by an original two-story portico with stately Tuscan columns and a delicate Federal cornice. It was one of Staunton's most conspicuous and elegant residences during the half century after its construction. Circuit Judge Lucas P. Thompson lived here from 1842 until his death in 1866. In 1872 the property was purchased from his estate by the Augusta Female Academy under the leadership of Mary Julia Baldwin, whose name the college now bears. A large wing designed by local architect T. J. Collins was added to the rear in 1904. Hill Top, now a residence hall, was restored in 1991. *(132–02) VLR: 12/19/78; NRHP: 06/19/79.*

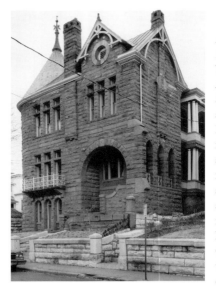

ARISTA HOGE HOUSE, *215 Kalorama Street.* The robust but romantic facade of the Arista Hoge house survives as Staunton's only domestic example of the Richardsonian Romanesque style, a style defined by rough-hewn brownstone ashlar and weighty Romanesque details. Commissioned by local businessman and public servant Arista Hoge in 1891 as a new front for a house built ca. 1882 for G. G. Gooch, it is an early work of the firm of Collins and Hackett. The juxtaposition of the two styles illustrates the swing in taste during the 1880s from the delicacy of the Italianate to the solidity of the Romanesque. Formed in 1891, the Collins and Hackett architectural firm lasted only three years, but its partner T. J. Collins on his own embellished Staunton with many of its finest buildings over the next several decades. *(132–15) VLR: 05/18/82; NRHP: 07/15/82.*

KABLE HOUSE, *310 Prospect Street.* The Kable house was built in 1873–74 for John W. Alby. This first building of the former Staunton Military Academy is now part of the Mary Baldwin College campus. In 1860 Capt. William Hartman Kable founded the Charles Town Male Academy in Charles Town (now West Virginia). After the Civil War, Kable decided to move his school to Virginia proper, and in 1883 he purchased this Italianate bracketed villa. Originally named the Staunton Male Academy, the school developed a military format in 1886. The house served as both a dormitory and the Kable family residence for many years and later was used for classrooms and offices. Its interior was remodeled in 1917 by the local firm of T. J. Collins & Son, but the exterior retains its Italianate flavor. Staunton Military Academy closed in 1976 and sold its campus to Mary Baldwin College, which uses the house for student services offices. *(132–22) VLR: 12/19/78; NRHP: 06/19/79.*

MARY BALDWIN COLLEGE ADMINISTRATION BUILDING, *Frederick and North New streets.* Established in 1842 by the Rev. Rufus W. Bailey as the Augusta Female Seminary, Mary Baldwin College is the nation's oldest women's college affiliated with the Presbyterian church. Construction of its first building, now the Administration Building, was completed in 1844, and wings were added in 1857. With its Doric portico and cream-painted brick walls, the Greek Revival edifice established an architectural image that the school has maintained for more than 150 years. Mary Julia Baldwin was principal in the difficult years following the Civil War. She introduced a university-level curriculum and was called "the best businessman in Staunton." The school prospered under her direction and was renamed in her honor in 1895. The building, now housing the office of the president and other administrative offices, underwent restoration in 1997–98. *(132–16) VLR: 06/19/73; NRHP: 07/26/73.*

J. C. M. MERRILLAT HOUSE, *521 East Beverley Street.* The J. C. M. Merrillat house is a proper mid-19th-century Gothic Revival cottage complete with steep gables, scrolled bargeboards, board-and-batten siding, and diamond-pane windows. It is situated against a steep hillside within spacious, picturesquely planted grounds. Although the Gothic cottage was a popular house type throughout the country, the Merrillat house is one of the few examples of the form in the Staunton area. It was built in 1851 for Dr. Jean Charles Martin Merrillat, a native of Bordeaux, France, who in 1839 was appointed first head of the Department of the Blind at the nearby Virginia School for the Deaf and the Blind. In 1852 he became administrator for the entire school. During the Civil War, when the school was used as a military hospital, Dr. Merrillat served there as a surgeon. *(132–28) VLR: 09/15/81; NRHP: 09/16/82.*

THOMAS J. MICHIE HOUSE, *324 East Beverley Street.* Built in 1847–48 for state delegate Thomas J. Michie, this well-mannered Greek Revival dwelling, one of the earliest houses on Staunton's East Beverley Street, also has been the home of Claiborne Rice Mason, a civil engineer; John Echols, founder of the National Valley Bank; Alan Caperton Braxton, a leader in the establishment of the State Corporation Commission; and Henry Winston Holt, chief justice of the Virginia Supreme Court of Appeals. With its brick construction, deck-on-hip roof, and wide plain entablature, the house typifies the conservative, solidly proportioned structures favored by local builders working in the Greek Revival idiom. A contrast to the clean lines is the delicately detailed Grecian-style iron railing topping the porch. *(132–33) VLR: 07/20/82; NRHP: 09/09/82.*

C. W. MILLER HOUSE, *210 North New Street.* Staunton architect T. J. Collins's experimentation with a broad range of styles endowed his city with marvelous variety in his many works. Of his surviving residential commissions, none is more elaborate than the large house he designed in the late 1890s for C. W. Miller, located adjacent to Mary Baldwin College. Drawing from the Châteauesque as well as Queen Anne style, Collins, with the buff brick, delicate ornamentation, and variety of curves, gave the house a grace and lightness not seen in the average domestic work of the period. Just as delightful is the interior, highlighted by a remarkable spindle and scrollwork screen framing a paneled stair. The Mary Baldwin music department was located here for many years. The house was carefully restored as a private residence in 1993 when the conservatory, removed in the 1930s, was reconstructed. *(132–18) VLR: 12/19/78; NRHP: 06/19/79.*

NATIONAL VALLEY BANK, *12–14 West Beverley Street.* The influence of the Neoclassical Revival on America's Main Street is well demonstrated in the facade of the National Valley Bank. Inspired by the triumphal arches of ancient Rome, the bank was designed by Staunton architect T. J. Collins and completed in 1903. The National Valley Bank was founded in 1865; its first president was former Confederate general John Echols. The present building was intended as a showcase for the bank's commercial success; craftsmen were brought from Baltimore to execute the impressive coffered ceiling, and furnishings and fittings were brought from Cincinnati. Despite some later remodeling, much of the original character of the grand interior has been brought out through restoration; the facade stands unaltered. The building continues to function as a bank. *(132–23) VLR: 12/19/78; NRHP: 06/19/79.*

NEWTOWN HISTORIC DISTRICT. Begun in 1781 as a twenty-five-acre annexation known as the Newtown Addition and since expanded, the Newtown Historic District is a large and varied neighborhood whose development spans over a century and a half. On the east, where Newtown joins Staunton's two commercial historic districts, warehouses coexist with richly detailed brick houses. The neighborhood's steep hills are a mix of 19th- and early 20th-century houses with individual examples of late 18th-century architecture such as the Stuart house of 1791. Three girls' schools were located in the district, of which Stuart Hall School remains. The religious buildings include Trinity Church (1855); the chapel of the city's first black church, organized in 1865; and several late 19th-century churches. An important but contrasting component of the district is the romantically landscaped Thornrose Cemetery, filled with Victorian funerary monuments. *(132–34) VLR: 06/21/83; NRHP: 09/08/83.*

OAKDENE, *605 East Beverley Street.* This complex house shows the late 19th-century Queen Anne style at its most imaginative. It was designed in 1893 by the Philadelphia firm of Yarnell and Goforth, which borrowed forms and motifs from 16th- and 17th-century European precedents and combined them into a structure uniquely American, employing outstanding craftsmanship and fine materials. Defining characteristics of the style are the asymmetrical facade, a multiplicity of roof forms, a mixture of surface materials, and the many different window types. The American touch is the neighborly front porch and terrace. Oakdene's conical tower is topped by an owl finial whose eyes were originally gas lit. The house was built in 1893 for Edward Echols, president of the local National Valley Bank and Virginia's lieutenant governor from 1898 to 1902. *(132–27) VLR: 09/15/81; NRHP: 11/24/82.*

THE OAKS, *437 East Beverley Street.* Against a wooded hillside on Staunton's East Beverley Street, this singular house was built by Maj. Jedediah Hotchkiss, Confederate cartographer and aide to Gen. Stonewall Jackson. Hotchkiss's Virginia campaign maps, often produced under dangerous conditions, are now in the Library of Congress and are considered by Civil War historians to be among the finest of their type. After the war Hotchkiss successfully speculated in land and minerals. He also wrote on Virginia geology, geography, and Civil War history. The rear wing of Hotchkiss's house was built in the 1840s as a wing of an earlier dwelling and features the deep bracketed eaves characteristic of the chalet style. The irregular Queen Anne–style front section was Hotchkiss's own design, drafted by the Boston firm of Winslow and Wetherell and erected in 1888–89. The interior contains intricately detailed woodwork typical of the period. *(132–21) VLR: 12/19/78; NRHP: 06/19/79.*

OLD WESTERN STATE HOSPITAL, *Greenville Avenue at U.S. Route 250.* First known as Western Lunatic Asylum of Virginia, this institution was founded in 1825 to serve Virginia's western region. Baltimore architect William Small designed the 1828 main building. The five-part structure, one of the nation's finest examples of early 19th-century institutional architecture, remains remarkably unaltered. It acquired a more monumental aspect in 1847 with the addition of porticoes. Flanking it are large annex buildings, both designed by Robert Cary Long, Jr., of Baltimore and completed in the early 1840s by contractor William B. Phillips. Behind the main building is the refectory and chapel building constructed in 1851 by Thomas Blackburn. A small ward of 1842 completes the antebellum complex. The buildings are a testament to Virginia's early effort to provide enlightened care to the mentally ill. The hospital relocated in the 1970s; the complex is currently a state prison. *(132–09) VLR: 05/13/69; NRHP: 11/25/69.*

ROSE TERRACE, *150 North Market Street.* Built ca. 1875 as a residence for Holmes Erwin, Rose Terrace illustrates the prosperity enjoyed by Staunton following the Civil War. Near the top of the city's highest hill, the L-shaped, two-and-a-half-story structure is in a freely interpreted Italianate style. It is an outstanding example of Victorian-era taste, with decorative brickwork and fancy chimney stacks. Rose Terrace was purchased in 1919 by Mary Baldwin Seminary (now College) and served as the president's home for many years. More recently, it has served as a residence hall and home of the college admissions office. Towering above the college's lower campus, the dwelling provides a lively architectural foil for Mary Baldwin's cream-colored Greek Revival academic structures and serves as a link between the upper and lower portions of the campus. *(132–17) VLR: 12/19/78; NRHP: 06/19/79.*

SEARS HOUSE, *400 Marquis Street.* On a wooded hilltop overlooking Staunton's downtown, this board-and-batten cottage was once the home of the educator Barnas Sears, chosen in 1867 by philanthropist George Peabody to administer the Peabody Educational Fund for the war-devastated South. Sears selected Staunton as his base of operation because of its convenience to transportation lines. He purchased the house erected a year earlier for Dr. Robert Madison, physician for the VMI cadets in the battle of New Market. He subsequently enlarged it with a polygonal tower to contain his library. The house conforms to the "bracketed cottage," promoted by Andrew Jackson Downing as the most pleasant, economical, and practical dwelling for middle-class Americans. It was long owned by the city but was acquired and restored in the 1970s by the Historic Staunton Foundation and resold as a private residence. *(132–12) VLR: 11/16/71; NRHP: 02/23/72; BHR EASEMENT.*

STAUNTON NATIONAL CEMETERY, *901 Richmond Avenue.* The superintendent's lodge at Staunton National Cemetery was built about 1871 in the Second Empire style from a design by Quartermaster General Montgomery C. Meigs. The cemetery itself was established in 1866. More than 750 Union soldiers are buried here, mostly casualties from the Shenandoah Valley battles of 1862 and 1865, including Cross Keys, Port Republic, and Waynesboro. Sixty-seven Union prisoners of war also are interred in the cemetery. One of the men killed at Cross Keys on June 8, 1862, Nicolae Dunca, was a Romanian who served as a captain on the staff of Maj. Gen. John C. Frémont, the Union commander at this battle. Cross Keys was the second-to-last battle in Gen. Stonewall Jackson's great Shenandoah Valley campaign. *(132–19) VLR: 10/18/95; NRHP: 02/26/96.*

STEEPHILL, *200 Park Boulevard.* Steephill was built in 1877–78 as a Gothic-style suburban villa for Col. John Lewis Peyton, author of *The History of Augusta County, Virginia* (1882) and other works of local and regional history. In 1926–27 the house was deftly remodeled in the Georgian Revival style by Staunton architect Samuel Collins for Peyton's son, Lawrence Washington Peyton. Collins was the son of T. J. Collins, founder of Stanton's most prominent architectural firm. The remodeling resulted in one of the city's best examples of this dignified 20th-century mode. Adding interest to the place is its dramatic setting on a steep, terraced hill within a spacious yard near the city's Gypsy Hill Park. During the remodeling the extensive landscaping, including a boxwood maze, was redesigned to be more compatible with Steephill's new look. *(132–31) VLR: 01/17/84; NRHP: 02/23/84.*

STUART ADDITION HISTORIC DISTRICT. The Stuart Addition Historic District generally conforms to a tract deeded to the city in 1803 by Judge Archibald Stuart. The neighborhood developed gradually but steadily and was well established by the Civil War. As with all of Staunton's older areas, it experienced its greatest growth from the 1870s to World War I. The district thus has great diversity of both architectural styles and forms. Intermingled with some of Staunton's oldest residences, some dating before 1825, are characteristic examples of later styles such as Italianate, Queen Anne, and Georgian Revival. Only a fraction of its 105 structures are modern intrusions. Traditionally a racially mixed neighborhood, the district contains three historic black churches and a 1915 black elementary school. A principal architectural landmark is the Victorian Gothic–style St. Francis of Assisi Roman Catholic Church designed by Staunton architect T. J. Collins. *(132–36) VLR: 03/20/84; NRHP: 05/03/84.*

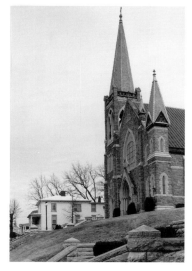

STUART HALL SCHOOL, OLD MAIN, *235 West Frederick Street.* Tracing its origins to 1827 and chartered in 1844 as the Virginia Female Institute, Stuart Hall is the oldest preparatory school for girls in the state. Its central building, "Old Main," was designed and built by Edwin Taylor and completed in 1846. The Greek Revival structure, dominated by a strong portico of Doric piers, is one of the earliest instances of a building erected specifically for the education of women. The school became affiliated with the Episcopal church in 1843. From 1880 to 1898 it gained stature under the direction of its principal, Flora Stuart, widow of Gen. J. E. B. Stuart, and was renamed in her honor in 1907. The school's physical plant has been greatly expanded since 1846, but Old Main remains the visual symbol of this enduring institution. *(132–11) VLR: 02/19/74; NRHP: 08/13/74.*

STUART HOUSE, *120 Church Street.* Archibald Stuart's imposing 1791 residence is one of Virginia's earliest expressions of the Classical Revival mode popularized by Thomas Jefferson. Its temple form and two-story portico broke with tradition and followed a format that was to be used for many houses and public buildings in subsequent decades. Stuart, a Virginia legislator and judge, was a close friend of Jefferson, and family tradition has it that Jefferson suggested the design. That Jefferson was its architect is unlikely, for the naive interpretation of the classical forms, especially the portico, is inconsistent with Jefferson's strict adherence to Roman precedent. Contrasting with the somewhat austere exterior is richly carved interior woodwork. On the grounds are a rare original Chinese lattice gate and Stuart's gambrel-roof office. Stuart's son, Alexander H. H. Stuart, who was born in the house in 1807, was secretary of the interior under Millard Fillmore. *(132–06) VLR: 01/18/72; NRHP: 05/05/72.*

TRINITY EPISCOPAL CHURCH, *West Beverley and South Lewis streets.* With its ascetic medievalism, Staunton's Trinity Church well demonstrates the more serious side of mid-19th-century America's Gothic Revival. Built in 1855–57 as the third church of Augusta Parish, founded in 1746, the dark red brick building with its angle-buttressed tower stands in a tree-shaded colonial burying ground. Its original architect was J. W. Johns, who designed a library for the Virginia Theological Seminary. The church was enlarged in 1870 under architect William A. Pratt who also drew the plans for the 1872 rectory. Charles E. Cassell of Baltimore was engaged to make further alterations in the 1880s. The interior contains a noteworthy collection of stained-glass windows including works by the Tiffany Studios. The parish's first church, formerly on this same parcel, temporarily housed the Virginia General Assembly after it fled Richmond during the Revolution. *(132–07) VLR: 01/18/72; NRHP: 05/05/72.*

VIRGINIA SCHOOL FOR THE DEAF AND THE BLIND, MAIN BUILDING, *East Beverley Street.* The high quality of the early architecture of many of Virginia's state-supported institutions is exemplified in the splendid main building of the Virginia School for the Deaf and the Blind. Founded in 1838, the institution did not see the final touches put on its huge central structure until 1846. Staunton was selected for the school because of its central location and because it was in the midst of "cheap and abundant country." Its designer was Robert Cary Long, Jr., a Baltimore architect whose mastery of the Greek Revival idiom is evident in the powerful hexastyle Greek Doric portico and in the proportions and detailing of the rest of the building. The contractor for the ambitious undertaking was William Donoho of Albemarle County. The building remains the principal structure of this pioneering humanitarian institution. *(132–08) VLR: 09/09/69; NRHP: 11/17/69.*

WAVERLEY HILL, *3001 North Augusta Street.* This elegant expression of the Georgian Revival was designed by William Lawrence Bottomley, a New York architect who maintained an extensive Virginia clientele in the 1920s and 1930s. Drawing from Palladian, English, and colonial Virginia precedents, Bottomley fashioned imaginative and functional dwellings and set a standard of excellence in domestic architecture. Bottomley stated his philosophy in a magazine interview: "I believe we should do everything possible to preserve this old southern ideal of country house architecture because it is one of the finest things we have and it is still vital." Waverley Hill was commissioned in 1928 by Mr. and Mrs. Herbert McKelden Smith. The five-part form is reminiscent of Carter's Grove, although the main doorway was inspired by the Hammond-Harwood house in Annapolis. From its elevated site the house commands stunning views of the surrounding countryside. *(132–29) VLR: 02/16/82; NRHP: 07/08/82; BHR EASEMENT.*

WHARF AREA HISTORIC DISTRICT. The completion of the Virginia Central Railroad to Staunton in 1854 made this Valley community an active shipping point. The area around the depot, along Middlebrook Avenue, became a busy commercial area; its importance was signaled by the construction of the extant Greek Revival American Hotel in 1857. The colorful range of warehouses lining the tracks today dates mostly from the last quarter of the 19th century and served commission merchants, wholesale grocers, saloon keepers, and liveries. The district's eastern end is marked by the turn-of-the-century White Star Mill, now remodeled as a restaurant. The small but well-defined neighborhood has been the scene of considerable preservation activity, which has protected its character and enhanced the economy of downtown Staunton. The area was named the Wharf because it was a shipping point; there is no body of water. *(132–14) VLR: 12/21/71; NRHP: 11/09/72.*

WOODROW WILSON BIRTHPLACE, *24 North Coalter Street.* Thomas Woodrow Wilson, twenty-eighth president of the United States, was born in this Greek Revival manse in 1856. Built in 1846 to house the pastors of Staunton's First Presbyterian Church, the manse's second occupants were Dr. and Mrs. Joseph Ruggles Wilson, Wilson's parents, who moved here in 1855. Although his family left Staunton while he was still a baby, it was in this forthright dwelling that the seeds of Wilson's firm moral and intellectual training were planted. He carried these precepts into his adult life as a professor, president of Princeton University, governor of New Jersey, and finally president of the United States. Wilson conceived the League of Nations, for which he was awarded the Nobel Peace Prize in 1919. The manse was acquired by the Woodrow Wilson Birthplace Foundation in 1938 and was dedicated as a museum by President Franklin D. Roosevelt in 1941. *(132–04) VLR: 09/09/69; NRHP: 10/15/66; NHL: 07/19/64.*

CITY OF SUFFOLK

Probably named for the English shire, Suffolk was established in 1742 on the site of John Constant's warehouse. It was incorporated as a town in 1808 and as a city 1910. Its size was greatly expanded in 1974 when it was merged with Nansemond County, which thereby became extinct.

CHUCKATUCK HISTORIC DISTRICT. Chuckatuck is one of the oldest communities in the modern city of Suffolk, formerly Nansemond County. The settlement developed in the mid–17th century and was supported by the agricultural economy of the surrounding plantations. The name Chuckatuck is of Indian origin and means "crooked creek." Chuckatuck in the 19th century was a commercial center with its water and land transportation arteries serving the tobacco industry. Little growth has occurred in this century. The historic district consists of some sixty-two contributing buildings, the dominant ones being freestanding weatherboarded dwellings mostly dating from the 19th century and generally situated in large, level yards dotted with trees. Only one of its three early store buildings survives—Gwaltney Store, built in 1823 as a residence and later converted. Though Chuckatuck remains essentially a dormant crossroads community, it still exudes an old-fashioned ambience. *(133–692) VLR: 09/15/92; NRHP: 04/07/95.*

DRIVER HISTORIC DISTRICT. Centered on the main intersection of this Tidewater village, the Driver Historic District is an interesting collection of small country stores and several examples of domestic types that reflect the continuing influence of earlier Tidewater dwellings. The earliest structure is the Parker house, a side-passage, two-story frame dwelling built between 1820 and 1840. The majority of Driver's buildings were constructed in the late 1880s, after the completion of the Norfolk and Carolina Railroad. The railroad expanded the market for local farm products and created new jobs in the area. At that time the settlement was named after E. J. Driver who operated a general store here. Punctuating the district are two Gothic-style churches built between 1890 and 1910. This district also has two school buildings built in 1926. The tiny community maintains a simple unassertive character typical of an eastern Virginia crossroads community. *(133–693) VLR: 09/15/92; NRHP: 04/07/95.*

GLEBE CHURCH, *Driver vicinity.* This chaste colonial church takes its present name from the fact that its parish was one of the few in Virginia that managed to retain its colonial glebe—property owned by the parish used to produce income—following the Revolution and the disestablishment. The 300-acre glebe is still in the possession of the parish. The church, known in colonial times as Bennett's Creek Church, was constructed in 1737–38 as the lower church of Suffolk Parish. It was made L-shaped by the addition of a wing in 1759. The church fell into ruin after the Revolution but was restored to use in 1850 when the wing was demolished and the bricks were used in the repair. The church received its last extensive renovation in 1900. Today only the 1738 Flemish bond walls are original. *(133–61) VLR: 09/19/72; NRHP: 05/25/73.*

GODWIN-KNIGHT HOUSE, *Chuckatuck.* Chuckatuck's most conspicuous landmark, the Godwin-Knight house was the childhood home of Mills E. Godwin, Jr., who served as governor of Virginia for two terms, 1966–70 and 1974–78. The house displays architectural features from two distinct eras. Edward F. Wicks built what was a traditional side-passage house in 1856 on land he bought from Jennette Godwin. The house was remodeled in the Queen Anne style in 1900 by Charles B. Godwin, great-uncle of the governor. The most striking features of the change are the corner tower and the elaborate wraparound front porch. Other additions include a tile vestibule and plaster embellishments in the parlor. Despite the exterior alterations, the original design is discernible and can be compared to a nearby Federal-period house that was a near twin to the earlier form. *(133–576) VLR: 02/28/92; NRHP: 08/24/92.*

HOLLAND HISTORIC DISTRICT. Originally known as Holland's Corner, this linear village was reputedly settled by descendants of Gabriel Holland who came to Virginia in 1621. The Hollands were prosperous farmers and owned a general merchandise store here for generations. Despite its early origins, the town's fabric dates mainly from the late 19th century. Its growth was spurred by the completion in 1888 of the Atlantic and Danville Railroad, which served the local agricultural and lumber industries. Much of the town was destroyed by fire on January 1, 1910. The replacement structures were rebuilt in brick. Holland's residences, both pre- and postfire, are a mixture of small-town types common to eastern Virginia. One of the earliest houses is the William T. Holland farmhouse, built between 1860 and 1880. The town's principal architectural work is the 1918 Holland Christian Church, a forceful classical design by R. H. Riedel, a German immigrant who settled here. *(133–691) VLR: 09/15/92; NRHP: 05/18/95.*

HOLLAND HOUSE APARTMENTS, *216 Bank Street.* The former Edward Holland house is a model example of America's Second Empire style—a more neighborly interpretation of the French imperial fashion that inspired the mode. It was built in 1885 for Col. Edward Holland, a native of Nansemond County who was Suffolk's mayor in 1886–87. Holland later served in the Virginia senate and the U.S. House of Representatives. He continued an active civic life

until his death in 1940. Between 1940 and 1965 Holland's residence was a meeting place for the Suffolk Elks Lodge No. 685. It now accommodates six apartments. Dominated by its concave mansard roof highlighted by patterned slates, the stylish dwelling retains much of its original architectural fabric, including a lacy front porch. Though northern states abound in Second Empire–style dwellings, the economic deprivation of the Reconstruction era makes them rare in Virginia. *(133–07) VLR: 08/13/85; NRHP: 11/07/85.*

PHOENIX BANK OF NANSEMOND, *339 East Washington Street.* The straightforward commercial building erected in 1921 for the Phoenix Bank of Nansemond represents the effort of Virginia blacks to establish, out of necessity, their own business enterprises. Because white-run banks resisted extending credit to blacks, black businessmen created lending institutions to serve their community. Between 1900 and 1920 twenty black banks opened in Virginia. During this period Suffolk was gaining recognition as the "Peanut Capital of the United States." This thriving industry brought economic gain to black workers and the need for financial services. The bank was founded in 1917 by Dr. W. T. Fuller; the present building was erected by his successor, John W. Richardson. Though compact, the building was well appointed. In 1921 the *Norfolk Journal and Guide* described its vault as "second to none in the city as to security." The bank closed in 1931, a victim of the Great Depression. *(133–86) VLR: 08/21/90; NRHP: 01/24/91.*

ST. JOHN'S EPISCOPAL CHURCH, *Chuckatuck vicinity.* Originally known as Chuckatuck Church after a nearby Indian village, St. John's was built in 1755 and is the third church at its location. Its rectangular form with gable roof was the most popular one for Virginia's smaller colonial churches. Like most of the state's early ecclesiastical buildings, it is constructed of Flemish bond brickwork highlighted by glazed headers and gauged-brick round arches. The church was abandoned for a half century after the Revolution but was reconsecrated by the Episcopalians with its present name in 1826. Union troops desecrated the building during the Civil War. The interior woodwork dates from an 1888 renovation. Despite the urbanization of Suffolk, the church retains a scenic rural setting overlooking a lake at the headwaters of Cedar Creek. *(133–17) VLR: 10/17/72; NRHP: 04/11/73.*

MILLS RIDDICK HOUSE (RIDDICK'S FOLLY), *510 North Main Street.* This Greek Revival mansion is Suffolk's most distinguished historic residence and an outstanding example of Greek Revival urban residential architecture. The formality of its exterior is emphasized by its large scale, fine brickwork, and stone lintels. The large airy rooms are decorated with bold Greek Revival trim and ornamental ceiling medallions. Mills Riddick, a member of a prominent area family, began construction of the house, next to the Nansemond County Courthouse, in 1837 after the fire that consumed much of the town. Maj. Gen. John J. Peck and his staff of Union officers occupied the house during the Civil War. Penciled messages written by Union soldiers remain on the third floor. The house stayed in the Riddick family until the 1960s when it was sold to Nansemond County. It subsequently was restored and is now a museum and cultural center. *(133–03) VLR: 11/20/73; NRHP: 05/02/74.*

SUFFOLK HISTORIC DISTRICT. Although modern Suffolk now includes Nansemond County, the original city is a historic Tidewater community with an individual identity. Established in 1742, Suffolk grew as a port on the Nansemond River trading in wood products from the Dismal Swamp. The commercial center was destroyed by the British during the Revolution and again was swept away in an 1837 fire. The majority of the earliest buildings are Federal-period frame residences north of the downtown. Significant growth, facilitated by the railroads, occurred after the Civil War. Suffolk later became home of the nation's largest peanut industry. While encompassing the earlier houses on North Main Street, the historic district is primarily a large residential area known as New Town. Its streets are tightly packed with a rich mixture of over 200 late 1800s and early 1900s houses in a variety of styles, a reflection of the city's prosperity at that time. *(133–72) VLR: 12/09/86; NRHP: 06/22/87.*

WHALEYVILLE HISTORIC DISTRICT. Whaleyville's some 100 contributing structures are mainly stretched along U.S. Route 13 (Whaleyville Boulevard) in the southern end of what was Nansemond County, now the city of Suffolk. Whaleyville was named after Samuel Whaley, who purchased a farm here in 1877 and established a sawmill. Major development came after Whaley sold his timber rights to the Jackson Brothers of Maryland. Most of the subsequent dwellings were built for timber industry employees. The architectural fabric reflects the town's boom years, 1880–1920, and consists mostly of residences. The modest houses, nearly all frame, are a mixture of vernacular types common to the region. Each house generally has an individual character; the repetitive quality of northern mill-town housing is lacking. Whaleyville's three churches, built between 1870 and 1920, are all vernacular Gothic buildings. The town's period of ascendancy ended when the Jackson Brothers lumber business closed in 1919. *(133–694) VLR: 09/15/92; NRHP: 04/07/95.*

SURRY COUNTY

On the south side of the James River, this rural Tidewater county was formed from James City County ca. 1652 and was named for the county of Surrey in England. The county seat is Surry.

BACON'S CASTLE, *Bacon's Castle.* The nation's outstanding example of high-style 17th-century domestic architecture and the oldest documented house in Virginia, Bacon's Castle was erected in 1665 for Arthur Allen. Pure Jacobean in form and detail, the house is distinguished by its cruciform plan, curvilinear gables, and diagonal chimney stacks. It acquired its present name in 1676 during Bacon's Rebellion when the house was fortified by a group of Nathaniel Bacon's followers. The house was modified in the 18th century when the first-floor paneling was installed and the windows were changed from casements to wooden sash. Further alterations occurred in the 1840s when a Greek Revival wing was added. The Association for the Preservation of Virginia Antiquities purchased the property in 1973 and exhibits it as a museum. On the grounds is a vast formal garden, reconstructed from archaeological evidence of the original 17th-century garden. *(90–01) VLR: 09/09/69; NRHP: 10/15/66; NHL: 10/09/60.*

CHIPPOKES PLANTATION HISTORIC DISTRICT (CHIPPOKES STATE PARK), *Bacon's Castle vicinity.* This 1,400-acre plantation opposite Jamestown Island has been a working farm for nearly four centuries. Named for Choupocke, a friendly Indian chief, Chippokes was acquired in 1671 by Governor Sir William Berkeley and passed into the Ludwell family, who owned it until 1824. The main dwelling is an Italianate house erected ca. 1855 for Albert C. Jones. The River House (shown), a vernacular frame house doubled in size in the 1840s, served as Jones's residence until he built the later house. An extensive collection of early outbuildings and farm buildings sustains the plantation atmosphere. Purchased by Mr. and Mrs. Victor Stewart in 1917, Chippokes was presented to the Commonwealth by Mrs. Stewart in 1967 to serve as a center focusing on the history of Virginia agriculture. On the property are various colonial-period archaeological sites. *(90–03) VLR: 11/05/68 (REREGISTERED AS A HISTORIC DISTRICT 07/15/86); NRHP: 10/01/69.*

ENOS HOUSE, *Surry vicinity.* Erected before 1820 by the Warren family and last used as a private residence by the Enos family, this Surry County homestead is the sort of house occupied by middling farmers of the early Republican era in Southside Virginia. A distinguishing aspect of the otherwise simple dwelling is its double-pile, hall-parlor plan, a regional peculiarity reflecting the infiltration of Georgian layout into the vernacular architecture of an area which clung tenaciously to traditional forms well into the 19th century. The steep gable roof and narrow dormers are features common to most small houses of the period. The front porch is a later addition. The building stood neglected for many years but has been stabilized by Surry County with eventual restoration planned to complement the programs of an adjacent county recreational center. *(90–39) VLR: 05/17/77; NRHP: 12/07/77.*

FOUR MILE TREE, *Surry vicinity.* Named for a tree marking its distance by water from Jamestown, this plantation has been an established unit since the early 17th century. It was first settled by the Browne family, who occupied it for over a century and a half. The present house, dating from the mid–18th century, shows the application of formal Georgian planning and detailing to a building with a more unassuming native quality. The visual character of the exterior is defined by its jerkinhead gambrel roof pierced by five dormers on each front. The house was remodeled in the 19th century when its brick walls were stuccoed, its sashes replaced, and the portico added. Much of the early paneled woodwork and a Georgian stair were left untouched. A family graveyard contains Virginia's oldest legible tombstone, dated 1650. *(90–09) VLR: 10/06/70; NRHP: 12/28/70.*

GLEBE OF SOUTHWARK PARISH, *Surry vicinity.* One of Virginia's rare collection of glebe houses, this dwelling was first occupied by the Rev. John Cargill, a leading colonial cleric. Cargill was a delegate to the 1719 convention that considered Commissary James Blair's request that the clergy side with him in a political dispute with Lieutenant Governor Alexander Spotswood. Cargill began his ministry in Southwark Parish in 1708. In 1724 he complained to the bishop of London that "my glebe house is in very bad condition and the parish will not repair it." Architectural evidence suggests that the present house was built soon after the complaint. The glebe was sold into private ownership in 1802, and the house underwent extensive remodeling. Exterior chimneys were added, the gable roof was rebuilt as a gambrel, and much of the present woodwork was installed. Despite these changes, the simple straightforwardness that characterized these glebe houses is intact. *(90–12) VLR: 10/21/75; NRHP: 05/17/76.*

LOWER SOUTHWARK PARISH CHURCH RUINS, *Bacon's Castle.* The walls of these romantic ruins date from 1754 when the Anglican Southwark Parish vestry completed a brick church to serve the lower part of the parish. The church fell into a long period of disuse after the Revolutionary War, but other denominations occasionally held services here. Episcopalians established a mission at the church in 1847 but were forced by the other groups using the building to erect their own church nearby. Before it was gutted by fire in 1868, Lower Church followed the format of the standard colonial rectangular church, with a single doorway on the west end and five bays on either side, including a side entrance. The surviving walls retain evidence of the location of many of the building's original fittings. The ruins are owned and maintained by the Bacon's Castle Cemetery Association. *(90–34) VLR: 09/16/82; NRHP: 01/02/86.*

MELVILLE, *Alliance vicinity.* The refinement that colonial builders could impart to even the smallest plantation dwellings is demonstrated in Melville, an engaging but otherwise simple hall-parlor house in the Surry County countryside. Setting the compact dwelling apart from its more humble contemporaries are its detailing and brickwork. The clipped-gable roof and the decorative chevron pattern with glazed headers on the gable ends were treatments usually reserved for more pretentious houses of the period. The property was patented by Thomas Binns is 1653. It was purchased in 1723 by the Faulcon family, who likely built the present house. The Faulcons held the place into the 19th century. The name Melville was first used in court records about 1813. *(90–13) VLR: 12/21/76; NRHP: 05/06/80.*

MONTPELIER, *Cabin Point vicinity.* The closet windows in the wide exterior end chimneys of this colonial dwelling give singularity to a relatively standard plantation house of the period. Closets in colonial houses were not used strictly for storage but often served as pantries, dressing rooms, or toilet areas, uses requiring daylight and benefiting from the warmth of the chimney. The deceptively large-scale dwelling has original weatherboarding and exceptionally tall windows with original sash. The house probably was built in the third quarter of the 18th century by Charles Harrison on property inherited in 1744. The roof originally had clipped gables, but they were covered over during an early 19th-century remodeling which included the installation of much of the present interior woodwork. The house stood neglected for a number of years but was restored in the late 1970s. *(90–14) VLR: 02/21/78; NRHP: 03/26/80.*

PLEASANT POINT, *Scotland vicinity.* Atop a bluff overlooking the James River opposite Jamestown Island, Pleasant Point illustrates the formality found in many of Virginia's lesser colonial seats. The complex consists of a compact story-and-a-half, brick-ended manor house flanked by the perpendicularly set laundry and reconstructed kitchen. A smokehouse and dairy on the river side define a symmetrical forecourt. A series of five terraces leads down to the James. The buildings and terracing form a unified piece, probably accomplished ca. 1735–45 during the ownership of Benjamin Edwards, sheriff of Surry County. Pleasant Point was included in a 1624 grant to George Sandys, treasurer of the Virginia Company, who upon his return to England ca. 1628 gained fame as a poet and translator of classical literature. Archaeological investigation may reveal the sites of Sandys's paled fort and other building known to have existed here. *(90–20) VLR: 09/17/74; NRHP: 07/16/76; BHR EASEMENT.*

RICH NECK FARM, *Bacon's Castle vicinity.* This striking early 19th-century farmhouse was built for William E. B. Ruffin in the second or third decade of the 19th century as the core of a prosperous Southside plantation. Rich Neck was acquired by the Ruffin family ca. 1675 and remained in its ownership until 1865. The exterior is dominated by large windows and a high gambrel roof framed by sloping parapets and paired chimneys with pent closets. The use of parapets terminated by corbeled shoulders illustrates the reversion to pre-Georgian vernacular forms that occurred in Virginia during the Federal period. Though the house has been unoccupied for a number of years, the interior preserves its original restrained Federal trim. Flanking the axial avenue leading to it are two granaries nearly as old as the house. *(90–21) VLR: 06/17/75; NRHP: 05/19/80.*

SECOND SOUTHWARK CHURCH ARCHAEOLOGICAL SITE, *Surry vicinity.* Although historical records suggest that more than eighty churches and chapels were constructed in Virginia during the 17th century, only St. Luke's Church in Isle of Wight County, Grace Church in Yorktown, and the Jamestown Church tower have survived from that time. Accordingly, the archaeological remains at the Second Southwark Church could reveal new information on the architecture and settings of Virginia's 17th-century ecclesiastical structures. This church was the second to serve Southwark Parish, which encompassed land south of the James River between Upper Chippokes Creek and College Run. The second church was probably standing by 1673, replacing the earlier Southwark Church, constructed before 1655. Abandoned shortly after the Revolution, the building stood in ruins until the Civil War. The site is marked by a monument erected in 1927. *(90–69) VLR: 01/17/84; NRHP: 02/23/84.*

SMITH'S FORT, *Surry vicinity.* A barely discernible earthwork on a steep finger of land above Gray's Creek is the remnant of what is likely the oldest extant construction of English origin in Virginia. The fort was begun in 1608 by order of Capt. John Smith as a refuge for the Jamestown settlers should the island be attacked. Destruction of supplies by rats forced the abandonment of the project, leaving only the one earthwork completed. In 1614 the site was included in a parcel presented by Chief Powhatan to his son-in-law John Rolfe, husband of Pocahontas. Three centuries later, in 1933, Smith's Fort was acquired by the Association for the Preservation of Virginia Antiquities along with the nearby Smith's Fort plantation house. The much-worn earthwork today is some 2 feet high and approximately 120 feet long with an opening in the center, possibly the location of an extended entrance. *(90–28) VLR: 12/02/69; NRHP: 06/15/70.*

SMITH'S FORT PLANTATION, *Surry vicinity.* This classic example of colonial Virginia architecture has been the inspiration for numerous 20th-century replicas. The house was long thought to have been the 17th-century home of either John Rolfe or Thomas Warren, but recent dendrochronological study indicates that it was built ca. 1763. Its first occupant was most likely Jacob Faulcon, who lived on a plantation at this location owned by his father. Faulcon became the Surry County clerk in 1781 and inherited the property in 1783. It remained in the Faulcon family until 1835. In 1928 it was acquired by the Williamsburg Holding Company, predecessor of the Colonial Williamsburg Foundation. Williamsburg gave the property in 1934 to the Association for the Preservation of Virginia Antiquities, which has since exhibited the house as a museum. The name Smith's Fort derives from an earthwork on the property constructed under the order of Capt. John Smith. *(90–22) VLR: 10/16/73; NRHP: 11/14/73.*

SNOW HILL, *Gwaltney Corner vicinity.* This frame farmhouse is an illustration of the persistence of Georgian forms in rural Southside Virginia well into the 19th century. It is also a demonstration of the formality that could be instilled in vernacular architecture with the use of symmetry and carefully calculated geometric proportions. Appearing older than its construction date of 1836, Snow Hill was first the home of Samuel Booth, a captain in the local militia. Though it has been unoccupied for many years, the regular five-bay structure is well preserved, even retaining its early beaded weatherboarding. Adding a liveliness to its otherwise restrained interior woodwork is an important decorative painting scheme of graining and marbleizing. Such fancy painting was a craft widely employed in the Virginia countryside in the 19th century but often covered by later coats of paint. *(90–40) VLR: 09/18/79; NRHP: 12/28/79.*

SURRY COUNTY COURTHOUSE COMPLEX, *Surry Court House.* The authority of local government is handsomely symbolized in Surry County's neoclassical courthouse, the dominant landmark of this crossroads county seat. The two-story brick building, highlighted by a stately Ionic portico, was erected in 1923 after a fire destroyed a 1907 courthouse on the same site. Designed by architect George R. Berryman to resemble the building that it replaced, the courthouse is the seventh structure to serve the county since its formation in 1652. A small clerk's office building erected in 1825–26 stands on the edge of the tree-shaded courthouse square. Several small later structures housing county offices are clustered around the courthouse. A 1909 monument to the county's Confederate dead completes this county-seat grouping. *(308–08) VLR: 12/17/85; NRHP: 04/10/86.*

SWANN'S POINT ARCHAEOLOGICAL SITE, *Scotland vicinity.* Test excavations conducted by the Virginia Department of Historic Resources at Swann's Point in 1973 revealed two abutting brick domestic foundations measuring 60 by 20 feet total. The related artifacts strongly suggest that the structure was built for either William Swann, who patented the land in 1635, or his son Thomas. Thomas Swann held numerous public offices including local justice and member of the governor's council. The fact that his residence was used for a meeting of royal commissioners in 1677 indicates that it was likely one of the colony's better houses. Swann took the side of Nathaniel Bacon during the latter's rebellion against Governor Berkeley but was spared punishment. His slab grave marker, carved with his coat of arms, remains at the site. Full archaeological investigation here should reveal much information on the architecture and objects associated with a member of Virginia's 17th-century ruling class. *(90–66) VLR: 12/17/74; NRHP: 04/01/75.*

❧ SUSSEX COUNTY

Named for the English shire, this rural southern Tidewater county was formed from Surry County in 1753. Its county seat is Sussex Court House.

MILES B. CARPENTER HOUSE, *U.S. 460, Waverly.* Miles B. Carpenter, one of America's foremost folk artists, purchased this 1890 frame house in 1912 and lived here until his death in 1985. Through his ownership of a local sawmill and planing mill, Carpenter acquired a familiarity with wood. This appreciation for the material, together with an artist's eye for figures suggested by the shapes of branches and stumps, led him to carve folk sculpture as his lumber business declined. Using his backyard and kitchen for his studio, Carpenter fashioned figures that ranged from the whimsical to the frightening. His carved and painted watermelons, monkeys, monsters, and humans attracted widespread attention and earned him the respect of museums. After his death Carpenter's house became a museum displaying his sculptures and tools. In addition to celebrating Carpenter's unique art, the museum exhibits the work of young area artists. *(91–73) VLR: 04/18/89; NRHP: 11/14/89.*

CHESTER, *Homeville vicinity.* The massive exterior end chimney structure, complete with windowed pent closets, lends architectural potency to this late 18th-century plantation house. This type of chimney construction served a practical function by accommodating several fireplaces of a relatively large timber-frame house in a single structure. Chester was built for Capt. William Harrison in 1793, a date found on five inscribed bricks. Consistent with the quality of the exterior is the Georgian interior woodwork, nearly all of which is intact. The principal first-floor rooms are embellished with paneled chimneypieces flanked by fluted pilasters. Except for the addition of a two-story ca. 1820 wing, Chester remains little changed. The house stood in neglected condition for many years but was purchased by a descendant of the builder in 1969 and has since been carefully restored. *(91–21) VLR: 10/06/70; NRHP: 12/18/70.*

FORTSVILLE, *Grizzard vicinity.* Fortsville was the home of John Young Mason (1799–1859), who served in Congress and held the offices of U.S. secretary of the navy, attorney general, and minister to France. He helped draw up the 1854 Ostend Manifesto, which stated the necessity for the United States to take possession of Cuba. The early 19th-century house apparently was built by Mason's father-in-law, Lewis Fort. John Young Mason and his wife, Mary Ann Fort Mason, made Fortsville their home following their marriage in 1821. The three-part composition is a local interpretation of the Palladian format favored by more architecturally literate Virginians in the early 19th century. Fortsville has a larger scale and finer detailing than most of this type. Its sophistication is emphasized by the starkness of its setting in Sussex County's flat fields. Fortsville stood neglected for many years but has since been restored. *(91–08) VLR: 06/02/70; NRHP: 09/15/70.*

HUNTING QUARTER, *Sussex Court House vicinity.* An example of traditional 18th-century plantation architecture, Hunting Quarter was built sometime after 1745, when Capt.

Henry Harrison inherited the property from his father, Benjamin Harrison of Berkeley. Henry Harrison was the brother of Benjamin Harrison, signer of the Declaration of Independence, and participated in the French and Indian War, serving at Fort Duquesne. The property remained in the Harrison family until 1887. Little altered over the past two centuries, the exterior is given visual character by its gambrel roof, a form favored for midsize plantation houses. The interior, with its paneled mantels and doors and an unusual modillion cornice in the principal room, preserves its colonial flavor. On the grounds are an early smokehouse and a family cemetery. Surrounding the curtilage are the level fields characteristic of the southeastern Virginia countryside. *(91–31) VLR: 04/28/95; NRHP: 04/07/95.*

LITTLE TOWN, *Littleton vicinity.* A strikingly dignified specimen of an eastern Virginia gentry homestead, Little Town was built in 1811 for James C. Bailey, the county clerk. An 1820 tax assessment gave Little Town the highest value of any house in the county. The Flemish bond brickwork and fine joinery of the windows, cornice, and pedimented porch are marks of a building of quality. A folk painting of the national seal on the parlor chimneypiece has led to the claim that Bailey used the room for court sessions. More likely, the seal represented the owner's patriotic fervor. Elsewhere in the interior are sections of original graining and marbleizing. The dining room mantel has a delicately molded frame decorated with reliefs of exotic animals—two camels, a rhinoceros, and an elephant. The house and surrounding farm remain in the ownership of the builder's family. *(91–11) VLR: 09/21/76; NRHP: 11/18/76.*

NOTTOWAY RIVER ARCHAEOLOGICAL SITE, *Stony Creek vicinity.* Included in this site is a series of spatially overlapping Indian components on a terrace above the Nottoway River. Dating from the Paleo-Indian (9200 B.C.) through the Late Woodland (A.D. 1600) periods, the site contains artifacts, deeply stratified deposits, and hearth features that could significantly contribute to the limited research available for Native American inhabitants of the interior coastal plain of southern Virginia. The heavy concentration of stone spear points, knives, and hide scrapers, as well as ceramic potsherds, has provided data on chronological sequences and the cultural history of the region. *(91–75) VLR: 09/20/88; NRHP: 11/03/88.*

SUSSEX COURT HOUSE HISTORIC DISTRICT. The tiny settlement of Sussex Court House typifies the early 19th-century Virginia county seat, consisting of a scattering of court structures with a few law offices and dwellings. The district is dominated by its Jeffersonian courthouse, completed in 1828 by Dabney Cosby, Sr., who built several court structures in the classical style he mastered while employed at the University of Virginia. For the courthouse Cosby made use of a pedimented pavilion with an arcaded ground floor instead of the usual columned portico. Across the road is the 1817 former treasurer's office, a story-and-a-half brick structure. Immediately north of the courthouse is the ca. 1800 Dillard house, a two-story weatherboarded dwelling which likely served as the courthouse tavern. Nearby is the John Bannister house, a two-story wood-frame house which at one time housed a girls' school. *(91–72) VLR: 10/17/72; NRHP: 07/24/73.*

TAZEWELL COUNTY

Tazewell County was formed from Wythe and Russell counties in 1799 and named for Henry Tazewell, U.S. senator from Virginia from 1794 until his death in 1799. It was later enlarged with parts of Russell, Wythe, Washington, and Logan (now in West Virginia) counties. Its county seat is Tazewell.

BIG CRAB ORCHARD HISTORIC AND ARCHAEO-LOGICAL COMPLEX, *Pisgah vicinity.* Patented in 1750, the Crab Orchard site was one of the first European settlements in Southwest Virginia. Parts of the tract were later owned by Morriss Griffith and William Ingles and then acquired by Thomas Witten, Sr., who settled here ca. 1760. In 1774 Witten's log house was reinforced and became known as Witten's Crab Orchard Fort, serving as a defense against Indians. In 1793 the first Pisgah Methodist Episcopal Church, a log building, was erected nearby. The archaeological sites of both structures remain. Big Crab Orchard also preserves various Late Woodland–period Indian sites (A.D. 800–1600), including those of a palisaded village, burial cave, campsite, and rockshelter. Part of the area is now owned by the Historic Crab Orchard Museum and Pioneer Park, Inc., and includes a museum, a 1926 replication of Witten's Fort, and a reconstructed pioneer settlement. *(92–13) VLR: 02/21/78; NRHP: 08/11/80.*

BULL THISTLE CAVE ARCHAEOLOGICAL SITE, *Tazewell vicinity.* The Bull Thistle Cave holds an undisturbed archaeological deposit containing human osteological remains and artifacts relating to its use as a place of burial during the latter half of the Late Woodland period (ca. A.D. 1300–1700). The site is the best-preserved example of a Late Woodland–period vertical drop burial cave known in Virginia. The burial deposit should contribute valuable data on the age, sex, stature, health, and genetic relationship, as well as religious practices, of the Indians of Southwest Virginia. It is likely that the cave also contains intact deposits useful for determining the prehistoric environment of the region. *(92–22) VLR: 03/17/87; NRHP: 09/10/87.*

BURKE'S GARDEN CENTRAL CHURCH AND CEMETERY, *Burke's Garden.* Settlers of German origin migrated from Pennsylvania to Southwest Virginia in the late 18th century, settling in Burke's Garden, a bowl-shaped valley atop Garden Mountain, now the Burke's Garden Rural Historic District. Here the Central Church and its cemetery were established in the 1820s. The cemetery is studded with German-style grave markers dating from the 1830s. The stars, pinwheels, sunflowers, and hearts decorating the stones are similar to those created by an unidentified carver for gravestones at Sharon Lutheran Church in Bland County and the Zion and Kimberling churches in Wythe County. Also here are some uninscribed, uncarved fieldstone markers and a rare wooden marker. The church and its cemetery were long shared by several denominations, but the property was owned by the Lutherans. The present wood-frame church was built in 1875 to replace the original 1820s building. *(92–14) VLR: 11/21/78; NRHP: 05/07/79.*

BURKE'S GARDEN RURAL HISTORIC DISTRICT. Encompassing nearly forty square miles, Burke's Garden is a topographically unique elongated basin rimmed entirely by Garden Mountain, a continuous mountain system which protects the area from modern intrusion. Originally surveyed by James Burke in the mid–18th century, the first permanent settlement took place here in the late 18th century by German Lutherans. The valley is one of the most productive grazing areas in Southwest Virginia. The many pastures in its network of farms allow for spectacular views across the valley to the encircling mountains. Accenting the landscape are groups of farm buildings clustered around associated dwelling houses; the more substantial farmhouses date from the late 19th century. Circulation patterns have changed little over the past 150 years. The valley is also rich in prehistoric archaeological sites reflecting continuous Indian occupation from the Early Archaic period. *(92–20) VLR: 10/15/85; NRHP: 02/25/86*

CHIMNEY ROCK FARM, *Witten Valley.* Chimney Rock Farm, also known as the Willows, is a strikingly sophisticated example of the three-part Palladian-type house in Southwest Virginia. Although this form was employed extensively in the Tidewater and Piedmont regions, such houses are rarely found in the farther upland reaches of the state. On the west fork of Plum Creek, in the shadow of a wooded mountain range, the house was built ca. 1843 for Maj. Hervey George, a lawyer and farmer who served as a delegate to the General Assembly during the Civil War. Finely crafted, the brick dwelling retains its delicate Federal interior woodwork, including some painted wood graining. Local tradition asserts that the house was the work of a Bedford County builder who erected four brick houses in Tazewell County. *(92–03) VLR: 03/17/81; NRHP: 07/08/82.*

CLINCH VALLEY ROLLER MILLS, *Cedar Bluff.* The Clinch Valley Roller Mills is one of the oldest and most significant industrial structures in Tazewell County. The mill was originally built in the late 1850s and was probably rebuilt after an 1884 fire. Expanded several times over subsequent decades, the complex at first operated as one of a group of grain, lumber, and woolen mills clustered along the Clinch River. The central and earliest section resembles many of Virginia's moderate-size custom mills of the 19th century. As altered in 1896, it became one of the region's largest producers of patent, high-grade flour. It continued as the chief supplier of flour, meal, and feed for the Tazewell area well into the mid–20th century. Last renovated in the 1980s, the mill, in working condition, is now a visitor attraction and an important symbol of the locale's historic continuity. *(92–17) VLR: 08/21/84; NRHP: 10/04/84.*

INDIAN PAINTINGS PREHISTORIC SITE, *Cove vicinity.* These pictographs are on a rock face high on Paint Lick Mountain. Stretched in a horizontal line along the irregular exposure is a series of simple images representing thunderbirds, human figures, deer, arrows, trees, and the sun, all painted in a red medium using iron oxide. Among the few prehistoric paintings extant in eastern North America, the images were executed by Indians before European settlement. Although some weathering and vandalism have occurred, these enigmatic works remain in relatively legible condition. The site is privately owned. *(92–07) VLR: 05/13/69; NRHP: 12/02/69.*

MAIDEN SPRING, *Ward's Cove.* Maiden Spring is among Southwest Virginia's most intact antebellum homesteads. The house is set off by its intricately detailed trim, two-level porticoes, and well-preserved interiors. Clustered about is a group of outbuildings and farm buildings dating from the mid–19th century into the 1900s. The original layout of the fields is intact, still served by a mid-19th-century barn. The Bowen family home for seven generations, the main portion of the house was built in 1838 for Rees Tate Bowen. Family tradition maintains that portions of an early frame house built by Bowen's uncle, Rees Bowen, Jr., are incorporated in the rear ell. Rees Tate Bowen served in the Virginia House of Delegates during the Civil War and later was elected to the U.S. Congress. In 1862 Confederate troops used Maiden Spring as a camp while defending the saltworks at Saltville. *(92–02) VLR: 06/15/94; NRHP: 08/16/94.*

OLD KENTUCKY TURNPIKE HISTORIC DISTRICT, *Cedar Bluff.* Cedar Bluff thrived commercially in the 19th and early 20th centuries as a milling center, benefiting from its location at the falls of the Clinch River on the mid-19th-century Tazewell Courthouse and Richlands Turnpike, now known as the Old Kentucky Turnpike. The community's historic district consists of an interesting and varied collection of primarily vernacular houses along the course of the turnpike. Among the most significant buildings are the Clinch Valley Roller Mills and the Peery house (shown), birthplace and childhood home of Virginia governor George C. Peery (1872–1952). Several of the more ornate late 19th-century structures, decorated with two-level porches and sawn-work detailing, are attributed to the local builder Thomas McChesney Cubine. A conspicuous landmark is the 1874 Cedar Bluff High School, atop a hill overlooking the district. *(184–01) VLR: 04/28/95; NRHP: 07/07/95.*

POCAHONTAS HISTORIC DISTRICT. Nestled in the Laurel Creek valley, this mountain community's mining structures, ornate commercial buildings, and rows of wooden workers' houses preserve the image of a late 19th-century coal-mining company town. Pocahontas was founded in 1881 and developed by the Southwest Virginia Improvement Co. as a company headquarters and miners' residential community at a terminus of the Norfolk and Western Railroad. Unlike most early mining towns, Pocahontas was from the start a model company town with orderly rows of company-built housing and a downtown embellished with richly decorated sheet-metal store fronts. The Victorian combination town hall and opera house is an architectural contrast to the prosaic company store, the miners' bathhouse, and the tiny brick coal sheds in front of many dwellings. A period of decline in recent decades has generated efforts to preserve the town's distinct character. *(92–11) VLR: 03/21/72; NRHP: 11/03/72.*

POCAHONTAS MINE NO. 1, *Route 659, Pocahontas vicinity.* The coal industry has had a profound impact on Virginia's economy, especially that of Southwest Virginia. A leading symbol of this enterprise is the Pocahontas Mine No. 1, the first mine to tap the great Pocahontas–Flat Top Coal Field of 1882. The high quality of the coal in this huge seam created a demand for Pocahontas coal and ushered in a long period of regional prosperity. A rail spur linked the mine with the Norfolk and Western Railroad by March 1883, and the shipyards and commercial areas of Norfolk and Newport News expanded from coal exporting. At the same time the town of Pocahontas developed near the mine and became a regional commercial center as well as a "company town" housing the coal miners. The mine closed in 1955 after producing forty-four million tons and has since been made a public attraction. *(92–11) VLR: 03/19/97; NHL: 10/12/94.*

ALEXANDER ST. CLAIR HOUSE, *St. Clair vicinity.* Built in 1879–80 for Alexander St. Clair, a county banker and farmer, this robust, finely appointed dwelling is a documented work of local builder Thomas M. Hawkins, who was responsible for the construction of approximately twenty-five houses in the area. The modified Italianate dwelling, the only known brick house built by Hawkins, illustrates the introduction of stylish catalog-ordered wood trim into traditional house forms in the state's southwestern arm. The marbleized interior woodwork is signed by Frank T. Wall and O. T. Jones, skilled local artisans and painters. Surviving on the property are several early outbuildings erected to serve the main house. Across the road is a horse stable constructed with logs from the original farm residence. *(92–16) VLR: 10/21/80; NRHP: 06/28/82.*

GEORGE OSCAR THOMPSON HOUSE, *Thompson Valley vicinity.* Thomas M. Hawkins, Tazewell County's talented master builder, erected this solidly crafted house in 1886–87 for George Oscar Thompson. With unusual sophistication of detail and composition, the dwelling blends traditional forms with more stylish late 19th-century features. Typical of Hawkins's work, the house is ornamented with the richly molded Italianate detailing popularized by catalogs of woodworking companies of the period. Two earlier dwellings also survive on the property: a ca. 1800 log house and a small frame farmhouse erected in three stages between 1831 and 1851. Each built for the Thompson family, pioneers in the late 18th-century settlement of the area, the three houses illustrate nearly two centuries of domestic occupation in this mountainous region. *(92–18) VLR: 11/18/80; NRHP: 06/28/82.*

WILLIAMS HOUSE, *102 Suffolk Avenue, Richlands.* The Williams house of 1890 was one of the first buildings constructed in the town of Richlands and originally served as the main office of the investment group that planned and founded the community. With high hopes of developing Richlands into the "Pittsburgh of the South," the company made its headquarters a conspicuous example of the popular Colonial Revival style as a demonstration that it intended to bring prosperity and sophistication to the area. The building was later purchased by Dr. W. R. Williams and used as Richlands's first hospital as well as the Williams family residence. In 1994 the Williams family donated the house to the town, whereupon it was restored to house the local public library. *(92–15) VLR: 09/16/82; NRHP: 07/07/83.*

JAMES WYNN HOUSE, *408 South Elk Street, Tazewell.* Built around 1828, this brick I-house is a document of the architectural requirements of one of the area's more outstanding citizens. While seemingly plain, it was, compared to ordinary housing here, a substantial dwelling for its time and place, having a Flemish bond facade and Federal woodwork within. James Wynn was the son of William Wynn, a Quaker pioneer. After his marriage to Sophia Peery, daughter of a prominent settler, he became a successful entrepreneur. Wynn's household consisted of seventeen people including four black servants. Along with his other activities, Wynn ran a tannery next to the house. This enterprise was continued by William Owen Yost, who purchased the property in 1858. The house has since undergone various modifications, but it preserves its historic character and maintains a semirural setting within the town of Tazewell. *(158–07) VLR: 10/09/91; NRHP: 10/28/92.*

CITY OF
VIRGINIA BEACH

Begun as an oceanfront resort community, Virginia Beach was incorporated as a town in 1906 and as a city in 1952. Its area was greatly expanded in 1963 by consolidation with the rapidly urbanizing Princess Anne County, which thereby became extinct.

BAYVILLE FARM, *First Court Road and Shore Drive.*
Bayville's broad, level fields, on a peninsula framed by Pleasure House Creek and Bayville Creek, remain one of the last open spaces in the northern part of what was formerly Princess Anne County, some of the earliest agricultural land in the country. The Federal plantation house was begun in 1826 as a side-passage dwelling built for John Singleton by the contractor Jacob Hunter. Sold two years later to pay debts, the house was expanded to its present five-bay form by its next owner, James Garrison. Bayville's brick ends are an architectural feature characteristic of many houses in the Chesapeake region. Preserved on the property is a series of undisturbed prehistoric and historic archaeological sites. The farmland has since been developed into a golf course sensitive to the historic integrity of the landscape and carefully preserving archaeological features. *(134–02) VLR: 06/17/75; NRHP: 05/19/80; BHR EASEMENT.*

CAPE HENRY LIGHT-HOUSE, *Fort Story.* This landmark commanding the entrance to Hampton Roads was the first lighthouse authorized, fully completed, and lighted by the newly organized federal government. The bid for its construction was approved by President George Washington. Put into operation in October 1792, the tapered octagonal structure faced with hammer-dressed sandstone ashlar was the first of three lighthouses designed and built by John McComb, Jr., of New York. McComb's original drawings for the structure are in the New-York Historical Society. The lighthouse function was taken over by a new tower erected nearby in 1881. The old lighthouse was deeded to the Association for the Preservation of Virginia Antiquities in 1930 and is now a museum. It stands near the spot where English colonists first set foot on Virginia soil in 1607. *(134–07) VLR: 09/09/69; NRHP: 10/15/66; NHL: 01/29/64.*

DE WITT COTTAGE, *1106 Atlantic Avenue.* Bernard Peabody Holland, the first mayor and postmaster of Virginia Beach, built this Queen Anne beach cottage in 1895. Its present name comes from Norfolk banker and cotton broker Cornelius de Witt, who purchased the property in 1909. The cottage remains the sole surviving example of the oceanfront dwellings constructed at Virginia Beach during its first period of development (1883–1906). Typical of early resort residences, it has a wraparound front porch and a small cupola. The interior is sheathed with beaded wooden boards. The last of the de Witt family moved from the cottage in the late 1980s. The property was acquired by the city of Virginia Beach and is now used as the Atlantic Wildfowl Heritage Museum. The picturesque cottage and its naturalistic landscaped grounds vividly contrast with the adjacent high-density development, serving as a reminder of the city's historic resort character. *(134–66) VLR: 04/19/88; NRHP: 06/16/88.*

FRANCIS LAND HOUSE, *3131 Virginia Beach Boulevard.* Also known by its more recent name Rose Hall, the Francis Land house is typical of the dwellings built by the more prosperous 18th-century planters of old Princess Anne County. Its gambrel roof was a form much favored in the area and gives a homey character to an otherwise formal and quite substantial house. The building probably dates from the last quarter of the 18th century or the early 19th century. The Land family, many of whom served as vestrymen and county justices, lived on the property from the 1630s to the 1830s. Threatened by encroaching development, the house was acquired by the city of Virginia Beach in 1975 for preservation. It was subsequently restored and opened for exhibition in 1986. Part of the surrounding seven acres have been landscaped to protect a sense of the dwelling's former rural context. *(134–31) VLR: 04/15/75; NRHP: 05/12/75.*

KEELING HOUSE, *3157 Adam Keeling Drive.* One of Virginia's rare vernacular manor houses, the Keeling house preserves the distinctive but rare decorative device of chevroning, a feature associated with pre-Georgian vernacular brick architecture. The chevrons are formed by parallel rows of glazed header bricks following the angle of the gables, made possible by the use of interior end chimneys. The house probably was erected ca. 1700 for Thomas Keeling on property originally acquired in 1635 by his immigrant grandfather, Thomas Keeling. The property remained in the Keeling family until 1881. Not unexpectedly for such vernacular dwellings, the entrance front has a regular five-bay facade while the rear has three irregularly spaced windows and a door. The closed-string stair and paneled parlor chimney wall appear to have been installed later in the 18th century. The house is at the head of a cove on the Lynnhaven River. *(134–18) VLR: 04/17/73; NRHP: 06/19/73.*

LYNNHAVEN HOUSE, *4405 Wishart Road.* Erected in 1724 for Francis Thelabell II, this time-enduring dwelling is a rare surviving example of the type of house favored by prosperous farmers immediately before colonial Virginia's Golden Age. With its irregularly spaced openings, exposed rafter ends, hall-parlor plan, and massive chimneys, the house is a holdover of English vernacular traditions of the 17th century. The survival of many of the interior features,

most notably the closed-string Jacobean-type stair and molded ceiling joists, makes Lynnhaven House particularly instructive. Long known as the Wishart house, it now bears a modern name derived from the nearby Lynnhaven River. Following years of neglect, the house was donated in 1971 by the Oliver family to the Association for the Preservation of Virginia Antiquities. The painstakingly restored structure is now a museum. *(134–37) VLR: 05/13/69; NRHP: 11/12/69.*

DR. JOHN MILLER-MASURY HOUSE (GREYSTONE MANOR), *515 Wilder Point.* Influenced by the 19th-century Scottish Baronial style, this arresting architectural pile, complete with crenellated tower, was the creation of Dr. John Miller-Masury, heir to the Masury Paint fortune. The house was finished in 1908 and was originally the centerpiece of a well-appointed estate called Lakeside, equipped with an electric power plant, gardens, orchard, and stables. The architect, Arnold E. Eberhard of Norfolk, and the interior decorator, E. G. Potter & Co. of New York, produced what was acknowledged at the time to be the largest and finest residence in southeastern Virginia. From 1936 to 1939 the estate housed the Crystal Club, a gambling casino and night club for which the interior was altered to create a ballroom. Later renamed Greystone Manor, most of the estate has since been developed, but the house remains an imposing vestige of Gilded Age hubris. *(134–532) VLR: 03/19/97; NRHP: 05/23/97.*

OLD COAST GUARD STATION MUSEUM (SEATACK/VIRGINIA BEACH LIFE-SAVING/COAST GUARD STATION), *Twenty-fourth Street and Atlantic Avenue.* The U.S. Life-Saving Service was established in 1871 to rescue victims of shipwrecks and other maritime disasters. The first-generation Seatack Life-Saving Station was one of five stations built in Virginia Beach and was constructed in 1878. It was replaced by the current structure built in 1903. The facility came under the jurisdiction of the U.S. Coast Guard in 1915 and was renovated in 1933 for a new generation of service. Decommissioned in 1969, the station was acquired by the city of Virginia Beach in 1979. In 1981 the building was moved 200 feet to its present location, also on the oceanfront, and restored as a museum. Distinguishing original features are the boat doors, lookout tower, and cedar-shingled walls. *(134–47) VLR: 03/20/79; NRHP: 07/11/79.*

OLD DONATION CHURCH, *4449 North Witch Duck Road.* Built in 1736 by Peter Malbone, Old Donation is the third building to serve the colonial Lynnhaven Parish, created soon after 1640. It was first called Lynnhaven Parish Church but received its present name in the early 19th century in commemoration of a gift of land to the parish. Curiously placed windows on the side walls indicate that the church was outfitted during colonial times with private galleries, or "hanging pews," high on the side walls. Old Donation suffered neglect during the first half of the 19th century and finally was gutted in an 1882 forest fire. It stood a roofless ruin until its restoration in 1916 and received parish church status once more in 1943. Although only its walls are original, Old Donation, in its wooded setting, is a reminder of the historic roots of the modern city of Virginia Beach. *(134–25) VLR: 11/16/71; NRHP: 04/13/72.*

PEMBROKE, *Constitution Drive.* This example of formal Georgian architecture was built in 1764 for Capt. Jonathan Saunders and his wife, Elizabeth Thoroughgood Saunders. During the Revolutionary War the state confiscated the property from Saunders's son John because he remained an avowed Loyalist. Pembroke is related architecturally to such formal mid-18th-century mansions as Carter's Grove, Wilton, Elsing Green, and especially the George Wythe house, which

Pembroke closely resembles. It was long overlooked by architectural scholars because the exterior for years was hidden by surrounding two-story galleries. Despite later interior alterations, some colonial wainscoting, window cases, and doorframes remain. The house was given to the Princess Anne Historical Society when the farmland was developed in the 1960s. Since sold, Pembroke has been restored and now serves as a private elementary school. *(134–26) VLR: 12/02/69; NRHP: 02/16/70; BHR EASEMENT.*

PLEASANT HALL, *5184 Princess Anne Road, Kempsville.* Pleasant Hall, among the last old houses in the all but totally redeveloped village of Kempsville, was built in 1763 for George Logan, a Scottish merchant. An outstanding example of Virginia's Georgian architecture, the house was used in 1775 as a headquarters for Lord Dunmore who later wrote: "I saw Mr. Logan's house and have never seen better in Virginia." Logan, a Loyalist, returned to Britain, whereupon Pleasant Hall escheated to the Commonwealth and eventually was sold to Peter Singleton. The formality of the exterior is carried to the interior with its exceptionally fine woodwork including a fully paneled parlor with a chimneypiece framed by pilasters in the rarely used Corinthian order. The massive king-post trusses supporting the roof are an important example of colonial carpentry. The house has been carefully restored for use as a funeral home. *(134–27) VLR: 10/17/72; NRHP: 01/25/73; BHR EASEMENT.*

ADAM THOROUGHGOOD HOUSE, *1636 Parish Road.* This famous brick dwelling illustrates the transition from Virginia's temporary frontier structures of the early 17th century to the more permanent, albeit informal, gentry houses of the early 18th century. The massive end chimney, irregular spacing of the openings, and lack of classical influences make the house a characteristic example of Virginia's pre-Georgian architecture. It was altered ca. 1720 when the casement windows were converted to sliding sash and paneled woodwork was installed. The exterior and part of the interior were returned to their original appearance after the Adam Thoroughgood House Foundation acquired the property. The house is on land obtained by Adam Thoroughgood in 1636 and was built ca. 1680 by either Thoroughgood's son or grandson. It is now exhibited by the Chrysler Museum of Art as a museum of Virginia's late 17th-century lifestyle and architecture. *(134–33) VLR: 09/09/69; NRHP: 10/15/66; NHL: 10/09/60.*

UPPER WOLFSNARE, *Potters Road, London Bridge vicinity.* Maj. Thomas Walke's will of 1759 bequeathed to his son Thomas a plantation house described as being under construction, a house presumed to be this brick dwelling. In 1788 the younger Thomas Walke served as one of Princess Anne County's two delegates to the Virginia convention that ratified the U.S. Constitution. Features of Walke's house parallel those in several other colonial houses of the area. The double-pile plan with a corner staircase is similar to Pleasant Hall. The style of the paneling, bereft of molding, seems to be a regional type. Known for many years as Brick House Farm, the property has been called by its present name since 1939, derived from Wolfsnare Creek, which ran nearby until obliterated by the Virginia Beach Expressway. The house has been in the custodianship of the Princess Anne Historical Society since 1966. *(134–34) VLR: 11/19/74; NRHP: 03/26/75.*

WEBLIN HOUSE, *Moore's Pond Road.* Despite its rapid transformation into a highly developed metropolitan area, the city of Virginia Beach preserves several pre-Georgian vernacular houses documenting the lifestyles of the more prosperous farmers around the end of the 17th century. With its hall-parlor plan and massive end chimney, the Weblin house is a representative of the "Virginia style," a vernacular house type evolved from the postmedieval farmhouses of the western and upland regions of England and employed by Virginia settlers from those areas. The house probably was built ca. 1700 for John Weblin, Jr., who inherited the property from his father in 1686. The steep gable roof was changed to a gambrel roof in the mid–18th century. The interior has undergone modifications, but the original floor plan survives, as does a second-floor bolection fireplace surround. *(134–35) VLR: 02/19/74; NRHP: 11/08/74; BHR EASEMENT.*

WARREN COUNTY

Formed from Shenandoah and Frederick counties in 1836, this lower Shenandoah Valley county was named for Joseph Warren, a Boston Revolutionary patriot killed in the battle of Bunker Hill. The county seat is Front Royal.

COMPTON GAP ARCHAEOLOGICAL SITE, *Compton Gap, Shenandoah National Park.* Identified through surface examination, the Compton Gap site dates from the Late Archaic period (ca. 2500–1000 B.C.). At the crest of the Blue Ridge, the site is likely a valuable source of information about the relationship between cultural and environmental zones in the prehistory of the mid-Atlantic region. One of the northernmost prehistoric sites identified in the Shenandoah National Park, the Compton Gap site should provide comparative data complementing the more familiar picture of Native American development in the Shenandoah Valley and the Piedmont. Because of its strategic location, the site may also provide information on the north-south and east-west movements of Native Americans. *(93–168) VLR: 09/16/82; NRHP: 12/13/85.*

ERIN, *Nineveh vicinity.* Built in 1848 for David Funsten, farmer, lawyer, and politician, Erin is the work of a talented but unidentified master housewright. The design is a sophisticated illustration of the influence of American architectural pattern books on an antebellum rural house. Such books instructed the builder on how to translate classical forms into wooden construction. Although the three-part format had been used in Virginia since the 18th century, the scheme here likely was inspired by a design for a three-part house published in Minard Lafever's *Modern Builder's Guide* (1833). Moreover, its elegant Greek Revival detailing, particularly its richly ornamented entrance, is derived from illustrations in Asher Benjamin's *The Practice of Architecture* (1833). The house is set off by an interesting range of outbuildings, from a limestone kitchen to Funsten's law office, a one-room wood-frame structure fronted by a simple portico. *(93–03) VLR: 10/16/79; NRHP: 12/28/79; BHR EASEMENT.*

FAIRVIEW FARM, *Rockland vicinity.* Fairview Farm's importance as a document of indigenous late 18th-century forms and details was long clouded by an early 20th-century remodeling that gave the house a hybrid foursquare-bungaloid appearance. Despite the changes, much original fabric was left intact, including the superb interior trim. Evidence for missing features was abundant. A comprehensive restoration, directed by furniture maker Peter Kramer, was undertaken in 1984 during which the stucco was removed and the portico reconstructed. As originally completed for Samuel Shackelford, member of a prosperous area family, the house combined Continental and English features. The Continental character is seen in the three-room plan, related to the three-room *Flurküchenhaus* plan employed by German settlers. The English influence is evident in the exterior chimneys, the richly detailed provincial Federal woodwork, and the king-post-truss framing of the roof. *(93–171) VLR: 12/17/85; NRHP: 06/05/86.*

FRONT ROYAL RECREATIONAL PARK, *Riverton vicinity.* Known today as the Front Royal Country Club, this park was the inspiration of William E. Carson, the first director of the Virginia Conservation and Development Commission. As such, Carson was a key figure in the establishment of the Shenandoah National Park and was instrumental in founding Virginia's state park system. In the last years of the depression, Carson saw the need for recreational facilities for his hometown Front Royal. In 1938 he and his wife, Agnes H. Carson, donated 63 acres of the Riverton Lime and Stone Co. quarry, which the Carsons owned, to the Front Royal Recreational Center Corp. He arranged for the Civilian Conservation Corps (CCC) to build the park facilities, including the golf course and rustic clubhouse. A living monument to the Carsons and to the CCC, one of the New Deal's most creative programs, the park still serves the area's citizens. *(93–63) VLR: 08/21/91; NRHP: 10/27/92.*

FLINT RUN ARCHAEOLOGICAL DISTRICT (INCLUDES THUNDERBIRD ARCHAEOLOGICAL DISTRICT), *Limeton vicinity.* This 2,300-acre complex of sites is one of North America's most significant archaeological areas. Research conducted by the Department of Anthropology of the Catholic University of America and the Thunderbird Research Corp. in the 1970s recorded prehistoric sites dating from the Paleo-Indian (9500 B.C.) through the Late Woodland (A.D. 1600) periods. Several stratified Paleo-Indian sites have been investigated, and some of the Western Hemisphere's earliest evidence of structures was discovered. The project, one of America's few fully documented Paleo-Indian settlement patterns, has led to the development of chronological sequences for the middle Shenandoah Valley with ramifications for eastern North American regions in general. Two sites within the district, the Thunderbird Site and Site Fifty, have been named a National Historic Landmark with the designation Thunderbird Archaeological District. *(93–165, 169) VLR: 12/16/75; 12/22/76; NHL (THUNDERBIRD ARCHAEOLOGICAL DISTRICT): 05/05/77; BHR EASEMENTS.*

KILLAHEVLIN, *1401 North Royal Avenue.* An arrestingly unconventional Queen Anne mansion, Killahevlin was designed by the Washington, D.C., firm of Alfred B. Mullett and Co. for the prominent Virginia conservationist William E. Carson. Born in 1870 in Northern Ireland, Carson came to America as a teenager and joined his father's lime company near Front Royal. He became active in Virginia business and politics and in 1926 was appointed the first director of the Virginia Conservation and Development Commission. He supervised the formation of Virginia's recreational parks system, helped to establish the state's system of historical road markers, and was instrumental in the creation of the Shenandoah National Park and Skyline Drive. He lived in Killahevlin from the time it was completed in 1905 until his death in 1942. Carson changed its appearance in 1926 by adding an enclosed sleeping porch across the front. The property was the scene of Civil War activity. *(112–24) VLR: 08/18/93; NRHP: 10/14/93.*

LONG MEADOW, *Strasburg vicinity.* On the North Fork of the Shenandoah River, this historic farm was established and occupied in the 1700s by Jost Hite and his family, early settlers in the area. The original house, Traveler's Hall, burned ca. 1840, and the present structure was built on its site by George W. Bowman, a Hite descendant. The formal brick dwelling illustrates the transition from the Federal to the Greek Revival styles. The earlier character is found in the five-bay facade with its central pedimented pavilion and hipped roof. The Greek Revival influences are seen primarily in the interior woodwork. Near the house is a grouping of late 18th- and 19th-century farm buildings. The Hite family cemetery at Long Meadow contains the graves of Isaac Hite, Sr., and Isaac Hite, Jr., builder of Belle Grove in Frederick County. *(93–06) VLR: 08/28/95; NRHP: 10/12/95.*

MOUNT ZION, *Milldale.* The Georgian style of Virginia's Tidewater plantation houses was given a regional interpretation in this massive Shenandoah Valley farmhouse. Built of native limestone, Mount Zion's fortresslike exterior contrasts with the ambitious provincial woodwork of the lofty interior. The parlor chimneypiece, decorated with carved pendants, swags, animal heads, and rope moldings, motifs based on published designs by Abraham Swan, is an extraordinary example of the area's 18th-century craftsmanship. The house was built ca. 1771 for the Rev. Charles Mynn Thruston, an Anglican minister and native of Gloucester County who raised a company of troops during the Revolution. Wounded in the battle of Piscataway, he was known as the "Fighting Parson." A later owner, Alexander Earle, served as a quartermaster in the Confederate army and was elected to the House of Delegates in 1881. *(93–08) VLR: 12/02/69; NRHP: 02/26/70.*

RIVERSIDE, *1315 Old Winchester Pike, Riverton.* On the point between the North and South Fork of the Shenandoah River, this massive residence was built in the 1840s by Samuel S. Spengler. Because Spengler and his wife were not congenial, the room arrangement departed from the norm. Their bedrooms were accessible only by separate staircases, with a large central stair for family and guests. The property was sold in 1849 to Maj. J. R. Richards who connected the bedrooms. Riverside was the scene of constant activity during the Civil War. Gen. Stonewall Jackson occupied Riverside the night of the battle of Front Royal, May 24, 1862. Union general Philip Sheridan stayed at Riverside twice in 1864. A trapdoor to a subbasement where the family hid valuables is intact in a first-floor closet. The present hipped roof and dormers were added around 1900, giving the house a Colonial Revival character. *(93–11) VLR: 08/28/95; NRHP: 10/12/95.*

ROSE HILL, *900 block of North Royal Avenue, Front Royal.* One of the early landmarks of Front Royal, Rose Hill was built as a center-passage single-pile frame farmhouse in 1830 for George C. Blakemore and his wife Elizabeth. A brick ell was added in 1845, after the property was conveyed to Elizabeth Blakemore's cousin William Richardson. The house was modernized in a 1937 remodeling which included the stuccoing of the exterior. The property was caught in the crossfire of considerable Civil War activity and served as a Confederate headquarters during the 1862 battle of Front Royal. In 1864 it became a Confederate hospital and was later pillaged by Union troops who destroyed the farm buildings and stole the livestock. Although now in a residential neighborhood, Rose Hill's eight-acre yard preserves an open-space setting for the house. *(112–32) VLR: 03/20/96; NRHP: 05/23/96.*

SKYLINE DRIVE HISTORIC DISTRICT, *Shenandoah National Park.* Extending through eight counties, the world-famous Skyline Drive is a testament to the expanding movement for natural-area conservation, public outdoor recreation, and regional planning that became a hallmark of 1930s New Deal federal policy. The concept of a scenic highway along the crest of the Blue Ridge Mountains in the Shenandoah National Park was first proposed in 1924 and promoted by William Carson, the influential director of the Virginia Conservation and Development Commission. Harvey Benson, National Park Service landscape architect, provided the initial design for the 105-mile highway. Describing the scheme, Benson stated: "Macadamized and smooth, with easy gradient and wide sweeping curves, the drive unfolds to view innumerable panoramas of lofty peaks, forested ravines and the patchwork patterns of valley farms." Using over 4,000 laborers, this monumental engineering and landscape project, with numerous associated buildings, was completed in 1939. *(93–01); VLR: 12/04/96; NRHP: 04/28/97.*

SONNER-PAYNE HALL, *200 Academy Drive, Front Royal.* Sonner-Payne Hall is the signature architectural piece for Randolph-Macon Academy, a coeducational preparatory school founded in 1892. Topped by a dome and fronted by a portico articulating a lengthy facade, the Georgian Revival structure is also a visually prominent landmark for Front Royal. Randolph-Macon began as preparatory school of the former Randolph-Macon system of colleges and academies. The system was established by the Methodist church in 1890 and at one time embraced three preparatory schools and two colleges. The Front Royal school has offered military training since 1917. Sonner-Payne Hall was designed built by J. P. Pettyjohn of Lynchburg as a multipurpose structure, originally providing faculty and student housing, classrooms, administration offices, dining room, and library. Although it remains affiliated with the United Methodist church, Randolph-Macon is now operated as an independent entity. *(112–57) VLR: 10/14/86; NRHP: 01/29/87.*

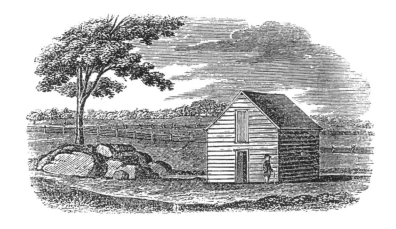

WASHINGTON COUNTY

At the southern end of western Virginia's chain of valleys, Washington County was formed from the extinct Fincastle County in 1776, with part of Montgomery County added later. It was the first county in the United States named for George Washington. Its county seat is Abingdon.

ABINGDON BANK, *225 East Main Street, Abingdon.* Early 19th-century bank buildings often were barely distinguishable from fine town houses because they incorporated the residence of the cashier, a respected local figure. These banks usually had two entrances, one for the banking area and one leading to the private quarters. Most banks had three stories because the residential section usually had two levels. The Abingdon Bank, erected in 1858 for Robert Preston, first resident cashier, is an excellent illustration of this early commercial type. The banking area retains its large windows with iron bars and its vault. The plain interior trim of the residential section contrasts with the elaborate brick cornice and belt course of the exterior. No longer a bank, the building has been restored to serve as a private residence and remains an important element of the facade of Abingdon's historic Main Street. *(140–01) VLR: 05/13/69; NRHP: 11/12/69.*

ABINGDON HISTORIC DISTRICT. Abingdon is the best preserved of the numerous linear communities that developed in the late 18th century along the Great Valley Road. The town is unusual for its large quantity of brick Federal and antebellum buildings, which served to give the community an air of permanence and prosperity. Abingdon was founded in 1778 and flourished almost immediately. Secretary of the Treasury John Campbell, Confederate general Joseph E. Johnston, and three Virginia governors, Wyndham Robinson, David Campbell, and John Buchanan Floyd, all lived in Abingdon. Gen. Francis Preston built one of the largest houses in Virginia here in the 1830s; it later was converted to Martha Washington College and is now the Martha Washington Inn (shown). Another architectural highlight is the imposing 1868 Washington County Courthouse. In recent times Abingdon has been the home of the Barter Theatre, a nationally prominent repertory theater founded in 1933 by Robert Porterfield. *(140–37) VLR: 12/02/69 (EXPANDED 04/15/86); NRHP: 02/26/70.*

BROOK HALL, *Old Glade Spring vicinity.* A proud statement of the prominence and prosperity of its first owner, Brook Hall was completed in 1826 for William Byars, a colonel in the local militia, a member of the Virginia General Assembly, and later a U.S. congressman. By 1830 Byars's landholdings included over 1,700 acres. One of the largest Federal-period houses in the region, Byars's twenty-four-room structure exhibits a high level of craftsmanship inside and out. A dominant interior element is the main stair, finished to the third level. The mantels are delicately ornamented with regionalized Federal motifs. An important feature is the array of original painted finishes, both decorative and plain. The Byars family entertained many prominent guests here, among them presidents Andrew Jackson and James K. Polk, as well as several Virginia governors. The property is currently being rehabilitated as a country inn. *(95–04) VLR: 03/19/97; NRHP: 06/05/97.*

CRABTREE-BLACKWELL FARM, *Blackwell vicinity.* The Crabtree-Blackwell farm complex forms a remarkably undisturbed picture of the folk culture of the Southwest Virginia uplands, a region settled by Tidewater English, Scotch-Irish, and Pennsylvania Germans. The resulting cultural mix is evident in the area's vernacular buildings. The earliest section of the Crabtree-Blackwell dwelling is the half-dovetail square-cabin form evolved from late medieval English prototypes. The later rectangular section, with its half story and V-notched corners, is more typical of the Scotch-Irish building traditions. The springhouse, with its cantilevered overhang, follows Central European vernacular building practices. The double-crib log barn is a common Appalachian form. The oldest portion of the house was probably built by the Crabtree family, who bought the land in 1818. The later section likely came after 1824 when the farm was purchased by the Davenport family. *(95–76) VLR: 12/17/74; NRHP: 04/01/75.*

EMORY AND HENRY COLLEGE, *Emory.* Emory and Henry College, founded in 1838 by the Holston Conference of the Methodist Episcopal Church, is the oldest college in Southwest Virginia and one of the few colleges of its period in the South that has operated with continued affiliation with its founding organization. The hilly, tree-shaded campus includes several structures from its early days. Among these are the Charles C. Collins house (1845; shown), home of the first president; the Emily Williams house (1848), home of the second president; and the J. Stewart French house (1852), home of seven successive college presidents. In addition to these, the college possesses a fine collection of Georgian Revival buildings. Dominating the complex is Ephraim Emerson Wiley Hall, the Georgian Revival administration building built in 1912. With their brick construction and classical trim, the buildings, both 19th and 20th century, form a cohesive architectural assemblage. *(95–98) VLR: 01/18/83; NRHP: 01/30/89.*

MONT CALM, *Cummings Street, S.W., Abingdon.* On a ridge overlooking the historic district of Abingdon, Mont Calm stands as one of the best examples of Federal domestic architecture in this historic Southwest Virginia community. The generously proportioned dwelling, with its formal facade, finely jointed brickwork, and Doric cornice, is tangible evidence of the sophisticated lifestyle enjoyed in the early days of the region. Completed in 1827, Mont Calm has been the home of the Campbell, Cummings, and Mingea families. It was built for David Campbell, who served as Virginia's governor in 1837–40 and was an early champion of public education. The interior was remodeled by Mr. and Mrs. Wilton Egerton Mingea after they purchased the property in 1905. Mr. Mingea started the Virginia-Carolina Railroad following his move to Abingdon. *(140–18) VLR: 01/15/74; NRHP: 07/18/74.*

WHITE'S MILL, *White's Mill.* A mill was established here in Toole Creek's narrow valley ca. 1797 by Thomas Moffett. Col. James White acquired the property in 1838. The present mill was built ca. 1840 by his son, William Y. C. White, and is one of the state's handful of operable gristmills powered by an overshot wheel. The mill's mechanism followed mill theorist Oliver Evans's guidelines published in *The Young Millwright and Miller's Guide* (1795). The structure was expanded to include the late 19th-century innovations in roller mill machinery, making it a demonstration of the technological evolution of gristmilling operation. The original wooden wheel has been replaced by the current 20-foot-diameter metal Fitz wheel. Most of the original wooden gears and workings remain intact. The mill, one of the most picturesque in the state, was in regular use until recent years. *(95–27) VLR: 04/16/74; NRHP: 09/10/74.*

CITY OF WAYNESBORO

Named for Anthony Wayne, a Revolutionary War general, and originally spelled Waynesborough, this Shenandoah Valley community was laid out in 1797 and established as a town in 1801. Incorporated in 1834, it was consolidated with Basic City in 1923. Waynesboro became a city in 1948.

COINER-QUESEN-BERY HOUSE, *332 West Main Street.* Built in 1806, this Federal town house, one of the city's few remaining early structures, is believed to be Waynesboro's first brick dwelling. Its original owner was Casper Coiner, who was of Pennsylvania German origin. With its elegant Georgian cornice, Coiner's residence is an unusually sophisticated representative of the houses found in the linear villages of the Shenandoah Valley. Following the practice of densely settled communities, particularly Philadelphia, the Valley settlers placed their houses at the front of their lots, giving their villages an urban character. The house originally had a center entrance, but an alteration of 1832 gave it a more conventional side-passage plan. The house was restored to its mid-19th-century appearance in 1972 by the Quesenbery family who had owned it for many years. *(136–01) VLR: 06/15/76; NRHP: 11/07/76.*

FAIRFAX HALL, *Winchester Avenue.* Fairfax Hall, originally the Brandon Hotel, is one of only two remaining of the many late Victorian resort hotel buildings for which the Shenandoah Valley was famed. Most of these establishments were built in conjunction with the coming of the Norfolk and Western Railroad, which made them easily accessible to eastern and northern cities. Opened in 1890 in what was originally Basic City, later consolidated with Waynesboro, the hotel was designed by Washington, D.C., architect William M. Poindexter. Poindexter produced a noteworthy Queen Anne scheme in the shingled mode, employing a central cupola and corner towers. A relaxed atmosphere was conveyed by the use of a long front porch. In 1920 the building became Fairfax Hall, a preparatory school and junior college for girls which operated for some fifty years. It later became a training center but now stands vacant. *(136–10) VLR: 07/20/82; NRHP: 09/09/82.*

FISHBURNE MILITARY SCHOOL, *225 South Wayne Avenue.* Fishburne Military School was founded in 1878 by James A. Fishburne, a student and protégé of Robert E. Lee. It was while attending Washington College that Fishburne was inspired by Lee to become an educator. The school flourished, and in 1916 Staunton architect T. J. Collins was commissioned to design a new barracks. Following the precedent of A. J. Davis's Virginia Military Institute, the barracks employed a castellated Gothic style. The composition has since become downtown Waynesboro's chief architectural landmark. Collins's sons, Samuel and William, continued the tradition with their designs for the administration-gymnasium building and barracks additions. Fishburne has developed into one of the state's most distinguished military academies, continuously rated an honor military school under the U.S. Junior Army Reserve Officers Training Corps since 1924. It is one of the few military schools in Virginia to continue in operation. *(136–04) VLR: 08/21/84; NRHP: 10/04/84.*

PLUMB HOUSE, *1012 West Main Street.* Built between 1802 and 1806 for Daniel West, the Plumb house is believed to be the only surviving early log building in the city of Waynesboro. The two-story structure originally had a hall-parlor plan and was sheathed in weatherboards. It later was given a center passage and was covered with shingles in the 20th century. Distinguishing features of the remarkably preserved interior include its fine Federal mantels, chevron-pattern door, and enclosed winder stair. The east chimney is a rare example for the region of the use of Flemish bond with glazed headers. Behind the house is an early smokehouse-kitchen. The property was purchased in 1838 by Alfred Plumb, a local tavern owner, and remained in the Plumb family until 1994 when it was acquired for preservation by the city of Waynesboro. *(136–03) VLR: 02/20/90; NRHP: 01/24/91.*

WESTMORELAND COUNTY

Named for the English shire, this Northern Neck county was formed from Northumberland County in 1653, with part of King George County added later. Its county seat is Montross.

BELL HOUSE, *821 King Avenue, Colonial Beach.* Alexander Graham Bell, inventor of the telephone, owned this riverside summer cottage from the time he inherited it from his father, Alexander Melville Bell, in 1907 until in 1918 when he deeded it to his private secretary, Arthur McCurdy. The elder Bell, a distinguished British elocutionist, purchased the house as a retreat in 1886, after his 1881 move to Washington, D.C. Although the younger Bell normally summered in Canada, he made visits here during his thirteen years of ownership. Local tradition has it that Bell experimented with kites or "flying machines," launching them from the balcony here. Built ca. 1883 for Col. J. O. P. Burnside, the house is a classic example of Stick-style residential architecture, a style popular in the Northeast but relatively rare in Virginia. The Stick style is characterized by its use of various lumber elements for decorative effects. *(199–03) VLR: 03/17/87; NRHP: 09/21/87.*

BLENHEIM, *Wakefield Corner vicinity.* Blenheim is the plantation next to Pope's Creek (Wakefield), birthplace of George Washington. The simple late Georgian dwelling here was built in 1781 for William Augustine Washington, son of George Washington's half brother, as a successor to the Pope's Creek house, which burned on Christmas Day, 1779. Washington vacated Blenheim sometime between 1787 and 1795, possibly when he married Sarah Tayloe, a younger daughter of John Tayloe of Mount Airy. The property eventually passed to Washington's daughter, Sarah Tayloe Washington, who was married to her cousin Lawrence Washington. Except for one break, Blenheim has remained in the ownership of Washington family descendants. The house was restored from near-ruinous condition in the 1970s by Lawrence Washington Latane, Jr. The wood-frame south wing is an earlier structure, said to have been an overseer's house. *(96–03) VLR: 02/18/75; NRHP: 06/05/75; BHR EASEMENT.*

CHANTILLY ARCHAEOLOGICAL SITE, *Montross vicinity.* Chantilly, part of the John Hallowes patent of 1650, was leased from Col. Philip Ludwell Lee by Richard Henry Lee in 1763 and remained Richard Henry Lee's home until his death in 1794. Raised at nearby Stratford, the Lee family seat, Richard Henry Lee was a Revolutionary leader of major stature. He wrote the Westmoreland Resolves, and as a delegate to the Continental Congress in 1776, he moved the resolution for American independence from Great Britain. Lee was also one of Virginia's signers of the Declaration of Independence. His house at Chantilly, described by Thomas Lee Shippen as more commodious than elegant, was destroyed early in the 19th century, possibly during the War of 1812. The house site and its immediate environs remain an important tangible relic of the domestic life of an American Revolutionary patriot. *(96–05) VLR: 10/06/70; NRHP: 12/16/71.*

INGLESIDE, *Oak Grove vicinity.* Ingleside was erected in 1834 as the Washington Academy, one of the numerous private preparatory schools established in Virginia during the antebellum period to educate the sons of the plantation society. The porticoed structure, with its plain detailing, is a rare example of rural institutional architecture of the period. Tradition has it that the school's founders patterned the building along the lines of Thomas Jefferson's temple-form Capitol in Richmond. The academy operated for a decade before decreased enrollment forced it to close. After the sale of the property in 1847, the building was converted to a private residence and received its present name. Following many changes of ownership, Ingleside was purchased in 1890 by nurseryman Carl Henry Flemer of Washington, D.C., and has since become the nucleus of the well-known Ingleside Plantation, Inc., a nursery and winery operated by the Flemer family. *(96–12) VLR: 12/21/76; NRHP: 03/15/79.*

MORGAN JONES POTTERY KILN ARCHAEOLOGICAL SITE, *Glebe Harbor.* Archaeological evidence and historical documents combine to make the site of Morgan Jones's pottery kiln a unique relic of a 17th-century American craft industry. According to Westmoreland County records, on August 28, 1677, Morgan Jones entered into a partnership with Dennis White for the "making and selling of Earthen warre" from a kiln on the western side of Lower Machotick (Machodoc) Creek. Investigation of the site in 1973 by archaeologists of the Department of Historic Resources uncovered the kiln's remains and unearthed many fragmentary samples of pottery manufactured here. Shards of wares similar to those found at the kiln site have been found in numerous archaeological sites in the Tidewater region, making the kiln excavations a valuable tool for dating and identifying Virginia pottery of the period. The site is preserved under county ownership. *(96–81) VLR: 06/18/74; NRHP: 10/16/74.*

JAMES MONROE BIRTHPLACE ARCHAEOLOGICAL SITE, *Monroe Hall.* James Monroe, fifth president of the United States, was born in 1758 in a modest wood-frame house near the tiny settlement of Monroe Hall. Archaeological investigation of the site revealed the foundation of a 57-by-18-foot structure which conforms to a print of the Monroe house in Robert Sears's *A Pictorial History of the American Revolution* (1845). Associated artifacts indicate a construction date of 1750. The artifacts, house plan, and a 1774 inventory made after the death of Monroe's father, Spence Monroe, a carpenter or joiner, indicate that the family was relatively prosperous but modest in terms of material circumstances. James Monroe lived here until 1774 when he enrolled in the College of William and Mary. Monroe inherited the property and sold it in 1781. The site is now preserved in a county-owned park. *(96–46) VLR: 12/21/76; NRHP: 07/24/79.*

ROCHESTER HOUSE, *Lyells vicinity.* This tiny vernacular farmhouse is an excellent albeit rare example of a mid-18th-century hall-plan dwelling, a once-prevalent Tidewater house type during the colonial period. Employing a sturdy braced-frame system, the 20-by-16-foot structure has but two bays and one main room, with a full basement and what was originally a finished loft, used as the bedchamber. A conspicuous feature, and one indicating that the house was of above-average quality, is the large exterior chimney with its T-shaped stack. The property was acquired by the English immigrant Nicholas Rochester in 1689. The present house was built by his son William, a successful planter. William's grandson, John Rochester, was influential in Westmoreland County affairs, holding positions in the militia, the church, and local government. John's younger brother, Nathaniel, settled in New York State and founded the city of Rochester. *(96–87) VLR: 12/11/90; NRHP: 01/25/91.*

SPENCE'S POINT, *Sandy Point vicinity.* Writer John Dos Passos (1896–1970) lived on this Potomac River farm for a portion of every year from 1949 until his death. Here he wrote many of his later works. The property was purchased in the late 19th century by Dos Passos's father, John Randolph Dos Passos, a Portuguese shoemaker's son who became a successful New York lawyer. As a youth Dos Passos lived with his mother but made frequent visits to Spence's Point with both parents. The plain three-bay farmhouse was built in 1806 for Alexander Spence. Dos Passos added the brick wing and much interior woodwork after making the house his principal residence. Among his writings are *Three Soldiers* (1921) and his trilogy *U.S.A.,* which includes *The 42nd Parallel* (1930), *1919* (1932), and *The Big Money* (1936). Spence's Point remains the property of Dos Passos's family; his second-floor office is much as he left it. *(96–22) VLR: 02/20/73; NHL: 11/11/71.*

SPRING GROVE, *Mount Holly vicinity.* This gracefully proportioned Federal farmhouse was erected in 1834 for Robert Murphy, a post-Revolutionary newcomer to the Northern Neck. It is one of a small group of formal brick residences built in the region in the early 19th century and reflects the local prosperity in its size and refinements. A conspicuous exterior feature is the academically detailed dwarf Ionic portico sheltering the entrance. Inside, the principal rooms are set off by woodwork and decorative plasterwork derived from pattern books by Boston architect Asher Benjamin. William Rogers, a later owner, thoroughly recorded the house in the 1870s with a set of drawings currently in the possession of the present owners, a rare instance of pictorial documentation of the period. The house survives with few alterations and enjoys a rural setting on the high, flat ground above Nomini Creek. *(96–23) VLR: 06/21/83; NRHP: 10/10/85.*

ROXBURY, *Oak Grove vicinity.* Roxbury's 1861 Victorian villa was the home of Dabney Carr Wirt, a son of the jurist, statesman, and author William Wirt. The Gothic-style dwelling, with its asymmetrical plan, multigable roofline, and long veranda, closely parallels "Design XX—A Villa Farm-House in the Bracketed Style" published in Andrew Jackson Downing's *Architecture of Country Houses* (1850), a design which Downing described as intended for the country home of a farmer of wealth. Such houses are relatively common in the North but rare in Virginia. No architect has been associated with Roxbury, suggesting that a talented local builder had access to Downing's popular pattern book. Around the turn of the century, Roxbury was the home of F. W. Alexander, who inaugurated the movement to acquire and restore Stratford as a memorial to the Lee family. Since 1960 it has been owned by Ingleside Plantation, Inc. *(96–20) VLR: 12/21/76; NRHP: 03/15/79.*

STRATFORD, *Montross vicinity.* Few places in America equal Stratford in architectural interest or historical associations. The great colonial mansion, with its complex of outbuildings and dependencies, was built in the 1730s by Thomas Lee. Although Stratford is best known as the birthplace of Confederate general Robert E. Lee, it was also the boyhood home of Richard Henry Lee and Francis Lightfoot Lee, the only brothers to sign the Declaration of Independence. With its H-shaped plan, clustered chimney stacks, and elegantly paneled great hall, the mansion is unique among colonial plantation houses. Enhancing the architecture is its rural setting with vistas to the Potomac River. Stratford left the Lees in 1822 and was acquired for preservation in 1929 by the Robert E. Lee Memorial Association, Inc. The restored plantation is now a historic site interpreting colonial plantation life and the Lee family. *(96–24) VLR: 09/09/69; NRHP: 10/15/66; NHL: 10/07/60.*

GEORGE WASHINGTON BIRTHPLACE NATIONAL MONUMENT (WAKEFIELD), *Oak Grove vicinity.* The site of George Washington's birthplace is a tract on Pope's Creek, just off the Potomac River, purchased in 1718 by Washington's father, Augustine. Born on February 22, 1732, Washington spent only his first three years here but returned at age eleven to study surveying with his half brother Augustine, Jr., who inherited the property. The original Washington home burned on Christmas Day, 1779. Its site was excavated in 1930 and 1936, revealing the foundations of a U-shaped timber-frame house. The present brick dwelling, the Memorial House, erected in 1930–31, reflects a typical medium-size planter's house of the period. First known as Pope's Creek, the property had been renamed Wakefield when the Washington family sold it in 1813. It was acquired by the Wakefield National Memorial Association in 1923, which transferred it to the National Park Service in 1932. *(96–26) VLR: 10/18/83; NRHP: 10/15/66.*

WIRTLAND, *Oak Grove vicinity.* Wirtland was erected in 1850 for Dr. William Wirt, Jr., one of the sons of the Virginia jurist, statesman, and author. Its romantically landscaped park and fanciful Gothic Revival mansion together conform to the mid-19th-century ideal of an American villa as defined by Andrew Jackson Downing. For Downing, a villa was "the most refined home of America," where "amid the serenity and peace of sylvan scenes . . . the artistic knowledge and feeling has full play." Downing recommended various historic styles for villas but was partial to Gothic. Although such a sophisticated house was normally custom-designed, no architect has been associated with it. More likely the design was based on published illustrations. After Dr. Wirt's death in 1898, Wirtland housed a female academy. The property is now part of the Ingleside Plantation, Inc., nursery and winery, with the house and its grounds a private residence. *(96–29) VLR: 12/21/76; NRHP: 03/15/79.*

YEOCOMICO CHURCH, *Tucker Hill.* Its blending of artisan-vernacular and classical elements make this singular colonial building an illustration of early 18th-century transitional architecture. The side entrance porch, possibly an early addition, with its wicket door (a smaller door cut into a larger door), is a common feature of English parish churches built through the postmedieval period but is a unique American example. The classical modillion cornice is a harbinger of the Georgian style. Adding interest is the strangely inconsistent brick bonding. Inscribed in the brickwork are fifteen sets of initials representing the participation of many workmen. The inscribed date 1706 may be a construction date; however, the present form is the result of a T-wing added ca. 1730–40. The church was used to house soldiers in three wars and left vacant at times. It has, nonetheless, survived remarkably intact and is still in service. *(96–31) VLR: 09/09/69; NRHP: 11/12/69; NHL: 04/15/70.*

CITY OF WILLIAMSBURG

Virginia's second colonial capital was established as Middle Plantation in 1633. The seat of government was moved here from Jamestown in 1698. It was renamed in honor of King William III in 1699. Williamsburg became a borough in 1722 and remained the capital until 1780. It was incorporated as a city in 1884.

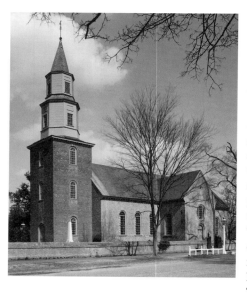

BRUTON PARISH CHURCH, *Duke of Gloucester Street.* Bruton Parish Church, the official house of worship of Virginia's former capital, remains one of the state's most ambitious representatives of colonial ecclesiastical architecture. It was constructed in 1711–15 to replace an earlier structure that stood nearby. The assembly voted part of the cost because its members worshiped here while in session. The design is credited to Lieutenant Governor Alexander Spotswood, who called for a cruciform-plan building, the colony's first. The builder was James Morris. The chancel was extended in 1752, and the tower, with its two-tiered steeple, was added in 1769 by Benjamin Powell. The removal of the capital to Richmond ended Bruton Parish's role as Virginia's leading church and ushered in a long stagnant period. The interior was rearranged in the 19th century but was restored in 1905. A more complete restoration was undertaken in 1939 under the guidance of Colonial Williamsburg architects. *(137–07) VLR: 09/18/73; NHL: 04/15/70.*

CAPITOL LANDING ARCHAEOLOGICAL SITE, *Capitol Landing Road, Williamsburg vicinity.* Williamsburg in the 18th century was served by two inland ports. South of town was College Landing on College Creek. To the north was Capitol Landing, officially known as Queen Mary's Port, linking Williamsburg to the York River. Established in 1699, Capitol Landing was on Queen's Creek at the end of what was then known as Queen's Road. Around its wharf grew a small settlement of shops, houses, and light industries. A succession of tobacco inspection warehouses stood at the wharf, regulating the colony's chief cash crop. A popular tavern, started by ferryman Giles Moody in 1717, served workers and travelers at the port for many years. All of the buildings vanished during the 19th century, leaving behind a series of yet unexcavated archaeological sites holding a rich store of knowledge relating to colonial Virginia's commerce and transportation. *(137–56) VLR: 06/21/77.*

CHANDLER COURT AND POLLARD PARK

HISTORIC DISTRICT. These connected neighborhoods are an intimate interpretation of the garden suburb ideal developed in late 19th-century Britain. They were the creation of John Garland Pollard, lawyer, educator, and Virginia governor 1929–33. Chandler Court was laid out on a tight scale, on level land, in 1924. Pollard Park was laid out more loosely around a wooded ravine. The two developments incorporated such design amenities as curved roadways, brick pathways, minimum setbacks, and common open space. The houses are generally small to medium-size middle-class dwellings typical of the 1920s to 1940s using various historical references. Some employ the more specific grammar of the Williamsburg colonial style. Architects whose work is represented here include Eimer Cappelmann, Clarence Huff, Jr., Charles M. Robinson, and Thomas T. Waterman. Prominent residents have included Governor Pollard, college librarian Earl Gregg Swem, and historian Richard L. Morton. *(137–478) VLR: 03/20/96; NRHP: 10/03/96.*

COLLEGE LANDING ARCHAEOLOGICAL SITE, *Route 132, Williamsburg vicinity.* South of Williamsburg at the confluence of College and Paper Mill creeks, College Landing was a principal port for the colonial capital, connecting it with shipping on the James River. Warehouses and wharves as well as a tavern and some light industrial structures, including a brewery, sprang up here. The landing also became an important military supply center during the Revolution. The small port remained a busy place throughout the 18th century, but after the removal of the capital to Richmond, its activity began to ebb. By the 20th century the site was completely abandoned. What remains is a series of archaeological sites relating to colonial Virginia's transportation, commercial, and industrial life, as well as to the material culture of the transients who worked and lived near the landing. Several sites were salvaged when threatened by highway construction in 1976. *(137–57) VLR: 12/21/76; NRHP: 07/12/78.*

WILLIAM FINNIE HOUSE (JAMES SEMPLE HOUSE), *Francis Street.* Among the most architecturally distinguished dwellings in Virginia's former capital is this three-part structure, which in 1809 St. George Tucker called "the handsomest house in town." It was built before 1782 for Col. William Finnie who served as quartermaster general of the Southern Department during the Revolution. In 1800 it was acquired by James Semple, a judge and professor of law at the College of William and Mary. With its pedimented center section and one-story wings, the house follows a Palladian format as interpreted in published designs by English architects such as Robert Morris and William Halfpenny. The house is also a prototype of the many tripartite houses erected throughout Virginia and neighboring southern states in the early national era. The William Finnie house was among the first to be acquired by the Colonial Williamsburg Foundation and was restored in 1932. *(137–33) VLR: 09/18/73; NHL: 04/15/70.*

PEYTON RANDOLPH HOUSE, *Nicholson Street.* Peyton Randolph, Speaker of the House of Burgesses for nine years, lived here from 1745 until his death in 1775. A leading champion of independence, Randolph served as president of nearly every important Revolutionary assemblage of Virginia and was president of both the first and second Continental Congresses. The house served as headquarters for the comte de Rochambeau in the Yorktown campaign; Lafayette stayed here in 1824 during his tour of America. The three-bay western section was built ca. 1716 for William Robertson, clerk of the council. A story-and-a-half tenement to the east was erected by 1724 and was later connected to the older part by a two-story, four-bay section probably built by Peyton Randolph. A marble chimney-piece and paneled woodwork distinguish the Randolph addition. The east wing was reconstructed when the house was restored by the Colonial Williamsburg Foundation in 1939–40. *(137–32) VLR: 09/18/73; NHL: 04/15/70.*

WILLIAMSBURG HISTORIC DISTRICT. Williamsburg served as the capital of the Virginia colony from 1699 until 1776 and as the capital of the Commonwealth of Virginia until 1780. Laid out by Governor Francis Nicholson, Williamsburg was one of North America's first planned towns. In its golden era Williamsburg was the colony's social and cultural center, and its institutions included the College of William and Mary and the Public Hospital. Virginia's political leaders, George Washington, Thomas Jefferson, and Patrick Henry among them, began discussions in Williamsburg that led the Old Dominion to revolution. After removal of the capital, Williamsburg fell dormant until the late 1920s when restoration of its colonial appearance was undertaken with the support of John D. Rockefeller, Jr. Over eighty colonial buildings have been restored, and numerous others reconstructed by the Colonial Williamsburg Foundation. The project has long set a national standard for architectural scholarship, historic preservation, and museum interpretation. *(134–50) VLR: 09/09/69; NHL: 10/09/60.*

WILLIAMSBURG INN, *136 East Francis Street.* The Williamsburg Inn was built in 1936–37 under the patronage of John D. Rockefeller, Jr., as a vehicle to advance the message of the restored colonial capital to a larger audience. Inspired by early 19th-century models, the Boston firm of Perry, Shaw and Hepburn departed from the strict interpretation of the colonial style of the restored area to create a premier resort hotel. The resulting complex reflects the intimate involvement of Rockefeller himself who influenced the design to embody his demand for exacting levels of comfort and service. With regard to its planning he wrote: "Careful brooding study of every detail of a bedroom, particularly where small, is, in my experience, the only way in which to get a satisfactory result." In its decades of service, the Williamsburg Inn has hosted numerous heads of state and international conferences. *(137–79) VLR: 03/19/97; NRHP: 06/04/97.*

WREN BUILDING, *College of William and Mary.* The main building of the nation's second-oldest seat of higher learning was begun in 1695 and completed four years later. Hugh Jones in his *Present State of Virginia* (1724) stated that the building was "first modelled by Sir Christopher Wren, adapted to the nature of the country by the gentlemen there." It was gutted by fire in 1705 and rebuilt in modified form within the original walls. It again burned in 1859 and 1862, but in each case the walls survived and were incorporated in the rebuildings. The Wren Building's 1705 exterior appearance is well documented, and it was to that form that it was returned during the restoration of 1928–31 directed by Colonial Williamsburg architects. Defining a forecourt are the President's House (1732–33) and the Brafferton, built in 1723 as an Indian school. William and Mary was chartered in 1693. It is now a state-owned university. *(137–13) VLR: 09/09/69; NHL: 10/09/60.*

GEORGE WYTHE HOUSE, *Palace Green.* Few colonial Virginia houses are so admired or have spawned so many imitations as this restrained Georgian dwelling in the heart of Williamsburg. The house was erected ca. 1750 by the builder Richard Taliaferro, who most likely was its designer. Taliaferro received public acclaim as an architect when he directed the 1754 addition of the ballroom to the Governor's Palace. For many years the house was the home of Taliaferro's son-in-law, George Wythe, a signer of the Declaration of Independence and first law professor at the College of William and Mary. It also served as George Washington's headquarters during the Yorktown campaign. The complex geometry of its proportions, combined with its subtle brickwork, demonstrates how Virginia's otherwise plain colonial architecture could transcend provinciality and achieve stateliness. Restored by the Colonial Williamsburg Foundation in 1939–40, the house serves as an exhibition building. *(137–58) VLR: 09/18/73; NHL: 04/15/70.*

CITY OF WINCHESTER

In the lower Shenandoah Valley, the county seat of Frederick County was originally known as Opequon and then Frederick's Town. It was renamed Winchester, for the English cathedral city, upon its establishment as a town in 1752. The town was incorporated in 1779 and became a city in 1874.

ABRAM'S DELIGHT, *1340 South Pleasant Valley Road.* The region's easily worked blue-gray limestone made an ideal building material for some of the Shenandoah Valley's earliest houses. Among these solid structures is the dwelling erected in 1754 for Isaac Hollingsworth on property settled in 1732 by his father, Abraham Hollingsworth, and named in his honor. The stonemason was Simon Taylor, who also is credited with Springdale, the 1753 home of John Hite south of Winchester. The house employs a two-over-two floor plan with center passage, a plan favored by the area's Scotch-Irish settlers. A two-story wing was added ca. 1800, and the original woodwork was replaced with Greek Revival trim in the mid–19th century. Acquired by the city of Winchester in 1943, the house is exhibited as a museum of early life by the Winchester–Frederick County Historical Society. *(138–29) VLR: 11/09/72; NRHP: 04/11/73.*

GLEN BURNIE, *801 Amherst Street.* Glen Burnie was part of a 1735 grant to James Wood, who founded Winchester in 1752 and platted its lots. Wood's log and stone house was replaced by the present brick dwelling, built ca. 1794 by his son Robert. Glen Burnie remained the home of Wood's descendants through the seventh generation. Although now within Winchester's city limits, the estate preserves its rural character. Extensive gardens were laid out by Julian Wood Glass, Jr., the last of Wood's descendants to live here, after he inherited the property in 1952. Within the gardens is the Wood family cemetery. The first floor of the oldest section, containing the stair hall and dining room, features some of the area's most sophisticated Federal woodwork. The stair hall cornice is decorated with gouge work and stars. Since 1992 the property has been a museum administered by the Glass–Glen Burnie Foundation. *(138–08) VLR: 06/19/79; NRHP: 09/10/79.*

HANDLEY LIBRARY, *100 West Piccadilly Street.* Judge John Handley of Scranton, Pa., who made a fortune in coal investments, late in life developed a warm affection for Winchester and its Scotch-Irish heritage. In 1895 he left funds for the construction of a library "for the free use of the people of the city of Winchester." The result of this munificence is perhaps Virginia's purest expression of the regal and florid Beaux Arts classicism. Its architects were J. Stewart Barney and Henry Otis Chapman of New York. Begun in 1908 and completed in 1913, the library was a model for its time. The dome, colonnades, and esplanades encased the most modern facilities, including an auditorium, well-appointed reading rooms, and five levels of glass-floored stacks, all in fireproof construction. Still an efficient facility, the Handley Library is an illustration of the long-lasting benefits of architectural quality. *(138–28) VLR: 09/09/69; NRHP: 11/12/69.*

STONEWALL JACKSON'S HEAD-QUARTERS, *415 North Braddock Street.* Winchester's storybook Gothic Revival cottage served as the headquarters of Gen. Stonewall Jackson from November 1861 to March 1862. Jackson's firm stand during the first battle of Manassas earned him his famous nickname and the rank of major general with the task of defending the Shenandoah Valley. He established his headquarters in Winchester and the following spring began a series of diversions to take pressure off Confederate forces to the east. The house that served as his headquarters was built in 1854 for William McP. Fuller. With its diamond-pane windows and scrolled bargeboards, the house follows the Gothic mode popularized by Andrew Jackson Downing. Mrs. Jackson, who resided here during the winter of 1861–62, described the dwelling as being in the cottage style and papered with elegant gilt paper. It is owned by the city and operated as a museum by the Winchester–Frederick County Historical Society. *(138–33) VLR: 09/09/69; NHL: 05/28/67.*

OLD STONE CHURCH, *304 East Piccadilly Street.* Old Stone Church exemplifies the sober architecture favored by the 18th-century Scotch-Irish settlers, many of whom came to the region from Pennsylvania's Cumberland Valley. It was built in 1788 as a branch of Frederick County's Opequon Church, organized in 1736. The Winchester Presbytery, covering parts of what is now West Virginia, southern Pennsylvania, western Maryland, and northwestern Virginia, was organized in the church in 1794. The congregation merged with another in 1834, and the building was sold to the Baptists. In 1875 the Baptists leased the building to the city as a school for black children; it later was used as an armory by the local militia. The Presbyterians reacquired the church in 1932 and restored it to its original appearance between 1941 and 1950. The building is now a museum. *(138–19) VLR: 12/21/76; NRHP: 08/18/77.*

THE HEXAGON HOUSE, *530 Amherst Street.* This unconventional structure, Virginia's only known hexagonal dwelling, was built in 1871–73 for James W. Burgess. Its polygonal form was likely influenced by Orson S. Fowler's *A Home for All* (1853), a theoretical architectural work which advocated the octagon as the most practical, economical, and healthful form for American dwellings. In keeping with Fowler's recommendation, each of the principal rooms in the Hexagon House has ventilators to remove "bad" air. James W. Burgess was a successful furniture dealer and also sold caskets. The house and its sloping parklike grounds, a vestige of 19th-century romantic landscaping, is owned by the Glass–Glen Burnie Foundation. *(138–34) VLR: 04/21/87; NRHP: 09/10/87.*

WASHINGTON'S HEADQUARTERS (ADAM KURTZ HOUSE), *Braddock and Cork streets.* Employing frame, log, and stone construction, this stern building is one of the oldest structures in Winchester. The frame center portion likely was standing in 1764 when Thomas Rutherford occupied the lot. Persistent local tradition has it that it was used by George Washington as a surveyor's office in 1749–52 and that it later was his headquarters in 1756–57 when he supervised the construction of Fort Loudoun, a frontier defense work. Washington's associations are not documented, but the strong belief in the connection has made the structure a relic of 19th-century patriotic Washington lore. A factual occupant is Adam Kurtz, one of Daniel Morgan's riflemen, who bought the building from Rutherford in 1778. The stone section appears to be of 18th-century origin, while the log portion probably dates to the early 19th century. *(138–25) VLR: 12/16/75; NRHP: 05/17/76.*

WINCHESTER HISTORIC DISTRICT. Founded by James Wood in 1752, Winchester began as a small farming community and prospered as the county seat and as a trading center at the junction of several turnpikes. Its strategic location in the Shenandoah Valley contributed to Winchester's involvement in the French and Indian, Revolutionary, and Civil wars. From the 1870s to the 1920s, the community served as the Valley's leading commercial and industrial center. During the present century Winchester has been the hub of Virginia's apple industry. The historic district incorporates approximately forty-five blocks of both commercial and residential properties along its grid-plan streets. The area is particularly rich in early vernacular log buildings, early stone houses, and Federal town houses. It also boasts an important collection of Victorian commercial buildings and large residences. The heart of the district is marked by the 1840 Greek Revival Frederick County Courthouse. *(138–42) VLR: 04/17/79; NRHP: 03/04/80.*

WINCHESTER NATIONAL CEMETERY, *401 National Avenue.* The Winchester National Cemetery was established on April 9, 1866, and contains more than 5,400 graves of U.S. soldiers. The cemetery is notable for its fourteen commemorative monuments dedicated to Union regiments that fought in the Shenandoah Valley battles of 1862–64. After the war, Union dead were reinterred from their temporary burial sites in the Valley as well as from the West Virginia towns of Harpers Ferry, Martinsburg, and Romney. The superintendent's lodge was built in 1871 as a one-story stone structure from a design by Quartermaster General Montgomery C. Meigs. The frame second floor was added about 1914. *(138–35) VLR: 10/18/95; NRHP: 02/26/96.*

WISE COUNTY

Formed in 1856 from Lee, Scott, and Russell counties, this coal-mining Southwest Virginia county was named for Henry Alexander Wise, governor of Virginia from 1856 to 1860. Its county seat is the town of Wise.

CHRIST EPISCOPAL CHURCH, *100 Clinton Avenue, Big Stone Gap.* Graced by an able design, Christ Church reflects the attention to architectural character usually found in late Victorian Episcopal churches, both large and small. The design was supplied by Baltimore architect T. Buckler Ghequiere, whose skill at adapting the Gothic style to small wooden buildings is also evident in St. Stephen's Church, Northumberland County. Completed in 1892, Christ Church served the well-to-do citizens of Big Stone Gap, a newly laid-out boomtown in the coalfields of Southwest Virginia. With its vaulted interior sheathed in tongue-and-groove boards, the church shows the influence of the British Arts and Crafts movement. Insufficient funds prevented the exterior from being painted its intended dark straw color, so a parishioner donated leftover red barn paint. His family continues the regular donation of red paint for the exterior to this day. *(101–05) VLR: 04/18/89; NRHP: 12/19/90.*

COLONIAL HOTEL (THE INN AT WISE COURTHOUSE), *Main and Spring streets, Wise.* The Colonial Hotel was erected in 1910 on a site that had been used for hotel purposes since just after the Civil War. In the tradition of inns and taverns in courthouse towns since colonial times, the hotel served those having business with the Wise County court. When its predecessor, the Dotson Hotel, burned in 1909, a group of local businessmen founded the Wise Hotel Corporation and purchased the site for a new hotel. The corporation was initially headed by future Virginia governor George C. Peery. A local builder, D. J. Phipps, was awarded the contract to erect the twenty-two-room structure for which he employed a modified Colonial Revival style. This prominent local landmark was recently reopened as a hotel and restaurant, renamed the Inn at Wise Courthouse. *(392–02) VLR: 12/11/90; NRHP: 02/05/91.*

COUNTRY CABIN, *U.S. Route 23, Norton.* Nestled in a mountain setting, this neorustic structure is a tangible symbol of Wise County's cultural heritage. The cabin was built around 1937 when Katherine ("Kate") O'Neil Peters Sturgill wanted to create a community center. Her father, William O'Neil, an Irish immigrant, donated the site. The Works Progress Administration program provided funds for the center. Local young men erected the log building, and Kate taught guitar lessons, conducted musical programs, and organized community gatherings here. A local banjo player, Doc Boggs, who later performed at Carnegie Hall, often joined her. Today, Country Cabin, owned by Appalachian Traditions, Inc., features cultural exchange programs with touring artists and hosts regular Saturday evening events aired on local radio and television stations. Traditional mountain music, dances, and crafts continue to fill the cabin. *(97–59) VLR: 04/22/92; NRHP: 10/27/92.*

JOHN FOX, JR., HOUSE, *Big Stone Gap.* John Fox, Jr., novelist of the mountaineers' struggle to cope with the mining era and a more modern lifestyle, lived and wrote here from 1890 until his death in 1919, drawing inspiration from the people and culture of the region. He is best remembered for two best-seller works: *The Little Shepherd of Kingdom Come* and *The Trail of the Lonesome Pine.* The shingled house was begun ca. 1890 for Fox's two eldest brothers, who came to Big Stone Gap from Kentucky as investors in mining options. Several additions were made to accommodate more of the family, including John Fox, Jr., and his wife, Viennese prima donna Fritzi Scheff. Throughout their ownership, which lasted until 1971, the Foxes made the rambling homeplace a cultural and social center. The property is now maintained as a museum by the Lonesome Pine Arts and Crafts Association. *(101–01) VLR: 11/20/73; NRHP: 06/07/74.*

JUNE TOLLIVER HOUSE, *Big Stone Gap.* This modified Queen Anne–style house, typical of Southwest Virginia's late 19th-century boom architecture, was the residence of June Morris during the time of her schooling at Big Stone Gap. She was the local woman after whom the writer John Fox, Jr., patterned June Tolliver, heroine of his novel *The Trail of the Lonesome Pine,* published in 1908. In the book this sheltered daughter of a local family falls in love with a mining engineer. Portraying the cultural clash that came with the region's mining boom, the book was one of the most popular of its time. The house is preserved as a literary landmark, with the novel that made it famous reenacted here seasonally as an outdoor drama. *(101–03) VLR: 07/17/73; NRHP: 08/28/73.*

U.S. POST OFFICE AND COURTHOUSE, *Main Street, Big Stone Gap.* Reflecting the prosperity brought by the coal industry to this mountain community, the federal post office and courthouse ranks with the state's most architecturally sophisticated federal buildings. A polished example of the 20th-century Renaissance Revival, the stone-faced exterior, with its deep bracketed cornice, shallow hipped roof, and rusticated ground floor, references the architecture of Florentine palaces. Its architect, James Knox Taylor, was responsible for numerous government buildings across the nation. Taylor resigned his federal post in 1912, and the building was completed under the supervision of Oscar Wenderoth. It survives with few alterations and preserves a great quantity of early wood trim, metalwork, electrical fixtures, and custom-designed furniture. Noteworthy is the courtroom, decorated with a coffered ceiling, ornamental plasterwork, and mahogany woodwork. The building still serves its original use. *(101–04) VLR: 10/21/75; NRHP: 12/23/75.*

WISE COUNTY COURTHOUSE, *Wise.* The Wise County Courthouse reflects the wealth reaped by the county from the expansion of the railroads and the increased mining of coal in the region at the turn of the century. A rare use in Virginia of the Renaissance Revival style for a county courthouse, the building was completed in 1896 after plans by the prolific Washington, D.C., architect Frank P. Milburn, who worked throughout the South. Milburn's courthouse is the third to serve the county. With its paired towers, lively massing, and well-articulated masonry detailing, the building has a palatial air and is perhaps the most successful of the several courthouses Milburn designed for Southwest Virginia counties. *(329–01)* *VLR: 10/21/80; NRHP: 03/02/81.*

WYTHE COUNTY

Named for George Wythe, a signer of the Declaration of Independence, this Southwest Virginia county was formed from Montgomery County in 1789, with part of Grayson County added later. Its county seat is Wytheville.

CORNETT ARCHAEOLOGICAL SITE, *Austinville vicinity.* Dating to the Late Woodland period, the Cornett site has proved to be significant in ceramic studies related to the prehistory of Southwest Virginia and neighboring regions. Further study of the site's ceramics is likely to enable archaeologists to define better the nature of cultural interactions with societies farther to the south in North Carolina and adjacent areas. The site is also significant for regional studies on Late Woodland period demography, subsistence, community organization, and settlement patterns. Such studies are possible because of the presence of a variety of documented features here including human burials and preserved organic materials within the site's sharply defined boundaries, which include a village site possibly with a palisade and central plaza. *(98–54) VLR: 08/16/83; NRHP: 09/29/83.*

CROCKETT'S COVE PRESBYTERIAN CHURCH, *Crockett's Cove.* Crockett's Cove was named for John Crockett, who settled in this pastoral vale in the 1770s. Crockett's daughter-in-law, Nancy Graham Crockett, the pious daughter of a Presbyterian elder, became concerned for the religious welfare of the area. At her death in 1853 she left funds to build a church for the community. Completed in 1858, the church was constructed by Wesley Johnson of Wytheville. The plain rectangular structure is typical of country Presbyterian meetinghouses, being basically functional and devoid of religious iconography. Lewis Miller, the Pennsylvania folk artist, sketched the church at its dedication. During the 1864 battle of Cove Mountain, the church was used as a Union hospital. Seventeen soldiers died here, and bloodstains from the wounded remain inside. The church closed in 1903 but was restored to occasional use in 1941. Buttresses were added in 1959 to halt splaying of the walls. *(98–27) VLR: 04/22/92; NRHP: 10/15/92.*

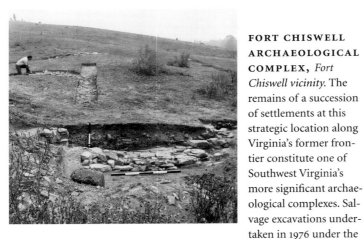

FORT CHISWELL ARCHAEOLOGICAL COMPLEX, *Fort Chiswell vicinity.* The remains of a succession of settlements at this strategic location along Virginia's former frontier constitute one of Southwest Virginia's more significant archaeological complexes. Salvage excavations undertaken in 1976 under the direction of the Virginia Department of Historic Resources in the path of interstate highway construction revealed prehistoric remains dating from the Middle Archaic period along with remnants of three successive periods of 18th-century occupation. Of the latter were chimney bases from two log cabins erected ca. 1752 by Alexander Sayers, as well as evidence of the military outpost established by Col. William Byrd III in 1760. Also uncovered were remains of the settlement started here in the early 1770s by James McGavock, Sr. Although some of Fort Chiswell's sites were destroyed by highway construction, other areas remain untouched and hold potential information important to the study of the region's early history. *(98–26) VLR: 12/21/76; NRHP: 08/29/78.*

FORT CHISWELL MANSION, *Fort Chiswell.* Fort Chiswell Mansion was built for two brothers, Stephen McGavock and Joseph Cloyd McGavock, overlooking the McGavocks' original homestead, since destroyed. The McGavocks were early settlers of the area and acquired large tracts of land. Their first home was at Fort Chiswell, a defense post on the Great Wilderness Road. Here they maintained a commercial establishment serving the many pioneers moving west. In 1839 the two McGavock brothers contracted with Lorain Thorn and James Johnson to build this brick house on a bluff above the Fort Chiswell settlement. The provincially interpreted Classical Revival structure has a two-column portico and paired semiexterior end chimneys, between which on either end is a large Palladian attic window. A series of brick service buildings remains. The imposing dwelling long served to signal the importance of the McGavocks to area newcomers. *(98–05) VLR: 03/02/71; NRHP: 05/06/71.*

MAJ. DAVID GRAHAM HOUSE, *Fosters Falls vicinity.* The various parts of the unforgettably eccentric Maj. David Graham house provide a chronicle of the architectural taste of a successful Southwest Virginia family. The house began ca. 1840 as a frame, two-story regionalized Federal-style dwelling with an elaborately carved entry. Its original owner, David Graham, was a prominent figure in the development of the local iron industry. Around 1855, Graham added an Italianate section of brick. The place was inherited in 1870 by Graham's son, Maj. David Pierce Graham, a former Confederate officer. Major Graham continued the tradition of embellishing the house by adding a tower and deck-on-hip roof. He further elaborated the building at the turn of the century with two enormous three-part bays connected by galleries. The exotic pile was owned by the Graham family until 1944. *(98–08) VLR: 12/11/84; NRHP: 02/14/85.*

HALLER-GIBBONEY ROCK HOUSE, *Monroe and Tazewell streets, Wytheville.* In the heart of Wytheville, the Haller-Gibboney Rock House is one of the simple but well-ordered stone vernacular houses that once marked many of western Virginia's linear towns. The region's limestone proved to be a plentiful and easily worked material and gave texture and character to the otherwise plain architecture. The house is thought to have been started in 1822 by Adam Saftly. It was sold unfinished in 1823 to Dr. John Haller, a native of York, Pa., and Wytheville's first resident physician. Dr. Haller made the Rock House his home until his death in 1840. The house was riddled by bullets in a Union raid during the Civil War but survived in an otherwise good state of preservation. Purchased by the town of Wytheville in 1967, the dwelling is now a museum. *(139–06) VLR: 04/18/72; NRHP: 11/09/72.*

KIMBERLING LUTHERAN CEMETERY, *Rural Retreat vicinity.* On a steep hillside looking over the countryside and mountains of western Wythe County, this early burying ground has a large collection of traditional German gravestones. Approximately fifty monuments date from the period 1800–1850 and are embellished, in most instances, with a single, high-relief motif—a heart, a cross, a six-pointed star, or some vegetal form—nearly always framed by a double band. Most of the inscriptions are in English, illustrating the acculturation of the German settlers. The use of these distinctly German-style gravestones halted in the 1850s; those erected from then on are indistinguishable from those in non-German cemeteries. The present twin-towered church, dating from 1913, is the third on the site. *(98–49) VLR: 12/20/77; NRHP: 03/26/80.*

LORETTO, *190 Peppers Ferry Road, Wytheville.* One of Wythe County's most eminent historic residences, Loretto is the product of three phases of development. The core is a single-pile brick house probably built around 1852 for William Alexander Stuart, older brother of Confederate general J. E. B. Stuart. Stuart was the county clerk and a developer of the salt industry in Saltville. Stuart sold Loretto to Benjamin Rush Floyd, son of Governor John B. Floyd, who himself served in the Virginia senate. The house was enlarged and remodeled in the Second Empire style in the 1880s when it was owned by Robert Crockett. In 1888 Loretto became the home of Archibald A. Campbell and his wife Susie, daughter of William Alexander Stuart. The Campbells made many changes, the most conspicuous being the Doric portico, added in 1911. A double-crib log barn and a rare log slave quarters stand nearby. *(139–15) VLR: 06/15/94; NRHP: 09/08/94.*

MARTIN ARCHAEOLOGICAL SITE, *Draper vicinity.* On the banks of the New River, this Indian site was occupied during the Late Woodland period (A.D. 900–1600). Test excavations on the site have established the presence of an Indian village, probably consisting of a cluster of domelike structures and perhaps enclosed by a palisade. Evidence of a succession of earlier occupations is preserved in the stratigraphy beneath the village remains. Artifacts found on the site include pottery sherds, stone tools, ceramic and shell trade items, and floral and faunal remains. A rare shell gorget is among the more interesting items to have been unearthed. *(98–46) VLR: 04/16/74; NRHP: 08/13/74.*

McGAVOCK FAMILY CEMETERY, *Fort Chiswell vicinity.* Atop a hill overlooking the Fort Chiswell mansion, a former McGavock home, this family cemetery contains an exceptionally rich collection of 19th-century funerary art, including an important group of Germanic stones, the only ones of their type found in a family burying ground. These crisply carved markers, dating from 1812 to the late 1830s, are attributed to Lawrence Krone, the county's most skillful stone carver. Like most German-style grave markers, these are double-sided with differing designs on the obverse and reverse. Each stone is highlighted by a single central motif—a tulip, a fern, or a sunflower—and most have footstones. The first McGavock in the region was James McGavock, Sr., born in County Antrim, Ireland. He came to Fort Chiswell from Fincastle in 1771 and was buried here in 1812 with a Germanic headstone marking his grave. *(98–22) VLR: 03/20/79; NRHP: 06/22/79.*

ST. JOHN'S LUTHERAN CHURCH AND CEMETERY, *Wytheville vicinity.* During the late 18th century, German settlers were concentrated near the present town of Wytheville. In 1798 St. John's Church, recently organized, adopted a common "Order of Agreement" with three other Wythe County German congregations under the leadership of German Reformed minister Bernard Willy. In 1799 Lutheran minister George Daniel Flohr became the congregation's first pastor. Flohr's 1826 gravestone in St. John's cemetery was executed by Lawrence Krone, perhaps the most accomplished of the region's German stone carvers. The marker is one of some thirty early 19th-century German-style stones remaining here. At the cemetery is the 1854 weatherboarded church, a massive, austere structure. Its heavy roof framing, now exposed, draws upon Continental framing systems practiced by German settlers in Pennsylvania, Maryland, and Virginia. The church, the mother church of the Wytheville-area Lutherans, replaced the original building of ca. 1800. *(98–18) VLR: 04/19/77; NRHP: 01/26/78.*

WYTHEVILLE HISTORIC DISTRICT. Incorporating the center of town, Wytheville's historic district has accommodated the town's commercial, civil, educational, and residential functions since the late 18th century. Dominating the area is the classical 1901 Wythe County Courthouse designed by Frank P. Milburn. A hint of the town's early 19th-century character is seen in a concentration of log buildings on East Main Street. The Main Street commercial buildings date from the 18th century through the 1940s and include a commercial block where Edith Bolling Wilson, second wife of President Woodrow Wilson, was born. During the 19th century Wytheville was celebrated for its moderate summer climate, attracting visitors from the Deep South. Many residences doubled as summer boardinghouses. The Supreme Court of Virginia held summer sessions here from 1870 to 1946. In the late 19th century Wytheville's merchants and attorneys built substantial and architecturally varied brick dwellings on its quiet residential streets. *(139–29) VLR: 08/17/94; NRHP: 09/30/94.*

SHOT TOWER, *Fosters Falls vicinity.* Thomas Jackson erected this imposing tower on a bluff of the New River ca. 1807 to manufacture shot for the firearms of the frontier settlers. The enterprise was supplied with lead from the Austinville mines several miles away. Shot was produced by dripping the molten lead from the top of the tower through a hole in the floor at the bottom and then down a seventy-five-foot shaft sunk into the cliff, where it fell into a kettle of water. While falling, the drops of lead cooled and developed into shot pellets; the water served to cushion the fall. The shaft was connected to the riverbank by a tunnel through which the shot was carried and loaded on boats. The shot tower, one of the few remaining in the country, is now owned and exhibited by the Virginia Department of Conservation and Recreation. *(98–16) VLR: 11/05/68; NRHP: 10/01/69.*

ZION EVANGELICAL LUTHERAN CHURCH CEMETERY, *Speedwell vicinity.* Forty-two well-preserved German-style gravestones, similar to those found in lesser numbers and in poorer condition in several other outlying Lutheran cemeteries around Wytheville, survive in the Zion Church graveyard. Like the other markers of the region, the Zion group is composed of thick sandstone slabs carved on

both sides and often decorated on the edges. The fanciest have undulating tops and faces carved with petaled flowers or pinwheel motifs, often framed by spiral pilasters. The inscriptions are in English, most in a flowing script. The stones seem to have been produced by a single carver between 1835 and 1840, some to replace earlier markers. Zion's simple Gothic-style church was built in 1940 and is the third church on the site. *(98–28) VLR: 11/21/78; NRHP: 02/01/79.*

YORK COUNTY

First named Charles River County, York County was one of Virginia's eight original shires formed by 1634. The present name was given in 1643, probably in honor of James, duke of York and later James II, the second son of King Charles I. The county seat is Yorktown.

BRUTON PARISH POORHOUSE ARCHAEOLOGICAL SITE, *Williamsburg vicinity.* This archaeological site consists of the remains of an 18th-century workhouse for indigents built by Williamsburg's Bruton Parish Church. By the mid–18th century, the colony's poor constituted a significant social problem. A 1755 act of the assembly empowered all of the colony's parishes to erect poorhouses; the Bruton Parish poorhouse is one of the few known to have been built. A survey of the site, conducted by the Virginia Department of Historic Resources in 1978, located the foundations of one of the four buildings identified by the French cartographer Desandrouin in 1781–82 as the poorhouse complex. Shown is a sampling of the variety of 18th-century artifacts associated with daily life found in the surface investigation. More intense archaeological activity could produce revealing data about the lives of a predominantly inarticulate portion of the colonial population. *(99–70) VLR: 11/18/80; NRHP: 09/02/82.*

BRYAN MANOR ARCHAEOLOGICAL SITE, *Williamsburg vicinity.* Frederick Bryan, deputy sheriff of York County, purchased a 500-acre plantation near Williamsburg in 1757 from John Fergason and Lewis Hansford and established his residence here. According to the Desandrouin map of 1781–82, the plantation complex then consisted of five buildings. Bryan had other landholdings and received considerable income from the sale of tobacco, pork, veal, and other commodities produced on his properties. Preserved in the York County records is a highly detailed household inventory made at Bryan's death in 1771, documentation that could possibly be matched with artifactual findings. A 1976 survey of the house site revealed an unusual footing made of sections of bog iron bonded together with shell mortar. Also at the site is a stone slab over the grave of Bryan's one-year-old son, John, who died in 1760. *(99–65) VLR: 06/21/77; NRHP: 11/14/78.*

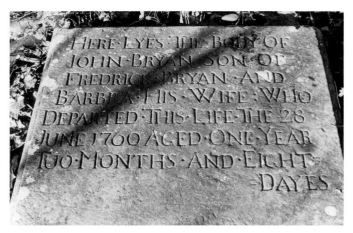

GOOCH TOMB AND YORK VILLAGE ARCHAEOLOG-ICAL SITE, *U.S. Coast Guard Reserve Training Center.* The village of York, on the York River near Wormeley Creek, was established before 1635. It remained the area's principal community until the early 1690s when Yorktown was established two miles west. A church was built at York ca. 1638, and within its walls in 1655 was buried Maj. William Gooch, a burgess from York County and uncle of Sir William Gooch, acting governor of the colony. Major Gooch's armorial slab is one of the oldest legible tombstones in Virginia. The village was abandoned by the late 18th century and ultimately disappeared. The church site is marked by a small park maintained by the U.S. Coast Guard with the tombstone protected by a special cover. The village site likely holds significant archaeological material relating to Virginia's 17th-century settlement. *(99–60) VLR: 10/16/73; NRHP: 01/18/74.*

GRACE CHURCH, *Yorktown.* Grace Church, originally known as York-Hampton Parish Church, was built ca. 1697. It is probably the state's only remaining colonial structure built of marl, a locally quarried soft material composed largely of shell matter which hardens almost to stone when exposed to air. The building was used as a magazine by Lord Cornwallis during the Revolutionary War. It was accidentally burned in 1814 and stood as a ruin until rebuilt in 1848. Further damage was done in the Civil War when Union troops put a signal tower on the roof and used the interior for a hospital. The church was returned to service in 1870 and received a thorough renovation in 1926 when the belfry was added. In its churchyard is the magnificent 1745 English table tomb of Thomas Nelson, as well as the grave of his grandson Thomas Nelson, Jr., a signer of the Declaration of Independence. *(99–10) VLR: 06/02/70; NRHP: 09/15/70.*

KISKIACK, *Yorktown Naval Weapons Station.* Named for an Indian tribe, Kiskiack is among Virginia's oldest works of vernacular architecture. The even spacing of its bays is a demonstration of the regularity that was to become a hallmark of colonial design. Although claims have been made for a 17th-century date, the house more likely was built in the early decades of the succeeding century for William Lee, who owned the property from 1696 to 1728. Lee was the grandson of the immigrant Henry Lee who patented the land in 1641. The house burned in 1915, and only the Flemish bond brick walls and the T-shaped chimneys are original. Rebuilt within the walls, the house remained a Lee home until 1918 when the property was acquired by the U.S. Navy for a high-security military installation. Now inaccessible to the public, the house has been sealed up for long-term preservation. *(99–12) VLR: 09/09/69; NRHP: 11/12/69.*

PORTO BELLO, *Camp Peary, Williamsburg vicinity.* During his short term as Virginia's last royal governor, Lord Dunmore acquired a York River plantation six miles from Williamsburg called Porto Bello where he maintained a country home. Here Dunmore sought refuge in 1775 when the hostility of the patriots forced him from the Governor's Palace. Historical documents indicate that Dunmore maintained at Porto Bello two dwellings and approximately ten outbuildings and farm buildings, none of which survives above ground. A small, much-altered brick house, probably built ca. 1800 for the Bright family, is all that is visible. The site of Dunmore's complex could be of considerable archaeological interest. At the beginning of World War II, the property was acquired by the federal government as a Seabee base. It is now a high-security training facility inaccessible to the public. *(99–50) VLR: 11/09/72; NRHP: 04/13/73.*

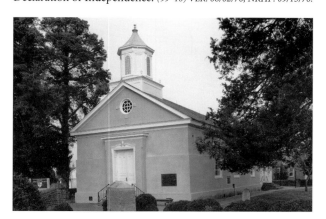

YORKTOWN HISTORIC DISTRICT. Yorktown was established in 1691 and became a thriving center of commerce and trade. It is chiefly remembered, however, as the scene of the final battle of the American Revolution. Here, on October 19, 1781, Lord Cornwallis surrendered his British forces, thus ending America's colonial era. Yorktown declined after the victory, and much of the lower part of the town burned in 1814. The town was held by both sides during the Civil War. Important landmarks include the Nelson house (shown) built about 1730 and later the home of Thomas Nelson, Jr., a signer of the Declaration of Independence. Near the battlefield is the Moore house where the surrender terms were negotiated. The Yorktown victory monument, designed by Richard Morris Hunt, was erected in 1881–84. The battlefield, the Moore house, and the Nelson house are exhibited by the National Park Service as part of the Colonial National Historical Park. *(99–57) VLR: 04/17/73; NRHP: 10/15/66.*

YORKTOWN SHIPWRECKS MARITIME ARCHAEO-LOGICAL SITE, *York River off Yorktown.* In October 1781, when the British army of Lord Cornwallis was bottled up at Yorktown by the Allied army and the French fleet was blockading the Chesapeake Bay, as many as twenty-six British vessels were scuttled off Yorktown. This prevented a landing by the French fleet. Cornwallis attempted to evacuate his troops across the York, but a violent squall prevented their escape. A British flag of truce was flown the next day, and on October 19, 1781, the surrender was signed, ending the Revolutionary War. Investigations by the Virginia Department of Historic Resources located nine ships dating to the wartime period. In 1982 a cofferdam was erected around one of the best-preserved wrecks, a British supply ship. The systematic excavation of the site by department archaeologists was a precedent-setting demonstration of underwater archaeological techniques. *(99–58) VLR: 02/20/73; NRHP: 10/09/73.*

APPENDIX I
Properties Removed From the Virginia Landmarks Register

The Board of Historic Resources has officially removed the following properties from the Virginia Landmarks Register because of destruction, loss of integrity, or legislative direction. The National Park Service has also removed from the National Register of Historic Places those properties listed below that were so designated.

ATHLONE, *Clifford vicinity, Amherst County.* A dignified Piedmont homestead, Athlone boasted a dwelling house built in two distinct phases. The earliest portion was erected ca. 1815 or earlier. The later part, a large country Greek Revival structure, dated from 1856. The house burned in 1996. The chimneys and several early outbuildings remain. *(05–119) VLR: 12/11/91; NRHP: 08/24/92.*

BENTFIELD, *Lawrenceville vicinity, Brunswick County.* This Federal plantation house near the Meherrin River was built in 1810 by the Revolutionary War colonel John ("Hellcat") Jones, Jr. It was noted for its fine brickwork and intricately detailed Federal woodwork. A fire of unknown origin destroyed it in 1974 while it was undergoing restoration. *(12–72) VLR: 11/20/73; NRHP: 01/24/74.*

BLADENSFIELD, *Lyells vicinity, Richmond County.* An imposing colonial mansion, Bladensfield was built in the third quarter of the 18th century by Robert ("Councillor") Carter, who in 1790 gave the place to his son-in-law John C. Peck. It was purchased in 1847 by the Rev. William N. Ward, whose descendants owned it when it burned in 1996. *(79–02) VLR: 02/19/80; NRHP: 10/31/80.*

BRANDY STATION BATTLEFIELD RURAL HISTORIC DISTRICT, *Brandy Station vicinity, Culpeper County.* On June 9, 1863, in these broad stretches of Culpeper and western Fauquier counties, Gen. J. E. B. Stuart, screening Gen. Lee's move to Gettysburg, fought the Union cavalry under Brig. Gen. Alfred Pleasonton. Though the outcome was indecisive, the engagement was the largest cavalry battle ever fought in North America. The battlefield was removed from the Virginia Landmarks Register by legislative direction in 1993. *(23–53) VLR: 10/30/89.*

BOTETOURT COUNTY COURTHOUSE, *Fincastle, Botetourt County.* Built in 1841–48, the Greek Revival Botetourt County Courthouse was the architectural centerpiece of Fincastle until it burned in 1970. The original walls were subsequently dismantled, and the four columns were incorporated into a modern copy of the courthouse. *(218–25) VLR: 04/06/71.*

BRIDGE OVER THE NORTH FORK OF THE ROANOKE RIVER, *Ironto vicinity, Montgomery County.* Employing a pin-connected Pratt through truss, this metal bridge was manufac-

tured in 1892 by the King Iron Bridge and Manufacturing Co. of Cleveland, Ohio. An example of a fast-disappearing form, the bridge was replaced by a concrete bridge in the early 1990s. *(60–394) VLR: 06/20/89; NRHP: 01/10/89.*

BRISTOE BATTLEFIELD, *Bristow vicinity, Prince William County.* The battle of Bristow Station was fought on October 14, 1863, in the aftermath of the battle of Gettysburg. The Confederates suffered severe losses, with the Union forces gaining a clear victory. The battlefield was removed from the Virginia Landmarks Register by legislative direction in 1993. *(76–24) VLR: 04/17/91.*

WILLIAM A. BOWERS HOUSE, *254 North Sycamore Street, Petersburg.* One of the state's outstanding examples of urban Federal architecture, this elegantly detailed building was erected in 1828–29. Threatened with collapse because of serious structural weakness, the building was demolished in 1977. *(123–52) VLR: 07/19/77.*

CASERTA, *Eastville vicinity, Northampton County.* A typical gentry-class Eastern Shore plantation house, Caserta, built ca. 1840, was originally the home of George P. Upshur. It was noted for its impressive open-well staircase. The house was struck by lightning and burned in 1975. *(65–51) VLR: 12/02/69; NRHP: 02/26/70.*

ENNISCORTHY, *Keene vicinity, Albemarle County.* Long associated with the Coles family, Enniscorthy boasted an important 1850 Greek Revival mansion and an outstanding collection of early outbuildings and farm building, many of which predated the house. The property lost its landmark designation in 1997 because of the removal of all the ancillary structures and the extensive architectural modification of the mansion. *(02–28) VLR: 04/22/92; NRHP: 09/24/92.*

CHRIST CHURCH, *West Freemason Street, Norfolk.* Designed by Levi Swain and built in 1828, Christ Church was a sophisticated Classical Revival edifice. Until 1910 it housed Norfolk's oldest Episcopal congregation. The building was demolished in 1973 by the Norfolk Redevelopment and Housing Authority. *(122–04) VLR: 04/06/71; NRHP 08/19/71.*

EXETER, *Leesburg, Loudoun County.* Dating from the 1790s, this unusual several-sectioned Federal plantation house was built by Dr. Wilson Cary Selden. Its portico and varied roof forms gave it particular distinction. It stood abandoned for many years and was finally destroyed by fire in 1980. *(53–77) VLR: 02/20/73; NRHP: 08/14/73.*

CRAWFORD HOUSE HOTEL, *450–454 Crawford Street, Portsmouth.* Completed in 1835 and named for William Crawford, founder of Portsmouth, the Crawford House was Portsmouth's first hotel. It stood essentially unaltered when it was demolished in 1970 for urban renewal by the Portsmouth Redevelopment and Housing Authority. *(124–26) VLR: 05/05/70.*

FIRST BAPTIST CHURCH, *407 North Jefferson Street, N.W., Roanoke.* Designed by the prolific Roanoke architect H. H. Huggins, First Baptist housed what was at the time the largest and most prominent black congregation west of Richmond. Completed in 1900, the building was gutted by fire in 1995, and the ruins were subsequently demolished. *(128–37) VLR: 08/21/90; NRHP: 12/06/90.*

FORT RODES, *Luray vicinity, Page County.* Probably built by John Rodes II in the fourth quarter of the 18th century, Fort Rodes was a rare German-style log house anglicized in the mid–19th century with the removal of the center chimney and the addition of end chimneys. It succumbed to fire in 1990. *(69–18) VLR: 11/12/77; NRHP: 05/22/78.*

HAYES HALL, *DeWitt Street, Lynchburg.* Hayes Hall was formerly the main building of Virginia College and Virginia Seminary, founded in 1886 as an institution espousing the self-help educational principles for blacks advocated by Booker T. Washington. Completed in 1888, the prodigious though deteriorated structure was demolished in 1988. *(118–59) VLR: 02/26/79 NRHP: 06/19/79.*

HARRISON-HANCOCK HARDWARE CO. BUILDING, *24 East Main Street, Christiansburg, Montgomery County.* The four-story Harrison-Hancock Hardware Co. Building was Christiansburg's chief example of small-town, turn-of-the-century commercial architecture. It was built in 1910 to supply the community with essential dry goods. It was demolished for a parking lot between 1989 and 1996. *(154–29) VLR: 06/20/89; NRHP: 11/13/89.*

MANCHESTER COTTON AND WOOL MANUFACTURING CO. BUILDING, *Hull Street at Manchester Bridge, Richmond.* Dating from the late 1830s, this impressive brick structure with its stepped-gable ends was one of Richmond's oldest industrial buildings and a conspicuous landmark on the south bank of the James River. It was demolished around 1990 for the construction of Richmond's flood wall. *(127–56) VLR: 04/19/83; NRHP: 07/21/83.*

NATHANIEL BURWELL HARVEY HOUSE, *Dublin vicinity, Pulaski County.* This dignified Colonial Revival house was built in 1909 for Nathaniel Burwell Harvey. Harvey employed James D. Chapman, an itinerant artisan, to embellish the entire interior with elaborate stenciled decoration. The rare decorative treatment was lost when the house was demolished in 1996. *(77–49) VLR: 10/15/85; NRHP: 02/13/86.*

MAUPIN-MAURY HOUSE, *formerly at 1105 East Clay Street, Richmond.* Dr. Socrates Maupin, a founder of what became the Medical College of Virginia, built this Greek Revival town house in 1846. Here, Matthew Fontaine Maury developed plans for a torpedo for the Confederate navy. In 1993 the house was dismantled and reerected a block away using only selected elements of the woodwork. *(127–74) VLR: 11/05/68; NRHP: 04/16/69.*

MONTGOMERY WHITE SULPHUR SPRINGS COTTAGE, *Depot and New streets, Christiansburg, Montgomery County.* This two-room cottage was a relic of Montgomery White Sulphur Springs, a popular spa begun in the 1850s. The resort closed in 1904, and the cottage was moved to Christiansburg. It was demolished in the early 1990s. *(154–08)* VLR: 06/20/89; NRHP: 11/13/89.

ELIJAH MURDOCK HOUSE, *Yellow Sulphur Springs vicinity, Montgomery County.* Dating mainly from the second quarter of the 19th century, the Elijah Murdock house exhibited many features characteristic of the vernacular traditions of the region. The hall-parlor dwelling combined log and frame construction with stone chimneys. Acquired by the county in the 1970s, it was demolished in the early 1990s. *(60–547)* VLR: 06/20/89; NRHP: 11/13/89.

MORRISON HOUSE, *West Market and Liberty streets, Harrisonburg.* Constructed between 1820 and 1824 for Joseph Thornton, the Morrison house was one of the few early dwellings remaining in downtown Harrisonburg. It stood in an excellent state of preservation until 1982 when the Wetsel Seed Company demolished the house for a parking lot. *(115–06)* VLR: 11/03/70; NRHP: 09/22/71.

OAK HILL, *Oak Ridge vicinity, Pittsylvania County.* Oak Hill, an ambitious Federal plantation house erected in 1823–25 by Samuel Hairston, was the work of James Dejarnett, a prominent area builder, and was noted for its fine woodwork. It was gutted by fire in 1988. *(71–26)* VLR: 09/18/79; NRHP: 12/28/79.

MOSS TOBACCO FACTORY, *Clarksville, Mecklenburg County.* An impressive relic of the antebellum tobacco industry, the Moss Tobacco Factory was erected in two stages during the 1830s. It housed a manufacturing operation until 1862. The building was demolished in 1980. *(192–13)* VLR: 05/21/79.

PRESTON HOUSE, *Saltville, Smyth County.* The Preston house was originally the home of Francis Preston, who represented the area in Congress and controlled the salt-producing lands in the vicinity. Begun in 1795 and later expanded, the house was demolished for a new dwelling in 1978. *(86–06)* VLR: 04/10/76; NRHP: 07/03/76.

RICHMOND VIEW, *Willis Road, Chesterfield County.* One of eastern Virginia's rare examples of a center-chimney vernacular house, Richmond View dated from around 1803 and was named for its view of the distant city of Richmond. The house was dismantled around 1994 and rebuilt in Charles City County. *(20–122) VLR: 05/20/75; NRHP: 09/18/75.*

ROSELAND MANOR, *Strawberry Banks, Hampton.* Overlooking Hampton Roads, Roseland Manor was a salient example of a Queen Anne mansion. The huge dwelling was designed by Arthur Crooks and built in 1888–87 for Harrison Phoebus, for whom the community of Phoebus was named. It was destroyed by fire in 1985. *(114–03) VLR: 07/18/78.*

SCOTT-CLARKE HOUSE, *9 South Fifth Street, Richmond.* One of the few freestanding Greek Revival houses remaining in downtown Richmond, the Scott-Clarke house was distinguished by its rare two-tiered portico on the garden side. The house lost its landmark status in 1986 after the removal of the portico and most of the original interior in a remodeling by the Virginia Chamber of Commerce. *(127–93) VLR: 11/16/74; NRHP: 04/13/72.*

SPRINGWOOD TRUSS BRIDGE, *Springwood, Botetourt County.* This three-span bridge upstream from Buchanan was Virginia's last major wooden bridge across the James River. It was constructed in 1884 by the Richmond and Alleghany Railroad Co. and acquired by the state in 1932. It was demolished following damage from a 1985 flood. *(11–103) VLR: 11/15/77; NRHP: 04/15/78.*

WESTOVER, *Eastville vicinity, Northampton County.* One of Virginia's earliest gambrel-roof houses, Westover was erected ca. 1750, probably for Michael Christian, Jr. The brick-ended dwelling featured outstanding colonial paneling. Long abandoned and deteriorating, the house was dismantled in 1997 for eventual reconstruction elsewhere. *(64–38) VLR: 11/18/80; NRHP: 06/28/82.*

WHITEHURST HOUSE, *North Muddy Creek Road, Virginia Beach.* A distinctive example an early 19th-century vernacular farmhouse, the Whitehurst house was occupied by Traynor Whitehurst as early as 1822. The compact dwelling had an unusual two-story, one-room plan. A fire destroyed the house in 1993. *(134–246) VLR: 09/15/92.*

APPENDIX II
Recently Registered Landmarks in the Virginia Landmarks Register

The following places were added to the Virginia Landmarks Register between March 19, 1997, and June 17, 1998, while this volume was in preparation.

"A" Fort and Battery Hill Redoubt, Camp Early, Fairfax County (06/17/98)

The Academy, Northampton County (09/17/97)

Anderson House, Botetourt County (09/17/97)

Ballard-Maupin House, Albemarle County (06/17/98)

Ballard-Worsham House, Bedford (09/17/97)

Ben Dover, Goochland County (06/17/98)

Buffalo Springs Historic Archaeological District, Mecklenburg County (12/03/97)

Burrland Farm Historic District, Fauquier County (07/02/97)

Calvert Manor, Arlington County (09/17/97)

Chase City High School, Mecklenburg County (09/17/97)

Davis and Kimpton Brickyard, Newport News (04/22/98)

Dumpling Island Archaeological Site, Suffolk (09/17/97)

Jubal A. Early Homeplace, Franklin County (09/17/97)

Earlysville Union Church, Albemarle County (09/17/97)

Echols Farm, Rockbridge County (06/17/98)

Edinburg Historic District, Shenandoah County (12/03/97)

Edmondson Hall, Washington County (09/17/97)

Fairview Historic District, Pulaski County (07/02/97)

Fancy Hill Historic District, Rockbridge County (07/02/97)

Flint Hill Baptist Church, Rappahannock County (07/02/97)

Grace Street Commercial Historic District, Richmond (12/03/97)

Grelen, Orange County (07/02/97)

Halwyck, Radford (07/02/97)

John Handley High School, Winchester (06/17/98)

Holbrook-Ross Historic District, Danville (07/02/97)

Hopewell Municipal Building, Hopewell (12/03/97)

Ingleside, Amelia County (07/02/97)

Jackson Blacksmith Shop, Goochland County (09/17/97)

Armstead T. Johnston High School, Westmoreland County (06/17/98)

King and Queen County Court House Historic District, King and Queen County (06/17/98)

LaVista, Spotsylvania County (09/17/97)

Luke's Mountain Historic District, Alleghany County (12/03/97)

Manchester Courthouse, Richmond (12/03/97)

Maple Springs, Culpeper County (09/17/97)

Martinsville Historic District, Martinsville (04/22/98)

Monterey, Salem (04/22/98)

Mount Calvary Lutheran Church, Page County (06/17/98)

Mount Zion Old School Baptist Church, Loudoun County (09/17/97)

No. 18 School, Fauquier County (07/02/97)

The Phillips Farm, Suffolk (06/17/98)

Red Hills, Albemarle County (12/03/97)

Rosedale Historic District, Alleghany County (12/03/97)

J. E. B. Stuart Birthplace, Patrick County (12/03/97)

Tacoma School, Wise County (07/02/97)

Walter Herron Taylor Elementary School, Norfolk (04/22/98)

Thermo-Con House, Fairfax County (07/02/97)

Maggie L. Walker High School, Richmond (06/17/98)

John Whitworth House, Richmond (12/03/97)

Woodbourne, Madison County (06/17/98)

PICTURE CREDITS

Unless noted in the following credits, all pictures in this volume were taken by Virginia Department of Historic Resources staff members or consultants or are otherwise the property of the department. Negatives of photographs by staff members and consultants are maintained in the department's collections. The historic prints used for vignettes are from *Historical Collection of Virginia* by Henry Howe (1856).

Ash Lawn–Highland
Ash Lawn–Highland 7

William Edmund Barrett
Ashleigh 164
Ball-Sellers House 41
Bank of Alexandria 24
Barboursville 362
Berry Hill 363
Beverley Mill 402
Birch House 162
Charles Richard Drew
    House 42
Christ Church 564
Fairfax County
    Courthouse 152
Farley 130
Frascati 364
Gadsby's Tavern 26
Green Springs 279
Greenville 130
Hawkwood 280
Hope Park Mill and Miller's
    House 157
Hume School 43
Ionia 280
Lloyd House 27
John Marshall House 433
Maupin-Maury House 565
Mitchell's Presbyterian
    Church 132
Montpelier 417
Nokesville Metal-Truss
    Bridge 406

Oak Ridge Railroad
    Overpass 332
St. Mary's Roman Catholic
    Church 160
St. Paul's Episcopal
    Church 408
St. Thomas's Episcopal
    Church 367
Scott-Clarke House 567
Stearns Block 443
Washington Historic
    District 418
Winchester Historic
    District 551

Bedford Historical Society
Bedford Historic Meeting
    House 61

Michael J. Bednar
The Farm 105

R. W. Cabaniss
Williamsville 222

Richard Cheek
Allmand-Archer House 342
Basilica of St. Mary of
    the Immaculate
    Conception 343
Baxter House 470
Beers House 420
Caroline County
    Courthouse 87

Castlewood 112
Christ Episcopal Church,
    Glendower 10
Commonwealth Club
    Historic District 425
Elmwood 149
Fancy Farm 63
Fire Station No. 1 455
Fortsville 522
Gay Mont 88
Ghent Historic District 345
Exchange Building 377
Glebe House of St. Anne's
    Parish 149
Greene County
    Courthouse 199
Keeling House 530
MacArthur Memorial 346
Madison County
    Courthouse 295
Morrison House 566
Masonic Temple 433
Old Mansion 89
Old Norfolk Academy
    Building 347
St. Sophia Home of the
    Little Sisters of the
    Poor 440
Spring Grove 90
Three Otters 65
Tinkling Spring Presbyterian
    Church 55
U. S. Customs House 348
Vauter's Church 150

West Freemason Street
    Historic District 34
Weston Manor 234
Willoughby-Baylor
    House 349
Woodbourne 66

*Charles Clemmer, courtesy of
    Frazier Associates*
Mount Ida 17

*Colonial Williamsburg
    Foundation*
Bruton Parish Church 546
Carter's Grove 239
Tutter's Neck Archaeological
    Site 243
Williamsburg Historic
    District 548
Williamsburg Inn 548

*Corporation for Jefferson's
    Poplar Forest*
Poplar Forest 65

*Matthew Cuda; courtesy of
    Liberty University*
Montview 289

Gene Dalton
Michie Tavern 15

Dan River Inc.
Dan River Inc. 137

INDEX

All places are in Virginia unless otherwise noted.

Southern Fireproof Company, 146

Southern Planter Publishing Company, 435

Southern Railway, 138, 332, 406

Southern Seminary Main Building, 83

Southside Land Company, 324

Southwark Parish, 517, 519

Southwest Historic District, Roanoke, 459

Southwest Mountains Historic District, 20

Southwest Turnpike, 327

Southwest Virginia: Female Institute, 74; Holiness Association Camp Meeting, 480; Improvement Co., 526

Southwestern State Hospital, 491

Southwestern Turnpike, 323

Sparks Brothers Building, 365

Spear, John, 464

Spears family, 114

Spence, Alexander, 544

Spencer, Anne, 291; House, 291

Spence's Point, 544

Spengler, Samuel S., 535

Sperryville Historic District, 418

Spiers, W. E., 224

Spilman, Edward M., 165

Spilman family, 165

Spilman-Mosby House, 165

Spitler, Isaac, 372; Homeplace, 372

Spitler, John, 372

Spooner, George Wallace, 106

Spotswood, Alexander, 75, 165, 200, 251, 295, 363, 499, 517, 546

Spotsylvania County Courthouse, 498

Spotsylvania Court House: battle of, 182, 367, 497, 498; Historic District, 498

Spratling, James, 198

Spring Grove: Caroline Co., 90; Westmoreland Co., 544

Spring Hill: Albemarle Co., 20; Greensville Co., 202

Springdale, 179, 549; Mill Complex, 179

Springfield: Hanover Co., 221; Northumberland Co., 359; School, Richmond, 442

Springs and resorts, 32, 58, 59, 128, 314, 318, 330, 366, 468, 487, 566

Springwood Truss Bridge, 567

Stabler, Edward, 28

Stabler-Leadbeater Apothecary Museum, 28

Stanard, William, 200

Stanley, Anne Pocahontas Bassett, 231

Stanley, Thomas B., 231

Stanton, Daniel, 81

Stanton, Edwin M., 40, 297

Stanton, Nancy, 81

Stanton Family Cemetery, 81

Staples, Abram, 374

Starkweather, Norris G., 29, 87, 365

State Arboretum of Virginia, 117

State Planters Bank, Richmond, 437

State Teachers College, Farmville, 397

Staunton and James River Turnpike, 11, 15

Staunton Hill, 103, 208

Staunton Male Academy, 506

Staunton Military Academy, 506

Staunton National Cemetery, 509

Staunton River Bridge, battle of, 203

Steamer Company No. 5, Richmond, 442

Stearns, Franklin P., 130, 443

Stearns Block, 443

Steele, William, 464

Steephill, 509

Stenett, M. McClung, 467

Stephens, Samuel, 337

Stephens City, 178

Stephenson, Percy S., 346

Steptoe, James, 85

Stern, Richard, 88, 247, 249

Stern, Yelverton, 88, 247, 249

Stevens, Benjamin F., 301

Stevens, Edna, 372

Stevens, Edward, 129, 133

Stevens, Mrs. George W., 469

Stevens, Mary, 372

Stevens Cottage, 372

Stevenson, Andrew, 8

Stevenson, Carter Littlepage, 182

Stewart, John, 443

Stewart, Norman, 443

Stewart, Thomas S., 426, 440

Stewart, Mr. and Mrs. Victor, 516

Stewart family, 443

Stewart-Lee House, 443

Stickler family, 371

Stijnen, Leon, 420

Stirling, 498

Stockdon, George H., 363

Stockley, Alexander II, 1

Stockley, Joseph, 1

Stockton, David, 11

Stoddart, William Lee, 457

Stone, Charles A., 17

Stone, Mrs. Charles A., 17

Stone, Frank, 453

Stone House: Archaeological Site, 242; Prince William Co., 405

Stoneburner House, 486

Stonehouse Farm, 47

Stoneleigh, 231

Stoner, R. D., 71

Stono, 264, 468

Stores, 28, 37, 72, 88, 110, 174, 183, 190, 285, 322, 480, 482, 565; general, 98, 132, 159, 204, 403, 468, 512; mill, 115

Stott, John, 237

Stoven, Charles, 367

Stover family, 370

Strasburg Historic District, 488

Strasburg Museum, 489

Strasburg Stone and Earthenware Manufacturing Company, 489

Stratford, 14, 20, 543, 544, 545

Stratton, Benjamin, 353

Stratton Major Parish, 245

Stratton Manor, 353

Strawberry Hill, 381

"A Streetcar Named Desire," Chatham, 382

Sarah Stribling House, 116

Strickland, William, 14

Strickler, Abraham, 369

Strickler family, 370

Strider, John P., 132

Strouse, Demetrius Bittle, 480

Stuart, Alexander H. H., 510

Stuart, Archibald, 509, 510

Stuart, David, 158

Stuart, Flora Cooke, 510

Stuart, James, 289

Stuart, James Ewell Brown, 81, 95, 216, 217, 271, 275, 293, 510, 557, 563; Birthplace, 569; equestrian statue, 435; Hollywood Cemetery, 430

Stuart, Levi U., 343

Stuart, Richard H., 247

Stuart, William Alexander, 557

Stuart Addition Historic District, 509

Stuart Hall School, Old Main, 507, 510

Stuart House, Staunton, 510

Stubblefield, John S., 98

Stubbs, John, 100

Sturgill, Katherine O'Neil, 553

Suarez-Galban, Mr. and Mrs. Julio, 14

Sudley, 401

Suffolk: Elks Lodge No. 685, 513; Historic District, 514; Parish, 513

Sugar Loaf Farm, 55

Sullivan, Louis, 411

Sully, 161

Summers, David, 55

Sunken Road, Fredericksburg, 182

Sunny Bank, 20

Sunnyfields, 21

Sunnyside: Loudoun Co., 276; Mecklenburg Co., 309; Northumberland Co., 359; Southampton Co., 495

Sunrise, 180

Surface, Frank, 328

Surface House, 328

Surface-Lee Block, 317

Surface Mill, Riner Historic District, 327

Surry County Courthouse Complex, 520

Sussex County Courthouse, 206, 523

Sussex Court House Historic District, 523

Sutherland, C. C., 11

Sutherlin, William T., 138, 140

Sutherlin House (Danville Museum of Fine Arts and History), 140

Sutton, William S., 164

Swain, Levi, 421, 564

Swan, Abraham, 149, 249, 535

Swan Tavern, 104

Swann, Thomas, 26, 273, 520

Swann, Thomas, Jr., 273

Swann, William, 520

Swannanoa, 333

Swann's Point Archaeological Site, 520

Swart, William, 164

Sweet Briar: College Historic District, 38; House, 38

Sweet Chalybeate Springs, 32

Sweet Hall, 254

Swem, Earl Gregg, 547

Swift Creek: battle of, 125, 126; Manufacturing Company, 115; Mill, 115

Swoope, William M., 81

Sycamore Tavern, 222

Sydnor family, 220

Sylvania, 279

Syme, John, 218

Tabb, John, 34

Tabb, Philip, 193

Tabb, Thomas, 34

Tabb family, 34, 35

Tabb Street Presbyterian Church, 379, 381

Tacoma School, 569

Taft, William Howard, 376

Taliaferro, Baldwin, 368

Taliaferro, Elizabeth Eggleston, 242

Taliaferro, Nathan, 37, 333

Taliaferro, Philip Alexander, 189

Taliaferro, Richard, 242, 548

Tankersley family, 468

Tankersley Tavern, 468

Tannenburg, David, 295

Tappahannock Historic District, 150

Tarleton, Banastre, 9, 80, 142, 171, 196, 278

Tarover, 208

Tarry, George, 307

Tarry, George B., 307

Tarry, Samuel, 307

Tastee 29 Diner, 153

Tate, Benjamin, 429

Tate, Joseph, 429

Tate, Robert, 47

Taverns and ordinaries: Andrews Tavern, 496; Boswell's Tavern, 278; The Boyd Tavern, 305; Boykin's Tavern, 235; Buckland Historic District, 402; Burke's Tavern, 360; Carter's Tavern, 205; Cartersville Tavern, 135; The Cedars, 9; Courthouse Tavern, Powhatan Court House, 394; Crossroads Tavern, 11; Cuckoo Tavern, 279; Dragon Ordinary, 190; Dranesville Tavern, 155; D. S. Tavern, 11; Eagle Tavern, 104; Eastville Inn, 352; Fairfax Arms, 156; French's Tavern, 392; Gadsby's Tavern, 26; Galbraith Tavern, 468; Germantown Tavern, 165; Gloucester Woman's Club, 190; Golden Eagle Tavern, 184; Hallsborough Tavern, 114; Hanover Tavern, 217; Ingles Ferry Tavern, 411; Johnston's Tavern, 88; Kentucky Hotel, 287; Kingsmill Plantation Archaeological District, 241; Lancaster Court House Historic District, 257; Langley Ordinary, 158; The Lockkeeper's House,

The Virginia Landmarks Register was designed and typeset in Minion
by Kachergis Book Design, Pittsboro, North Carolina; and printed
on 70-pound Fortune Matte and bound by Thomson-Shore,
Dexter, Michigan.